T0214286

Lecture Notes in Computer Science   11280

Commenced Publication in 1973
Founding and Former Series Editors:
Gerhard Goos, Juris Hartmanis, and Jan van Leeuwen

More information about this series at http://www.springer.com/series/7407

Xuemin Chen · Arunabha Sen
Wei Wayne Li · My T. Thai (Eds.)

Computational Data and Social Networks

7th International Conference, CSoNet 2018
Shanghai, China, December 18–20, 2018
Proceedings

 Springer

Editors
Xuemin Chen 🄳
Texas Southern University
Houston, TX, USA

Wei Wayne Li
Texas Southern University
Houston, TX, USA

Arunabha Sen
Ira A. Fulton School of Engineering
Tempe, AZ, USA

My T. Thai 🄳
University of Florida
Gainesville, AL, USA

ISSN 0302-9743   ISSN 1611-3349   (electronic)
Lecture Notes in Computer Science
ISBN 978-3-030-04647-7   ISBN 978-3-030-04648-4   (eBook)
https://doi.org/10.1007/978-3-030-04648-4

Library of Congress Control Number: 2018962150

LNCS Sublibrary: SL1 – Theoretical Computer Science and General Issues

This Springer imprint is published by the registered company Springer Nature Switzerland AG
The registered company address is: Gewerbestrasse 11, 6330 Cham, Switzerland

Preface

This book constitutes the refereed proceedings of the 7th International Conference on Computational Data and Social Networks Social Networks, CSoNet 2018, held in Shanghai, China, during December 18–20, 2018. This conference provides a premier interdisciplinary forum to bring together researchers and practitioners from all fields of complex networks, i.e., social networks, communication networks, and senor networks, working on various fundamental and emerging issues such as network computing, modeling, social network analysis, and data mining for presentation of original research results, as well as the exchange and dissemination of innovative, practical development experiences.

The topics cover the fundamental background, theoretical technology development, and real-world applications associated with complex and data network analysis, minimizing influence of rumors on social networks, blockchain Markov modeling, fraud detection, data mining, Internet of Things (IoT), Internet of Vehicles (IoV), and others. Selected papers will be published in special issues of *Journal of Combinatorial Optimization, IEEE Transactions on Network Science and Engineering, and Computational Social Networks*.

The intended audience of this book mainly consists of researchers, research students, and practitioners in complex networks and data mining, focused more on social networks and wireless sensor networks. The book is also of interest to researchers and industrial practitioners in emerging areas such as artificial intelligence, big data, blockchain, cloud computing, fraud detection, intelligent transportation system, spam detection, and rumor blocker.

We would like to express our appreciation to all contributors and the conference committee members. A special appreciation goes to Shanghai Polytechnic University (SPU) for its support of this conference. Furthermore, without the unlimited efforts from the local chair, Dr. Chuang Ma, and his team members, publicity co-chairs, Drs. Xiang Li, Mugeng Peng, and Wenan Tan, financial chair, Dr. Thang Dinh, and website chair, David Smith, our conference would not have been so success in its seventh anniversary year. We would also like to recognize Dr. Jian Wang's contribution in editing the final proceedings document. In addition, we sincerely appreciate the consistent support and great effort in the publication process of these proceedings by Anna Kramer and Alfred Hofmann from Springer.

December 2018

Xuemin Chen
Arunabha Sen
Wei Wayne Li
My T. Thai

Organization

General Chairs

Wei Wayne Li	Texas Southern University, USA
My T. Thai	University of Florida, USA

Technical Program Co-chairs

Xuemin Chen	Texas Southern University, USA
Arunabha Sen	Arizona State University, USA

Technical Program Committee

Leman Akoglu	Carnegie Mellon University, USA
Yuming Bo	Nanjing University of Science and Technology, China
Lin Chen	Shanghai Polytechnic University, China
Hocine Cherifi	Université de Bourgogne, France
Arun Das	Arizona State University, USA
Jinyoung Han	Hanyang University, South Korea
Xiaoming Hu	Shanghai Polytechnic University, China
Yo-Ping Huang	National Taipei University of Technology, Taiwan
Taekyoung Kwon	Seoul National University, South Korea
Donghyun Kim	Kennesaw State University, USA
Xiaoyan Kui	Central South University, China
Demin Li	Donghua University, China
Huaizhong Li	Lishui University, China
Quan-Lin Li	Yanshan University, China
Xiaoou Li	National Polytechnic Institute, Mexico
Hong Lu	Shanghai Polytechnic University, China
Zaixin Lu	Washington State University, USA
Mingzhang Luo	Yangtze University, China
Anisha Mazumder	Arizona State University, USA
Bivas Mitra	Indian Institute of Technology Kharagpur, India
Hien Nguyen	Ton Duc Thang University, Vietnam
Nam Nguyen	Towson University, USA
Wenlong Ni	JiangXi Normal University, China
NhatHai Phan	New Jersey Institute of Technology, USA
Shahrzad Shirazipourazad	Arizona State University, USA
Shensheng Tang	Missouri Western State University, USA
Nguyen Tran	The University of Sydney, Australia
Gaocai Wang	Guangxi University, China

Jiacun Wang	Monmouth University, USA
Jian Wang	Shanghai Polytechnic University, China
Jinting Wang	Beijing Jiaotong University, China
Ning Wang	Texas Southern University, USA
Zecheng Wang	Anhui University of Finance and Economics, China
Zhije Wang	Donghua University, China
Zidong Wang	Brunel University, UK
Xiaodong Xiong	Yangtze University, China
Zhen Xu	Beihang University, China
Guanglin Zhang	Donghua University, China
Xianzhong Zhou	Nanjing University, China
Jihong Zhu	Tsinghua University, China

Publicity Co-chairs

Xiang Li	Santa Clara University, USA
Mugen Peng	Beijing University of Posts and Telecommunications, China
Wenan Tan	Shanghai Polytechnic University, China

Local Organizing Committee Chair

| Chuang Ma | Shanghai Polytechnic University, China |

Financial Chair

| Thang Dinh | Virginia Commonwealth University, USA |

Web Chair

| J. David Smith | University of Florida, USA |

Contents

Short Papers

Minimizing Influence of Rumors
by Blockers on Social Networks

Ruidong Yan[1], Deying Li[1(✉)], Weili Wu[2], and Ding-Zhu Du[2]

[1] School of Information, Renmin University of China, Beijing 100872, China
{yanruidong,deyingli}@ruc.edu.cn
[2] Department of Computer Science, University of Texas at Dallas,
Richardson, TX 75080, USA
{weiliwu,dzdu}@utdallas.edu

Abstract. In recent years, with the rapid development of Internet technology, social networks such as Facebook, Twitter and Google+ have been integrated into daily life. These social networks not only help users stay in touch with family and friends, but also keep abreast of breaking news and emerging contents. However, in some scenarios, we need to take measures to control or limit the spread of negative information such as rumors. In this paper, we first propose the *Minimizing Influence of Rumor* (MIR) problem, i.e., selecting a blocker set $\mathcal{B}$ with k nodes such that the users' total activation probability from rumor source S is minimized on the network. Then we use classical *Independent Cascade* (IC) model as information diffusion model. Based on this model, we prove that the objective function is monotone decreasing and non-submodular. In order to solve MIR problem effectively, we propose a two-stages method named GCSSB that includes *Generating Candidate Set* and *Selecting Blockers* stages. Finally, we evaluate proposed method by simulations on synthetic and real-life social networks. Furthermore, we also compare with other heuristic methods such as Out-Degree, Betweenness Centrality and PageRank. Experimental results show that our method is superior to comparison approaches.

Keywords: Social influence · Rumor blocking · Social network
Submodularity · Greedy algorithm

1 Introduction

With the advance of the internet and computer technology, some significant social networks have been widely integrated into our daily life, such as Facebook, Twitter and Google+. Social networks can usually be represented as complex networks of nodes and edges, where nodes denote the individuals (people, organizations, or other social entities) and edges denote the social relationships

This work is partly supported by National Natural Science Foundation of China under grant 11671400 and National Science Foundation under grant 1747818.

between individuals (friendship, collaboration, or information interaction). These online social networks have become significant platforms that not only disseminate positive contents (ideas, opinions, innovations, interests and so on) but also negative contents such as rumors. It has been shown that rumors spread very fast and cause serious consequences [3]. For example, when the devastating wild-fires happens in California in October 2017, at the time the officers were evacuating residents and searching through the burned ruins of homes for missing persons they still had to deal with the fake news. Although the rumor was shot down by the officers and was debunked by some government websites afterwards, the original story was shared 60,000 times and similar stories was shared 75,000 times on Facebook.

In order to provide better service and accurate information, it is crucial to have an effective strategy to block or limit the negative effect of such rumors. Currently, the literature related to rumor blocking on social networks can be roughly divided into the following three categories: (1) Block rumors at influential nodes. This method usually selects the most influential nodes in the network based on certain criteria and remove these influential nodes from network such that rumor spreading is limited such as [6,10,14]; (2) Block rumors by deleting edges. This method usually removes a set of edges from network such that rumor spreading is as less as possible [8,9,13]; (3) Spread positive information (truth) to clarify rumors. It is based on the assumption that users will not adopt rumors once they adopt positive messages. Specifically, this method identifies a subset of nodes and disseminates positive information such that the positive information is adopted by as many individuals as possible [2,12].

In this paper, we study the novel problem how to control or limit the rumors spread (*Minimizing Influence of Rumors* (MIR)), i.e., identify a set $\mathcal{B}$ with k nodes and remove this set from network such that the total activation probability of nodes on the network is minimized. We call a node $v \in \mathcal{B}$ as a *blocker*. In order to solve MIR problem effectively, we propose a two-stages method named GCSSB that includes *generating candidate set* and *selecting blockers* stages. Specifically, in the first stage, we sort the nodes on the network to find top $\alpha * k$ nodes that have strong ability to disseminate the rumor, where α is a threshold parameter. And we generate a candidate set of blockers $\mathcal{C}$ by these $\alpha * k$ nodes. In the second stage, we design a basic greedy algorithm and select k nodes from the candidate set $\mathcal{C}$ according to the maximum marginal gain. Unlike previous researches, we have a preprocessing stage before we design the basic greedy algorithm. The advantage is that it can effectively reduce the time consumption of the greedy algorithm. In other words, we identify the blocker set based on the subgraph of these $\alpha * k$ nodes instead of the original network. We summarize our main contributions as follows:

- We formalize the *Minimizing Influence of Rumors* (MIR) problem and prove the objective function is not submodular under the *Independent Cascade* (IC) model.
- We propose a two-stages strategy named GCSSB to solve the MIR problem on social networks for the first time.

– In order to evaluate proposed algorithm, we use a synthetic and three real-life social networks with various scales in experiments. The extensive simulations conducted on these networks. Furthermore, we compare proposed method with other heuristic approaches. Experimental results validate that our method is superior to other approaches.

The rest of this paper is organized as follows. We first begin by recalling some existing related work of rumor blocking in Sect. 2. Then we introduce information diffusion model in Sect. 3. And we show the problem description and properties in Sect. 4. Algorithm is presented in Sect. 5. We analyze and discuss the results of the experiments in Sect. 6. Finally, we draw our conclusions in Sect. 7.

2   Related Work

Domingos et al. [4] first study the influence between users for marketing in social networks. Kempe et al. [7] model viral marketing as a discrete optimization problem, which is named *Influence Maximization* (IM). They propose a greedy algorithm with $(1 - 1/e)$-approximation ratio since the function is submodular under *Independent Cascade* (IC) or *Linear Threshold* (LT) model. Based on Kempe's contributions, there have been substantial efforts in modeling the propagation of information in recent years such as [15–17].

2.1   Blocking Nodes for Rumor

In [6], Fan et al. study the problem that identifies a minimal subset of individuals as initial protectors (the nodes are used to limit the bad influence of rumors.) to minimize the number of people infected in neighbor communities at the end of both diffusion processes. Authors propose algorithms under *Opportunistic One-Activate-One* and *Deterministic One-Activate-Many* models and show the theoretical analysis in detail. In [14], Wang et al. address the problem of minimizing the influence of rumor. In their paper, they assume a rumor emerges in the social network and part of users have already adopted it, their goal is to minimize the size of ultimately contaminated users by discovering and blocking k uninfected users. A greedy method for efficiently finding a good approximate solution to this problem is proposed. Unfortunately, they have no theoretical analysis. In social networks, how to identify the influential spreaders is crucial for rumors. Ma et al. in [10] propose a gravity centrality index to identify the influential spreaders in complex networks and compare with some well-known centralities, such as degree, betweenness, closeness, and so forth.

2.2   Blocking Links for Rumor

In [9], Kimura et al. propose a method (by blocking a limited number of links) for efficiently finding a good approximate solution to rumor blocking. In [8], Khalil et al. propose a edge deletion problem and optimize the topology of a networked system to bring a flu under control. They show this problem is supermodular under the LT model. And this surprising property allows them to design efficient data structures and scalable algorithms with provable approximation guarantees. In [13], Tong et al. propose effective and scalable algorithms to solve dissemination problems and answer which edges should be deleted in order to contain a rumor.

2.3 Spreading Positive Truth for Rumor

In [2], Budak et al. propose the problem that identifying a subset of individuals that need to be convinced to adopt the competing (or good) campaign so as to minimize the number of people that adopt the bad campaign at the end of both propagation processes. And they show this problem is NP-hard and provide a greedy algorithm. In [12], Tong et al. study the rumor blocking problem that asks for k seed users to trigger the spread of a positive cascade such that the number of the users who are not influenced by rumor can be maximized. They present a randomized approximation algorithm which is provably superior to the state-of-the art methods with respect to running time.

3   Information Diffusion Model

In this section, we briefly introduce influence diffusion model: *Independent Cascade* (IC) model which is first proposed by [7]. Given a directed social network that can be denoted by a graph $G = (V, E, p)$, where V represents users (node set), $E \subseteq V \times V$ represents the relationships between users (edge set), and p_{uv} of edge (u, v) denotes the probability that node u can activate v successfully. We call a node as *active* if it adopts the information (rumor) from other nodes, *inactive* otherwise. Influence propagation process unfolds discrete time steps t_i, where $i = 0, 1, ...$ Initial source nodes of rumor $S_{t_0} = S$ (seed set). Let S_{t_i} denote *active* nodes in time step t_i, and each node u in S_{t_i} has single chance to activate each *inactive* neighbor v through its out-edge with probability p_{uv} at time step t_{i+1}. Repeat this process until no more new nodes can be activated. Note that a node can only switch from *inactive* to *active*, but not in the reverse direction.

4   Problem Description and Properties

4.1   Problem Description

Given a directed social network $G = (V, E, p)$, an information diffusion model $\mathcal{M}$, a rumor source set S and a positive integer budget k, where V denotes user set, $E \subseteq V \times V$ denotes the relationships between users, and p_{uv} of edge (u, v) denotes the probability that u activates v successfully. We define the activation probability of a node $v \in V$ when given S under model $\mathcal{M}$ as follow

$$Pr_{\mathcal{M}}(v, S) = \begin{cases} 1, & \text{if } v \in S \\ 0, & \text{if } N^{in}(v) = \emptyset \\ 1 - \displaystyle\prod_{u \in N^{in}(v)} (1 - Pr_{\mathcal{M}}(u, S)p_{uv}), & \text{otherwise.} \end{cases} \quad (1)$$

Where $N^{in}(v)$ is the set of in-neighbors of v and $Pr_{\mathcal{M}}(u, S)p_{uv}$ represents the probability u successfully activates v under the diffusion model $\mathcal{M}$ (Here, $\mathcal{M}$ is IC model). As we can clearly see the activation probability of a node v depends on the its in-neighbors u. Then we give the problem description as follow

Definition 1. *Minimizing Influence of Rumor (MIR). Given a directed social network $G = (V, E, p)$, a rumor source set S, a positive integer budget k, and the IC model $\mathcal{M}$, MIR aims to find a blocker set $\mathcal{B}$ with k nodes such that*

$$\mathcal{B}^* = \arg \min_{\mathcal{B} \subseteq V \setminus S, |\mathcal{B}| = k} \sum_{v \in V \setminus \{S \cup \mathcal{B}\}} Pr_{\mathcal{M}}(v, S). \quad (2)$$

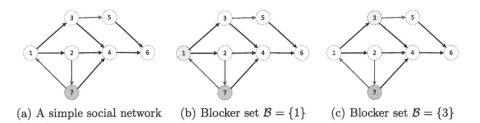

(a) A simple social network   (b) Blocker set $\mathcal{B} = \{1\}$ (c) Blocker set $\mathcal{B} = \{3\}$

Fig. 1. An example shows calculating the value of objective function when $k = 1$. Figure 1(a) shows a simple social network where green node indicates the rumor source $S = \{7\}$. Figure 1(b) shows that selecting node 1 as a blocker. Figure 1(c) shows that selecting node 3 as a blocker. (Color figure online)

Figure 1 shows how to calculate the objective function value when $k = 1$ under the IC model. In Fig. 1, in order to simplify the calculation, we set all the propagation probabilities to be 1. And green node is rumor source $S = \{7\}$. On one hand, S can activate two nodes (node 4 and 6) when we select node 1 as a blocker. Therefore $\sum_{v \in V \setminus \{S \cup \mathcal{B}\}} Pr_{\mathcal{M}}(v, S) = 2$. On the other hand, S can activate four nodes (node 1, 2, 4 and 6) when we select node 3 as a blocker. Therefore $\sum_{v \in V \setminus \{S \cup \mathcal{B}\}} Pr_{\mathcal{M}}(v, S) = 4$. Obviously, in the above two cases, it is more appropriate to select node 1 as a blocker instead of node 3.

4.2   Properties of Objective Function

Theorem 1. *The objective function (2) is monotone decreasing and not submodular under the IC model.*

Proof. A set function f is monotone decreasing if $f(A) \geq f(B)$ whenever $A \subseteq B$. It is obvious that the objective function is monotone decreasing in our MIR problem, because the more blockers we choose, the smaller the objective function will be. We omit its proof.

Then we show the objective function is not submodular. If V is a finite set, a submodular function is a set function $f : 2^V \to \Re$, where 2^V denotes the power set of V, satisfies the following condition: for every $A \subseteq B \subseteq V$ and $x \in V \backslash B$, $f(A \cup \{x\}) - f(A) \geq f(B \cup \{x\}) - f(B)$. Going back to the example mentioned in Fig. 1, we let $S = \{7\}$, $f = \sum_{v \in V \backslash \{S \cup B\}} Pr_{\mathcal{M}}(v, S)$, $A = \{4\}$, $B = \{3, 4\}$ and $x = \{1\}$. Thus $f(A) = 5$ and $f(A \cup \{x\}) = 0$. And $f(B) = 2$ and $f(B \cup \{x\}) = 0$. Therefore $f(A \cup \{x\}) - f(A) < f(B \cup \{x\}) - f(B)$. It indicates non-submodularity.

5   Algorithm

In this section, we propose a two-stages method GCSSB which includes generating candidate set and selecting blockers stages. We introduce them in Sects. 5.1 and 5.2 respectively.

$$
A = \begin{bmatrix} 0 & 0.5 & 0.5 & 0 & 0 & 0 & 0 \\ 0 & 0 & 0 & 0.5 & 0 & 0 & 0.5 \\ 0 & 0 & 0 & 0.5 & 0.5 & 0 & 0 \\ 0 & 0 & 0 & 0 & 0 & 0.5 & 0 \\ 0 & 0 & 0 & 0 & 0 & 0.5 & 0 \\ 0 & 0 & 0 & 0 & 0 & 0 & 0 \\ 0.5 & 0 & 0 & 0.5 & 0 & 0 & 0 \end{bmatrix} I = \begin{bmatrix} 1 \\ 1 \\ 1 \\ 1 \\ 1 \\ 1 \\ 1 \end{bmatrix}, AI = \begin{bmatrix} 1 \\ 1 \\ 1 \\ 0.5 \\ 0.5 \\ 0 \\ 1 \end{bmatrix}, A^2 I = \begin{bmatrix} 1 \\ 0.75 \\ 0.5 \\ 0 \\ 0 \\ 0 \\ 0.75 \end{bmatrix} \dots A^5 I = \begin{bmatrix} 0.125 \\ 0.156 \\ 0 \\ 0 \\ 0 \\ 0 \\ 0.094 \end{bmatrix}, \sigma = I + AI \dots + A^5 I = \begin{bmatrix} 3.938 \\ 3.531 \\ 2.5 \\ 1.5 \\ 1.5 \\ 1 \\ 3.656 \end{bmatrix}
$$

(a) Adjacent matrix   (b) $\sigma = I + AI + \dots A^5 I$

Fig. 2. An example with propagation probability $p = 0.5$. Figure 2(a) shows the adjacent matrix where $A_{ij} = 0.5$ means there is a directed edge from i to j. Figure 2(b) shows how to calculate σ.

5.1   Generating Candidate Set

Given a directed social network $G = (V, E, p)$ and a rumor source set S, we first sort nodes on the network. The purpose of sorting is to determine the candidate set of blockers and reduce time consuming by the greedy algorithm in second stage. Intuitively, we will choose the nodes with strong spreading ability as blockers rather than those nodes with weak spreading ability. Therefore, how to measure the spreading ability of nodes becomes a key issue.

Here, we define $\sigma = I + AI + \dots A^r I$, where A denotes the adjacent matrix of network, I denotes unit column vector and $1 \leq r \leq |V|$. As we all know, A_{ij}^r denotes the approximation probability that i activates j through a path of length r. Therefore σ denotes its total probability. For example, Fig. 2(a) shows the adjacent matrix of the network in Fig. 1 when propagation probability $p = 0.5$.

Figure 2(b) shows $\sigma = I + AI + ...A^r I = (3.938, 3.531, 2.5, 1.5, 1.5, 1, 3.656)^T$ where $r = 5$. And we sort σ in descending order. Then we obtain permutation $\Pi = (3.938, 3.656, 3.531, 2.5, 1.5, 1.5, 1)^T$ and choose the top $\alpha * k$ nodes as the candidate set of blockers $\mathcal{C}$ where α is a threshold parameter. Consistent with the example mentioned earlier, we choose node 1 instead of node 3 because $\sigma_1 = 3.938 > \sigma_3 = 2.5$ when $k = 1$.

5.2 Selecting Blockers

In Subsect. 5.1, we determine the candidate set of the blockers $\mathcal{C}$. And, in this subsection, we introduce how to accurately select k blockers. Specifically, we propose a greedy algorithm based on maximum marginal gain. We first give the definition of marginal gain.

Definition 2. *(Marginal Gain). Given a directed social network $G = (V, E, p)$, a rumor source set S and information diffusion model $\mathcal{M}$, for any node $x \in V \backslash S$, let*

$$\Delta(x|S) = \sum_{v \in V \backslash S} Pr_{\mathcal{M}}(v, S) - \sum_{v \in V \backslash \{S \cup \{x\}\}} Pr_{\mathcal{M}}(v, S) \tag{3}$$

be marginal gain of S with respect to x.

Obviously, our algorithm focuses on the maximum marginal gain of nodes in candidate $\mathcal{C}$. We define following

Definition 3. *(Maximum Marginal Gain). For any node $x \in \mathcal{C}$, let*

$$x^* = \arg\max_{x \in \mathcal{C}} \Delta(x|S) = \arg\max_{x \in \mathcal{C}} (\sum_{v \in V \backslash S} Pr_{\mathcal{M}}(v, S) - \sum_{v \in V \backslash \{S \cup \{x\}\}} Pr_{\mathcal{M}}(v, S)) \tag{4}$$

be the maximum marginal gain of S with respect to x.

Based on the above definitions, we propose our greedy algorithm. We first start with the empty set, i.e., $\mathcal{B} = \emptyset$. Then, in the t-th iteration, we add the node x_t with the maximum marginal gain. The algorithm executes k times until k blockers are selected. The greedy algorithm is shown in Algorithm 1.

Let us analyze the complexity of the Algorithm 1. The loop from line 2 to 9 at most runs k times. In each iteration, the inner loop runs at most $|\mathcal{C}|$ times and it takes at most $O(|E|)$ time to calculate $\Delta(x|S)$. Therefore, the total time complexity is $O(k|\mathcal{C}||E|)$ in the worst case.

6 Experiment

In this section, we evaluate proposed algorithm on synthetic and real-life networks. First, we describe the data sets and experiment setup. Second, we analyze and discuss experimental results from different perspectives. Finally, we compare with other heuristic approaches.

Algorithm 1 . Greedy Algorithm (GA)

Input: $G = (V, E, p)$, $\mathcal{M}$, S, $\mathcal{C}$ and k.
Output: $\mathcal{B}$.
1: $\mathcal{B}_0 \leftarrow \emptyset$, $\Delta(x|S) = 0$ for $x \in \mathcal{C}$;
2: **for** $t = 1$ to k **do**
3:    **for** each $x \in \mathcal{C}$ **do**
4:        $\Delta(x|S) = \sum_{v \in V \setminus \{S \cup \mathcal{B}_t\}} Pr_{\mathcal{M}}(v, S) - \sum_{v \in V \setminus \{S \cup \mathcal{B}_t \cup \{x\}\}} Pr_{\mathcal{M}}(v, S)$;
5:    **end for**
6:    $x^* = \arg \max_{x \in \mathcal{C}} \Delta(x|S)$;
7:    $\mathcal{B}_t \leftarrow \mathcal{B}_t \cup \{x^*\}$;
8:    $\mathcal{C} \leftarrow \mathcal{C} \setminus \{x^*\}$;
9: **end for**
10: **return** $\mathcal{B} \leftarrow \mathcal{B}_t$.

6.1   Data Sets

We generate a random network and collect three real-life social networks with various scale from *Stanford Large Network Dataset Collection* (SNAP)[1] and the *Koblenz Network Collection* (KONECT)[2] respectively. Table 1 provides the details of these data sets. In table, 'CC' represents clustering coefficient and 'MD' represents the maximum degree.

Table 1. The details of synthetic and real-life social data sets.

Data Sets	Relationship	#Node	#Edge	CC	MD	Diameter
Synthetic	Synthetic	2000	10000	-	62	6
Wiki Vote	Voting	7,115	103,663	0.14	875	7
Twitter Lists	Following	23,370	33,101	0.02	239	15
Google+	Friend sharing	23,628	39,242	0.03	2,771	8

- **Synthetic** (SYN). We randomly generate a graph using Erdos-Renyi model [5] which assigns equal probability η to all nodes. The higher assigned probability is, the more dense the graph is. In experiments, we let $\eta = 0.5$.
- **Wiki Vote** (WV). This network contains all the Wikipedia voting data from the inception of Wikipedia till January 2008. Nodes in the network represent wikipedia users and a directed edge from node u to node v represents that user u voted on user v.
- **Twitter Lists** (TL). This directed network contains Twitter user-user following information. A node represents a user. An edge indicates that the user represented by the left node follows the user represented by the right node.

---

[1] http://snap.stanford.edu/data.
[2] http://konect.uni-koblenz.de.

– **Google+** (G+). This directed network contains Google+ user-user links. A node represents a user, and a directed edge denotes that one user has the other user in his circles.

6.2   Experiment Setup

We make the following setup for rumor spreading process: Given a directed social network $G = (V, E, p)$, 1% of nodes are selected randomly and uniformly from V as rumor source set S. In our all experiments, we adopt *Independent Cascade* (IC) model as information diffusion model. In particular, we assign p in two ways since the data sets lack propagation probability p. One assigns a uniform probability $p = 0.5$ for each edge on the networks. Another assigns a trivalency model $p = TRI$ for each edge, i.e., we uniformly select a value from $\{0.1, 0.01, 0.01\}$ at random that corresponds to high, medium and low propagation probabilities. Notice that all networks are simple networks[3].

Comparison Methods: To compare with existing methods, other heuristic methods such as **Out-Degree**, **Betweenness Centrality** and **PageRank** are selected as comparison methods. Our two-stage approach is abbreviated as GCSSB.

– **Out-Degree** (OD) [7]. The out-degree of a node v is the number of outgoing edges from the node v. Kempe et al. shows high degree nodes may outperform other centrality-based heuristics in terms of influential identification.
– **Betweenness Centrality** (BC) [1]. A nodes betweenness is equal to the number of shortest paths from all nodes to all others that pass through that node. Recently, betweenness centrality has become an important centrality measure in social networks.
– **PageRank** (PR) [11]. This is widely known Google Page-Rank measure. The pagerank score indicates the importance of a node. There is a damping factor parameter and we set it to 0.9 in all experiments.

Evaluation Criteria: The experimental evaluation is carried out from the following aspects: (1) parameter α study. In our GCSSB method, we need to generate candidate set $\mathcal{C}$ with $\alpha * k$ nodes. (2) parameter k study. We study the relationship between the size of the blocker set and the objective function value. (3) Compare with other methods. We compare GCSSB with other heuristic methods such as Out-Degree, Betweenness Centrality and PageRank. Our evaluation criteria is objective function value (total activation probability). A smaller function value indicates that the algorithm is better.

---

[3]   Self-loops and multiple edges are not allowed.

6.3   Results

Parameter α Study: We study the effect of candidate set size (parameter α) on the objective function value (total activation probability). The experimental results are shown in Fig. 3. Figure 3(a) and (b) show the propagation probability $p = 0.5$ and $p = TRI$, respectively. The results on each network show the same trends in both subgraphs. Taking Fig. 3(a) as an example, the horizontal axis and the vertical axis represent the parameter α and the total activation probability, respectively. The total activation probability decreases as the parameter α increases. In particular, the total acceptance probability remains essentially the same when $\alpha \geq 6$. Therefore we let $\alpha = 6$ in latter experiments.

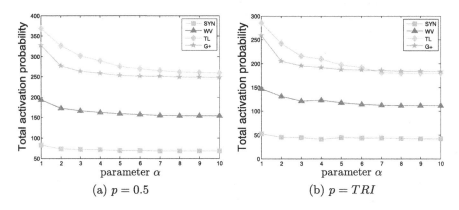

(a) $p = 0.5$ (b) $p = TRI$

Fig. 3. Total activation probability Vs. Parameter α under IC model: rumor source $|S| = 1\%|V|$ on each network, $p = 0.5$ or $p = TRI$, and $k = 50$.

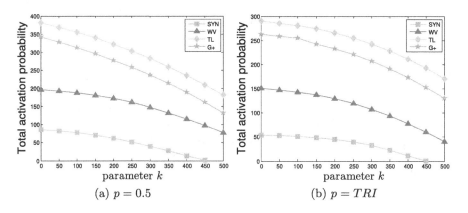

(a) $p = 0.5$ (b) $p = TRI$

Fig. 4. Total activation probability Vs. Parameter k under IC model: rumor source $|S| = 1\%|V|$ on each network, $p = 0.5$ or $p = TRI$, and $\alpha = 6$.

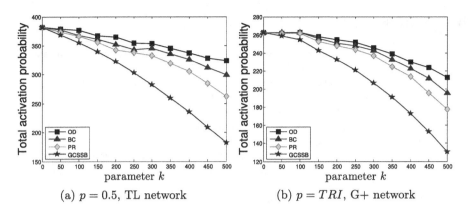

(a) $p = 0.5$, TL network   (b) $p = TRI$, G+ network

Fig. 5. Compare with other methods: rumor source $|S| = 1\%|V|$, $p = 0.5$ on TL network or $p = TRI$ on G+ network, and $\alpha = 6$.

Parameter k Study: We study the relationship between the size of the blocker set and the total activation probability. The experimental results are shown in Fig. 4. In the subfigures, the horizontal and vertical axes represent the parameter k and the total activation probability, respectively. Through experiments, we observe that the total activation probability decreases as k increases. In particular, it is drastically reduced when $k > 300$ on each network.

Comparing with Other Methods: We compare our GCSSB with other methods (OD, BC and PR). The experimental results are shown in Fig. 5. The horizontal and vertical axes represent the parameter k and the total activation probability, respectively. In both subfigures, The total activation probability decreases as k increases. We observe that the proposed method is the best since the total activation probability is the smallest. Moreover, in comparison methods, the PR's performance is the best but the OD is the worst.

7 Conclusions

In this paper, we study a novel problem called *Minimizing Influence of Rumor* (MIR) problem that finds a small size blocker set such that the activation probability of users on network is minimized. Based on IC model, we prove objective function satisfies non-submodularity. We develop a two-stages method GCSSB to identify blocker set. Furthermore, in order to evaluate our proposed method, extensive experiments have been conducted. The experiment results show that our method outperforms comparison approaches.

References

1. Brandes, U.: On variants of shortest-path betweenness centrality and their generic computation. Soc. Netw. **30**(2), 136–145 (2008)
2. Budak, C., Agrawal, D., El Abbadi, A.: Limiting the spread of misinformation in social networks. In: Proceedings of the 20th International Conference on World Wide Web, pp. 665–674. ACM (2011)
3. Doerr, B., Fouz, M., Friedrich, T.: Why rumors spread so quickly in social networks. Commun. ACM **55**(6), 70–75 (2012)
4. Domingos, P., Richardson, M.: Mining the network value of customers. In: Proceedings of the Seventh ACM SIGKDD International Conference on Knowledge Discovery and Data Mining, pp. 57–66. ACM (2001)
5. ERDdS, P., R&WI, A.: On random graphs i. Publ. Math. Debrecen **6**, 290–297 (1959)
6. Fan, L., Lu, Z., Wu, W., Thuraisingham, B., Ma, H., Bi, Y.: Least cost rumor blocking in social networks. In: 2013 IEEE 33rd International Conference on Distributed Computing Systems (ICDCS), pp. 540–549. IEEE (2013)
7. Kempe, D., Kleinberg, J., Tardos, É.: Maximizing the spread of influence through a social network. In: Proceedings of the Ninth ACM SIGKDD International Conference on Knowledge Discovery and Data Mining, pp. 137–146. ACM (2003)
8. Khalil, E.B., Dilkina, B., Song, L.: Scalable diffusion-aware optimization of network topology. In: Proceedings of the 20th ACM SIGKDD International Conference on Knowledge Discovery and Data Mining, pp. 1226–1235. ACM (2014)
9. Kimura, M., Saito, K., Motoda, H.: Minimizing the spread of contamination by blocking links in a network. In: AAAI, vol. 8, pp. 1175–1180 (2008)
10. Ma, L.L., Ma, C., Zhang, H.F., Wang, B.H.: Identifying influential spreaders in complex networks based on gravity formula. Phys. A Stat. Mech. Appl. **451**, 205–212 (2016)
11. Page, L., Brin, S., Motwani, R., Winograd, T., et al.: The PageRank citation ranking: bringing order to the web (1998)
12. Tong, G., et al.: An efficient randomized algorithm for rumor blocking in online social networks. IEEE Trans. Netw. Sci. Eng. (2017)
13. Tong, H., Prakash, B.A., Eliassi-Rad, T., Faloutsos, M., Faloutsos, C.: Gelling, and melting, large graphs by edge manipulation. In: Proceedings of the 21st ACM International Conference on Information and Knowledge Management, pp. 245–254. ACM (2012)
14. Wang, S., Zhao, X., Chen, Y., Li, Z., Zhang, K., Xia, J.: Negative influence minimizing by blocking nodes in social networks. In: AAAI (Late-Breaking Developments), pp. 134–136 (2013)
15. Wen, S., Haghighi, M.S., Chen, C., Xiang, Y., Zhou, W., Jia, W.: A sword with two edges: propagation studies on both positive and negative information in online social networks. IEEE Trans. Comput. **64**(3), 640–653 (2015)
16. Yan, R., Zhu, Y., Li, D., Ye, Z.: Minimum cost seed set for threshold influence problem under competitive models. World Wide Web 1–20 (2018)
17. Zhu, Y., Li, D., Zhang, Z.: Minimum cost seed set for competitive social influence. In: IEEE INFOCOM 2016-The 35th Annual IEEE International Conference on Computer Communications, pp. 1–9. IEEE (2016)

Budgeted Competitive Influence Maximization on Online Social Networks

Canh V. Pham$^{1,2(\boxtimes)}$, Hieu V. Duong^2, Bao Q. Bui^2, and My T. Thai^3

^{1} University of Engineering and Technology, Vietnam National University,
Hanoi, Viet Nam
maicanhki@gmail.com
^{2} Faculty of Information and Security, People's Security Academy, Hanoi, Viet Nam
dvhieubg95@gmail.com, buiquybao.c500@gmail.com
^{3} Department of Computer and Information Science and Engineering,
University of Florida, Gainesville, FL 32611, USA
mythai@cise.ufl.edu

Abstract. Influence Maximization (IM) is one of the key problems in viral marketing which has been paid much attention recently. Basically, IM focuses on finding a set of k seed users on a social network to maximize the expected number of influenced nodes. However, most of related works consider only one player without competitors. In this paper, we investigate the Budgeted Competitive Influence Maximization (BCIM) problem within limited budget and time constraints which seeks a seed set nodes of a player or a company to propagate their products's information while at the same time their competitors are conducting a similar strategy. We first analyze the complexity of this problem and show that the objective function is neither submodular nor suppermodular. We then apply Sandwich framework to design SPBA, a randomized algorithm that guarantees a data dependent approximation factor.

Keywords: Social network · Competitive Influence Maximization
Approximation algorithm

1 Introduction

Online social network (OSN) has recently been a very effective mean in diffusing information, propagating opinions or ideas. Many companies have leveraged word-of-mouth effect in OSNs to promote their products. The key problem of viral marketing is Influence Maximization (IM), which aims to select a set of k users (called *seed set*) in a social networks with maximum influence spread. Kempe *et al.* [8] first formulated IM problem in two diffusion models, named Linear Threshold (LT) and Independent Cascade (IC), which simulated the propagation of influence through social networks. This problem has been widely studied due to its important role in viral marketing [2, 10, 14, 16, 17].

© Springer Nature Switzerland AG 2018
X. Chen et al. (Eds.): CSoNet 2018, LNCS 11280, pp. 13–24, 2018.
https://doi.org/10.1007/978-3-030-04648-4_2

However, all of above mentioned studies only focus on studying influence propagation of single player or company in social networks. In the context of competing in product promotions, there are many competitors simultaneously implement the same strategy of marketing spread on OSNs. This phenomenon requires the task of maximizing a product's influences under competitive circumstances, called Competitive Influence Maximization (CIM) problem, thus it has been received much attention recently [1, 3, 4, 11–13, 18].

Bharathi *et al.* [1] first proposed CIM problem, which seeks a seed set to maximize the propagation of their products information while their competitors carry out the same strategy. Since then, related works have tried to investigate CIM in different contexts. Some authors proposed algorithms to solve CIM problem base on the *submodularity* of the objective function. It provided a $(1 - 1/e)$-approximation when applying natural greedy algorithm. For example, Lu *et al.* [12] studied the problem in context of fair competitive influence from the host perspective. Chen *et al.* [4] proposed independent cascade model with negative opinions by extend IC model and showed a greedy algorithm with the approximation ratio of $1 - 1/e$. Lui *et al.* [11] consider CIM problem under Diffusion-Containment model and present a $(1 - 1/e)$-approximation algorithm. Recently, some works approached in other directions, including: design community-based algorithm [3], find the seed set with minimum cost set for threshold competitive influence problem [18], and proposed competition and complementary approaches by extending IC model [13].

Although previous works tried to solve the CIM problem in many circumstances, the feasibility of the existing works is limited due to following reasons. Firstly, they do not take into account time constraint and cost to initialize a user as seed for CIM. In a more realistic scenario, the effectiveness of competitive influence process depends very much on these two factors. Secondly, for the problems related to information diffusion the complexity of calculating the objective function is enormous. Some works using Mote-Carlo method to estimate the objective value for any seed set [3, 4, 8]. However, the method requires high complexity, and it takes several hours even on very small networks.

In this paper, we introduce the problem named *Budgeted Competitive Influence Maximization* (BCIM) which takes into account both arbitrary cost for selecting a node in set seed and time constraint for competitive influence process. The BCIM problem is more general than CIM. To simulate the competitive influence propagation process, we propose Time constraint Competitive Linear Threshold (TCLT), which extend Competitive Competitive Linear Threshold [5, 7] with incorporation propagation hop.

The main challenges of this problem lie in following aspects. Firstly, under TCLT, BCIM problem is NP-hard problem and it is #P-Hard to calculate the objective function. Secondly, we point out the objective function is neither submodular nor supermodular. It makes BCIM cannot be easily solved using greedy-based algorithms, as well as methods for influence maximization. To address the above challenges, in this article, we present SPBA, an efficient randomized algorithm based on polling method and Sandwich approximation framework [13]. Our main contributions are summarized as follows:

- We formulate TCLT model by extending Competitive Competitive Linear Threshold model in [5,7] to simulate competitive influence within time constraint τ. Given two competitors A and B who need to advertise their productions on OSNs, assume that we know nodes which are activated by B (B-seed set), with the limited budget L and heterogeneous costs for nodes in a social network, we propose BCIM problem which aims to seek A-seed set nodes within limited budget L and time constraint τ to maximize influence nodes by A under TCLT model. We then show that BCIM is NP-hard and the objective function is not *submodular* nor *supermodular*.
- We propose SPBA, an efficient randomize algorithm based on Sandwich approximation and polling method. We first design a *upper* bound submodular function of the objective function and develop a polling-based approximation algorithm to find the solution of bound functions. Next, we apply Sandwich framework in [13], which give a data-dependent approximation factor.

Road Map. The rest of paper is organized as follows. We introduce propagation models, problem definition and its properties in Sect. 2. Section 3 present our proposed algorithm. Finally, we give some tasks for future work and conclusion in Sect. 4.

2   Models and Problem Definition

In this section, we first define the TCLT model, which is an extension of CLT model in [5,7]. The main difference between our model and CLT model is that we only consider propagation process in limited propagation hop (step) τ. Based on that, we define the BCIM problem. Table 1 summarizes the frequently used notations.

Table 1. Notations

Notations	Descriptions
n, m	the number of nodes and the number of edges
$N_-(v), N_+(v)$	the sets of incoming, and outgoing neighbor nodes of v
$\mathbb{I}(\cdot), \mathbb{U}(\cdot)$	The expected number of A-active nodes, and its upper bound, respectively
S^*, S_U^*	Optimal solution for BCIM, maximum $\mathbb{I}(\cdot)$, and $\mathbb{U}(\cdot)$
OPT, OPT$_u$	$\mathbb{I}(S^*), \mathbb{U}(S_U^*)$
$\Upsilon(\epsilon, \delta)$	$(1+\epsilon)(2+\frac{2}{3}\epsilon)\ln\frac{2}{\delta}\frac{1}{\epsilon^2}$
$\mathsf{Cov}_{\mathcal{R}}(S)$	the number of URR sets R_j be covered by S
$\hat{\mathbb{U}}(S)$	$\hat{\mathbb{U}}(S) = \frac{1}{|\mathcal{R}|}\mathsf{Cov}_{\mathcal{R}}(S)$ an estimation of $\mathbb{U}$ over URR sets $\mathcal{R}$
k_{max}	$\max\{k : \exists A \subseteq V, c(A) \leq L\}$

2.1   Time Constraint Competitive Influence Model

In this model, a social network is abstracted by a directed graph $G = (V, E)$, where V is the set of nodes (or vertices) representing users and E is the set of edges representing links among users. There are two competitors A and B want to promote their products in a social network G. Each edge $(u, v) \in E$ has two weights $w_A(u, v)$ and $w_B(u, v)$ represent the influence of A and B on edge (u, v), respectively. The weights satisfies condition $\sum_{u \in V} w_A(u, v) \leq 1$, $\sum_{u \in V} w_B(u, v) \leq 1, \forall v \in V$. Each node can chose one of three status: A-active, B-active, and inactive which represent the node is successfully activated by A, activated by B, and has not been activated by both A and B, respectively. Each node v picks two independent thresholds $\theta_A(v), \theta_B(v)$ uniformly from $[0, 1]$, called A-threshold and B-threshold.

Given a limited propagation hop τ, the propagation happen in discrete steps $t = 0, 1, \ldots, \tau$. Denote S_A and S_B are the seed sets of competitors A and B (called A-seed set and B-seed set). A_t and B_t are the set of A-active and B-active nodes at step t, respectively. The process of propagation operates as follow:

– At step $t = 0$, $A_0 = S_A, B_0 = S_B$.
– At step $t \geq 1$, each node $v \notin A_{t-1} \cap B_{t-1}$ becomes A-active if

$$\sum_{u \in N_-(v) \cap A_{t-1}} w_A(u, v) \geq \theta_A(v) \text{ and } \sum_{u \in N_-(v) \cap B_{t-1}} w_B(u, v) < \theta_B(v) \quad (1)$$

Node v becomes B-active if

$$\sum_{u \in N_-(v) \cap B_{t-1}} w_B(u, v) \geq \theta_B(v) \text{ and } \sum_{u \in N_-(v) \cap A_{t-1}} w_A(u, v) < \theta_A(v) \quad (2)$$

– If in step t, a node v has

$$\sum_{u \in N_-(v) \cap A_{t-1}} w_A(u, v) \geq \theta_A(v) \text{ and } \sum_{u \in N_-(v) \cap B_{t-1}} w_B(u, v) \geq \theta_B(v) \quad (3)$$

We use tie-breaking rule to determine its state. Accordingly, v is A-activated with probability

$$p_A(v|A_{t-1}, B_{t-1}) = \frac{\sum_{u \in N_-(v) \cap A_{t-1}} w_A(u, v)}{\sum_{u \in N_-(v) \cap A_{t-1}} w_A(u, v) + \sum_{u \in N_-(v) \cap B_{t-1}} w_B(u, v)}$$

and v is B-activated with probability

$$p_B(v|A_{t-1}, B_{t-1}) = \frac{\sum_{u \in N_-(v) \cap B_{t-1}} w_B(u, v)}{\sum_{u \in N_-(v) \cap A_{t-1}} w_A(u, v) + \sum_{u \in N_-(v) \cap B_{t-1}} w_B(u, v)}$$

– Once a node becomes activated (A-active or B-active), it remain status in next steps. The propagation process ends after τ hops of propagation.

2.2   Live-Edge Model

We follow the method in [7] to construct a *live-edge* model and prove this model is equivalent to TCLT model.

Live-Edge Construction. From original graph $G = (V, E)$ and weights w_A and w_B, respectively, we construct *sample* graph (or *realization*) g from G as follows: For each $v \in V$, we randomly select one in-edge (u, v) with probability $w_A(u, v)$, and do not select any in-edge with probability $1 - \sum_{u \in V} w_A(u, v)$. The selected edge is called *A-edge*. On the other hand, we also randomly select one in-edge (u, v) (called *B*-edge) with probability $w_B(u, v)$, and do not select any in-edge with probability $1 - \sum_{u \in V} w_B(u, v)$. Let g_A, g_B be the sub-graph including only *A*-edges and *B*-edges, respectively. Finally, we return g as union of g_A and g_B.

A-*active* Nodes and B-*active* Nodes Distribution on Live-Edge Model. On a live-edge g, we denote A'_t and B'_t are set of *A*-active and *B*-active nodes on g at step t. The distribution of *A*-active and *B*-active nodes in g was be happen in discrete steps t as follows:

- At step $t = 0$, $A'_t = S_A$ and $B'_t = S_B$
- At step $t \geq 1$, a node $v \notin A'_{t-1} \cup B'_{t-1}$ becomes *A-active* if v reachable from A'_{t-1} in one step in g_A (i.e., $d_A(A'_{t-1}, v) = 1$) and but not reachable from B'_{t-1} in one step in g_B (i.e., $d_B(B'_{t-1}, v) > 1$), then v is in A'_t. Symmetrically, if v reachable from B'_{t-1} in one step in g_A but not reachable from A'_{t-1} in one step in g_B, then v is in B'_t.
- If at step $t \geq 1$, v is reachable from A'_{t-1} in one step in g_B and reachable from B'_{t-1} in one step in g_B, v is *A*-activated with probability

$$p_A(v|A'_{t-1}, B'_{t-1}) = \frac{\sum_{u \in N_-(v) \cap A'_{t-1}} w_A(u, v)}{\sum_{u \in N_-(v) \cap A'_{t-1}} w_A(u, v) + \sum_{u \in N_-(v) \cap B'_{t-1}} w_B(u, v)}$$

and v is *B*-activated with probability

$$p_B(v|A'_{t-1}, B'_{t-1}) = \frac{\sum_{u \in N_-(v) \cap B'_{t-1}} w_A(u, v)}{\sum_{u \in N_-(v) \cap A'_{t-1}} w_A(u, v) + \sum_{u \in N_-(v) \cap B'_{t-1}} w_B(u, v)}$$

- The process of propagation ends after hop $t = \tau$ or no more nodes be activated.

We demonstrate the equivalence of two models through the following theorem

Theorem 1. *For a given A-seed set S_A and B-seed set S_B, the distribution over A-active sets and B-active node sets at hop t for any $t = 1, 2.., \tau$ on TCLT model and live-edge model are equivalent.*

The proof of Theorems and Lemmas were presented in Appendix due to space constraint. Denote X_G is the set of sample graphs generated from G and $\Pr[g|G]$ denotes the probability of generating sample graph g in G, we have:

$$\Pr[g|G] = \Pr[g_A|G] \cdot \Pr[g_B|G] = \prod_{v \in V} p_A(v, G, g) \cdot \prod_{v \in V} p_B(v, G, g) \quad (4)$$

where

$$p_A(v, G, g) = \begin{cases} w_A(u, v), & \text{If } \exists u : (u, v) \in E(g_A) \\ 1 - \sum_{u:(u,v) \in E} w_A(u, v), & \text{Otherwise} \end{cases} \quad (5)$$

$$p_B(v, G, g) = \begin{cases} w_B(u, v), & \text{If } \exists u : (u, v) \in E(g_B) \\ 1 - \sum_{u:(u,v) \in E} w_B(u, v), & \text{Otherwise} \end{cases} \quad (6)$$

$E(g_A)$ and $E(g_B)$ are the set edges of g_A and g_B, respectively. Denote $\mathbb{I}_B^\tau(A)$ is the expected number of A-active nodes after τ hops with B is given. For convenience, we simply $\mathbb{I}_B^\tau(S_A)$ as $\mathbb{I}(S_A)$ due to B and τ are constants in this work. Based on result of Theorem 1, we have $\mathbb{I}(A) = \sum_{g \in X_G} \Pr[g|G]\mathbb{I}(g, A)$. Where $\mathbb{I}(g, S_A)$ is the expected number of A-*active* nodes in g under live-edge model.

2.3   Budgeted Competitive Influence Maximization Problem

In this paper, we assume that we know B-seed set $S_B \subset V$ and each node is associated with an arbitrary cost $c(v)$ to add in A-seed set S_A. We define *Budgeted Competitive Influence Maximization* (BCIM) as follow:

Definition 1 (BCIM problem). *Given a directed graph $G = (V, E)$ representing a social network under* TCLT *model, B-seed set $S_B \subset V$, a budget $L > 0$, and time constraint τ. Find A-seed set $S \subset V$ with total cost $\sum_{u \in A} c(u) \leq L$ to maximize $\mathbb{I}(S)$.*

We see that when $B = \emptyset$ and $\tau = n$, the TCLT model becomes to well-known LT model and BCIM becomes IM problem [8]. In other word, IM is a special case of BCIM. This leads to BCIM is NP-hard problem and calculate influence $\mathbb{I}(A)$ is #P-hard. Although the objective function in IM problem is *monotone* and *submodular* function, unfortunately, the objective function in BCIM is neither *submodular* nor *supermodular*. Therefore, we can not use the nature greedy for optimizing submodular and supermodular function to get an approximation guarantee.

Theorem 2. *The function $\mathbb{I}(\cdot)$ is neither submodular nor supermodular under* TCLT *model*

3 Randomized Approximation Algorithm

In this section, we present an approximation algorithm for BCIM problem. Due to the $\mathbb{I}(\cdot)$ is not submodular, we use the *Sandwich Approximation* (SA) method [13] for maximizing the combinatorial optimization with the objective function is non-submodular. We first devise *upper bound* submodular function of $\mathbb{I}$, namely $\mathbb{U}(\cdot)$. We then design a $(1 - \frac{1}{\sqrt{e}} - \epsilon)$-approximation with high probability to find solution for maximizing function $\mathbb{U}$, namely PBA. Finally, we apply SA method and PBA algorithm to find solution for maximizing $\mathbb{I}(\cdot)$ with data-dependent approximation guarantee.

Estimating the Influence Function. We first estimate function $\mathbb{I}(\cdot)$ based on the concept of live-edge model. For a node v is randomly selected (called *source* node) and a random sample graph g, we denote function

$$\gamma_g^u(S) = \begin{cases} 1, & \text{If } u \text{ is } A\text{-activated when run live-edge model in } g \\ 0, & \text{Otherwise} \end{cases} \tag{7}$$

We denote $\gamma(S)$ is expectation of $\gamma_g^u(S)$ over random sources and sample graphs. Lemma 1 show that we can use $\gamma(\cdot)$ to estimate objective function.

Lemma 1. *For any $S \subset V$, we have $\mathbb{I}(S) = n \cdot \mathbb{E}[\gamma(S)]$*

Upper Bound Function. For a random source node v and a sample graph g, denote $\mathsf{P}_A^\tau(g, v)$ is the simple path end at v with the length at most τ on g_A. We found that the set nodes S can A-active v, i.e, $\gamma_g^v(S) = 1$ with probability > 0, has at least a node belongs to $\mathsf{P}_A^\tau(g, v)$. We chose the set nodes on $\mathsf{P}_A^\tau(g, v)$ as a candidate nodes to active node v and define *Upper bound Reachable Reversal* (URR) set as follows:

Definition 2 (URR set). *Given graph $G = (V, E, w_A, w_B)$, a random URR set R_j is generate from G by: (1) picking a random node $v \in V$; (2) generate a sample graph g from G by live-edge model, and adding each node $u \in \mathsf{P}_S^\tau(v)$ into R_j*

For any $S \subseteq V$, denote a random variable $X_j = 1$ if $R_j \cap S \neq \emptyset$, $X_j = 0$ otherwise, and $R_j(g, u)$ is a URR set with source node u, and $X_j(g, u)$ is value of X_j corresponding to $R_j(g, u)$, the following Lemma shows the upper bound of X_j.

Lemma 2. *For any set $S \subseteq V$, we have $X_j(g, u) \geq \gamma_g^u(S)$*

Define $\mathbb{U}(S) = n \cdot \mathbb{E}[X_j]$ and $\mathcal{R}$ be a set of URR, we define an estimation of $\mathbb{U}(S)$ is $\hat{\mathbb{U}}(S) = \frac{n}{|\mathcal{R}|} \sum_{R_j \in \mathcal{R}} X_j$. Lemma 3 shows the properties of $\mathbb{U}$ function.

Lemma 3. *For any set of nodes $S \subseteq V$, we have: $\mathbb{U}(S) \geq \mathbb{I}(S)$ and $\mathbb{U}(\cdot)$ is a monotone and submodular function.*

Lemma 3 suggests that we can use $\mathbb{U}$ as a upper bound submodular function of $\mathbb{I}$. We devise an algorithm, which is summarized in Algorithm 1, to generate a URR set. We first randomly selected a source node u with uniform distribution in $[0, 1]$ (line 1). After that, it attempts to select an in-neighbor u of v on g_A according to the live-edge model (line 4). Then it moves from v to u and repeats process. The algorithm stops within τ steps (line 3), or no edge is selected (line 10), or the selected node belongs to R_j (line 7).

Algorithm 1. Generate URR set

Data: Graph $G = (V, E, w_A, w_B)$, B-seed set $S_B \subseteq V$, τ
Result: a URR set R_j
1. Select randomly a node $v \in V$
2. $R_j \leftarrow v$; $d_A \leftarrow 0$
3. **while** $d_A \leq \tau$ **do**
4.   Select an A-edge (u, v) by using live-edge model
5.   **if** *An edge (u, v) is selected* **then**
6. $v \leftarrow u$; $d_A \leftarrow d_A + 1$
7.   If $v \in R_j$ break
8.   Add v into R_j
9.   **else**
10.   break
11.   **end**
12. **end**
13. **return** R_j;

3.1   Polling-Based Algorithm for Maximum Bound Functions

Now we introduce an approximation algorithm for finding maximum upper bound function $\mathbb{U}$ in which all nodes have heterogeneous cost, named PBA. Our algorithm based on polling method which was proposed for IM problem [2,14,16,17]. The details of our algorithm were depicted in Algorithm 2.

Algorithm Description. PBA first generates a collection $\mathcal{R}_1$ contains Λ URR sets. The main phrase of PBA contain several iterators (at most t_{max}). In each iterator, the algorithm first finds the candidate solution S by using Greedy algorithm to solve Budgeted Maximum Coverage (BMC) problem [9] (line 5). It provides an approximation ratio of $(1 - \frac{1}{\sqrt{e}})$. We denote Greedy$(\mathcal{R}, L)$ is Greedy algorithm with the input data is a collection URR sets $\mathcal{R}$ and budget $L > 0$. Then, it calls 3 algorithm which independently generates more at most $|\mathcal{R}_t|$ URR sets to estimate $\mathbb{U}(S)$ with a (ϵ_1, δ_1)-approximation (line 6). If the check does not pass, PBA use $\hat{\mathbb{U}}_c(S)$ and $\hat{\mathbb{U}}_t(S)$ to chose the parameters $\epsilon_1', \epsilon_2, \epsilon_3, \epsilon_t$ (line 7 in Algorithm 3). If current solution S meets approximation guarantee condition $\epsilon_t \geq \epsilon$ (line 9 in Algorithm 3), the main algorithm returns S. If not, it moves to next iterator and stops the number of URR sets at least N_{max}.

Theoretical Analysis. Now, we shall prove that PBA returns a $(1 - 1/\sqrt{e} - \epsilon)$-approximation solution with probability at least $1 - \delta$. We observe that $X_j \in [0, 1]$. Let randomly variable $Z_i = \sum_{j=1}^{i}(X_j - \mu), \forall i \geq 1$, where $\mu = \mathbb{E}[X_j]$.

For a sequence random variables $Z_1, Z_2, \ldots$ we have $\mathbb{E}[Z_i | Z_1, \ldots, Z_{j-1}] = \mathbb{E}[Z_{i-1}] + \mathbb{E}[X_i - \mu] = \mathbb{E}[Z_{i-1}]$. Hence, $Z_1, Z_2, \ldots$ be a form of martingale [6]. Therefore, we obtain the same results in [16].

Lemma 4 ([16]). *For any $T > 0, \epsilon > 0$, μ is the mean of X_j, and an estimation of μ is $\hat{\mu} = \frac{\sum_{i=1}^{T} X_i}{T}$ we have:*

$$\Pr[\hat{\mu} \geq (1+\epsilon)\mu] \leq e^{\frac{-T\mu\epsilon^2}{2+\frac{2}{3}\epsilon}} \tag{8}$$

$$\Pr[\hat{\mu} \leq (1-\epsilon)\mu] \leq e^{\frac{-T\mu\epsilon^2}{2}} \tag{9}$$

Algorithm 2. Polling-Based Approximation algorithm (PBA)

Data: Graph $G = (V, E, w_A, w_B)$, budget $L > 0$, and $\epsilon, \delta \in (0, 1)$
Result: A-seed S
1. $\Lambda = \Upsilon(\epsilon, \frac{\delta}{6}), t \leftarrow 1$
2. Generate Λ URR set by alg. 1 and add them into $\mathcal{R}_1$
3. $N_{max} \leftarrow N(\epsilon, \frac{\delta}{3}) \frac{\mathsf{OPT}_u}{k}, t_{max} = \left\lceil \log_2 \frac{2N_{max}}{\Upsilon(\epsilon, \frac{\delta}{6})} \right\rceil$
4. **repeat**
5. $< A, \mathsf{Cov}_{\mathcal{R}_t}(A) > \leftarrow$ Greedy$(\mathcal{R}_t, L)$
6.   **if** *(CheckQS$(\mathcal{R}_t, \mathsf{Cov}_{\mathcal{R}_t}(S_t), \delta, \epsilon) = True)$ or $(|\mathcal{R}_t| \geq N_{max})$* **then**
7. | **return** S
8.   **else**
9. | $t \leftarrow t+1$, $\mathcal{R}_t \leftarrow$ CheckQS$(\mathcal{R}_t, \mathsf{Cov}_{\mathcal{R}_t}(A_t), \delta, \epsilon)$
10.   **end**
11. **until** $|\mathcal{R}_t| \geq N_{max}$;
12. **return** S;

Tang *et al.* [16] proposed IMM algorithm based on RIS process for solving IM problem [2,14,16,17]. They show that the number of random *Reverse Reachable* (RR) sets, which ensures RIS process returns a $(1 - 1/e - \epsilon)$-approximation with probability $1 - \delta$, is

$$\theta_{max} = 2n \left(\left(1 - \frac{1}{e}\right) \sqrt{\ln\left(\frac{2}{\delta}\right)} + \sqrt{\left(1 - \frac{1}{e}\right)\left(\ln\frac{2}{\delta} + \ln\binom{n}{k}\right)} \right)^2 \frac{1}{\epsilon^2 k} \tag{10}$$

This threshold also be used as a stopping condition on IM algorithms [14,15]. However, it does not guarantee that the candidate solution S is a $(1 - 1/\sqrt{e})$-approximation under the heterogeneous selecting costs into seed set. To address this challenge, we provide another threshold which can guarantee a $(1 - 1/\sqrt{e} - \epsilon)$ approximation ratio by following Theorem.

Algorithm 3. Check quality of solution (CheckQS)

Data: $\mathcal{R}_t, \mathrm{Cov}_{\mathcal{R}_t}(A_t), \delta, \epsilon$

Result: True or (False and $\mathcal{R}_{t+1}$)

1. $\delta_1 = \frac{\delta}{3t_{max}}$, $\epsilon_1 = \frac{\epsilon}{4}$, $\Lambda_1 \leftarrow \Upsilon(\epsilon_1, \delta_1)$, $cov \leftarrow \mathrm{Cov}_{\mathcal{R}_t}(A)$, $\mathcal{R}_c \leftarrow \mathcal{R}_t$

2. **while** $cov < \Lambda_1$ **do**

3. $\quad$ | $\quad$ Generate a URR set R_j by alg. 1 and add it to $\mathcal{R}_c$

4. $\quad$ | $\quad$ If $R_j \cap A \neq 0$, then $cov \leftarrow cov + 1$

5. $\quad$ | $\quad$ If $|\mathcal{R}_c| > 2|\mathcal{R}_t|$, then **return** False and $\mathcal{R}_t$

6. **end**

7. $\hat{\mathbb{U}}_c(A) \leftarrow n \cdot \frac{cov}{|\mathcal{R}_c|}$; $\epsilon_2 \leftarrow \frac{\hat{\mathbb{U}}_c(A)}{\hat{\mathbb{U}}_t(A)} - 1$; $\epsilon_1' = \frac{\epsilon_1}{1+\epsilon_1}$; $\epsilon_3 \leftarrow \sqrt{\frac{3\ln\frac{t_{max}}{\delta_1}}{|\mathcal{R}_t|(1-\epsilon_1')\hat{\mathbb{U}}_c(A)}}$

8. $\epsilon_t = (1 - 1/\sqrt{e})(1 - \epsilon_1'\epsilon_2 + \epsilon_1'\epsilon_3 - \epsilon_2\epsilon_3 + \epsilon_1'\epsilon_2\epsilon_3)$

9. **if** $\epsilon_t \leq \epsilon$ **then**

10. $\quad$ | $\quad$ **return** True

11. **else**

12. $\quad$ | $\quad$ If $|\mathcal{R}_c| < 2|\mathcal{R}_t|$, then generate more $2|\mathcal{R}_t| - |\mathcal{R}_c|$ URR sets and add them into $\mathcal{R}_c$

13. $\quad$ | $\quad$ **return** False and $\mathcal{R}_c$

14. **end**

15. **return** False;

Theorem 3. *For $\epsilon > 0$, $\delta \in (0,1)$ be the parameters. In* Greedy *algorithm, if the number of samples $T = |\mathcal{R}|$ greater or equal to*

$$N(\epsilon, \delta) = \frac{2n(1 - \frac{1}{\sqrt{e}})^2 \ln(1/\delta)}{\mathsf{OPT}_u \epsilon^2} \tag{11}$$

, this algorithm return a $(1 - 1/\sqrt{e} - \epsilon)$-approximation solution with probability at lest $1 - \delta$.

Lemma 5. *Let event $B_t^1 = \left(|\mathcal{R}_t| \geq N_{max}\right) \cup \left(\mathbb{U}(S) < (1 - 1/\sqrt{e} - \epsilon)\mathsf{OPT}_u)\right)$ then, $\Pr[B_t^1] < \frac{\delta}{3}$*

Lemma 6. *For each $1 \leq t \leq t_{max}$, Let B_2 be the bed event that $B_t^2 = \left(\mathbb{U}(S) < \frac{1}{1+\epsilon_1}\mathbb{U}_c(S)\right)$. We have: $\Pr[B_t^2] < \delta_1$*

Lemma 7. *For any $t = 1,2\ldots t_{max}$, we let the bad event $B_t^3 = \mathbb{U}_t(S_U^*) < (1 - \epsilon_3')\mathbb{U}(S_u^*)$, where $\epsilon_3' = \sqrt{\frac{2n\ln\frac{3t_{max}}{\delta}}{|\mathcal{R}_t|\mathsf{OPT}_u}}$. We have $\Pr[B_3^t] \leq \delta_1$*

Theorem 4 (Main result). *Given $0 \leq \epsilon, \delta \leq 1$, the main algorithm returns the set node S satisfying: $\Pr[\mathbb{U}(S) \geq (1 - 1/\sqrt{e} - \epsilon)\mathbb{U}(S_l^*)] \geq 1 - \delta$*

3.2   Sandwich Approximation

We apply Sandwich Approximation framework in [13] to design our algorithm, namely SA-PBA. Let S_u are solutions selected by PBA algorithm for maximizing $\mathbb{U}$ within the total cost at most L and A' is a solution for original problem. Denote $\hat{\mathbb{I}}(S)$ is a (δ', ϵ')-approximation of $\mathbb{I}(A)$, i.e,

$$\Pr[(1 - \epsilon')\mathbb{I}(S) \leq \hat{\mathbb{I}}(S) \leq (1 + \epsilon')\mathbb{I}(S)] \geq 1 - \delta' \tag{12}$$

We chose $S_{sa} = \arg\max_{S\in\{S',S_u\}} \hat{\mathbb{I}}(S)$ as the solution of SPBA algorithm. The details of our algorithm were showed in Algorithm 4. The following Theorem show approximation ratio of our algorithm.

Algorithm 4. Sandwich Approximation base on PBA algorithm (SPBA)

   Data: Graph $G = (V, E, w_A, w_B)$, budget $L > 0$, and $\epsilon, \delta, \epsilon', \delta' \in (0, 1)$
   Result: seed S
1. $S_u \leftarrow$ PBA$(\mathbb{U}, G, L, \epsilon, \delta)$
2. $S_0 \leftarrow$ a solution for maximizing $\mathbb{I}$ by any algorithm.
3. $S \leftarrow \arg\max_{A'\in\{S_u,S'\}} \hat{\mathbb{I}}(S')$
4. **return** S;

Theorem 5. *Let S^* is optimal solution, and S_{sa} is a solution return by Algorithm 4. We have:* $\mathbb{I}(S_{sa}) \geq \frac{\hat{\mathbb{I}}(S_U)}{\mathbb{U}(S_U)}\cdot(1-1/\sqrt{e}-\epsilon)(1-\epsilon')\cdot$OPT *with probability at least* $1 - \delta - \delta'$.

4   Conclusion

In this paper, we investigate the BCIM problem, which finds the seed set of a player to maximize their influence while with opposite players within budget and time constraints. We first proposed TCLT model to capture the competitive influence of two competitors on a social network and formulate BCIM in this model. We provide the hardness results, properties of objective function. To solve this problem, we proposed a randomized algorithm that guarantees a data-dependent approximation factor, called SPBA.

Acknowledgements. This work is partially supported by NSF EFRI 1441231 grant.

References

1. Bharathi, S., Kempe, D., Salek, M.: Competitive influence maximization in social networks. In: Deng, X., Graham, F.C. (eds.) WINE 2007. LNCS, vol. 4858, pp. 306–311. Springer, Heidelberg (2007). https://doi.org/10.1007/978-3-540-77105-0_31
2. Borgs, C., Brautbar, M., Chayes, J.T., Lucier, B.: Maximizing social influence in nearly optimal time. In: Proceedings of the ACM-SIAM, pp. 946–957 (2014)
3. Bozorgi, A., Samet, S., Kwisthout, J., Wareham, T.: Community-based influence maximization in social networks under a competitive linear threshold model. Knowl. Based Syst. **134**, 149–158 (2017)
4. Chen, W., et al.: Influence maximization in social networks when negative opinions may emerge and propagate. In: Proceedings of the SDM, pp. 379–390 (2011)
5. Chen, W., Lakshmanan, L.V.S., Castillo, C.: Information and Influence Propagation in Social Networks. Synthesis Lectures on Data Management. Morgan & Claypool Publishers, San Rafael (2013)
6. Chung, F.R.K., Lu, L.: Survey: concentration inequalities and martingale inequalities: a survey. Internet Math. **3**(1), 79–127 (2006)
7. He, X., Song, G., Chen, W., Jiang, Q.: Influence blocking maximization in social networks under the competitive linear threshold model. In: Proceedings of the SDM, pp. 463–474 (2012)
8. Kempe, D., Kleinberg, J.M., Tardos, É.: Maximizing the spread of influence through a social network. In: Proceedings of the KDD, pp. 137–146 (2003)
9. Khuller, S., Moss, A., Naor, J.: The budgeted maximum coverage problem. Inf. Process. Lett. **70**(1), 39–45 (1999)
10. Leskovec, J., Krause, A., Guestrin, C., Faloutsos, C., VanBriesen, J.M., Glance, N.S.: Cost-effective outbreak detection in networks. In: Proceedings of the KDD, pp. 420–429 (2007)
11. Liu, W., Yue, K., Wu, H., Li, J., Liu, D., Tang, D.: Containment of competitive influence spread in social networks. Knowl. Based Syst. **109**, 266–275 (2016)
12. Lu, W., Bonchi, F., Goyal, A., Lakshmanan, L.V.S.: The bang for the buck: fair competitive viral marketing from the host perspective. In: Proceedings of the KDD, pp. 928–936 (2013)
13. Lu, W., Chen, W., Lakshmanan, L.V.S.: From competition to complementarity: comparative influence diffusion and maximization. PVLDB **9**(2), 60–71 (2015)
14. Nguyen, H.T., Thai, M.T., Dinh, T.N.: Stop-and-stare: optimal sampling algorithms for viral marketing in billion-scale networks. In: Proceedings of the SIGMOD, pp. 695–710 (2016)
15. Nguyen, H.T., Thai, M.T., Dinh, T.N.: A billion-scale approximation algorithm for maximizing benefit in viral marketing. IEEE/ACM Trans. Netw. **25**(4), 2419–2429 (2017)
16. Tang, Y., Shi, Y., Xiao, X.: Influence maximization in near-linear time: a martingale approach. In: Proceedings of the SIGMOD, pp. 1539–1554 (2015)
17. Tang, Y., Xiao, X., Shi, Y.: Influence maximization: near-optimal time complexity meets practical efficiency. In: Proceedings of the SIGMOD, pp. 75–86 (2014)
18. Yan, R., Zhu, Y., Li, D., Ye, Z.: Minimum cost seed set for threshold influence problem under competitive models. World Wide Web (2018)

Blockchain Queue Theory

Quan-Lin Li[1]($\boxtimes$), Jing-Yu Ma[1], and Yan-Xia Chang[2]

[1] School of Economics and Management Sciences, Yanshan University,
Qinhuangdao 066004, China
`liquanlin@tsinghua.edu.cn`
[2] School of Science, Yanshan University, Qinhuangdao 066004, China

Abstract. Blockchain has many benefits including decentralization, availability, persistency, consistency, anonymity, auditability and accountability, and it also covers a wide spectrum of applications ranging from cryptocurrency, financial services, reputation system, Internet of Things, sharing economy to public and social services. Not only may blockchain be regarded as a by-product of Bitcoin cryptocurrency systems, but also it is a type of distributed ledger technologies through using a trustworthy, decentralized log of totally ordered transactions. By summarizing the literature of blockchain, it is found that more and more important research is to develop basic theory, for example, mathematical models (Markov processes, queueing theory and game models) for mining management and consensus mechanism, performance analysis and optimization of blockchain systems. In this paper, we develop queueing theory of blockchain systems and provide system performance evaluation. To do this, we design a Markovian batch-service queueing system with two different service stages, which are suitable to well express the mining process in the miners pool and the building of a new blockchain. By using the matrix-geometric solution, we obtain a system stable condition and express three key performance measures: (a) The average number of transactions in the queue, (b) the average number of transactions in a block, and (c) the average transaction-confirmation time. Finally, we use numerical examples to verify computability of our theoretical results. Although our queueing model here is simple only under exponential or Poisson assumptions, our analytic method will open a series of potentially promising research in queueing theory of blockchain systems.

Keywords: Blockchain · Bitcoin · Queueing theory
Matrix-geometric solutions · Mining process
Block-generation process · Blockchain-building process

1 Introduction

In this paper, we develop queueing theory of blockchain systems under a dynamic behavior setting. Such a blockchain queue in general is very necessary and useful

Quan-Lin Li was supported by the National Natural Science Foundation of China under grant No. 71671158 and No. 71471160, and by the Natural Science Foundation of Hebei province under grant No. G2017203277.

in performance analysis and optimization of blockchain systems, and it will also be helpful in optimal design of blockchain technologies. To this end, we propose and analyze a Markovian batch-service queueing system with two different service stages, which are suitable to well express the mining process in the miners pool and the building of a new blockchain. By using the matrix-geometric solution, we obtain a system stable condition and express three key measures: The average number of transactions in the queue, the average number of transactions in a block, and the average transaction-confirmation time. At the same time, we use some numerical examples to verify effective computability of our theoretical results. Different from the previous works in the literature, this paper is the first one to give a complete solution with respect to analysis of blockchain queues. We hope that our approach opens a new avenue to queueing analysis of more general blockchain systems in practice, and can motivate a series of promising future research on development of blockchain technologies.

Blockchain is one of the most popular issues discussed extensively in recent years, and it has already changed people's lifestyle in some real areas due to its great impact on finance, business, industry, transportation, heathcare and so forth. Since the introduction of Bitcoin by Nakamoto [23], blockchain technologies have become widely adopted in many real applications, for example, survey work of applications by NRI [25] and Foroglou and Tsilidou [10]; finance by Tsai et al. [30]; business and information systems by Beck et al. [1]; applications to companies by Montemayor et al. [22]; Internet of Things and shared economy by Huckle et al. [12]; healthcare by Mettler [21]; and the others.

So far blockchain research has obtained many important advances, readers may refer to a book by Swan [29]; survey papers by Tschorsch and Scheuermann [31], Zheng et al. [35,36], Lin and Liao [19] and Constantinides et al. [6]; a key research framework by Yli-Huumo et al. [34], Plansky et al. [27], Lindman et al. [20] and Risius and Spohrer [28]; consensus mechanisms by Wang et al. [33] and Debus [8]; blockchain economics by Catalini and Gans [5] and Davidson et al. [7]; and the others by Vranken [32] and Dinh et al. [9].

However, little work has been done on basic theory of blockchain systems so far, for example, developing mathematical models (e.g., Markov processes, queueing theory, game models, optimal methods, and decision making), providing performance analysis and optimization, and setting up useful relations among key factors or basic parameters (e.g., block size, transaction fee, mining reward, solving difficulty, throughput, and efficiency).

Our blockchain queueing model focuses on analysis of the block-generation and blockchain-building processes in the mining management, in which the sum of the block-generation and blockchain-building times is regarded as the transaction-confirmation time of a block. For convenience of reader's understanding, it is necessary to simply recall some papers which discussed the miner pools and the mining processes. A blockchain is maintained and updated by the mining processes in which many nodes, called miners, compete for finding answers of a very difficult puzzle-like problem. While the transactions are grouped into a block, and then the block is pegged to the blockchain once the key nonce is

provided by means of a mining competition that an algorithmic puzzle specialized for this block is solved. For such a mining process, readers may refer to, for
example, Bitcoin by Nakamoto [23], Bhaskar and Chuen [2] and Böhme et al. [4];
and blockchain by Sect. 2 in Zheng et al. [35] and Sect. 2 in Dinh et al. [9]. At the
same time, the mining processes are well supported by mining reward methods
and consensus mechanism whose detailed analysis was given in Debus [8] as well
as an excellent overview by Wang et al. [33]. In addition, it may be useful to
see transaction graph and transaction network by Ober et al. [26] and Kondor
et al. [16]. Finally, the mining processes are also discussed by game theory, e.g.,
see Houy [11], Lewenberg et al. [17], Kiayias et al. [15] and Biais et al. [3].

Kasahara, Kawahara and Kawase provided an early research (in fact, so far
there have been only their two papers in the literature) on applying queueing
theory to deal with the transaction-confirmation time for Bitcoin, in which they
gave some interesting idea and useful simulations to heuristically motivate future
promising research. See Kasahara and Kawahara [13] and Kawase and Kasahara
[14] for more details. In those two papers, Kasahara, Kawahara and Kawase first
assumed that the transaction-confirmation times follow a continuous probability
distribution function. Then they used the supplementary variable method to set
up a system of differential-difference equations (see Sect. 3 of Kawase and Kasahara [14]) by using the elapsed service time. However, they have not correctly
given the unique solution of the system of differential-difference equations yet,
although they used the generating function technique to provide some formal-
ized computation. For example, the average number $E[N]$ of transactions in the
system and the average transaction-confirmation time: $E[T] = E[N]/\lambda$ given
in (17) of Kawase and Kasahara [14], while it is worth noting that they still
directly depend on the infinitely-many unknown numbers: α_n for $n = 0, 1, 2, \ldots$.
However, those unknown numbers α_n defined in their paper are impossible to be
obtained by such an ordinary technique. In fact, we also believe that analysis of
the Bitcoin queueing system with general transaction-confirmation times, given
in Kawase and Kasahara [14], is still an interesting open problem in the future
queueing research.

To overcome the difficulties involved in Kawase and Kasahara [14], this paper
introduce two different exponential service stages corresponding to the block-
generation and blockchain-building times. As seen in Sect. 2, such two service
stages are very reasonable in description of the block-generation and blockchain-
building processes. Although our blockchain queueing model is simple only under
exponential or Poisson assumptions, it is easy to see that this model is still very
interesting due to its two stages of batch services: a block of transactions is
generated and then a new blockchain is built. At the same time, we obtain
several new useful results as follows:

(a) **Stability:** This system is positive recurrent if and only if

$$\frac{b\mu_1\mu_2}{\mu_1 + \mu_2} > \lambda.$$

Note that this stable condition is not intuitive, and it can not be obtained by means of some simple observation. In addition, since our transaction-confirmation time S is the sum of the block-generation time S_1 and the blockchain-building time S_2, it is clear that our transaction-confirmation time obeys a generalized Erlang distribution of order 2 with the mean $E[S] = E[S_1] + E[S_2] = 1/\mu_1 + 1/\mu_2$. Thus our stable condition is the same as that condition: $\lambda E[S] < b$ given in Page 77 of Kawase and Kasahara [14].

(b) **Expressions:** By means of the matrix-geometric solution, we use the rate matrix to provide simple expressions for the average number of transactions in the queue, the average number of transactions in a block, and the average transaction-confirmation time. At the same time, we use numerical examples to verify computability of our theoretical results.

The structure of this paper is organized as follows. Section 2 describes an interesting blockchain queue. Section 3 establishes a continuous-time Markov process of GI/M/1 type, and derives a system stable condition and the stationary probability vector by means of the matrix-geometric solution. Section 4 provides simple expressions for three key performance measures, and uses some numerical examples to verify computability of our theoretical results. Finally, some concluding remarks are given in Sect. 5.

2   Model Description for a Blockchain Queue

In this section, based on the real background of blockchain, we design an interesting blockchain queue, in which the block-generation and blockchain-building processes are expressed as a two stages of batch services.

When using a queueing system to model the blockchain, it is a key to set up the service process by means of analysis of the mining management which is related to the consensus mechanism. Here, we take a service time as the transaction-confirmation time which is the sum of the block-generation and blockchain-building times, that is, our service time is two stages: the first one is generated from the mining processes, while another comes from the network latency. In the block-generation stage, a newly generated block is confirmed by solving a computational intensive problem by means of a cryptographic Hash algorithm, called *mining*; while a number of nodes who compete for finding the answer is called *miners*. The winner will be awarded reward, which consists of some fixed values and fees of transactions included in the block, and he still has the right to peg a new block to the blockchain. In addition, a block is a list of transactions, together with metadata including the timestamp of the current block, the timestamp of the most previous block, and a field called a nonce which is given by the mining winner. Therefore, it is seen that the block-generation and blockchain-building processes, the two stages of services, can be easily understand from the real background of blockchain, e.g., see Bitcoin networks by Nakamoto [23] and Bhaskar and Chuen [2]; and blockchain by Sect. 2 in Zheng et al. [35] and Sect. 2 in Dinh et al. [9]. Based on this, we can abstract the mining processes to set up the two stages of services: the block-generation and blockchain-building processes, so that the blockchain system is described as a Markovian batch service queue with two different service stages, which is depicted in Fig. 1.

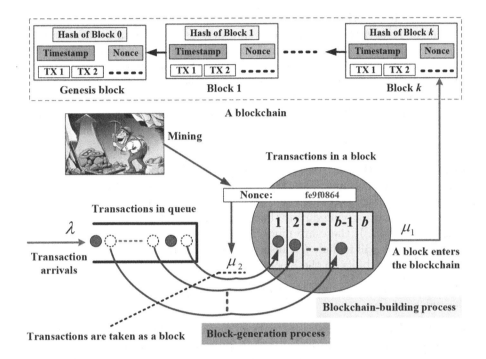

Fig. 1. A blockchain queueing system

Now, from Fig. 1 we provide some model descriptions as follows:

Arrival Process: Transactions arrive at the blockchain system according to a Poisson process with arrival rate λ. Each transaction must first enter and queue up in an waiting room of infinite size. Note that the arrival process of transactions is denoted in the lower left corner of Fig. 1.

Service Process: Each arrival transaction first queues up in the waiting room. Then it waits for being successfully mined into a block, this is regarded as the first stage of service, called block generation. Up to the block-generation time, a group of transactions are chosen as a block and simultaneously, a nonce is appended to the block by the mining winner. See the lower middle part of Fig. 1 for more details. Finally, the block with the group of transactions will be pegged to a blockchain, this is regarded as the second stage of service due to the network latency, called blockchain building, see the right and lower part of Fig. 1. In addition, the upper part of Fig. 1 also outlines the blockchain and the internal structure of every block.

In the blockchain system, for the two stages of services, we assume that the block-generation times in the first stage are i.i.d and exponential with service rate μ_2; the blockchain-building times in the second stage are i.i.d and exponential with the service rate μ_1.

The block-Generation Discipline: A block can consist of several transactions but at most b transactions. The transactions mined into a block are not completely based on the First Come First Service (FCFS) with respect to the transaction arrivals. Thus some transactions in the back of this queue may be preferentially first chosen into the block, seen in the lower middle part of Fig. 1.

For simplification of description, our later computation will be based on the FCFS discipline. This may be a better approximation in analysis of the blockchain queueing system if the transactions are regarded as the indistinctive ones under a dynamic behavior setting.

The Maximum Block Size: To avoid the spam attack, the maximum block size is limited. We assume that there are at most b transactions in each block. If the resulting block size is smaller than the maximum block size b , then the transactions newly arriving during the mining process of a block can be accepted in the block again. If there are more than b transactions in the waiting room, then a new block will include b transactions through the full blocks to maximize the batch service ability in the blockchain system.

Independence: We assume that all the random variables defined above are independent of each other.

Remark 1: The arrival process of transactions at the blockchain system may be non-Poisson (for example, Markov arrival process, renewal process and nonhomogeneous Poisson process). On the other hand, the two stages of batch service times may be non-exponential (for example, phase-type distribution and general distribution). However, so far analysis of the blockchain queues with renewal arrival process or with general service time distribution has still been an interesting open problem in queueing research of blockchain systems.

Remark 2: In the blockchain system, there are key factors, such as the maximum block size, mining reward, transaction fee, mining strategy, security of blockchain and so on. Based on some of them, we may develop reward queueing models, decision queueing models, and game queueing models in the study of blockchain systems. Analysis for these key factors will be very necessary and useful in improving blockchain technologies in many future applications.

3   A Markov Process of GI/M/1 Type

In this section, for the blockchain queueing system, we establish a continuous-time Markov process of GI/M/1 type. Based on this, we derive a system stable condition and the stationary probability vector of this system by means of the matrix-geometric solution.

Let $I(t)$ and $J(t)$ be the numbers of transactions in the block and in the queue at time t, respectively. Then, $(I(t), J(t))$ may be regarded as a state of the blockchain queueing system at time t. Note that $i = 0, 1, \ldots, b$ and $j = 0, 1, 2, \ldots$, for various cases of $(I(t), J(t))$ we write

$$
\begin{aligned}
\Omega &= \{(i, j) : i = 0, 1, \ldots, b, \quad j = 0, 1, 2, \ldots\} \\
&= \{(0,0), (1,0), \ldots, (b,0); (0,1), (1,1), \ldots, (b,1); \ldots; \\
&\quad (0,b), (1,b), \ldots, (b,b); (0,b+1), (1,b+1), \ldots, (b,b+1); \ldots\}. \quad (1)
\end{aligned}
$$

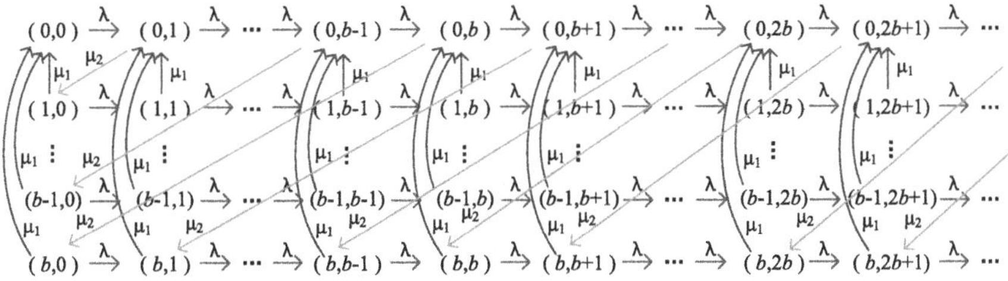

Fig. 2. State transition relation of a Markov process

Let $X(t) = (I(t), J(t))$. Then $\{X(t) : t \geq 0\}$ is a continuous-time Markov process of GI/M/1 type on the state space Ω. Figure 2 denotes the state transition relation of the Markov process $\{X(t) : t \geq 0\}$, thus its infinitesimal generator is given by

$$
Q = \begin{pmatrix}
B_0 & A_0 & & & & & \\
B_1 & A_1 & A_0 & & & & \\
B_2 & & A_1 & A_0 & & & \\
\vdots & & & \ddots & \ddots & & \\
B_b & & & & A_1 & A_0 & \\
& A_b & & & & A_1 & A_0 \\
& & A_b & & & & A_1 & A_0 \\
& & & \ddots & & & & \ddots & \ddots
\end{pmatrix}, \quad (2)
$$

where

$$
A_0 = \lambda I, \quad A_1 = \begin{pmatrix}
-(\lambda + \mu_2) & & & \\
\mu_1 & -(\lambda + \mu_1) & & \\
\vdots & & \ddots & \\
\mu_1 & & & -(\lambda + \mu_1)
\end{pmatrix}, \quad A_b = \begin{pmatrix}
0 & \cdots & 0 & \mu_2 \\
& & & \\
& & &
\end{pmatrix},
$$

and

$$
B_0 = \begin{pmatrix}
-\lambda & & & \\
\mu_1 & -(\lambda + \mu_1) & & \\
\vdots & & \ddots & \\
\mu_1 & & & -(\lambda + \mu_1)
\end{pmatrix},
$$

$$B_1 = \begin{pmatrix} 0 & \mu_2 & 0 & \cdots & 0 \\ & & & & \\ & & & & \\ & & & & \end{pmatrix}, \quad B_2 = \begin{pmatrix} 0 & 0 & \mu_2 & \cdots & 0 \\ & & & & \\ & & & & \\ & & & & \end{pmatrix}, \quad \ldots, \quad B_b = \begin{pmatrix} 0 & \cdots & 0 & \mu_2 \\ & & & \\ & & & \\ & & & \end{pmatrix}.$$

For the continuous-time Markov process of GI/M/1 type, now we use the mean drift method to discuss its system stable condition. Note that the mean drift method for checking system stability is given a detailed introduction in Chap. 3 of Li [18] (e.g., Theorem 3.19 and the continuous-time case in Page 172).

From Chap. 1 of Neuts [24] or Chap. 3 of Li [18], for the Markov process of GI/M/1 type, we write

$$A = A_0 + A_1 + A_b = \begin{pmatrix} -\mu_2 & & & & \mu_2 \\ \mu_1 & -\mu_1 & & & \\ \vdots & & \ddots & & \\ \mu_1 & & & -\mu_1 & \\ \mu_1 & & & & -\mu_1 \end{pmatrix}.$$

Clearly, the matrix A is an irreducible, aperiodic and positive recurrent Markov process with two states (i.e., States 0 and b), together with $b - 1$ instantaneous states (i.e., States $1, 2, \ldots, b-1$) which will vanish as the time t goes to infinity. Note that such a special Markov process A can not influence applications of the matrix-geometric solution because it is only related to the mean drift method for establishing system stable conditions. In this case, let $\boldsymbol{\theta} = (\theta_0, \theta_1, \ldots, \theta_b)$ be the unique solution to the system of linear equations: $\boldsymbol{\theta} A = \mathbf{0}$ and $\boldsymbol{\theta} e = 1$, where e is a column vector of ones with proper dimension. It is easy to check that

$$\boldsymbol{\theta} = \left(\frac{\mu_1}{\mu_1 + \mu_2}, 0, \ldots, 0, \frac{\mu_2}{\mu_1 + \mu_2} \right).$$

The following theorem provides a necessary and sufficient condition under which the Markov process Q is positive recurrent.

Theorem 1. *The Markov process Q of GI/M/1 type is positive recurrent if and only if*

$$\frac{b\mu_1\mu_2}{\mu_1 + \mu_2} > \lambda.$$

Proof. By using the mean drift method given in Chap. 3 of Li [18] (e.g., Theorem 3.19 and the continuous-time case in Page 172), it is easy to see that the Markov process Q of GI/M/1 type is positive recurrent if and only if

$$\boldsymbol{\theta} A_0 e < b \boldsymbol{\theta} A_b e. \tag{3}$$

Note that

$$\boldsymbol{\theta} A_0 e = \lambda, \tag{4}$$

and
$$b\boldsymbol{\theta} A_b e = b\theta_0 \mu_2 = \frac{b\mu_1\mu_2}{\mu_1 + \mu_2}, \tag{5}$$

thus we obtain
$$\frac{b\mu_1\mu_2}{\mu_1 + \mu_2} > \lambda.$$

This completes the proof. ∎

When the Markov process $\boldsymbol{Q}$ of GI/M/1 type is positive recurrent, we write its stationary probability vector as
$$\boldsymbol{\pi} = (\boldsymbol{\pi}_0, \boldsymbol{\pi}_1, \boldsymbol{\pi}_2, \ldots),$$

where
$$\boldsymbol{\pi}_0 = (\pi_{0,0}, \pi_{1,0}, \ldots, \pi_{b,0}),$$
$$\boldsymbol{\pi}_1 = (\pi_{0,1}, \pi_{1,1}, \ldots, \pi_{b,1}),$$
$$\boldsymbol{\pi}_k = (\pi_{0,k}, \pi_{1,k}, \ldots, \pi_{b,k}), \quad k \geq 2.$$

For the Markov process $\boldsymbol{Q}$ of GI/M/1 type, to compute its stationary probability vector, we need to first obtain the rate matrix R, which is the minimal nonnegative solution to the following nonlinear matrix equation
$$R^b A_b + R A_1 + A_0 = \boldsymbol{0}. \tag{6}$$

In general, it is very complicated to provide expression for the unique solution to this nonlinear matrix equation due to the term $R^b A_b$ of size $b + 1$. In fact, for the blockchain queueing system, here we can not also provide an explicit expression for the rate matrix R. For example, we consider a special case with $b = 2$. For this simple case, we have
$$A_0 = \lambda I, A_1 = \begin{pmatrix} -(\lambda + \mu_2) & & \\ \mu_1 & -(\lambda + \mu_1) & \\ \mu_1 & & -(\lambda + \mu_1) \end{pmatrix}, A_2 = \begin{pmatrix} 0 & 0 & \mu_2 \\ & & \end{pmatrix}.$$

From computing $R^2 A_2 + R A_1 + A_0 = \boldsymbol{0}$, it is easy to see that for the simple case with the maximal block size $b = 2$, we can not provide an explicit expression for the rate matrix R of size 3 yet.

Although the rate matrix R has not an explicit expression, we can use some iterative algorithms, given in Chaps. 1 and 2 of Neuts [24], to give its numerical solution. Here, an effective iterative algorithm is described as
$$R_0 = \boldsymbol{0},$$
$$R_{N+1} = \left(R_N^b A_b + A_0 \right) (-A_1)^{-1}.$$

Note that this algorithm is fast convergent, that is, after a finite number of iterative steps, we can numerically given a solution of higher precision for the rate matrix R.

The following theorem directly comes from Theorem 1.2.1 of Chap. 1 in Neuts [24]. Here, we restate it without a proof.

Theorem 2. *If the Markov process Q of GI/M/1 type is positive recurrent, then the stationary probability vector $\boldsymbol{\pi} = (\boldsymbol{\pi}_0, \boldsymbol{\pi}_1, \boldsymbol{\pi}_2, \ldots)$ is given by*

$$\boldsymbol{\pi}_k = \boldsymbol{\pi}_0 R^k, \quad k \geq 1, \tag{7}$$

where the vector $\boldsymbol{\pi}_0$ is positive, and it is the unique solution to the following system of linear equations:

$$\boldsymbol{\pi}_0 B[R] = \boldsymbol{\pi}_0, \tag{8}$$
$$\boldsymbol{\pi}_0 (I - R)^{-1} \boldsymbol{e} = 1,$$

and the matrix $B[R] = \sum_{k=0}^{b} R^k B_k$ is irreducible and stochastic.

4   Performance Analysis

In this section, we provide performance analysis of the blockchain queueing system. To this end, we provide three key performance measures and give their simple expressions by means of the vector $\boldsymbol{\pi}_0$ and the rate matrix R. Finally, we use numerical examples to verify computability of our theoretical results, and show how the performance measures depend on some key parameters of this system.

When the blockchain queueing system is stable, we write

$$I = \lim_{t \to +\infty} I(t), \quad J = \lim_{t \to +\infty} J(t).$$

(a) The average number of transactions in the queue
It follows from (8) and (7) that

$$E[J] = \sum_{j=0}^{\infty} j \sum_{i=0}^{b} \pi_{i,j} = \sum_{j=0}^{\infty} j \boldsymbol{\pi}_j \boldsymbol{e} = \boldsymbol{\pi}_0 R (I - R)^{-2} \boldsymbol{e}.$$

(b) The average number of transactions in the block
Let $\boldsymbol{h} = (0, 1, 2, \ldots, b)^T$. Then

$$E[I] = \sum_{j=0}^{\infty} \sum_{i=0}^{b} i \pi_{i,j} = \sum_{j=0}^{\infty} \boldsymbol{\pi}_j \boldsymbol{h} = \boldsymbol{\pi}_0 (I - R)^{-1} \boldsymbol{h}.$$

(c) The average transaction-confirmation time
In the blockchain system, the transaction-confirmation time is the time interval from the time epoch that a transaction arrives at the waiting room to the point that the blockchain pegs a block with this transaction. In fact, the transaction-confirmation time is the sojourn time of the transaction in the blockchain system, and it is also the sum of the block-generation and blockchain-building times of a block with this transaction.

Let T denote the transaction-confirmation time of any transaction when the blockchain system is stable.

The following theorem provides expression for the average transaction-confirmation time by means of the stationary probability vector.

Theorem 3. *If the blockchain queueing system is stable, then the average transaction-confirmation time* $E[T]$ *is given by*

$$E[T] = \sum_{k=0}^{\infty}\sum_{l=0}^{b-1}\pi_{0,kb+l}\,(k+1)\left(\frac{1}{\mu_1}+\frac{1}{\mu_2}\right) + \sum_{i=1}^{b}\sum_{k=0}^{\infty}\sum_{l=0}^{b-1}\pi_{i,kb+l}\left[\frac{1}{\mu_1}+(k+1)\left(\frac{1}{\mu_1}+\frac{1}{\mu_2}\right)\right].$$

Proof. It is clear that $(i, kb + l)$ is a state of the blockchain system for $i = 0, 1, \ldots, b, k = 0, 1, \ldots,$ and $l = 0, 1, \ldots, b - 1$.

When a transaction arrives at the blockchain system at time t, it observes and finds that there are i transactions in the block and $kb+l$ transactions in the queue. Based on the two stages of exponential service times and by using the stationary probability vector $\boldsymbol{\pi}$, we apply the law of total probability to be able to compute the average transaction-confirmation time. For this, our computation will have two different cases as follows:

Case One: $i = 0$. In this case, the transaction finds that there is no transaction in the block at the beginning moment, thus its transaction-confirmation time includes $k + 1$ block-generation times $(k + 1)/\mu_2$ and $k + 1$ blockchain-building times $(k + 1)/\mu_1$. Thus we obtain

$$E[T_{|i=0}] = \sum_{k=0}^{\infty}\sum_{l=0}^{b-1}\pi_{0,kb+l}\,(k+1)\left(\frac{1}{\mu_1}+\frac{1}{\mu_2}\right).$$

Case Two: $i = 1, 2, \ldots, b$. In this case, the transaction finds that there are i transactions in the block, thus its transaction-confirmation time includes $k + 1$ block-generation times $(k+1)/\mu_2$ and $k+2$ blockchain-building times $(k+2)/\mu_1$. We obtain

$$E[T_{|i\neq0}] = \sum_{i=1}^{b}\sum_{k=0}^{\infty}\sum_{l=0}^{b-1}\pi_{i,kb+l}\left[\frac{1}{\mu_1}+(k+1)\left(\frac{1}{\mu_1}+\frac{1}{\mu_2}\right)\right].$$

Therefore, by means of considering all the different cases, the average transaction-confirmation time $E[T]$ is given by

$$E[T] = \sum_{k=0}^{\infty}\sum_{l=0}^{b-1}\pi_{0,kb+l}\,(k+1)\left(\frac{1}{\mu_1}+\frac{1}{\mu_2}\right) + \sum_{i=1}^{b}\sum_{k=0}^{\infty}\sum_{l=0}^{b-1}\pi_{i,kb+l}\left[\frac{1}{\mu_1}+(k+1)\left(\frac{1}{\mu_1}+\frac{1}{\mu_2}\right)\right].$$

This completes the proof. ∎

Let $\langle \mathbf{x}\rangle_{|i=0}$ be the 1st element of the vector $\mathbf{x}$. The following theorem provides a simple expression for the average transaction-confirmation time $E[T]$ by means of the vector $\boldsymbol{\pi}_0$ and the rate matrix R.

Theorem 4. *If the blockchain queueing system is stable, then the average transaction-confirmation time* $E[T]$ *is given by*

$$E[T] = \frac{1}{\mu_1}\left[\boldsymbol{\pi}_0\,(I-R)^{-1}\,\boldsymbol{e} - \left\langle \boldsymbol{\pi}_0\,(I-R)^{-1}\right\rangle_{|i=0}\right]$$
$$+ \left(\frac{1}{\mu_1}+\frac{1}{\mu_2}\right)\boldsymbol{\pi}_0\,(I-R^b)^{-1}\,(I-R)^{-1}\,\boldsymbol{e}.$$

Proof. By using Theorem 3, we give some corresponding computation. Note that

$$\frac{1}{\mu_1}\sum_{i=1}^{b}\sum_{k=0}^{\infty}\sum_{l=0}^{b-1}\pi_{i,kb+l} = \frac{1}{\mu_1}\left[\sum_{k=0}^{\infty}\sum_{l=0}^{b-1}\pi_{kb+l}e - \sum_{k=0}^{\infty}\sum_{l=0}^{b-1}\pi_{0,kb+l}\right],$$

$$\sum_{k=0}^{\infty}\sum_{l=0}^{b-1}\pi_{kb+l}e = \sum_{k=0}^{\infty}\sum_{l=0}^{b-1}\pi_0 R^{kb+l}e = \pi_0\left(I - R\right)^{-1}e,$$

$$\sum_{k=0}^{\infty}\sum_{l=0}^{b-1}\pi_{0,kb+l} = \left\langle\sum_{k=0}^{\infty}\sum_{l=0}^{b-1}\pi_{kb+l}\right\rangle_{|i=0} = \left\langle\pi_0\left(I - R\right)^{-1}\right\rangle_{|i=0},$$

we obtain

$$\frac{1}{\mu_1}\sum_{i=1}^{b}\sum_{k=0}^{\infty}\sum_{l=0}^{b-1}\pi_{i,kb+l} = \frac{1}{\mu_1}\left[\pi_0\left(I - R\right)^{-1}e - \left\langle\pi_0\left(I - R\right)^{-1}\right\rangle_{|i=0}\right].$$

On the other hand, since

$$\sum_{i=0}^{b}\sum_{k=0}^{\infty}\sum_{l=0}^{b-1}\pi_{i,kb+l}\left(k + 1\right)\left(\frac{1}{\mu_1} + \frac{1}{\mu_2}\right) = \left(\frac{1}{\mu_1} + \frac{1}{\mu_2}\right)\sum_{k=0}^{\infty}\sum_{l=0}^{b-1}\left(k + 1\right)\pi_{kb+l}e,$$

we get

$$\sum_{k=0}^{\infty}\sum_{l=0}^{b-1}\left(k + 1\right)\pi_{kb+l} = \sum_{k=0}^{\infty}\sum_{l=0}^{b-1}\left(k + 1\right)\pi_0 R^{kb+l}$$

$$= \pi_0\sum_{k=0}^{\infty}\left(k + 1\right)R^{kb}\left(I - R^b\right)\left(I - R\right)^{-1}$$

$$= \pi_0\left(I - R^b\right)^{-1}\left(I - R\right)^{-1}.$$

This leads our desired result. The proof is completed.   ∎

In the remainder of this section, we provide some numerical examples to verify computability of our theoretical results and to analyze how the three performance measures $E\left[J\right]$, $E\left[I\right]$ and $E\left[T\right]$ depend on some crucial parameters of the blockchain queueing system.

In the numerical examples, we take some common parameters: Block-generation service rate $\mu_1 \in [0.05, 1.5]$, blockchain-building service rate $\mu_2 = 2$, arrival rate $\lambda = 0.3$, maximum block size $b_1 = 40, b_2 = 80, b_3 = 320$.

From the left part of Fig. 3, it is seen that $E\left[J\right]$ and $E\left[I\right]$ decrease, as μ_1 increases. At the same time, from the right part of Fig. 3, $E\left[J\right]$ decreases as b increases, but $E\left[I\right]$ increases as b increases.

From Fig. 4, it is seen that $E\left[T\right]$ decreases, as μ_1 increases; while it decreases, as b increases.

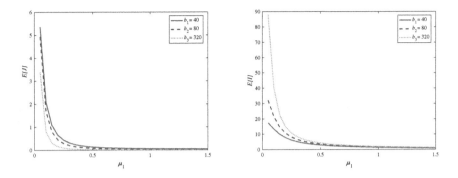

Fig. 3. $E[J]$, $E[I]$ vs. μ_1 for three different b_1, b_2, b_3.

Finally, we specifically observe the impact of the maximal block size b on the $E[T]$. Comparing with the parameters given in Figs. 3 and 4, we only change the two parameters b and λ: $b = 40, 41, 42, \ldots, 500$, $\lambda_1 = 0.1, \lambda_2 = 0.9, \lambda_3 = 1.5$. From Fig. 5, it is seen that $E[T]$ decreases, as b increases. In addition, it is observed that there exists a critical value η such that when $b \leq \eta$, $E[T]$ increases, as λ increases. On the contrary, when $b > \eta$, $E[T]$ increases, as λ decreases. In fact, such a difference is also intuitive that the block generation time becomes bigger as λ decreases.

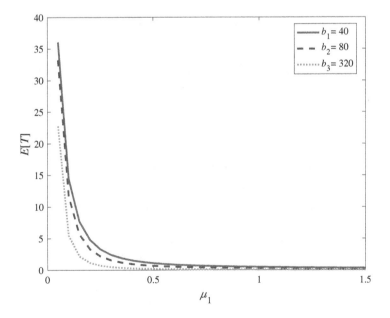

Fig. 4. $E[T]$ vs. μ_1 for three different b_1, b_2, b_3.

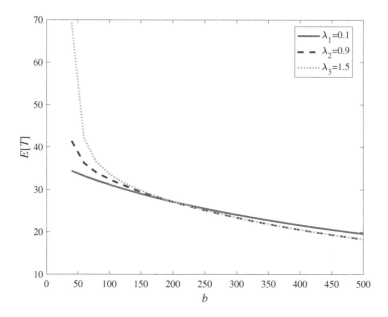

Fig. 5. $E[T]$ vs. b for three different $\lambda_1, \lambda_2, \lambda_3$.

5 Concluding Remarks

In this paper, our aim is to focus on how to develop queueing theory of blockchain systems. To do this, we design an interesting Markovian batch-service queueing system with two different service stages, while the two stages can well express the mining process in the miners pool and the building of a new blockchain. By using the matrix-geometric solution, we not only obtain a system stable condition but also simply express three key performance measures: The average number of transactions in the queue, the average number of transactions in a block, and the average transaction-confirmation time. Finally, we use numerical examples to verify computability of our theoretical results. Along these lines, we will continue our future research on the following directions:

– Considering more general blockchain queueing systems, for example, the Markov arrival process of transactions, and two stages of phase-type batch services.
– Analyzing multiple classes of transactions in the blockchain systems. Also, the transactions are dealt with in the block-generation and blockchain-building processes according to a priority service discipline.
– When the arrivals of transactions are a renewal process, and the block-generation times or the blockchain-building times follow general probability distributions, an interesting research work is to focus on fluid and diffusion approximations of the blockchain systems.

- Setting up reward function with respect to cost structures, transaction fees, mining reward, consensus mechanism, security and so forth. Our aim is to find optimal policies in the blockchain systems.
- Further developing stochastic optimization and control, Markov decision processes and stochastic game theory in the blockchain systems.

References

1. Beck, R., Avital, M., Rossi, M., Thatcher, J.B.: Blockchain technology in business and information systems research. Bus. Inf. Syst. Eng. **59**(6), 381–384 (2017)
2. Bhaskar, N.D., Chuen, D.L.K.: Bitcoin mining technology. In: Handbook of Digital Currency, pp. 45–65 (2015)
3. Biais, B., Bisiere, C., Bouvard, M., Casamatta, C.: The blockchain folk theorem. Working paper, Toulouse School of Economics, Université Toulouse Capitole, pp. 1–71 (2018)
4. Böhme, R., Christin, N., Edelman, B., Moore, T.: Bitcoin: economics, technology, and governance. J. Econ. Perspect. **29**(2), 213–38 (2015)
5. Catalini, C., Gans, J.S.: Some simple economics of the blockchain. National Bureau of Economic Research, No. w22952, pp. 1–29 (2016)
6. Constantinides, P., Henfridsson, O., Parker, G.G.: Introduction - platforms and infrastructures in the digital age. Inf. Syst. Res. **29**(2), 381–400 (2018)
7. Davidson, S., De Filippi, P., Potts, J.: Economics of blockchain. Online Available: HAL Id: hal-01382002, pp. 1–23 (2016)
8. Debus, J.: Consensus methods in blockchain systems, pp. 1–58. Frankfurt School of Finance & Management, Blockchain Center, Technical report (2017)
9. Dinh, T.T.A., Liu, R., Zhang, M., Chen, G., Ooi, B.C., Wang, J.: Untangling blockchain: a data processing view of blockchain systems. IEEE Trans. Knowl. Data Eng. **30**(7), 1366–1385 (2018)
10. Foroglou, G., Tsilidou, A.L.: Further applications of the blockchain. Abgerufen Am 3, 1–9 (2015)
11. Houy, N.: The bitcoin mining game. Online Available: HAL Id: halshs-00958224, pp. 1–17 (2014)
12. Huckle, S., Bhattacharya, R., White, M., Beloff, N.: Internet of Things, blockchain and shared economy applications. Procedia Comput. Sci. **98**, 461–466 (2016)
13. Kasahara, S., Kawahara, J.: Effect of Bitcoin fee on transaction-confirmation process. arXiv preprint arXiv:1604.00103, pp. 1–24 (2016)
14. Kawase, Y., Kasahara, S.: Transaction-confirmation time for bitcoin: a queueing analytical approach to blockchain mechanism. In: Yue, W., Li, Q.-L., Jin, S., Ma, Z. (eds.) QTNA 2017. LNCS, vol. 10591, pp. 75–88. Springer, Cham (2017). https://doi.org/10.1007/978-3-319-68520-5_5
15. Kiayias, A., Koutsoupias, E., Kyropoulou, M., Tselekounis, Y.; Blockchain mining games. In: Proceedings of the 2016 ACM Conference on Economics and Computation, pp. 365–382. ACM (2016)
16. Kondor, D., Pósfai, M., Csabai, I., Vattay, G.: Do the rich get richer? An empirical analysis of the Bitcoin transaction network. PloS ONE **9**(2), 1–10 (2014)
17. Lewenberg, Y., Bachrach, Y., Sompolinsky, Y., Zohar, A., Rosenschein, J.S.: Bitcoin mining pools: a cooperative game theoretic analysis. In: Proceedings of the 2015 International Conference on Autonomous Agents and Multiagent Systems, pp. 919–927 (2015)

18. Li, Q.L.: Constructive Computation in Stochastic Models with Applications: The RG-Factorizations. Springer, Heidelberg (2010). https://doi.org/10.1007/978-3-642-11492-2
19. Lin, I.C., Liao, T.C.: A survey of blockchain security issues and challenges. Int. J. Netw. Secur. **19**(5), 653–659 (2017)
20. Lindman, J., Tuunainen, V.K., Rossi, M.: Opportunities and risks of blockchain technologies - a research agenda. In: Proceedings of the 50th Hawaii International Conference on System Sciences, pp. 1533–1542 (2017)
21. Mettler, M.: Blockchain technology in healthcare: the revolution starts here. In: The 18th International IEEE Conference on e-Health Networking, Applications and Services, pp. 1–3. IEEE (2016)
22. Montemayor, L., Boersma, T., van Dorp, T.: Comprehensive guide to companies involved in blockchain and energy. Blockchain Business (2018)
23. Nakamoto, S.: Bitcoin: a peer-to-peer electronic cash system, pp. 1–9 (2008). https://bitcoin.org/bitcoin.pdf
24. Neuts, M.F.: Matrix-Geometric Solutions in Stochastic Models. Johns Hopkins University Press, Baltimore (1981)
25. NRI, Survey on blockchain technologies and related services. FY2015 Report, Nomura Research Institute, pp. 1–78 (2015). http://www.meti.go.jp/english/press/2016/pdf/053101f.pdf
26. Ober, M., Katzenbeisser, S., Hamacher, K.: Structure and anonymity of the Bitcoin transaction graph. Future Internet **5**(2), 237–250 (2013)
27. Plansky, J., O'Donnell, T., Richards, K.: A strategist's guide to blockchain. Strateg. + Bus. Mag. **82**, 1–12 (2016)
28. Risius, M., Spohrer, K.: A blockchain research framework. Bus. Inf. Syst. Eng. **59**(6), 385–409 (2017)
29. Swan, M.: Blockchain: Blueprint for a New Economy. O'Reilly Media Inc., Newton (2015)
30. Tsai, W.T., Blower, R., Zhu, Y., Yu, L.: A system view of financial blockchains. In: The IEEE Symposium on Service-Oriented System Engineering, pp. 450–457. IEEE (2016)
31. Tschorsch, F., Scheuermann, B.: Bitcoin and beyond: a technical survey on decentralized digital currencies. IEEE Commun. Surv. Tutor. **18**(3), 2084–2123 (2016)
32. Vranken, H.: Sustainability of bitcoin and blockchains. Curr. Opin. Environ. Sustain. **28**, 1–9 (2017)
33. Wang, W., et al.: A survey on consensus mechanisms and mining management in blockchain networks. arXiv preprint arXiv:1805.02707, pp. 1–33 (2018)
34. Yli-Huumo, J., Ko, D., Choi, S., Park, S., Smolander, K.: Where is current research on blockchain technology? – A systematic review. PloS ONE **11**(10), 1–27 (2016)
35. Zheng, Z., Xie, S., Dai, H.N., Chen, X., Wang, H.: An overview of blockchain technology: architecture, consensus, and future trends. In: The IEEE International Congress on Big Data, pp. 557–564. IEEE (2017)
36. Zheng, Z., Xie, S., Dai, H.N., Wang, H.: Blockchain challenges and opportunities: a survey. Int. J. Web Grid Serv. **13**(2), 1–25 (2017)

Optimal Energy Efficiency Data Dissemination Strategy Based on Optimal Stopping Theory in Mobile Network

Gaocai Wang$^{(\boxtimes)}$, Ying Peng, and Qifei Zhao

Guangxi University, Nanning 53004, China
wanggcgx@163.com, 623833@qq.com, feigefeixiang@163.com

Abstract. Data dissemination application has become popular in mobile networks, which made energy consumed by mobile terminals growing rapidly. It is becoming an important research topic to reduce energy consumption for data dissemination in mobile networks. This paper studies the energy consumption optimization problem in mobile networks with Time-Varying channel quality, when multiple sending terminals use the same channel for data dissemination. Sending terminal transmits data with a certain probability for competing channel. After getting channel successfully, the sending terminal decides whether to distribute data according to channel quality, thereby saving energy. The maximization problem of average energy efficiency for distributing data with delay demand is constructed firstly in this paper. Then this maximization problem is transformed into an optimal stopping rule problem, and the optimal myopic stopping rule is obtained. Finally, the optimal transmission rate thresholds at each period are solved by optimal stopping theory, and then the optimal energy efficiency data dissemination strategy based on optimal stopping theory is realized. Simulation results show that the strategy proposed in this paper has bigger average energy efficiency and higher average delivery than other strategies, and achieves better energy optimization effect and network performance.

Keywords: Mobile networks · Data dissemination
Optimal energy efficiency · Optimal stopping · Optimal rate

1 Introduction

With the fast development of mobile networks, various mobile terminals are rapidly becoming popular. In particular, mobile smart phones have become a necessity for people's daily lives. Mobile terminals equipped with various wireless interfaces such as Bluetooth, Wi-Fi, and cellular networks have strong wireless communication capabilities. A user carrying a mobile terminal can perform

This study was funded by the National Natural Science Foundation of China under Grant No. 61562006 and 61632009, 61772233, in part by the Natural Science Foundation of Guangxi Province under Grant No. 2016GXNSFBA380181.

© Springer Nature Switzerland AG 2018
X. Chen et al. (Eds.): CSoNet 2018, LNCS 11280, pp. 41–52, 2018.
https://doi.org/10.1007/978-3-030-04648-4_4

various types of data communication with other mobile terminals such as audio, video, images, text, etc. And it can also distribute shared data to other mobile terminals within the transmission range, such as video conference information, major Real-Time news, and online traffic information and so on. The mobile terminal realizes information sharing efficiently by disseminating data, which has become an important application of mobile networks. However, the battery life of the mo-bile terminal is limited. Disseminating a large amount of data will quickly exhaust the power and affect the normal operation of the mobile terminal, especially in an environment where the power cannot be supplemented in time. Therefore, researching data dissemination strategies to save energy on the basis of guaranteed performance is an important topic in the study of energy consumption and performance optimization in mobile networks.

In mobile networks, the quality of the wireless channel randomly changes over time due to user mobility, environmental interference and multipath propagation and so on. The energy consumption for data dissemination will effectively reduce if the sending terminal chooses to disseminate data when the channel quality is good. In scenarios where multiple sending terminals use the same channel to disseminate data, the channel is only allowed to be used by one sending terminal at the same time. It will result in transmission collisions and data dissemination fails if multiple (more than one) sending terminals use a channel to disseminate data at the same time. In order to reduce energy waste caused by transmission collisions of a plurality of transmitting terminals, the sending terminal detects the channel usage condition through whether successfully receiving a response signal from the receiving terminal within a certain time when it disseminates data to the receiving terminal [1,6]. And the channel quality is estimated based on the power value of the signal. When only one terminal is detected to use the channel, the transmitting terminal decides whether to continue to disseminate data according to the quality of the channel so as to avoid increasing the energy consumption of the transmission data when the channel quality is poor. The process is called channel competition when the sending terminal detects the channel usage status. It is a key for saving energy consumption that the sending terminal selects the optimal channel quality to disseminate data on the premise of successfully competing to the channel.

The paper is organized as follows. Section 2 reviews the related research work. Section 3 describes the system model and optimization problems. Section 4 describes the optimal energy efficiency data dissemination strategy based on the optimal stopping theory. Section 5 gives simulation results and analysis. Finally, we summarize the full text and look forward to further work in Sect. 6.

2 Related Research Work

In [1], the authors assume that multiple sending terminals participate in channel competition with equal probability and transmit data for a given length of time. The optimal stopping theory is used to derive the optimal transmission rate of the data dissemination by the sending terminal so as to increase the amount of data dissemination per unit of energy consumption and improve energy efficiency. In [2], the authors study the energy optimization problem of data dissemination from the perspective of the probability of participating in channel competition in mobile networks. This paper uses game theory to derive the optimal probability that multiple sending terminals participate in channel competition to reduce the energy consumption of data transmission collision and save the energy consumption of data dissemination. In [3], the authors study the optimal control problem for flood data dissemination in mobile social networks. This paper assumes that the control ability is a function of time dissemination. It studies the optimal control strategy of data dissemination and proposes an Easy-to-Handle data dissemination analysis model. It also solves the time dissemination problem of the optimal control signal through the dynamic programming to minimize the total network cost. In [4,5], the authors study the energy optimization problem of data transmission over randomly varying channel quality. This paper uses the optimal stopping theory to solve the optimal transmission rate threshold when the rate of data generation on the link is constant and changing respectively. It improves energy efficiency and increases transmission rate on the premise of guaranteeing data transmission delay. In [6], the authors study the distributed opportunity scheduling problem that a plurality of sending terminals compete for the same channel for data dissemination in mobile ad hoc networks. This paper uses the optimal stopping theory to construct an optimal stopping problem that maximizes network throughput. And it also solves the optimal transmission rate of the sending terminal by a backward induction method to maximize the throughput of the entire network. But this paper does not consider the data transmission delay requirements and it assumes that the sending terminal always has enough data to be distributed all the time. In [7], the authors study the data dissemination problem when the channel quality changes randomly in mobile networks. This paper uses the optimal stopping theory to solve the optimal transmission rate threshold for maximizing network throughput. And it also uses Non-cooperative games to solve users' best response strategy to improve throughput. In [8], the authors study the problem of effectively disseminating data to a given number of receiving terminals in the vehicular ad hoc networks. This paper uses the vehicular network's mobile features to design heuristic algorithms so as to reduce data dissemination overhead and delay. In [9], the authors study the problem of minimizing the delay when multiple mobile users download different data contents due to their interests in heterogeneous cellular networks. The optimal distributed caching algorithm is designed by using the confidence level to minimize the download time of data dissemination. In [10], the authors study the problem of distributing different data contents according to different user needs in Vehicle-Based opportunistic networks.

3 Network Model and Problem Description

3.1 Network Model

In a mobile network with a base station support, the base station sends a Q_d data to mobile terminals at intervals of T_{diss}. Mobile terminals that are not within the transmission range of the base station cannot directly receive the data, and other mobile terminals that receive the data need to distribute data to them. The data dissemination model in mobile networks is shown in Fig. 1. On the other hand, one round of channel competition and data dissemination process is shown in Fig. 2.

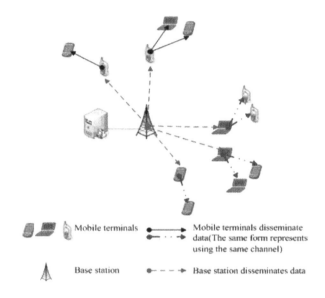

Fig. 1. Mobile network model

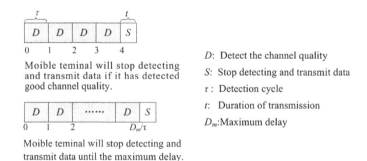

Fig. 2. One round of channel competition and data dissemination process

3.2 Problem Description

Assume that the number of transmitting terminals using the same channel is K in the transmission interference range. Sending terminals contend for the channel with an equal probability p, and the value is $1/K$. At the beginning of each round of channel contention, K transmitting terminals participate in channel competition with probability p. When only one terminal contends for the channel, it is called channel competition success. This success is called the first round channel competition success, and assuming that the sending terminal is A. If the current channel quality is good, A continues to disseminate data, and other sending terminals wait to participate in the next round of channel contention. Otherwise, the A gives up disseminating data, exits this round of channel competition, and waits for participation in the next round of channel competition, while the remaining $K-1$ transmitting terminals continue to contend for the channel. When there is only one terminal competing channel, the second round is successfully contested, and the sending terminal is called B. In addition, B performs the same operation as A. Obviously, the terminal A successfully competing for the first round continues to disseminate data if the channel quality in the current cycle is good. Otherwise, each terminal that successfully obtaining the channel has to give up the use of the channel, and the channel is successfully contending for K times. Therefore, the probability that the channel will compete successfully in the i-th round is:

$$\rho_i^s = \binom{1}{K-i+1}p(1-p)^{K-i} \tag{1}$$

The total competition expected times of the channel is $b_i = \frac{1}{\rho_i^s}$ in the i-th round successful competition process. The number of competition expectations for each sending terminal is $b_i \cdot p$ in the i-th competition. And the total number of competition expectations is $\sum_{i=1}^{K} b_i \cdot p$ in each round of K-time competition. The transmission power consumption of the sending terminal is P, and the duration of each competition is τ. Indeed, the competition energy consumption is $P \cdot \tau$. Therefore, the expected competition power consumption of the sending terminal is $\sum_{i=1}^{K} b_i \cdot p \cdot P \cdot \tau$ in each round of channel competition. The sending terminal which successfully contends for the channel disseminates data in the 1-th round if the channel quality is good. The expected duration of competition is $b_1 \cdot \tau$ and the length of the remaining transmission time is $T - b_1 \cdot \tau$.

In an actual data dissemination service application, the data has a certain deadline. And the data that has not been transmitted within the deadline will be discarded. This paper assumes that the maximum delay of data is D_m. If a sending terminal successfully contends for the channel and carries the data to be distributed which is about to reach the maximum delay D_m, then it distributes data without selecting the channel quality, so as to avoid the data being discarded for exceeding delay. Obviously, the total number of competing expectations of the sending terminal is $b_1 \cdot p$. The expected competition energy is $b_1 \cdot p \cdot P \cdot \tau$. The expected competition time is $b_1 \cdot \tau$. And the length of the remaining transmission time is $T - b_1 \cdot \tau$.

4   Optimal Energy Efficiency Data Dissemination Strategy Based on Optimal Stopping Theory

4.1   The Formation of Optimal Energy Efficiency Problems

Assuming that the sending terminal successfully obtains the channel in the i-th competition of one round channel contention. And the channel transmission rate is R. Then the energy efficiency of the terminal disseminating data is:

$$\gamma = \frac{Rt}{Pt - E_{total}} \tag{2}$$

Among them, E_{total} is the sum of all competing energy consumption and reference energy consumption before the sending terminal obtains the i-th transmission opportunity. And it is abbreviated to the total energy consumption for detection, which is calculated from the next round of channel competition after the last successful data transmission, including competitive energy consumption and reference energy consumption in this round. The reference energy consumption is the basic energy consumed by each current device of the transmitting terminal in the Non-off state (including the idle state and the transmission state). Among them, t represents the actual transmission time length, whose value is determined by the amount of data to be distributed and the transmission rate. It is defined as:

$$t = \begin{cases} Q_d/R, Q_d/R \leq T - b_1 \cdot \tau \\ T - b_1 \cdot \tau, Q_d/R > T - b_1 \cdot \tau \end{cases} \tag{3}$$

In order to save energy consumption, each sending terminal maximizes its own energy efficiency to achieve optimal energy efficiency. Therefore, the optimal energy efficiency γ_{op} of the sending terminal is defined as:

$$\gamma_{op} = max[\frac{Rt}{Pt - E_{total}}] \tag{4}$$

4.2   Optimal Stopping Rule Problem of Optimal Energy Efficiency

After receiving the data with the maximum delay of D_m, the transmitting terminal starts participating in channel competition and observes the quality of the successfully committed channel. The sending terminal will disseminate data if the channel quality reaches the optimal energy efficiency standard. Otherwise, it waits to participate in the next round of channel competition. If the sending terminal keeps observing until the maximum delay D_m while carrying the data, it must perform data dissemination after obtaining the channel, so as to avoid the data being discarded due to the excessive delay. Therefore, the transmitting terminal participates in channel competition with $M = \lfloor \frac{D_m}{t} \rfloor$ rounds.

If the sending terminal obtains the channel and distributes the data in the N-th $(1 \leq N < M)$ round, its energy efficiency is

$$\gamma_N = \frac{R_N t_N}{P t_N + \sum_{n=1}^{N}(\sum_{i=1}^{K} b_i p P \tau + P_0 T)} \tag{5}$$

Among them, R_N is the transmission rate obtained by the transmitting terminal in the N-th round; t_N represents the actual time length of data dissemination at this moment, which is defined in (3); $\sum_{i=1}^{K} b_i p P \tau$ represents the expected competitive energy consumption. P_0 is the reference power consumption of the transmitting terminal. And $P_0 \cdot T$ is the reference energy consumption. Since the transmitting terminal must disseminate data after successfully competing to the channel in the M-th round, the energy efficiency of the M round is:

$$\gamma_M = \frac{R_M t_M}{P t_M + \sum_{n=1}^{M-1}(\sum_{i=1}^{K} b_i p P \tau + b_1 p P \tau + M P_0 T)} \tag{6}$$

It is called one data dissemination that the sending terminal from participating in the channel competition to successfully competing to the channel and disseminating data. Indeed, one data distribution includes one or more rounds of channel competition and one data dissemination. N_y is defined as the number of channel competition rounds of data dissemination in the y-th. That is, the time when channel competition stops and data dissemination starts, which is referred to as the stop time. If the sending terminal repeatedly performs data dissemination for Y times, the corresponding stop time sequence is $\{N_1, N_2, \cdots, N_y, \cdots, N_Y\}$. The transmission rate sequence is $\{R_{N_1}, R_{N_2}, \cdots, R_{N_y}, \cdots, R_{N_Y}\}$. The actual transmission time length sequence is $\{t/N_1, t/N_2, \cdots, t/N_y, \cdots, t/N_Y\}$. And the detected total energy consumption sequence is $\{E_{total,N_1}, E_{total,N_2}, \cdots, E_{total,N_y}, \cdots, E_{total,N_Y}\}$.

Combining (5) and (6), the average energy efficiency of the sending terminal is:

$$\chi = \sum_{y=1}^{Y} \gamma_{N_y} = \frac{\sum_{y=1}^{Y} R_{N_y} t_{N_y}}{\sum_{y=1}^{Y}(P t_{N_y} + E_{total,N_y})} \tag{7}$$

According to the law of large numbers, furthermore, (7) transforms the following

$$\chi = \frac{E[R_N t_N]}{E[P t_N + E_{total,N}]} \tag{8}$$

Here, $E[\cdot]$ represents the mathematical expectation. N represents the number of competition rounds before disseminating data, which is also the stop time of the channel competition. Since the data to be disseminated has the maximum delay D_m, the maximum stop time of the channel contention is M.

Define the stop time set for channel contention as $= \{N : 1 \leq N \leq M\}$. So the biggest problem with the average energy efficiency of this paper is

$$max_{N\in} \frac{E[R_N t_N]}{E[Pt_N + E_{total,N}]} \tag{9}$$

According to (8) and (9), the optimal average energy efficiency (The average value of the maximum amount of data per unit energy transmission) is:

$$\chi^* = sup_{N\in} \frac{E[R_N t_N]}{E[Pt_N + E_{total,N}]} \tag{10}$$

Further, the Formula (10) is transformed by an equation transformation into:

$$sup_{N\in}(E[R_N t_N] - \chi^*(E[Pt_N + E_{total,N}])) = 0 \tag{11}$$

The formula (11) is an average energy efficiency maximization problem concerning the maximization of expected reward $E[\phi_N(\chi)]$ about χ, where the reward function $\phi_N(\chi)$ is:

$$\phi_N(\chi) = R_N t_N - \chi(Pt_N + E_{total,N}) \tag{12}$$

Therefore, the average energy efficiency maximization problem of (9) is converted into an optimal stopping problem:

$$\psi(\chi) = max_{N\in}E[\phi_N(\chi)] \tag{13}$$

The goal of (13) is to obtain the optimal stopping time $N^* = N(\chi^*)$ of the channel competition, so as to obtain the optimal average energy efficiency $\chi*$. So there is:

$$N^* = \arg\sup_{N\in} \frac{E[R_N t_N]}{E[pt_N + E_{total,N}]} \tag{14}$$

The average energy efficiency maximization problem of (14) is a Limited-Range optimal stopping problem. This problem has an optimal stopping rule (shown in [4]). In this paper, the optimal myopia stopping problem is solved by inverse induction. And the transmitting terminal obtains an optimal transmission rate threshold when stops channel contention and disseminates data in each period T.

4.3   Optimal Stopping Rule of Optimal Energy Efficiency

The sending terminal's reward for stopping channel competition and disseminating data is $\phi_n(\chi) = R_n t_n - \chi(Pt_n + E_{total,n})$ when successfully competing to the channel at time n. If it does not disseminate data, the sending terminal will expect to receive reward:

$$E[\phi_{n+1}(\chi)|F_n] = E[R_{n+1}t_{n+1} - \chi(Pt_{n+1} + E_{total,n+1})|F_n] \tag{15}$$

Here, $n = 1, 2, \cdots, M - 1$ and F_n represents that the transmission rate sequence values $R_1, \cdots, R_n$. According to the optimal stopping rule [5,11], if the actual reward $\phi_N(\chi)$ of the data dissemination is greater than or equal to the expected reward $E[\phi_N(\chi)|Fn]$ after the transmitting terminal successfully competes with the channel at time n, the data will be disseminated. Instead, the sending terminal abandons the use of the channel and continues to participate in the next round of channel competition. Therefore, the condition that the transmitting terminal disseminates data after obtaining the channel at time n satisfies:

$$\phi_n(\chi) \geq E[\phi_{n+1}(\chi)|F_n], n = 1, 2, \cdots, M - 1 \tag{16}$$

5   Experimental Results and Analysis

This section compares the Optimal Energy Efficiency Data Dissemination Strategy based on optimal stopping theory proposed by us with other data dissemination strategies of related literatures, then analyzes and evaluates the average energy efficiency and the average transmission rate of each strategy. The strategies used in this paper for comparison include the following three: (1)Energy-Efficient Optimization for Distributed Opportunistic Scheduling Strategy (EEO-DOS);

(2) Energy Efficient Data Dissemination Strategy Based on Game Theory (EEDDBG);

(3) Randomly competing data dissemination strategy (Random).

The value of each parameter in the simulation experiment is shown in Table 1.

Table 1. Simulation experiment parameter values

Parameters	Description	Value
W	Bandwidth [HZ]	225.944 5
N_0	Noise power spectral density [W/HZ]	10^7
σ^2	Channel gain variance correlation value8	10^{-7}
P	Transmission power [W]	1
g	Channel gain	0.1
A	Peak of main signal amplitude	$0 \sim 4$
K	Number of sending terminals	5
T_{diss}	Cycle of base station dissemination data [s]	4
Q_d	Amount of data distributed by the base station at each time [KB]	144
D_m	The maximum delay of data [s]	10
T	Channel quality holding time [s]	$0.7 \times D_m$
τ	Channel competition period [s]	$0.001 \times T$
T_{trans}	Transmission time length of EEODOS [s]	$3 \times \tau$
Pe	Reference power consumption [W]	$0.1 \times P$

Energy efficiency is the ratio of the total amount of data disseminated by the sending terminal to the total energy consumption. And the average energy efficiency is the average of the energy efficiency of each sending terminal. The average energy efficiency represents the average amount of data dissemination per unit of energy consumption. It also represents the data dissemination efficiency by the unit energy consumption. The larger the average energy efficiency, the greater the amount of data dissemination per unit of energy consumption and the more energy saved. Figure 3 shows the comparison of the average energy efficiency of each strategy when the Rayleigh and Rician distributions have different parameters.

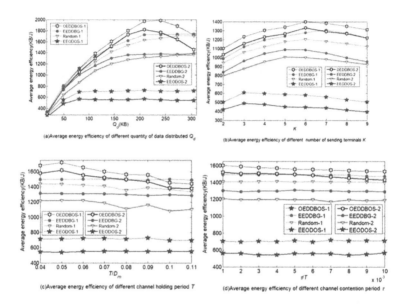

Fig. 3. The comparison of the average energy efficiency of different strategy

Figure 3 The comparison of the average energy efficiency of different strategy In Fig. 3, OEDDBOS-1 indicates the OEDDBOS situation under the Rician distribution, and OEDDBOS-2 suggests that the OEDDBOS condition under the Rayleigh distribution. And the other three strategies are the same. From Fig. 3, OEDDBOS has the greatest average energy efficiency. That is, it has the best saving effect. OEDDBOS obtains the optimal transmission rate threshold of the sending terminal by using the optimal stopping theory at each period T, which is based on the quantity of data to be distributed Qd, the number of terminals participating in the competition K, the channel holding period T, the channel contention period, and the value of the reference power consumption P0. Indeed, this threshold ensures the maximum average energy efficiency. EEDDBG obtains the optimal probability that the sending terminal participates in the competition by game theory. This strategy mainly reduces the conflict energy consumption of channel competition. But, it does not consider the random variation of channel quality and its average energy efficiency is related to the probability distribution of channel transmission rate. Random has neither obtained the optimal probability of participating in the competition, nor selected the transmission rate when the channel quality is good, and its average energy efficiency is lower. EEODOS obtains the optimal transmission rate threshold through the optimal stopping theory.

6 Conclusion

In this paper, firstly, the optimal stopping problem of the maximum average energy efficiency with maximum delay requirement is constructed. Then, the optimal stopping theory is used to solve the optimal transmission rate threshold of the data dissemination after the transmitting terminal successfully competes to the channel in each channel competition period. Finally, the sending terminal that successfully competes to the channel selects the time when the average energy efficiency is optimal to transmit data by comparing the transmission rate of the current channel period with the corresponding optimal rate threshold. Simulation results show that Optimal Energy Efficiency Data Dissemination Strategy Based on the Optimal Stopping Theory proposed in this paper effectively improves the average energy efficiency and the average transmission rate when the sending terminal disseminates data, and saves network energy consumption on the premise of ensuring network performance.

References

1. Garcia-Saavedra, A., Serrano, P., Banchs, A.: Energy-efficient optimization for distributed opportunistic scheduling. IEEE Commun. Lett. **18**(6), 1083–1086 (2014)
2. Antonopoulos, A., Verikoukis, C.: Multi-player game theoretic MAC strategies for energy efficient data dissemination. IEEE Trans. Wirel. Commun. **13**(2), 592–603 (2014)
3. Chen, P.Y., Cheng, S.M., Chen, K.C.: Optimal control of epidemic information dissemination over networks. IEEE Trans. Cybern. **44**(12), 2316–2328 (2014)
4. Peng, Y., Wang, G., Huang, S., et al.: An energy consumption optimization strategy for data transmission based on optimal stopping theory in mobile networks. Chin. J. Comput. **39**(6), 1162–1175 (2016). (in Chinese)
5. Peng, Y., Wang, G., Wang, N., et al.: Energy consumption optimization strategy for data transmission based on data arrival rate in mobile networks. Comput. Sci. **44**(1), 117–122 (2017). (in Chinese)
6. Chen, H., Baras, J.S.: Distributed opportunistic scheduling for wireless ad-hoc networks with block-fading model. IEEE J. Sel. Areas Commun. **31**(11), 2324–2337 (2013)
7. Zheng, D., Ge, W.Y., Zhang, J.S.: Distributed opportunistic scheduling for ad hoc networks with random access: an optimal stopping approach. IEEE Trans. Inf. Theor. **55**(1), 205–222 (2009)
8. Yan, T., Zhang, W., Wang, G.: DOVE: data dissemination to a desired number of receivers in VANET. IEEE Trans. Veh. Technol. **63**(4), 1903–1916 (2014)

9. Li, J., Chen, Y., Lin, Z., et al.: Distributed caching for data dissemination in the downlink of heterogeneous networks. IEEE Trans. Commun. **63**(10), 3553–3568 (2015)
10. Li, Y., Zhu, X., Jin, D.: Multiple content dissemination in roadside-unit-aided vehicular opportunistic networks. IEEE Trans. Veh. Technol. **63**(8), 3947–3956 (2014)
11. Ferguson, T.S.: Optimal Stopping and Applications. http://www.math.ucla.edu/~tom/Stopping/Contents.html. Accessed 29 June 2018

Cease with Bass: A Framework for Real-Time Topic Detection and Popularity Prediction Based on Long-Text Contents

Quanquan Chu[1], Zhenhao Cao[1], Xiaofeng Gao[1(✉)], Peng He[2], Qianni Deng[1], and Guihai Chen[1]

[1] Shanghai Key laboratory of Scalable Computing and Systems, Department of Computer Science and Engineering, Shanghai Jiao Tong University, Shanghai, China
{spring_chu,Hazelnut}@sjtu.edu.cn, {gao-xf,deng-qn,gchen}@cs.sjtu.edu.cn
[2] Tencent, Shenzhen, China
paulhe@tencent.com

Abstract. Nowadays, social network has become a powerful information source. At the advent of new services like WeChat Official Account, long-text contents have been embedded into social network. Compared with tweet-style contents, long-text contents are better-organized and less prone to noise. However, existing methods for real-time topic detection leveraging long-textual data do not produce satisfactory performance on sensitivity and scalability, and long-text based trend prediction methods are also facing absence of stronger rationales. In this paper, we propose a framework specifically adapted for long-text based topic analysis, covering both topic detection and popularity prediction. For topic detection, we design a novel real-time topic model dubbed as a **C**ost-**E**ffective **A**nd **S**calable **E**mbedding model (**CEASE**) based on improved GloVe Models and keyword frequency clustering algorithm. We then propose strategies for topic tracking and renewal by taking topic abortion, mergence and neologies into account. For popularity prediction, we propose **F**eature-**C**ombined **B**ass model with **A**ssociation Analysis (**FCA-Bass**) with a strong rationale transplanted from economic fields. Our methods are validated by experiments on real-world dataset from WeChat and are proved to outperform several currently existing mainstream methods.

Keywords: Topic detection · Popularity prediction · Social network

1 Introduction

Studies on social network analysis are prevalent nowadays, ranging from popularity prediction to text-based sentiment analysis. As a highly-organized information pattern, *Topic* deserves our attentions because they normally have close connections with real-world events. Accurate detection on topics can help sense

X. Chen et al. (Eds.): CSoNet 2018, LNCS 11280, pp. 53–65, 2018.
https://doi.org/10.1007/978-3-030-04648-4_5

important events efficiently, which has great significance for many services such as marketing, advertisement, recommendation systems and search engines. By detecting and tracking topics at an early stage, we can capture textual or temporal features of hot topics. This further enables us to predict their future popularity. For example, news media aims at accurate detection and trend prediction of events to maximize their news visibilities. More importantly, detecting topics and predicting popularity help us get in-depth understanding of information diffusion.

Topics are extracted from texts in social network, which is largely dependent on Natural Language Processing (NLP) techniques. Online textual contents are classified into short-text and long-text with distinct tactics. Recently, some newly-emerging services like WeChat Official Accounts bring about a new type of long-text items. Operators of official accounts publish articles on social network, and then wait for readers to like, comment or share these articles. Embedded in social networks to an unprecedented degree, these long-text items are endowed a stronger diffusion power. This new service pattern has aroused a burst in long-text contents, greatly raising the necessity of long-text based and real-time studies. Moreover, topics of long-text are inherently more implicit and complex in comparison with short-text, bringing more challenging problems for analysis. However, most existing studies on topic analysis based on long-text are not cost-effective or scalable, ignoring real-time requirements from industrial application.

In this paper, we focus on real-time topic detection and topic popularity prediction, and propose an integrated model specially adapted to scenarios for long-text items. The performance of our model has been proven to outperform current existing methods on both detection sensitivity and prediction accuracy.

Topic Detection. In this work, *topic* is formally defined as a set of keywords with weights. Most current methods statically maintain all topics once they emerged. Actually, topics can evolve or fade away as time goes, and different events may have intrinsic connections or similarities that may lead multiple topics to merge. More importantly, new concepts or neologies could be brought by new events, which induces vibrations in latent semantic space both globally and locally. Most existing studies provide no strategy for detection and modification in response to semantic vibration. **CEASE** handles detection task dynamically, by considering not only topic abortion and mergence but also cost-effective semantic modification for neologies. These will be discussed in detail in Sect. 3.

Popularity Prediction. Numerous researches on popularity prediction simply focus on trials of different feature sets without a strong rationale or interpretablity. We find the underlying similarity between a topic and a product, and then transplant the Bass Model, one of the most widely applied models in the management science, into social network analysis. Therefore, we develop a novel model with a strong rationale towards popularity prediction. To the best of our knowledge, this is the first research embedding the Bass Model to topic-oriented studies, which proves its effectiveness.

Our Contributions. We summarize our contributions as follows:

- We propose a novel real-time topic model dubbed as a **C**ost-**E**ffective **A**nd **S**calable **E**mbedding model (**CEASE**) based on global word vectors. Given data streams containing corpus, **CEASE** automatically detects semantic vibrations both locally (word-level) and globally (topic-level). **CEASE** maintains the most valuable topics dynamically and promises the clustering quality by controlling internal homophily and external distinction.
- We transplant the underlying idea of Bass Model, a widely applied model in management science, into topic-related area of social network analysis. We extend the strong rationale behind the Bass Model and adapt it to our long-text topic scenarios.

The remainder of this article is organized as follows. In Sect. 2, we list some researches related to our work. In Sect. 3, we illustrate our topic-detecting method in detail. Section 4 further demonstrates our popularity prediction model. In Sect. 5, we explain our experiment procedure and present the experimental outcomes. Finally, we conclude the paper in Sect. 6.

2   Related Work

In this section, we introduce the most relevant literature in two areas: topic detection and popularity prediction.

2.1   Topic Detection

Topic detection has been an active area of research for a long time. Some online topic models, such as OHDP [19] and ciDTM [4], get a pretty good performance in topic detection tasks. However, the long texts in WeChat contain inappropriate content, which contains numerous inspirational articles. Those online topic models are based on co-occurrence relationship between keywords and text, which are difficult to give accurate topic results. At the same time, those methods always have complex parameters, which lead to long training time. Therefore, we consider detecting topic from a word-level methods, which can distinguish those noise in data. Typically, a topic can be represented by a word-level distribution, a set of weighted keywords, and a low-rank embedding. In this work, we adopt the keyword representation for its interpretability. Keyword extraction [3,12], word embedding [13,15,16], and text clustering algorithm [7] are usually the most commonly-used procedures for topic detection. Typical keyword extraction algorithms include TF-IDF [3] and TextRank [12]. Word embedding learns low-dimensional and dense representation, which contains local semantic meaning and relationships among texts. The most practical word embedding algorithms are Word2Vec [13] and GloVe [15]. Text clustering algorithms normally obtain topic sets by computing text similarities [18] or using probabilistic models [7].

2.2   Topic Popularity Prediction

Popularity prediction, as one of the most common prediction problems in social network analysis, has drawn researchers' attention. As pioneers of researchers on topic trend, Naaman et al. [14] focused on the taxonomy and important factors of emerging trends in massive data. Thereafter, Becher et al. [2] further studied more diverse feature spaces for topic analysis. Researches exclusively on certain type of feature also proliferate over time. Temporal features have proven to be strong predictors when it comes to popularity predictions in social network [6,8,11]. Time series, as the most simple but powerful predictor, has been studied for a long time in trend learning. SEISMIC [21] are successful applications of time series as a discretized predictor. In [5,9,10], temporal features were used as hyper-features for machine learning. Our proposed **FCA-Bass** Model is also based on time series, with the assistance of some other extractable metadata features.

3   Topic Detection: The CEASE Model

In this section, we present a novel real-time topic model dubbed as **CEASE** based on improved GloVe model and word frequency clustering algorithm, covering both detection and tracking tasks.

3.1   Word-Embedding

Learning representations for words in vector space is a key step to bridge textual objects to numeric feature space. The GloVe Model [15] sets a good example to learn global word representations, combining the merits of global matrix factorization and local context window methods. GloVe leverages the matrix of word-word co-occurrence counts denoted by X and defines the probability that word j appears in the context of word i by X_{ij}/X_i. By manipulating the appearance probability and selecting self-consistent functions, GloVe obtains its object function in the form of factorizing the logarithm of the co-occurrence matrix X. However, GloVe orients static corpus and requires re-learning each time the corpus is updated. In other words, it is not scalable. The learning process is unacceptably time-consuming for real-time topic detection task since we aim to detect an unexpected event as early as possible. Thus, we propose an improved GloVe model.

$$J = \frac{1}{2} f(X_{i,j}) [\sum_{i,j=0}^{n} J_{ij} + e^{-J_i^t} (\mathbf{w}_i^t - \mathbf{w}_i^{t-1})^2 + e^{-J_j^t} (\mathbf{w}_j^t - \mathbf{w}_j^{t-1})^2]$$

where

$$J_{ij} = (\mathbf{w}_i^T \mathbf{w}_j + b_i + b_j - \log(X_{ij}))^2$$

$$J_i^t = \frac{1}{n} \sum_{i=0}^{n} J_{ij}, J_j^t = \frac{1}{n} \sum_{j=0}^{n} J_{ij}$$

The part related to J_{ij} adopts the idea of GloVe and essentially aim to factorize the logarithm of the co-occurrence matrix X. $\mathbf{w}_i$ is the vector representation of word k_i and b_i act as bias. The latter terms $(e^{-J_i^t}(\mathbf{w}_i^t - \mathbf{w}_i^{t-1})^2)$ in J are penalty terms introduced to detect semantic vibrations and carry out modifications. Note that the model should be run at the initialization stage and each time new data arrive. In other words, the penalty terms only play a role when semantic vibrations are detected and updating is needed. f is set to weigh different co-occurrences distinctively. We adopt the setting of GloVe and set f as

$$f(X_{i,j}) = \begin{cases} (\frac{X_{i,j}}{X_{max}})^{c_3} & \text{if } X_{i,j} < X_{max} \\ 1 & \text{otherwise} \end{cases}$$

At the very beginning of launching **CEASE** model, we train the model using the whole training corpus. At this time, there are no real-time requirements and the initialization can be done anytime before a detection task arrives. After initialization, we heuristically run **CEASE** each time new articles arrive and initialize $\mathbf{w}_i$ with the previous states instead of random vectors. In the training process, we sample a small number articles from the original corpus and new articles, and train the new vectors together. **CEASE** can automatically detect semantic vibrations in the hybrid training sets and carry out adjustments on relevant word vectors, while leaving irrelevant ones unaffected. The penalty terms in the object function J play a role to detect significant semantic vibrations. The vibration is essentially triggered by the inconsistent context information brought by new articles. In detail, $w_i^T w_j$ based on empirical knowledge could diverge dramatically from the new statistical information X_{ij}. The semantic divergence of word w_i is depicted by the average loss related to it J_i. When the divergence is nonnegligible, the penalty efficient in exponential form will decrease to allow for a divergence between the former and the new vector $w_i^t - w_i^{t-1}$. After each training, we will replace w_i^{t-1} with w_i^t and recalculate the vector representations of the topics that word w_i gets involved in.

3.2 Keyword Extraction

This part presents a procedure of keyword extraction for long text contents. For each article, we assign higher weights (doubly in our experiments) to the words from subtitles and obtain the weights of all words by TextRank [12]. After sorting the words by weight, we select a specific number of nouns, verbs, gerunds, toponyms, names and other entities with greatest weights as keywords of this article. In this way, an article can be represented by a set of weighted keywords. We denote the jth keyword of article A_i by k_j^i. Correspondingly, its weight is denoted by wg_j^i.

3.3 Keyword-Based Clustering

Topic detection task is commonly deemed as a clustering problem because the unsupervised learning mechanism adapts well to the evolution process of a topic, that is, each object ranged into a classification will modify it in turn. Based on a standard word-vector lexicon obtained beforehand, we carry out article clustering and accomplish detection task. Throughout the process of clustering, we maintain a topic set recording top-k most prevalent topics. We denote the topic set by T. T is an empty set at the very beginning, the keywords of the first article will be set as the first topic.

When an article emerges and gets captured, we calculate the cosine similarity between the newly-crawled article and each existing topic in T. Select the greatest similarity Sim_{max} among all existing topics and compare it with a threshold $Sim_{threshold}$ set beforehand. If Sim_{max} reaches $Sim_{threshold}$, then we classify this article to the topic that maximize the similarity. Otherwise, the keywords set of this article is deemed to constitute a new topic. Once we decide to classify an article A_i to an existing topic t in T, the feature vector of t should be modified with respect to A_i. For the common words in both the keyword sets of A_i and t, we alter the weights of these words, which take into consideration of the word frequency. The formula is below

$$wg_{fk} = \begin{cases} wg_t & fre_{key} > fre_c \\ wg_t + \dfrac{\alpha_1}{\beta_1 + \gamma_1^{\frac{1}{fre_{key}}}} & fre_{key} \leq fre_c \end{cases}$$

where wg_{fk} represents the weight of keyword k after modification, wg_t is the origin weight of k with respect to topic t, fre_{key} is the frequency of k in corpus and fre_c is the frequency threshold which is manually set. Note that a word is regarded as a high-frequency word if its frequency in corpus surpasses this threshold. After modifying the weights of the common words, we merge the common words and obtain a united keyword set of t and A_i without repetitive words. Sort the words by weight and take the top-k words as modified keywords of topic t. Therefrom, new keyword set and feature vector of a topic in T can be obtained each time a new article is appended and clustered.

3.4 Topic Mergence

It is mentionable that as new articles are added constantly, topics may come close to each other in feature space. It may happen that originally distinctive topics have a cosine similarity over $Sim_{threshold}$ as new articles are continuously classified into these topics and modify them in turn. In a bad situation, the same topic may be clustered into two or more topics. To avoid this, topic mergence mechanism is introduced into our model. Topics in T are examined periodically to find out whether excessive similarity exists in the current topic set. Cosine similarity values are calculated between each pair of topics and compared with $Sim_{threshold}$. Similar topics will be merged if necessary. We alter the weights of common words by the formula

$$wg_{fk} = wg_{t1} + wg_{t2}$$

where wg_{fk} is still the final weight of keyword k after modification, wg_{t_1} is the origin weight of k with respect to topic t_1 and wg_{t_2} is the origin weight of k with respect to topic t_2.

4 Popularity Prediction: FCA-BASS

In this section, we first give the definition of the popularity. The popularity of a topic mainly consists of read count and share count for each articles. Therefore, we define the popularity count $Y(\tau)$ at time τ as:

$$Y(\tau) = \sum_{\mathbf{A}} (wg_1^I \cdot r(\tau) + wg_2^I \cdot \frac{\overline{r_t}}{\overline{s_t}} \cdot s(\tau))$$

where $0 < \tau \leq \tau_s$, τ_s is the determination time of hot topics. $r(\tau)$ and $s(\tau)$ represent the read count and share count at time τ, wg_1^I and wg_2^I is the corresponding weight, and $\mathbf{A}$ is the article set in a topic. $\overline{r_t}$ and $\overline{s_t}$ represent the average count in the whole dataset at time τ in read and share respectively.

The Bass model [1] is one of the most widely applied models in management sciences, which is put forward to predict the sales volume of a new product when it is launched on the market.

Given the sale records of a new product in the first several days or months, it can easily predict the performance of the product later via only two parameters, *innovators* p and *imitators* q. *Innovators* p is the probability of an initial purchase at $\tau = 0$, and *imitators* q reflects the pressures operating as the numbers of previous buyers increases.

Yan et al. [20] introduced the Bass model into social network at the first time. They proposed STH-Bass that relaxed Bass model to individual-level heterogeneity, which allows everyone to favorite or repost a tweet with distinctive possibilities. However, STH-Bass cannot distinguish the effects of publisher features and topic features, which have different meaning for popularity. To better fit the topic scenario, we put forward **FCA-Bass**, which enroll topic features and associations among different topics into the original bass model.

4.1 FC-Bass Model

The spread of a topic is always influenced by the publishers and the topic itself, therefore, it is necessary to take advantage of these features for prediction. Uniting the specificity of publisher features and topic features, it is easy to relax the limitation of the original Bass model. In the way, to combine the effect of these two kinds of features, we propose the FC-Bass model. Topic features affect the popularity count through the characteristics of articles in the topic. To a certain degree, they are similar to the *innovators* in the original Bass model. Analogously, the publisher features are similar to the *imitators* which reflect the propagation of the topic to some extent. In this way, we can combine the topic features and the parameter *innovators* p as $p = \beta \mathbf{y}$. Meanwhile, combining the publisher features and the parameter *imitators* q as $q = \alpha \mathbf{x}$. Here $\mathbf{x}$ is the vector of topic features, which such as accumulative views and average number of sharing. $\mathbf{y}$ is the vector of publisher features, which such as follower number and average number of posts. Those features will be ruled out by Principal Component Analysis (PCA) and Index Correlation Matrix.

In the original Bass model [1], it has a basic assumption: the probability that the purchase will be made at τ which has not been made, denoted as $P(\tau)$, is a linear function of the number of previous buyers $Y(\tau)$, which represent as:

$$\frac{f(\tau)}{1 - F(\tau)} = P(\tau) = p + \frac{q}{m} Y(\tau)$$

In that $F(\tau) = \frac{Y(\tau)}{m}$, we have

$$f(\tau) = [p + qF(\tau)][1 - F(\tau)] = p + (q - p)F(\tau_s) - q[F(\tau)]^2$$

To obtain the $F(t)$, we have to solve the non-linear differential equation:

$$dT = \frac{dF}{p + (q - p)F - qF^2}$$

The solution is: $F(\tau) = \frac{q - pe^{-(\tau + C)(p+q)}}{q(1 + e^{-(\tau + C)(p+q)})}$.

Since $F(0) = 0$, the integration constant may be evaluated: $-C = \frac{\ln \frac{q}{p}}{p + q}$.

Hence, $F(\tau) = \frac{1 - e^{-(p+q)\tau}}{1 + \frac{q}{p} e^{-(p+q)\tau}}$.

Then, $Y(\tau) = mF(\tau) = \frac{m(1 - e^{-(p+q)\tau})}{1 + \frac{q}{p} e^{-(p+q)\tau}}$.

Then the solution is:

$$Y(\tau) = \frac{m(1 - e^{-(\beta y + \alpha x)\tau})}{1 + \frac{\alpha \mathbf{x}}{\beta \mathbf{y}} e^{-(\beta y + \alpha x)\tau}} \tag{1}$$

As a result, we get the Feature-Combined Bass model.

4.2   Association Analysis

In reality, there is always a variety of associations among different topics. Obviously, a hot topic always leads to the rise of another topic, and the rise of the topic can increase this hot topic in turn. At the same time, the rise of a topic always leads to the decline of another topic. We call those associations as promotive association and recessionary association respectively.

As for the promotive association, when a hot topic appears, people would like to create a relative topic to express their viewpoints. Those topics always increase the propagation of the original topic. On the other hand, as for recessionary association, people always interested in several topics during a period. In this way, a topic might reduce it's popularity by other topics. Thus, the final popularity of the topic ought to consider those association, which can be represented as:

$$Y(\tau) = \frac{m(1 - e^{-(\beta y + \alpha x)\tau})}{1 + \frac{\alpha x}{\beta y}e^{-(\beta y + \alpha x)\tau}} + \lambda_1 - \lambda_2$$

where $Y'(\tau)$ is the final popularity. λ_1 represents the parameter of promotive association, which indicates the popularity from other topics, and λ_2 represents the parameter of recessionary association, which express the popularity transferred to similar topics.

Moreover, we adopt the **Least Square Method** [1], which is one of the recommended mathematical methods to solve the original Bass model, to get the parameters. With the parameters, we can easily predict the popularity count of a topic at any time τ, where $1h < \tau \leq \tau_s$.

5   Experiments

In this section, we show the experimental results of our proposed **CEASE** and **FCA-Bass** models on the real-world datasets. We conduct comparisons with several baseline prediction methods in setting determination time τ_s ranging from 12th hour to 72nd hour.

5.1   Dataset Description

WeChat. The dataset contains 183,638 articles among 159,659 Official Accounts from 4th, Nov, 2017 to 24th, Nov, 2017. We first cluster all the text with our **CEASE** and then manually correct the texts into corresponding topics. Totally 354 topics have been extracted from the whole corpus with 78 hot topics and 276 non-hot topics, which divided by threshold γ. It also contains 309,794 read records and 96,102 share records.

5.2   Parameter Calculation

Based on experience and some fine-tuning, we set $\alpha_1 = 0.1$, $\beta_1 = \beta_2 = 1$, $\gamma_1 = \gamma_2 = 1.01$, $\alpha_2 = 0.5$, $c_1 = 250$, $c_2 = 1.01$, $wg_1^I = wg_2^I = 0.5$ and $\gamma = 846286$.

Table 1. The result of cluster with training and test set in different corpus

Model	Precision	Recall	F-score	Accuracy
ciDTM [4]	0.8605	0.8737	0.8670	0.9295
GloVe-based	0.6063	0.7151	0.6562	0.8303
CEASE	**0.9792**	**0.9468**	**0.9627**	**0.9797**

5.3   Topic Detection

To further evaluate the performance for topic detection, we randomly select some articles from Nov. 11th, 2017 to Nov. 17th, 2017 as training set, and then randomly choose some articles on 24th, Nov, 2017 as test set. That is to say, the training set and test set are extracted from the different corpuses. The result of clustering is shown in Table 1. As we can see, **CEASE** completely defeats other baselines. ciDTM [4] is obviously unsuitable for this WeChat dataset with many inspirational articles, which *Precision* is 12% worse than **CEASE**. The GloVe-based method can perform good when it in a corpus. However, when a new corpus comes, the GloVe-based method cannot accept the neologies, it only keeps the original semantics of the word, so that it always makes mistakes. **CEASE** can adapt to different changes in WeChat corpus and get a pretty good performance.

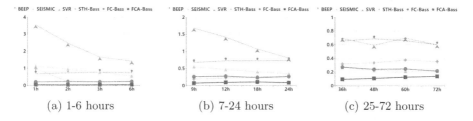

(a) 1-6 hours   (b) 7-24 hours   (c) 25-72 hours

Fig. 1. The *MAPE* of different models at different time

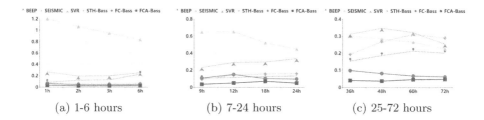

(a) 1-6 hours   (b) 7-24 hours   (c) 25-72 hours

Fig. 2. The *MdAPE* of different models at different time

5.4   Popularity Prediction

To better evaluate **FCA-Bass** model, we divide the active time of topics into 3 time windows, the early stage $(1\,h\text{--}6\,h)$, the middle stage $(7\,h\text{--}24\,h)$ and the latter stage $(25\text{--}72\,h)$. We set the earlier time data as the training set to train the parameters and each time stage data as the test set to evaluate trained models. In other words, at the early stage, we use the features before $1\,h$, and to evaluate the performance of our model at the early stage. At the middle stage, we use the features at the early stage to evaluate the performance at the middle stage successively. Given the features in early time, we can predict the popularity of the topic for a long time period.

Figures 1 and 2 respectively show the Mean APE and Median APE of our **FC-Bass**, **FCA-Bass**, and four baselines at the early, middle and latter stage. Our **FCA-Bass** and **FC-Bass** get a pretty good performance. The **FCA-Bass** performs absolutely better than other models at any stage especially at the early stage. In addition, the **FCA-Bass**, **FC-Bass**, **STH-Bass** [20] and **BEEP** [11] have the same tendency in both $MdAPE$ and $MAPE$, which get stable performances. However, when the first hour, **STH-Bass** has unusual performance due to the limits of time points. In addition, **SEISMIC** [21] and Support Vector Regression (**SVR**) [17] have unstable performance. **SVR** has a low $MdAPE$ but a high $MAPE$, and **SEISMIC** has a low $MAPE$ and a high $MdAPE$, which may be due to the effect by some extreme points.

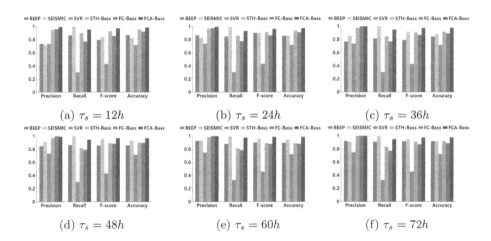

Fig. 3. The result of popularity status classification at different τ_s

5.5   Hot Topic Prediction

We can get the popular status based on a suitable threshold γ and the final popularity count $Y(\tau_s)$. Figure 3 shows the performance of hot topic prediction by our **FCA-Bass**, **FC-Bass** and four other baselines. The **FCA-Bass**, **STH-Bass** and **FC-Bass** have decent performance. Particularly, **FCA-Bass** model has the best performance in *Precision*, *F-score* and *Accuracy*, and much higher than other models. **STH-Bass** and **FC-Bass** perform in the second place, which **SEISMIC** has the best performance in *Recall*, but its *Precision* and *Accuracy* are relatively low. **BEEP** has a more balanced performance in all metrics. However, **SVR** has the worst performance. As a whole, **FCA-Bass** has the best performance in hot topic prediction without additional models.

6   Conclusions

Topic detection is meaningful as an indicative tool for real-world events, and popularity prediction also has great significance for advertisement, marketing and recommendation systems. In this paper, we propose an integrated model for both real-time topic detection and popularity prediction in the context of online social network, specially adapted to long-text contents. For topic detection, we propose a novel model dubbed as **C**ost-**E**ffective **A**nd **S**calable **E**mbedding model (**CEASE**) based on improved GloVe Models and keyword frequency clustering algorithm adapted for textual feature space. Moreover, neologies can be well handled by **CEASE**. For popularity prediction, we transplant the key idea of Bass, a most famous and widely-applied model in economic fields, to the context of social network analysis, and develop **F**eature-**C**ombined **Bass** model with **A**ssociation **A**nalysis (**FCA-Bass**) based on time series as well as elaborately selected feature sets.

We experiment on real-world dataset from WeChat, a most prevalent social network service at present. Our model is proved to outperform several currently mainstream methods, on both topic detection and popularity prediction.

Acknowledgements. This work is supported by the National Key R&D Program of China (2018YFB1004703), the National Natural Science Foundation of China (61872238, 61672348, 61672353), the Shanghai Science and Technology Fund (17510740200), the CCF-Tencent Open Research Fund (RAGR20170114), and Huawei Innovation Research Program (HO2018085286), and the National Key Research of China (2018YFB1003800). Quanquan Chu finished the experiments in this paper when he was an intern at Tencent Shenzhen. The authors also would like to thank Chunxia Jia, Yiming Zhang, Chao Wang, and Tianxiang Gao for their contributions on this paper.

References

1. Bass, F.M.: A new product growth for model consumer durables. MS **15**(5), 215–227 (1969)
2. Becker, H., Naaman, M., Gravano, L.: Beyond trending topics: real-world event identification on twitter. ICWS **11**, 438–441 (2011)
3. Brants, T., Chen, F.: A system for new event detection. In: SIGIR, pp. 330–337 (2003)
4. Elshamy, W.: Continuous-time infinite dynamic topic models. arXiv:1302.7088 (2013)
5. Figueiredo, F., Almeida, J.M., Gonçalves, M.A., Benevenuto, F.: TrendLearner: early prediction of popularity trends of user generated content. IS **349**, 172–187 (2016)
6. Gao, S., Ma, J., Chen, Z.: Effective and effortless features for popularity prediction in microblogging network. In: WWW, pp. 269–270 (2014)
7. Kasiviswanathan, S., Melville, P., Banerjee, A., Sindhwani, V.: Emerging topic detection using dictionary learning. In: CIKM, pp. 745–754 (2011)
8. Kong, S., Mei, Q., Feng, L., Ye, F., Zhao, Z.: Predicting bursts and popularity of hashtags in real-time. In: SIGIR, pp. 927–930 (2014)

9. Kong, S., Ye, F., Feng, L., Zhao, Z.: Towards the prediction problems of bursting hashtags on twitter. JASIST **66**(12), 2566–2579 (2015)
10. Kupavskii, A., et al.: Prediction of retweet cascade size over time. In: CIKM, pp. 2335–2338 (2012)
11. Ma, X., Gao, X., Chen, G.: Beep: a Bayesian perspective early stage event prediction model for online social networks. In: ICDM, pp. 973–978 (2017)
12. Mihalcea, R., Tarau, P.: TextRank: bringing order into text. In: EMNLP, pp. 1–8 (2004)
13. Mikolov, T., Chen, K., Corrado, G., Dean, J.: Efficient estimation of word representations in vector space. arXiv:1301.3781 (2013)
14. Naaman, M., Becker, H., Gravano, L.: Hip and Trendy: characterizing emerging trends on twitter. JASIST **62**(5), 902–918 (2011)
15. Pennington, J., Socher, R., Manning, C.: Glove: Global vectors for word representation. In: EMNLP, pp. 1532–1543 (2014)
16. Proskurnia, J., Mavlyutov, R., Castillo, C., Aberer, K., Mauroux, P.: Efficient document filtering using vector space topic expansion and pattern-mining: the case of event detection in microposts. In: CIKM, pp. 457–466 (2017)
17. Rosenfeld, N., Nitzan, M., Globerson, A.: Discriminative learning of infection models. In: WSDM, pp. 563–572 (2016)
18. Tang, X., Yang, C.: Tut: a statistical model for detecting trends, topics and user interests in social media. In: CIKM, pp. 972–981 (2012)
19. Wang, C., Paisley, J., Blei, D.: Online variational inference for the hierarchical Dirichlet process. In: AISTATS, pp. 752–760 (2011)
20. Yan, Y., Tan, Z., Gao, X., Tang, S., Chen, G.: STH-Bass: a spatial-temporal heterogeneous bass model to predict single-tweet popularity. In: DASFAA, pp. 18–32 (2016)
21. Zhao, Q., Erdogdu, M.A., He, H.Y., Rajaraman, A., Leskovec, J.: SEISMIC: a self-exciting point process model for predicting tweet popularity. In: KDD, pp. 1513–1522 (2015)

Application of SIRUS in Credit Card Fraud Detection

Yuwei Zhang[1,2], Guanjun Liu[1,2(✉)], Wenjing Luan[1,2], Chungang Yan[1,2],
and Changjun Jiang[1,2]

[1] Department of Computer Science and Technology, Tongji University,
Shanghai 201804, China
{zyw,liuguanjun,cjjiang}@tongji.edu.cn, wenjingmengjing@163.com,
cgyan2@163.com
[2] Key Laboratory of Embedded System and Service Computing,
Ministry of Education, Shanghai 201804, China

Abstract. Credit card fraud problem is very common in recent years. It not only causes economic loss to people, but also causes trust crisis to enterprises. Due to the imbalance of data, fraud detection has always been tricky. In our previous work, we proposed a method of dealing with the class imbalance problem based on stacking ensemble learning and inverse random undersampling method (SIRUS). First, the inverse random undersampling method is used to generate multiple data subsets from the original data set. Then we use the stacking ensemble learning method for each data subset to train several different learners (also called first-level learners), and then the results generated by each first-level learner are taken as features to train a meta learner. We apply SIRUS to detect the credit card fraud in this paper. Our dataset comes from a financial company in China. A variety of measurements such as recall, precision, accuracy, *F-measure*, and *G-mean* to illustrate the effectiveness of our method in fraud detection.

Keywords: Fraud detection · Stacking
Inverse random undersampling · Class imbalance problem

1 Introduction

With the development of science and technology and the improvement of the economic level, the use of credit cards and debit cards has grown tremendously in recent years. In the meantime, billions of dollars are lost every year because of credit card fraud [1]. According to the statistics of the European Central Bank, during 2012, the single Euro payments fraud reached 1.33 billion Euros, which has increased by 14.8% compared with 2011. Among them, non-traditional channels (such as electronic transactions) account for 60%, which was only 46% in 2008 [2]. The sharp increase in fraud not only causes huge economic losses to individuals, but also makes people lose confidence in enterprises [3]. Therefore, credit card fraud problem needs to be solved urgently.

© Springer Nature Switzerland AG 2018
X. Chen et al. (Eds.): CSoNet 2018, LNCS 11280, pp. 66–78, 2018.
https://doi.org/10.1007/978-3-030-04648-4_6

Machine learning has proved to be a good method to solve the fraud problem. Many machine learning algorithms have been applied to fraud detection before, such as Support Vector Machine(SVM) [4] and Random Forest (RF)[5]. However, progress in fraud detection is not very fast, the main two reasons are as follows: (1) credit card data involves user privacy and is often not disclosed. (2) results are usually not exposed to the public [6]. Due to the serious imbalance of data (the number of fraudulent transactions is much less than that of legal transactions), the traditional machine learning algorithms cannot achieve a good performance. The imbalanced data processing method and the ensemble learning method have been proved to be two effective methods to solve the problem. This paper mainly focus on these two aspects.

Although balanced class distribution is a frequently used method to solve imbalanced data problems, a balanced class distribution (which means that the ratio of the legal transactions to fraudulent transactions is 1:1) is not an optimal distribution [7], especially for fraud detection. The fraudulent transactions should be identified as much as possible to reduce economic losses. In other words, the goal of fraud detection is to increase true positive rate (TPR) while controlling false positive rate (FPR) at the same time. Recently, the IRUS method proposed by Tahir et al. [8] has proved to be an excellent method to deal with imbalanced data problems. It generates several data subsets, the ratio of majority class to minority one in each data subset is opposite to that in the original dataset. After that, each subset generates a base classifier, and then fuses them into an ensemble classifier through some kind of combination strategy [10], which is also called bagging ensemble learning method [9]. IRUS, which based on inverse random under sampling and bagging method, has been proved to have better performance than many existing methods [8]. However, the base classifiers in bagging are homogeneous, which means that it cannot get a good generalization accuracy. Moreover, the method of voting or mean value is usually adopted to fuse the base classifiers, so the performance of different classifiers cannot be distinguished. As we all know, stacking ensemble learning method can improve generalization accuracy as high as possible [11] and make the classifier with good performance has higher weight. Therefore, we proposed a method called SIRUS to deal with the class imbalance problem [12]. In this paper we use SIRUS to solve credit card fraud problem.

This paper compares the proposed method with other excellent methods through the real data provided by a large financial company in China. The results show that SIRUS is very competitive in fraud detection. The main work of this paper is summarized as follows:

*(1)*The method combining inverse random under sampling method and stacking (SIRUS) is reviewed.
- The inverse random under sampling method is used to generate training subsets;
- Different classification algorithms are used on each training subset to obtain different component learners
- The result of each classifier is taken as a feature to train an ensemble learner.

*(2)*The proposed method is compared with other excellent algorithms on the real fraud data, and the effectiveness of SIURS is proved.

The rest of the paper is organized as follows: In Sect. 2, we review some fraud detection methods as well as imbalanced data processing methods and ensemble learning methods. Sect. 3 presents the details of SIRUS. Section 4 describes the source and attributes of the data, as well as the settings and metrics for the experiment. Results of the experiment and discussion are provided in Sect. 5. Finally, Sect. 6 concludes the paper.

2   Related Work

Fraud detection has been a hot research area in recent decades both in academia and industry. There are many popular machine learning methods used in fraud detection. Logistic regression, support vector machine and random forest are compared in [13]. The Hidden Markov Model is used for Fraud Detection in [1]. Chan et al. [25] propose a scalable technology combined with Stacking ensemble learning method to solve the fraud detection problem, and use a novel cost model to analyze the experimental results. [14] summarizes the application of the existing classification methods in fraud detection comprehensively.

However, few of these methods mention the difficulty of dealing with imbalanced data. In fact, the ratio of fraudulent transactions to legal transactions in financial data is extremely imbalanced, and the imbalance in financial data is a normal situation. The common methods for solving imbalanced data problem are sampling methods and ensemble learning methods.

2.1   Sampling Methods

Sampling methods mainly include oversampling and undersampling. [15] gives a comprehensive summary of various sampling methods. There are two forms of Sampling methods: heuristic and non-heuristic.

The two most common non-heuristic methods are random undersampling method (RUS) and random oversampling method (ROS), the former randomly eliminates samples from majority class while the latter randomly replicates samples from minority class to balance data distribution. Both of these methods have drawbacks, ROS may lead to overfitting, and RUS may discard useful data.

In order to improve the disadvantages of non-heuristic methods, many heuristic methods are proposed. Tomek 's links [16] is a common heuristic method for undersampling. Synthetic Minority Over-Sampling Technique (SMOTE) [17] is a heuristic method for oversampling and proved to be very effective, but SMOTE does not consider the distribution of adjacent samples, which may increase the probability of repetition between majority samples and minority samples [26]. Therefore, some improved SMOTE algorithms are proposed, such as borderline-smote [18]. Tahir et al. [8] proposed the inverse random undersampling method (IRUS), which has achieved good results in comparison with the above-mentioned methods on multiple public data sets.

2.2   Ensemble Learning Methods

Ensemble learning is a very important field in machine learning and has been proved to be a very effective way to solve imbalanced data problems [19]. Ensemble learning methods mainly include Boosting [20], Bagging [9], Stacking [11] and some of their variants [21, 22]. A large number of ensemble learning methods for dealing with imbalanced data problems are summarized in [27].

As far as we know, previous fraud detection researches seldom deal with imbalanced data. Even if some are processed, they only balance class distribution. IRUS [8] further improves minority classes by inversing the majority and minority class samples and combining bagging. IRUS improves the recognition rate of minority class samples by inversing the ratio of samples from majority class to those from minority class and combining bagging ensemble learning method. However bagging can't reach a high generalization accuracy because of two reasons: 1. To get a good ensemble, it is generally believed that the base classifiers should be as diverse as possible [23], but in bagging classifier is homogenous. 2. Bagging fuses classifiers with some kind of combination strategy [10], which often cannot distinguish the performance among different classifiers. In [11], stacking method is used to obtain a generalization accuracy as high as possible. Thus we combine IRUS and stacking. To the best of our knowledge, no one has combined them for fraud detection before.

3   The SIRUS Method

This section will introduce the specific details of SIRUS [12] and pseudo code implementation. SIRUS is a combination of inverse random undersampling and Stacking. First, we will introduce the two parts.

3.1   Inverse Random Undersampling

Tahir et al. [8] first propose inverse random undersampling method to solve imbalanced data problem. IRUS was inspired by the phenomenon: the probability of misclassifying samples from the majority class will be lower than the probability of error for the minority class. Inverse random undersampling generates multiple data subsets by drastically reducing majority class samples, so the ratio of minority class to majority one in each data subset is opposite to that of the original data set. Figure 1 shows the inverse random undersampling method.

D is the original data set, where A is the collection of majority class samples and B is the collection of minority class samples. A_i (i=1, 2,..., k) is the data subset obtained by undersampling A. Each A_i and B form a training subset and $|B|/|A_i| \approx |A|/|B|$.

3.2   Inverse Random Undersampling

Stacking was first proposed by Wolpert [11], in which a learner was trained to combine individual classifiers [23]. The individual classifier is usually called as the first-level learner, and the learner is usually called as the meta-learner.

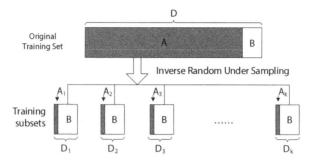

Fig. 1. An example of inverse random undersampling.

The main idea of stacking is that using the original data set to train the first-level learner, and then generate a new data set, and then train the meta learner on the new data set. The first-level learners are usually different learning algorithms. In other words, they are all heterogeneous. The stacking pseudo code shows in Algorithm 1:

Algorithm 1. Stacking algorithm

Input: Data set $D=(x_1,y_1),(x_2,y_2),...,(x_n,y_n)$
   First-level learning algorithms $c_1,c_2,...,c_m$
   Meta learning algorithm c'
   Test sample x'
Output: y': the label for x'
  Process:
  for $i = 1 \rightarrow m$ **do**
     $h_i \leftarrow c_i(D)$ //Train first-level learners
  end for
  $D' \leftarrow \varnothing$ //Generate a new data set
  for $j = 1 \rightarrow n$ **do**
     for $i = 1 \rightarrow m$ **do**
     $z_{ji} \leftarrow h_i(x_j)$
     end for
        $D' \leftarrow D' \cup ((z_{j1},...,z_{jm}),y_j)$
  end for
  $h' \leftarrow c'(D')$ //Train the meta learner
  $y' \leftarrow h'(h_1(x'),...,h_m(x'))$

3.3 SIRUS Method

The SIRUS method combines the Inverse random undersampling method and stacking ensemble learning method to improve the performance on imbalanced data sets. The main process of SIRUS is as follows:

(1) First of all, the original training set is divided into a training data set and a validation data set, then using inverse random undersampling method on the training data set to produce multiple data subsets, each data subset contains a few samples from the majority class and all samples from the minority class.

(2) For each data subset, various learning algorithms are used to train different classifiers. So the first-level learners are obtained.

(3) Use all the first-level learners to predict the validation data set and generate the new data set which contains the output of each learner. Then the meta classifier is trained on the new data set.

The SIRUS algorithm is shown in Fig. 2. The SIRUS algorithm pseudo code is illustrated in Algorithm 2.

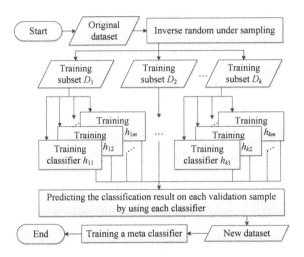

Fig. 2. The procedure of SIRUS.

The symbols in the Algorithm 2 are described as follows: D and V represent the training set and the validation set, respectively. A and B are the set of samples from majority class and those from minority class in the training set. F ($|F|=m$) is a collection of learning algorithms. f' is the algorithm used for training meta-learner. n' denotes the number of samples sampling from the majority class, and k represents the times of undersampling. D_i is the subset contains A_i and B. C ($|C|=c$) is a collection of first-level learners, and Z is the new data set. When a test sample x needs to be classified, each first-level learner gives a classification value on x, and then all values are combined to generate a new sample x'. Finally, use the meta classifier to classify x' and get the final result.

Algorithm 2. SIRUS algorithm

Input: D, V, A, B, k, n', F, f', x
Output: y: the label for x
  Step 1: Initialization
      $C \leftarrow \varnothing$, $Z \leftarrow \varnothing$
  Step 2: Training component classifiers
  for $i = 1 \rightarrow k$ **do**
      $A_i \leftarrow$ randomly pick n' samples without replacement from A
      $D_i \leftarrow A_i \cup B$
      for $j = 1 \rightarrow m$ **do**
          Training component classifier h_{ij} on D_i using classification algorithm j
          $C \leftarrow C \cup h_{ij}$
      end for
  end for
  Step 3: Training meta classifiers
  for $i = 1 \rightarrow v$ **do**
      $v_i \leftarrow$ the ith sample in V
      for $j = 1 \rightarrow c$ **do**
      $c_j \leftarrow$ the jth classifier in C
      $z_{ij} \leftarrow$ the prediction result of v_i assigned by c_j
      z_{ij} is taken as a feature to construct vector v'_i
      end for
      $Z \leftarrow Z \cup (v'_i, y_i)$
  end for
      Training meta classifier c' on Z by classification algorithm f'
  Step 4: Prediction
  for $i = 1 \rightarrow c$ **do**
      $c_i \leftarrow$ the ith classifier in C
      $z_i \leftarrow$ the prediction result of x assigned by c_i
  end for
  $x' \leftarrow$ the new sample formed by prediction results for x
  $y=$ the prediction result of x' assigned by c'
  Output y

---

4 Experiments

4.1 Experimental Setup

The data of this experiment was provided by a financial company in China. There are about 5 million transaction information from November 2016 to January 2017 and April 2017 to June 2017, including 4,977,278 normal transactions and 147,829 fraud transactions. It can be found that the ratio between normal transactions and fraud transactions is extremely imbalanced, and the number of normal transactions is about 33 times than that of fraud transactions. Therefore, traditional machine learning algorithms do not work well in this data set. We randomly selected 250,000 normal transactions and 50,000 fraud transactions as the training set, and the rest as the test set. All experimental results are obtained through a 10 × 10-fold cross validation.

4.2   Benchmark Methods

Decision tree is a very common machine learning method, and the tree-structured learner often has a good effect on imbalanced data. Therefore, we chose the decision tree as a baseline for our experiment. IRUS uses inverse random undersampling method combined with bagging ensemble learning method and has proven to be better than most imbalanced data processing methods (including RUS, ROS, SMOTE, EasyEnsemble and Asymmetric) [8]. Therefore, we chose IRUS as the second comparison. Chan [25] also uses the Stacking for fraud detection, we chose Chan's method as the third comparison. All of the above algorithms are implemented based on weka [24], which is a collection of machine learning algorithms for data mining tasks. The four methods involved in the experiment are described as follows:

(1) *The decision tree*: which is the baseline for the experiment, uses the original training set to train the decision tree. For highly imbalanced data, pruning may reduce the coverage of the minority class in the decision tree, therefore, all experiments based on decision tree set the parameter of no pruning(including IRUS, SIRUS, Chan's method).

(2) *IRUS*: using inverse random undersampling method to divide the original train set into a number of different subsets, then training each data subset to get a decision tree classifier, finally combining all decision tree classifiers through soft voting (MEAN rule) [8].

(3) *SIRUS*: SIRUS is similar to IRUS in the data processing stage. The original train set is divided into multiple different subsets by using inverse random undersampling method. For each subset, we will train four different classifiers (including decision tree, naive bayes, support vector machine (SVM), and logistic regression), all of which will constitute the first-level learners. To determine the meta-learner, we use the same four classifiers to learn the new data set, and then select the classifier with the highest AUC value as the final meta-learner.

(4) *Chan's method (Chan)* [25]: Chan's method firstly samples majority class without replacement to generate multiple data subsets, the number of majority samples is the same as that of minority samples in each subset. For each subset, four classifiers same as those in SIRUS are trained, and these classifiers are then fused using the same stacking method as SIRUS.

4.3   Performance Measures

We use a variety of measurements to measure the final performance of the proposed method. After the classification, a confusion matrix as shown in Table 1 can be obtained. Accuracy is the most commonly used measurement of classifiers performance. Although it is not suitable for imbalanced data, we still use accuracy as one of the measurements to judge the performance of the classifier across all samples. In addition, there are 5 measurements as follows:

Table 1. Confusion matrix

	Predicted Positive Class	Predicted Negative Class
Actual Positive Class	TP (True Positive)	FN (False Negative)
Actual Negative Class	FP (False Positive)	TN (True Negative)

Specificity, tnr $= \frac{TN}{TN+FP}$

Recall, tpr $= \frac{TP}{TP+FN}$

Precision $= \frac{TP}{TP+FP}$

$G\text{-}mean = \sqrt{tnr \times tpr}$

$F\text{-}measure = \frac{2 \times Precision \times Recall}{Precision + Recall}$

The five indicators are all the bigger the better. Their meanings are as follows: Specificity indicates the accuracy of the normal samples, recall indicates the accuracy of the abnormal samples, precision represents the accuracy of samples predicted as fraud, $G\text{-}mean$ is the geometric average of Specificity and Recall, indicating the comprehensive performance of classifier to the two classes. Since single Recall or Precision cannot truely describe the performance of the classifier, for example, assume that test set has a total of (m + n) samples, including m normal samples and n abnormal samples (m >> n), if predict all samples as abnormal, then we can get the following confusion matrix: $TP = $ n, $FP = $ m−n, $TN = 0$, $FN = 0$, we can get recall $= 1$, if we look at the recall alone, the classifier works well but Precision $= $ n/m$\approx$0. Similarly, if all samples are predicted as normal and only one abnormal sample is predicted as abnormal, then the following confusion matrix can be obtained: $TP = 1$, $FP = 0$, $TN = $ m, $FN = $ n−1, we can obtain the precision $= 1$, however the Recall $= 1/$n ≈ 0. Therefore, a comprehensive evaluation indicator of Recall and precision is needed. This indicators is the $F\text{-}measure$, and $F\text{-}measure$ is the harmonic average of recall and precision. The larger the $F\text{-}measure$, the better the performance of the classifier.

5   Results and Discussion

In this chapter, we first present the results of the four methods by using the above measurements. Then the results and time complexity will be analyzed.

5.1   Performance Analysis

The results of all indicators are presented in Table 2.

Table 2. The results of all indicators

Method	TP	FP	TN	FN
The decision tree	49174	323605	4453673	48655
IRUS	92616	267225	4510053	5213
Chan's method	91472	174438	4602840	6357
SIRUS	**93680**	**172472**	**4604806**	**4149**

Method	Recall	Precision	Accuracy	Specificity	G-mean	F-measure
The decision tree	0.502	0.132	0.923	0.932	0.684	0.209
IRUS	0.946	0.257	0.944	0.944	0.945	0.404
Chan's method	0.935	0.344	0.962	**0.964**	0.949	0.502
SIRUS	**0.958**	**0.352**	**0.964**	**0.964**	**0.961**	**0.515**

The optimal value of each indicator is marked in bold. We can find that whether using *G-mean* or *F-measure* as measurement, SIRUS can achieve the highest value, which means that SIRUS can obtain a good classification performance for both normal samples and abnormal samples. Comparing the SIRUS and the baseline decision trees, it can be seen that there are significant improvements in all indicators.

Comparing SIRUS and IRUS can find that the *TP* is not much different, but as for *FP*, IRUS is 55% more than SIRUS. Since both of them use the inverse random undersampling method for data processing, it can be believed that Stacking significantly reduces the misclassification rate of normal samples than Bagging. Through analysis, this is mainly because after inverse random undersampling, the number of abnormal samples in each data subset is larger than that of the normal samples. Stacking uses heterogeneous first-level learners and meta classifier, which makes the learners with better performance have higher weights. However, bagging uses homogenous classifiers and simple voting fusion rules, which can easily cause the sample to be predicted as the majority sample (now is the abnormal sample). As a result, the precision of IRUS is very low, and the misclassification rate of normal samples is higher.

Comparing with SIRUS and Chan, we can find that the *FP* of the two method are similar, but the *TP* of SIRUS is higher. This means that using the inverse random undersampling method can effectively improve the recognition rate of the minority samples, so as to enhance the overall performance of the classifier. At the same time, we have an interesting discovery. In the case of using the same classification algorithm, a balanced data distribution may not obtain the optimal classifier performance, similar conclusions are mentioned in [7]: when the ratio of two classes is 3:1, the best classifier performance can be obtained.

5.2   Time Complexity Analysis

The time of the above methods is mainly spent on training classifier, and the testing time is almost negligible. The training for each subset can be parallel, so the training time is only related to the subset with the largest size. Similarly, different classifiers for the same subset can be trained in parallel, so only the classifier with the longest training time should be considered. Since SIRUS and IRUS use the same inverse random undersampling method, we assume that the size of data subset in SIRUS and IRUS is S_1, and that in Chan's method is S_2, so we can get that $S_1 = (A_i+B)$ and $S_2 = (A'_i+B)$, where B is a set of all minority class samples, and A_i and A'_i are sets of majority class samples extracted by inverse random undersampling method and Chan's method, respectively, then $|S_2| > |S_1|$ because $|A'_i| > |A_i|$. Assume that the size of the validation set is $|V|$, and the training time of the decision tree on $|V|$ is $T_1(|V|)$, among the several classification algorithms(decision tree, naive bayes, support vector machine (SVM), and logistic regression) used, the longest training time on $|V|$ is $T_{max}(|V|)$, obviously, $T_{max}(|V|) >= T_1(|V|)$. The time complexity of the three methods is show in Table 3.

Table 3. The time complexity of the three methods

Method	Time Complexity
IRUS	$O(T_1(|S_1|))$
SIRUS	$O(T_{max}(|S_1|)+T_{max}(|V|))$
Chan's method	$O(T_{max}(|S_2|)+T_{max}(|V|))$

We can conclude that the time consumption of the three methods is Chan>SIRUS>IRUS.

6   Conclusion

In this paper, we propose a fraud detection method based on inverse random undersampling method and stacking ensemble learning method. Since the data used are from real financial company, we cannot discuss features in detail as well as the impact of each feature. By conducting experiments on the real transaction data, a comprehensive evaluation are obtained through using a variety of measurements, including Specificity, Recall, Precision, *G-mean*, and *F-measure*. The results all show that SIRUS is very competitive.

References

1. Srivastava, A., et al.: Credit card fraud detection using Hidden Markov Model. IEEE Trans. Dependable Secur. Comput. **5**(1), 37–48 (2008)
2. Bahnsen, A.C., Aouada, D., Stojanovic, A.: Feature engineering strategies for credit card fraud detection. Expert Syst. Appl. Int. J. **51**(C), 134–142 (2016)
3. Albrecht, W.S., Albrecht, C., Albrecht, C.C.: Current trends in fraud and its detection. Inf. Syst. Secur. **17**(1), 2–12 (2008)
4. Yong-Hua, X.U.: Detection of credit card fraud based on support vector machine. Comput. Simul. **28**(8), 371–376 (2011)
5. Whitrow, C., et al.: Transaction aggregation as a strategy for credit card fraud detection. Data Min. Knowl. Disc. **18**(1), 30–55 (2009)
6. Kou, Y., et al.: Survey of fraud detection techniques. In: IEEE International Conference on Networking, Sensing and Control IEEE, vol. 2, 749–754 (2004)
7. Khoshgoftaar, T.M., et al.: Learning with limited minority class data. In: International Conference on Machine Learning and Applications, pp. 348–353. IEEE (2007)
8. Tahir, M.A., Kittler, J., Yan, F.: Inverse random under sampling for class imbalance problem and its application to multi-label classification. Pattern Recogn. **45**(10), pp. 3738–3750 (2012)
9. Breiman, L.: Bagging predictors. Mach. Learn. **24**(2), 123–140 (1996)
10. Kittler, J., et al.: On combining classifiers. IEEE Trans. Pattern Anal. Mach. Intell. **20**(3), 226–239 (1998)
11. Wolpert, D.H.: Stacked generalization *. Neural Netw. **5**(2), 241–259 (1992)
12. Zhang, Y., Liu, G., Luan, W., Yan, C., Jiang, C.: An approach to class imbalance problem based on stacking and inverse random under sampling methods, pp. 1–6 (2018). https://doi.org/10.1109/ICNSC.2018.8361344
13. Bhattacharyya, S., et al.: Data mining for credit card fraud: a comparative study. Decis. Support. Syst. **50**(3), 602–613 (2011)
14. Abbasi, A., et al.: Metafraud: a meta-learning framework for detecting financial fraud. MIS Q. **36**(4), 1293–1327 (2012)
15. He, H., Garcia, E.A.: Learning from imbalanced data. IEEE Trans. Knowl. Data Eng. **21**(9), 1263–1284 (2009)
16. Tomek, I.: Two modifications of CNN. IEEE Trans. Syst. Man Cybern. SMC **6**(11), 769–772 (1976)
17. Chawla, N.V., et al.: SMOTE: synthetic minority over-sampling technique. J. Artif. Intell. Res. **16**(1), 321–357 (2002)
18. Han, H., Wang, W.-Y., Mao, B.-H.: Borderline-SMOTE: a new over-sampling method in imbalanced data sets learning. In: Huang, D.-S., Zhang, X.-P., Huang, G.-B. (eds.) ICIC 2005. LNCS, vol. 3644, pp. 878–887. Springer, Heidelberg (2005). https://doi.org/10.1007/11538059_91
19. Weiss, G.M.: Mining with rarity: a unifying framework. ACM SIGKDD Explor. Newslett. **6**(1), 7–19 (2004)
20. Freund, Y., Schapire, R.E.: A desicion-theoretic generalization of on-line learning and an application to boosting. In: Vitányi, P. (ed.) EuroCOLT 1995. LNCS, vol. 904, pp. 23–37. Springer, Heidelberg (1995). https://doi.org/10.1007/3-540-59119-2_166
21. Nanni, L., Lumini, A.: FuzzyBagging: a novel ensemble of classifiers. Pattern Recogn. **39**(3), 488–490 (2006)

22. Zhang, P.B., Yang, Z.X.: A Novel AdaBoost framework with robust threshold and structural optimization. IEEE Trans. Cybern. **PP**(99), 1–13 (2016)
23. Zhou, Z.H.: Ensemble Methods: Foundations and Algorithms. Taylor & Francis (2012)
24. Hall, M., et al.: The WEKA data mining software: an update. ACM SIGKDD Explor. Newslett. **11**(1), 10–18 (2009)
25. Chan, P.K., Stolfo, S.J.: Toward scalable learning with non-uniform class and cost distributions: a case study in credit card fraud detection. In: International Conference on Knowledge Discovery and Data Mining AAAI Press, pp. 164–168 (1998)
26. Wang, B.X., Japkowicz, N.: Imbalanced Data Set Learning with Synthetic Examples. IRIS Machine Learning Workshop, N.p. (2004). Print
27. Galar, M., et al.: A review on ensembles for the class imbalance problem: bagging-, boosting-, and hybrid-based approaches. IEEE Trans. Syst. Man Cybern. Part C Appl. Rev. **42**(4), 463–484 (2012)

Graph Convolutional Networks: Algorithms, Applications and Open Challenges

Si Zhang[1(✉)], Hanghang Tong[1], Jiejun Xu[2], and Ross Maciejewski[1]

[1] Arizona State University, Tempe, USA
{szhan172,hanghang.tong,rmacieje}@asu.edu
[2] HRL Laboratories, Malibu, USA
jxu@hrl.com

Abstract. Graph-structured data naturally appear in numerous application domains, ranging from social analysis, bioinformatics to computer vision. The unique capability of graphs enables capturing the structural relations among data, and thus allows to harvest more insights compared to analyzing data in isolation. However, graph mining is a challenging task due to the underlying complex and diverse connectivity patterns. A potential solution is to learn the representation of a graph in a low-dimensional Euclidean space via embedding techniques that preserve the graph properties. Although tremendous efforts have been made to address the graph representation learning problem, many of them still suffer from their shallow learning mechanisms. On the other hand, deep learning models on graphs have recently emerged in both machine learning and data mining areas and demonstrated superior performance for various problems. In this survey, we conduct a comprehensive review specifically on the emerging field of graph convolutional networks, which is one of the most prominent graph deep learning models. We first introduce two taxonomies to group the existing works based on the types of convolutions and the areas of applications, then highlight some graph convolutional network models in details. Finally, we present several challenges in this area and discuss potential directions for future research.

Keywords: Graph convolutional networks · Spectral · Spatial

1 Introduction

Graphs naturally arise in many real-world applications, including social analysis [3], fraud detection [1,45], traffic prediction [28], computer vision [31] and many more. By representing the data as graphs, the structural information can be encoded to model the relations among entities, and furnish more promising insights underlying the data. For example, in a transportation network, nodes are often the sensors and edges represent the spatial proximity among sensors. In addition to the temporal information provided by the sensors themselves, the graph structure

© Springer Nature Switzerland AG 2018
X. Chen et al. (Eds.): CSoNet 2018, LNCS 11280, pp. 79–91, 2018.
https://doi.org/10.1007/978-3-030-04648-4_7

modeled by the spatial correlations leads to a prominent improvement in the traffic prediction problem [28]. Moreover, by modeling the transactions among people as a graph, the complex transaction patterns can be mined for synthetic identity detection [45] and money laundering detection [46].

However, the complex structure of graphs [5] often hampers the capability of gaining the true insights underlying the graphs. Such complexity, for example, resides in the non-Euclidean nature of the graph-structured data. A potential solution to deal with the complex patterns is to learn the graph representations in a low-dimensional Euclidean space via embedding techniques, including the traditional graph embedding methods [4,34,37] and the recent network embedding methods [21,33]. Once the low-dimensional representations are learned, many graph-related problems can be easily done, such as the classic node classification and link prediction [21]. There exist many thorough reviews on both traditional graph embedding and recent network embedding methods. For example, [40] reviews several well-established traditional graph embedding methods and discusses the general framework for graph dimensionality reduction. Hamilton et al. review the general graph representation learning methods, including node embedding and subgraph embedding [23]. Furthermore, [11] discusses the differences between the traditional graph embedding and the recent network embedding methods. One notable difference is that the recent network embedding is more suitable for the task-specific network inference. Other existing literature reviews on network embedding include [8,20].

Despite some successes of these embedding methods, many of them suffer from the limitations of the shallow learning mechanisms [21,33] and might fail to discover the more complex patterns behind the graphs. Deep learning models, on the other hand, have been demonstrated their power in many applications. For example, convolution neural networks (CNN) achieve a promising performance in many computer vision [19] and natural language processing [18] applications. In particular, due to the grid-like nature of images, the convolution layers in CNN enable to learn different trainable localized filters which scan every pixel in the images, combining with the surrounding pixels. The basic components are the convolution and pooling operators, as well as the trainable localized filters.

However, the non-Euclidean characteristic of graphs (e.g., the irregular structure) makes the graph convolutions and graph filtering not as well-defined as on images. In the past decades, researchers have been working on the graph signal operations, such as graph filtering, graph wavelets, etc. Shuman et al. give a comprehensive overview of graph signal processing, including the common operations on graphs [36]. To be brief, spectral graph convolutions are defined in the graph Fourier domain, which is considered as an analogy of 1-D signal Fourier transform. Graph filtering can be defined in the spectral and vertex domains. The emergence of these operators open a door to graph convolutional networks. Note that in the past few years, many other graph deep learning models have been proposed, including (but are not limited to): (1) graph auto-encoder [26], (2) graph generative adversarial model [14,44], (3) graph attention model [27,39], (4) graph recurrent neural networks [43]. But in this survey, we focus specifically on reviewing the existing literature of the graph convolutional networks. The main contributions of this survey are summarized as following:

1. We introduce two taxonomies to group the existing graph convolutional network models by the types of filtering and the areas of applications.
2. We motivate each taxonomy by surveying and discussing the state-of-the-art graph convolutional network models.
3. We discuss the challenges of the current models that need to be addressed and highlight some promising directions for the future work.

The rest of the paper is organized as follows. We start by summarizing the notations and introducing some preliminaries of graph convolutional networks in Sect. 2. Then in Sect. 3 and Sect. 4, we categorize the existing models into the spectral based methods and the spatial based methods by the types of graph filtering with some detailed examples. Section 5 presents the methods from a view of applications. In Sect. 6, we conclude our survey, discuss some of the challenges and provide some directions for the future work.

2   Notations and Preliminary

In this section, we present the notations and some preliminaries for the graph convolutional networks. In general, we use bold uppercase letters for matrices, bold lowercase letters for vectors, and lowercase letters for scalars. For matrix indexing, we use $\mathbf{A}(i, j)$ to denote the entry at the intersection of the i-th row and j-th column. We denote the transpose of a matrix $\mathbf{A}$ as $\mathbf{A}^T$.

Graphs and Graph Signals. In this survey, we are interested in the graph convolutional network models on an undirected connected graph $\mathcal{G} = \{\mathcal{V}, \mathcal{E}, \mathbf{A}\}$, which consists of a set of nodes $\mathcal{V}$ with $|\mathcal{V}| = n$, a set of edges $\mathcal{E}$ with $|\mathcal{E}| = m$ and the adjacency matrix $\mathbf{A}$. If there is an edge between node i and node j, the entry $\mathbf{A}(i, j)$ denotes the weight of the edge; otherwise, $\mathbf{A}(i, j) = 0$. For unweighted graphs, we simply set $\mathbf{A}(i, j) = 1$. We denote the degree matrix of $\mathbf{A}$ as a diagonal matrix $\mathbf{D}$ where $\mathbf{D}(i, i) = \sum_{j=1}^{n} \mathbf{A}(i, j)$. Then the Laplacian matrix of $\mathbf{A}$ is denoted as $\mathbf{L} = \mathbf{D} - \mathbf{A}$. The corresponding symmetrically normalized Laplacian matrix is $\tilde{\mathbf{L}} = \mathbf{I} - \mathbf{D}^{-\frac{1}{2}}\mathbf{A}\mathbf{D}^{-\frac{1}{2}}$ where $\mathbf{I}$ is an identity matrix.

A graph signal defined on the nodes is represented as a vector $\mathbf{x} \in \mathbb{R}^n$ where $\mathbf{x}(i)$ is the signal value on the node i [36]. Node attributes, for instance, can be considered as the graph signals. Denote $\mathbf{X} \in \mathbb{R}^{n \times d}$ as the node attribute matrix of an attributed graph, then the columns of $\mathbf{X}$ are the d signals of the graph.

Graph Fourier Transform. It is well-known that the classic Fourier transform of an 1-D signal f is computed by $\hat{f}(\xi) = \langle f, e^{2\pi i \xi t} \rangle$ where ξ is the frequency of $\hat{f}$ in the spectral domain and the complex exponential is the eigenfunction of the Laplace operator. Analogously, the graph Laplacian matrix $\mathbf{L}$ is the Laplace operator defined on a graph, and hence an eigenvector of $\mathbf{L}$ associated with its corresponding eigenvalue is an analog to the complex exponential at a certain frequency. Note that the symmetrically normalized Laplacian matrix $\tilde{\mathbf{L}}$ and the random-walk transition matrix can be also used as the graph Laplace operator. In particular, denote the eigenvalue decomposition of $\tilde{\mathbf{L}}$ as $\tilde{\mathbf{L}} = \mathbf{U}\boldsymbol{\Lambda}\mathbf{U}^T$ where the l-th column of $\mathbf{U}$ is the eigenvector $\mathbf{u}_l$ and $\boldsymbol{\Lambda}(l,l)$ is the corresponding eigenvalue λ_l, then we can compute the Fourier transform of a graph signal $\mathbf{x}$ as

$$\hat{\mathbf{x}}(\lambda_l) = \langle \mathbf{x}, \mathbf{u}_l \rangle = \sum_{i=1}^{n} \mathbf{x}(i)\mathbf{u}_l^*(i) \tag{1}$$

The above equation represents in the spectral domain a graph signal defined in the vertex domain. Then the inverse graph Fourier transform can be written as

$$\mathbf{x}(i) = \sum_{l=1}^{n} \hat{\mathbf{x}}(\lambda_l)\mathbf{u}_l(i) \tag{2}$$

Graph Filtering. Graph filtering is a localized operation on graph signals. Analogous to the classic signal filtering in the time or spectral domain, one can localize a graph signal in its vertex domain or spectral domain as well.

(1) Frequency filtering: Recall that the frequency filtering of a classic signal is often represented as the convolution with the filter signal in the time domain. However, due to the irregular structure of the graphs (e.g., different nodes having different numbers of neighbors), graph convolution in the vertex domain is not as straightforward as the classic signal convolution in the time domain. Note that for classic signals, the convolution in the time domain is equivalent to the inverse Fourier transform of the multiplication between the spectral representations of two signals. Therefore, the spectral graph convolution is defined analogously as

$$(\mathbf{x} *_{\mathcal{G}} \mathbf{y})(i) = \sum_{l=1}^{n} \hat{\mathbf{x}}(\lambda_l)\hat{\mathbf{y}}(\lambda_l)\mathbf{u}_l(i) \tag{3}$$

Note that $\hat{\mathbf{x}}(\lambda_l)\hat{\mathbf{y}}(\lambda_l)$ indicates the filtering in the spectral domain. Thus, the frequency filtering of a signal $\mathbf{x}$ on graph $\mathcal{G}$ with a filter $\mathbf{y}$ is exactly same as Eq. (3) and is further re-written as

$$\mathbf{x}_{out} = \mathbf{x} *_{\mathcal{G}} \mathbf{y} = \mathbf{U} \begin{bmatrix} \hat{\mathbf{y}}(\lambda_1) & & 0 \\ & \ddots & \\ 0 & & \hat{\mathbf{y}}(\lambda_n) \end{bmatrix} \mathbf{U}^T \mathbf{x} \tag{4}$$

(2) Vertex filtering: The graph filtering of a signal $\mathbf{x}$ in the vertex domain is generally defined as a linear combination of the signal components in the nodes neighborhood. Mathematically, the vertex filtering of a signal $\mathbf{x}$ at node i is

$$\mathbf{x}_{out}(i) = w_{i,i}\mathbf{x}(i) + \sum_{j \in \mathcal{N}(i,K)} w_{i,j}\mathbf{x}(j) \tag{5}$$

where $\mathcal{N}(i,K)$ represents the K-hop neighborhood of node i in the graph and the parameters $\{w_{i,j}\}$ are the weights used for the combination. It can be shown that by using a K-polynomial filter, the frequency filtering can be interpreted from the vertex filtering perspective [36].

3   Spectral Graph Convolutional Networks

In this section and the subsequent Sect. 4, we categorize the graph convolutional neural networks into the spectral based methods and the spatial based methods respectively. We consider the spectral based methods to be those methods that start with constructing the frequency filtering.

The first notable spectral based graph convolutional network is proposed by Bruna et al. [7]. Motivated by the classic CNN, this deep model on graphs contains several spectral convolutional layers that take a vector $\mathbf{X}_p$ of size $n \times d_p$ as the input feature map and output a feature map $\mathbf{X}_{p+1}$ of size $n \times d_{p+1}$ by:

$$\mathbf{X}_{p+1}(:,j) = \sigma \left(\sum_{i=1}^{d_p} \mathbf{V} \begin{bmatrix} (\boldsymbol{\theta}_i^j)(1) & & 0 \\ & \ddots & \\ 0 & & (\boldsymbol{\theta}_i^j)(n) \end{bmatrix} \mathbf{V}^T \mathbf{X}_p(:,i) \right), \ \forall j = 1, \cdots, d_{p+1}$$

(6)

where $\mathbf{X}_p(:,i)$ ($\mathbf{X}_{p+1}(:,j)$) is the i-th (j-th) dimension of the input (output) feature map respectively, $\boldsymbol{\theta}_i^j$ denotes a vector of learnable parameters of the filter $\boldsymbol{\theta}_i^j$. Each column of $\mathbf{V}$ is the eigenvector of $\mathbf{L}$ and $\sigma(\cdot)$ is the activation function. However, there are several issues with this convolutional structure. First, the eigenvector matrix $\mathbf{V}$ requires the explicit computation of the eigenvalue decomposition of the graph Laplacian matrix, and hence suffers from the $O(n^3)$ time complexity which is impractical for large-scale graphs. Second, though the eigenvectors can be pre-computed, the time complexity of Eq. (6) is still $O(n^2)$. Third, there are $O(n)$ parameters to be learned in each layer. Besides, these non-parametric filters are not localized in the vertex domain. To overcome the limitations, the authors also propose to use a rank-r approximation of eigenvalue decomposition. To be specific, they use the first r eigenvectors of $\mathbf{V}$ that carry the most smooth geometry of the graph and consequently reduce the number of parameters of each filter to $O(1)$ [7]. Moreover, if the graph contains the clustering structure that can be explored via such a rank-r factorization, the filters are potentially localized. However, it still requires $O(n^2)$ time complexity.

To address these limitations, Defferrard et al. propose to use K-polynomial filters in the convolutional layers for localization [12]. Such a K-polynomial filter is represented by $\hat{\mathbf{y}}(\lambda_l) = \sum_{k=1}^{K} \theta_k \lambda_l^k$. As mentioned in Sect. 2, the K-polynomial filters achieve a good localization by integrating the node features within the K hop neighborhood [36], and the number of the trainable parameters decreases to $O(K) = O(1)$. In addition, to further reduce the computational complexity, the Chebyshev polynomial approximation [24] is used to compute the spectral graph convolution. Mathematically, the Chebyshev polynomial $T_k(x)$ of order k can be recursively computed by $T_k(x) = 2xT_{k-1}(x) - T_{k-2}(x)$ with $T_0 = 1$, $T_1(x) = x$. They normalize the filters by $\tilde{\lambda}_l = 2\frac{\lambda_l}{\lambda_{\max}} - 1$ to make the scaled eigenvalues lie within $[-1, 1]$ [12]. As a result, the convolution layer is

$$\mathbf{X}_{p+1}(:,j) = \sigma \left(\sum_{i=1}^{d_p} \sum_{k=0}^{K-1} (\boldsymbol{\theta}_i^j)(k+1) T_k(\tilde{\mathbf{L}}) \mathbf{X}_p(:,i) \right), \ \forall j = 1, \cdots, d_{p+1} \quad (7)$$

where $\boldsymbol{\theta}_i^j$ is a K-dimensional parameter vector for the i-th column of input feature map and the j-th column of output feature map. The authors also design a max pooling operation [12] with the multilevel clustering method Graclus [13] which is quite efficient to uncover the hierarchical structure of the graphs.

As a special variant, the graph convolutional network proposed by Kipf et al. (named as GCN) aims at the semi-supervised node classification task on graphs [25]. In this model, the authors truncate the Chebyshev polynomial to first-order (i.e., $K = 2$ in Eq. (7)) and specifically set $(\boldsymbol{\theta})_i^j(1) = -(\boldsymbol{\theta})_i^j(2) = \theta_i^j$. Besides, since the eigenvalues of $\tilde{\mathbf{L}}$ are within $[0, 2]$, relaxing $\lambda_{\max} = 2$ still guarantees $-1 \leq \tilde{\lambda}_l \leq 1$, $\forall l = 1, \cdots, n$. This leads to the simplified convolution layer as

$$\mathbf{X}_{p+1} = \sigma \left(\tilde{\mathbf{D}}^{-\frac{1}{2}} \tilde{\mathbf{A}} \tilde{\mathbf{D}}^{-\frac{1}{2}} \mathbf{X}_p \mathbf{\Theta}_p \right) \tag{8}$$

where $\tilde{\mathbf{A}} = \mathbf{I} + \mathbf{D}^{-\frac{1}{2}} \mathbf{A} \mathbf{D}^{-\frac{1}{2}}$ and $\tilde{\mathbf{D}}$ is the diagonal degree matrix of $\tilde{\mathbf{A}}$, $\mathbf{\Theta}_p$ is a $d_{p+1} \times d_p$ parameter matrix. Besides, Eq. (8) has a close relationship with the Weisfeiler-Lehman isomorphism test [35]. The last layer outputs the node representations. A softmax classifier is then added after the last spectral convolutional layer and the objective is to minimize the cross-entropy error over the labeled nodes. The objective function is then minimized in a gradient descent manner. However, the training process could be costly (in terms of memory) for large-scale graphs. Moreover, the transduction of GCN interferes with the generalization, making the learning of representations of the unseen nodes in the same graph and the nodes in an entirely different graph more difficult [25].

To address the issues of GCN [25], FastGCN [10] improves the original GCN model by viewing the spectral graph convolution as an integral of embedding functions under some probability measure. It first assumes the input graph $\mathcal{G}$ is an induced subgraph of a possibly infinite graph $\mathcal{G}'$ such that the nodes $\mathcal{V}$ of $\mathcal{G}$ are i.i.d. samples of the nodes of $\mathcal{G}'$ (denoted as $\mathcal{V}'$) under some probability measure $\mathcal{P}$. This way, the original convolution layer represented by Eq. (8) can be illustrated by an embedding function of independent vertices. Denote the embedding function at the p-th layer as $\mathbf{x}_p$, then we have

$$\mathbf{x}_{p+1}(v) = \sigma \left(\int \tilde{\mathbf{A}}(v, u) \mathbf{x}_p(u) \mathbf{\Theta}_p d\mathcal{P}(u) \right) \tag{9}$$

where u, v are some independent nodes. Now, Eq. (9) can be approximated by Monte Carlo sampling. Denote some i.i.d. samples $u_1^p, \cdots, u_{t_p}^p$ at layer-p, the integral can be estimated by

$$\mathbf{x}_{p+1}(v) = \sigma \left(\frac{1}{t_p} \sum_{i=1}^{t_p} \tilde{\mathbf{A}}(v, u_i^p) \mathbf{x}_p(u_i^p) \mathbf{\Theta}_p \right) \tag{10}$$

Denote P as the number of layers of the deep architecture, and $u_1^P, \cdots, u_{t_P}^P$ as a batch of nodes. At each layer p, they uniformly sample with replacement the nodes $u_1^p, \cdots, u_{t_p}^p$, then the output feature map is computed by

$$\mathbf{X}_{p+1}(v,:) = \sigma \left(\frac{n}{t_p} \sum_{i=1}^{t_p} \tilde{\mathbf{A}}(v, u_i^p) \mathbf{X}_p(u_i^p, :) \mathbf{\Theta}_p \right) \tag{11}$$

and the batch loss w.r.t. the output of the last layer is

$$\mathcal{L} = \frac{1}{t_P} \sum_{i=1}^{t_P} g\left(\mathbf{X}_P(u_i^P, :) \right) \tag{12}$$

where $g(\cdot)$ is some loss function. Note that this Monte Carlo estimator of the original convolution could lead to a high variance of estimation. To reduce the variance, the authors also formalize the variance and solve for a sampling distribution $\mathcal{P}$ of nodes. Due to the space limitation, we suggest the readers of interests to refer to [10]. In addition, [9] is another recent work on the stochastic training of GCN [25]. To reduce the variance of the estimator, the authors use the historical activations of nodes as a control variate and propose an efficient sampling-based stochastic algorithm. Besides, the authors theoretically prove the convergence of the algorithm regardless of the sampling size in the training phase, and also the exact predictions in the testing phase in [9].

4   Spatial Graph Convolutional Networks

As the spectral graph convolution relies on the specific eigenfunctions of Laplacian matrix, it is nontrivial to transfer the spectral based graph convolutional network models learned on one graph to another graph whose eigenfunctions are different. Spatial based methods, on the other hand, alternatively generalize the convolution to the combinations of the graph signal within the nodes neighborhood and define the learnable filters in the vertex domain.

Monti et al. propose a generic graph convolution network framework named MoNet [31] by designing a universe patch operator which integrates the signals within the node neighborhood. In particular, for a node i and its neighboring node $j \in \mathcal{N}(i)$, they define a d-dimensional pseudo-coordinates $\mathbf{u}(i,j)$ and feed it into P learnable kernel functions $(w_1(\mathbf{u}), \cdots, w_P(\mathbf{u}))$. Then the patch operator is formulated as $D_p(i) = \sum_{j \in \mathcal{N}(i)} w_p(\mathbf{u}(i,j)) \mathbf{x}(j)$, $p = 1, \cdots, P$ where $\mathbf{x}(j)$ is the signal value at the node j. The graph convolution in the spatial domain is then based on the patch operator as

$$(\mathbf{x} *_s \mathbf{y})(i) = \sum_{l=1}^{P} \mathbf{g}(p) D_p(i) \mathbf{x} \tag{13}$$

It is shown that by carefully selection of $\mathbf{u}(i,j)$ and the kernel function $w_p(\mathbf{u})$, many existing graph convolutional network models [2,25] can be viewed as a specific case of MoNet. SplineCNN [15] follows the same framework (i.e., Eq. (13)) but uses a different convolution kernel based on B-splines.

From a more general perspective, the graph convolution in the spatial domain can be alternatively thought of as an aggregation of a subset of nodes. Hamilton et al. propose an aggregation based representation learning, named GraphSAGE [22]. The full batch version of the algorithm is straightforward: for a node i, one (1) aggregates the representation vectors of all its immediate neighbors in the current layer via some learnable aggregator; (2) concatenates the representation vector of node i with the aggregated representation; (3) then feeds the concatenated vector to a fully connected layer with some nonlinear activation function $\sigma(\cdot)$, followed by a normalization step. The output of the last layer is considered as the final representations of nodes, which can be followed by some loss function. The authors provide some choices of the aggregator functions, including the mean aggregator, LSTM aggregator and the pooling aggregator. Among others, using the mean aggregator makes the whole algorithm approximately resemble the GCN model [25]. In addition, for training efficiency, they also provide a minibatch variant by uniformly sampling the neighboring nodes [22].

Velickovic et al. design a novel attention layer that aggregates the features of the neighboring nodes weighted by some learnable importance [39]. Consider the input node attribute matrix $\mathbf{X}$ with each row as the feature vector of a node. The attention layer contains a shared learnable weight matrix $\mathbf{W}$ and computes the attention coefficients between node i and its neighbor node $j \in \mathcal{N}(i)$ by

$$\alpha_{ij} = \frac{\exp\left(\mathbf{a}^T[\mathbf{W}\mathbf{X}(i,:)^T \| \mathbf{W}\mathbf{X}(j,:)^T]\right)}{\sum_{q \in \mathcal{N}(i)} \exp\left(\mathbf{a}^T[\mathbf{W}\mathbf{X}(i,:)^T \| \mathbf{W}\mathbf{X}(q,:)^T]\right)} \tag{14}$$

where $\|$ denotes the concatenation operation and $\mathbf{a}$ is a single-layer feedforward neural network. This attention coefficient acts as a weight to encode the importance of feature vector of the neighboring node j for node i. And the final output of the feature vector is computed by a linear combination $\mathbf{X}_{out}(i,:) = \sigma\left(\sum_{j \in \mathcal{N}(i)} \alpha_{ij} \mathbf{W}\mathbf{X}(j,:)^T\right)$. To stabilize the learning process, the authors apply the multi-head attention [38] (i.e., L independent attention mechanism as Eq. (14)), and then feed the average of the output of all heads to a nonlinearity. Compared to the GCN model [25], more flexibility is achieved thanks to the learnable importance of the nodes within the neighborhood.

Note that despite the inherent differences among the models above, all of them can be viewed as an instance of using vertex filtering. It is just the strategy of how to decide the weights w_{ij} in Eq. (5) that differentiates the models.

5   Applications of Graph Convolutional Networks

The different graph convolutional network models can be also divided by what kind of data they are applied to. Although a substantial amount of applications exist, we generally categorize them into (1) applications on graph data, (2) applications on image and manifold, and (3) applications on other data.

Applications on Graph Data. A number of works have been proposed to solve the tasks on graphs. The majority of them are for node classification, including [10,17,22,25,31,39]. A commonality among them is that the output feature map of these methods can be considered as the node representations, and thus these methods can be also naturally generalized to other node-level problems, such as link prediction, node clustering and visualization. Another application is the graph classification. One straightforward way is to aggregate the learned node representations as the graph representations and then feed to some classifiers (e.g., fully connected network). However, this may not be a quite promising strategy since the simple aggregation of the isolated node representations may not represent the graph in its entirety. [7,12,42] leverages the graph coarsening and pooling operator to explore the hierarchical representations of graphs. In particular, [42] recently designs a differential pooling operator that can generate the graph hierarchical representations. There are some other adapted graph convolutional network models that aim to solve problems in specific domains. For example, Li et al. [28] propose a diffusion convolutional recurrent neural network for traffic forecasting by exploring spatial and temporal dependencies. [16] introduces a special graph convolutional network architecture for protein interface prediction.

Applications on Images and Manifolds. Image classification problems have been studied for decades. Traditional CNN based methods directly consider the images as a grid-like structure. The recent graph convolutional network models allow to consider image classification as a classification on the non-Euclidean structures (e.g., graphs that encode the relations among pixels). Briefly speaking, k-NN similarity graphs with pixels of the images as the nodes need to be constructed and the image classification problem is then converted to a graph classification problem. Existing works on this problem include [7,12,31], etc. In addition, another application of the graph convolutional network models in the computer vision area is to learn the correspondence between the collections of 3D shapes represented by the discrete manifolds. This problem is roughly cast as a labelling problem, i.e., to label each node on a query shape with the index of the node on the target shape [31].

Applications on Other Data. In addition to the applications on graphs and manifolds, graph convolutional network models are also widely used for natural language processing. For example, [30] deals with the semantic role labelling by encoding sentences with the graph convolutional network. Marcheggiani et al. attempt to use graph convolutional network models for machine translation problems [29]. Besides, they can also be used for recommender systems. In particular, Monti et al. cast the recommender system problem as a matrix completion problem with two graphs as side information, then define a multiple graph convolution operator of the convolution layer to adapt the graph convolutional network model to solve the matrix completion problem [32]. Another notable work [41] deploys a random-walk-based graph convolutional network model for high-quality recommendations. Besides, the authors develop an on-the-fly convolution computation for efficient training process and a MapReduce pipeline for efficient inferences.

6   Concluding Remarks

Graph convolutional network models, as one category of the graph deep learning (or geometric deep learning) models, have become a very hot topic in both machine learning and data mining areas, and a substantial amount of models have been proposed to solve different problems. In this survey, we conduct a comprehensive literature review on the emerging field of graph convolutional networks. Specifically, we introduce two intuitive taxonomies to group the existing works. These are based on the types of graph filtering operations, and based on the areas of applications. For each taxomony, we highlight with some detailed examples from a unique standpoint. In addition to our survey, another comprehensive tutorial on geometric deep learning [6] may help readers step into this area Meanwhile, despite the advancements made by the recent works, there still exist some potential issues in the current graph convolutional network models. This way we discuss some challenges and provide some potential future directions.

Multiple Graph Convolutional Networks. As already mentioned before, the major drawback of the spectral graph convolutional networks is its inability of adaptation from one graph to another graph if two graphs have different Fourier basis (i.e., eigenfunctions of the Laplacian matrix). The existing work [32] alternatively learns the filter parameters by generalizing the eigenfunctions of a single graph to the eigenfunctions of the Kronecker product graph of multiple input graphs. As a different track, the spatial graph convolutional network models attempt to learn the a rule of how to combine neighboring nodes in the vertex domain which could be used on different graphs. However, a drawback of these methods is the inability of modeling the interactions (e.g., anchor links) or correlations (e.g., correlations among multiple views) across multiple graphs. In fact, given multiple graphs, the representation learning of a unique node should be able to benefit from more information provided across graphs or views. However, to our best knowledge, there is no existing model aiming at the problems in this setting.

Hybrid Spectral-Spatial Graph Convolutional Networks. Note that the graph convolutional network models reviewed in this survey start with either the spectral filtering in the frequency domain or the spatial filtering in the vertex domain. This raises the issue that the existing graph convolutional network models may not fully exploit the insights simultaneously from both the spectral and spatial perspectives of the graph. Recall that the anomaly detection on some classic 1-D signals requires the knowledge in both time domain and frequency domain. In this way, a hybrid spectral-spatial graph convolution operator may provide more comprehensive representations of nodes and hence help some tasks, such as anomaly detection on graphs.

Deep Graph Convolutional Networks. Although the initial objective of graph convolutional network models is to leverage the deep architecture for better representation learning, most of the current models still suffer from their shallow structure. For example, GCN [25] in practice only uses two layers. And as the authors analyzed, more convolution layers may even hurt the performance [25].

This is also intuitive due to its simple propagation procedure. As deeper the architecture is, the representations of nodes may become smoother even for those nodes that are distinct and far from each other. This issue violates the purpose of using deep models. Consequently, how to build a deep architecture that exploits the deeper structural patterns of graphs is another possible research direction.

Acknowledgement. This material is supported by the National Science Foundation under Grant No. IIS-1651203, IIS-1715385, IIS-1743040, and CNS-1629888, by DTRA under the grant number HDTRA1-16-0017, by the United States Air Force and DARPA under contract number FA8750-17-C-0153 (Distribution Statement "A" (Approved for Public Release, Distribution Unlimited)), by Army Research Office under the contract number W911NF-16-1-0168, and by the U.S. Department of Homeland Security under Grant Award Number 2017-ST-061-QA0001. The content of the information in this document does not necessarily reflect the position or the policy of the Government, and no official endorsement should be inferred. The U.S. Government is authorized to reproduce and distribute reprints for Government purposes notwithstanding any copyright notation here on.

References

1. Akoglu, L., Tong, H., Koutra, D.: Graph based anomaly detection and description: a survey. Data Min. Knowl. Disc. **29**(3), 626–688 (2015)
2. Atwood, J., Towsley, D.: Diffusion-convolutional neural networks. In: NIPS (2016)
3. Backstrom, L., Leskovec, J.: Supervised random walks: predicting and recommending links in social networks. In: WSDM, pp. 635–644. ACM (2011)
4. Belkin, M., Niyogi, P.: Laplacian eigenmaps and spectral techniques for embedding and clustering. In: NIPS, pp. 585–591 (2002)
5. Boccaletti, S., Latora, V., Moreno, Y., Chavez, M., Hwang, D.U.: Complex networks: structure and dynamics. Phys. Rep. **424**(4–5), 175–308 (2006)
6. Bronstein, M.M., Bruna, J., LeCun, Y., Szlam, A., Vandergheynst, P.: Geometric deep learning: going beyond euclidean data. IEEE Signal Process. Mag. **34**(4), 18–42 (2017)
7. Bruna, J., Zaremba, W., Szlam, A., LeCun, Y.: Spectral networks and locally connected networks on graphs. arXiv preprint arXiv:1312.6203 (2013)
8. Cai, H., Zheng, V.W., Chang, K.: A comprehensive survey of graph embedding: problems, techniques and applications. TKDE (2018)
9. Chen, J., Zhu, J., Song, L.: Stochastic training of graph convolutional networks with variance reduction. In: ICML, pp. 941–949 (2018)
10. Chen, J., Ma, T., Xiao, C.: FastGCN: fast learning with graph convolutional networks via importance sampling. arXiv preprint arXiv:1801.10247 (2018)
11. Cui, P., Wang, X., Pei, J., Zhu, W.: A survey on network embedding. TKDE (2018)
12. Defferrard, M., Bresson, X., Vandergheynst, P.: Convolutional neural networks on graphs with fast localized spectral filtering. In: NIPS, pp. 3844–3852 (2016)
13. Dhillon, I.S., Guan, Y., Kulis, B.: Weighted graph cuts without eigenvectors a multilevel approach. IEEE Trans. Pattern Anal. Mach. Intell. **29**(11) (2007)
14. Ding, M., Tang, J., Zhang, J.: Semi-supervised learning on graphs with generative adversarial nets. arXiv preprint arXiv:1809.00130 (2018)
15. Fey, M., Lenssen, J.E., Weichert, F., Müller, H.: SplineCNN: fast geometric deep learning with continuous b-spline kernels. In: CVPR, pp. 869–877 (2018)

16. Fout, A., Byrd, J., Shariat, B., Ben-Hur, A.: Protein interface prediction using graph convolutional networks. In: NIPS, pp. 6530–6539 (2017)
17. Gao, H., Wang, Z., Ji, S.: Large-scale learnable graph convolutional networks. In: KDD, pp. 1416–1424. ACM (2018)
18. Gehring, J., Auli, M., Grangier, D., Dauphin, Y.N.: A convolutional encoder model for neural machine translation. arXiv preprint arXiv:1611.02344 (2016)
19. Girshick, R., Donahue, J., Darrell, T., Malik, J.: Rich feature hierarchies for accurate object detection and semantic segmentation. In: CVPR, pp. 580–587 (2014)
20. Goyal, P., Ferrara, E.: Graph embedding techniques, applications, and performance: a survey. Knowl. Based Syst. **151**, 78–94 (2018)
21. Grover, A., Leskovec, J.: node2vec: Scalable feature learning for networks. In: KDD, pp. 855–864. ACM (2016)
22. Hamilton, W., Ying, Z., Leskovec, J.: Inductive representation learning on large graphs. In: NIPS, pp. 1024–1034 (2017)
23. Hamilton, W.L., Ying, R., Leskovec, J.: Representation learning on graphs: methods and applications. arXiv preprint arXiv:1709.05584 (2017)
24. Hammond, D.K., Vandergheynst, P., Gribonval, R.: Wavelets on graphs via spectral graph theory. Appl. Comput. Harmonic Anal. **30**(2), 129–150 (2011)
25. Kipf, T.N., Welling, M.: Semi-supervised classification with graph convolutional networks. arXiv preprint arXiv:1609.02907 (2016)
26. Kipf, T.N., Welling, M.: Variational graph auto-encoders. arXiv preprint arXiv:1611.07308 (2016)
27. Lee, J.B., Rossi, R., Kong, X.: Graph classification using structural attention. In: KDD, pp. 1666–1674. ACM (2018)
28. Li, Y., Yu, R., Shahabi, C., Liu, Y.: Diffusion convolutional recurrent neural network: data-driven traffic forecasting (2018)
29. Marcheggiani, D., Bastings, J., Titov, I.: Exploiting semantics in neural machine translation with graph convolutional networks. arXiv preprint arXiv:1804.08313 (2018)
30. Marcheggiani, D., Titov, I.: Encoding sentences with graph convolutional networks for semantic role labeling. arXiv preprint arXiv:1703.04826 (2017)
31. Monti, F., Boscaini, D., Masci, J., Rodola, E., Svoboda, J., Bronstein, M.M.: Geometric deep learning on graphs and manifolds using mixture model CNNs. In: CVPR, vol. 1, p. 3 (2017)
32. Monti, F., Bronstein, M., Bresson, X.: Geometric matrix completion with recurrent multi-graph neural networks. In: NIPS, pp. 3697–3707 (2017)
33. Perozzi, B., Al-Rfou, R., Skiena, S.: DeepWalk: online learning of social representations. In: KDD, pp. 701–710. ACM (2014)
34. Roweis, S.T., Saul, L.K.: Nonlinear dimensionality reduction by locally linear embedding. Science **290**(5500), 2323–2326 (2000)
35. Shervashidze, N., Schweitzer, P., Leeuwen, E.J.V., Mehlhorn, K., Borgwardt, K.M.: Weisfeiler-lehman graph kernels. JMLR **12**(Sep), 2539–2561 (2011)
36. Shuman, D.I., Narang, S.K., Frossard, P., Ortega, A., Vandergheynst, P.: The emerging field of signal processing on graphs: extending high-dimensional data analysis to networks and other irregular domains. IEEE Signal Process. Mag. **30**(3), 83–98 (2013)
37. Tenenbaum, J.B., De Silva, V., Langford, J.C.: A global geometric framework for nonlinear dimensionality reduction. Science **290**(5500), 2319–2323 (2000)
38. Vaswani, A., et al.: Attention is all you need. In: NIPS, pp. 5998–6008 (2017)
39. Velickovic, P., Cucurull, G., Casanova, A., Romero, A., Lio, P., Bengio, Y.: Graph attention networks. arXiv preprint arXiv:1710.10903 (2017)

40. Yan, S., Xu, D., Zhang, B., Zhang, H.J., Yang, Q., Lin, S.: Graph embedding and extensions: a general framework for dimensionality reduction. IEEE Trans. Pattern Anal. Mach. Intell. **29**(1), 40–51 (2007)
41. Ying, R., He, R., Chen, K., Eksombatchai, P., Hamilton, W.L., Leskovec, J.: Graph convolutional neural networks for web-scale recommender systems. arXiv preprint arXiv:1806.01973 (2018)
42. Ying, R., You, J., Morris, C., Ren, X., Hamilton, W.L., Leskovec, J.: Hierarchical graph representation learning with differentiable pooling. arXiv preprint arXiv:1806.08804 (2018)
43. You, J., Ying, R., Ren, X., Hamilton, W.L., Leskovec, J.: GraphRNN: a deep generative model for graphs. arXiv preprint arXiv:1802.08773 (2018)
44. Yu, W., et al.: Learning deep network representations with adversarially regularized autoencoders. In: KDD, pp. 2663–2671. ACM (2018)
45. Zhang, S., et al.: Hidden: hierarchical dense subgraph detection with application to financial fraud detection. In: SDM, pp. 570–578. SIAM (2017)
46. Zhou, D., et al.: A local algorithm for structure-preserving graph cut. In: KDD, pp. 655–664. ACM (2017)

A Path Planning Approach with Maximum Traffic Flow and Minimum Breakdown Probability in Complex Road Network

Mengran Xu[1,2], Demin Li[1,2(✉)], Guanglin Zhang[1,2], Mengqi Cao[1,2], and Shuya Liao[1,2]

[1] College of Information Science and Technology, Donghua University, Shanghai, China
mengranxu@mail.dhu.edu.cn, {deminli,glzhang}@dhu.edu.cn
[2] Engineering Research Center of Digitized Textile and Apparel Technology, Ministry of Education, Shanghai 201620, China

Abstract. In urban scenarios, the issues of traffic congestion keep disturbing governments and individuals, especially in complex road networks. It seems urgent to improve road utilization for alleviating the traffic congestion. In this paper, we first propose an optimization model to improve the road utilization, which not only considers the traffic breakdown probability but also the spontaneous traffic flow. Traffic breakdown occurs during the transition from free flow to spontaneous flow and may probably cause traffic congestion. By considering traffic flow, more drivers can avoid traffic breakdown and the road utilization will be increasing. Secondly, in order to decrease the complexity and redundancy, this paper uses a big traffic flow condition and Taylor series to simplify the objective function and obtain an optimal result with accuracy. Finally, the simulations that use real urban traffic scenario of Songjiang University Town in ShangHai evaluate the proposed algorithm's performance. Our proposed algorithm outperforms other existing path-planning algorithm.

Keywords: Breakdown probability · Traffic flow · Road utilization

1 Introduction

With the increasing amount of vehicles, the road network becomes more complex and the problem of congestion keeps disturbing traffic operations, especially in the metropolitan areas such as: Shanghai, Beijing and Guangzhou [2].

This work is supported by the NSF of China under Grant No. 71171045, No. 61772130, and No. 61301118; the Innovation Program of Shanghai Municipal Education Commission under Grant No. 14YZ130; and the International S&T Cooperation Program of Shanghai Science and Technology Commission under Grant No. 15220710600.

X. Chen et al. (Eds.): CSoNet 2018, LNCS 11280, pp. 92–102, 2018.
https://doi.org/10.1007/978-3-030-04648-4_8

What's more, these traffic problems will increase not only driver's travel time, but also the additional travel cost, it is necessary to relieve the situation caused by increasing vehicles. Therefore, optimal path planning should be developed to reduce the travel time and alleviate the traffic congestion [11].

However, in most cases, drivers prefer to choose according to the distance and arrival time, among which, more travelers tend to filter by the length of distance [1]. Although drivers pick the shortest way to reduce their travel time, the travel time will increase due to greater amounts of cars in this shortest path. Consequently, imbalanced traffic flow may bring about traffic congestion [9], to avoid that, measures should be taken. For example, the local officials improve road construction through broadening road and collecting tolls for main roads. These methods are unable to solve the traffic problems fundamentally and the velocity of road construction can not catch up the increasing number of cars. Hence, as a better solution, improve road utilization such as planning path appropriately should be applied to alleviate traffic congestion.

The traffic breakdown condition means a road becomes congested spontaneously. The concept of traffic breakdown was developed by Kerner, after that he proposed a breakdown minimization principle in [6]. The three-phase traffic theory identified by Kerner in [5] revealed the principle of traffic breakdown. To be specific, three phases are free flow, synchronized flow and wide moving jam. Traffic breakdown was a local first-order phase transforms from free flow to synchronized flow. In [10], Wardrop principle mentioned that, if drivers who are travelling in the road network only consider their own travel time, the total traffic time of system is not minimization. Hongliang Guo and his team proposed a multiple vehicles routing approach in [3]. Guo et al. used a matrix to choose an optimal route with minimize breakdown probability which can usefully reduce the total road network traffic time. The algorithm provided an efficient distributed path-planning method for the large scale road network which drivers can benefit a lot from. In [7], dynamic control of traffic breakdown at network bottlenecks is proposed, Kerner thought traffic flow and road capacity should be take into account.

However, the model which consider both the breakdown probability and the traffic flow is seldom discussed. There is no effective method to simplify the model which can largely reduce the travel time and travel cost. The contributions of this paper are as follows:

- First, we propose an optimal vehicle allocation model to improve the road utilization, which not only minimum the traffic breakdown probability but also maximum the spontaneous traffic flow.
- Second, we simplify the system model through big traffic flow condition and Taylor series remains two or three terms, which largely reduce the computational complexity of existing algorithm in path-planning and have an optimal result with accuracy.

The remainder of this paper is organized as follows. In Sect. 1, it presents the system model of the breakdown probability's improvement and explains in detail.

In Sect. 2, the methodology of algorithm is illustrated. Section 3 demonstrates the performance of our proposed breakdown probability based on simulations. The final, Sect. 4 concludes the final results.

2   System Model

To allocate an optimal path for each vehicle with control, a path-planning method is proposed to help more drivers to avoid congestion and improve road utilization in road network.

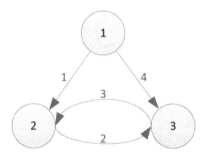

Fig. 1. Road network example

Figure 1 is an simple road network example. In [3], a matrix W is provided to denote a concise road network topology structure. Each row and column of the matrix represent node and edge in sequence. In the real network, node means intersection and edge means the road segment between two intersections. W is given beforehand in accordance with the actual urban map. The map can be simplified in a road network which can be described as a matrix W:

$$W = \begin{bmatrix} 1 & 0 & 0 & 1 \\ -1 & 1 & -1 & 0 \\ 0 & -1 & 1 & -1 \end{bmatrix} \tag{1}$$

There are three nodes and four edges in this example, which means m = 3, n = 4. The '1' in matrix means traffic outflow in this node and the '−1' means traffic inflow. The objective of $Wx = b$ is to choose some available routes from origin to destination, x is a vector which presents the way. The origin-destination (O-D) pair is described as vector b.

When we choose the first and the third node as the origin and destination, the vector which represents the O-D can be described as $b = (1, 0, -1)^T$. With constraint of condition Eq. (4), there are two available paths can be calculated. The path takes edge 1 and edge 2 in order, which can be encoded as $x = (1, 1, 0, 0)$. And another path $x = (0, 0, 0, 1)$ only uses the edge 4. Matrix W is used to find paths as the alternative set.

Breakdown probability is the probability for spontaneous traffic breakdown which may cause traffic jam. System allocates an optimal path with the lowest breakdown probability of the whole road network, but some drivers do not like to accept our assignment of a slightly longer road. Increasing the number of vehicles in optimal path is a effective measure which can let more vehicles accept assignment. Under the breakdown probability minimum condition, the proposed algorithm makes the traffic flow in this selected segment maximum. The maximize traffic flow formula can be calculated as:

$$max \sum_{i=1}^{n}(a_i \cdot x_i + r_i) \tag{2}$$

Here, a_i is the number of vehicles which allocated by system in the edge i. x_i represents the probability that the path will be chosen by the system in edge i. The number of vehicles which system can't control is r_i. The number of edges are describe as n. The sum of controlled vehicles $a_i \cdot x_i$ and uncontrolled vehicles r_i presents the total number of vehicles in the road edge i. Sum up the total road segments' vehicles we get the traffic flow of the path we chose. Increasing the traffic flow in optimal path can improve road utilization.

Because x_i is the probability, the value of x_i has its restrictions which is described as follow:

$$0 \le x_i \le 1 \tag{3}$$

In order to improve the road utilization, the Eq. (2) aims to find out the maximum value of the traffic flow and the minimum value of the breakdown probability. When breakdown probability subtracts Eq. (2), it is now equivalent to find out the minimum value of its opposite number. This combined formula can be stated as follows:

$$\min_{x} \sum_{i=1}^{n}[\ln(1 + e^{w(a_i \cdot x_i + r_i)+c}) - (a_i \cdot x_i + r_i)]$$
$$s.t. \quad Wx = b$$
$$0 \le x \le 1 \tag{4}$$

Here, we combined Eq. (3) and matrix as the constraint conditions. w and c are used to represent the influence in breakdown probability. The solution to the problem as given in Eq. (4) will be described in next section.

3   Methodology and Complexity

In this section, we discuss several methods to simplify this model, including transformation into a linear function in big traffic flow condition and Taylor Series. Furthermore, we analysis the complexity of the methods.

The objective function of Eq. (4) is the sum of every edge in the selected path. In this section, in order to consider the easiest case in edge i, we omit the subscript to ease the transition. A generic function is defined as follow:

$$g(x) = \ln(1 + e^{w(a \cdot x+r)+c}) - (a \cdot x + r) \tag{5}$$

As shown in Algorithm 1, we outline the pseudo code of the optimal path-planning method, which explains how to choose the right feasible road and choose the optimal road with the highest traffic flow and the lowest breakdown probability.

Algorithm 1. Optimize path planning algorithm

1: BEGIN
2: /*Initialization*/
3: Input the road network matrix W
4: Input origin-destination vector b
5: Find available path x
6: **for** edge i in road network **do**
7:     Calculates the sum of generic function $g(x)$
8:     **if** the sum is minimum **then**
9:       Output the optimal path
10:     **end if**
11: **end for**
12: END

3.1 Simplification Based on Big Traffic Flow Condition

The breakdown probability can be simplified by logarithmic function. The exponential function rises quickly when the base number is a positive integer $(e > 0)$. When the index t is big enough, logarithmic function can be reduced to a single function.

$$\ln(1 + e^t) \approx t \tag{6}$$

When $t = w(a \cdot x + r) + c$ which means traffic flow is big enough, the index t of e is big enough to ignore some constant. According to generic function $g(x)$ in Eq. (5), we can simplify the $g(x)$ as follows:

$$g(x) \approx c + (w - 1)(a \cdot x + r) \tag{7}$$

Thus, our model can be simplified as:

$$\min_x \sum_{i=1}^{n} [c + (w - 1)(a \cdot x + r)]$$
$$s.t. \quad Wx = b \tag{8}$$
$$0 \leq x \leq 1$$

We can see the complex objective function in this model is simplified as a linear function of one variable x. This assumption holds when traffic is heavy. Based on the heavy traffic volume of urban area in peak hours, this situation can be achieved.

3.2   Simplification Based on Taylor Series

Then we apply Taylor series to simplify this problem. In mathematics, Taylor series consists of an infinite sum of terms and calculates from the value of the derivative of the function at a point [8]. The generic function $g(x)$ is simplified by Taylor series and remains two or three terms which means the napierian logarithm is simplified into unary primary function or unary quadratic function.

Remain Two Terms. Taylor series is a famous math tool of calculation and is used to simplify complex mathematical problem. In this condition, Taylor series is used to simplify the objective function. The simplification of generic function and remains two terms is described as follow:

$$g(x) \approx (\frac{w}{2} - 1)(a \cdot x + r) + \frac{c}{2} + ln2 + R_1[w(a \cdot x + r) + c] \tag{9}$$

Thus, our model can be simplified as:

$$\min_x \sum_{i=1}^n [(\frac{w}{2} - 1)(a \cdot x + r) + \frac{c}{2} + ln2] \tag{10}$$
$$s.t. \quad Wx = b$$
$$0 \leq x \leq 1$$

Here, $R_1[w(a \cdot x + r) + c]$ is the remainder of Taylor series that is a higher order infinitesimal which can be omitted. In this formula, the breakdown probability is simplified by Taylor series as a linear function of one variable.

Remain Three Terms. In this condition, Taylor series is used to simplify the objective function with three terms remain. Theoretically speaking, the more terms remain, the more accuracy result can be reached. The simplification is described as follow:

$$g(x) \approx \frac{w^2}{8}(a \cdot x + r)^2 + (\frac{wc}{4} + \frac{w}{2} - 1)(a \cdot x + r) + \frac{c^2}{8} + \frac{c}{2}$$
$$+ ln2 + R_2[w(a \cdot x + r) + c] \tag{11}$$

Thus, our model can be simplified as:

$$\min_x \sum_{i=1}^n [\frac{w^2}{8}(a \cdot x + r)^2 + (\frac{wc}{4} + \frac{w}{2} - 1)(a \cdot x + r) + \frac{c^2}{8} + \frac{c}{2} + ln2]$$
$$s.t. \quad Wx = b \tag{12}$$
$$0 \leq x \leq 1$$

Here, $R_2[w(a \cdot x + r) + c]$ is the remainder of Taylor series that is a higher order infinitesimal which can be omitted. When breakdown probability is simplified by Taylor Series with three series remain, it can be proposed as a quadratic function of one variable.

3.3   Complexity Analysis

Compare all methods mentioned above, it is obvious that they have the same time complexity. The complexity is represented by iterations of the algorithm that the simplification based on big traffic flow condition and Taylor series remains two or three terms are all $O(n)$. Simplification based on big traffic flow condition and Taylor series remains two terms are both unary primary function which is simpler than Taylor series remains three terms. With the terms of Taylor series increasing, the accuracy of result can be increased and error can be reduced. Taylor series remained three terms is more accuracy than remained two terms.

When objective function is simplified, the simplification model can make the proposed algorithm find the optimal solutions more quickly with accuracy. In complex traffic network, reduce the model's allocation time can largely reduce drivers' travel time and cost.

4   Simulation

4.1   Parameters Setting

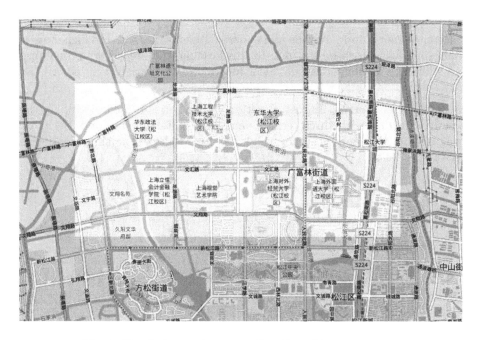

Fig. 2. Simulation environment: Songjiang University Town

We use the Open Street Map to download a real map of Songjiang University Town, covering an area of about $4000\,\mathrm{m} \times 2000\,\mathrm{m}$, which is showed in Fig. 2. The real-map is simplified and extracts the main road via JOSM [4] in Fig. 3. The simplified road network contains 18 nodes and 50 edges, which represents the matrix W's size is $18 * 50$.

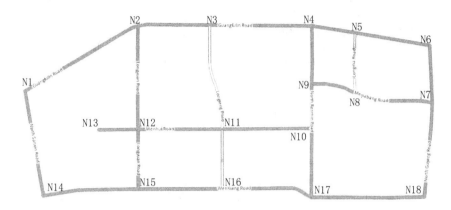

Fig. 3. Simplified road network of Songjiang University Town

The parameters in Eq. (4) are set as follows: $c = -30$, $w = 0.1$. The Taylor series in Sect. 3 is centered at zero. In order to satisfy Taylor series' and big traffic flow condition's remand, the total number of vehicles in this simulation environment is 100. r_i is set as a random sample and the number of it is significantly greater than x_i. Ten vehicles are controlled by our traffic system.

4.2   Simulation Results and Analysis

Table 1. Performances of path planning algorithms

Algorithm	Average calculation time (s)	Complexity
Inter point method	0.207601	$O(mn^2)$
Big traffic flow condition	0.057165	$O(n)$
Taylor series (2 terms)	0.081964	$O(n)$
Taylor series (3 terms)	0.082250	$O(n)$

Complexity. The comparison of four methods in computational complexity and average calculated time mentioned before are showed in Table 1. With the same restricted condition, the complexity of path planning algorithms depend on their objective function. According to [3], the evaluation of IPM's computational complexity in ordinary case is $O(mn^2)$, where m and n are the number of nodes and edges. IPM needs multiple internal iterations (Newton iterations) and external iterations which lead to high complexity. The computational complexity of our algorithm mentioned in Sect. 3 is all $O(n)$, which are simpler than the IPM. The n represents the number of iterations of algorithm. According to Algorithm 1, the number of iterations is equal to the number of road edges. The computational complexity of our algorithm is $n = 50$ times. By multiplying the required number of IPM, the computational complexity of it is $18 \times 50^2 = 45000$ flops. As indicated above, our methods are significantly better in computational complexity.

Table 2. Experimental result of path planning

O-D	Algorithm	Path (Node ID)	Cost time (s)
$1 \to 18$	Inter point method	$1 - 14 - 15 - 16 - 17 - 18$	0.273515
	Big traffic flow condition	$1 - 14 - 15 - 16 - 17 - 18$	0.041528
	Taylor series (2 terms)	$1 - 14 - 15 - 16 - 17 - 18$	0.088665
	Taylor series (3 terms)	$1 - 14 - 15 - 16 - 17 - 18$	0.093706
$3 \to 7$	Inter point method	$3 - 4 - 5 - 8 - 7$	0.198964
	Big traffic flow condition	$3 - 4 - 5 - 8 - 7$	0.038057
	Taylor series (2 terms)	$3 - 4 - 5 - 8 - 7$	0.060439
	Taylor series (3 terms)	$3 - 4 - 5 - 8 - 7$	0.068879
$17 \to 2$	Inter point method	$17 - 10 - 11 - 3 - 2$ (38.30%)	0.180324
		$17 - 16 - 11 - 12 - 2$ (30.59%)	
		$17 - 16 - 15 - 12 - 2$ (31.11%)	
	Big traffic flow condition	$17 - 10 - 11 - 3 - 2$ (36.56%)	0.091911
		$17 - 16 - 11 - 12 - 2$ (33.23%)	
		$17 - 16 - 15 - 12 - 2$ (30.21%)	
	Taylor series(2 terms)	$17 - 10 - 11 - 3 - 2$ (41.27%)	0.096788
		$17 - 16 - 11 - 12 - 2$ (28.95%)	
		$17 - 16 - 15 - 12 - 2$ (29.78%)	
	Taylor series(3 terms)	$17 - 10 - 11 - 3 - 2$ (39.83%)	0.094166
		$17 - 16 - 11 - 12 - 2$ (30.44%)	
		$17 - 16 - 15 - 12 - 2$ (29.73%)	

Accuracy. The Table 2 shows the path planning results' detail of simulation by listing selected path and calculation time of algorithms. Three different origin-destination (O-D) pairs are selected. For example, when other roads have high traffic flow, in the path from intersection $N1$ to intersection $N18$, methods choose the same and only one path with no traffic jam. If the available paths all have nearing heavy traffic, vehicles will be allocated proportionally according to existing traffic. It can be seen from intersection $N17$ to intersection $N2$, the result of four methods are similar. The interior point method (IPM) has a high accuracy because it is used to optimize the iterative process to find the optimal solution. So the IPM is chose as the accuracy criterion. As the result shows in Table 2, the other three methods only have single-digit-percentages error. Compared this four methods, the method of remains 3 terms in Taylor series has a highest accuracy result and the method of remains 2 terms in Taylor series has the worst result. They all choose the same road with IPM. What's more, with few cooperatively vehicles, the gap between these methods are even smaller.

5   Conclusion and Future Work

In this paper, we propose an optimization model which improves road utilization via increasing the traffic flow and avoiding the traffic breakdown congestion. The algorithm uses the real-map simulation environment with a big traffic data. Two methods which simplified by big traffic flow condition and Taylor series are proposed to reduce computational complexity from $O(mn^2)$ to $O(n)$. Finally, the real urban traffic scenario is used in the simulation. Compared with other existing path-planning algorithm, our algorithm reduce about 50–70% of computation time and also has good accuracy and validity.

In the future, we would like to consider the drivers' behavior into the model, which proposes the available arrangement to encourage drivers to choose the alternative path. Additionally, we would like to set the flow via real traffic data.

References

1. Bosch, A.V.D., Arem, B.V., Mahmod, M., Misener, J.: Reducing time delays on congested road networks using social navigation. In: Integrated and Sustainable Transportation System, pp. 26–31 (2011)
2. Guo, C., Li, D., Zhang, G., Zhai, M.: Real-time path planning in urban area via vanet-assisted traffic information sharing. IEEE Trans. Veh. Technol. **PP**(99), 1–1 (2018)
3. Guo, H., Cao, Z., Seshadri, M., Zhang, J., Niyato, D., Fastenrath, U.: Routing multiple vehicles cooperatively: minimizing road network breakdown probability. IEEE Trans. Emerg. Top. Comput. Intell. **1**(2), 112–124 (2017)
4. Huber, S., Rust, C.: osrmtime: Calculate travel time and distance with open-StreetMap data using the open source routing machine (OSRM). Stata J. **16**(Number 2), 416–423 (2016)
5. Kerner, B.S.: Experimental features of self-organization in traffic flow. Phys. Rev. Lett. **81**(17), 3797–3800 (1998)
6. Kerner, B.S.: Optimum principle for a vehicular traffic network: minimum probability of congestion. J. Phys. A **44**(9), 092001 (2011)
7. Kerner, B.S.: Breakdown minimization principle versus wardrops equilibria for dynamic traffic assignment and control in traffic and transportation networks: A critical mini-review. Phys. Stat. Mech. Appl. **466**, 626–662 (2017)
8. Lavrakas, P.J., Williams, R.L.: Taylor series linearization. In: Lavrakas, P.J. (ed.) Encyclopedia of Survey Research Methods. Sage Publications, Newbury Park (2008)

9. Souza, A.M.D., Yokoyama, R.S., Maia, G., Loureiro, A., Villas, L.: Real-time path planning to prevent traffic jam through an intelligent transportation system. In: Computers and Communication, pp. 726–731 (2016)
10. Wardrop, J.G.: Road paper. Some theoretical aspects of road traffic research, vol. 1, no. 3, pp. 325–362 (1952)
11. Zhu, M., et al.: Public vehicles for future urban transportation. IEEE Trans. Intell. Transp. Syst. **17**(12), 3344–3353 (2016)

Optimal Resource Allocation for Brokers in Media Cloud

Wenlong Ni[1(✉)] and Wei Wayne Li[2(✉)]

[1] School of Computer Information Engineering, JiangXi Normal University,
NanChang, China
`wni@jxnu.edu.cn`
[2] Department of Computer Science, Texas Southern University, Houston, USA
`Wei.Li@tsu.edu`

Abstract. Due to the rapid increases in the population of mobile social users, providing the users with satisfied multimedia services has become an important issue. Media cloud has been shown to be an efficient solution to resolve the above issue, by allowing mobile social users to connect to it through a group of distributed brokers. However, as the resource (like bandwidth, servers, computing power, etc.) in media cloud is limited, how to allocate resource among media cloud with brokers becomes a challenge. Media cloud can determine the price of the resource and a broker can decide whether it will pay the price for the resource when there is an incoming multimedia task (simplified as task). A broker can collect the revenues from the mobile social users by providing the multimedia services. Since resource is limited, the price will generally go up as the resource becomes more and more consumed. Therefore, in this paper, by assuming that accepting each task a broker can get a reward (by collecting revenues from mobile social users like online ads, etc.) and it needs pay some price (to the media cloud) for each task in the network, we concentrate on the optimization problems of when to admit or reject a task for a broker in order to achieve the maximum total discounted expected reward for any initial state. By establishing a discounted Continuous-Time Markov Decision Process (CTMDP) model, we verify that the optimal policies for admitting tasks are state-related control limit policies. Our numerical results with explanations in both tables and diagrams are consistent with our theoretic results.

Keywords: Media cloud · Cloud broker · Mobile social user
Resource allocation · Optimal control policy
Continuous-Time Markov Decision Process (CTMDP)

1 Introduction

WITH the advent of 4G mobile technologies and coming soon 5G mobile technologies, the number of hours spent per adult on mobile devices per day has

This work was supported in part by Natural Science Foundation of China under Grant No. 61463033 and US National Science Foundation under Grant No. 1137732.

increased dramatically in the past ten years. Beginning in 2014, mobile devices have surpassed desktop/laptops as the most used device per day for internet usage. A steady increase of mobile application usage over the past few years has contributed to the rise of mobile social networks (MSNs), more and more mobile social users can obtain various multimedia content by having interaction with each other [1]. Especially, with the popularity of shared data plan and unlimited data plan, mobile social users may not only obtain and but also share more multimedia contents with others who have social relations with them. Therefore, providing mobile social users with efficient multimedia services becomes more and more challenging than before.

However, to provide mobile social users with satisfied multimedia services, there exist some new problems to be resolved. On one hand, due to the explosive growth of volume of multimedia, providing mobile social users with multimedia services needs a large amount of resources. But, the local mobile devices in mobile social users generally only have a limited resource such as, CPU capacity, memory, bandwidth etc. On the other hand, multimedia content servers are remotely placed from mobile social users making mobile social users to obtain the requested multimedia content with a longer time. For example, if a mobile social user wants to watch a movie with his mobile device, the content of movie has to be retrieved from a remote multimedia content server through a large number of routing nodes.

To resolve the above issues, media cloud has been advocated with the following reasons [3]. Firstly, media cloud can deploy cloud resource to process multimedia tasks. Some complicated computations or large-sized multimedia content storage which need extra resource can be performed at the side of media cloud, where the required resource can be reduced for mobile social users. Therefore, the media cloud can help mobile social users to save their resource. Secondly, a cloud broker [5] can be placed between media cloud and mobile social users. As the broker can act as a proxy which is close to mobile social users, mobile social users can connect media cloud through the broker for multimedia services. With the high-speed communication links between media cloud and the broker, mobile social users can obtain multimedia services faster than contacting the remote multimedia content servers directly by themselves. Although some related studies have been carried out to study resource allocation about cloud computing and mobile networks [4,7,8], few of works have studied the resource allocation problem based on the social features in media cloud [2]. Therefore, it is still a new and open problem to design resource allocation scheme for brokers in media cloud with mobile social users.

In this paper, based on the competitions among brokers in the media cloud on cloud resource, we propose a novel resource allocation scheme in media cloud for a broker to maximize its total discounted expected reward for any initial state. Specifically, media cloud sells the cloud resource to brokers to obtain revenue. The brokers employ the cloud resource to process media tasks for mobile social users. Assuming the arrival processes of tasks as poisson process [10], their departure process follows negative exponential distribution, the major contribution of this paper is that we established a discounted Continuous Time Markov Decision Process (CTMDP) model for the MSNs, by doing so we can concentrate on the optimization problems for a broker of when to admit or reject a task in order to achieve the maximum total discounted expected reward for any initial state, making the problem be an admission control problem for tasks. So far as we know this is the first time that the MSN is modeled as a CTMDP model defined in this paper. We verify that the optimal policies for admitting tasks are state-related control limit policies. Our numerical results explained in both tables and diagrams are consistent with our theoretic results.

The rest of this paper is organized as follows. Section 2 discusses the modeling, Sect. 3 describes the structure of optimal policy which is a control limit policy and the verification process. Section 4 deals with the numerical analysis with some tables and diagrams that verifies the theoretical results. Finally in Sect. 5 we offers conclusion remarks.

2 Model Formulation

In this section we build the models on the mobile social network. In the first part we introduce the system model, and in the second part we define the CTMDP model based on the system model assumptions.

2.1 System Model

There are three parties which are media cloud, brokers, and mobile social users within the communities, respectively. The media cloud is composed of a large number of servers which can be used to compute, store, and provide media contents and media application. The brokers can be seen as proxies to process the media tasks of mobile social users, where the brokers receive the media tasks from mobile social users and then buy the corresponding resources to process the tasks. Mobile social users with the similar interest can form a community.

The advantages of introducing cloud brokers are as follows. Firstly, due to the high speed communications between media cloud and cloud brokers, the service response time can be significantly reduced so that mobile social users can obtain the media services quickly. Secondly, for media cloud, as it directly connects cloud brokers and the number of brokers is less than mobile social users, media cloud can decrease the cost of access control and transmission.

Mobile devices can connect with brokers through wireless connection. Firstly, the brokers buy the resource from the media cloud after determining the price of resource. Next, mobile social users send the corresponding tasks to brokers with wireless communication. In addition, the brokers deliver the tasks to media cloud by wired module. At last, the results of tasks are delivered back to mobile social users.

In this paper we consider a Mobile Social Network with multiple types of tasks, without loss of generality in this paper we assume that there are two types of tasks, each of them would require the resources in the media cloud for service. The other basic assumptions in the MSN are given as follows:

1. The resources for a task is defined as a channel. The number of channels defines the capacity of resources from the media cloud. There are C channels in the system.
2. There are two types of *Tasks* (T_1 and T_2) in the system, each needs a channel for service. The arrival process of tasks T_1 and T_2 are Poisson processes with rates λ_1 and λ_2. The channel holding time for tasks follow negative exponential distributions with rates μ_1 and μ_2.
3. When a task comes to the system, if there are free channels, the broker will decide whether to admit/reject the task based on the current state of the system. If the system is full, which means there is no free channel, the task will leave the system.
4. Serving a task $T_1(T_2)$ would contribute $R_1(R_2)$ units of reward to the broker. However, for each task, the broker needs to pay a price at rate $f(n_1, n_2)$ to buy a channel (resources) from media cloud when there are already n_1 (T_1 tasks) and n_2 (T_2 tasks) in service.

2.2   CTMDP Model

First, let us introduce some concepts in the CTMDP models. Each model has a state space S with states s, Action space, Transition Probabilities between states, reward functions and decision epochs. Also in CTMDP models, a decision rule prescribes a procedure for action selection in each state at a specified decision epoch. Decision rules range in general from deterministic Markovian to randomized History Dependent, depending on how they incorporate past information and how they select actions. Deterministic Markovian decision rules specify the action choice when the system occupies a state s at decision epoch t. A policy π specifies the decision rule to be used at every decision epoch. It provides the decision maker with a prescription for action selection under any possible future system state or history. For each policy π, let $v_\gamma^\pi(s)$ denote the total expected infinite-horizon discounted reward with γ as the discount factor, given that the process occupies state s at the first decision epoch. In this paper, our objective is to find an optimal policy π that can bring the maximum total expected discounted reward $v_\gamma^\pi(s)$ from a sensor for every initial state s.

$$v_\gamma^\pi(s) = E_s^\pi \left\{ \int_0^\infty e^{-\gamma t} r(s_t, a_t) dt \right\}, \tag{1}$$

where s_t stands for the state at time t, a_t is the action to take at state s_t, and $r(s_t, a_t)$ is the reward obtained when action a_t is selected at state s_t. We now introduce the CTMDP model as follows:

1. Let state space be $S = \{s : s = (n_1, n_2)\}$, where $n_1 \in \{0, 1, \ldots, C\}$ and $n_2 \in \{0, 1, \ldots, C\}$, event space be $E = \{D_1, D_2, A_1, A_2\}$, where D_1 and D_2 means a T_1 and T_2 departure from the system after service, while A_1 means an arrival of a T_1 task, A_2 is an arrival of T_2 task. Since the states migration not only depends on the number of tasks in the system but also depends

on the happening departure and arrival events, for this model we define a new state space as $\hat{S} = S \times E$. By doing so a state could be written as $\hat{s} = \langle s, e \rangle = \langle (n_1, n_2), e \rangle$, where n_1 and n_2 are the numbers for T_1 and T_2 tasks, e stands for the event which will probably happen on state (n_1, n_2), $e \in \{D_1, D_2, A_1, A_2\}$. Please be noticed that the specification of the event in this paper is one of major technical differences from that in paper [6].

2. In states $\langle (n_1, n_2), D_1 \rangle$ and $\langle (n_1, n_2), D_2 \rangle$, if denote by a_C as the action to continue, thus the action space

$$A_{\langle (n_1,n_2),D_1 \rangle} = \{a_C\}, n_1 > 0, n_2 \geq 0, n_1 + n_2 \leq C,$$

$$A_{\langle (n_1,n_2),D_2 \rangle} = \{a_C\}, n_1 \geq 0, n_2 > 0, n_1 + n_2 \leq C.$$

In states $\langle (n_1, n_2), A_1 \rangle$ and $\langle (n_1, n_2), A_2 \rangle$, if denote by a_R as the action to reject the request and a_A as the action to admit, the action space will be

$$A_{\langle (n_1,n_2),A_1 \rangle} = \{a_R, a_A\}, n_1 \geq 0, n_2 \geq 0, n_1 + n_2 \leq C,$$

$$A_{\langle (n_1,n_2),A_2 \rangle} = \{a_R, a_A\}, n_1 \geq 0, n_2 \geq 0, n_1 + n_2 \leq C.$$

In this model we focus on the admission control for tasks.

3. The decision epochs are those time points when a call arriving or leaving the system. Based on our assumption, it is not too hard to know that the distribution of time between two epochs is

$$F(t|\hat{s}, a) = 1 - e^{-\beta(\hat{s},a)t}, t \geq 0.$$

where for each state $\hat{s} = \langle ((n_1, n_2)), b \rangle$ and action a, $\beta_0(s) = \lambda_1 + \lambda_2 + n_1\mu_1 + n_2\mu_2$, since a departure event only happens when there is a task in the system, the $\beta(\hat{s}, a)$ will be represented as

$$\beta(\hat{s}, a) = \begin{cases} \beta_0(s) - \mu_1, & b = D_1, a = a_C, n_1 > 0, \\ \beta_0(s) - \mu_2, & b = D_2, a = a_C, n_2 > 0, \\ \beta_0(s) + \mu_1, & b = A_1, a = a_A, n_1 \geq 0, n_2 \geq 0, n_1 + n_2 < C, \\ \beta_0(s) + \mu_2, & b = A_2, a = a_A, n_1 \geq 0, n_2 \geq 0, n_1 + n_2 < C, \\ \beta_0(s), & b = \{A_1, A_2\}, a = a_R, n_1 \geq 0, n_2 \geq 0, n_1 + n_2 \leq C. \end{cases}$$

4. Let $q(j|\hat{s}, a)$ denote the probability that the system occupies state j in the next epoch, if at the current epoch the system is at state $\hat{s}$ and the decision maker takes action $a \in A_{\hat{s}}$. For the cases of departure events, e.g. for a departure event of D_1 under the condition of $(n_1 > 0, n_2 \geq 0, n_1 + n_2 \leq C)$, $(\hat{s}, a) = (\langle (n_1, n_2), D_1 \rangle, a_C)$, if denote by $s_n = (n_1 - 1, n_2)$, then we will have $q(j|\hat{s}, a)$ as

$$q(j|\hat{s}, a) = \begin{cases} \lambda_1/\beta_0(s_n), & j = \langle (n_1 - 1, n_2), A_1 \rangle, \\ \lambda_2/\beta_0(s_n), & j = \langle (n_1 - 1, n_2), A_2 \rangle, \\ (n_1 - 1)\mu_1/\beta_0(s_n), & j = \langle (n_1 - 1, n_2), D_1 \rangle, \\ n_2\mu_2/\beta_0(s_n), & j = \langle (n_1 - 1, n_2), D_2 \rangle. \end{cases}$$

Similar equations can be derived for cases like $(\hat{s}, a) = (\langle(n_1, n_2), D_2\rangle, a_C)$. For the cases of arrival events, $(\hat{s}, a) = (\langle(n_1, n_2), A_1\rangle, a_A)$, $(\hat{s}, a) = (\langle(n_1, n_2), A_2\rangle, a_A)$, since admitting an incoming call migrates the system state immediately (adding one user or not), with $n_1 \geq 0, n_2 \geq 0, n_1 + n_2 < C$ we will get $q(j|\hat{s}, a)$ as

$$
q(j|\hat{s}, a) = \begin{cases}
q(j|\langle(n_1 + 2, n_2), D_1\rangle, a_C), & b = A_1, a = a_A, \\
q(j|\langle(n_1 + 1, n_2), D_1\rangle, a_C), & b = A_1, a = a_R, \\
q(j|\langle(n_1, n_2 + 2), D_2\rangle, a_C), & b = A_2, a = a_A, \\
q(j|\langle(n_1, n_2 + 1), D_2\rangle, a_C), & b = A_2, a = a_R.
\end{cases}
$$

5. Because the system state does not change between decision epochs, from Chp 11.5.2 [9] and our assumptions, the expected discounted reward between epochs satisfies

$$
\begin{aligned}
r(\hat{s}, a) &= k(\hat{s}, a) + c(\hat{s}, a)E_{\hat{s}}^a \left\{ \int_0^{\tau_1} e^{-\alpha t} dt \right\} \\
&= k(\hat{s}, a) + c(\hat{s}, a)E_{\hat{s}}^a \left\{ [1 - e^{-\alpha \tau_1}]/\alpha \right\} \\
&= k(\hat{s}, a) + \frac{c(\hat{s}, a)}{\alpha + \beta(\hat{s}, a)},
\end{aligned}
$$

where

$$
k(\hat{s}, a) = \begin{cases}
0, & b = \{D_1, D_2\}, a = a_C, \\
0, & b = \{A_1, A_2\}, a = a_R, \\
R_1, & b = A_1, a = a_A, \\
R_2, & b = A_2, a = a_A.
\end{cases}
$$

Here, since we will get $R_1(R_2)$ unites of reward after the service of a $T_1(T_2)$ task, we can treat this as that we get the reward at the time of accepting the task, thus making the problem to be an admission control problem. Also, we have the cost function $c(\hat{s}, a) =$ as

$$
\begin{cases}
f(n_1 - 1, n_2), & b = D_1, a = a_C, n_1 > 0, n_2 \geq 0, n_1 + n_2 \leq C, \\
f(n_1, n_2 - 1), & b = D_2, a = a_C, n_1 \geq 0, n_2 > 0, n_1 + n_2 \leq C, \\
f(n_1 + 1, n_2), & b = A_1, a = a_A, n_1 \geq 0, n_2 \geq 0, n_1 + n_2 < C, \\
f(n_1, n_2 + 1), & b = A_2, a = a_A, n_1 \geq 0, n_2 \geq 0, n_1 + n_2 < C, \\
f(n_1, n_2), & b = \{A_1, A_2\}, a = a_R, n_1 \geq 0, n_2 \geq 0, n_1 + n_2 \leq C.
\end{cases}
$$

In the next section we will prove that there exists a state-related threshold for accepting the tasks if the cost function has some special properties.

3   Control Limit Policy

In our CTMDP model, an optimal policy π means that it can bring the maximum total expected discounted reward $v_\alpha^\pi(\hat{s})$ for every initial state $\hat{s}$. A policy is stationary if, for each decision epoch t, $d_t = d$ is the same, which can be denoted by d^∞. In our CTMDP model, since both the state space $\hat{S}$ and the action space A are finite, the reward function $r(\hat{s}, a)$ is also finite, then from Theorem 11.3.2 of [9], the optimal policy is a stationary deterministic policy d^∞, so our problem can be reduced to find a deterministic decision rule d. For each deterministic decision rule d, let $q_d(j|\hat{s}) = q(j|\hat{s}, d(\hat{s}))$, $r_d(\hat{s}) = r(\hat{s}, d(\hat{s}))$ and $\beta_d(\hat{s}) = \beta(\hat{s}, d(\hat{s}))$, from Chp 11.5.2 [9],

$$v_\alpha^{d^\infty}(\hat{s}) = r_d(\hat{s}) + \frac{\beta_d(\hat{s})}{\alpha + \beta_d(\hat{s})} \sum_{j \in \hat{S}} q_d(j|\hat{s}) v_\alpha^{d^\infty}(j). \tag{2}$$

From Eq. (2), it is seen that if $\beta_d(\hat{s})$ is a constant for all state $\hat{s}$, the calculation for $v_\alpha^{d^\infty}(\hat{s})$ could be simplified. This is the idea of rate uniformization technique. Based on the assumptions, our process fits the condition of Assumption 11.5.1 of [9], which is $[1 - q(\hat{s}|\hat{s}, a)]\beta(\hat{s}, a) \leq c, \forall \hat{s} \in \hat{S}, a \in A$, here c is a constant. So, we can define a uniformization of our process with components denoted by $\sim$. Let $c = \lambda_1 + \lambda_2 + C * \max(\mu_1, \mu_2)$, from Chp 11.5.2 [9], we have

$$\tilde{q}(j|\hat{s}, a) = \begin{cases} 1 - \frac{[1 - q(\hat{s}|\hat{s}, a)]\beta(\hat{s}, a)}{c}, & j = s, \\ \frac{q(j|\hat{s}, a)\beta(\hat{s}, a)}{c}, & j \neq \hat{s}. \end{cases}$$

Furthermore, for the reward functions, we have $\tilde{r}(\hat{s}, a) \equiv r(\hat{s}, a)\frac{\alpha + \beta(\hat{s}, a)}{\alpha + c}$. From Proposition 11.5.1 [9], for each d^∞ policy and $\hat{s} \in \hat{S}$, we have

$$\tilde{v}_\alpha^{d^\infty}(\hat{s}) = v_\alpha^{d^\infty}(\hat{s}). \tag{3}$$

From Eqs. (2) and (5), the optimal equation of $v(\hat{s})$ for maximum $v_\alpha^\pi(\hat{s})$ would have the form of

$$v(\hat{s}) = \max_{a \in A_{\hat{s}}} \left\{ \tilde{r}(\hat{s}, a) + \lambda \sum_{j \in \hat{S}} \tilde{q}(j|\hat{s}, a)v(j) \right\},$$

where $\lambda \equiv \frac{c}{c+\alpha}$.

For our admission problem, a policy is called a control limit policy for a given number of **Tasks** n_1 and n_2 in the system, say for T_1 task, is there existing a constant or threshold $D(n_2) \geq 0$ such that the system will accept the **arriving** T_1 whenever the number of T_1 currently in the system is less than $D(n_2)$, that means the decision rule for T_1 is:

$$d(n_1, n_2) = \begin{cases} Admit, \; n_1 \leq D(n_2), n_2 \geq 0, \\ Reject, \; n_1 > D(n_2), n_2 \geq 0. \end{cases} \tag{4}$$

Similar definitions can be found with T_2 tasks. It is observed that a control limit policy is a stationary deterministic policy.

In our CTMDP model, the newly introduced state space $\hat{S}$ is finite, the action space is finite, so is the reward functions, so the rate uniformizaiton technique can be applied. Let $c = \lambda_1 + \lambda_2 + C * \max(\mu_1, \mu_2)$, with $s = (n_1, n_2), n_1 \geq 0, n_2 \geq 0$, we get

$$v(\langle\langle(n_1 + 1, n_2), D_1\rangle\rangle)$$
$$= \frac{1}{\alpha + c}[-f(n_1, n_2) + \lambda_1 v(\langle\langle(n_1, n_2), A_1\rangle\rangle) + \lambda_2 v(\langle\langle(n_1, n_2), A_2\rangle\rangle)$$
$$+ n_1\mu_1 v(\langle\langle(n_1, n_2), D_1\rangle\rangle) + n_2\mu_2 v(\langle\langle(n_1, n_2), D_2\rangle\rangle)$$
$$+ (c - \beta_0(s))v(\langle\langle(n_1 + 1, n_2), D_1\rangle\rangle)].$$

This means that

$$v(\langle\langle(n_1 + 1, n_2), D_1\rangle\rangle)$$
$$= \frac{1}{\alpha + \beta_0(n_1, n_2)}[-f(n_1, n_2) + \lambda_1 v(\langle\langle(n_1, n_2), A_1\rangle\rangle) + \lambda_2 v(\langle\langle(n_1, n_2), A_2\rangle\rangle)$$
$$+ n_1\mu_1 v(\langle\langle(n_1, n_2), D_1\rangle\rangle) + n_2\mu_2 v(\langle\langle(n_1, n_2), D_2\rangle\rangle)]. \tag{5}$$

Similarly, It is easily seen that

$$v(\langle\langle(n_1 + 1, n_2), D_1\rangle\rangle) = v(\langle\langle(n_1, n_2 + 1), D_2\rangle\rangle),$$

which shows the equality between different departure events, similar results can also be seen among arrival events or even between departure and arrival events. This leads us to define a new function $X(s), s = (n_1, n_2), n_1 \geq 0, n_2 \geq 0$ which is

$$X(s) = v(\langle\langle(n_1 + 1, n_2), D_1\rangle\rangle) = v(\langle\langle(n_1, n_2 + 1), D_2\rangle\rangle).$$

It is noticed that $X(s)$ is only related to the state, but not with the happening event, which can greatly simplify the proof process. Since admitting a call migrates the system state immediately, we get

$$v(\langle\langle(n_1, n_2), A_1\rangle, a_A) \geq R_1 + X((n_1 + 1, n_2)),$$
$$v(\langle\langle(n_1, n_2), A_1\rangle, a_R) \geq X((n_1, n_2)),$$
$$v(\langle\langle(n_1, n_2), A_2\rangle, a_A) \geq R_2 + X((n_1, n_2 + 1)),$$
$$v(\langle\langle(n_1, n_2), A_2\rangle, a_R) \geq X((n_1, n_2)).$$

And furthermore, the above inequalities will be the equality when the corresponding action a_A (whenever an A_1 arrives), a_R (whenever an A_1 arrives), a_A (whenever an A_2 arrives) and a_R (whenever an A_2 arrives), is the best action, respectively. This also includes the situation when $n_1 + n_2 = C$, the action a_R is the the best action for any arrival of A_1 and A_2.

From these analysis, it is not too hard to verify that

$$v(\langle\langle(n_1, n_2), A_1\rangle\rangle) = \max\left[X((n_1, n_2)), R_1 + X((n_1 + 1, n_2))\right], \tag{6}$$

$$v(\langle\langle(n_1, n_2), A_2\rangle\rangle) = \max\left[X((n_1, n_2)), R_2 + X((n_1, n_2 + 1))\right]. \tag{7}$$

For the cost function $f(n_1, n_2)$ $(n_1 \geq 0, n_2 \geq 0)$, if denote by

$$\Delta_{n_1} f(n_1, n_2) = f(n_1 + 1, n_2) - f(n_1, n_2),$$
$$\Delta_{n_2} f(n_1, n_2) = f(n_1, n_2 + 1) - f(n_1, n_2),$$

then from the Eqs. (6) and (7), we have the following theorem.

Theorem: If $f(n_1, n_2)$ is convex and increasing for nonnegative integers n_1 and n_2, respectively, and

$$\Delta_{n_1} f(n_1, n_2) \geq 0, \quad \text{and} \quad \Delta_{n_2} f(n_1, n_2) \geq 0,$$

the optimal policy is a control limit policy.

Proof: We use Value Iteration Method to show that for all states $X(n_1, n_2)$ is concave and nonincreasing for nonnegative integers n_1 and n_2, respectively.

1. Set $X^0(n_1, n_2) = 0$, and substitute this into Eq. (2), we will have

$$X^1(n_1, n_2) = -\frac{f(n_1, n_2)}{\alpha + c}, \qquad n_1 \geq 0, n_2 \geq 0.$$

By concavity and monotony of $f(n_1, n_2)$, $X^1(n_1, n_2)$ is therefore concave nonincreasing for n_1 and n_2, respectively.
2. Set n=n+1, it is not hard to verify $X^{n+1}(n_1, n_2)$ is also concave nonincreasing for n_1 and n_2, respectively
3. As the iteration continues, with n goes to ∞, $X(n_1, n_2)$ is always concave nonincreasing for n_1 and n_2, respectively.

By the Theorem 11.3.2 of [9], the solution of $v(\hat{s})$ is unique, so the value iteration $X(s)$ converges to $v(\hat{s})$, thus $v(\hat{s})$ is concave nonincreasing.

4   Numerical Analysis

We start the numerical analysis with following parameter settings, let the channel Capacity $C = 6$, Discount Factor $\gamma = 0.1$, set other parameters for T_1 and T_2 tasks as shown in Table 1 to study the performance of our CTMDP model.

Table 1. Parameter values

	λ	μ	R
T_1	4	10	0.2
T_2	2	4	0.3

It can be seen from the Table 1 that the loads for T_1 and T_2 tasks are $\rho_1 = \frac{\lambda_1}{\mu_1} = 0.4$ and $\rho_2 = \frac{\lambda_2}{\mu_2} = 0.5$, which means the system are medium loaded, and the rewards for T_2 is a little higher than the T_1 task.

Table 2. State related actions for A_1 arrivals with cost function f_1

	1			$n_2 \rightarrow$			6
1	1	1	1	1	1	1	0
	1	1	1	1	1	0	−1
	1	1	1	1	0	−1	−1
$n_1 \downarrow$	1	1	1	0	−1	−1	−1
	1	1	0	−1	−1	−1	−1
	1	0	−1	−1	−1	−1	−1
6	0	−1	−1	−1	−1	−1	−1

Table 3. State related actions for A_2 arrivals with cost function f_1

	1			$n_2 \rightarrow$			6
1	1	1	1	1	1	1	0
	1	1	1	1	1	0	−1
	1	1	1	1	0	−1	−1
$n_1 \downarrow$	1	1	1	0	−1	−1	−1
	1	1	0	−1	−1	−1	−1
	1	0	−1	−1	−1	−1	−1
6	0	−1	−1	−1	−1	−1	−1

First, we set the cost function be

$$f_1(x, y) = x + y$$

Here in Tables 2 and 3, '1' means the model would accept the arrival, '0' means the model would reject the task, '−1' means the model has no such state in the system. It can be seen from Tables 2 and 3 that for both the arrivals of T_1

Table 4. $v(s)$ values for cost function f_1

	1			$n_2 \rightarrow$			6
1	5.216	4.9719	4.7276	4.4824	4.2332	3.968	3.668
	5.1169	4.8728	4.628	4.3804	4.1186	3.8186	0
	5.0179	4.7734	4.5268	4.2678	3.9678	0	0
$n_1 \downarrow$	4.9186	4.6727	4.4158	4.1158	0	0	0
	4.8182	4.563	4.263	0	0	0	0
	4.7097	4.4097	0	0	0	0	0
6	4.556	0	0	0	0	0	0

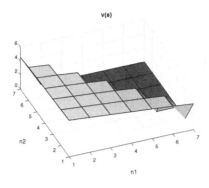

Fig. 1. Total discounted expected reward $v(s)$ with cost function f_1

and T_2 tasks, the broker would accept them until it reaches the system capacity limit.

Table 4 shows the values of $v(s)$ for all the states, which means the total expected discounted reward the broker can get from each initial state.

As seen in Fig. 1, the values of $v(s)$ drops linearly along the n_1 and n_2 due to the fact that the holding cost function f_1 is a linear function.

Next, we set the cost function be

$$f_2(x, y) = 2x + y.$$

In the cost function f_2, the holding cost for T_1 arrivals is doubled, with everything else unchanged, let us see the difference with the first cost function f_1.

It is seen from Table 5 that due to the doubled holding cost, the broker would stop accepting T_1 arrival even there is one free channel in the system, which means at that state it is better for the broker to reject the T_1 arrival to get more revenues other than paying the holding cost.

As seen from the Table 6, due to the more reward T_2 has, the broker still accept T_2 arrivals until it reaches the system capacity limit.

It is seen from Table 7 that due to the doubled holding cost, the total expected discounted reward the broker can get drops largely, like for the initial $(0, 0)$ state, the $v(s)$ values drops from 5.216 to 1.257.

Table 5. State related actions for A_1 arrivals with cost function f_2

	1			$n_2 \rightarrow$			6
1	1	1	1	1	1	0	0
	1	1	1	1	0	0	−1
	1	1	1	0	0	−1	−1
$n_1 \downarrow$	1	1	0	0	−1	−1	−1
	1	0	0	−1	−1	−1	−1
	0	0	−1	−1	−1	−1	−1
6	0	−1	−1	−1	−1	−1	−1

Table 6. State related actions for A_2 arrivals with cost function f_2

	1			$n_2 \rightarrow$			6
1	1	1	1	1	1	1	0
	1	1	1	1	1	0	-1
	1	1	1	1	0	-1	-1
$n_1 \downarrow$	1	1	1	0	-1	-1	-1
	1	1	0	-1	-1	-1	-1
	1	0	-1	-1	-1	-1	-1
6	0	-1	-1	-1	-1	-1	-1

Table 7. $v(s)$ values for cost function f_2

	1		$n_2 \rightarrow$				6
1	1.2568	1.0129	0.7689	0.5248	0.28	0.0311	-0.2689
	1.0588	0.8149	0.5708	0.3262	0.0782	-0.2218	0
	0.8608	0.6168	0.3723	0.125	-0.175	0	0
$n_1 \downarrow$	0.6627	0.4184	0.1715	-0.1285	0	0	0
	0.4644	0.2179	-0.0821	0	0	0	0
	0.2641	-0.0359	0	0	0	0	0
6	0.0103	0	0	0	0	0	0

5 Conclusion

In this paper, we studied a Mobile Social Network providing multimedia services with multiple types of multimedia tasks. There are three parties in the network: media cloud, broker and mobile social users. The broker works as a proxy between mobile social users and multimedia content on the media cloud. Admitting each task would bring a reward (by collecting revenues from mobile social users) to the broker and at the same time holding each task in the system would also incur some expenses (or cost) to the broker, like the prices it pays to the media cloud for the resources it occupied. We have assumed that the task services follows an exponential distribution, their arrival processes are Poisson processes. This leads to an optimization control problem of when to admit/reject the Tasks in order to achieve the maximum reward. By using CTMDP technique, we have found that the optimal admission control policy for Tasks is a control limit policy if the holding cost function for Tasks is convex nondecreasing. The numerical analysis has proven our theoretical conclusion and described the relationship between parameters. The result of this paper could easily be used in helping brokers to behave in an economically optimal way for proving multimedia services to the mobile social users.

References

1. Su, Z., Xu, Q., Zhu, H., Wang, Y.: A novel design for content delivery over software defined mobile social networks. IEEE Netw. **29**(4), 62–67 (2015)
2. Su, Z., Xu, Q., Fei, M., Dong, M.: Game theoretic resource allocation in media cloud with mobile social users. IEEE Trans. Multimed. **18**(8), 1650–1660 (2016)
3. Wu, Y., Wu, C., Li, B., Zhang, L.: Scaling social media applications into geo-distributed clouds. IEEE/ACM Trans. Netw. **23**(3), 689–702 (2015)
4. Ren, J., Zhang, Y., Zhang, K., Shen, X.: Exploiting mobile crowdsourcing for pervasive cloud services: Challenges and solutions. IEEE Commun. Mag. **53**(3), 98–105 (2015)
5. Qiu, X., Wu, C., Li, H., Li, Z., Lau, F.: Federated private clouds via brokers marketplace: a Stackelberg-game perspective. In: IEEE 7th International Conference on Cloud Computing, pp. 296–303, June 2014
6. Ni, W., Li, W., Alam, M.: Determination of optimal call admission control policy in wireless networks. IEEE Trans. Wirel. Commun. **8**(2), 1038–1044 (2009)
7. Li, W., Chao, X.: Call admission control for an adaptive heterogeneous multimedia mobile network. IEEE Trans. Wirel. Commun. **6**(2), 515–525 (2007)
8. Chao, X., Chen, H., Li, W.: Optimal control for a tandem network of queues with blocking. ACTA Math. Appl. Sin. **13**(4), 425–437 (1997)
9. Puterman, M.L.: Markov Decision Process: Discrete Stochastic Dynamic Programming. Wiley, New York (2005)
10. Ross, S.M.: Stochastic Process. Wiley, New York (1983)

Towards a New Evolutionary Algorithm for the Minimum Tollbooth Problem

Pavel Krömer[1]($\boxtimes$), Jana Nowaková[1], and Martin Hasal[2]

[1] Department of Computer Science, VŠB Technical University of Ostrava,
Ostrava, Czech Republic
{pavel.kromer,jana.nowakova}@vsb.cz
[2] IT4Innovations, VŠB Technical University of Ostrava, Ostrava, Czech Republic
martin.hasal@vsb.cz

Abstract. Minimum tollbooth problem is a well–known hard optimization problem from the area of intelligent transportation systems. It consists in the search for a set of optimum locations of a fixed number of tollbooths in a road network so that the behaviour of road users is affected in a way that mitigates the congestions in the network. In this short paper, we summarize the problem, outline the design of an evolutionary algorithm to solve it, and provide an initial computational evaluation of the feasibility of the proposed approach.

1 Introduction

The minimum tollbooth problem (MINTB) is a traditional problem from the area of transportation management and planning with a wide application potential. It consists in the search for optimum locations of a fixed number of tollbooths that are placed within a transportation network. The tollbooths represent fees associated with the passing of a road segment and are considered a cost that road users, travelling from one location to another, will consider. A road user is expected to select his/her path from the origin to the destination so that the total cost (sum of fees) of the travel is minimized.

From a theoretical point of view, the MINTB can be seen as a combinatorial optimization problem that involves the selection of a fixed subset of unique objects from a larger superset. In more formal terms, a combinatorial optimization (CO) problem, $\mathbb{P} = \{I, \{sol(i)\}_{i \in I}, m\}$, can be defined as a minimization or maximization problem that consists of a set of problem instances, I, a set of feasible solutions, $sol(i)$, for every instance $i \in I$, and a function, $m : \{(i, q) | i \in I, q \in sol(i)\} \rightarrow \mathbb{Q}_+$, where $\mathbb{Q}_+$ is the set of positive rational numbers and $m(i, q)$ is the value of solution q for the problem instance i [17]. An optimal solution to an instance of a combinatorial optimization problem is a solution that has maximum (or minimum) value among all other solutions.

The remainder of this paper is organized in the following way: the minimum tollbooth problem is introduced, defined, and discussed in Sect. 2. The proposed

© Springer Nature Switzerland AG 2018
X. Chen et al. (Eds.): CSoNet 2018, LNCS 11280, pp. 116–125, 2018.
https://doi.org/10.1007/978-3-030-04648-4_10

nature–inspired approach is described in Sect. 3 and initial computational evaluation is provided in Sect. 4. The conclusions are drawn and future wark is outlined in Sect. 5.

2   Minimum Tollbooth Problem

The MINTB is a problem motivated by real–world needs. It was first formulated in the Port Authority of New York and New Jersey, a traffic hub established in 1921. The authority manages tunnels, bridges, seaports, and airports and has to deal with every day heavy traffic. In 1954, L.C. Edie formulated the first definition of MINTB as a schedule of tollbooths [8]. The problem asked for the optimum number of toll collectors that have to be at work to serve enough tollbooths to assure the appropriately fast service without traffic delays with predefined restrictions based on working rules for employees and was addressed by integer linear programming. From the beginning, it was known as a multi–objective optimization problem with conflicting economical and operational (service) objectives.

The MINTB has since its inception evolved into a problem where to place tollbooths for optimal traffic run and/or toll pricing problem for setting the pricing strategy. It reflects the evolution in technology as the tollbooths have changed to be automatic, without the necessity of human work. The placement of tollbooths is supposed to motivate road users to choose alternative roads and paths. In summary, the general MINTB is very complex and includes both, tollbooth localization and toll pricing strategy determination.

2.1   Definition

The MINTB can be defined as an integer linear programming problem and graph problem [5, 24]. Consider a weighted graph, $\mathcal{G} = (N, A)$ with a set of nodes, N, and a set of weighted arcs, A. Let L be the number of tariff levels and R be the number of tollbooths to allocate. Each arc, $a \in A$, and tariff level, $p = \{0, 1, \ldots, L\}$, has an associated unit travel cost, c_a^p, tariff cost, tf_a^p, and flow capacity, u_a^p. Moreover, each link has two link–tuning parameters, α_a and β_a, and free flow time, t_a. Assume the set of commodities, K, set of origin nodes, $o(k) \in A$, destination nodes, $d(k) \in A$, and demands, d^k.

The objective of the MINTB is to minimize the travel an tariff costs, $c_a^p + tf_a^p$ by the allocation of R tollbooths with associated toll tariff levels. Various linear programming formulations of the MINTB can be found e.g. in [24, 25].

2.2   Related Work

MINTB was first defined in [8] as a scheduling problem and further developed in [7]. The original formulation assumed the following restrictions:

– the toll collector has a predefined working period, which should be no shorter than one hour and no longer than three hours without a break,

– the toll collector must have a meal break every four hours within the working period, and
– the collector cannot start the work before 6 A.M. and stop the work later than 12:30 A.M.

The second version of the MINTB [7] eliminated some of the requirements (e.g. meal breaks) and later led to an optimization problem dealing with complex tolling strategies. The optimization target shifted to the search for the minimum number and optimum locations of tollbooths that are required to streamline the traffic so that the traffic delays (congestions) are minimized. This section summarizes relevant works that dealt with the MINTB in different contexts.

The placing of tollbooths in Stockholm road network was addressed in [13]. The study sought the minimum number of tollbooths needed and evaluated five alternative pricing strategies for a nine–node network. The socio–economical aspects of the problem were considered in [11]. The work formulated an optimization problem with an equilibrium constraint that dealt with the partitioning of road construction and road maintenance costs.

Two methods for fixed demands toll pricing were presented in [14]. The first one was based on [13] and the second one was a cutting plane method for the minimum toll revenue problem. Both methods were evaluated on computational experiments on the nine–node problem and the Sioux Falls problem. A similar method with elastic toll pricing demand was proposed in [15] and further discussed in [21]. A nature–inspired method for tolling strategy selection based on genetic algorithms was presented in [12]. It aimed at the use of the least number of tollbooths and efficient use of the network but was not able to scale to large transportation networks.

An equilibrium–based algorithm for the search for first best toll pricing strategy was presented in [28]. It was further developed and theoretically analyzed in [2,12]. Another approach based on modified max–algebra was used as a part of traffic simulations with tandem tollbooths. The analysis showed that the efficiency of the method depended in particular on the number of available tollbooths, driver reaction time, and service time [16]

A metaheuristic algorithm for MINTB was proposed in [1]. The use of metaheuristics was motivated by the NP–hardness of the problem and tested on 30 randomly generated and three real–world transportation networks. The algorithm also utilized a local search technique, where the neighborhood function employed a dynamic slope scaling procedure to deal with the fixed charge nature of the objective function.

A privacy–preserving Electronic Toll Pricing (PrETP) system by Balasch and Geuens [3] was based on on–board units sending location data to the tollbooth operator in order to ensure fast operation and short service times. Stefanello et al. [10], [25] defined a mathematical formulation for several types of the MINTB with only two piecewise linear functions to approximate the costs.

The risk–neutral second best toll pricing (SBTP) strategy was addressed in [4]. The algorithm consisted of three steps – the characterization of the solution set; random sampling over the solution set; and a two–phase simulation optimization. A network formulation of the optimum–flow problem can be found e.g. in [6]. The optimal flow was considered as a network equilibrium and the MINTB as an NP–hard problem to approximate within a factor 1.1377 through a reduction from the minimum vertex cover problem.

The main research focus of [20] was the design of a dynamic toll pricing assignment under real–world conditions. A real–world application of tollbooth scheduling and placement problem was recently solved in Jakarta. The optimization became an important part of the planning of new roads. The location of tollbooths was in [24] determined by a hybrid heuristic method. The work provided two new formulations of the MINTB that were computationally expensive but had linear relaxation bounds close to the best integer solution. The authors also presented two hybrid MINTB algorithms, where the first one is better for smaller networks and the second one gave a good ratio between the computation time and the solution quality.

3   Differential Evolution for Fixed–Length Subset Selection

The DE is a versatile and easy to use stochastic evolutionary optimization algorithm [22]. It is a population-based optimizer that evolves a population of real encoded vectors representing the solutions to given problem. The DE was introduced by Storn and Price in 1995 [26, 27] and it quickly became a popular alternative to the more traditional types of evolutionary algorithms. It evolves a population of candidate solutions by iterative modification of candidate solutions by the application of the differential mutation and crossover [22]. In each iteration, so called trial vectors are created from current population by the differential mutation and further modified by various types of crossover operator. At the end, the trial vectors compete with existing candidate solutions for survival in the population.

The DE starts with an initial population of N real-valued vectors. The vectors are initialized with real values either randomly or so, that they are evenly spread over the problem space. The latter initialization leads to better results of the optimization [22].

During the optimization, the DE generates new vectors that are scaled perturbations of existing population vectors. The algorithm perturbs selected base vectors with the scaled difference of two (or more) other population vectors in order to produce the trial vectors. The trial vectors compete with members of the current population with the same index called the target vectors. If a trial vector represents a better solution than the corresponding target vector, it takes its place in the population [22].

There are two most significant parameters of the DE [22]. The scaling factor $F \in [0, \infty]$ controls the rate at which the population evolves and the crossover probability $C \in [0, 1]$ determines the ratio of bits that are transferred to the trial vector from its opponent. The size of the population and the choice of operators are another important parameters of the optimization process.

The basic operations of the classic DE can be summarized using the following formulas [22]: the random initialization of the ith vector with N parameters is defined by

$$x_i[j] = rand(b_j^L, b_j^U), \quad j \in \{0, \ldots, N-1\} \tag{1}$$

where b_j^L is the lower bound of jth parameter, b_j^U is the upper bound of jth parameter and $rand(a, b)$ is a function generating a random number from the range $[a, b]$. A simple form of the differential mutation is given by

$$v_i^t = v_{r1} + F(v_{r2} - v_{r3}) \tag{2}$$

where F is the scaling factor and v_{r1}, v_{r2} and v_{r3} are three random vectors from the population. The vector v_{r1} is the base vector, v_{r2} and v_{r3} are the difference vectors, and the ith vector in the population is the target vector. It is required that $i \neq r1 \neq r2 \neq r3$. The differential mutation in 2D (i.e. for $N = 2$) is illustrated in Fig. 1.

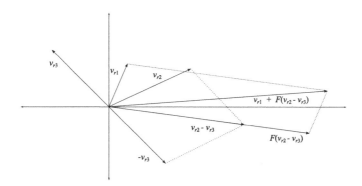

Fig. 1. The differential mutation.

The uniform crossover that combines the target vector with the trial vector is given by

$$l = rand(0, N-1) \tag{3}$$

$$v_i^t[m] = \begin{cases} v_i^t[m] & \text{if}(rand(0,1) < C) \text{ or } m = l \\ x_i[m] \end{cases} \tag{4}$$

for each $m \in \{1, \ldots, N\}$. The uniform crossover replaces with probability $1 - C$ the parameters in v_i^t by the parameters from the target vector x_i.

The outline of the classic DE according to [9,22] is summarized in Algorithm 1.

The DE is a successful evolutionary algorithm designed for continuous parameter optimization driven by the idea of scaled vector differentials. That makes it

```
 1 Initialize the population P consisting of M vectors using Eq. (1);
 2 Evaluate an objective function ranking the vectors in the population;
 3 while Termination criteria not satisfied do
 4    for i ∈ {1, . . . , M} do
 5       Differential mutation: Create trial vector v_i^t according to Eq. (2);
 6       Validate the range of coordinates of v_i^t. Optionally adjust coordinates of
         v_i^t so, that v_i^t is valid solution to given problem;
 7       Perform uniform crossover. Select randomly one parameter l in v_i^t and
         modify the trial vector using Eq. (3);
 8       Evaluate the trial vector.;
 9       if trial vector v_i^t represent a better solution than population vector v^i
         then
10          add v_i^t to P^{t+1}
11       else
12          add v^i to P^{t+1}
13       end
14    end
15 end
```

Algorithm 1. A summary of classic Differential Evolution

an interesting alternative to the wide spread genetic algorithms that are designed to work primarily with discrete encoding of the candidate solutions. As well as GA, it represents a highly parallel population based stochastic search meta-heuristic. In contrast to the GA, the differential evolution uses the real encoding of candidate solutions and different operations to evolve the population. It results in different search strategy and different directions found by DE when crawling a fitness landscape of the problem domain.

3.1 DE for Fixed–Length Subset Selection

The DE for fixed–length subset selection, used in this work to solve the MINTB, is based on the $/DE/rand/1$ version of the algorithm [22] and uses the traditional DE crossover and mutation operators. It translates the combinatorial optimization problem into the continuous domain using an intuitive candidate representation.

A candidate solution is in this approach represented by a real-valued vector, c, of the size k. Each vector, c, is decoded into a set of k feature indices, B. Every floating-point coordinate of c, c_i, is in this process truncated and added to B. If $trunc(c_i)$ already belongs to B, the next available feature that is not in B yet is added to the subset.

This general nature–inspired fixed–length subset selection approach was previously employed to solve e.g. the p-Median problem [18] and the feature subset selection problem [19]. In this work, it is used to address the MINTB.

```
1  B = ∅;
2  for i ∈ {0, . . . , k − 1} do
3  |   j = trunc(i);
4  |   while c_j ∈ B do
5  |   |   j = (j + 1)  mod k;
6  |   end
7  |   B = B ∪ {j}
8  end
```

Algorithm 2. Candidate vector decoding

4   Experiments

To evaluate the ability of the DE for fixed–length subset selection to solve the MINTB, a series of initial computational experiments was performed. The experiments were done over the well–known Sioux Falls road transportation network. It is a network with 24 nodes that is often used to evaluate novel MINTB algorithms [23]. For simplicity, the toll amount was considered as the be solely the travel cost and only a single commodity and one tariff level were assumed. The experimental evaluation was conducted for 5, 10, and 15 tollbooths, respectively.

The DE was the traditional $/DE/rand/1$ version of the algorithm with population size 100, scaling factor, F, and crossover probability, C, equal to 0.9, and the maximum number of DE generations set to 1,000. The fitness function was network congestion, Φ, computed according to [25] as

$$\Phi = \sum_{a \in A} \frac{l_a}{S} t_a \left(1 + \beta_a \left(\frac{l_a}{c_a} \right)^{\alpha_a} \right), \tag{5}$$

where S is the total sum of demands and l_a is the total flow on the arc, a. Because the algorithm is stochastic, each experiment was repeated 31 times independently.

Table 1. The congestion (fitness) in the Sioux Falls road network. Lower is better.

No. of tollbooths	Fitness of randomly placed tollbooths (avg. of 31 random placements)	Fitness		
		Min	Mean	Max
5	277.692	149.354	155.710	164.802
10	445.910	170.736	178.411	187.609
15	875.033	174.854	212.230	238.615

The results of the optimization are summarized in Table 1. The table summarizes the average congestion (fitness) of 31 random problem solutions as well as the results of the proposed algorithm. It shows that the proposed novel approach is indeed able to find reasonable tollbooth locations. For all three numbers of tollbooths, the algorithm was able to evolve location assignments that improved the congestion (i.e. fitness function) when compared with randomly placed tollbooths. The average improvement was 46.22% for 5 tollbooths, 61.71% for 10 tollbooths, and more than 80% for 15 tollbooths.

The results are illustrated in Fig. 2, where blue dots represent the random solutions, green line the average solution, found by the proposed approach, and green area the interval between the worst and best solution found by the proposed approach.

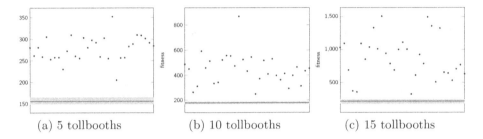

(a) 5 tollbooths   (b) 10 tollbooths   (c) 15 tollbooths

Fig. 2. The fitness of random problem solutions (dots) and evolved problem solutions (lines). (Color figure online)

5 Conclusions and Future Work

This paper outlined a new evolutionary algorithm for the minimum tollbooth problem. It is based on a recent differential evolution for fixed–length subset selection and allows the use of this efficient metaheuristic for the MINTB. In contrast to previous approaches, it uses a real–parameter optimization strategy to address the MINTB which is a combinatorial optimization problem. Initial computational experiments show that the proposed approach is feasible and can evolve tollbooth location assignments with respect to the selected optimization criteria.

Future work will include the evaluation of the proposed method on a more complex MINTB variant (multiple toll levels, more complex travel costs, multiple commodities etc.). It will be also studied on more MINTB instances and compared to other existing heuristic and metaheuristic (especially nature–inspired) methods for the MINTB.

Acknowledgement. This work was supported by the Czech Science Foundation under the grant no. GJ16-25694Y, by the European Regional Development Fund under the project AI&Reasoning (reg. no. CZ.02.1.01/0.0/0.0/15_003/0000466), and by the project SP2018/126 of the Student Grant System, VŠB-Technical University of Ostrava.

References

1. Bai, L., Hearn, D.W., Lawphongpanich, S.: A heuristic method for the minimum toll booth problem. J. Glob. Optim. **48**(4), 533–548 (2010)
2. Bai, L., Stamps, M.T., Harwood, R.C., Kollmann, C.J.: An evolutionary method for the minimum toll booth problem: the methodology. J. Manag. Inf. Decis. Sci. **11**(2), 33 (2008)
3. Balasch, J., Rial, A., Troncoso, C., Preneel, B., Verbauwhede, I., Geuens, C.: Pretp: privacy-preserving electronic toll pricing. In: USENIX Security Symposium, vol. 10, pp. 63–78 (2010)
4. Ban, X.J., Ferris, M.C., Tang, L., Lu, S.: Risk-neutral second best toll pricing. Transp. Res. Part B Methodol. **48**, 67–87 (2013)
5. Basu, S., Lianeas, T., Nikolova, E.: New complexity results and algorithms for the minimum tollbooth problem. CoRR abs/1509.07260 (2015)
6. Basu, S., Lianeas, T., Nikolova, E.: New complexity results and algorithms for the minimum tollbooth problem. In: Markakis, E., Schäfer, G. (eds.) WINE 2015. LNCS, vol. 9470, pp. 89–103. Springer, Heidelberg (2015). https://doi.org/10.1007/978-3-662-48995-6_7
7. Dantzig, G.B.: Letter to the editor - a comment on edie's "traffic delays at toll booths". J. Oper. Res. Soc. Am. **2**(3), 339–341 (1954)
8. Edie, L.C.: Traffic delays at toll booths. J. Oper. Res. Soc. Am. **2**(2), 107–138 (1954)
9. Engelbrecht, A.: Computational Intelligence: An Introduction, 2nd edn. Wiley, New York (2007)
10. Fernando, S., et al.: Routing in road networks: the toll booth problem (2012)
11. Ferrari, P.: Road network toll pricing and social welfare. Transp. Res. Part B Methodol. **36**(5), 471–483 (2002)
12. Harwood, R.C., Kollmann, C.J., Stamps, M.T.: A genetic algorithm for the minimum tollbooth problem (2005)
13. Hearn, D.W., Ramana, M.V.: Solving congestion toll pricing models. In: Marcotte, P., Nguyen, S. (eds.) Equilibrium and Advanced Transportation Modelling, pp. 109–124. Springer, Boston (1998). https://doi.org/10.1007/978-1-4615-5757-9_6
14. Hearn, D.W., Yidirim, M., Ramana, M., Bai, L.: Computational methods for congestion toll pricing models. In: Proceedings of the Intelligent Transportation Systems, pp. 257–262. IEEE (2001)
15. Hearn, D.W., Yildirim, M.B.: A toll pricing framework for traffic assignment problems with elastic demand. In: Gendreau, M., Marcotte, P. (eds.) Transportation and Network Analysis: Current Trends, pp. 135–145. Springer, Boston (2002). https://doi.org/10.1007/978-1-4757-6871-8_9
16. Hong, Y.-C., Kim, D.-K., Kho, S.-Y., Kim, S.W., Yang, H.: Modeling and simulation of tandem tollbooth operations with max-algebra approach. In: Lee, Y., Kim, T., Fang, W., Ślęzak, D. (eds.) FGIT 2009. LNCS, vol. 5899, pp. 138–150. Springer, Heidelberg (2009). https://doi.org/10.1007/978-3-642-10509-8_17
17. Jongen, H., Meer, K., Triesch, E.: Optimization Theory. Springer, New York (2007). https://doi.org/10.1007/b130886
18. Kromer, P., Platos, J., Snasel, V.: Traditional and self-adaptive differential evolution for the p-median problem. In: IEEE 2nd International Conference on Cybernetics (CYBCONF), pp. 299–304, June 2015
19. Krömer, P., Platos, J.: Evolutionary feature subset selection with compression-based entropy estimation. In: Proceedings of the 2016 on Genetic and Evolutionary Computation Conference, Denver, 20–24 July 2016, pp. 933–940 (2016)

20. Laval, J.A., Cho, H.W., Muñoz, J.C., Yin, Y.: Real-time congestion pricing strate-
    gies for toll facilities. Transp. Res. Part B Methodol. **71**, 19–31 (2015)
21. Lawphongpanich, S., Hearn, D.W.: An MPEC approach to second-best toll pricing.
    Math. Program. **101**(1), 33–55 (2004)
22. Price, K.V., Storn, R.M., Lampinen, J.A.: Differential Evolution A Practical App-
    roach to Global Optimization. Natural Computing Series. Springer, Heidelberg
    (2005). https://doi.org/10.1007/3-540-31306-0
23. Schofer, J., Morlok, E.: Development and Application of a Highway Network
    Design Model: Transportation Center Research Report, vol. 2. Environmental
    Planning Branch, Federal Highway Administration, U.S. Department of Trans-
    portation (1973). Type: Report
24. Silva, A., Mateus, G.R.: Hybrid heuristics for the minimum tollbooth problem. In:
    IEEE 19th International Conference on Intelligent Transportation Systems (ITSC),
    pp. 913–918. IEEE (2016)
25. Stefanello, F., et al.: On the minimization of traffic congestion in road networks
    with tolls. Ann. Oper. Res. **249**(1–2), 119–139 (2017)
26. Storn, R.: Differential evolution design of an IIR-filter. In: Proceeding of the IEEE
    Conference on Evolutionary Computation ICEC, pp. 268–273. IEEE Press (1996)
27. Storn, R., Price, K.: Differential Evolution- A Simple and Efficient Adaptive
    Scheme for Global Optimization over Continuous Spaces. Technical report (1995)
28. Yildirim, M.B., Hearn, D.W.: A first best toll pricing framework for variable
    demand traffic assignment problems. Transp. Res. Part B Methodol. **39**(8), 659–
    678 (2005)

Methods for Optimal Resource Allocation on Cooperative Task Scheduling in Cross-Organizational Business Process

Wenan Tan[1,2]([⊠]), Lu Zhao[2], Na Xie[2], Anqiong Tang[1],
Xiaoming Hu[1], and Shan Tang[1]

[1] School of Computer and Information Engineering,
Shanghai Polytechnic University, Shanghai 201209, China
watan@sspu.edu.cn
[2] College of Computer Science and Technology, Nanjing University of Aeronautics
and Astronautics, Nanjing 211106, China
{lzhao,xiena}@nuaa.edu.cn

Abstract. The optimal resource allocation (ORA) strategy for cooperative task scheduling is very important to form an efficient execution team to complete an instance in cross-organizational business processes (COBPs). In team formation, members of a team refer to the performers with specific skills and knowledge, and accomplish various tasks by cooperation and collaboration of corresponding resource roles. The team as a whole should focus on the overall comprehensive ability, which includes professional ability (PA) of members and cooperative ability (CA) between them, instead of individual combat. To address the resource allocation issue of COBPs for social networking cooperation, this paper proposes an ORA model for cooperative task scheduling based on the PA of performer who is qualified to complete task and the CA between performers whose roles require cooperation. In the proposed model, the tabu search (TS) algorithm is utilized to address the objective function solution, which outputs the optimal solutions mapping on resource allocation strategies. Finally, experiments show that the proposed optimization model for resource allocation supporting cooperative task scheduling is more in line with modern enterprise resource management models and it provides a new way for resource allocation during the cooperative task scheduling in COBPs.

Keywords: Cross-organizational business process
Resource allocation · Cooperative task scheduling
Tabu search algorithm · Interaction and cooperation

Supported by the Graduate Innovation Program (A01Gy17F022), the National Natural Science Foundation, China (61672022,61272036), the Key Discipline Foundation of Shanghai Polytechnic University (XXKZD1604).

X. Chen et al. (Eds.): CSoNet 2018, LNCS 11280, pp. 126–138, 2018.
https://doi.org/10.1007/978-3-030-04648-4_11

1   Introduction

The cooperative model for socialized network has evolved from the interaction among members within an enterprise to the cooperation among different organizations. In actual practice, much work inside or outside organizations takes place in teams, orderly teamwork is one of the guarantees to ensure the smooth operations and efficient completion of business. Therefore, it is very important to build an efficient team with optimal resource allocation (ORA) to solve the cooperative tasks scheduling issue in cross-organizational business processes (COBPs) operation. In COBPs management, the resource allocation strategy is based on the role or organization model to assign tasks from the adaptability and usability of the resource allocation, and the consistency between roles and performers [1, 2]. Researchers address it from the perspective of teamwork using service-based group-intelligence cooperative techniques. Such as, crowdsource computing based on social networking [3, 4] and expert social networks-oriented team discovery [5, 6]. However, the resource allocation issues for cooperative task scheduling have been proved to be an NP-hard problem [7–9].

The traditional resource allocation requires only a group of roles and specific performers who are qualified to perform various tasks, that is, the professional ability (PA) of the performer (e.g. the skill level of completing the task) [10]. However, the success of a project depends not only on the PA of the performers, but also on the effective communication between the performers, and even on the many factors such as the interests and political positions among partners. Specifically, the better the inter-performers cooperative ability (CA) is, the higher efficiency of execution between tasks performed by them is. So, in order to optimize the execution performance of the team, some researchers utilize the social relationships of the candidates to optimize team formation supporting resource allocation of workflow task [8, 11–15].

The social relationship between performers can be measured by the network knowledge transfer, which provides a new perspective for human resource management in modern enterprises [16]. So, social networks are an important way to realize complex knowledge sharing across organizations [17]. Although most of the existing works on the methods formed task team by considering the social relationships among performers (e.g., the minimum communication cost [9, 11, 14, 15]), their goal is to maximize overall CA of team without considering whether their roles require collaboration and cooperation. If there is non-cooperation between performers who have the powerful CA, it will result in wasting productivity. So, it is necessary to consider the powerful CA between specific performers whose roles require collaboration and cooperation. While some work has considered the impact of the performers social relationships and cooperation on the process operation [8, 13–15], but they are limited to candidates who possess the appropriate skills and have the same professional skills.

Actually, a performer can often be involved in multiple roles to complete multiple tasks in COBPs, and whose PA is also an important influencing factor for task allocation. According to above, this paper will fully consider the impact of the PA of performers and their CA on task allocation. Through the analysis of historical event log information, the performer's PA and their CA may be calculated out. Based on this, considering the interactive relationship between collaboration tasks comprehensively, a combination optimization team model that supports the cooperative tasks allocation in COBPs will be proposed. Finally, the optimal solution can be obtained by using tabu search algorithm, and a reasonable resource allocation strategy to address cooperative task scheduling will be discussed.

2   Concepts and Definitions

2.1   Professional Ability (PA) of Performers

In COBPs, a task can be completed by multiple role users, and a performer can also assume multiple roles to perform multiple tasks. For a specific task, actually, different performers who are qualified to perform it may have different PA. Thus, the PA of performer in completing a certain task is defined and the specific description is as follows.

Definition 1 (The familiarity of performer). Given a set of performers P, such that $P_i : P_i \in P, i \in m$, and $t_k : t_k \in T, k \in n$ is a set of tasks T. Assume that $numb(p_i, t_k)$ represents the number of times task t_k successfully executed by performer p_i, then the familiarity of p_i with t_k can be described as

$$fami(p_i, t_k) = \frac{numb(p_i, t_k)}{\sum_{t_k \in T} numb(p_i, t_k)} \tag{1}$$

Where, the larger the value of $fami(p_i, t_k)$, the higher level of familiarity of p_i with t_k is. Subject to $\sum_{t_k \in T} fami(p, t_k) = 1 : \forall p \in P$.

In actual practice, however, there may be more than one performer with the same familiarity in specific domain. So, in order to select the best candidate to complete task t_k, we not only need to consider the familiarity of each performer with the skills required for t_k, but also the competitiveness of p_i with respect to other performers on t_k should be considered. Then the competitiveness of performer is defined as follows.

Definition 2 (The competitiveness of performer). Given a set of performers P, such that $P_i : P_i \in P, i \in m$, and $t_k : t_k \in T, k \in n$ is a set of tasks T. Assume that $numb(p_i, t_k)$ represents the number of times task t_k successfully executed by performer p_i, then the competitiveness between p_i and other performers qualified to complete t_k can be described as

$$comp(p_i, t_k) = \frac{numb(p_i, t_k)}{\sum_{p_i \in P} numb(p_i, t_k)} \tag{2}$$

Where, the larger the value of $comp(p_i, t_k)$, the more competitive of the performer p_i, and p_i is more suit for the candidate performer set of task t_k. Subject to $\sum_{p_i \in P} comp(p_i, t) = 1 : \forall t \in T$.

Considering that the familiarity of the performer in completing a task has a positive correlation with his or her peers' competitiveness, this paper utilizes a multiplicative model to evaluate professional ability (PA) of p_i in t_k.

$$PA(p_i, t_k) = fami(p_i, t_k)comp(p_i, t_k) \tag{3}$$

Where, the larger the value of $PA(p_i, t_k)$, the greater the chance of that p_i is responsible for performing t_k.

2.2 Cooperative Ability (CA) Between Performers

Based on our previous work [18], the social relationship between performers can be calculated by using the handover of social network described as a weighted directed graph as $G = (P, E, SC)$. Where, P is the set of performers, E represents the set of connected edges between vertices and SC is the weight set of connected edge.

Definition 3 (The weight of social relations). Given the handover of social network $G = (P, E, SC)$ presented in [18]. Assume that the handover of work between performers is successful, let $numb(p_i, p_j)$ indicates the number of times p_i handed over to p_j, then the weight of social relations between performers p_i and p_j can be defined as

$$SC(p_i, p_j) = \frac{numb(p_i, p_j)}{\sum_{p_r \in P} numb(p_i, p_r)} \tag{4}$$

Where, the larger the value of $SC(p_i, p_j)$, the smaller the cost of communication between p_i and p_j is, and subjects to $\sum_{p_r \in P} SC(p, p_r) = 1 : \forall p \in P$. It means that the more opportunities for them to participate in teamwork.

For a team, however, it should consider the effect of skill overlap between performers on cooperative interaction, in addition to their social relations. Because of the complementary resources between performers, it will play a better synergy.

Definition 4 (The skill level similarity). Assume that different skills are required for different tasks, i.e. how many types of tasks the performer completes represent how many different skills they have. Given performers $p_i, p_j \in P : i, j \in m \wedge i \neq j$, and let $T(p_i) = \{t_k \mid t_k \in T : k \in h \to N^+ \leq n\}$ is the skill set owned by p_i. Then the skill level similarity (SLS) between p_i and p_j is defined as follows.

$$SLS(p_i, p_j) = \frac{\mid T(p_i) \bigcap T(p_j) \mid}{\mid T(p_i) \bigcup T(p_j) \mid} \tag{5}$$

The lower SLS among performers is, the more types of tasks with minimal dominant resources are accomplished, which realizes maximize resource utilization. Meanwhile, it is also necessary to meet the minimum cost of teamwork communication and to achieve the maximum working efficiency of team. Hence, the cooperative ability (CA) between performers can be calculated by Eq. (6).

$$CA(p_i, p_j) = SC(p_i, p_j)[1 - SLS(p_i, p_j)] \tag{6}$$

Where, the larger the value of $CA(p_i, p_j)$, the stronger the CA between p_i and p_j is. It means that with relatively little communication cost, its integrated resources cover a relatively wide range.

3   Optimal Resource Allocation (ORA) Model

A high-quality team is the core force for the development of organizations (such as enterprises, departments, and working groups). The team as a whole should pay attention to the overall comprehensive ability instead of individual combat. For the members of team, of course, they should not only have personal ability, but also need to have the ability to do their best in different positions and coordinate with other members. Therefore, an efficient execution team for cooperative tasks can be formed from the next three perspectives in COBPs.

3.1   ORA Model with the Strongest Professional Ability (TSPA)

Given a cooperative task set $\{t_k \in T : k \in n\}$ and candidate performer set $\{p_i \in P : i \in m\}$. The ORA model can be described as

$$Team_1 = arg \max_{\{p_i \in P : i \in m\}} \sum_{t_k \in T} A_{ki} PA(p_i, t_k) \tag{7}$$

Subject to:

$$\sum_{i=1}^{m} A_{ki} = 1, k = 1, 2, \cdots, n \tag{8}$$

$$A_{ki} \leq Q_{ki}, 1 \leq k \leq n, 1 \leq i \leq m \tag{9}$$

Where, when performer p_i is assigned to perform task t_k, $A_{ki} = 1$, otherwise, $A_{ki} = 0$. If performer p_i is qualified to perform task t_k, then $Q_{ki} = 1$, if not, $Q_{ki} = 0$. The constraint (8) means that every task t_k must be assigned to exactly one performer p_i. The constraint (9) represents that the performer p_i assigned to perform task t_k must be qualified to perform it.

The core idea of TSPA is to traverse all candidate performers who are qualified to perform the task, and select the performer with the maximum PA to complete each task in the cooperative task allocation. Finally, a team with the TSPA will be assigned to perform the entire cooperative task. It means that TSPA strategy is to search a set of candidate feasible solutions (i.e., a random set of candidate performers) in performer domain by one-to-one matching with tasks until a set of solutions satisfying TSPA is found. Its time complexity is $O(mn)$.

3.2 ORA Model with the Strongest Cooperative Ability (TSCA)

As presented in [8], that is to say that the goal of this TSCA strategy is to maximize overall ability of team by considering the CA between performers whose roles require cooperation. Given a cooperative task set and candidate performer set. The description of the ORA model is shown as

$$Team_2 = arg \max_{\{p_i \in P: i \in m\}} \sum_{k,v=1}^{n} \sum_{i,j=1}^{m} A_{ki} A_{vj} CT_{kv} CA(p_i, p_j) \qquad (10)$$

Subject to:

$$\sum_{i=1}^{m} A_{ki} = 1, k = 1, 2, \cdots, n \qquad (11)$$

$$A_{ki} \leq Q_{ki}, 1 \leq k \leq n, 1 \leq i \leq m \qquad (12)$$

$$Q_{ki} + Q_{vj} - CP_{ij} \leq 1, CT_{kv} = 1, 1 \leq k, v \leq n, 1 \leq i, j \leq m \qquad (13)$$

Where, $A_{ki} = \{0,1\}$ and $Q_{ki} = \{0,1\}$ are described above. If an cooperation is required between tasks t_k and t_v, then $CT_{kv} = 1$, if not, $CT_{kv} = 0$. When performers p_i and p_j are assigned to perform tasks t_k and t_v respectively, $CP_{ij} = 1$, otherwise, $CP_{ij} = 0$. The constraint (13) means that if there is an cooperation between tasks t_k and t_v, then the $CA(p_i, p_j)$ between performers p_i and p_j who are qualified to perform these two tasks respectively within required constraints (11) and (12), is the element of the target optimization function. So, TSCA strategy needs to traverse the interactions between the cooperative tasks and all the candidate performers.

The idea of TSCA is to pay attention to the CA between performers. It also traverses all candidate performers who are qualified to perform the task, but it assumes that all candidates are qualified with the same PA. Based on this, its goal is to capture notions of CA (i.e., compatibility) between performers who will perform the collaboration tasks, and obtain a group with maximizing overall the CA to accomplish the entire cooperative task. Thus, its time complexity $O(m^2 n^2)$.

3.3 ORA Model with the Strongest Integrative Objective (TSIO)

Improved ORA model based on TSPA and TSCA, denoted as the strongest integrative objective (TSIO), in other words, it comprehensively considers both PA of performers who are qualified to perform tasks and CA between performers whose roles require cooperation, but it requires a trade-off between PA and CA. Specifically, Given a cooperative task set $\{t_k \in T : k \in n\}$ and candidate performer set $\{p_i \in P : i \in m\}$, then the optimization model of resource allocation for cooperative tasks can be described as

$$Team_3 = arg \max_{\{p_i \in P: i \in m\}} \sum_{k,v=1}^{n} \sum_{i,j=1}^{m} A_{ki} A_{vj} CT_{kv} [PA(p_i, t_k) + PA(p_j, t_v)] CA(p_i, p_j)$$

$$(14)$$

Subject to:

$$\sum_{i=1}^{m} A_{ki} = 1, k = 1, 2, \cdots, n \tag{15}$$

$$A_{ki} \leq Q_{ki}, 1 \leq k \leq n, 1 \leq i \leq m \tag{16}$$

$$Q_{ki} + Q_{vj} - CP_{ij} \leq 1, CT_{kv} = 1, 1 \leq k, v \leq n, 1 \leq i, j \leq m \tag{17}$$

Where, A_{ki}, Q_{ki}, CT_{kv} and CP_{ij} belong to {0, 1}, which are described in Subsect. 3.1 and 3.2. Compared with TSPA, TSCA strategy, TSIO strategy presented in above fully considers the PA and CA among performers and utilizes the combinatorial optimization method to address the cooperative task scheduling, which is improved based on them. Obviously, TSIO strategy is basically similar to TSCA strategy presented in Eq. (10), but it considers the impact of performers with different PA on ORA and its time complexity is $O(m^2 n^2)$.

3.4   Comparative Analysis with Different ORA Model

In COBPs, tasks or activities are performed by various types of computing resources (such as human resources, network resources, or applications, etc.) in the scheduling resource model [2]. Where human resource refers to the performers with specific skills and knowledge, to accomplish various tasks by cooperation and collaboration of corresponding resource roles. For the high-quality teamwork, the performer's PA and the CA with each other are very important to the smooth and efficient of the entire business process execution.

The ORA model based on TSPA strategy only considers the performer with maximum PA. When there is a need for interaction between tasks during business execution, the powerful cooperation efficiency between performers can reduce the cost of knowledge flow between them and reduce the duration of the services. It means that good cooperation between performers can effectively improve the efficiency of cooperative tasks. So, TSCA strategy is better than TSPA strategy. But the TSCA strategy is assumed that all performers are qualified with the same PA. Due to the difference in the cultural level and project experience of each performer, in actual practice, there is a difference in their PA. In addition, the role for a simple task do not need the highly qualified PA, rather, the role of important positions requires professional performer, e.g., accountant.

Based on this, this paper improves the TSCA strategy for ORA model, which quantifies the PA of each performer and constructs improved ORA model with TSIO strategy. It not only considers the individual's own PA, but focuses on the CA among individuals. Compared with the TSPA strategy and TSCA strategy, it is more in line with the modern enterprise human resource management model.

3.5   ORA Based on Tabu Search (TS) Algorithm

Based on our previous work [19], this paper utilizes the TS algorithm to solve the resource allocation issue on cooperative task scheduling in ORA model based on TSPA, TSCA and TSIO strategy. For solving the ORA model, the data in the Q, CT, PA and CA matrices can be taken directly from the historical event log and calculated by the definitions described above.

The basic idea of the TS algorithm is to generate a feasible domain solution for the current solution from an initial feasible solution. It may select a series of specific search directions as a probe, to implement a movement that allows a specific objective function value to change the most. In order to avoid falling into the local optimal solution, the TS algorithm utilizes the tabu list technology to record and select the process that has been optimized to guide the next search direction. Furthermore, the results output the optimal solution, and give the ORA strategy.

4   Experimental Analysis

To validate the proposed ORA algorithm for cooperative task, we utilize the data sets of a real-life event log provided by BPIC 2012[1]. This event log at hand consists of 262,200 events. In the complete data set, 13,087 process instances are found, which consisted on average of 20 events. There are a total number of 36 event classes (i.e. tasks), with a total number of 69 resource. In the data pre-processing, the input event log results in a total of 244,190 noiseless activity-supporter pairs, which includes 24 tasks and 68 resources with no repetition.

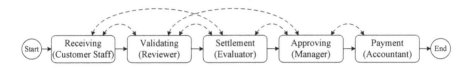

Fig. 1. A simple insurance business model for claim process.

According to the simulation experiments, we will present the comparative analysis of the rationality of the cooperative tasks scheduling in COBPs from three strategies: TSPA, TSCA, TSIO. Since the data set is anonymized to private data, it is assumed that the data set contains the insurance business claim process, as shown in Fig. 1.

Figure 1 is a simple insurance business claims process that includes receiving, validating, settlement, approving, and payment. Where the solid line indicates the business logic relationship and the dotted line indicates that the cooperation between roles is required in performing tasks. From Fig. 1, we utilize binary numbers to describe the cooperative relationships between tasks. Specifically, 1 represents handover of work, 0 indicates no handover.

By analyzing historical event logs, 10 qualified candidate performers involved in this business process are obtained. Next, we extract 1000 complete execution

---

[1]   http://www.win.tue.nl/bpi/doku.php?id=2012:challenge&redirect=1id=2012/
challenge.

procedures as input for this experiment and calculate the PA between tasks and performers and the CA between performers. In the following, we will utilize the TS algorithm to address the cooperative tasks scheduling issues from three perspectives presented in Sect. 3, and the details of optimal resource allocation are as follows.

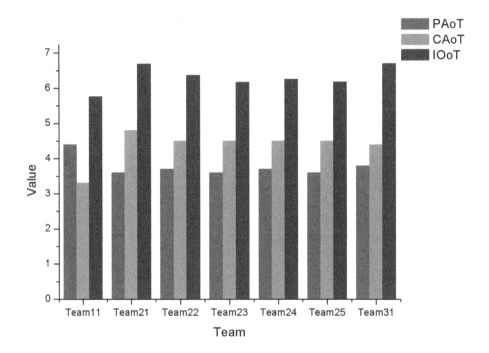

Fig. 2. Team performance in different ORA solutions.

(1) If ORA strategy only requires that the team members have the strongest PA, then TSPA allocation strategy can be obtained by Eq. (7). The result is shown as $Team_{11}$ = {Receiving: 10910; Validating: 10939; Settlement: 10931; Approving: 10932; Payment: 10881}, and the PA of $Team_{11}$ (denoted as PAoT) is 4.4 as shown in Fig. 2. Meanwhile, the CA of $Team_{11}$ (CAoT) can be calculated by using Eq. (6), its value is 3.5.

(2) According to the Eq. (10) presented in [8], the optimal solution of TSCA allocation strategy is shown as $Team_{21}$ = {Receiving: 10912; Validating: 10932; Settlement: 10931; Approving: 10912; Payment: 10899} whose value of CAoT is 4.6 and the PAoT is 3.6. Note that the performer 10912 in $Team_{21}$ serves two roles as customer and manager respectively. However, when an organization addresses tasks scheduling from roles perspective, it is impossible an enterprise to allow a manager to work full-time as a customer service agent. In addition, when enterprise resources are in short supply, an individual is also not allowed

to appear in multiple organization within across organizations. So, $Team_{21}$ does not accord with the enterprise human resource management model.

Fortunately, we find two satisfactory resource allocation strategies qualified for resource management model in the suboptimal solution, which are $Team_{22}$ = {Receiving: 10910; Validating: 10939; Settlement: 10932; Approving: 10912; Payment: 10899} and $Team_{23}$ = {Receiving: 10912; Validating: 10939; Settlement: 10932; Approving: 10910; Payment: 10881}. As shown in Fig. 2, they have the same CAoT with the value at 4.5. But the value of their PA is different, and the result is 3.7 and 3.6 respectively. If the ORA issue of cooperative task is analyzed from the perspective of teams PA, then $Team_{22}$ is better than $Team_{23}$ for cooperative tasks (because of 3.7 > 3.6). Compared the team strategy with TSPA, $Team_{21}$, $Team_{22}$ and $Team_{23}$ have strong CA, but their PA is somewhat inadequate, while the CA of $Team_{11}$ is relatively poor. From the above analysis, the optimal team supporting cooperative task scheduling is $Team_{22}$.

For the suboptimal solutions, there are multiple optimal teams with the same CAoT as $Team_{22}$ and $Team_{23}$, such as $Team_{24}$ = {Receiving: 10910; Validating: 10939; Settlement: 10932; Approving: 10910; Payment: 10881}, $Team_{25}$ = {Receiving: 10912; Validating: 10939; Settlement: 10932; Approving: 10912; Payment: 10899}. But they are contrary to human resource management model in the modern enterprise, just like $Team_{21}$.

(3) To balance the impact of team members' PA and CA on tasks scheduling, we propose TSIO strategy presented in Eq. (14). Furthermore, the optimal solution of ORA model based on TSIO strategy can be obtained, which is shown as $Team_{31}$ = {Receiving: 10932; Validating: 10929; Settlement: 10931; Approving: 10935; Payment: 10881}, and the value of its integrative objective (IOoT) is 6.7. Similarly, the value of PA and CA of $Team_{31}$ are calculated by using Eqs. (3) and (6), and their results are 3.9, 4.4 respectively, as shown in Fig. 2.

Compared with TSPA and TSCA strategy, we can see from Fig. 2 that its comprehensive ability is stronger, such that $IOoT_{31} = 6.7 > IOoT_{22} = 6.4 > IOoT_{11} = 5.8$. Meanwhile, it is easily to be seen that the PA of $Team_{31}$ is better than $Team_{22}$ (3.9 > 3.7), and its CA is also better than $Team_{11}$ (4.4 > 3.5).

In addition, the TSIO strategy is to assign performers with different capabilities based on the roles required for different tasks. As shown in Fig. 3, the PA of members in $Team_{31}$ in their respective roles is in line with the modern enterprise human resources management model. Specifically, customer service personnel only need to record insurance business claims and do not need the highly qualified PA, where, the performer 10932 in $Team_{31}$ has the PA with the value at 0.5. In contrast, the three roles of reviewer, evaluator and accountant must require highly qualified people. Because, the first two roles are the review and evaluation of materials to verify the true or false nature and the amount of claims, and the last role is accountant that it is faced with enterprise financial projects so to have highly qualified PA. The value of their PA are 0.8, 0.9, and 0.9 respectively. What's more, the manager is the core role in this team, he/she needs to approve, sign, and confirm the submitted materials, and also has the

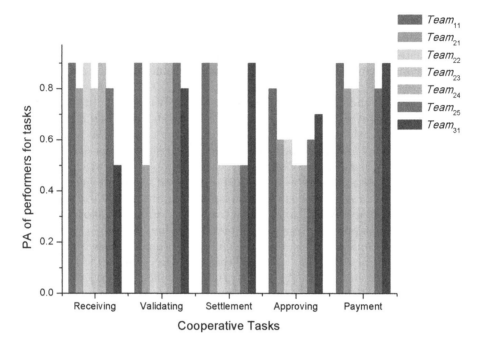

Fig. 3. The PA of performers in different ORA solutions.

ability to coordinate the team. So, the performer 10935 with the value of PA at 0.8 is selected as manager in $Team_{31}$.

As shown in Fig. 4, moreover, it can be seen that when the task needs cooperation, the CA between 10935 and other members in $Team_{31}$ is strong and the values of their CA are all above 0.7. In $Team_{22}$ formed by TSCA strategy proposed by [8], however, the PA of performers 10932 and 10912 who are involved in roles of evaluator and manager respectively is obviously insufficient, which are 0.5 and 0.6. What's more, the CA of 10912 is lower than that of 10935 in the position of manager. Thus, the performer 10935 is qualified to be competent to department manager.

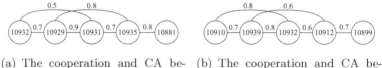

(a) The cooperation and CA between performers in $Team_{31}$

(b) The cooperation and CA between performers in $Team_{22}$

Fig. 4. Comparing $Team_{31}$ with $Team_{22}$ in CA.

5   Conclusions

In this paper, we discuss the resource allocation issues for cooperative task in COBPs and propose an improved ORA algorithm. Specifically, the contribution of this paper is mainly as follows: (1) The PA of performers who are qualified to perform the cooperative tasks and the CA between performers whose roles require cooperation are calculated based on event logs information. (2) are effectively described. According to the cooperative relationship between interactive tasks, an improved team optimization model for cooperative task assignment is proposed by combining the individual attributes (skills, competitiveness) and social attributes (social relations, domain knowledge) of the performers. (3) We comprehensively consider the adaptability of resource allocation and the collaborative cooperation among performers to optimize goal with maximizing the integrative ability of team. Finally, the optimal solution is obtained by using tabu search algorithm, which achieves the effective and reasonable resource allocation. Furthermore, experiments show that the ORA model based on combinatorial optimization effectively can address the issue of cooperative task scheduling in COBPs, and it is suitable for resource management in complex large-scale social network cooperative projects.

However, due to the multiple and complex factors involved in resource allocation in COBPs management, our approach proposed in this paper does not provide a complete solution and has also the limitation. In the future, we will study the optimal cooperative tasks scheduling in COBPs from the perspective of resource workload.

References

1. Alotaibi, Y., Liu, F.: Survey of business process management: challenges and solutions. Enterp. Inf. Syst. **11**(8), 1119–1153 (2017). https://doi.org/10.1080/17517575.2016.1161238
2. Tan, W., Xu, W., Yang, F., et al.: A framework for service enterprise workflow simulation with multi-agents cooperation. Enterp. Inf. Syst. **7**(4), 523–542 (2013). https://doi.org/10.1080/17517575.2012.660503
3. Gadiraju, U., Demartini, G., Kawase, R., et al.: Human beyond the machine: Challenges and opportunities of microtask crowdsourcing. IEEE Intell. Syst. **30**(4), 81–85 (2015). http://doi.ieeecomputersociety.org/10.1109/MIS.2015.66
4. Schall, D., Satzger, B., Psaier, H.: Crowdsourcing tasks to social networks in BPEL4People. World Wide Web **17**(1), 1–32 (2014). https://doi.org/10.1007/s11280-012-0180-6
5. Yin, H., Cui, B., Huang, Y.: Finding a wise group of experts in social networks. In: Tang, J., King, I., Chen, L., Wang, J. (eds.) ADMA 2011. LNCS (LNAI), vol. 7120, pp. 381–394. Springer, Heidelberg (2011). https://doi.org/10.1007/978-3-642-25853-4_29
6. Juang, M.C., Huang, C.C., Huang, J.L.: Efficient algorithms for team formation with a leader in social networks. J. Supercomput. **66**(2), 721–737 (2013). https://doi.org/10.1007/s11227-013-0907-x

7. Reijers, H.A., Jansen-Vullers, M.H., zur Muehlen, M., Appl, W.: Workflow management systems + swarm intelligence = dynamic task assignment for emergency management applications. In: Alonso, G., Dadam, P., Rosemann, M. (eds.) BPM 2007. LNCS, vol. 4714, pp. 125–140. Springer, Heidelberg (2007). https://doi.org/10.1007/978-3-540-75183-0_10

8. Kumar, A., Dijkman, R., Song, M.: Optimal resource assignment in workflows for maximizing cooperation. In: Daniel, F., Wang, J., Weber, B. (eds.) BPM 2013. LNCS, vol. 8094, pp. 235–250. Springer, Heidelberg (2013). https://doi.org/10.1007/978-3-642-40176-3_20

9. Kittur, A., Nickerson, J.V., Bernstein, M., et al.: The future of crowd work. In: Proceedings of the 2013 Conference on Computer Supported Cooperative Work, pp. 1301–1318. ACM (2013). https://doi.org/10.1145/2441776.2441923

10. Anagnostopoulos, A., Becchetti, L., Castillo, C., et al.: Online team formation in social networks. In: Proceedings of the 21st International Conference on World Wide Web, pp. 839-848. ACM (2012). https://doi.org/10.1145/2187836.2187950

11. Lappas, T., Liu, K., Terzi, E.: Finding a team of experts in social networks. In: Proceedings of the 15th ACM SIGKDD International Conference on Knowledge Discovery and Data Mining, pp. 467–476. ACM (2009). https://doi.org/10.1145/1557019.1557074

12. Xu, J., Huang, Z., Yu, Y., et al.: A performance analysis on task allocation using social context. In: Proceedings of the 2012 Second International Conference on Cloud and Green Computing, pp. 637–644. IEEE (2012). https://doi.org/10.1109/CGC.2012.88

13. Bajaj, A., Russell, R.: AWSM: allocation of workflows utilizing social network metrics. Decis. Support Syst. **50**(1), 191–202 (2010). https://doi.org/10.1016/j.dss.2010.07.014

14. Wang, X., Zhao, Z., Ng, W.: A comparative study of team formation in social networks. In: Renz, M., Shahabi, C., Zhou, X., Cheema, M.A. (eds.) DASFAA 2015. LNCS, vol. 9049, pp. 389–404. Springer, Cham (2015). https://doi.org/10.1007/978-3-319-18120-2_23

15. Basiri, J., Taghiyareh, F., Ghorbani, A.: Collaborative team formation using brain drain optimization: a practical and effective solution. World Wide Web **20**(6), 1385–1407 (2017). https://doi.org/10.1007/s11280-017-0440-6

16. Cross, R., Parker, A., Prusak, L., et al.: Knowing what we know: supporting knowledge creation and sharing in social networks. Organ. Dyn. **30**(2), 100–120 (2001). https://doi.org/10.1016/S0090-2616(01)00046-8

17. Wi, H., Oh, S., Mun, J., et al.: A team formation model based on knowledge and collaboration. Expert Syst. Appl. **36**(5), 9121–9134 (2009). https://doi.org/10.1016/j.eswa.2008.12.031

18. Zhao, L., Tan, W., Fang, X.: Role identification to discover potential opportunity information in business process. In: Proceedings of the 14th International Conference on e-Business Engineering (ICEBE), pp. 70–75. IEEE (2017). http://doi.ieeecomputersociety.org/10.1109/ICEBE.2017.20

19. Tan, W., Zhang, Q., Sun, Y.: Proactive scheduling optimization of emergency rescue based on hybrid genetic-tabu optimization algorithm. In: Zu, Q., Hu, B. (eds.) HCC 2016. LNCS, vol. 9567, pp. 400–408. Springer, Cham (2016). https://doi.org/10.1007/978-3-319-31854-7_36

A Vehicular Collision Avoidance Routing Algorithm based on V2V

Aiping Zhang[1,2], Demin Li[1,2(✉)], Guanglin Zhang[1,2], Junjie Wang[1,2], and Mengqi Cao[1,2]

[1] College of Information Science and Technology,
Donghua University, Shanghai, China
`aipingzhang@mail.dhu.edu.cn`, {`deminli,glzhang`}`@dhu.edu.cn`
[2] Engineering Research Center of Digitized Textile and Apparel Technology,
Ministry of Education, Shanghai 201620, China

Abstract. Vehicle to vehicle (V2V) communication can give us better results by avoiding the major problems in road like collision of vehicle, better route selection in case of traffic congestion etc. In this paper, we propose a vehicular collision avoidance routing algorithm based on V2V communication to deal with the issue of collision of vehicles in urban scenarios. We first investigate vehicular collision cases at intersection, which is influenced by status of traffic light and driving state of vehicle and determine alternative collision sets based on the remaining time of traffic lights. Furthermore, we provide an information acquisition method that takes into account priority of the driving state function and formulize the collision detection. Moreover, by using Network Simulation version 2 (NS-2), compared with Vehicular Ad-hoc on-demand Distance Vector (VAODV), the algorithm proposed in this paper outperforms in network throughput and message delivery time.

Keywords: Collision avoidance routing algorithm
Alternative collision sets · Driving state function
Collision time difference · V2V

1 Introduction

With the rapid development of economy and the constantly rising standard of living, the number of private cars has increased sharply, which has brought a lot of traffic problems, especially the traffic safety issue. According to World Health Organization (WHO), about 1.25 million people worldwide lose their living in traffic accidents each year [8]. In the urban scenario, especially, intersections are

Supported by the NSF of China under Grant No. 71171045, No. 61772130, and No. 61301118; the Innovation Program of Shanghai Municipal Education Commission under Grant No. 14YZ130; and the International S&T Cooperation Program of Shanghai Science and Technology Commission under Grant No. 15220710600.

ⓒ Springer Nature Switzerland AG 2018
X. Chen et al. (Eds.): CSoNet 2018, LNCS 11280, pp. 139–151, 2018.
https://doi.org/10.1007/978-3-030-04648-4_12

considered as high frequency areas for traffic accidents [3]. With the development of wireless communication technologies and applications, Vehicular ad hoc network (VANET) [11] is a candidate for improving the traffic conditions and servicing to drivers and passengers. Therefore, combined with the advanced vehicle network technology, it has attracted wide attention of researchers to propose a method to solve the problem of vehicle collision by obtaining and sharing road and vehicle information.

In the current research, many researchers have proposed corresponding methods to deal with the problem of vehicle collision in different application scenarios. Benedetto et al. [1] applied telecommunications methodologies to road safety for avoiding rear-end collisions. Huang et al. [4] presented a vector-based cooperative collision warning system (VCCW) to deal with collision of vehicles on curve road condition and improve the accuracy of warning. Li et al. [5] proposed a time-to-collision (TTC) based vehicular collision warning algorithm under considering the traffic safety with the scenario of arterial road. The warning message can be calculated and forwarded to vehicles through the road side unit (RSU) device. Roy et al. [6] presented a protocol called VAODV to avoid the collision of vehicles, which was a modification of AODV routing protocol. The proposed protocol continuously checked the distance and speed of each vehicle. Thangaraj et al. [10] analysed the performance of the proposed VAODV protocol and latter extended for OSPF in different metrics.

Those researches mentioned above are efficient, but there are some challenges to investigate vehicle collision at intersection. The conventional researches ignore the impact of the traffic lights on vehicle collision and lack of analysis of alternative collision sets under different status of traffic lights. The contributions of this paper are as follows:

- First, we investigate the collision of vehicles at intersection, and determinate alternative collision sets based on the remaining time of traffic lights, which can shrink the range of sending packets.
- Second, we provide a method which takes the priority of the driving state function for next-hop selection and use the collision time difference of vehicles to estimate the collision risk, which is greatly effective.
- Finally, we simulate collision detection, delay and throughput by using proposed algorithm in this paper, which not only avoids collision of vehicles at the intersection, but also has greater network throughput and shorter data delivery delay.

2   System Model

2.1   The System Scenario

In our system, we suppose that the distance from vehicle to intersection can be acquired, all vehicles are equipped with wireless communication device to acquire the information about traffic light and vehicle. And in this paper, traffic

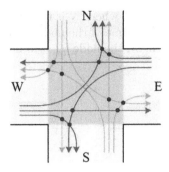

Fig. 1. Illustration of traffic flow and collision (Color figure online)

lights are synchronized and green time is the same as red time regardless of the yellow time.

The Fig. 1. illustrates the driving direction of vehicles and collision at the single road intersection by considering the influence of traffic light. The green and red arrow mean the driving direction of vehicles when the current traffic light is green. Every intersection has four directions (e.g. East, West, South and North). The vehicle has three behaviors which are turn-left, turn-right and going straight crossing the road intersection. When the vehicle passes the intersection according to the vehicular driving behaviors, it may collide with other vehicles from different directions. As illustrated in Fig. 1, it may have 12 collision points at intersection during a period of traffic light. As we can know that the driving behaviors influence vehicular collision. Therefore, we will discuss alternative sets of dynamic collision nodes on the basic of the driving behaviors.

2.2   Alternative Sets of Dynamic Collision Nodes

This part will be classified by the different driving behaviors of vehicles and the status of traffic lights for each driving behavior to analyze alternative sets of dynamic collision nodes. The alternative sets of dynamic collision nodes will be given by the remaining time of traffic light. The vehicular collision may occur at the intersection under the following scenarios.

Case 1: The host vehicle (HV) turns left across the road intersection.

In this case, it will be discussed when the status of traffic light is green on HV's direction. Because the HV can not pass intersection when the status of traffic light is red. As shown in Fig. 2, the traffic light on latitude is green and the longitude is opposite. The HV intents to turn left across the intersection and the opposite vehicles may pass intersection by turning right or going straight. When the opposite vehicle turns right, two vehicles travel on different paths, but they have the same target path and pass the same point. When the opposite vehicle goes straight, two vehicles have different target paths, but they meet at the same point. The blue dotted oval is defined as the range of the collision node set $S_L = \{n_{o_1}, n_{o_2}, \ldots, n_{o_i} | i \leq N\}$, where N is the maximum number of vehicles of collision node set. If the travel time of the node n_{o_i} to intersection is less than the remaining time of traffic light, the node n_{o_i} will be a member of S_L, and the vehicle may collide with HV.

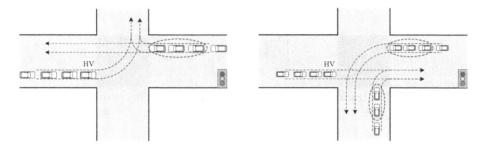

Fig. 2. Host vehicle on turn-left (Color figure online)

Fig. 3. Host vehicle on straight (Color figure online)

Case 2: The HV goes straight through the road intersection.

In this case, it will be discussed when the status of traffic lights is green on HV's direction. As shown in Fig. 3, the traffic light on latitude is green and the longitude is opposite. The HV goes straight through the intersection, the opposite vehicles turns left and the vehicles on HV's right side turn right across the intersection. The HV and opposite vehicles have different target paths, however, they have the same junction when they pass the intersection. The HV has the same target path with the vehicles on HV's right side, and they have a certain probability of collision at one point of the intersection. In this condition, there are two collision node sets located in different segments in Fig. 3, which are the opposite collision node set $S_{SO} = \{n_{o_1}, n_{o_2}, \ldots, n_{o_j} | j \leq N\}$ and the right collision node set $S_{SR} = \{n_{r_1}, n_{r_2}, \ldots, n_{r_k} | k \leq N\}$ respectively. Therefore, the collision node set can be expressed by $S_S = S_{SO} \bigcup S_{SR}$ in this case.

Case 3: The HV turns right across the road intersection

In this case, the right-turn vehicles are not affected by traffic lights, that is, no matter whether the status of traffic light is green or red, vehicles can pass through the intersection. There are different sets of collision nodes under different status of traffic light.

Case 3.1 The traffic light is green

As shown in Fig. 4(a), the traffic light on HV's direction (latitude) is green and the longitude is red. The HV intents to turn right across the intersection. The opposite vehicles turn left to pass the intersection. They have the same target path and pass the same point. So, they will collide according to the driving behaviors at intersection. The blue dotted oval is the collision node set $S_{RG} = \{n_{g_1}, n_{g_2}, \ldots, n_{g_m} | m \leq N\}$ in this condition.

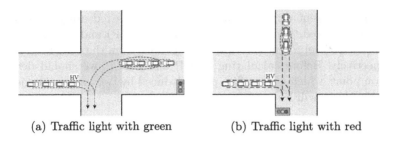

(a) Traffic light with green   (b) Traffic light with red

Fig. 4. Host vehicle on turn-right (Color figure online)

Case 3.2 The traffic light is red

As shown in Fig. 4(b), the traffic light on HV's direction (latitude) is red and the longitude is green. And the HV can't go straight and turn left except turning right. And the vehicle on longitude can pass the intersection with going straight, they will collide as they have the same target path and meet the same point. The blue dotted oval is the collision node set $S_{RR} = \{n_{r_1}, n_{r_2}, \ldots, n_{r_p} | p \leq N\}$.

The collision node set can be expressed by

$$S_R = \begin{cases} S_{RG} \text{ when the traffic light is green} \\ S_{RR} \text{ when the traffic light is red} \end{cases}$$

Above, the range of collision node sets is analyzed according to the driving behaviors and traffic lights at intersection, then we will calculate and compare the time of the vehicle to intersection with the remaining time of traffic light to estimate whether the vehicle is a member of the collision node sets. The time t_i of the vehicle i to intersection can be formulized by Eq. (1).

$$t_i = \frac{d_i}{v_i} \tag{1}$$

Where d_i and v_i represent the distance of the vehicle i to intersection and the speed of the vehicle i respectively. The vehicle i will be regarded as a member of collision node sets if the t_i is no more than the remaining time of traffic light T_{lr}. The maximum number N of vehicles in the blue dotted oval is

$$N = \frac{T_{lr} \cdot \bar{v}}{l_v} \tag{2}$$

where $\bar{v}$ and l_v denote the average velocity of vehicles and the average length of vehicles in the blue dotted oval respectively.

2.3 Collision Detection

In this part, we will illustrate the collision detection with the difference of time to collision point of two vehicles. As depicted in Fig. 5, there are two vehicles running along different directions and meeting in the red area, then the collision will be occurred. Time to collision point (TTCP) and distance to collision point (DTCP) represent the time and distance from the vehicle to collision point respectively. Before calculating TTCP and DTCP, we should determine the collision point, which is a conflict point deduced by two vehicles' trajectories assuming that they will keep going straight [7].

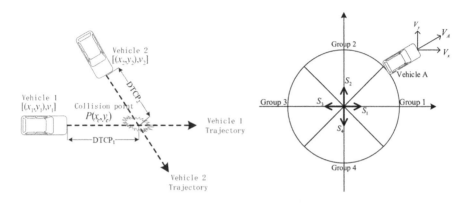

Fig. 5. Illustration of vehicular collision   **Fig. 6.** Illustration of grouping of vehicles

The TTCP can be calculated based on the DTCP and velocity of vehicle which are obtained through the vehicle's sensors by

$$TTCP_1 = \frac{DTCP_1}{v_1} \tag{3}$$

$$TTCP_2 = \frac{DTCP_2}{v_2} \tag{4}$$

where the v_1, v_2 are the velocity of vehicle 1 and vehicle 2. Therefore, the difference of time T_d used to trigger the collision warning is estimated by

$$T_d = |TTCP_1 - TTCP_2| \tag{5}$$

The collision will occur at the intersection, when the T_d satisfies $T_d < \varepsilon$, where ε represents the packets delivery delay in VANETs.

3   Collision Avoidance Routing Algorithm

3.1   Indexes for Next-hop Selection

In urban scenario, the road is usually straight or nearly perpendicular, so the velocity vector of vehicle is depicted by using a Rectangular Plane Coordinates System [9]. Vehicles are classified into four different groups based on their velocity vectors, which are expressed by unit vectors respectively, $S_1 = (1,0)$, $S_2 = (0,1)$, $S_3 = (-1,0)$, $S_4 = (0,-1)$ in Fig. 6. Let $V_A = (V_x, V_y)$ denotes the speed of vehicle A, the vehicle A belongs to Group i, if $V_A \cdot S_i$ takes maximum value. We set up the vehicle driving state function $f(s,n,d)$ under the inspiration of grouping thought, where s, n, d represent the source vehicle, neighbor vehicle and destination vehicle respectively. Let $f(s,n,d)$ denotes the relationship of driving state between vehicles. When HV's state, namely source node's state, is $state_L$ or $state_S$, the driving state function can be defined by

$$f_1(s,n,d) = \begin{cases} 0 & \text{when } s \text{ and } n \text{ own different states} \\ 1 & \text{when } s \text{ and } n \text{ own same state} \end{cases} \tag{6}$$

When the HV's state is $state_R$, the driving state function can be given by

$$f_2(s,n,d) = \begin{cases} 0 & \text{when } d \text{ and } n \text{ own different states} \\ 1 & \text{when } d \text{ and } n \text{ own same state} \end{cases} \tag{7}$$

The state function $f(s,n,d)$ is a prior index of next hop selection. It is not enough to just consider $f(s,n,d)$ when more than one neighbor node makes $f(s,n,d) = 1$. Hence, the distance between vehicles is a crucial factor for next hop selection.

In this paper, assume that $s(x_s, y_s)$ and $n(x_n, y_n)$ are the coordinates of the source vehicle and neighbor vehicle, respectively. The distance between s and n can be expressed as

$$d_{sn} = \sqrt{(x_s - x_n)^2 + (y_s - y_n)^2} \tag{8}$$

Considering the transmission delay, we choose the neighbor node owning the maximum distance as relay node. The angle $\alpha = <\overrightarrow{sn}, \overrightarrow{sd}>$ is also a significant factor besides state function and distance when $f(s,n,d)$ is 0.

3.2 Algorithm Details

In order to preferably illustrate routing selection algorithm for collision warning at the road intersection, we investigate the process of delivering packets in different scenarios in Fig. 7. on the basis of the driving state of vehicle. Further, the scenarios are classified as two categories depending on whether the neighbor vehicle has the same state as the source vehicle or destination vehicle. As shown in Fig. 7, vehicle A and vehicle D(F) represent source node and destination node respectively, other vehicles represent neighbor node.

When vehicle A turns left or go straight in Fig. 7(a), (b), vehicle B owning the same driving state with the vehicle A is chosen as next hop node to relay packets to destination node if there is only one neighbor vehicle owning the same state with vehicle A in R of the vehicle A. If there are more than one vehicles owning the same state with the vehicle A, neighbor node which owns the maximum distance in R is chosen as relay node to transmit packets to destination node. Hence, the prior transmission path of packets from source node to destination

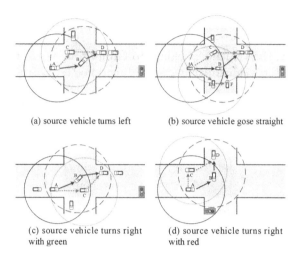

(a) source vehicle turns left   (b) source vehicle gose straight

(c) source vehicle turns right
with green

(d) source vehicle turns right
with red

Fig. 7. Illustration of delivering packets in different scenarios

node is $A \rightarrow B \rightarrow D$ in Fig. 7(a), when the vehicle A turn left. When the vehicle A goes straight, there are two destination nodes (D and F in Fig. 7(b)) located in different collision sets. Therefore, two prior paths are $A \rightarrow B \rightarrow D$ and $A \rightarrow B \rightarrow F$ respectively. In this condition, the vehicle B is used fully to send packets to two vehicles at the same time. However, sometimes there is no the vehicle owning the same state with source node in R, we may consider alternative vehicle to be relay node to transmit packets. The alternative path can be generated on the basis of the angle α and maximum of d_{sn}. In Fig. 7(a), the path $A \rightarrow C \rightarrow D$ is a suboptimal path for transmitting packets to destination node. In Fig. 7(b), the suboptimal paths $A \rightarrow C \rightarrow D$ and $A \rightarrow E \rightarrow F$ are given for different destination nodes.

We will discuss the process of transmission of packets in different traffic light, as the vehicle A is not affected by the traffic light when the vehicle A turns right. In this condition, the vehicle B which owns the same driving state with destination node (vehicle D) is chosen as relay node if only one neighbor node owning the same state with vehicle D in R of vehicle A in Fig. 7(c), (d). When more than one node owning the same state with destination node, the maximum d_{sn} is used for next-hop selection to relay packets to destination node. The path $A \rightarrow B \rightarrow D$ is priority used for transmission packets from source node to destination node. There is no neighbor node which owns the same state with destination node in R, alternative path is consider for transmission of packets on the basis of the angle α and maximum of d_{sn}. The suboptimal path $A \rightarrow C \rightarrow D$ is used for relaying the packets when the prior path does not exist.

Based on the discussion above, we outline the pseudo-code of next hop selection in Algorithm 1. Using Algorithm 1, the source node can obtain the information of destination node in different scenarios such as vehicular ID, speed, location and trajectory etc. and computes the time difference T_d between source

---

Algorithm 1. Next-hop selection routing algorithm

1: **Notation:**
2: s-source node, d-destination node, n-neighbor node, R-transmission range of vehicle
3: r-relay node, α-angle of $\overrightarrow{sr}$ and $\overrightarrow{sd}$, f-driving state function
4: $count$-number of vehicle owning same state as s or d, $state$-travel state of vehicle
5: **if** d in R of s **then**
6:     s relay packets to d to acquire information
7: **else**
8:     **Process**: next hop selection
9: **end if**
10: **Process**: next hop selection
11: **if** $state_s == state_L \| state_s == state_S$ **then**
12:     calculate f_1 by Eq. (6)
13:     $f \leftarrow f_1$
14: **else**
15:     calculate f_2 by Eq. (7)
16:     $f \leftarrow f_2$
17: **end if**
18: **if** $f == 1$ **then**
19:     **if** $count == 1$ **then**
20:         add n as r, relay packets to r to acquire information
21:     **else**
22:         calculate the distance by Eq. (8)
23:         add n of maximum distance as r, relay packets to r to acquire information
24:     **end if**
25: **else**
26:     **if** $\alpha \in [0, \frac{\pi}{2}]$ **then**
27:         calculate the distance by Eq. (8)
28:         add n of maximum distance as r, relay packets to r to acquire information
29:     **else**
30:         carry the packets
31:     **end if**
32: **end if**

---

node and destination node. Compare T_d with ε to determine whether collision will occur between source node and destination node. As show in Algorithm 2, we briefly outline the pseudo-code of vehicular collision avoidance algorithm.

Algorithm 2. Vehicular collision avoidance algorithm

1: /*Initialization*/
2: **Input:** Acquired information about destination node
3: s calculates the difference of time T_d by Eq. (5)
4: **if** $T_d < \varepsilon$ **then**
5:     s sends warning message to d
6: **end if**

---

4   Simulation

4.1   Simulation Parameters

The performance of our proposed collision avoidance routing algorithm is evaluated by NS-2 [2] installed in Ubuntu 16.04. There are 3 nodes $(10 \, \text{m/s}{-}15 \text{m/s})$ in our simulation scenario which is $600 \times 500 \, \text{m}^2$. UDP and CBR are Transport Agent and Application Agent respectively. The Queue length is 50 packets. The simulation time lasts $40 \, \text{s}$.

4.2   Simulation Results and Analysis

The simulation experiments are conducted for comparing with the performance between the paper [10] and our method. In addition, we also simulate the vehicular collision with or without V2V communication to verify our method.

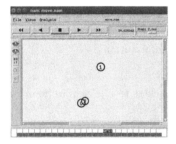

Fig. 8. Collision without V2V communication

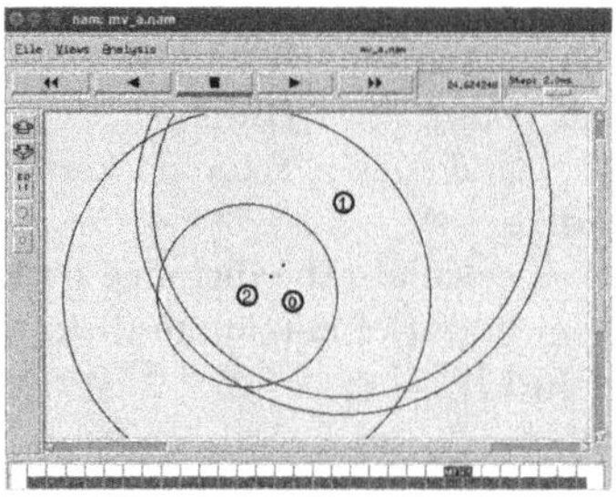

Fig. 9. Collision avoidance with V2V communication

(1) Collision detection: we use simulation tool NS-2 to generate the moving model of vehicles, whose speed is in range of $10 \, \text{m/s}$–$15 \, \text{m/s}$. NS-2 produces a trace file recording the information of packets and NAM file recording the dynamic process of vehicles and packets. As shown in Figs. 8 and 9, they are dynamic display windows to reveal the moving process of vehicles according to NAM file. In two graphs, node 0, node 1, node 2 represent source node, relay node and destination node. We simulate the moving process of nodes without V2V communication in Fig. 8. As the simulation time constantly increases, node 0 and node 2 intersect gradually at the simulation time reaching about 24.62 s. In other words, node 0 and node 2 may collide without V2V communication when simulation time is 24.62 s.

The moving process of nodes with V2V communication is simulated to display in the Fig. 9. Obviously, node 2 eschews node 0 at the same simulation time 24.62 s. Because node 0 can perceive the risk of collision and inform node 2 adjusting speed to avoid the risk of collision through the data packets. The method proposed in this paper can effectively perceive the risk and then take actions to avoid the risk of collision.

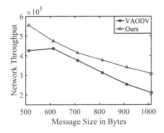

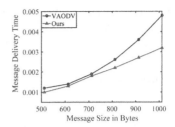

Fig. 10. Throughput at different message size of packets (Color figure online)

Fig. 11. Message delivery time at different message size of packets (Color figure online)

(2) Throughput [6, 10]: as shown in Fig. 10, the graph of the network throughput is given by comparing VAODV with our method at the different message sizes. The blue curve with a circle and red curve with a triangle represent change of network throughput of VAODV and our method respectively. The network throughput is declining as message sizes increases, however, the network throughput of the method in our paper outperforms that of VAODV.

(3) Message delivery time (MDT) [10]: the output curve in Fig. 11. represents the comparison of message delivery time at the different message size in case of VAODV and our method. The blue curve with a circle corresponds to the MDT for VAODV and the red curve with a triangle corresponds to the MDT for our method in this paper. With the message size gradually increasing, the curve of MDT smoothly rises. However, the MDT of our proposed method is shorter than that of VAODV.

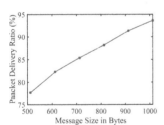

Fig. 12. Packet delivery ratio at different message size of packets (Color figure online)

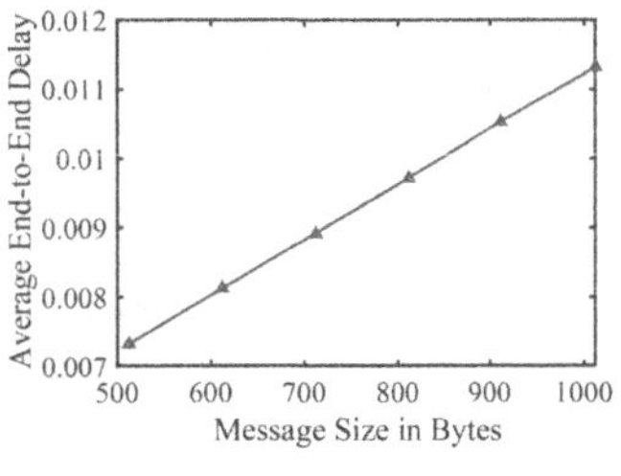

Fig. 13. Average end-to-end delay at different message size of packets (Color figure online)

(4) Packet delivery ratio and average end-to-end delay [6, 10]: those are two important metrics of performance for vehicular ad hoc network. As shown in Figs. 12 and 13, two graphs are displayed to account for the changes in the successful packets reception and end to end delay at the different message sizes. The output red curve with star in Fig. 12. gradually rises as the message size

increases. The packet delivery ratio is close to 95%. The red curve with triangle in Fig. 13. illustrates the behavior of delay with increasing message size. The average end-to-end delay is less than 0.012 when the message size reach 1012.

5 Conclusion

In this paper, a collision avoidance routing algorithm based on V2V communication is proposed, which effectively solves the issue of vehicle collision at urban intersections and improves driving safety. We investigate the collision of urban traffic, classify the collision scenario according to the driving states of vehicles and the status of traffic light. Alternative sets of dynamic collision nodes can be determined by using the remaining time of traffic light. We establish an information acquisition mechanism that takes priority of the driving state function and uses the collision time difference of vehicles to determine whether there is a collision risk between vehicles, thereby achieving collision avoidance. According to the simulation results, the algorithm proposed in this paper can detect the collision risk in advance and avoid collision. At the same time, compared with VAODV, our algorithm has a greater network throughput and shorter message delivery time. In future work, we will focus on research and improvement of collision avoidance algorithms in urban environments.

References

1. Benedetto, F., Calvi, A., D'Amico, F., Giunta, G.: Applying telecommunications methodology to road safety for rear-end collision avoidance. Transp. Res. Part C Emerg. Technol. **50**, 150–159 (2015)
2. Chen, Q., Schmidt-Eisenlohr, F., Jiang, D., Torrent-Moreno, M., Delgrossi, L., Hartenstein, H.: Overhaul of IEEE 802.11 modeling and simulation in NS-2. In: Proceedings of the 10th ACM Symposium on Modeling, Analysis, and Simulation of Wireless and Mobile Systems, pp. 159–168. ACM (2007)
3. Colombo, A., Del Vecchio, D.: Least restrictive supervisors for intersection collision avoidance: a scheduling approach. IEEE Trans. Autom. Control **60**(6), 1515–1527 (2015)
4. Huang, C.M., Lin, S.Y.: Cooperative vehicle collision warning system using the vector-based approach with dedicated short range communication data transmission. IET Intell. Transp. Syst. **8**(2), 124–134 (2014)
5. Li, Y., Zhang, L., Song, Y.: A vehicular collision warning algorithm based on the time-to-collision estimation under connected environment. In: 14th International Conference on Control, Automation, Robotics and Vision (ICARCV), pp. 1–4. IEEE (2016)
6. Roy, D., Das, P.: Collision avoidance protocol for inter vehicular communication. Int. J. Comput. Appl. Technol. Res. **4**(10), 767–776 (2015)
7. Sengupta, R., Rezaei, S., Shladover, S.E., Cody, D., Dickey, S., Krishnan, H.: Cooperative collision warning systems: concept definition and experimental implementation. J. Intell. Transp. Syst. **11**(3), 143–155 (2007)
8. Stanchev, P., Geske, J.: Autonomous cars. History. State of art. Research problems. In: Vishnevsky, V., Kozyrev, D. (eds.) DCCN 2015. CCIS, vol. 601, pp. 1–10. Springer, Cham (2016). https://doi.org/10.1007/978-3-319-30843-2_1

9. Taleb, T., Ochi, M., Jamalipour, A., Kato, N., Nemoto, Y.: An efficient vehicle-heading based routing protocol for VANET networks. In: Wireless Communications and Networking Conference, WCNC 2006, vol. 4, pp. 2199–2204. IEEE (2006)
10. Thangaraj, J., Ravi, B., Kumari, S.: Performance analysis of collision avoidance routing protocol for inter-vehicular communication. Cluster Comput. 1–7 (2017)
11. Wang, Y., Li, F.: Vehicular ad hoc networks. In: Misra, S., Woungang, I., Chandra Misra, S. (eds.) Guide to Wireless Ad Hoc Networks, pp. 503–525. Springer, London (2009). https://doi.org/10.1007/978-1-84800-328-6_20

Embedded Software-Define Radio for Wearable Microware Detection

Yizhi Wu[1,2(✉)], Biao Luo[1,2(✉)], and Hairui Zhu[1,2]

[1] College of Information Science and Technology,
Donghua University, Shanghai, China
yz_wu@dhu.edu.cn, biao_luo@mail.dhu.edu.cn
[2] Engineering Research Center of Digitized Textile and Apparel Technology,
Ministry of Education, Shanghai 201620, China

Abstract. Microwave imaging (MWI) based breast cancer detection has attracted widespread attentions because it has great advantages of non-ionization and low price. However, the current MWI systems require huge and expensive hardware, and complex signal calibration and present substantial challenges to the application of MWI system. For this reason, the embedded MW imaging (E-MWI) method is proposed for breast cancer detection. Firstly, the Software Define Radio (SDR) software is implemented on an embedded platform to reduce cost and miniaturize system. Secondly, an amplitude-based spatial domain confocal algorithm is used in E-MWI system to simplify the system calibration by avoiding signal phase acquisition. To verify the proposed method, experiments platform is set up using the E-MWI prototype system and a liquid breast phantom. The results show that the system successfully detects the target with different sizes.

Keywords: Embedded MW imaging · Software Defined Radio
Confocal algorithm

1   Introduction

Non-refracting electromagnetic attenuation based on electromagnetic attenuation has brought about a medical revolution through computed tomography (CT). Currently, diffraction MW detection has triggered new interest in breast cancer, brain stroke and even blood glucose detection due to its non-ionization and low price [4,9,12].

Most current microwave imaging systems for medical applications are using vector network analyzers (VNA) as the microwave transceiver to generate stable ultra-wideband signals. But the equipment using the VNA is bulky and expensive and is hard to be applied in emergency diagnosis and daily monitoring. To solve

Supported by the Science and technology commission of Shanghai, China (SSTEC). No. 14510711600; the Fundamental Research Funds for Central Universities. No. 17D110417.

that, researchers have made a lot of efforts. Dedicated CMOS integrated circuit for ultra-wideband microwave medical imaging is designed [2,14], but the early-stage cost of CMOS circuit manufacturing is high. The Software Defined Radio (SDR) implements the RF function blocks such as the modulator, waveform generator, demodulator and signal processor in software instead of in hardware and has advantages of fast development for signal processing module, and convenient debugging and maintenance [6]. Recently SDR based MW medial system has been adopted and greatly reduce the cost of the system [7]. But its versatile SDR software is still running in PC/laptop platform, which is prevented the microwave detection systems from being portable and wearable. In this study, we design a low-cost embedded microware imaging (E-MWI) system in which SDR software is transported to run on an ARM based microcontroller to control the MW signal collection implemented in SDR hardware. Instead of using costly and bulky VNA and PC/laptop, the presented E-MWI is not only convenient to be used in empirical medical application, but also is easily embedded in wearable MW based system and thus has good prospect for future application. On the other hand, it is difficult to obtain a stable and continuous phase signal because the phase is random and its very sensitive to device performance [7].

This paper is organized as follows: In Sect. 2, the hardware platform design. A space-domain confocal algorithm is discussed in Sect. 3. Then, the E-MWI based on experimental platform is introduced, and experimental results are discussed in Sect. 4. The Sect. 5 part is the conclusion.

2 System Architecture and Implementation

The E-MWI home monitoring system for breast cancer detection is composed of the embedded SDR based MW signal imaging (E-MWI) subsystem and the space domain confocal algorithm based on MW amplitude signal subsystem running on workstation as shown in Fig. 1.

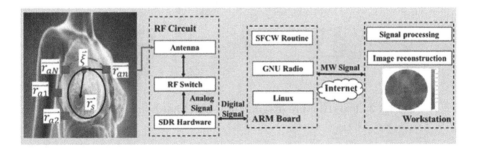

Fig. 1. The architecture of the E-MWI home monitoring system for breast cancer detection

The MW data acquisition is completed by wearable antenna array controlled by RF switch and SDR hardware. The E-MWI system has adopted monostatic method that transmit and receive signals simultaneously with an antenna. When a breast scan recorded begins, a short-duration excitation signal of stepped frequency continuous wave (SFCW) is generated by SFCW routine and SDR software running on top of Linux in ARM board. The stepped sine RF waves with specific baseline offset is amplified and then input into an automated $Nx2$ switching matrix that selects each antenna as the transmitter and each antenna as the receiver in turn. The signal is scattered off of the breast tissues, i.e., at all interfaces between complex breast tissue types, and is then collected by the selected receiving antenna. The received MW signal is then digitized and the amplitude extracted by the SDR and send to the workstation via Internet by network interface integrated in ARM board. The workstation conducted the functions of signal processing and image reconstruction. In practical use, the user starts MW based breast cancer detection, download and check the diagnostic results made by browse his history records by the application on his smart phone.

2.1   E-MWI Hardware System

The SDR hardware is mainly composed of RF transceiver, ARM processor and UWB antenna. Details are shown in Fig. 2.

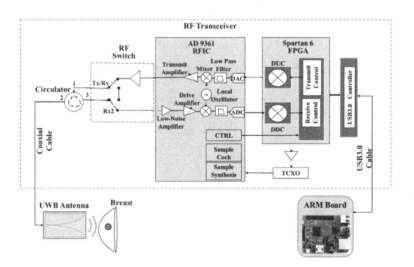

Fig. 2. The structure diagram of E-MWI hardware system

E-MWI RF Transceiver. The E-MWI radio frequency (RF) transceiver consists of a transmitter, a receiver and a controller, which is implemented in a FPGA chip to control the streaming and synchronization of transceivers to send and receive wideband signals via the antenna. The transmitter includes a tunable amplifier, mixer, and an adjustable low pass filter. The receiver includes a low-noise filter, a tunable drive amplifier mixer and low pass filter. In E-MWI, we choose AD9361 RF agility transceiver integrated circuit (RFIC) to transmit excitation RF signal and receive the scatted MW signals with the operating frequency in the 70 MHz to 6.0 GHz [1,3]. On the other hand, Spartan6 FPGA supports 8-bit low-power 3.2G/s serial transmission and 1.2 V core voltage, which is achieved fast transmission and low power requirements of wearable medical devices. Then, a circulator connects Tx and Rx to collect the reflected signal, an RF switch that allows transmitted signals and received signals simultaneously. Moreover, USB3.0 controller and USB3.0 cable integrate the host's power supply and control, performs data acquisition at a very high speed.

E-MWI Controller Board. The typical setup for SDR is running software on a computer to control the SDR hardware [11]. This approach works well for many applications but it is inconvenient for a wearable medical device which is implemented on PC/laptop platform. The single-board computers Raspberry Pi has powerful performance with a 64-bit quad-core, 1.2 GHz ARM Cortex processor in a compact dimension of 85 × 56 × 17 mm. We choose tiny and powerful Raspberry Pi to run GNU Radio. By using USB connectivity and the UHD (USRP Hardware Driver) software, The GNU radio running on the Raspberry Pi can control the RF transceiver to complete the transmission and reception of the MW signal.

Ultra-wideband Antenna. The suitable microwave band for the breast cancer MW detection is reported as 1.5 GHz–6.0 GHz [10]. In our experiment platform, a vivaldi antenna is fabricated and shown in the lower middle of Fig. 3, the geometric parameters of the antenna structure are: length 105 mm, width 90 mm, and thickness 1.28 mm. The antenna return loss is measured by the vector network analyzer is compared with the result of simulation, as shown in Fig. 3. The measured operating frequency is 3 GHz to 5 GHz along the boresight direction. The return loss of the antenna is less than −10 dB in the operating bandwidth, it is fully in line with the standards for antenna production.

2.2 E-MWI Software System

SDR Software. The SDR software provides signal processing blocks to implement radio functions in software. It can be used with specialized radio hardware to capture, analyze, and transmit signals created in software on radio frequencies. We choose the GNU Radio to manipulate the SDR hardware to send and receive MW signals and perform the required signal processing. The GNU radio needs to run on specific Linux version, so it is important to configure the OS on the embedded board.

Embedded OS. Because GNU Radio generally runs on Linux system and the USRP driver UHD (USRP hardware driver) only supports the Linux, the

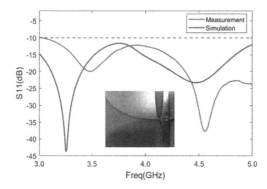

Fig. 3. Reflection coefficient curve of the simulation and measurement

operating system is definitely Linux. In order to make Ubuntu compatible to the Raspberry board, we chose an extended version of Ubuntu Linux 16.04. Firstly, this version has its kernel compiled for the Raspberry CPU, so it saves our work to compile the kernel. This is very important for the GNU Radio internal compiler, because GNU Radio built-in compiler is designed for the X86 hardware platform itself.

SFCW Transceiver. Stepped frequency continuous wave (SFCW) is widely used detection waveform and can be synthesized to wide band signal. A SFCW transceiver routine is designed written in Python in GNU radio, which is composed of a Tx block and a Rx block. The block diagram of the SFCW transceiver based on GNU Radio is shown in Fig. 4. The Tx block is a Signal Source connected to a USRP sink, the Rx block is designed using USRP Source, Stream to Vector, FFT, the three modules are connected in order. Then, a match filter is used between the received signal after FFT and the transmitted baseband signal. Finally, the data is transmitted through UDP Client to workstation. The single tone waveform of SFCW consists of a baseband signal with amplitude and sampling rate, from signal source block connected to USRP sink with Carrier Frequency. The SFCW transceiver is further modified to change the carrier frequency with a step frequency. The received power of SFCW depends on the Tx gain and Rx gain. The received signal stored in the disk of workstation.

3   Imaging Algorithm

3.1   Signal Processing

N is the number of antenna positions $(r_{a1}, \cdots, r_{an}, \cdots, r_{aN})$ as shown in Fig. 1, the E-MWI adopted (f_L, f_H) frequency bandwidth with M frequency points. Then, the frequency domain amplitude data, S_n, of nth antenna position collected by the E-MWI can be represented by the following vector.

$$S_n = [s_n(f_1), \cdots, s_n(f_m), \cdots, s_n(f_M)] \tag{1}$$

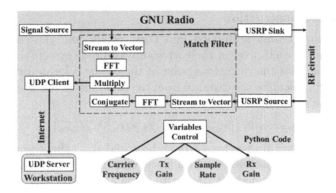

Fig. 4. The block diagram of the SFCW transceiver

Where $f_m = f_L + (m-1) \cdot \frac{f_H - f_L}{M-1}, m \in [1, M]$ is mth frequency point. For imaging, the data S_n is converted into space domain signal. First, we created a space computing domain $D \in (d_L, d_H)$ and discrete I equal parts: $(d_1, ..., d_i, ..., d_I)$, and get the following frequency-space conversion operator.

$$W = \begin{bmatrix} jk_b\left(f_1\right)d_1 & \cdots & jk_b\left(f_M\right)d_1 \\ \vdots & \ddots & \vdots \\ jk_b\left(f_1\right)d_I & \cdots & jk_b\left(f_M\right)d_I \end{bmatrix} \qquad (2)$$

Where $k_b\left(f_m\right) = \frac{2\pi f_m}{c}$ is the spatial wave number, c is free space speed of light. Second, a hamming window is used to attenuate signals on both sides to avoid oscillations in the space-domain.

$$H = \left[h\left(f_1\right), \cdots, h\left(f_m\right), \cdots, h\left(f_M\right)\right]^T \qquad (3)$$

Finally, the spatial signal can be obtained by the following expression.

$$\Gamma_n = exp\left(W\right) \times \left(S_n. \times H\right) \qquad (4)$$

Where Γ_n is the space-domain signal of the nth antenna. The received data contains effective clot reflection signals, but also more strong interference at the skin layer. The energy of these interfering signals is much stronger than that of the tumor, which makes it easy to get artifacts. Therefore, using rotational difference method to eliminate skin interference and common background noise.

$$\Delta_n = \begin{cases} \Gamma_n - \Gamma_N, n = 1 \\ \Gamma_n - \Gamma_{n-1}, n \neq 1 \end{cases} \qquad (5)$$

Where Δ_n is the spatial domain signal difference value of two adjacent antennas, when $n = 1$ the difference between the first antenna and the last antenna.

3.2   Image Reconstruction

The imaging target area is divided into UxV pixels, and the coordinates of the center point of each pixel in the cartesian coordinate system are defined as (x_u, y_v). Assume that the suspicious point of the tumor is located $\boldsymbol{r}_s = (x_p, y_q)$. According to [8], calculate the distance from the radiation to the suspicious point of each antenna's electromagnetic wave.

$$\gamma_n = min \left(\|\boldsymbol{r}_{an} - \boldsymbol{\xi}\| + \|\boldsymbol{r}_{\xi} - \boldsymbol{r}_s\| \cdot \sqrt{\epsilon_{bavg}} \right) \qquad (6)$$

Where $\boldsymbol{\xi}$ is a point on the breast boundary, and ϵ_{bavg} the average dielectric constant of normal breast tissue, which is calculated by the following formula.

Then, the antenna signals of the entire circle array are coherently accumulated and calculated and got the reconstructed image.

$$im\,(x_p, y_q) = \sum_{n=1}^{N} \sum_{d_i=d_1}^{d_I} \Delta_n \cdot 2\gamma_n \qquad (7)$$

Where $im\,(x_p, y_q)$ is the image intensity of suspicious point (x_p, y_q). The results of all antenna responses at the suspicious point have a large sum of coherence and a large concentration of energy. Then, calculating the value of each point $\boldsymbol{r}_s$ on the entire breast. And normalize the result with respect to the maximum value, produce a continuous color image by drawing. The high-intensity color indicates the location of suspected tumor points in the breast.

4   Experimental Setup

The simple liquid breast phantoms are created from a mixture of glycerol, peanut oil and water. According to paper [5,13], the dielectric constant of human breast tissue should satisfy the first-order Debye model $\epsilon_b\,(f) = \epsilon_\infty + \frac{\Delta\epsilon}{1+j2\pi f\tau}$, the average dielectric constant of normal tissues ranges from 4.2 to 4.9, and the tumor tissue is 58–68 at 0–5 GHz. Hence, we constructed two different mixtures: a mixture with an average dielectric constant of $\epsilon_{bavg} = 45$ is packed in a series of graduated cylinders, another mixture with an average dielectric constant of $\epsilon_{tavg} = 65$ is mounted on a large glass beaker with radius of 66 mm, thickness of 1.4 mm and height of 190 mm. Then, we inserted the graduated cylinders into the large glass beaker. Finally, we placed them all on the rotating test platform, and can simulate the different size of the tumor in the breast by adjusting the different size of the graduated cylinders in the glass beaker.

4.1   Data Acquisition

Our microwave experiment system has been described in detail in Sect. 2 and as shown in Fig. 5.

We are explored the bandwidth between 3.0 GHz and 5.0 GHz, in 3.0 MHz and used monostatic configuration mode to synthesized the array signal by rotating the platform, and the distance between the antenna and the glass beaker is 4 mm. We obtained N measurements by rotating the platform in $\left(\frac{360}{N}\right)^\circ$ steps, the acquired data of $N = 32$ with cylinders radius is 12.5 mm as shown in Fig. 6.

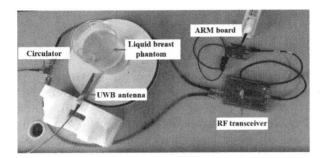

Fig. 5. The experiment platform of E-MWI

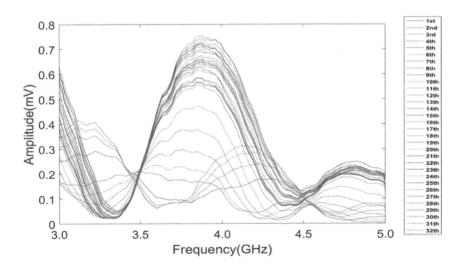

Fig. 6. The data acquired in experimental platform and each curve is the data of the nth antenna

4.2   Experimental Results

The images we obtained after running the amplitude-based confocal algorithm on the acquired data are reported in Fig. 7. The red dashed circle identifies the actual target, while the shaded hue highlights the scattering point detected by the E-MWI.

Figures 7(a) and (b) refer to the case where the radius the measuring cylinder embedded in the large beaker is 12.5 mm. Figures 7(a) and 7(b) are obtained with antenna number $N = 16$ and $N = 32$, respectively. In both case, the tumor can be detected by the constructed image. However, the target offsets more from the actual position in Fig. 7(a) than in Fig. 7(b) an it shows that the positioning is more correct with more antenna. Figure 7(c) and (d) are obtained with cylinder radius of 10 mm, and with the number of antennas $N = 16$ and $N = 32$, respectively. We can find the similar phenomenon still exists. In the above two examples, the E-MWI system can correctly detect the existence of the tumor.

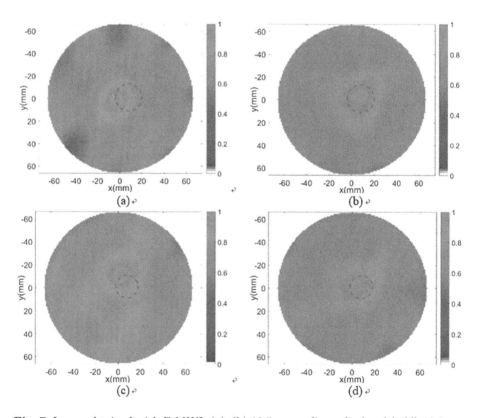

Fig. 7. Image obtained with E-MWI, (a)–(b) 12.5 mm radius cylinder, (c)–(d) 10.0 mm radius cylinder (Color figure online)

5   Conclusion

We designed a simplified and low-cost E-MWI system for breast cancer detection by integrating SDR software into an ARM embedded processor instead of PCs. Moreover, the amplitude-based space-domain confocal imaging is adopted to further simplify both the system hardware and signal acquisition. Finally, our experimental results show that the system is able to correctly detect whether the target exists and gives a position and approximate size with frequency band in 3.0 GHz–5.0 GHz and 32 antennas.

References

1. http://www.analog.com/cn/products/rf-microwave.html
2. Bassi, M., Caruso, M., Bevilacqua, A., Neviani, A.: A 65-nm CMOS 1.75–15 GHz stepped frequency radar receiver for early diagnosis of breast cancer. IEEE J. Solid-State Circuits **48**(7), 1741–1750 (2013)
3. Dubey, A., Vohra, D., Vachhani, K., Rao, A.: Demonstration of vulnerabilities in GSM security with USRP B200 and open-source penetration tools. In: Communications (2016)
4. Guo, L., Abbosh, A.M.: Optimization-based confocal microwave imaging in medical applications. IEEE Trans. Antennas Propag. **63**(8), 3531–3539 (2015)
5. Lazebnik, M., et al.: A large-scale study of the ultrawideband microwave dielectric properties of normal, benign and malignant breast tissues obtained from cancer surgeries. Phys. Med. Biol. **52**(10), 6093–6115 (2007)
6. Marimuthu, J., Bialkowski, K.S., Abbosh, A.M.: Stepped frequency continuous wave software defined radar for medical imaging. In: Antennas and Propagation Society International Symposium, pp. 1909–1910 (2014)
7. Marimuthu, J., Bialkowski, K.S., Abbosh, A.M.: Software-defined radar for medical imaging. IEEE Trans. Microw. Theor. Tech. **64**(2), 643–652 (2016)
8. Mobashsher, A.T., Bialkowski, K.S., Abbosh, A.M., Crozier, S.: Design and experimental evaluation of a non-invasive microwave head imaging system for intracranial haemorrhage detection. PLoS ONE **11**(4), e0152351 (2016)
9. Mohammed, B.J., Abbosh, A.M., Mustafa, S., Ireland, D.: Microwave system for head imaging. IEEE Trans. Instrum. Meas. **63**(1), 117–123 (2013)
10. Nepote, M.S., Herrera, D.R., Tapia, D.F., Latif, S., Pistorius, S.: A comparison study between horn and vivaldi antennas for 1.5–6 GHz breast microwave radar imaging. In: European Conference on Antennas and Propagation, pp. 59–62 (2014)
11. Patton, L.K.: A GNU radio based software-defined radar (2007)
12. Persson, M., Fhager, A., Trefna, D.T., Yu, Y.: Microwave-based stroke diagnosis making global prehospital thrombolytic treatment possible. IEEE Trans. Biomed. Eng. **61**(11), 2806–2817 (2014)
13. Ruvio, G., Solimene, R., D'Alterio, A., Ammann, M.J., Pierri, R.: RF breast cancer detection employing a noncharacterized vivaldi antenna and a music-inspired algorithm. Int. J. RF Microw. Comput. Aided Eng. **23**(5), 598–609 (2013)
14. Tan, K.W., Lo, A.H., Chu, T.S., Hsu, S.S.H.: A k-band reconfigurable pulse-compression automotive radar transmitter in 90-nm cmos. IEEE Trans. Microw. Theor. Tech. **63**(4), 1380–1387 (2015)

Group Based Immunization Strategy on Networks with Nonlinear Infectivity

Chandni Saxena$^{(\boxtimes)}$, M. N. Doja, and Tanvir Ahmad

Department of Computer Engineering, Jamia Millia Islamia, New Delhi 110025, India
cmooncs@gmail.com, mdoja@jmi.ac.in, tahmad2@jmi.ac.in

Abstract. Misinformation diffusion on network and its adverse effects are stimulus factors in designing efficient immunization strategies. We aim to study the node inoculation in the network which is exposed to nonlinear rumor propagation. In order to delimit the contagion on network the group based centrality is considered to order nodes according to their positional power and functional influence in the network. In the process of propagation dynamics, the strength of a node can be determined by the aspect of its connectivity to the other nodes in the network and the flow of contagion through edges depends on the strength of its two end nodes. Therefore, it is pertinent to study effect of immunization on network when misinformation propagation varies with tie strength between nodes. This paper considers degree dependent node strength which varies for every contact and determines nonlinear infectivity on the network. The competence of our proposed method can be established on empirical data sets which determines its adequacy to delimit rumor spread.

Keywords: Node inoculation · Nonlinear rumor propagation
Node strength · Group based centrality

1 Introduction

A large range of real world complex systems can be characterized as the complex networks of its components as nodes and their relationships as links. Dynamics associated with these networks can be studied as the topological evolution of networks under node-link dynamics and spreading on the networks as events of epidemic outbreak, opinion formation, rumor spread and viral marketing [6]. Investigating the dynamics of spread and the control of spread on complex networks has gained a momentous recognition in recent years due to its significance in finding assistance to the threat of propagation of virus, rumor or any misinformation over the network [15]. Modeling epidemiology plays an imperative role to design compelling control strategy and as a possible solution to these challenges. The SIR [6] spreading model is predominantly used to introduce rumor propagation on complex network. The recognized rumor model by Daley and Kendall (DK) [3] and another derived model by Maki-Thompson (MK) [10]

© Springer Nature Switzerland AG 2018
X. Chen et al. (Eds.): CSoNet 2018, LNCS 11280, pp. 162–173, 2018.
https://doi.org/10.1007/978-3-030-04648-4_14

have been the most general framework to investigate rumor-spread and its mathematical model on the networks. In this framework of rumor model, the network nodes are divided in one of the three states as ignorant (who has not notices the rumor yet), as spreader (who has confronted rumor and can spread that) and as strifler (who has confronted the rumor and choose not to spread that).The spreading can be characterized from initial sources to the neighboring nodes following Interactive Markov Chain (IMC) framework in the network. The nodes in network communicate among themselves and follow state transitions under the consequences of infecting rate λ, stifling rate σ, and recovery rate δ, which follow probabilistic behavior. In DK model when a spreader meets an adjacent ignorant, the ignorant transits state to spreader with probabilistic rule λ and when a spreader confronts another spreader or another stifler, the initiating spreader transits its state to stifler with probabilistic rule σ. In MK model an initiating spreader changes its state only when it meets an adjacent spreader and becomes stifler. Nekovee et al. [13] suggested that particular node spreader can stop spreading exclusively with recovery rate δ and transits to stifler state. Singh and Singh [19] considered a model where the state transition rates λ and σ varies for every contact and depends on interacting nodes. In general, there are two aids of controlling the transmission of rumor or misinformation: one method deals with transfiguring the network topology [14] and other is to mediate intervention strategies such as random and target immunization [16]. The process of immunization challenges the spread propagation on above defined rules and aims to design possible control strategy against rumor contagion. Targeted immunization is the control strategy to select nodes and inoculate some fraction of it to prevent further outbreak. There are different centrality measurements that rank the nodes and identify them for immunization scheme. The prevailing topology based centrality methods are based on degree, betweenness, closeness, eigenvector centrality etc. These methods are based upon individual characteristics of the nodes however group based centrality introduced by Everett and Borgatti [4] considers the ensemble effect of the criteria effectively for a set of nodes formed as group. The group based centrality provides a measure as combined effect of the participating entities (nodes here) in the group. In this paper, we aim to study the spread mitigation built on group based centrality on nonlinear rumor spreading model. A game theoretic formulation of Shapley value redivides the group based centrality among nodes as a function of its marginal input to the all possible groups. Our recently proposed metric SVIDA (Shapley Value based Information Delimiters in adaptive formulation) [17] is a group based centrality measure which can effectively immunize the network against contagion set up on SIR spreading model. In the present work we propose to investigate the effect of immunization based on SVIDA on nonlinear spread of misinformation propagation [19] build upon the tie strength as a function of the degrees of two end nodes.

In the subsequent Sect. 2 related studies are reported. Section 3 introduces group based centrality and describe its efficient computation. A nonlinear rumor spread model which determines the non-constant rate of states transition is described in Sect. 4. Section 5 points up evaluation metrics and experimental setup. Section 6 reviews the performance of proposed centrality in regards to existing methods using empirical data sets and Sect. 7 concludes the paper.

2   Related Work

Node immunization targeted to inhibit rumor or misinformation propagation in the network is to determine and amputate a set of nodes based on their importance in the network. A considerably effective criteria is to select immunization strategies based on structural importance of the nodes on various norms, such as degree and betweenesss. The degree based immunization strategies categorically select nodes based on the number of its immediate neighboring nodes [11]. It can be grouped based on selecting leaps of the neighbors and can be divided further based on targeted immunization [16] and based on acquaintance immunization approaches [2]. Other nodes importance metrics such as k-core [1] rely on the importance of nodes topological location and eigenvector centrality [7] is based on influences of neighboring nodes. However these criteria are important to ascertain the nodes structural features, but they do not aim to set up optimal solution to the issue of node immunization for information delimitation. Whereas, SVID [17] aims to assign nodes rank based upon its target role in immunization. The community based strategies [21] rely on community level structural information to detect leading nodes for immunization objective. With known structural information of nodes on community level, a balance of bridging and hub score is assigned to the nodes based on their inter and intra community connections. For network with non overlapping community structure connector-hubs can be detected using community level information [5]. For network with overlapping community structure with information of overlapping nodes among communities, the immediate neighbors of these nodes in communities [8] are expected to be community hubs and can be selected for immunization targets. Other analogous approaches to node immunization are based on spectral theoretic technique in graph [20] and dynamic activities of the nodes [9].

3   Group Based Centrality

The group based centrality (SVID) [17] targets to the issue of information delimitation in complex network. It is based on the game theoretic solution concept of Shapley value in cooperative games. This session introduces an overview of Shapley value [18] concept and its efficient computation for information delimitation problem. The Shapley value based coalition game is defined on the graph G having $N = \{p_1, p_2...p_{|N|}\}$ set of players of game and $\vartheta : 2^{(G)} \to \mathbb{R}$ denotes characteristic function which signifies the value created as a result of the nodes unions C formed where $C \subset N$ with $\vartheta(\varnothing) = 0$. A game for coalition N and characteristic function ϑ is defined as a tuple $\langle N, \vartheta \rangle$. We denote a graph G with $V(G)$ and $E(G)$ as nodes and edges respectively, where coalition C of nodes as players of game denotes any subset of $V(G)$. The main exploration of Shapley value is to assign the dividend attained as value created by group (coalition) formed to individual players or nodes. This is achieved by the criteria of marginal contribution in Shapley value as weighted average of payoff for a player that participates in all possible groups formed.

3.1 Shapley Value

The Shapley value of a player p_i is the marginal contribution that it makes to all the possible coalitions C given by:

$$\Theta(p_i) = \sum_{C \subseteq N \setminus \{p_i\}} \frac{|C|!(|N| - |C| - 1)!}{|N|!} [\vartheta(C \cup \{p_i\}) - \vartheta(C)]$$

The Shapley value fulfills the criteria of efficiency, symmetry, null player and additivity as explained in [18]. Next, we define estimated computation of the game (SVID) for information delimitation formulated on the concept of probabilistic approach of the solution as proposed by Michalak et al. [12].

3.2 SVID

We observe the game on unweighted and undirected network. The rationale behind objective criteria for the game of information delimiters is to find those players (nodes) whose elimination could increase the short term distances among remaining nodes of the network or decrease the count of distinct paths among nodes. Lesser the common neighborhood overlap, lower would be the possibility of alternative paths among nodes and increased distance among nodes would make infection die out quickly and this target could be achieved if we are aiming to find hubs and connector nodes. For any coalition C a node u would marginally contribute a neighbor v: in case one u, v are present in different connected component of the graph and have they have no neighbors in common, in case two both are connected and have an edge in common with K neighbors overlap. In case one the marginal contribution is 1 for the other case we define the probabilistic approach to find the desired number of permutations for such contribution. The precondition for node u is to join the coalition before its neighbor v and all the common neighbors of u, v must join after them. Therefore for K common neighbors between two nodes u and v, the requirement for positive contribution of node u to node v can be devised with given estimation of Shapley value:

$$\Theta(v) = \sum_{neighbors_v} \frac{1}{(K + 1)(K + 2)} \tag{1}$$

Where $K = neighbors_u \cap neigbhors_v$ and nodes u and v are linked by an edge. The above estimate of Shapley value can be established with following explanation:

(1) If we select K+2 positions in the line-up of v and u and their common neighbors K from a nodes N. The number of such selection can be done in $^N C_{K+2}$ ways.

Algorithm 1. SVID Adaptive algorithm

Input: Unweighted, undirected graph $G(V, E)$
Output: Shapley values of all nodes

1 **for** *each edge $e \in E(G)$* **do**
2   Remove the edge e connecting u and v from G
3      $S_v \leftarrow$ Nodes reachable from v upto one hop
4      $S_u \leftarrow$ Nodes reachable from u upto one hop
5      $K \leftarrow |S_v \cap S_u|$
6      $\Theta(u) + = \frac{1}{(K+1)(K+2)}$
7      $\Theta(v) + = \frac{1}{(K+1)(K+2)}$

8 delimiters $\leftarrow 0$; A $\leftarrow 0$; $k \leftarrow$ no. of top nodes
9 **for** *1 to k* **do**
10   **if** *not all nodes are immunized* **then**
11   top nodes $\leftarrow argmax_{v \notin delimetes}\{\Theta(v)\}$
12   delimiters $\leftarrow delimiters \cup \{topnodes\}$
13   A $\leftarrow$ A$\cup\{topnodes\}$
14   **for** *each $u \in N_{topnode}(G)$* **do**
15              $v \leftarrow N_u(G)$
16   **for** *each edge(u,v) and $K \leftarrow |S_u \cap S_v|$* **do**
17                  $\Theta(v) - = \frac{1}{(K+1)(K+2)}$

18   **else**
19   select a node $i \notin$ A with highest $\Theta(i)$ and add to A

20 **return** *(A containing top k delimiters)*

---

(2) u and v are to join the coalition prior to their common neighbors, therefore K picked positions are for common neighbors along with two positions occupied by u and v before them. $K!$ is such number of selections.
(3) The remaining components can be appointed in $(|N| - (K + 2))!$ ways.
(4) Total number of corresponding permutations are:

$$^{N}C_{K+2}(K!)(|N| - (K + 2))! = \frac{|N|!}{(K + 1)(K + 2)}$$

(5) The likelihood of occurrence of one of such permutations is $\frac{1}{(K+1)(K+2)}$

SVIDA (Algorithm 1) is a motivating criteria for immunization as it gives highest scores to the bridge nodes who has no or less edges among its neighbors therefore $1/(K + 1)(K + 2)$ takes up maximal value. It also tend to value hub nodes as well due to aggregated sum of neighbors contributions to the score. We consider the adaptive version of the Shapley value and remove the neighboring nodes of the target nodes selected with their contribution to the values of the top ranked target nodes. The Shapley value formulated as given in [17] assigns high rank order for the target nodes selected for immunization and adaptive SVID is entitled as SVIDA.

4   Nonlinear Rumor Spreading Model

We consider to investigate the rumor spreading model with non linear propagation of infection and stifling interactions of the nodes based on degree dependent edge strength proposed in [19]. In classical SIR model on the nodes population of network considered for rumor propagation, nodes are in one of the three state: ignorant, spreader and stifler. The ignorant node changes its state to spreader when it communicates with adjacent spreader at rate λ. The spreader node changes its state to stifler when it communicates with stifler neighbor at rate σ. The spreader node can change its state to stifler when it communicates with adjacent spreader at rate σ. The spreader node can also change its state to stifler according to rate δ. The rumor propagation and nodes interactions can be explained from Fig. 1. Considering expected values of ignorant, spreader and stifler population in the network at time t with degree k as: $I_k(t)$, $S_k(t)$ and $R_k(t)$. We analyze time evolution density for ignorant, spreader and stifler at time t with degree k as:

$$i_k(t) = \frac{I_k(t)}{N_k}; \quad s_k(t) = \frac{S_k(t)}{N_k}; \quad r_k(t) = \frac{R_k(t)}{N_k}$$

Where N_k is number of nodes in the network having degree k and $i_k(t) + s_k(t) + r_k(t) = 1$ holds true for degree k at time t. Considering complex networks to formulate interactive Markov chains with following set of differential equations:

$$\frac{di_k(t)}{dt} = -k \, i_k(t) \, \omega_1(t) \, \frac{\phi(l)}{l} \, \lambda_{lk}, \tag{2}$$

$$\frac{ds_k(t)}{dt} = k \, i_k(t) \, \omega_1(t) \, \frac{\phi(l)}{l} \, \lambda_{lk} \; - \; k \, s_k(t) \, \omega_2(t) \, \frac{\phi(l)}{l} \, \sigma_{lk} \; - \; \delta s_k(t) \tag{3}$$

$$\frac{dr_k(t)}{dt} = k \, s_k(t) \, \omega_2(t) \, \frac{\phi(l)}{l} \, \sigma_{lk} + \delta s_k(t) \tag{4}$$

Where $\omega_1(t) = \sum_l P(l|k) \, s_k(t)$ and $\omega_2(t) = \sum_l (s_k(t) + r_k(t)) \, P(l|k)$.

The network here considered to have no degree-degree correlation and $P(l|k)$ is the conditional probability for a node with degree l to connect with a node with degree k which is proportional to $\frac{lP(l)}{\langle k \rangle}$, where $P(l)$ denotes the degree distribution and $\langle k \rangle$ stands for mean degree of the network. The rumor spreadness of a node is considered as a function of its degree and given by $\phi(k) = k^\alpha$, where α is a infectivity parameter and grows with degree k. It determines that a spreader might contact with k^α adjacent nodes in a time interval, where $0 < \alpha \leqslant 1$. The spread transmission rate λ_{lk} is inconstant unlike λ and regarded as a function of connected nodes with degree l and k. Where $\lambda_{lk} = \lambda k^\beta \xi$ and $\xi = \frac{\langle k \rangle}{\langle k^{1+\beta} \rangle}$. The transmission exponent parameter β determines the inconstant nature of λ_{lk} such as: for $\beta > 0$ the higher degree neighbor receive the rumor, for $\beta < 0$ the lower neighbor receives it and for $\beta = 0$ the transmission of rumor is independent of nodes degree. Similarly, the stifling rate σ_{lk} also varies and with degrees

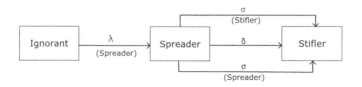

Fig. 1. Rumor propagation model

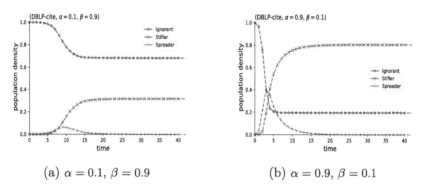

(a) $\alpha = 0.1$, $\beta = 0.9$ (b) $\alpha = 0.9$, $\beta = 0.1$

Fig. 2. The population density of ignorant, spreader and stifler with time, for simulation of rumor dynamics on DBLP-cite data set with tuning parameters $\alpha = 0.1$, $\beta = 0.9$ and $\alpha = 0.9$, $\beta = 0.1$, other parameters $\lambda = 0.75$, $\sigma = 0.15$, $\delta = 0.10$ are same for both simulations.

of contacting nodes l and k. The population density of ignorant, spreader and stifler in Dblp-cite data time plotted for tuning parameters $\alpha = 0.1$, $\beta = 0.9$ and $\alpha = 0.9$, $\beta = 0.1$ Fig. 2.

5   Experimental Setup

5.1   Data Sets

To evaluate effectiveness of SVIDA on nonlinear rumor dynamic as described in Sect. 6, we consider four empirical network data sets[1,2]. This work employs undirected and unweighted construction of all data sets. The statistical features of these data sets are given in Table 1. We consider FXM2-6 network dataset used for linear programming problem. Powergrid (Power-Grid) is an undirected network and it represents information about the power grid from Western States of USA. The edge in graph represents a power supply line and a node is either a transformer, a generator or a substation of the power-grid. Dblp-cite (DBLP-cite) represent a citation network of dblp which is a database of collection for scientific publications. A node represents a publication such as a book or a paper

---

[1] http://konect.uni-koblenz.de/networks/.
[2] http://networkrepository.com.

and each directed edge represents the citation of the publication by another publication. Digg is a communication network on the social news website Digg. A node in graph denotes a user of the website and an edge represents a communication reply from one user to another.

5.2   Performance Metric

In order to evaluate the competence of SVIDA we consider the performance of immunization process on four empirical data sets and analyze the same with benchmark immunization strategies. We consider immunization strategies based on Adaptive degree, betweenness, k-core and eigen vector centrality termed as DA, BWA, CNA and EVA in order. We simulate rumor dynamics with nonlinear infect rate and immunize network at q fractions of nodes selected due to SVIDA ranking. The fraction of infected nodes decreases as immunization faction of delimiters increases. The final absolute size of rumor $|r|$ at steady state with fraction q of immunized nodes signifies the effectiveness of immunization strategy. The fraction of size of giant connected cluster gcc (f) testifies the importance of nodes for the connectivity of network when the size of gcc reduces as a result of fraction of nodes (q) removal in the process of immunization.

6   Results and Analysis

To anticipate the efficacy of proposed strategy, four network data sets with given statistical features are studied (Table 1). The alternative strategies as DA, BWA, CNA and EVA are considered to compare the performance of SVIDA when fraction of gcc f is plotted with fraction of immunized nodes q as shown in Fig. 3. For FXM2-6 network Fig. 3(a) SVIDA is smaller than DA, BWA, CNA and EVA by 35%, 44%, 50%, and 54% respectively and takes ≈42% of nodes to remove for the network to collapse. In case of Power-Grid network Fig. 3(b), DA and SVIDA both require ≈35% of node removal for the loss of giant component however SVIDA shows up the advancement of 11% and 14% over DA and BWA. For DBLP-cite network Fig. 3(c), DA takes ≈25% node to amputate for loss of giant component and SVIDA takes ≈27% for the same. However, SVIDA

Table 1. Basic statistical characteristics of the empirical data sets having the number of network nodes and network edges, the average degree $\langle k \rangle$ and the average clustering coefficient c for the graph.

Networks	Nodes	Edges	$\langle k \rangle$	c
FXM2-6	2,845	12,812	9.0	0.0004
Power-Grid	4,951	6,594	2.6	0.0801
DBLP-cite	12,591	49,620	7.9	0.1168
Digg	30,398	85,155	5.6	0.0053

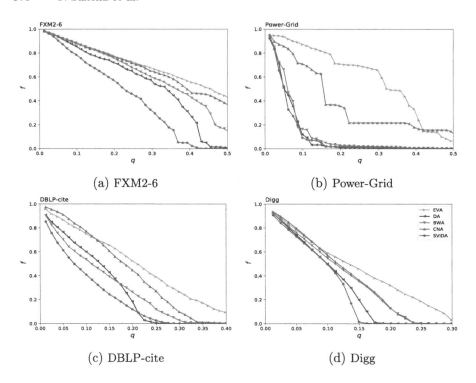

(a) FXM2-6   (b) Power-Grid

(c) DBLP-cite   (d) Digg

Fig. 3. The fraction of largest connected component nodes f vs fraction of removed nodes q.

informs advancements of 19%, 15%, 37% and 41% on DA, BWA, CNA and EVA in that order. For Digg network Fig. 3(d) SVIDA generates the lowest size of largest connected component for all proportions of the immunized nodes and achieves improvements of 18%, 34%, 35% and 44% from DA, BWA, CNA and EVA in that order. In order to estimate immunization on rumor dynamics with nonlinear infect propagation, the size of rumor $|r|$ in network against fraction of immunized population q can be examined from Fig. 4. The size of $|r|$ at steady state of the dynamics is investigated until no more spreader nodes appear in the network. Consider $\alpha = 0.9$, $\beta = 0.1$ and $\alpha = 0.1$, $\beta = 0.9$ as two frontier value sets of tuning parameters for nonlinear propagation and contagion variability in the network. The infection probability is $\lambda = 0.75$, stifling probability rate is $\sigma = 0.15$ and recovery probability rate is $\delta = 0.10$ in both cases. Immunizing high degree nodes lowers the density of network which can effect the range of infection. If nodes with high betweenness centrality are immunized, they tend to cut down the numbers of alternative routes among other nodes and hence affect contagion propagation. Nodes with highest coreness lie is the vital topological configuration hence immunizing them can bring useful criteria to isolate core from loosely connected periphery in network. Eigen vector centrality detects nodes with higher influence and removing them can effect transmission of spread.

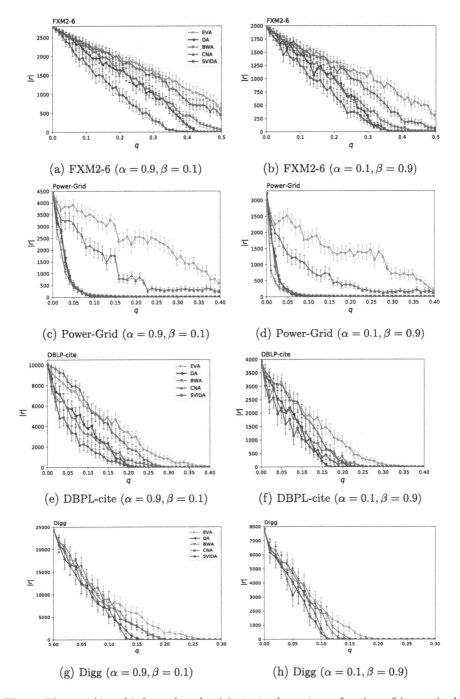

(a) FXM2-6 ($\alpha = 0.9, \beta = 0.1$)

(b) FXM2-6 ($\alpha = 0.1, \beta = 0.9$)

(c) Power-Grid ($\alpha = 0.9, \beta = 0.1$)

(d) Power-Grid ($\alpha = 0.1, \beta = 0.9$)

(e) DBPL-cite ($\alpha = 0.9, \beta = 0.1$)

(f) DBPL-cite ($\alpha = 0.1, \beta = 0.9$)

(g) Digg ($\alpha = 0.9, \beta = 0.1$)

(h) Digg ($\alpha = 0.1, \beta = 0.9$)

Fig. 4. The number of informed nodes $|r|$ at steady state vs fraction of immunized portion q of the network population for ($\alpha = 0.9, \beta = 0.1$) and ($\alpha = 0.1, \beta = 0.9$)

SVIDA is a motivating norm for immunization as it gives highest scores to the bridge nodes accounted to be hub nodes as well. With $\alpha = 0.9$, $\beta = 0.1$ we plot $|r|$ vs q for 100 simulation runs. We plot errors due to standard deviation of $|r|$ values for same value of q along with mean values of $|r|$ Fig. 4(a), (c), (e), (g). We find that SVIDA performs fairly good in terms of fraction of nodes require to cease the spread is lower as compare to all benchmark strategies. With $\alpha = 0.1$, $\beta = 0.9$ Fig. 4(b), (d), (f), (h) represent the similar results. In case of $\alpha = 0.9$ the spreading node gets more numbers of neighbors to infect due to high value for rumor spreadness $\phi = k^{\alpha}$, therefore it requires comparatively more fraction of nodes to remove to block contagion. Where as for $\alpha = 0.1$ requires lesser size of immunized fraction for the same. The SVIDA outplays in overall performance, DA and BWA show up next significant criteria.

7   Conclusion

We have investigated the proposed group based centrality for immunization strategy with order for the nodes according to the scores assigned by SVIDA. Using benchmark strategies for comparison with proposed method, we measure performance on the bases of low gcc size in the movement of node removal. The SVIDA established a denoting performance improvement upon comparable benchmark strategies. We speculated the nonlinear rumor dynamics on network and employed immunization according to the nodes centrality scores. The SVIDA demonstrated its effectiveness as scoring lowest size overall of rumor in network with immunization progress. Due to its fair balance in selecting hubs and connectors for immunization strategy our method outperforms the benchmark strategies. Configuring estimation of Shapley value for directed and weighted networks as extension can be progressed for this work. The nonlinear dynamic propagation based on varied topological criteria of nodes strength could be another interesting direction to explore for immunization approach.

References

1. Carmi, S., Havlin, S., Kirkpatrick, S., Shavitt, Y., Shir, E.: A model of internet topology using k-shell decomposition. Proc. Natl. Acad. Sci. **104**(27), 11150–11154 (2007)
2. Cohen, R., Havlin, S., Ben-Avraham, D.: Efficient immunization strategies for computer networks and populations. Phys. Rev. Lett. **91**(24), 247901 (2003)
3. Daley, D.J., Kendall, D.G.: Stochastic rumours. IMA J. Appl. Math. **1**(1), 42–55 (1965)
4. Everett, M.G., Borgatti, S.P.: The centrality of groups and classes. J. Math. Sociol. **23**(3), 181–201 (1999)
5. Ghalmane, Z., Hassouni, M.E., Cherifi, H.: Immunization of networks with non-overlapping community structure. arXiv preprint arXiv:1806.05637 (2018)
6. Guille, A., Hacid, H., Favre, C., Zighed, D.A.: Information diffusion in online social networks: a survey. ACM SIGMOD Record **42**(2), 17–28 (2013)

7. Khansari, M.: Centrality measures for immunization of weighted networks. Netw. Biol. **6**(1), 12 (2016)
8. Kumar, M., Singh, A., Cherifi, H.: An efficient immunization strategy using overlapping nodes and its neighborhoods. In: Companion of the the Web Conference 2018 on the Web Conference 2018, pp. 1269–1275. International World Wide Web Conferences Steering Committee (2018)
9. Li, X., Guo, J., Gao, C., Zhang, L., Zhang, Z.: A hybrid strategy for network immunization. Chaos Solitons Fractals **106**, 214–219 (2018)
10. Maki, D.P., Thompson, M.: Mathematical models and applications: with emphasis on the social life, and management sciences. Technical report (1973)
11. Mehta, A., Mukhoty, B., Gupta, R.: Controlling spread of rumor using neighbor centrality. Acta Physica Polonica B **47**(10), 2325–2339 (2016)
12. Michalak, T.P., Aadithya, K.V., Szczepanski, P.L., Ravindran, B., Jennings, N.R.: Efficient computation of the shapley value for game-theoretic network centrality. J. Artif. Intell. Res. **46**, 607–650 (2013)
13. Nekovee, M., Moreno, Y., Bianconi, G., Marsili, M.: Theory of rumour spreading in complex social networks. Phys. A Stat. Mech. Appl. **374**(1), 457–470 (2007)
14. Pan, Z.f., Wang, X.f., Li, X.: Simulation investigation on rumor spreading on scale-free network with tunable clustering. J. Syst. Simul. **18**(8), 2346–2348 (2006)
15. Pastor-Satorras, R., Castellano, C., Van Mieghem, P., Vespignani, A.: Epidemic processes in complex networks. Reviews of modern physics **87**(3), 925 (2015)
16. Pastor-Satorras, R., Vespignani, A.: Immunization of complex networks. Phys. Rev. E **65**(3), 036104 (2002)
17. Saxena, C., Doja, M., Ahmad, T.: Group based centrality for immunization of complex networks. Phys. A Stat. Mech. Appl. **508**, 35–47 (2018)
18. Shapley, L.S., Shubik, M.: A method for evaluating the distribution of power in a committee system. Am. Polit. Sci. Rev. **48**(3), 787–792 (1954)
19. Singh, A., Singh, Y.: Nonlinear spread of rumor and inoculation strategies in the nodes with degree dependent tie strength in complex networks. Acta Physica Polonica B **44**, 5 (2013)
20. Tariq, J., Ahmad, M., Khan, I., Shabbir, M.: Scalable approximation algorithm for network immunization. arXiv preprint arXiv:1711.00784 (2017)
21. Yamada, Y., Yoshida, T.: A comparative study of community structure based node scores for network immunization. In: Huang, R., Ghorbani, A.A., Pasi, G., Yamaguchi, T., Yen, N.Y., Jin, B. (eds.) AMT 2012. LNCS, vol. 7669, pp. 328–337. Springer, Heidelberg (2012). https://doi.org/10.1007/978-3-642-35236-2_33

Question Understanding in Community-Based Question Answering Systems

Phuc H. Duong[1], Hien T. Nguyen[1(✉)], and Hao T. Do[2]

[1] Artificial Intelligence Laboratory, Faculty of Information Technology,
Ton Duc Thang University, Ho Chi Minh City, Vietnam
{duonghuuphuc,nguyenthanhhien}@tdtu.edu.vn
[2] NewAI Research, Ho Chi Minh City, Vietnam
hao.do@newai.vn

Abstract. In this paper, we propose a novel method for community-based question answering task. The proposed method takes advantage of the bidirectional long short-term memory to represent questions and answers in combination with an attention mechanism. The attention model based on a multilayer perceptron captures important information in questions and their candidate sentences. We conduct experiments on public datasets, published by SemEval workshop. The experimental results show that our method achieves state-of-the-art performance.

Keywords: Answer selection · Community-based question answering

1 Introduction

Question answering is one of important tasks in natural language processing that automatically retrieves information to answer a given question. QA systems can be categorized into (1) closed-domain and (2) open-domain. A closed-domain QA system only deals with questions under a specific domain, *e.g.*, medical, space science. Since exploiting information from domain-specific knowledge sources, closed-domain QA systems are considered to be easier than open-domain QA systems. In contrast, an open-domain QA system deals with questions about anything and the data size is growing rapidly. An instance of open-domain QA system is community-based question answering (CQA). CQA is a crowd sourcing service, in which users can pose their questions and get answers from community. There are some advantages and disadvantages of CQA systems. On positive side, in CQA systems, users can freely ask questions about anything, and can inspect the data from community to find useful answers. On negative side, there are plenty of similar questions to the given ones, which have been already answered. Therefore, users either waste time to find answers or wait other users answer their questions. In order to address this problem, in this paper, we propose a

© Springer Nature Switzerland AG 2018
X. Chen et al. (Eds.): CSoNet 2018, LNCS 11280, pp. 174–185, 2018.
https://doi.org/10.1007/978-3-030-04648-4_15

method which scores candidate answers corresponding to a given question in CQA systems.

There have been many studies on QA and CQA systems, but the model presented by Ferrucci *et al.* [1] has become a widely adopted one. In [1], the proposed DeepQA architecture has an answer selection component, which is our focus in this study. This component is designed for open-domain QA systems, and is described as follows: given a question and a list of candidate sentences, the system will retrieve and return sentences which can answer the question. To illustrate this task, we take an example extracted from SemEval-2016 Task 3 [2] dataset:

- Q: *How long can I drive in Qatar with my international driver's permit ...?*
- A_1: *I think it depends on where your original drivers license is from.*
- A_2: *Is any member of this site is working with QP? How is their work culture?*

In this example, A_1 is a good sentence that can answer the question, but A_2 is not. In reality, in order to return relevance sentences to a given question, we need to assess much information, for instance, meta-data. For example, in SemEval datasets, besides questions and answers, they also include some meta-data, *i.e.*, date, user, and topic. Therefore, a QA system can take advantage of these information to assess the relevance between a question and its candidate sentences. However, in this study, instead of exploiting these meta-data, we propose a method which combines artificial neural networks with neural attention mechanism to represent both questions and answers, then measures semantic similarity between them.

The rest of this paper is organized as follows. Section 2 presents related work. Section 3 presents our proposed model. Section 4 presents our experiments. And our conclusion is in Sect. 5.

2 Related Work

There have been many proposed methods in literature to extract features from questions and answers for measuring the relevance between them, including manual and automated feature extraction methods. In this paper, we review related work at two aspects:

- Feature-based approaches, and
- Neural-based approaches.

2.1 Feature-Based Approaches

Wang *et al.* [3] apply a probabilistic quasi-synchronous grammar technique, together with three adjustments at a high level of the model. In order to choose the best candidate answer in a set of candidate sentences, the method applies Bayes' rule with three adjustments. The first one is marginal probability $\Pr(a)$

in $\Pr(a|q) = \Pr(q|a) \cdot \Pr(a)$[1]. To calculate $\Pr(a)$, the authors propose to ignore some information, *e.g.*, the reputability of answer source, grammaticality. The second adjustment is to take advantage of the directed dependency parse tree in representing sentences, and the last one is applying 1:1 words alignment between q and a sentences. Yao *et al.* [4] apply tree edit distance approach to compute the edit sequence needed to transform question tree to answer tree, by evaluating three operations, *i.e.*, insertion, deletion, and rename. Tymoshenko and Moschitti [5] exploit shallow syntactic tree and semantic dependency tree to represent questions/answers, enriched with external knowledge bases such as YAGO[2], DBpedia[3], or WordNet[4]. Besides representing structures of questions and answers, Li and Roth [6] exploit question types to find appropriate answers. They propose to categorize the question types into 6 coarse classes, *i.e.*, numeric, abbreviation, description, entity, human, location.

In answer selection task, given a question and a list of candidate answers, the system will return a ranked list of candidate answers. Some studies consider this task as measuring semantic similarity between questions and answers [7,8]. Nguyen *et al.* [9] propose a method exploiting both syntactic and semantic features to assess the similarity. The proposed model includes two phases; first, exploring named entities and finding their co-reference relations; then, measuring the semantic similarity by applying word-to-word similarity methods [10], together with determining the ordering of words between sentences. tau Yih *et al.* [7] present lexical semantic models and learning QA matching models to measure the similarity. With the limitation of surface-form matching methods, the authors explore multi-relationship between sentences' words, *i.e.*, general word semantic similarity, synonymy/antonymy, hypernymy/hyponymy. For learning QA matching models, the authors evaluate the bag-of-words model and learning latent structures.

2.2 Neural-Based Approaches

Recently, neural network models and deep learning also achieve promising results in question answering tasks. He *et al.* [11] propose a model consists of two components: (1) sentence model, and (2) similarity measurement layer. For sentence model, the authors apply CNN for modeling each sentence with different perspectives of the input and multiple types of pooling. Then, in similarity measurement layer, the authors perform structured comparisons over particular regions of the sentence representation. The reason for doing these comparisons is that flattening the sentence to vector (to measure the similarity between two vectors) may discard some useful information for measuring the similarity. Yu *et al.* [8] apply a bag-of-words model and bigram-CNN to represent the questions and answers. Yang *et al.* [12] propose a method combining QA matching matrix with

---

[1] Throughout this paper, we use q and a to denote questions and answers, respectively.
[2] https://github.com/yago-naga/yago3.
[3] https://wiki.dbpedia.org/.
[4] https://wordnet.princeton.edu/.

value-shared weights. Zhang *et al.* [13] apply attention mechanism to find useful sections in questions and answers in CQA systems. The method takes into account 4 types of information, *i.e.*, segment representation, interaction with other text, question topic, and question type. Tam *et al.* [14] present an idea that replacing Wh-words (focus on who-type, when-type, and where-type) in questions with prototypes. The authors consider a prototype as a representative. In particular, the method uses the 7-class model of Stanford NER to define the category. To decide which prototype to replace Wh-word, the authors propose to consider the interaction between NE list, answers list, and question list. Yin *et al.* [15] use Tree-LSTM model to represent question sentences, and then generate answers by considering two kinds of questions' outputs, *i.e.*, answer-type and triple. For both answer-type and triple, the authors apply attention-based neural networks and Freebase[5] triples. Xiong *et al.* [16] extend the Dynamic Co-attention Network [17] with a deep residual co-attention encoder to represent questions and answers. To train the model, the authors combine reinforcement learning (rewarded by word overlap) and cross entropy loss over positions. In [18], Min *et al.* improve the method in [16] by presenting a sentence selector module to select a minimal list of candidate answers from document, and to boost both training and inference time. The list size depends on question content, instead of a fixed number used in other methods. In [19], Yu *et al.* apply an attention mechanism with multi-layer which takes advantage of both convolutional neural network and long-short term memory in order to focus on the interrogative words.

By taking into account the strengths of feature-engineering and neural-based approaches, in [20], Duong *et al.* propose a hybrid method which exploiting the surface form and semantic of words, together with neural-based approach to learn deep features. In [21], in addition to apply neural-based approaches, the authors also apply feature-based approaches, *i.e.*, word matching, machine translation metric, topic model, and lexical semantic similarity features. In [22], Xie *et al.* consider both semantic features and heuristic rules. For semantic, the authors use various of features, *i.e.*, forming lexical semantics vectors and measuring the distance between question and comment, using latent Dirichlet allocation topic similarity. For heuristic rules, the authors exploit the meta-data, *e.g.*, the presence of question marks in answers, the lengths of questions and answers, whether a comment is written by the same author of a question.

3   Proposed Method

In this section, we describe the proposed attention-based neural architecture in answer selection task. In Fig. 1, we illustrate the general model of our proposed method. Given a pair of questions and answers, denoted by $s = \{w_1, w_2, \ldots, w_N\}$, first, we convert each word into word embedding and character embedding, denoted by $v_s = \{v_{w1}, v_{w2}, \ldots, v_{wN}\}$. Next, we input those

---

[5] https://developers.google.com/freebase/.

embeddings to an encoder layer, which is based on a bidirectional long short-term memory. We then apply an attention mechanism to calculate attention vector for question understanding, denoted by v_α. Finally, the attention vector together with the outputs from encoder layer are concatenated in order to represent the sentences. Denoted by v_s^α.

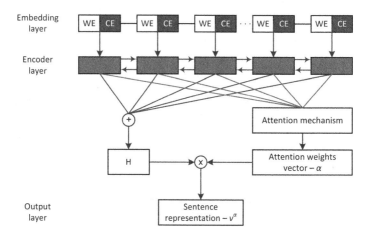

Fig. 1. A general model of our proposed method. The WE, CE denote word-embedding and character-embedding, respectively.

3.1 Embedding Layer

In the embedding layer, given a sentence, we convert each input word into word embedding and character embedding, and then concatenate them to form a v_s vector. For word embedding, we use the pre-trained word vectors, *i.e.*, GloVe[6] [23] and *word2vec*[7] [24] to represent word-level embedding. For character embedding, we apply CharCNN[8] method, proposed by Kim *et al.* [25], which feeds all characters of a word into a convolutional neural network with max-over-time pooling architecture to obtain character-level representation. The embedding layer is applied for both input questions and answers, resulting in two matrices $Q \in \mathbb{R}^{n \times d}$ and $A \in \mathbb{R}^{m \times d}$, where n and m are the length of questions and answers, respectively.

3.2 Encoder Layer

In the encoder layer, the input sentence is encoded by using a bidirectional long short-term memory (bi-LSTM). The LSTM was proposed by Hochreiter and Schmidhuber [26] in order to overcome the limitation of traditional recurrent

---

[6] https://nlp.stanford.edu/projects/glove/.
[7] https://code.google.com/archive/p/word2vec/.
[8] https://github.com/yoonkim/lstm-char-cnn.

neural networks in capturing a long-term dependencies, which leads to the vanishing and exploding gradient problems. A LSTM unit consists of three gates: an input gate, an output gate, and a forget gate. Equation 1 presents the equations of LSTM that we apply in our approach:

$$
\begin{aligned}
I_t &= \sigma \left(x_t W^I + h_{t-1} W^I + b_I \right) \\
F_t &= \sigma \left(x_t W^F + h_{t-1} W^F + b_F \right) \\
\tilde{C}_t &= \tanh \left(x_t W^C + h_{t-1} W^C + b_C \right) \\
C_t &= F_t * C_{t-1} + I_t * \tilde{C}_t \\
O_t &= \sigma \left(x_t W^O + h_{t-1} W^O + b_O \right) \\
h_t &= O_t * \tanh(C_t)
\end{aligned}
\tag{1}
$$

In Eq. 1, I_t, F_t, O_t are input gate, output gate, and forget gate of an LSTM unit at step t, respectively. Besides that, C_t is unit state, $\tilde{C}_t$ is candidate hidden state, h_t is hidden output, and b is bias. The vanilla LSTM encodes the input from one direction, thus we propose to stack the two LSTMs on top of each other to form a bi-LSTM architecture. The hidden output H, from bi-LSTM, is now computed based on the hidden output h_t of both LTSMs. Specifically, given a sentence $s = \{w_1, w_2, w_3, \ldots, w_N\}$, the bi-LSTM produces the hidden output H as shown in Eq. 2, which is the result of concatenating both forward and backward of LSTM units.

$$
H = \begin{bmatrix} \overrightarrow{h_1} \ \overrightarrow{h_2} \ \overrightarrow{h_3} \ \ldots \ \overrightarrow{h_N} \\ \overleftarrow{h_1} \ \overleftarrow{h_2} \ \overleftarrow{h_3} \ \ldots \ \overleftarrow{h_N} \end{bmatrix} = [h'_1, h'_2, h'_3, \ldots, h'_N]
\tag{2}
$$

3.3   Attention Component

In previous sections, we have presented how to represent a sentence by using word embedding and character embedding, then input to a bi-LSTM neural network. However, based on the characteristics of question answering tasks, representing a sentence through embedding and encoder layers is still not enough, since we can't capture much useful information from the question to determine which answer is the most appropriate. For instance, a question begins with *"Where"* should be answered by a location. Therefore, to overcome this drawback, we apply an attention mechanism to capture important information in questions and answers.

In Fig. 2, we present the architecture of an attention mechanism for question understanding. The input of this component is a sequence of hidden states from the encoder layer, and the output is a vector which provides weights corresponding to important elements in questions and answers. Before going further, for ease of presentation, we list the notations as follows:

- d is the dimension of each hidden state;
- m, n are the lengths of questions and answers, respectively;
- h is the sum of m, n and the separator, that means, $h = m + n + 1$;

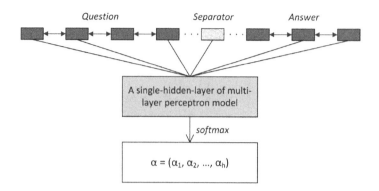

Fig. 2. An attention mechanism architecture. At top of the figure, we denote the hidden outputs from bi-LSTM model of questions and answers, together with a separator.

- $Q \in \mathbb{R}^{m \times d}$ is a matrix that represents the hidden states of question;
- $A \in \mathbb{R}^{n \times d}$ is a matrix that represents the hidden states of answer.

In the input layer of attention component, we concatenate the hidden output from the encoder layer of questions and answers, together with a separator vector ($\in \mathbb{R}^{1 \times d}$), so we form a matrix $H \in \mathbb{R}^{d \times h}$ as an input to the attention component. Next, to compute attention vector, denoted by $\alpha \in \mathbb{R}^{1 \times h}$, we feed H into a bi-layer perceptron neural network with a *tanh* activation function follows by a dense *softmax* layer, as shown in Eq. 3; where $W_\alpha^{(1)} \in \mathbb{R}^{h \times d}$ and $W_\alpha^{(2)} \in \mathbb{R}^{1 \times h}$.

$$\alpha = \text{softmax}\left(W_\alpha^{(2)} \times \tanh\left(H \times W_\alpha^{(1)}\right)\right) \tag{3}$$

To capture important information in questions and answers, we form the v_q^α and v_a^α by multiplying the hidden output from encoder layer by α. There is no problem with the difference between the lengths of hidden output and α, since we have included the separator in α, as explained in Eq. 4.

$$\begin{aligned} v_q^\alpha &= H_q \times \alpha_q^{\mathrm{T}} = H_q \times \alpha_{(1,\dots,m)}^{\mathrm{T}} \\ v_a^\alpha &= H_a \times \alpha_a^{\mathrm{T}} = H_a \times \alpha_{(m+2,\dots,h)}^{\mathrm{T}} \end{aligned} \tag{4}$$

where $H_q \in \mathbb{R}^{h \times m}$, $\alpha_q \in \mathbb{R}^{1 \times m}$, $H_a \in \mathbb{R}^{h \times n}$, $\alpha_a \in \mathbb{R}^{1 \times n}$, and T is transpose operation.

Summary. In this section, we have presented our proposed method for modeling questions and answers. Given a sentence, each input word is represented by word-embedding and character-embedding, then fed into a bi-LSTM neural model. In order to capture important information in questions and answers, we apply attention mechanism to compute the weighted tensor. Finally, combining the output from bi-LSTM neural model with weighted tensor, we get the representation of questions and answers.

4   Experiments

4.1   Datasets

We evaluate our proposed method on two datasets: SemEval-2016 Task 3 [2] and SemEval-2017 Task 3 [27]. SemEval is a series of evaluation tasks of computational semantic analysis systems, and Task-3 focuses on community-based question answering systems and includes 3 subtasks. In this study, we evaluate our method on subtask C, which assesses the question-external comment similarity systems. This subtask is described as follows: given a question q and 10 related questions to q, together with the first 10 comments for each of related question, the goal is to classify the 100 comments according to the given question.

Technically, in order to perform subtask C of Task-3, we need to perform one or both subtask A and subtask B. Since we only focus on subtask C, we just take an advantage of the SemEval datasets to train a classifier, then we use the test sets to evaluate our model. Therefore, in the test sets, we only take into account the gold label of each pair of questions and answers. In SemEval-2016, the subtask C requires to classify into 3 classes, *i.e.*, good, bad, and potentially-useful. However, in SemEval-2017, the potentially-useful label is merged with bad, thus it becomes a binary classification task.

The SemEval provides the datasets in 3 subsets, including training, development, and testing datasets. In practice, for training our model, we combine the training and development datasets. Table 1 shows the sizes of the training and testing datasets corresponding to Task 3 of SemEval-2016 and SemEval-2017.

Table 1. Statistics about Task-3 datasets of SemEval-2016 and SemEval-2017

	Training dataset	Testing dataset
SemEval-2016 Task 3	31,690	7,000
SemEval-2017 Task 3	31,690	8,800

4.2   Experiment Settings

We evaluate our method in two cases: (1) using different word-embedding datasets, and (2) augmenting the proposed method with convolutional neural network model. For case (1), we apply *word2vec* [24] and *GloVe* [23] to represent each input word. For case (2), after modeling questions and answers as two semantic vectors, we either compute the output by (i) applying cosine similarity, or (ii) applying a single-layer-CNN model. By practice, for SemEval-2016, we set the thresholds to determine the labels are $T_{Good} = 0.71448$ and $T_{Bad} = 0.36023$; for SemEval-2017, the thresholds are $T_{Good} = 0.70652$. Specifically, we perform the experiments by the following settings (for both datasets):

- Using *word2vec* with cosine similarity.
- Using *GloVe* with cosine similarity.

- Using *word2vec* with a single-layer-CNN model.
- Using *GloVe* with a single-layer-CNN model.

4.3   Experimental Results

Tables 2 and 3 show the experimental results corresponding to the presented experiment settings on SemEval-2016 and SemEval-2017 datasets, respectively. In order to measure the performance of our method, we use the following scores[9]: accuracy (Acc), and F_1. Besides that, we also compare the performance of our method among top-5 methods in SemEval-2016 and SemEval-2017, respectively.

The experimental results show that our method achieves better performance when combining GloVe with cosine similarity in both SemEval-2016 and SemEval-2017 datasets. The main differences between our method and the others are as follows:

- We only focus on subtask C, instead of training the system on subtask A and B.
- We do not consider the meta-data in measuring the relationship between questions and answers.
- We use the pretrained word embedding datasets. There are some other methods proposed to retrain the word embedding on the domain-specific datasets from Qatar Living and/or DohaNews, which are the data source of SemEval datasets.

Table 2. Experimental results on SemEval-2016 Task 3

Experiment settings	Acc	F1
word2vec + cosine similarity	87.46	**33.42**
word2vec + single-layer-CNN	87.27	15.68
GloVe + cosine similarity	**90.43**	31.72
GloVe + single-layer-CNN	90.11	23.19
ECNU	**91.07**	15.88
SLS	90.54	21.97
ConvKN	90.51	14.65
UH-PRHLT	88.56	35.87
Kelp	84.79	**44.21**

---

[9] Since we focus on classification task, we do not present the mean average precision (MAP) score, which is used for ranking task in SemEval Task 3.

Table 3. Experimental results on SemEval-2017 Task 3

Experiment settings	Acc	F1
word2vec + cosine similarity	90.87	15.69
word2vec + single-layer-CNN	91.26	12.33
GloVe + cosine similarity	**95.52**	21.71
GloVe + single-layer-CNN	95.39	**24.08**
EICA	**97.08**	0.77
bunji	95.64	**19.67**
ECNU	95.1	13.63
IIT-UHH	83.03	14.44
KeLP	63.75	12.07

5 Conclusion

In this paper, we present a novel method in answer sentence selection task on community-based question answering systems. We construct the model by taking into account the bidirectional long short-term memory in combination with an attention mechanism. To understand the question, we present an attention component, based on a multilayer perceptron neural network, to capture important information in questions and answers.

We then conduct the experiments on the Task 3 datasets of SemEval-2016 and SemEval-2017 workshop, which are the real-life datasets in community-based question answering systems. The experimental results show that our method achieves state-of-the-art performance.

References

1. Ferrucci, D.A., et al.: Building Watson: an overview of the DeepQA project. AI Mag. **31**(3), 59–79 (2010)
2. Nakov, P., Màrquez, L., Magdy, W., Moschitti, A., Glass, J., Randeree, B.: Semeval-2016 task 3: community question answering. In: Proceedings of the 10th International Workshop on Semantic Evaluation, SemEval 2016, San Diego. Association for Computational Linguistics, June 2016
3. Wang, M., Smith, N.A., Mitamura, T.: What is the jeopardy model? A quasi-synchronous grammar for QA. In: Eisner, J. (ed.) Proceedings of the 2007 Joint Conference on Empirical Methods in Natural Language Processing and Computational Natural Language Learning, EMNLP-CoNLL 2007, 28–30 June 2007, Prague, Czech Republic, pp. 22–32. ACL (2007)
4. Yao, X., Durme, B.V., Callison-Burch, C., Clark, P.: Answer extraction as sequence tagging with tree edit distance. In: Vanderwende, L., Daumé III, H., Kirchhoff, K. (eds.) HLT-NAACL, pp. 858–867. The Association for Computational Linguistics (2013)

5. Tymoshenko, K., Moschitti, A.: Assessing the impact of syntactic and semantic structures for answer passages reranking. In: Bailey, J., et al. (eds.) Proceedings of the 24th ACM International Conference on Information and Knowledge Management, CIKM 2015, Melbourne, 19–23 October 2015, pp. 1451–1460. ACM (2015)
6. Li, X., Roth, D.: Learning question classifiers. In: Proceedings of the 19th International Conference on Computational Linguistics - Volume 1. Association for Computational Linguistics (2002)
7. tau Yih, W., Chang, M.W., Meek, C., Pastusiak, A.: Question answering using enhanced lexical semantic models. In: The Association for Computer Linguistics, vol. 1, pp. 1744–1753. ACL (2013)
8. Yu, L., Hermann, K.M., Blunsom, P., Pulman, S.: Deep learning for answer sentence selection. In: NIPS Deep Learning Workshop (2014)
9. Nguyen, H.T., Duong, P.H., Le, T.Q.: A multifaceted approach to sentence similarity. In: Huynh, V.-N., Inuiguchi, M., Denoeux, T. (eds.) IUKM 2015. LNCS (LNAI), vol. 9376, pp. 303–314. Springer, Cham (2015). https://doi.org/10.1007/978-3-319-25135-6_29
10. Duong, P.H., Nguyen, H.T., Nguyen, V.P.: Evaluating semantic relatedness between concepts. In: IMCOM, pp. 20:1–20:8. ACM (2016)
11. He, H., Gimpel, K., Lin, J.J.: Multi-perspective sentence similarity modeling with convolutional neural networks. In: Màrquez, L., Callison-Burch, C., Su, J., Pighin, D., Marton, Y. (eds.) Proceedings of the 2015 Conference on Empirical Methods in Natural Language Processing, EMNLP 2015, Lisbon, 17–21 September 2015, pp. 1576–1586. The Association for Computational Linguistics (2015)
12. Yang, L., Ai, Q., Guo, J., Croft, W.B.: aNMM: ranking short answer texts with attention-based neural matching model. In: Proceedings of the 25th ACM International on Conference on Information and Knowledge Management, pp. 287–296. ACM (2016)
13. Zhang, X., Li, S., Sha, L., Wang, H.: Attentive interactive neural networks for answer selection in community question answering. In: Singh, S.P., Markovitch, S. (eds.) Proceedings of the Thirty-First AAAI Conference on Artificial Intelligence, 4–9 February 2017, San Francisco, pp. 3525–3531. AAAI Press (2017)
14. Tam, W.L., Han, N., Navarro-Horñiacek, J.I., Miyao, Y.: Finding prototypes of answers for improving answer sentence selection. In: Sierra, C. (ed.) Proceedings of the Twenty-Sixth International Joint Conference on Artificial Intelligence, IJCAI 2017, Melbourne, 19–25 August 2017, pp. 4103–4108. ijcai.org (2017)
15. Yin, J., Zhao, W.X., Li, X.: Type-aware question answering over knowledge base with attention-based tree-structured neural networks. J. Comput. Sci. Technol. **32**(4), 805–813 (2017)
16. Xiong, C., Zhong, V., Socher, R.: DCN+: mixed objective and deep residual coattention for question answering. CoRR abs/1711.00106 (2017)
17. Xiong, C., Zhong, V., Socher, R.: Dynamic coattention networks for question answering. In: Proceedings of ICLR (2017)
18. Min, S., Zhong, V., Socher, R., Xiong, C.: Efficient and robust question answering from minimal context over documents. In: Association for Computational Linguistics 2018 Conference. The Association for Computational Linguistics (2018)
19. Yu, B., Xu, Q., Zhang, P.: Question classification based on MAC-LSTM. In: IEEE Third International Conference on Data Science in Cyberspace (DSC), pp. 69–75, June 2018

20. Duong, P.H., Nguyen, H.T., Nguyen, D.D., Do, H.T.: A hybrid approach to answer selection in question answering systems. In: Huynh, V.-N., Inuiguchi, M., Tran, D.H., Denoeux, T. (eds.) IUKM 2018. LNCS (LNAI), vol. 10758, pp. 191–202. Springer, Cham (2018). https://doi.org/10.1007/978-3-319-75429-1_16

21. Wu, G., Lan, M.: ECNU at SemEval-2016 task 3: exploring traditional method and deep learning method for question retrieval and answer ranking in community question answering. In: Bethard, S., Cer, D.M., Carpuat, M., Jurgens, D., Nakov, P., Zesch, T. (eds.) Proceedings of the 10th International Workshop on Semantic Evaluation, SemEval@NAACL-HLT 2016, San Diego, 16–17 June 2016, pp. 872–878. The Association for Computer Linguistics (2016)

22. Xie, Y., Wang, M., Ma, J., Jiang, J., Lu, Z.: EICA team at SemEval-2017 task 3: semantic and metadata-based features for community question answering. In: Bethard, S., Carpuat, M., Apidianaki, M., Mohammad, S.M., Cer, D.M., Jurgens, D. (eds.) Proceedings of the 11th International Workshop on Semantic Evaluation, SemEval@ACL 2017, Vancouver, 3–4 August 2017. Association for Computational Linguistics, pp. 292–298 (2017)

23. Pennington, J., Socher, R., Manning, C.D.: Glove: global vectors for word representation. In: Empirical Methods in Natural Language Processing (EMNLP), pp. 1532–1543 (2014)

24. Mikolov, T., Sutskever, I., Chen, K., Corrado, G.S., Dean, J.: Distributed representations of words and phrases and their compositionality. In: Burges, C.J.C., Bottou, L., Ghahramani, Z., Weinberger, K.Q. (eds.) Advances in Neural Information Processing Systems 26: 27th Annual Conference on Neural Information Processing Systems 2013. Proceedings of a Meeting Held 5–8 December 2013, Lake Tahoe, pp. 3111–3119 (2013)

25. Kim, Y., Jernite, Y., Sontag, D., Rush, A.M.: Character-aware neural language models. In: Schuurmans, D., Wellman, M.P. (eds.) Proceedings of the Thirtieth AAAI Conference on Artificial Intelligence, 12–17 February 2016, Phoenix, pp. 2741–2749. AAAI Press (2016)

26. Hochreiter, S., Schmidhuber, J.: Long short-term memory. Neural Comput. **9**(8), 1735–1780 (1997)

27. Nakov, P., et al.: SemEval-2017 task 3: community question answering. In: Proceedings of the 11th International Workshop on Semantic Evaluation, SemEval 2017, Vancouver. Association for Computational Linguistics, August 2017

User Linkage Across Anonymizd Social Networks

Chao Kong$^{(\boxtimes)}$, Wan Tao, Sanmin Liu, and Qiang Zhang

School of Computer and Information, Anhui Polytechnic University, Wuhu, China
kongchao315@163.com, taowan@ahpu.edu.com, aqlsm@163.com, 15009673@qq.com

Abstract. Nowadays, the user linkage or link prediction task is usually based on user profile or some sensitive data (i.e., name, gender, ID, life or health insurance accounts, etc.). With the enhancement of laws and regulations, the difficulty of personal sensitive data acquisition is increasing. Moreover, the abnormal users called online water army often camouflage themselves to achieve specific goals. They often register false user information such as name, gender, age, etc. To protect privacy and satisfy the needs of camouflage, users and ISPs often hide those sensitive data (i.e., user profile). In this paper, we want to link same user in multiple social networks, which is formally defined as ULASN (User Linkage across Anonymized Social Networks) problem. ULASN is very challenging to address due to (1) the lack of enough ground-truth to build models and obtain accurate prediction results, (2) the studied networks are anonymized, where no user profile or sensitive data is available, and (3) the need of scalable algorithms for user linkage task in large-scale social nateworks, and (4) users in social network are interrelated. To resolve these challenges, a noval user linkage framework based on social structures called ULA is proposed in this paper. ULA tackles these problems by considering massive, low-quality and interrelated user information. It uses few ground-truth to partition users into blocks, which reduces the size of candidates. By extending Fellegi-Sunter methods, our proposed algorithm can handle social network similarity complying to continuous distributions. A probabilistic generative model is proposed and solved by EM algorithm. Simultaneously, missing value problem can also solved when we use EM algorithm to learning parameters. Extensive experiments conducted on two real-world social networks demonstrate that ULA can perform very well in solving ULASN problem.

Keywords: Link prediction · Privacy protection · Blocking method
Probabilistic generative models

This work is supported by the Initial Scientific Research Foud of Introduced Talents in Anhui Polytechnic University (No. 2017YQQ015) and Natural Science Foundation of Anhui Province (No. 1608085MF147).

X. Chen et al. (Eds.): CSoNet 2018, LNCS 11280, pp. 186–197, 2018.
https://doi.org/10.1007/978-3-030-04648-4_16

1 Introduction

As proposed in [1], people nowadays are normally involved in multiple social networks simultaneously to enjoy more social network services. User linkage is the problem of identifying which users in a social network link to the same users in the other social networks. It is a well known and paramount problem that arises in many research fields, including information retrieval, data integration, machine learning, etc. As a kind of typical social sensor, social network platforms can perceive a wide range of user behavior. So user linkage across the social networks is a necessary step for analyzing and mining user behavior. However, due to the increasing awareness of privacy and security, users' sensitive information is increasingly protected by law, which makes it paramount for researchers to obtain sensitive information. In addition, some users are disguised to perform specific tasks on the Internet (such as online water army) who usually provide false sensitive information deliberately to cause a very low quality of user sensitive information. Therefore, it is one of general problem to ignore sensitive information to implement user linkage across anonymized social networks based on the social network structures only.

In addition to its importance and novelty, the ULASN problem is very difficult to solve due to the following challenges:

- How to design and implement scalable user linkage algorithm is a really difficult problem.
- In ULASN problem, we used social network structure information only rather than more sensitive user profiles. How to ensure the performance of our algorithm is an arduous work.
- The nodes in social networks are interrelated, so how to make full use of this dependency is also a difficult problem.

In this article, we provide an approach called ULA to link users across anonymized social networks. We formulate user linkage task as a semi-supervised learning problem. Our proposed approach can be performed with accuracy with few ground-truth which are usually arduous and costly to collect in Web applications. With the provided method, we would like to address the three challenges highlighted earlier. To the best of our knowledge, there is so far no feasible approach to user linkage across anonymized social networks using social network structures only. We use few number of labeled linking users and Locality Sensitive Hash to block users, reducing the size of candidates. Moreover, we extend Fellegi-Sunter method to deal with continuous distribution of social similarity, construct probability generation model, learn parameters using EM algorithm and handle data quality simultaneously. In summary, our major contributions are as following.

- We proposed a semi-supervised method ULA based on probabilistic generation model to link prediction across anonymized social networks. ULA builds model only using social structure information. Besides, we define the social network similarity measurement across social platforms.

- We design the blocking method based on social network structure to improve the scalability of our proposed algorithm.
- For most continuous and discrete probability distributions, the EM algorithm is employed to estimate the parameters. Finally, a decision making method is proposed.
- We illustrate the performance of our algorithm against a comparable baseline on two real social networks. Empirical study results manifest that ULA outperforms baseline in user linkage across two anonymized social networks.

The rest of paper is organized as follows. We shortly discuss the related work in Sect. 2. We formally define the problem and describe the overview of our algorithm in Sect. 3. We present the user linkage method in Sect. 4. We report our empirical study in Sect. 5. Finally, we conclude this paper in Sect. 6.

2   Related Work

User linkage aims at detecting several linkages which link the same user from given social networks. The study of user linkage or link prediction problem has been a long time, and some earlier study can go back to 1950s [2]. However, user linkage is also an active research field presently and widely studied in multiple application fields. User linkage technology is most commonly employed to improve the selection of similar users in recommendation systems which follow a collaborative approach to obtain better recommendations [3,4]. Due to the rapid development of social networks, they have become very popular in modern society. Users on the social platforms need simple and effective mechanism to find acquaintances among a large number of registered users. The general approach is employing user linkage or link prediction technology to automatically find acquaintances with a high degree of accuracy [5,6].

In biology community, user linkage technology is applied to discover potential interactions between protein pairs in protein-protein interaction networks [7,8]. Another application in this filed is the disease prediction. Kaya used supervised and unsupervised learning approach respectively to link users for disease prevention [9,10].

In collaborative prediction community, the scientific cooperation networks are accessible easily. Therefore, we can better understand which research field will be prevalent by predicting which authors or groups may collaborate in the future [11]. Social network analysis has also been widely used to analyze criminal structures and terrorist networks to combat organized crime. For example, [12] propose a strategy to identify missing links in a criminal network on the basis of the topological analysis of the links classified as marginal.

Finally, the information network can be used to analyze the development tendency of the entire society. Network analysis can also be employed to stock market. Some researchers have shown how link forecasting can be used in the stock market to achieve a better share purchase plan [13].

As mentioned above, the existing studies of user linkage can be mainly divided into two categories: supervised learning approach and unsupervised learning approach [14]. For supervised method, [15] first proposed a series of new centrality indices for links in line graph. Then, utilizing these line graph indices, as well as a number of original graph indices, they designed three supervised learning methods to realize link weight prediction both in the networks of single layer and multiple layers. There are also some other researchers have used supervised learning methods to obtain delightful experimental results [16]. Due to the careful consideration of [17] ultimately leads to a completely general framework that outperforms unsupervised link prediction methods by more than 30% AUC.

For unsupervised learning method, Kaya [18] used an unsupervised learning strategy to design and implement experiments on a weighted directional citation network. The experimental results illustrate that the proposed approach can return satisfactory results. Wu et al. [19] proposed a weighted local naive Bayes (WLNB) probabilistic link prediction framework. Experimental results illustrate that their methods perform better than several link prediction methods in weighted complex networks.

In recent years, some scholars have begun to use semi-supervised learning or deep learning method to solve the link prediction problem [20–23]. The semi-supervised approach should be performed with accuracy with few ground-truth and social network structure information only. These are the focus of this work.

3   User Linkage Approach

To protect privacy, users or ISPs usually hide user profile. In this section, before we overview our proposed approach, we describe a formal definition of the ULASN problem.

3.1   The Problem Definition

Definition 1 *(Social network). Social network G is a tuple (V, E), where V represents node sets and $E = \{(v_1, v_2)|v_i \in V, i = 1, 2\}$ represent edge sets.*

Definition 2 *(Linked user pair). Given two social networks $G^A = (V^A, E^A)$ and $G^B = (V^B, E^B)$, the set $R = \{(\alpha(v_i^A), \alpha(v_j^B))|v_i^A \in V^A, v_j^B \in V^B\}$ is represented as linked user pair set, which any tuple $(\alpha(v_i^A), \alpha(v_j^B)) \in R$ is represented as a linked user pair.*

Actually, linked user pair set is Cartesian product of two node sets V^A and V^B, that is $R = \alpha(V^A) \times \alpha(V^B)$. Any element is represented as linked user pair.

As definition above, $v_i^A = v_j^B$ means that two users v_i^A and v_j^B from social networks A and B respectively are the same user. User linkage task should be aimed at mining linked user pair sets R. e need to linked node sets from linked user pair sets R whose size is $|V^A| \times |V^B|$. Besides, social networks G^A and G^B are isolated network structure. Therefore, it is not possible to infer the relationship of users from different networks directly. How to link users effectively and efficiently based on few linked users is our focus in this work.

Algorithm 1. ULA: User linkage algorithm

Require: Two social networks, G^A and G^B with partial ground-truth pairs GP, cautious parameter k;

Ensure: Linked pairs LP;

    $cp \leftarrow \emptyset; LP \leftarrow \emptyset$;

1: **while** convergence condition is not satisfied **do**

2:      $pl \leftarrow \emptyset$;

3:      //*Step 1: Candidate pair generation and similarity computation*;

4:    **for** each $a \in N^A(GP \cup MP)$ or $b \in N^B(GP \cup MP)$ **do**

5:      shingles each vertex a or b in terms of set GP;

6:      buckets $\leftarrow a($ or $b)$ //*Blocing with LSH*;

7:    **end for**

      $tempCP \leftarrow \emptyset$;

8:    **for** each bucket in LSH **do**

9:      **for** a, b exist in the bucket **do**

10:        $tempCP \leftarrow tempCP \cup \{(a, b)\}$;

11:      **end for**

12:    **end for**

      $cp \leftarrow cp \cup tempCP$;

13:    **for** each pair $r_j \in cp$ **do**

14:      computing social similarity γ_j for user pair r_j;

15:    **end for**

      //*Step 2: Probabilistic generation model and parameter learning*;

      building a generative model for user linkage problem;

16:    **while** parameter set Θ has not converged **do**

17:      $eStep(cp \cup GP \cup LP)$;

18:      $mStep(cp \cup GP \cup LP)$;

19:    **end while**

      //*Step 3: Linking score and decision making*;

20:    **for** $r_j \in cp$ **do**

21:      $sc_j \leftarrow \log \frac{P(r_j \in M | \gamma_j, \hat{\Theta})}{P(r_j \in U | \gamma_j, \hat{\Theta})}$;

22:    **end for**

      $pl \leftarrow k$ pairs in cp with the highest scores;

      $LP \leftarrow LP \cup pl$;

      remove pairs related matched pairs in pl from cp;

23: **end while**

24: **return** LP;

3.2   ULA Algorithm

We now present the full ULA algorithm in Algorithm 1. In this algorithm, $N^A(GP \cup LP) = \{a | \exists (b, c) \in GP \cup LP, (a, b) \in V^A\}$ are represented as neighbor sets of linked users in social network A. Meanwhile, neighbor sets of users in social network B are denoted as $N^B(GP \cup LP)$. Each iteration of ULA algorithm (lines 1–23) consists of three steps: In the step 1, we employ LSH to block the users in $N^A(GP \cup LP)$ and $N^B(GP \cup LP)$ first (lines 4–12), then compute the social network similarity γ_j of each candidate linked user pairs r_j; In the step 2, we construct the probabilistic generation model by employing latent variable to learn model parameters with EM algorithm (lines 16–19); In the step 3, we define the linking score as $\log \frac{P(r_i \in M | \gamma_i, \hat{\Theta})}{P(r_i \in U | \gamma_i, \hat{\Theta})}$ to calculate the score sc_j of each candidate pair and judge them link or not according to the score (lines 20–22). At the end of one iteration, the linked users pl which are found by the ULA will be added into the linked user sets LP. The loop body is executed again until no new candidate pairs are added to the candidate pair sets cp.

4   Parameters Learning and Decision Making

In this section, we will introduce how to construct probabilistic generation model, estimate model parameters with EM algorithm and judge the candidate pairs link or not.

4.1   Likelihood

Let's assume that the linking label is M and the unmatching label is U. For a candidate pair, we can not determine its label in advance. Given a user pair r_i, we need to calculate the probability of $P(r_i \in L|\gamma_i, \Theta)$ and $P(r_i \in U|\gamma_i, \Theta)$, and the expression of the log-likelihood function is:

$$
\begin{aligned}
L(\Theta|X) = &\sum_{i=1}^{N^2+M} L_i[logP(\gamma_i|r_i \in M, \Theta), logP(\gamma_i|r_i \in U, \Theta)]' \\
&+ \sum_{i=N^2+1}^{N^2+M} L_i[logp, log(1-p)]'
\end{aligned}
\tag{1}
$$

4.2   Maximum Likelihood Estimation

EM is an iterative algorithm whose each iteration consists of two steps: E-step and M-step. The algorithm runs until the parameters converge.

E-step: In this step, we look for the expectation of log-likelihood, remove the latent variable l_i and prepare for maximizing log-likelihood and parameter estimation in the next step. That means we can estimate the prior probability of latent variable based on the model parameters or initial parameters calculated in the previous iterations. The expectation of l_i is taken as current estimation. In the k-th iteration, the conditional distribution of l_i with γ_i and $\Theta^{(k-1)}$ is $l_i|\gamma_i, \Theta^{(k-1)} \sim B(1, p_i^{(k)})$, where

$$
\begin{aligned}
p_i^{(k)} = P(l_i = 1|\gamma_i, \Theta^{(k-1)}) &= \frac{P(r_i \in M, \gamma_i|\Theta^{(k-1)})}{P(\gamma_i|\Theta^{(k-1)})} \\
&= \frac{p^{(k-1)} \cdot f_1(\cdot; \cdot)}{p^{(k-1)} \cdot f_1(\cdot; \cdot) + (1 - p^{(k-1)}) \cdot f_0(\cdot; \cdot)}
\end{aligned}
\tag{2}
$$

Thus, we can obtain the equation of expectation substituting $p_i^{(k)}$ for l_i.

M-step: In this step, the expectation of latent variable calculated in E-step which is $l_j^{(k)} = p_j^{(k)} i = 1, \cdots, m$ is employed to maximize the log-likelihood and estimate the model parameters.

We can estimate the parameters in $(k+1)$-th step by solving equations above. Finally, the maximum likelihood estimation of similarity distribution of linked group and unmatched group are obtained.

4.3   Decision Making

On the one hand, we can compare the probability $P(r_i \in M|\gamma_i, \Theta)$ and $P(r_i \in U|\gamma_i, \Theta)$ to judge the candidate pair linking or not; on the other hand the probability $P(r_i \in M|\gamma_i, \Theta)$ and $P(r_i \in U|\gamma_i, \Theta)$ can also help us making decision. For simplicity, we define the *linking score* function as:

$$W_i = log(\frac{P(r_i \in M|\gamma_i, \hat{\Theta})}{P(r_i \in U|\gamma_i, \hat{\Theta})}) \tag{3}$$

where $P(r_i \in M|\gamma_i, \hat{\Theta}) > P(r_i \in U|\gamma_i, \hat{\Theta})$ when $W_i > 0$. Alternatively, we can assign r_i to the linked group if $W_i > W_0$ where $W_0 > 0$ is a threshold. We sort the score of each user pair r_i in descending order and consider the highest score k user pairs as the final linked user pair. In each iteration of algorithm 1, the candidate pairs with top-k highest probability will be assigned as linked nodes.

5   Empirical Study

This section will systematically evaluate ULA through experiment employing real social networks and different experimental settings. We design two groups of experiments based on real social networks to verify and evaluate the performance of ULA. First, we created a new dataset $T_N(\delta)$ for the self-linking task according to Twitter dataset, where $T_N(\delta)$ is the subnet of Twitter. In this experiment, 8 users with high social similarity and their ego-networks are selected as subnet. N represents the size of the subnet, and δ represents the probability that the social connections between users are erased, which is called interference probability. In the self-linking experiment, since the parameter settings can be easily modified, it can be used to more easily and deeply understanding the algorithm. In addition, the users are all from the same social network, so we can get one-to-one linked user pairs. In order to better evaluate the performance and efficiency of ULA, the we randomly erase the social connections between some users and modify the size of the training set; Second, according to the known 3520 ground-truth, we evaluate the performance of ULA in two real large-scale social networks.

Table 1. Statistical information of datasets

Social graph	# Vertexes	# Edges
Foursquare	205054	5128966
Twitter	73111	1376518

This experiment uses two real large-scale social networks. Their descriptive statistics are shown in Table 1.

5.1   Self-linking Evaluation

Firstly, we evaluate the performance of ULA through a node self-linking task. In this task, all users come from the same social network, so we can get complete one-to-one labeled data. In order to simulate data more accurately, the user's social connections will be randomly erased to better understanding the performance of the algorithm. For Twitter dataset, we create a new dataset $T_N(\delta)$, which is subnet of Twitter. In this experiment, we choose 8 users with high social relevance and their ego-network to construct subnet. The size of the subnet is denoted as N, and δ represents the probability of social connections be erased, which is called interference probability. In order to demonstrate the performance of the ULA algorithm, we choose 500 users as the training set from the subnet, and the remaining 564 users as the testing set.

In summary, the node self-matching task evaluates the performance of ULA from three aspects: (1) to evaluate performance of ULA by interfering user's social connections; (2) to observe the change of performance of ULA by modifying the size of training set; (3) to verify scalability of ULA by changing the size of social networks.

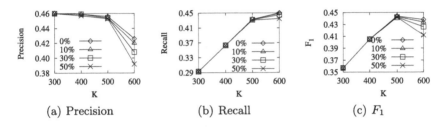

(a) Precision   (b) Recall   (c) F_1

Fig. 1. The validation of interference immunity to ULA

Interference Immunity to ULA: In this experiment, we observe the accuracy of ULA on $T_{564}(\delta)$ varying δ from 0 to 50%. As shown in Fig. 1(a)–(c), as more and more social connections are erased randomly, Precision@K, Recall@K, and F-measure@K drop dramatically. Even if δ increases to 30%, ULA still remains high accuracy. We observe that both of the Precision@K and Recall@K are about 41% in top-600 results. Even 50% noise is injected into the data, the precision is almost 40%.

Scalability of ULA: We performed node self-matching task on different size of social networks to evaluate the scalability of ULA. The dataset used in this experiment is $T_N(30\%)$. The users are randomly sampled from the complete user dataset while maintaining the social connections. Figure 2 manifests the changes in the number of candidate pairs on different size of social network and run time of the algorithm in the last iteration.

After each iteration of the algorithm, the predicted linked nodes added to the training set is the top-k pairs with the highest linking score, which is used for the next round of parameter learning, and repeat this processing until the parameter is stable or the algorithm terminates. When the iteration is terminated, the number of predicted linked nodes added to the training set almost reaches N^2. Therefore, LSH is not only to reduce the number of candidate pairs, but also to reduce the size of the training set to reduce the time and space overhead while maintaining high performance. The user linkage on large-scale social network with ULA employing LSH is denoted as ULA_H. While ULA_{nonH} means there is not blocking step with LSH in ULA algorithm. In Fig. 2, we can find that only less than 1‰ candidate pairs are remained after using LSH to block users. As shown in Fig. 2, ULA associated with LSH detects users within two hours. However, the elapsed time of ULA without LSH is more than 12 h when the size of social network is greater than 30000. In summary, LSH is helpful to reduce the number of candidate pairs and speed up the computation of ULA.

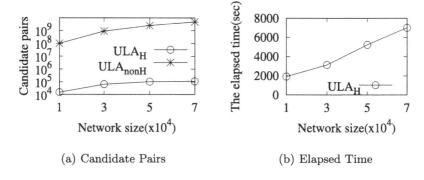

(a) Candidate Pairs   (b) Elapsed Time

Fig. 2. The scalability of ULA

Performance VS. the Size of Traing Set: Figure 3 illustrates the change of ULA performance varying the size of training set from 100 to 500. The users from training set and testing set maintain social connections in favor of enhancing performance. As shown in Fig. 3, with more and more training data are used to estimate models and parameters, the accuracy of ULA is also improved.

In summary, we verify the efficiency and effectiveness of ULA from interference immunity, scalability and the effect of performance varying the size of traing set in node self-linking task.

5.2   User Linkage Across Anonymizd Social Networks

In this experiment, we evaluate the performance of ULA across two real anonymizd social networks. We consider known 3520 linked user pairs as labeled data, we select 1520 pairs of ground truth as training set to train model and verify the performance with left 2000 user pairs.

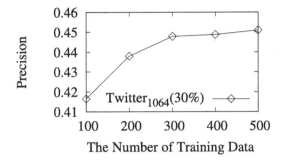

Fig. 3. Performance VS. the size of traing set

Varying Parameters in LSH Setting: Figure 4 illustrates the change of ULA performance varying the parameters in LSH setting. We can clearly observe that ULA is stability from Fig. 4(a) to (d) which illustrate the stable performance of ULA when we alter the parameters g and t for LSH building respectively, where g and t denote the number of groups and the length of a signature in a LSH. We can conclude that: (1) ULA possesses a promising tradeoff between scalability and effectiveness; (2) social connection is momentous feature for user linkage since performance does not show up as swing curve or sharp decrease when ULA only considers the pairs with high similarities of social connection as candidates.

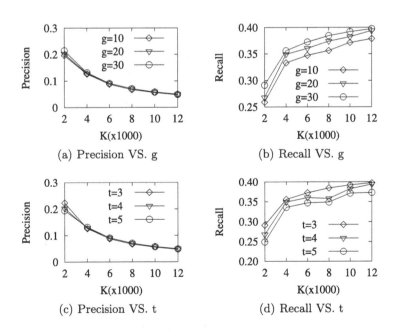

Fig. 4. Performance of ULA with different parameters of LSH

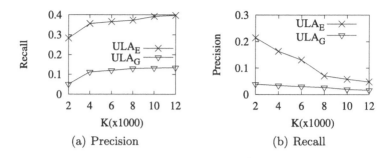

Fig. 5. Performance of linking Twitter and Foursquare

Performance of Different ULA Variants: Figure 5 illustrates performance of ULASN with different ULA variants. We observe that ULA_E outperforms ULA_G and using Exponential distribution is better than using Gaussian distribution.

6   Conclusion

This paper developed a novel algorithm ULA to address user linkage problem with semi-supervised model. It is an arduous work due to large size anonymizd social networks, few labeled data, privacy protection and extensibility for ULASN problem. To address the challenging task, our proposed algorithm ULA employs LSH and two-phrase blocking technic to scale up large-scale network, utilizes few labeled data to estimate parameters in a semi-supervised manner and considers only social network structure to handle ULASN problem. To best optimal point of our method, this work is the first one to use semi-supervised method for handling ULASN problem. Furthermore, extensive experiments on anonymizd Twitter and Foursquare networks demonstrate high-performance in solving the ULASN problem.

In our future work, we desire to extend our work to link users on multiple networks maturely and develop a distributed algorithm to support more efficient computation and win better performance.

References

1. Kong, X., Zhang, J., Yu, P.S.: Inferring anchor links across multiple heterogeneous social networks. In: CIKM 2013 Proceedings of the 22nd ACM International Conference on Information & Knowledge Management, pp. 179–188. ACM, San Francisco (2013)
2. Newcombe, H.B., et al.: Automatic linkage of vital records. Science **130**(3381), 954–959 (1959)
3. Wang, H., et al.: Nodes evolution diversity and link prediction in social networks. IEEE Trans. Knowl. Data Eng. **29**(10), 2263–2274 (2017)
4. Wu, L., et al.: Modeling the evolution of users' preferences and social links in social networking services. IEEE Trans. Knowl. Data Eng. **29**(6), 1240–1253 (2017)

5. Zhu, L., et al.: Scalable temporal latent space inference for link prediction in dynamic social networks. IEEE Trans. Knowl. Data Eng. **28**(10), 2765–2777 (2016)
6. Ermi, B., Acar, E., Cemgil, A.T.: Link prediction in heterogeneous data via generalized coupled tensor factorization. Data Min. Knowl. Discov. **29**(1), 203–236 (2015)
7. Zhao, L., et al.: Protein complexes prediction via positive and unlabeled learning of the PPI networks. In: Proceedings of International Conference on Service Systems and Service Management, pp. 1–6. IEEE, Kunming (2016)
8. Yang, Y., Lichtenwalter, R.N., Chawla, N.V.: Evaluating link prediction methods. Knowl. Inf. Syst. **45**(3), 751–782 (2015)
9. Kaya, B., Poyraz, M.: Finding relations between diseases by age-series based supervised link prediction. In: Proceedings of the 2015 IEEE/ACM International Conference on Advances in Social Networks Analysis and Mining, pp. 1097–1103. ACM/IEEE, Paris (2016)
10. Kaya, B., Poyraz, M.: Unsupervised link prediction in evolving abnormal medical parameter networks. Int. J. Mach. Learn. Cybern. **7**(1), 145–155 (2016)
11. Chuan, P.M., et al.: Link prediction in co-authorship networks based on hybrid content similarity metric. Appl. Intell. **2017**(3), 1–17 (2017)
12. Berlusconi, G, et al.: Link prediction in criminal networks: a tool for criminal intelligence analysis. Plos One **11**(4) (2016). https://doi.org/10.1371/journal.pone.0154244
13. Nayak, S.C., Misra, B.B., Behera, H.S.: ACFLN: artificial chemical functional link network for prediction of stock market index. Evol. Syst. **2018**(4), 1–26 (2018)
14. Martnez, V., Berzal, F., Cubero, F.: A survey of link prediction in complex networks. ACM Comput. Surv. **49**(4), 69 (2016)
15. Fu, C., Zhao, M., Fan, L., et al.: Link weight prediction using supervised learning methods and its application to Yelp layered network. IEEE Trans. Knowl. Data Eng. **30**(8), 1507–1518 (2018)
16. De, A., et al.: Discriminative link prediction using local, community, and global signals. IEEE Trans. Knowl. Data Eng. **28**(8), 2057–2070 (2016)
17. Lichtenwalter, R.N., Lussier, J.T., Chawla, N.V.: New perspectives and methods in link prediction. In: Proceedings of ACM SIGKDD International Conference on Knowledge Discovery and Data Mining, pp. 243–252. ACM, Washington, DC (2010)
18. Liu, J., Deng, G.: Link prediction in a userobject network based on time-weighted resource allocation. Phys. A Stat. Mech. Appl. **388**(17), 3643–3650 (2009)
19. Wu, J.H., et al.: Weighted local naive Bayes link prediction. J. Inf. Process. Syst. **13**(4), 914–927 (2017)
20. Chen, H., et al.: Scaling up Markov logic probabilistic inference for social graphs. IEEE Trans. Knowl. Data Eng. **29**(2), 433–445 (2017)
21. Liao, L., et al.: Attributed social network embedding. IEEE Trans. Knowl. Data Eng. (2017). https://doi.org/10.1109/TKDE.2018.2819980
22. Ozcan, A., Oguducu, S.G.: Link prediction in evolving heterogeneous networks using the NARX neural networks. Knowl. Inf. Syst. **2017**(3), 1–28 (2017)
23. Chen, K., et al.: A time-aware link prediction approach based on semi-supervised learning. J. Comput. Inf. Syst. **10**(11), 4593–4600 (2014)

K-Shell Rank Analysis Using Local Information

Akrati Saxena and S. R. S. Iyengar$^{(\boxtimes)}$

Computer Science and Engineering Department,
Indian Institute of Technology Ropar, Rupnagar, India
{akrati.saxena,sudarshan}@iitrpr.ac.in

Abstract. For network scientists, it has always been an interesting problem to identify the influential nodes in a given network. K-shell decomposition method is a widely used method which assigns a shell-index value to each node based on its influential power. K-shell method requires the entire network to compute the shell-index of a node that is infeasible for large-scale real-world dynamic networks. In the present work, first, we show that the shell-index of a node can be estimated using its $h^2 - index$ which can be computed using local neighborhood information. We further show that $h^2 - index$ has better monotonicity and correlation with the spreading power of the node than the shell-index. Next, we propose hill-climbing based methods to identify top-ranked nodes in a small number of steps. We further propose a heuristic method to estimate the percentile rank of a node without computing influential power of all the nodes.

1 Introduction

K-shell decomposition method is a well-known method in social network analysis to identify influential nodes in unweighted networks [1]. This algorithm works by recursively pruning the nodes from lower degree to higher degree. First, we recursively remove all nodes of degree 1, until there is no node of degree 1. All these nodes are assigned shell-index $k_s = 1$. Similarly, nodes of degree $2, 3, 4, 5, ...$ are pruned step by step. When we remove nodes of degree k, if there appears any node of degree less than k, it will also be removed in the same step. All these nodes are assigned shell-index k. This method thus divides the entire network into shells and assigns a shell-index to each node. The shell-index increases as we move from the periphery to the core of the network and higher shell-index represents higher coreness. The innermost shell has the highest shell-index k_{max} and is called the core of the network.

Many studies have shown that the core nodes are highly influential nodes in a network. During the entire discussion, influential nodes refer to the nodes having the higher spreading power. Kitsak et al. [2] showed that the information spreads faster if it is started from a core node than a periphery node. Saxena et al. [3] showed that the information becomes viral once it hits core nodes and spreads into multiple communities through the core. K-shell is a widely used

© Springer Nature Switzerland AG 2018
X. Chen et al. (Eds.): CSoNet 2018, LNCS 11280, pp. 198–210, 2018.
https://doi.org/10.1007/978-3-030-04648-4_17

method to compute the influential power of a node, but it has its disadvantages. Firstly, the k-shell method needs the entire network to compute the shell-index of a node which is infeasible for large-scale dynamic networks. Secondly, the k-shell method assigns the same index values to many nodes which actually might have different influential power as shown in [4,5].

Zeng et al. modified k-shell decomposition method and proposed a mixed degree decomposition (MDD) method which considers both the residual degree and the exhausted degree of nodes while assigning them index values [4]. Liu et al. proposed an improved ranking method that considers both the k-shell value of the node and its distance with the highest k-shell value nodes [5]. The proposed method computes the shortest distance of all nodes with the highest k-shell nodes, and has high computational complexity. Basaras et al. proposed a hybrid centrality measure based on degree and shell-index and showed that it works better than the traditional shell-index [6]. Bae and Kim proposed a method where the centrality value of a node is computed based on the shell-index value of its neighbors [7]. The proposed method outperforms other methods in scale-free networks with community structure. Tatti and Gionis proposed a graph decomposition method that considers both the connectivity as well as the local density while the k-shell decomposition method only considers connectivity of the nodes [8]. All the discussed centrality measures have better monotonicity but they require global information of the network to be computed, and so, they are not favorable in large-scale networks.

Lu et al. showed the relationship between degree, h-index, and coreness of a node [9]. They show that the h-index family of a node converges to the coreness of the node. In this work, we show that the shell-index value of a node can be estimated using its $h^2 - index$ that can be computed using local neighborhood information of the node. We further propose hill-climbing based algorithms using the proposed estimator to identify top-ranked nodes in a small number of steps. Next, we propose a heuristic method to estimate the influential rank of a node without computing the index value of all the nodes.

The rest of the paper is organized as follows. Section 2 covers preliminary definitions. In Sect. 3, we discuss the estimation of shell-index using $h^2 - index$ and experimental results. In Sect. 4, we discuss hill-climbing based approaches to identify the top-ranked nodes using local information and their simulation on real-world networks. In Sect. 5, we discuss a heuristic method to estimate the percentile rank of a node. Section 6 concludes the paper with future directions.

2   Preliminaries

2.1   H-Index

The h-index of a node u $(h - index(u))$ is h if h of its neighbors have degree at least h and there is no subset of $h + 1$ neighbors where each node belonging to that subset has the degree at least $h + 1$.

The $h^2 - index$ of a node u $(h^2 - index(u))$ is computed by taking its $h - index$ based on the $h - index$ of its neighbors and not their degrees.

2.2 Susceptible-Infected-Recovered (SIR) Model

We use the SIR model to compute the spreading power of each node. In SIR model a node can be in three possible states: 1. S (susceptible), 2. I (infected), and 3. R (recovered). Initially, all nodes are in the susceptible mode except one node which is infected and will start spreading the infection in the network. The infected node will infect each of its susceptible neighbor with infection probability (λ). If the neighbor gets infected, its status is changed to Infected. Once an infected node contacts all of its neighbors to infect them, its status is changed to Recovered with probability μ. For generality we set $\mu = 1$. Recovered nodes will neither be infected anymore nor infect others, and they remain in the Recovered state until the spreading stops. The spreading process stops when there is no infected node in the network. The number of recovered nodes is considered the spreading power or spreading capability of the original node.

3 Shell-Index Estimation

In this section, we discuss a method to estimate the shell-index using local neighborhood information.

Theorem 1. *The shell-index of a node u can be computed as $k_s(u) = h - index(k_s(v)|\forall v \in ngh(u))$, where $ngh(u)$ is the set of the neighbors of node u.*

Proof. Let's assume that h-index of $(k_s(v)|\forall v \in ngh(u))$ is h then there are at least h nodes having shell-index equal to or greater than h as per the definition of h-index.

Now, we will see how the shell-index of node u will be decided in k-shell decomposition method. In k-shell decomposition method, in i_{th} iteration all those nodes are removed who have exactly i connections with the nodes having the shell-index i or greater than i. Thus, the node u will be removed in h_{th} iteration as h of its neighbors have shell-index h or greater than h. This is nothing but the $h - index$ of node u based on the shell-indices of its neighbors as defined above. □

Next, we explain Theorem 1 using an example shown in Fig. 1(a) where node u has 8 neighbors having shell-indices 1, 2, 3, 3, 4, 6, 8, and 10. Now, we will see how the shell-index of node u will be determined during the k-shell decomposition method. In the 1_{st} iteration, first of its neighbor will be removed and node u will be left with seven connections with the nodes having the shell-indices greater than 1, so, the node u will not be removed in the first iteration. In the 2_{nd} iteration, its second neighbor will be removed as it has shell-index 2, but still, the node u has six connections with the higher shells, so, it will not be removed. In the third iteration, its third and fourth neighbors will be removed as both of these neighbors have shell-index 3. The node u still has four connections with the higher shells, so it will not be removed. In the fourth iteration, 5th of its neighbors having shell-index 4 will be removed, and now the node u has only

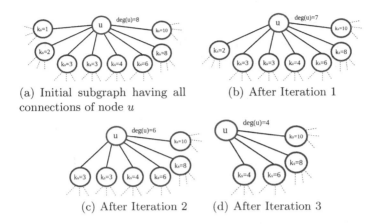

(a) Initial subgraph having all connections of node u

(b) After Iteration 1

(c) After Iteration 2

(d) After Iteration 3

Fig. 1. Example 1: Estimate shell-index of node u while applying k-shell decomposition algorithm

three connections with the higher shells, so, as per the k-shell decomposition method, node u will also be removed in the fourth iteration. So, the shell-index of node u is 4 that is nothing but the $h-index$ of the shell-indices of its neighbors.

Shell-Index Estimation

Using Theorem 1, the shell-index of a node can be estimated if the shell-indices of its neighbors are known. However, in real-life applications, the shell-indices of the neighbors are not known. We know that the shell-index of a node is bounded above by its degree, $k_s(u) \leq d(u)$. So, to estimate the shell-index of node u, we can consider the degrees of its neighbors in place of their shell-indices. This is nothing but the $h - index$ of node u as defined in Sect. 2.1. To further improve the estimation, we consider the $h - index$ of its neighbors as $k_s(v) \leq h - index(v) \leq d(v)$ and this is nothing but the $h^2 - index$ of the node. Thus the shell-index of a node can be estimated using its $h^2 - index$. The proposed estimator can be further improved if we compute the $h^3 - index$ of the node however in the Results section, we show that $h^2 - index$ is itself a good estimator. It can be computed faster and requires less neighborhood information than to compute the $h^3 - index$ of the node.

3.1 Results and Discussion

We study the performance of $h^2 - index$ versus shell-index on real-world networks and experimental results are shown in Table 1. First, we compute the monotonicity of shell-index and $h^2 - index$. In the k-shell decomposition method, all nodes which are pruned at one level are assigned the same shell-index value. Researchers have shown that they have different influential power and so, a better centrality measure will assign the same value to fewer nodes and will assign more unique values. This characteristic of the measure can be computed using the monotonicity that is defined as $M(R) = \left(1 - \frac{\sum_{r \in R} n_r(n_r-1)}{n(n-1)}\right)^2$ where R is the ranking values of all the nodes based on any given centrality measure, n is the number of nodes, and n_r is the number of nodes having rank r [7]. The results in Table 1 show that the monotonicity of $h^2 - index$ is either the same or slightly better than the shell-index.

We further study the correlation of shell-index and $h^2 - index$ with the spreading power of nodes using Kendall's Tau (τ), Pearson (r), and Spearman (ρ) correlation coefficients. The spreading power of a node is computed by executing the SIR model 100 times and taking the average of the spreading powers. In experiments, the infection probability λ is taken as $\lambda = \langle d \rangle / (\langle d^2 \rangle - \langle d \rangle) + 0.01$, where d represents degree of the node. Table 1 shows that the correlation of $h^2 - index$ with the spreading power is either as good as the correlation of shell-index with the spreading power or better.

Table 1. Performance of Shell-Index (k_s) and $h^2 - index$ using monotonicity and SIR spreading model

Network	Ref	Nodes	Edges	Monotonicity		k_s vs. SIR			$h^2 - index$ vs. SIR		
				k_s	$h^2 - Index$	Kendall	Pearson	Spearman	Kendall	Pearson	Spearman
Astro-Ph	[10]	14845	119652	0.89	0.89	0.51	0.67	0.67	0.52	0.67	0.68
Buzznet	[11]	101163	2763066	0.93	0.93	0.21	0.28	0.30	0.21	0.28	0.30
Cond-Mat	[10]	13861	44619	0.75	0.76	0.55	0.69	0.69	0.56	0.70	0.70
DBLP	[12]	317080	1049866	0.74	0.75	0.49	0.61	0.61	0.49	0.62	0.62
Digg	[13]	261489	1536577	0.45	0.45	0.48	0.60	0.59	0.48	0.60	0.59
Enron	[14]	84384	295889	0.30	0.30	0.45	0.58	0.55	0.45	0.58	0.55
Facebook	[15]	63392	816831	0.91	0.91	0.49	0.64	0.65	0.49	0.64	0.65
Fb-Wall	[15]	43953	182384	0.76	0.77	0.62	0.75	0.76	0.62	0.75	0.76
Foursquare	[11]	639014	3214985	0.50	0.50	0.54	0.66	0.65	0.54	0.66	0.65
Gowalla	[16]	196591	950327	0.73	0.74	0.59	0.71	0.72	0.59	0.71	0.72

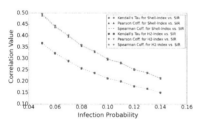

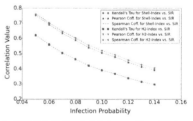

(a) Astro-Ph Collaboration Network   (b) FB-Wall Social Interaction Network

Fig. 2. The correlation of shell-Index and $h^2 - index$ with the spreading power for varying infection probability on (a) Astro-Ph and (b) FB-Wall network

We also study how the correlation of shell-index and $h^2 - index$ with the spreading power changes as we vary the infection probability. The plots are shown in Fig. 2 for Astro-physics collaboration network and FB-wall social interaction network. The results show that $h^2 - index$ has a good correlation with varying infection probabilities. Thus we observe that $h^2 - index$ is a better centrality measure and a good estimator of the shell-index in real-world networks. $h^2 - index$ has an advantage over shell-index that it is a local centrality measure and can be computed for a node using local neighborhood information without collecting the entire network.

4 Hill-Climbing Based Approach to Identify Top-Ranked Nodes

In many real-life applications, we need to identify top influential nodes to spread the information faster. For example, identify people to provide free samples for publicizing a product or infect a computer system to spread the virus using the Internet network. In large-scale networks, it is infeasible to collect the entire network to identify the top influential nodes. So, we need methods to identify these nodes using local information without having the global information. In [17], Gupta et al. proposed Hill-Climbing based methods that can be used to hit the highest shell-index nodes faster in a network. In the proposed method, the random walker starts from a periphery node and move to one of its neighbors having the highest shell-index until a top node is found. The proposed method cannot be applied in practice as the shell-index is a global centrality measure.

In this work, we have shown that the influential power of a node can be computed using its $h^2 - index$, i.e., a local measure. We modify the proposed methods to identify the highest $h^2 - index$ node in the network. In rest of the discussion, the *top-ranked nodes* refer to the nodes having the highest $h^2 - index$. The algorithm is called $IndexBasedHillClimbing(G, u, k, maxindex)$, and its pseudo code is given in Algorithm 1. The inputs of the algorithm are G, u, k, and $maxindex$ where G is the given network, u is the seed node from which the crawler starts crawling the network, k is the repeat-count that shows how many times the crawler will restart the walk from a randomly chosen neighbor of the current node if it is stuck to a local maxima, and $maxindex$ is the maximum $h^2 - index$ in the given network. A node is called local maxima if its $h^2 - index$ is higher than all of its neighbors. The nodes having the highest $h^2 - index$ in the network are called global maxima. For the clarification, a local maxima can also be the global maxima.

The algorithm works in the following manner. The crawler starts from a given node u, and it moves to one of its neighbors that has not been visited before and has the highest $h^2 - index$. The crawler keeps moving until it hits the local maxima. If this node has the highest $h^2 - index$, the algorithm exits, else, the crawler jumps to one of its non-visited neighbors uniformly at random, and the repeat-count is increased by one. The same procedure is repeated until the highest $h^2 - index$ node is identified or the repeat-count reaches its maximum

---

Algorithm 1. $IndexBasedHillClimbing(G, u, k, maxindex)$

Take a list $visited\_nodes$ and $visited\_nodes = [\,]$
$num\_of\_steps = 0$
$repeat\_count = 0$
$current\_node = u$
$next\_node = u$
add u in $visited\_nodes$
$flag = True$
while $flag == True$ **do**
    for each v in $ngh(current\_node)$ **do**
        if $h^2 - index(v) \geq h^2 - index(next\_node)$ and $v \notin visited\_nodes$ **then**
            $next\_node = v$
        end if
    end for
    if $next\_node == current\_node$ **then**
        if $h^2 - index(next\_node) == maxindex$ **then**
            $flag = False$
        else if $repeat\_count < k$ **then**
            $next\_node = randomchoice_{v \notin visited\_nodes} ngh(current\_node)$
            $repeat\_count = repeat\_count + 1$
        else
            Print "The algorithm is failed to find out the top-ranked node."
            $flag = False$
        end if
    end if
    if $flag == True$ **then**
        add $next\_node$ in $visited\_nodes$
        $current\_node = next\_node$
        $num\_of\_steps = num\_of\_steps + 1$
    end if
end while
return $h^2 - index(current\_node)$

---

value. If the algorithm reaches to maximum repeat-count without finding out the highest $h^2 - index$, it returns "The algorithm is failed to find out the top-ranked node." In Algorithm 1, $ngh(u)$ represents the set of all the neighbors of node u. $randomchoice(list)$ function returns a random element from the given list.

The proposed method is further modified using the degree of the nodes and named as $IndexAndDegreeBasedHillClimbing(G, u, k, maxindex)$. In this method, the crawler will move to one of the highest degree nodes among the non-visited neighbors having the highest $h^2 - index$. Except this, there is one more change; once the algorithm is stuck to local maxima, the crawler moves to one of its non-visited neighbors having the highest degree. Intuitively, it seems that the highest degree node has a high probability to be connected with top-ranked nodes, and so, this algorithm will work faster and better than the first one.

Discussion

We implement the proposed methods on real-world networks, and results are shown in Table 2. In experiments, the algorithm is executed from all non top-ranked nodes, and the number of steps taken to hit a top-ranked node are averaged to compute the average number of steps. In experiments, the value of repeat-count (k) is set to 50. In Table 2, the average and the standard deviation of the number of steps are shown in $Avg\,(steps)$ and $Std\,(steps)$ columns. The $Avg\,(count)$ shows the average of the number of repeat-count that algorithm takes before reaching a global maxima. The $Algo\ Failed(\%)$ shows how many times the algorithm is not succeeded to hit the top-ranked node in the given repeat-count. The algorithm might succeed if we increase the value of repeat-count.

The results show that on an average a top-ranked node can be reached in very few steps (3–213 in the considered datasets), and the average value of the repeat-count is 0–10. The algorithm is failed in few cases for repeat-count 50. In the case of $IndexAndDegreeBasedHillClimbing$ algorithm, the average number of steps and the average repeat-count is reduced but the probability to fail the algorithm is increased in the given repeat-count as the crawler always moves to higher degree nodes and ends up following the same path that leads to the local maxima. In DBLP network, the probability of failure is much higher when we apply degree based hill-climbing approach as the algorithm is mostly stuck to a local maxima due to following the same route and not able to hit the global maxima in the given repeat-count. This highly depends on the network structure and not on its size.

When we apply these algorithms in practice, we do not know the highest $h^2 - index\ (maxindex)$, so, the algorithms need to be repeated few more times to make sure that the node returned by the algorithm is the actual global maxima and not the local maxima. The results show that a smaller value of $repeat - count$ will suffice the purpose. The algorithms can be started from a few randomly chosen nodes to avoid the local maxima and hit the top-ranked nodes with a high probability.

The proposed methods can be further improved by only computing the $h^2 - index$ of the neighbors that can be considered for the next step of the crawler instead of computing the $h^2 - index$ of all of its neighbors. A node having the degree lower than the $h^2 - index$ of the current node cannot have the $h^2 - index$ higher than the current node, so, all such neighbors can be discarded. This further fastens up the proposed method.

In considered datasets, we observed that the induced subgraph of all top-ranked nodes is connected and once we hit one top node, all top nodes can be identified. All these nodes can be used to spread the information faster in the network.

Table 2. Results for $IndexBasedHillClimbing$ and $IndexAndDegreeBased$ - $HillClimbing$ Algorithms

Network	$Nodes$	$IndexBasedHillClimbing$				$IndexAndDegreeBasedHillClimbing$			
		Avg (steps)	Std (steps)	Avg (count)	Algo Failed(%)	Avg (steps)	Std (steps)	Avg (count)	Algo Failed(%)
Astro-Ph	14845	8.66	9.82	0.37	1.21	5.70	1.40	0.00	3.27
Buzznet	101163	3.20	0.69	0.00	0.00	3.20	0.69	0.00	0.00
Cond-Mat	13861	15.55	15.46	2.27	1.39	9.95	4.88	0.18	11.58
DBLP	317080	213.13	84.89	9.79	5.45	118.76	5.34	0.00	79.60
Digg	261489	4.09	1.50	0.02	0.03	4.03	0.85	0.00	0.15
Enron	84384	5.08	0.97	0.00	0.00	5.07	0.93	0.00	0.04
Facebook	63392	6.06	1.90	0.30	0.00	5.99	1.80	0.31	0.02
FB-Wall	43953	9.04	4.48	0.59	0.00	8.65	4.12	0.48	0.04
Foursquare	639014	10.84	0.38	0.00	0.00	10.84	0.38	0.00	0.00
Gowalla	196591	4.33	4.17	0.15	0.02	3.92	1.32	0.03	0.22

5   Rank Estimation of a Node

In real-life applications, researchers are interested in studying the relative importance of a node that is denoted by its rank based on the given centrality measure [18]. In large-scale networks, it is infeasible to compute the centrality value of all nodes to compute the rank of one node, so researchers have proposed efficient ranking methods for different centrality measures like degree [19–21], and closeness centrality [22,23].

In this section, we study the characteristics of $h^2 - index$ and based on that propose a fast rank estimation method. We observe that the percentile rank versus $h^2 - index$ follows a unique pattern in all the considered real-world networks as shown in Fig. 3. The percentile rank of a node is computed as $PercentileRank(u) = \frac{n - R(u) + 1}{n} * 100$, where n is the network size and $R(u)$ is the rank of node u based on its $h^2 - index$ value in the given network. We study this curve and find that 4-parameters logistic equation better fits the curve. The equation of the curve is given as $PercentileRank(u) = a_2 + \frac{a_1 - a_2}{1 + \left(\frac{h^2 - index(u)}{x_0}\right)^p}$, where a_1, a_2, x_0, and p are variables, and p denotes slope of the logistic curve (also called hill's slope).

The plots are shown in Fig. 3, where black colored circles show the actual percentile rank of the nodes and the red colored triangles show the best-fit curve using the 4-parameter logistic equation. The best fit curve is plotted using scaled Levenberg-Marquardt algorithm [24] with 1000 iterations and 0.0001 tolerance. It can be concluded from the plots that the logistic equation can be used to estimate the percentile rank of the node. Once we estimate the parameters of the equation, the rank of a node can be computed in $O(1)$ time without computing the index values of all the nodes.

Estimating Parameters of the Logistic Curve: We estimate the parameters of the logistic curve by analyzing the curves for different networks. In logistic curve, a_2 is the highest rank value, so, it can be estimated as $a_2 = 100$. Based on our analysis, we estimate $a_1 = 1$ and observe that the fitted curve is closed to the best fit. The value of p is taken as the average of the slopes of the considered datasets using the estimated value of a_1 and a_2. The value of p using the estimated parameters ($a_1 = 1$ and $a_2 = 100$) is shown in Table 3 and their average is $p = 1.44$. The estimation of x_0 is still an open question, and we have computed it using scaled Levenberg-Marquardt algorithm for the implementation.

Table 3. Networks versus their p values using the estimated values of a_1 and a_2

Network	p value	Network	p value	Network	p value	Network	p value	Network	p value
Astro-Ph	1.49	Buzznet	1.26	Cond-Mat	2.44	DBLP	2.08	Digg	0.91
Enron	0.90	Facebook	1.37	FB-Wall	1.56	Foursquare	0.97	Gowalla	1.40
								Average	1.44

Discussion

The plots for the actual rank, best-fit rank, and estimated rank are shown in Fig. 3 for some networks due to the space constraint. The estimated rank is computed using the estimated parameters ($a_1 = 1$, $a_2 = 100$, and $p = 1.44$). Next, we compute the absolute error ($|Actual\ Percentile\ Rank - Computed\ Percentile\ Rank|$) for each $h^2 - index$ value and then take the average to compute the average error. The average error and standard deviation of the estimated rank using the best-fit and estimated parameters are shown in Table 4. The results show that the logistic curve can be efficiently used to estimate the percentile rank.

Table 4. Absolute error for percentile ranking using best-fit and estimated curve

Network	Best-fit		Estimated	
	Avg. error	Std. dev	Avg. error	Std. dev
Astro-Ph	0.36	0.28	1.96	1.02
Buzznet	5.73	6.13	1.73	1.91
Cond-Mat	0.64	0.39	6.92	2.86
DBLP	0.18	0.14	2.83	2.05
Digg	0.36	0.29	0.95	1.31
Enron	0.57	0.31	1.48	1.74
Facebook	6.58	5.62	2.66	1.66
Fb-Wall	0.65	0.43	2.43	0.88
Foursquare	1.54	1.46	2.02	3.01
Gowalla	0.19	0.12	0.64	0.51

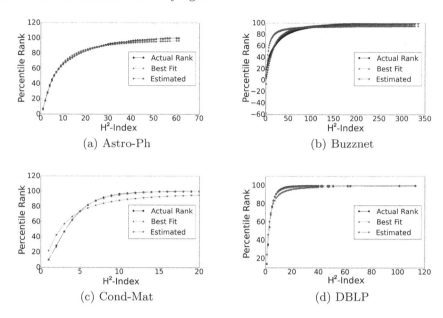

Fig. 3. Percentile Rank versus $h^2 - index$

6   Conclusion

In this work, we have shown that $h^2 - index$ is a good estimator of shell-index and can be used to identify influential nodes in real-world networks. We also observed that $h^2 - index$ has better monotonicity than the shell-index and has better correlation with the spreading power of the nodes. Next, we proposed hill climbing based methods to identify the top-ranked nodes. The results show that a top-ranked node can be found in a small number of steps. We observed that the induced subgraph of all the top-ranked nodes is connected and once we find one top node, all the top nodes can be identified. One can further propose mathematical bound to compute the required number of steps to hit a top node in the given scale-free real-world network. In the last section, we discussed a heuristic method to estimate the percentile rank of the node. One can further propose better methods for estimating the parameters of the logistic curve that will improve the accuracy of the rank estimation.

References

1. Seidman, S.B.: Network structure and minimum degree. Soc. Netw. **5**(3), 269–287 (1983)
2. Kitsak, M., et al.: Identification of influential spreaders in complex networks. Nat. Phys. **6**(11), 888–893 (2010)

3. Saxena, A., Iyengar, S.R.S., Gupta, Y.: Understanding spreading patterns on social networks based on network topology. In: 2015 IEEE/ACM International Conference on Advances in Social Networks Analysis and Mining (ASONAM), pp. 1616–1617. IEEE (2015)
4. Zeng, A., Zhang, C.-J.: Ranking spreaders by decomposing complex networks. Phys. Lett. A **377**(14), 1031–1035 (2013)
5. Liu, J.-G., Ren, Z.-M., Guo, Q.: Ranking the spreading influence in complex networks. Phys. A Stat. Mech. Appl. **392**(18), 4154–4159 (2013)
6. Basaras, P., Katsaros, D., Tassiulas, L.: Detecting influential spreaders in complex, dynamic networks. Computer **46**(4), 0024–29 (2013)
7. Bae, J., Kim, S.: Identifying and ranking influential spreaders in complex networks by neighborhood coreness. Phys. A Stat. Mech. Appl. **395**, 549–559 (2014)
8. Tatti, N., Gionis, A.: Density-friendly graph decomposition. In: Proceedings of the 24th International Conference on World Wide Web, pp. 1089–1099. International World Wide Web Conferences Steering Committee (2015)
9. Lü, L., Zhou, T., Zhang, Q.-M., Stanley, H.E.: The H-index of a network node and its relation to degree and coreness. Nat. Commun. **7** (2016)
10. Leskovec, J., Kleinberg, J., Faloutsos, C.: Graph evolution: densification and shrinking diameters. ACM Trans. Knowl. Discov. Data (TKDD) **1**(1), 2 (2007)
11. Zafarani, R., Liu, H.: Social computing data repository at ASU (2009)
12. Yang, J., Leskovec, J.: Defining and evaluating network communities based on ground-truth. Knowl. Inf. Syst. **42**(1), 181–213 (2015)
13. Hogg, T., Lerman, K.: Social dynamics of digg. EPJ Data Sci. **1**(1), 1–26 (2012)
14. Klimt, B., Yang, Y.: The Enron corpus: a new dataset for email classification research. In: Boulicaut, J.-F., Esposito, F., Giannotti, F., Pedreschi, D. (eds.) ECML 2004. LNCS (LNAI), vol. 3201, pp. 217–226. Springer, Heidelberg (2004). https://doi.org/10.1007/978-3-540-30115-8_22
15. Viswanath, B., Mislove, A., Cha, M., Gummadi, K.P.: On the evolution of user interaction in facebook. In: Proceedings of the 2nd ACM Workshop on Online Social Networks, pp. 37–42. ACM (2009)
16. Cho, E., Myers, S.A., Leskovec, J.: Friendship and mobility: user movement in location-based social networks. In Proceedings of the 17th ACM SIGKDD International Conference on Knowledge Discovery and Data Mining, pp. 1082–1090. ACM (2011)
17. Gupta, Y., Das, D., Iyengar, S.R.S.: Pseudo-cores: the terminus of an intelligent viral meme's trajectory. In: Cherifi, H., Gonçalves, B., Menezes, R., Sinatra, R. (eds.) Complex Networks VII. SCI, vol. 644, pp. 213–226. Springer, Cham (2016). https://doi.org/10.1007/978-3-319-30569-1_16
18. Saxena, A., Iyengar, S.R.S.: Global rank estimation. arXiv preprint arXiv:1710.11341 (2017)
19. Saxena, A., Malik, V., Iyengar, S.R.S.: Rank me thou shalln't compare me. arXiv preprint arXiv:1511.09050 (2015)
20. Saxena, A., Gera, R., Iyengar, S.R.S.: Observe locally rank globally. In: Proceedings of the 2017 IEEE/ACM International Conference on Advances in Social Networks Analysis and Mining 2017, pp. 139–144. ACM (2017)
21. Saxena, A., Gera, R., Iyengar, S.R.S.: Estimating degree rank in complex networks. Soc. Netw. Anal. Min. **8**(1), 42 (2018)

22. Saxena, A., Gera, R., Iyengar, S.R.S.: Fast estimation of closeness centrality ranking. In: Proceedings of the 2017 IEEE/ACM International Conference on Advances in Social Networks Analysis and Mining 2017, pp. 80–85. ACM (2017)
23. Saxena, A., Gera, R., Iyengar, S.R.S.: A faster method to estimate closeness centrality ranking. arXiv preprint arXiv:1706.02083 (2017)
24. Moré, J.J.: The Levenberg-Marquardt algorithm: implementation and theory. In: Watson, G.A. (ed.) Numerical Analysis. LNM, vol. 630, pp. 105–116. Springer, Heidelberg (1978). https://doi.org/10.1007/BFb0067700

Leveraging Blockchain to Enhance Data Privacy in IoT-Based Applications

Truc D. T. Nguyen[1(✉)], Hoang-Anh Pham[2], and My T. Thai[1]

[1] Department of Computer and Information Science and Engineering,
University of Florida, Gainesville, FL 32611, USA
truc.nguyen@ufl.edu, mythai@cise.ufl.edu
[2] Faculty of Computer Science and Engineering, HCMC University of Technology,
VNU-HCM, Ho Chi Minh City, Vietnam
anhpham@hcmut.edu.vn

Abstract. In this paper, we present how blockchain can be leveraged to tackle data privacy issues in Internet of Things (IoT). With the aid of smart contracts, we have developed a system model featuring a trustless access control management mechanism to ensure that users have full control over their data and can track how data are accessed by third-party services. Additionally, we propose a firmware update scheme using blockchain that helps prevent fraudulent data caused by IoT device tampering. Finally, we discuss how our proposed solution can strengthen the data privacy as well as tolerate common adversaries.

1 Introduction

With the great success of Bitcoin [1], the blockchain technology recently has become a trending research topic in both academic institutes and industries associations. In a simple manner, blockchain is a decentralized database that contains linked data blocks where each block is a group of valid and digitally signed transactions. The blockchain itself is maintained by nodes in a peer-to-peer network. What makes blockchain noticeable is the employment of a decentralized fashion in which applications can operate efficiently without the need of a central authority. In specific, it enables a trustless network where participants can transact although they do not trust one another. Smart contracts in the blockchain context are self-executing and self-enforcing contracts that are stored on chain. They are deployed with explicit terms and conditions that are publicly visible to all participants. Blockchain and smart contracts together have motivated numerous decentralized applications such as Golem [2], Augur [3], or Status [4]. Consequently, the blockchain technology has the potential to go beyond financial transactions and can be leveraged to tackle many problems in other domains, especially in Internet of Things (IoT), which is currently employing a centralized architecture.

© Springer Nature Switzerland AG 2018
X. Chen et al. (Eds.): CSoNet 2018, LNCS 11280, pp. 211–221, 2018.
https://doi.org/10.1007/978-3-030-04648-4_18

We are witnessing the incredible growth of smart and networked embedded devices that Cisco predicts to have about 50 billion connected devices by 2020 [5]. As such, there is an urgent need to shift toward a decentralized model with open-access networks and distributed cloud for sustaining the ever-expanding IoT ecosystem [6]. In a typical IoT system, IoT devices aggregate data from dedicated sensors, perform preprocessing, and push them to data center or cloud for storage. These data are then analyzed and processed for different applications. One critical concern with this type of architecture is the privacy as these data could be very sensitive and related to private information. In fact, by using a centralized cloud storage, data's owners have very limited control and awareness over their data. They have to put trust in cloud providers and would not know if the data were being used for bad purposes. In this paper, we propose an IoT-based system model that adopts blockchain and smart contracts as a solution for the privacy issue. Particularly, we emphasize the data ownership that users should have full control over their data and be aware of how they are being used.

Another problem in current IoT systems is that data are only as good as the IoT devices from which they are originated, there is no guarantee that they are accurate. In IoT, devices are subjected to be compromised in which a device's firmware can be replaced by a malicious one [7–9]. Various incidents about this type of attack have been recorded [10,11]. Such attack could take control of the IoT devices to perform illegal actions or produce false data. In the scope of this work, we leverage blockchain to help users detect malicious firmwares as well as make sure that devices are updated with legitimate ones. This solution will prevent fraudulent data from being published to the network.

Our contributions are summarized as follows:

1. Proposing an IoT system model based on blockchain and smart contracts that features a trustless access control management. Our solution makes sure that users are the owners of their data and third-party services can only access the data given users' consent.
2. Proposing a firmware update scheme using blockchain to ensure that IoT devices are programmed with legitimate firmwares. This will help prevent fraudulent data caused by IoT device tampering.

The remainder of this paper is organized in the following manners. Section 2 introduces the problems that are addressed in this work. The overall design of the system model is given in Sect. 3. We describe detailed implementation in Sect. 4. Section 5 analyzes the privacy and security of the model. Some related works are presented in Sect. 6, and Sect. 7 provides the final concluding remarks.

2   Problem Statement

This paper mainly tackles the data privacy issues when third-party services are involved. In specific, we concentrate on IoT-based applications in which data collected from IoT devices can be accessed by some third-party services given that the users have consented. Our solution aims to address the following privacy issues:

- Access control: the system recognizes users as the owners of their data and they can authorize other services to access the data. Users have the flexibility to modify the set of permissions at any given time.
- Data transparency: Third-party services who were granted permissions by users can easily access the published data; and the assurance that those published data are officially coming from the users.
- Access tracking: Users are fully aware over what data are being collected and how they are accessed by third-party services.

Furthermore, we address the attack in which adversaries can tamper with IoT devices and produce fraudulent data. Our solution makes sure that IoT devices can obtain the latest official firmware from their vendors and prevent fraudulent data from being published on blockchain, thereby maintaining the data integrity.

3 System Model

Figure 1 illustrates an overview of our system model. As can be seen, all entities interact with each other via a blockchain network. A set of *Aggregators* $A = \{a_1, a_2, ..., a_n\}$ represents users who own one or more IoT devices that generate data. An Aggregator can categorize data from IoT devices into slots so that it can permit third-party services to access only a subset of data. For example, an Aggregator a_1 wishing to categorize its data into temperature, humidity and location will result in having three slots, that is $SLOT_{a_1} = \{[temperature], [humidity], [location]\}$. Each Aggregator will issue transactions to the blockchain for granting permissions or publishing data.

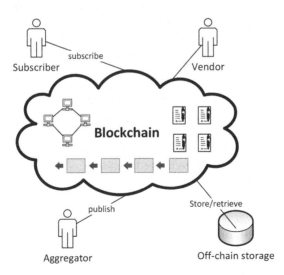

Fig. 1. System model

A set of *Subscribers* $S = \{s_1, s_2, ..., s_n\}$ represents third-party services who can issue transactions to access data published by Aggregators given appropriate permissions. A set of *Vendors* $V = \{v_1, v_2, ..., v_n\}$ represents manufacturers of IoT devices who are responsible for publishing official firmware images. Each of Aggregator, Subscriber and Vendor is identified by a set of public-private key to interact with the blockchain network, they are responsible for securing their own private keys to avoid being compromised.

Data published by Aggregators are stored in the off-chain storage. This component uses a content-based addressing scheme, that means for each piece of data, its hash corresponds to the address at which it is stored. Thus, this hash can be used as a pointer to retrieved the data. The off-chain storage could be either a distributed peer-to-peer filesystem platform where data are stored across a set of storage nodes such as IPFS [12], Swarm [13], and Storj [14]; or, even a centralized cloud with sufficient trust in a third-party service. In case of using a distributed platform, a node could serve as both a storage node and a blockchain's node. The off-chain storage only accepts requests originated from the blockchain's nodes.

The blockchain network is deployed with two smart contracts: *AccessControl* and *FirmwareUpdate* that are used for managing access permissions and updating new firmwares, respectively. We assume that all smart contracts are correctly deployed. For better understanding the workflow of our system, consider the following example: the Aggregator a_1 collects data from IoT devices and categorizes them into $SLOT_{a_1}$ as above, by issuing a *publish* transaction to the blockchain, $SLOT_{a_1}$ is stored in the off-chain storage and its hash is saved in the blockchain. Assume that a_1 wants to share the temperature data with s_1, location and humidity with s_2, a_1 will invoke the AccessControl contract to grant s_1 and s_2 access permissions to its specific data slots. The access control policy of a pair (a_i, s_j) is then saved in the AccessControl contract.

Consider that s_1 wants to access the temperature data of a_1, it will issue a *retrieve* transaction to the blockchain to retrieve the data from the off-chain storage. This transaction will invoke the AccessControl contract to check for (a_1, s_1)'s policy to see if s_1 has the right to access the temperature data of a_1.

Each Vendor v_i will publish the hash of its official firmware images to the blockchain by using the FirmwareUpdate contract. An Aggregator can monitor the firmware of its devices by comparing the image hash of the devices with the one published on the blockchain by Vendors. Therefore, it can update the new image or know which devices were being tampered.

4   Implementation

4.1   Encryption Scheme

Data stored in the off-chain storage are encrypted by the Aggregator. Since encrypting a large chunk of data using asymmetric encryption schemes is not known to be efficient, in this work, we employ a hybrid approach with a re-encryption scheme [15,16]. We denote $ENC(d, k)$ as encrypting data d using key k, $DEC(d_{enc}, k)$ as decrypting the encrypted data d_{enc} using key k, pk as public key and sk as private (or secret) key. Our encryption scheme is as follows:

1. An Aggregator a_i besides its permanent public/private key (pk_{a_i}, sk_{a_i}) will generate a temporary pair of $(pk_{a_i}^l, sk_{a_i}^l)$ for each of its slot $l \in SLOT_{a_i}$. With respect to a slot l, for each Subscriber s_j that a_i wants to grant access, a_i generates a uni-directional re-encryption key $K_{a_i \to s_j}^l$ from $sk_{a_i}^l$ and pk_{s_j}. This key allows a proxy server to convert from $ENC(m, pk_{a_i}^l)$ to $ENC(m, pk_{s_j}^l)$ for any message m without revealing the underlying text or $sk_{a_i}^l$ [16]. All re-encryption keys are kept in the AccessControl contract.
2. When a_i wants to publish a data slot l, it first signs the data using its private key sk_{a_i} to create a $sig_{a_i}^l$ which will also be added into l. Then it generates a new symmetric random key $rk_{a_i}^l$ and uses it to encrypt the data to create l_{enc} as follows:

$$l_{enc} = ENC(\langle sig_{a_i}^l | l \rangle, rk_{a_i}^l) \tag{1}$$

3. a_i encrypts that random key using its $pk_{a_i}^l$ and prepends it to the encrypted data, that means a_i will publish $\langle ENC(rk_{a_i}^l, pk_{a_i}^l) || l_{enc} \rangle$
4. When s_j is authorized to access that data published by a_i, the blockchain node will perform re-encryption:

$$ENC(rk_{a_i}^l, pk_{s_j}^l) = K_{a_i \to s_j}^l ENC(rk_{a_i}^l, pk_{a_i}^l) \tag{2}$$

and then it returns l_{enc} together with $ENC(rk_{a_i}^l, pk_{s_j}^l)$ to s_j.
5. Now, s_j can perform:

$$\begin{aligned} rk_{a_i}^l &= DEC(ENC(rk_{a_i}^l, pk_{s_j}^l), sk_{s_j}) \\ \langle sig_{a_i}^l | l \rangle &= DEC(l_{enc}, rk_{a_i}^l) \end{aligned} \tag{3}$$

At this time, s_j can read the published data l, and also verify the $sig_{a_i}^l$ using pk_{a_i} to confirm the data's origin.

Each time a_i wants to publish new data, it only needs to repeat from step 2. However, in case a_i wants to revoke the access permission of s_j to a specific slot l, it will repeat step 1 to generate a new pair of $(pk_{a_i}^l, sk_{a_i}^l)$ so that the re-encryption keys are now changed, s_j will not be able to decrypt any further l_{enc}.

4.2 Access Control Contract

Contract 1 presents the implementation of the AccessControl contract. It holds a state variable M which is a map between a pair of $(a_i \in A, s_j \in S)$ and a set of policies P. Each element in P is a pair of $(l_{id}, K_{a_i \to s_j}^l)$ where l is the slot identifier and $K_{a_i \to s_j}^l$ is the corresponding re-encryption key as in Sect. 4.1. Whenever an a_i wants to grant access to any s_j, it will issue a transaction that specifies the set P for each s_j to the *Share* procedure of the contract. At this time, the variable M will be updated with that new information.

Contract 1 AccessControl

M: map $(a_i, s_j) \rightarrow P$ ▷ P: a set of policies

$AccessLog$: record an attempt to access an a_i's slot by a 5-tuple $(s_j, a_i, l, time, stt)$

procedure SHARE(pk_t, PK_S, POL)   ▷ Share data slots with Subscribers

    Input

        pk_t public key of the transaction's issuer

        PK_S list of Subscribers' public keys

        POL set of policies for each Subscriber

    for $pk_{s_j} \in PK_S$ **do**

        $P \leftarrow POL[pk_{s_j}]$ ▷ Obtain P of s_j

        $M[(pk_t, pk_{s_j})] \leftarrow P$

    end for

end procedure

function ACCESS(pk_a, pk_t, l_{id})   ▷ Check if an Aggregator's slot is accessible

    Input

        pk_a public key of the Aggregator

        pk_t public key of the transaction's issuer

        l_{id} the slot that needs to be checked

    $P \leftarrow M[(pk_a, pk_t)]$

    if $l_{id} \in P$ **then**

        $AccessLog \leftarrow (pk_t, pk_a, l, time, True)$

        return True

    else

        $AccessLog \leftarrow (pk_t, pk_a, l, time, False)$

        return False

    end if

end function

In case an a_i wants to deny access from s_j to its slot l, a_i will generate a new $(pk_{a_i}^l, sk_{a_i}^l)$ as in Sect. 4.1 and do not create a re-encryption key for s_j. a_i then issues a transaction to the contract to update its policy including new re-encryption keys for other Subscribers.

Moreover, the contract also has a state variable $AccessLog$ that records an s_j's attempt to access a slot $l \in SLOT_{a_i}$. Each record is a 5-tuple $(s_j, a_i, l, time, stt)$ where $time$ and stt dictates the timestamp and status (True/False) of the access, respectively. When s_j issues a $retrieve$ transaction to access a_i's data, the function $Access$ of this contract will be activated to check if the slot is accessible, and the attempt, whether granted or denied, will be recorded on the blockchain. If a_i wants to see the past contents of this $AccessLog$ variable, it only needs to traverse back the blockchain history.

4.3   Data Publishing and Retrieval

For these operations, as they involve a large amount of data, they can only be executed off-chain. An Aggregator a_i who wants to publish a new data slot l will first sign and encrypt it as in Sect. 4.1. As above-mentioned, the published data will in fact be $\langle ENC(rk_{a_i}^l, pk_{a_i}^l)||l_{enc}\rangle$, we denote it as l_{pub}. a_i will issue a *publish* transaction to the blockchain that includes $H(l_{pub})$ (hash of l_{pub}) and the slot identifier l_{id}. Once the transaction is recorded on the blockchain, a_i will send l_{pub} to a blockchain node(s). This node can be randomly chosen or selected by proof-of-stake or a_i can even send to multiple nodes for redundancy. These nodes upon receiving l_{pub} first need to verify that $H(l_{pub})$ matches the hash included in the corresponding *publish* transaction. Then, they upload l_{pub} to the off-chain storage in which it can later be addressed by $H(l_{pub})$.

When a Subscriber s_j wants to access the published data of a_i, it will issue a *retrieve* transaction indicating the pk_{a_i} and l_{id}. This transaction will trigger the AccessControl contract at function *Access* as in Sect. 4.2. If the function returns false, no further actions will take place. If it returns true, the blockchain node will look into the records and find the most recent $H(l_{pub})$ associated with pk_{a_i} and l_{id}. Then it will use the hash to obtain l_{pub} from the off-chain storage, perform re-encryption using the key $K_{a_i \rightarrow s_j}^l$ stored in the AccessControl contract as in Sect. 4.1, and return the data to s_j. After decrypting, s_j can check the received data's hash against the record on blockchain.

4.4   Firmware Update Contract

Contract 2 illustrates the implementation of the FirmwareUpdate contract. This is a simple contract in which it records all firmwares' hash issued by Vendors. It has a state variable F that is a map between Vendor $v_i \in V$ and the hash of its latest firmware. For simplicity, we assume that each Vendor only issues one IoT device. Each time a v_i wants to publish a new firmware, it will issue a transaction to invoke the *NewFirmware* procedure to update the variable F.

An Aggregator a_i may use this contract to update its devices' firmware or check for device tampering. To update a device, a_i only needs to look for the corresponding Vendor in F for the latest hash, if this hash is different than its device's firmware hash, a_i can download the new firmware directly from the Vendor and then verify the downloaded file using the hash in this contract. To check if its device was tampered, a_i will traverse back the blockchain history of variable F to see whether any of the published hash matches the current firmware hash of the device. If the result is negative, that means the device's firmware was overwritten by attackers.

5   Privacy and Security Analysis

As opposed to the traditional cloud-centric IoT model in which data are susceptible to be manipulated and misused, the Aggregators in this system design have full control over their data. As can be seen from the AccessControl contract, an Aggregator may modify the set of permissions at any time without the need of any central authority. By combining with the encryption scheme, the system makes sure that Subscribers who are not granted permissions will not be able to access the Aggregator's data. An adversary may attempt to take control of the storage nodes to obtain data, however, the data are all encrypted, thus without having a re-encryption key issued by the Aggregator, the data cannot be decrypted. Furthermore, in case of using a distributed storage platform like *distributed hashtable* (DHT) [17], data are separated into chunks and are stored across different storage nodes, it would be hard for someone to assemble the data. Another way of attack is to have a malicious blockchain node query data from the off-chain storage or the node itself ignores the access control policy and gives data to unauthorized Subscribers. However, in the same manner, data are encrypted, only Subscribers who were granted permissions may be able to decrypt them.

Contract 2 FirmwareUpdate

F: map between a $v_i \in V$ to its latest firmware hash

    procedure NEWFIRMWARE(pk_t, h)   ▷ Publish new firmware
        Input
            pk_t public key of the transaction's issuer
            h hash of the firmware
        if $pk_t \in V$ **then**   ▷ Check if the issuer is a Vendor
            $F[t] \leftarrow h$
        end if
    end procedure

Subscribers who were given appropriate permission may easily access data published by the Aggregator. As the system guarantees the data integrity, Subscribers can make sure that the obtained data are accurate, untampered. This is due to the fact that the off-chain storage uses a content-based addressing scheme, therefore if the data were altered, it would not be addressable by the hash stored on blockchain. Additionally, as blockchain is immutable, hashes stored on chain remain permanently authentic. Thanks to that, even if an Aggregator's private key was stolen, data already stored on the off-chain storage could not be modified. By verifying the signature found in the data, Subscribers can firmly believe that they are originated from the official source.

Along with sharing data, the system also enables Aggregators to be fully aware of the shared data. Each time a Subscriber issues a *retrieve* transaction to obtain data, the attempt, either successful or failed, will be recorded by the AccessControl contract. By looking into the records, the Aggregator may track how its data are being collected by third-party services.

Moreover, by employing the firmware update scheme, we limit attempts to physically tamper IoT devices that overwrites the firmware in order to produce fraudulent data to the network. By traversing back all firmware's hashes stored on the blockchain, an Aggregator can detect if its devices were compromised, which also helps discovering some vulnerabilities resided within its system. Aggregators can set up a schedule to check or update new firmware images on a recurring basis (e.g., daily). In this way, users can assure that malicious firmwares will eventually be replaced with legitimate firmwares (given the assumption that the Vendor keeps its private key secured).

Even though data on chain are publicly accessible, an adversary will not be able to learn any essential information on the blockchain because it can only see the access control policy and some hashes. All sensitive data are encrypted and kept secured off-chain with restricted access. Nevertheless, since our proposed system relies on blockchain and smart contracts, it can only be as secured as the blockchain itself.

6   Related Work

Due to the attraction of blockchain and IoT, there are a lot of research efforts in both academic and industrial works that have addressed the integration of blockchain and IoT. In [18], the authors gave a detailed review on how blockchain and smart contracts make a good fit for IoT in which they concluded that the combination will cause important impact on several industries. Khan et al. [19] presented current security issues in IoT and asserted that blockchain would be a key solution. Some other works [20–22] outline aspects and use cases where blockchain can be combined with IoT. However, none of these works illustrates the integration in detail.

In [23], the authors presented an access control mechanism using blockchain. They described the system thoroughly with detailed designs and protocols. Nevertheless, all the operations are executed off-chain, that is, they did not exploit the smart contracts in their work. Therefore, they missed out some great advantages of smart contracts such as accuracy, transparency and trust. In our proposed system, we keep the access control management on-chain with smart contracts so that the operations are explicitly visible to all participants which eliminates the possibility of manipulation, bias or error.

The work by Shafagh et al. [24] is the most closely related to ours. They presented a blockchain-based system for IoT that enabled a secured data sharing without the need of any central authority. However, they also did not take the advantages of smart contracts. Furthermore, as they enabled third-party services to retrieve data directly from the off-chain storage, users could not track how their data were being accessed. In our proposed solution, all attempts to access users' data are all recorded permanently on the blockchain.

7   Conclusion and Discussion

In this paper, we have demonstrated how blockchain can be leveraged to strengthen data privacy in IoT-based applications. We proposed a system model based on smart contracts and blockchain that tackles the access control, data transparency and access tracking issues in IoT when third-party services are involved. Specifically, the system enables a trustless data sharing mechanism in which users have full control over their data that they can choose which services are allowed to access. Third-party services who were consented can easily access the data with the assurance that data are authentic and comes from the right user. Moreover, we also propose a firmware update scheme to limit the impact of IoT device tampering in which firmwares are overwritten by malicious ones to produce fraudulent data.

Since this paper only presents the concepts and modelings, further efforts should focus on conducting realistic experiments to evaluate the performance and robustness of the system, especially in terms of latency, throughput and stability as these are crucial criteria in any IoT application. The proposed system model can be implemented using some blockchain platforms such as Ethereum [25] or Hyperledger [26].

Acknowledgment. This paper is partially supported by NSF CNS-1443905 and NSF EFRI 1441231.

References

1. Nakamoto, S.: Bitcoin: A peer-to-peer electronic cash system (2008)
2. Golem: https://golem.network/
3. Augur — a decentralized oracle & prediction market protocol. https://www.augur.net/
4. Status, a mobile ethereum os. https://status.im/
5. Evans, D.: The internet of things: how the next evolution of the internet is changing everything. CISCO White Pap. **1**(2011), 1–11 (2011)
6. Brody, P., Pureswaran, V.: Device democracy: Saving the future of the internet of things. IBM, September 2014
7. Barcena, M.B., Wueest, C.: Insecurity in the internet of things. Security Response, Symantec (2015)
8. Mosenia, A., Jha, N.K.: A comprehensive study of security of internet-of-things. IEEE Trans. Emerg. Top. Comput. **5**(4), 586–602 (2017)
9. Arias, O., Wurm, J., Hoang, K., Jin, Y.: Privacy and security in internet of things and wearable devices. IEEE Trans. Multi-Scale Comput. Syst. **1**(2), 99–109 (2015)
10. Hernandez, G., Arias, O., Buentello, D., Jin, Y.: Smart nest thermostat: A smart spy in your home, Black Hat USA (2014)
11. Miller, C.: Battery firmware hacking, Black Hat USA, pp. 3–4 (2011)
12. Benet, J.: IPFS-content addressed, versioned, P2P file system (2014). https://github.com/ipfs/papers
13. Swarm. https://swarm-gateways.net/bzz:/theswarm.eth/
14. Wilkinson, S., Boshevski, T., Brandoff, J., Buterin, V.: Storj a peer-to-peer cloud storage network (2014)

15. Blaze, M., Bleumer, G., Strauss, M.: Divertible protocols and atomic proxy cryptography. In: Nyberg, K. (ed.) EUROCRYPT 1998. LNCS, vol. 1403, pp. 127–144. Springer, Heidelberg (1998). https://doi.org/10.1007/BFb0054122
16. Egorov, M., Wilkison, M., Nuñez, D.: Nucypher kms: decentralized key management system. arXiv preprint arXiv:1707.06140 (2017)
17. Maymounkov, P., Mazières, D.: Kademlia: a peer-to-peer information system based on the XOR metric. In: Druschel, P., Kaashoek, F., Rowstron, A. (eds.) IPTPS 2002. LNCS, vol. 2429, pp. 53–65. Springer, Heidelberg (2002). https://doi.org/10.1007/3-540-45748-8_5
18. Christidis, K., Devetsikiotis, M.: Blockchains and smart contracts for the internet of things. IEEE Access 4, 2292–2303 (2016)
19. Khan, M.A., Salah, K.: IoT security: review, blockchain solutions, and open challenges. Future Gener. Comput. Syst. 82, 395–411 (2018)
20. Kshetri, N.: Can blockchain strengthen the internet of things? IT Prof. 19(4), 68–72 (2017). https://doi.org/10.1109/MITP.2017.3051335
21. Dorri, A., Kanhere, S.S., Jurdak, R.: Towards an optimized blockchain for IoT. In: Proceedings of the Second International Conference on Internet-of-Things Design and Implementation, IoTDI 2017, pp. 173–178. ACM, New York (2017). https://doi.org/10.1145/3054977.3055003
22. Huckle, S., Bhattacharya, R., White, M., Beloff, N.: Internet of things, blockchain and shared economy applications. Procedia Comput. Sci. 98(C), 461–466 (2016)
23. Zyskind, G., Nathan, O., et al.: Decentralizing privacy: using blockchain to protect personal data. In: 2015 IEEE Security and Privacy Workshops (SPW), pp. 180–184. IEEE (2015)
24. Shafagh, H., Burkhalter, L., Hithnawi, A., Duquennoy, S.: Towards blockchain-based auditable storage and sharing of IoT data. In: Proceedings of the 2017 on Cloud Computing Security Workshop, pp. 45–50. ACM (2017)
25. Wood, G.: Ethereum: A secure decentralised generalised transaction ledger. Ethereum project yellow paper, vol. 151, pp. 1–32 (2014)
26. Cachin, C.: Architecture of the hyperledger blockchain fabric. In: Workshop on Distributed Cryptocurrencies and Consensus Ledgers, vol. 310 (2016)

A Formal Model for Temporal - Spatial Event in Internet of Vehicles

Na Wang[1](✉) and Xuemin Chen[2]

[1] Shanghai Polytechnic University, Shanghai 201209, China
wangna@sspu.edu.cn
[2] Texas Southern University, Houston, TX 77004, USA
xuemin.chen@tsu.edu

Abstract. In internet of vehicles (IoV), there are several events, e.g., location, speed, arriving time, that should be detected while the vehicle is running. Nowadays, formal description is becoming an effective method to describe and detect events. In this paper, we propose a temporal - spatial Petri net (TSPN) formal model which is deduced from Petri net. The rules of transition firing and marking updating are both defined in TSPN for further system analysis. In addition, an efficient TSPN analysis algorithm is developed for structured detection models. With a case study, we illustrate that TSPN can describe and detect events in advance for the IoV system.

Keywords: Formal model · Temporal and spatial · Petri net
Internet of vehicles · Event detection

1 Introduction

The internet of vehicles (IoV) is an important part of the intelligent transportation system (ITS) [1]. The related research of the internet of things (IoT) and information fusion system has been continuously developed which provide new theories, methods and technologies for IoV. The IoV which is based on the IoT is composed of units carried by vehicles, units deployed by the roadside, the control center and the smart equipment carried by individuals. Different from the general internet of things, there are a large number of moving objects in IoV. These objects carry a large number of sensing devices, so the data in IoV have an obvious temporal-spatial character. In IoV, all kinds of sensing devices continuously generate multi-source and multi-dimensional data. These data include time, location, behavior, speed, environment and so on.

An important application of IoV is traffic monitoring. Normally, vehicle drivers follow traffic rules. However, due to various reasons, abnormal events

The paper is supported in part by the National Natural Science Foundation of China under Grant No. 61672022, Key Disciplines of Software Engineering of Shanghai Polytechnic University under Grant No. XXKZD1604 and the U.S. National Science Foundation under Grant 1137732.

X. Chen et al. (Eds.): CSoNet 2018, LNCS 11280, pp. 222–234, 2018.
https://doi.org/10.1007/978-3-030-04648-4_19

in traffic systems may occur such as running red lights, illegal overtaking, speeding and so on. These abnormal traffic incidents will lead to traffic accidents which result in huge losses of life and property. Traffic monitoring system is a widely used traffic management tool for reducing traffic accidents.

Introducing IoV technology and event-driven method into the traffic monitoring system can help us to build a IoV event monitoring system with temporal - spatial constraints. The proposed system is shown in Fig. 1. In the event-driven IoV, all data are abstracted as events. Users only focus on events that meet specific conditions. Since different users may pay attention to different events, users need to express their concerns with a specific event processing model. In Fig. 1, users represent events of their own attention as an event processing model, then transform it into event handling rules by event processing engine. The temporal-spatial events of the vehicles are handled by the event processing rules, then results are obtained.

In order to describe the temporal-spatial events accurately so as to get the exact result of event, we will apply the Petri net processing model for the temporal-spatial event in IoV. Based on the Petri net processing model, the event processing algorithm is constructed to complete the task of temporal-spatial event confirmation in IoV.

The rest of the paper is organized as follows. Related work is introduced in Sect. 2. The temporal-spatial Petri net (TSPN) model is proposed in Sect. 3. The analysis of TSPN for traffic monitoring and a case study are depicted in Sect. 4. The conclusion and future work are drawn in Sect. 5.

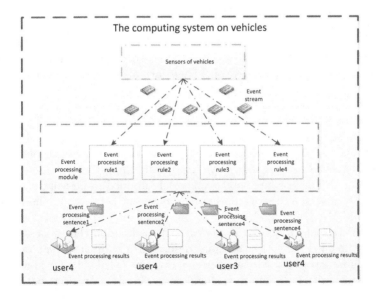

Fig. 1. The temporal spatial event detection system.

2   Related Work

Temporal and spatial features have been proposed and analyzed in wireless sensor networks (WSNs). In [2], authors aimed to detect anomalies at the sensor nodes with reducing energy and spectrum consumption. They evaluated the effects of neighborhood size and spatial-temporal correlation on the performance of their new neighborhood-based approach using a range of real-world network deployments and datasets. Their work paved the way towards understanding how distributed data fusion methods may help managing the complexity of wireless sensor networks, for instance in massive internet of things scenarios. In [3], the quality of a WSN service was assessed focusing on abnormal data derived from faulty sensors. It developed an effective strategy for locating faulty sensor nodes in WSNs. They proposed a fault detection strategy that is decentralized, coordinate-free, and node based which uses time series analysis and spatial correlations.

In order to get more precise data analysis and event detection results, formal methods are widely used. The formal method can provide languages with strict semantics and syntax, correspond techniques for the construction of models of systems under development, and verify these models against selected requirements [4]. As a consequence, quantitative and qualitative properties, such as faults or event detection rate, can be checked. In [5], authors develop an extension of temporal logic called timed multivariate statistical logic (TMSL) that can specify not only spatial features but also temporal dynamics of systems in a formal way. A purely data-based algorithm was presented to automatically learn the TMSL from process data for extracting spatial features and generating meaningful regions called Regions-of-Interest. Then, a temporally-annotated automaton for TMSL was generated with these discovered Regions-of-Interest. A PCA-based spatial monitor and a TMSL-based temporal monitor were further developed for on-line fault detection. There are also a few of formal methods that have been used for event specification in networks [6,7]. In [8–10], it has been shown that most of the popular formal approaches are based on theoretical models such as finite state machine, timed automata and process algebra.

Petri nets have advantages to describe events in workflow nets [11] and network applications [12] because it can handle non-determinism without suffering from state explosion. Petri nets have graphical supporting for users to operate easily. But Petri nets have not been widely applied in network applications because the temporal and spatial properties in sensor networks are hard to specify by simple Petri net models. If the models can be improved for complex attributes, Petri nets will be a powerful tool to describe the processes in networks including IoV. In [13], authors described a compact event description and analysis language for wireless sensor networks (MEDAL) for simultaneous monitoring of multiple events in a single network based on Petri net. MEDAL is a modified Petri net which provides a more compact formal language for event description. It can capture the structural, spatial, and temporal properties of a complex event detection system, so as to assist system designers identifying inconsistencies and potential problems. MEDAL is an improvement of formalization in WSNs, but it can only describe the attributes separately without relativity. In IoV, the correlations of spatial and temporal attributes of vehicles are crucial for event detection. So we need to develop an effective formal model for the special requirements in IoV.

In this paper, we propose a formal model for temporal - spatial Event in internet of vehicles. The main contributions of this paper are to:

- build structure units for temporal - spatial formal model;
- analyze temporal - spatial attributes in the formal model;
- propose a event detection algorithm based on the formal model.

3   TSPN Model

The basic structure of Petri nets consists of places (P), transitions (T), arcs and tokens. The circles represent the states; dots are used to model instances or objects; rectangles model various kinds of actions; and arcs represent changes between states. When a token represents an object with a variety of attributes, the token has a value that represents the specific characteristics of the object modeled by the token. For the sake of analysis, when time needs to be modeled, each token may have a time stamp. For specific application, we can extend Petri nets into most functional ones.

According to the requirements of temporal-spatial event, it is necessary for formal description to abstract items including current time of driving, current location of driving, current speed of driving and threshold for decision.

3.1   Definition of TSPN

Formally, a Petri net is defined as $PN = (P, T, I, O, M_0)$ where

$P = \{p_1, p_2, \ldots p_m\}$ is a finite set of places;

$T = \{t_1, t_2, \ldots t_n\}$ is a finite set of transitions, $P \cup T \neq \emptyset, and\, P \cap T \neq \emptyset$;

$I = T \times P \rightarrow N$ is an input function that defines directed arcs from places to transitions;

$O = T \times P \rightarrow N$ is an output function that defines directed arcs from transitions to places;

$M_0 = P \rightarrow N$ is the initial marking.

A marking in a Petri net is an assignment of tokens to the places of a Petri net. Tokens reside in the places of a Petri net. The number and location of tokens may change during the execution of a Petri net. The tokens are used to define the execution of a Petri net. A place containing one or more tokens is said to be marked [11].

TSPN can be described as a 8-tuple structure $(P, T, I, O, M_0, \delta, \iota, \theta)$ based on Petri nets, where P, T, I, O and M_0 are classic definitions in Petri net. In order to describe trust based detection, we extend the basic Petri net with three new items.

•ι is the spatial guard for transitions. For example, assume there is one arc a entering T, and one arc d comes out of T. $\iota(T) = s$ means T can only fire if the location of the token carried by a is at point s. In fact, after T is firing, the new token will be the succeeding of token in a. The details about token updating will be discussed later. This guard can be generalized to support more complex spatial constructs. It can also be triple, dual and single dimension. When the application concerns of the absolute location, ι will be as (x, y, z). When the application concerns of the relative location, ι will be as (x, y). Otherwise, it can be a point in a sequence.

•δ is a time guard for T, $\delta: T \rightarrow [t_1, t_2]$ and $t_1 \leq t_2$. For example, $\delta(T) = (a, b)$ means transition T can only fire during t_1 and t_2. Especially, if $t_1 = t_2$, that means the transition can only happen on t_1.

•θ is the threshold of token capacity in P, $\theta: P \rightarrow R$ and R is a real type data. For example, if $\theta(P) = r_1$, that means when the capacity of token in P is less than r_1, P can reach to a new station.

Tokens are abstract representations of sensed data. During transition, the values of a token will be updated according to the rules. In TSPN, the main data is speed.

3.2   Temporal-Spatial Event Modeling

In IoV, when the condition of location and time are consistent, a spatial event may be confirmed. For example, in a bus monitoring system, when the location is in the interval from spot a_1 to spot a_2, and the time is in the duration from t_1 to t_2, we can conclude that the bus will arrive on time. In the monitoring process, we use F^{in} to describe input token and F^{out} to describe output token. We use TP_k to represent an event confirmation unit, $F^{in}(TP_k)$ is associated with current condition and $F^{out}(TP_k)$ is associated with the next condition. The basic event confirmation unit can be described as shown in Fig. 2. Considering Fig. 2, P_1 is an input state. When there is a confirmation in TP_1, $F^{in}(TP_1)$ will be the current condition in state P_1 and $F^{out}(TP_1)$ will be the next condition which will be loaded into the next state according to spatial operations which will be introduced later.

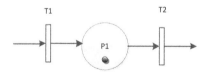

Fig. 2. TSPN unit.

3.3 Rules in TSPN

Rules for firing transitions:
A transition T_k under state marking M_i can be fired if and only if

$$t_k \in \delta(T_K) \tag{1}$$

$$F^{in}(TP_k) > 0 \tag{2}$$

$$F^{out}(TP_k) \le \theta(P_i) \tag{3}$$

$$M_i \ge I(t_k) \tag{4}$$

where $\delta(T_k)$ is current sensing time of a car in IoV and $F^{in}(TP_k)$ is current value of token in input place. $F^{out}(TP_k)$ is current value of token in output place and θ is the threshold for entering P_i. Noting that current value can be a set instead of a single value.

Condition (1) stands for time limit satisfaction, condition (2), (3) stand for valid value available and condition (4) stands for control ready. These conditions must be met trust factors simultaneously.

Rules for markings:
A token value may be changed when a transition fires and it will be held by new place due to threshold.

$$F^{out}(TP_k) = f(F^{in}(TP_k)) \tag{5}$$

where $f()$ represents a function on current set and $f()$ can be defined flexibly according to applications.

3.4 An Example for TSPN

In order to explain TSPN efficiently, we give an example here. When there is a requirement described as following, it says there is a bus monitoring system, each station has its arriving time duration and location ι. When the bus is running, it has a speed, say 30 km/h, which cannot exceed the maximum speed limitation. TP_1 represents the driving process of the fist station and $F^{in}(TP_1)$ means the token in the first station. $\theta(P_i)$ is the threshold of each state which means if current speed in token is less than it, the new state can be reached and the bus can go on driving without event. The example can be depicted as Fig. 3.

$\delta(T_1) = [4.9, 5.1], \delta(T_2) = [10.2, 10.5], \delta(T_3) = [15.5, 15.8];$
$\iota(T_1) = s_1, \iota(T_2) = s_2, \iota(T_3) = s_3;$
$M_0 = (1, 0, 0, 0);$
$\theta(P_2) = 0.45, \theta(P_3) = 0.4, \theta(P_4) = 0.35;$
$F^{in}(TP_1)$ is the initial parameters defined as time, station, avgspeed which is set as 0, s_0, 0.25. Here, 0 is current time, s_0 is current station, 25 is the average speed.

Fig. 3. An example for TSPN.

If the distances and time are specified as follows:
$d(s_0, s_1) = 2.1, time^{out}(TP_1) = 4.9;$
$d(s_1, s_2) = 1.9, time^{out}(TP_2) = 10.3;$
$d(s_2, s_3) = 1.7, time^{out}(TP_3) = 15.6;$

$f()$ is defined as recording current time as timeout, the next station of F^{in} and the average speed during the previous station. The average speed can be calculated by

$$avgspeed = d(s^{out} - s^{in})/(time^{out} - time^{in}) \qquad (6)$$

Then $F^{out}(TP_1) = (4.9, s_1, 0.42)$, and 4.9 meets $\delta(T_1)$, 0.42 meets $\theta(P_2)$, so T_1 fires and P_2 is reached. Similarly, $F^{out}(TP_2) = (10.3, s_2, 0.35)$ and $F^{out}(TP_3) = (15.6, s_3, 0.32)$. We can continue this process until we get to a state that no transitions are enabled.

3.5   Structured Model in TSPN

A temporal-spatial event can be modeled with multiple units of TSPN as shown in Fig. 2. In order to detects much more complex events, there must be some structured models based on basic unit. The first one is sequential structure shown in Fig. 4. There are two units TP_1 and TP_2, after TP_1 executed, TP_2 can be triggered. It can describe a sequential process such as bus driving.

The second is parallel structure that is shown in Fig. 5. There are two units TP_1 and TP_2, if and only if there are tokens in both P_1 and P_2, P_3 will be reached

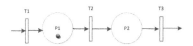

Fig. 4. Sequential structure.

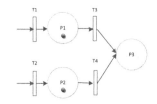

Fig. 5. Parallel structure.

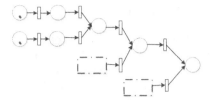

Fig. 6. Chained parallel structure.

when meeting threshold. In this case, TP_1 and TP_2 are the parallel units for P_3. This structure can be chained as shown in Fig. 6. A parallel structure can describe a process such as the interactivity of two vehicles. And the chained parallel structure can describe a system including much more vehicles that can communicate with each other for complex event detection.

The third is choice structure that is shown in Fig. 7. There are two choice units TP_2 and TP_3. Once there is token in P_1, T_2 or T_3 will fire. Then P_2 or P_3 will be marked if temporal, spatial and threshold conditions are all met. And choice structure can be nested as shown in Fig. 8. A choice structure can describe a process such as whether the vehicle is normally driven or speeding etc. And the chained parallel structure can describe different event detection of the vehicles.

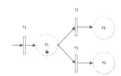

Fig. 7. Choice structure.

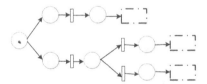

Fig. 8. Chained choice structure.

4   Analysis of TSPN

The purpose of using TSPN is to focus on how to check the events of vehicles and between vehicles according to the time constraints, spatial constraints and thresholds of new states. When the token meets threshold during the time constraint in a specific space, the TSPN model will go on. Otherwise, an event will be detected.

4.1   Analysis of Time Constraint

With regard of time constraints, δ is used to control the transition duration. If there is no requirement for time limit, the default of δ is $(-\infty, +\infty)$. For sequential and choice structures, firing time of each transition must be in δ. For parallel structures, firing role about time must be described specially.

Assume there are two transitions T_1 and T_2. The firing duration of a transition T_1 is $\delta(T_1) = [t_1, t_2]$, and $\delta(T_2) = [t_3, t_4]$. T_1 is enabled at time τ_1 where $t_1 \leq \tau_1 \leq t_2$. If it fires at time $\tau_1 + \phi_1$, according to the time rules in a timed Petri net, $\delta(T_2) = [max\{0, t_3 - \phi_1\}, t_4 - \phi_1]$.

If there are more parallel transitions in a system, the firing time of a transition will shift for times according to the number of transitions firing before it, which is shown in (7). If we use D to denote the set of time constraint δ, then where $D = \{\delta(T_j), j = 0 \ldots n\}$, n is the number of places.

$$\delta(T_j) = [max\{0, t_{j,1} - \sum_{i=2}^{j} \varphi_{i-1}\}, t_{j,2} - \sum_{i=2}^{j} \varphi_{i-1}] \tag{7}$$

For example, in Fig. 9, there are four units which are parallel. Assume the initial values of δ are available, they are indicated in Table 1.

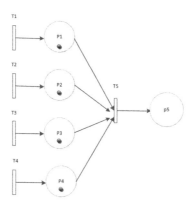

Fig. 9. A parallel example.

Table 1. Time of transition.

Transition	δ	Enabled time	Firing time	Firing order
T1	[1,5]	1	1.5	1
T2	[2,4]	2	1	3
T3	[2,5]	1	0.5	2
T4	[3,6]	2	1	4
T8	[1,2]	1	1	1

According to time constrain analysis, D will be:
$D_0 = \{1 \leq \delta(T_1) \leq 4, 2 \leq \delta(T_2) \leq 4, 2 \leq \delta(T_3) \leq 4, 3 \leq \delta(T_4) \leq 4\}$
$D_1 = \{0.5 \leq \delta(T_2) \leq 2.5, 0.5 \leq \delta(T_3) \leq 2.5, 1.5 \leq \delta(T_4) \leq 2.5\}$
$D_2 = \{0 \leq \delta(T_2) \leq 2, 1 \leq \delta(T_4) \leq 2\}$
$D_3 = \{0 \leq \delta(T_4) \leq 1\}$
$D_4 = \{1 \leq \delta(T_8) \leq 2\}$
$D_5 = \emptyset$

4.2   Analysis of TSPN Model

TSPN Analysis Algorithm

```
input:
   Bus station information including station name, distance;
   Thresholds for speed;
   Lower time of δ;
   Upper time of δ;
   Current time;
output:
   Event detection result;
initialization:
   Generate TSPN model according to bus station information;
while (M_j)
{
   for (i=0; i<n; i++)
   {
         calculate F^out(TP_j) using Eqs (7);
         if (D_i)
               calculate F^out_{j+1} using Eqs (5)
   }
   if (F^in_{j+1} ≤ θ_j)
      j++;
}
```

4.3   A Case Study

We use a part of the schedule of bus 64407 in Beijing [14] which is shown in Table 2 to build a case study for TSPN. The TSPN model can be described as shown in Fig. 10.

Suppose the stop duration is 20 seconds [15], and the deviation can be 10 seconds. Then δ should be set as from expected arriving time-10 to expected

Table 2. Schedule plan of bus 64407.

Station name	MGY	LLQB	GZFN	GZFD	JSBWG	MXDX	GHDL
Expected arriving time	7:33	7:36:46	7:40:20	7:44:58	7:49:39	7:51:20	7:54:21

Fig. 10. TSPN for bus 64407.

arriving time+30. θ is the max speed limit of each station. ι is the current station which is a point in a sequence. The constraints are set as that of in Table 3. According to the analysis algorithm, the tokens are updated as shown in Table 4.

Table 3. Constraints in TSPN for bus 64407.

$\delta(hh:mm:ss)$	[7:32:50, 7:33:30]	[7:36:36, 7:37:16]	[7:40:10, 7:40:50]	[7:44:48, 7:45:22]	[7:49:29, 7:50:09]	[7:51:10, 7:51:50]	[7:54:11, 7:54:51]
$\theta(km/h)$	30	35	35	40	45	35	30
ι	MGY	LLQB	GZFN	GZFD	JSBWG	MXDX	GHDL
Distance (km)	1.88	1.85	1.75	1.8	1.28	1.52	1.67

Table 4. Tokens updating.

$F^{in}(T_1)$	$F^{out}(T_1)$	$F^{in}(T_2)$	$F^{out}(T_2)$
7:33, MGY, 30	7:36:48, LLQB, 29.8	7:37:08, LLQB, 29.8	7:40:19, GZFN, 35.6
$F^{in}(T_3)$	$F^{out}(T_3)$	$F^{in}(T_4)$	$F^{out}(T_4)$
7:40:39, GZFN, 35.6	7:44:59, GZFD, 24.3	7:45:19, GZFD, 24.3	7:49:41, JSBWG, 24.7
$F^{in}(T_5)$	$F^{out}(T_5)$	$F^{in}(T_6)$	$F^{out}(T_6)$
7:50:01, JSBWG, 24.7	7:51:31, MXDX, 45.7	7:51:51, MXDX, 45.7	7:54:35, GHDL, 33.4

The TSPN model is a sequential one since it describes a bus driving process and captures events during driving. From the data in the two tables above, we can find the arriving time of each station which is indicated as time in $F^{out}(T_i)$ meets δ. The location of each station which is indicated as station name in $F^{out}(T_i)$ meets ι. The average speed of each station which is indicated as speed in $F^{out}(T_i)$ meets θ. So the process is going through until station GHDL. In other cases, once one of the constraints cannot be met, the process will abort so as to report an event. If δ or ι cannot be met, the report will be "Delay". Otherwise, the report will be "Speeding". TSPN can describe other applications relative to event detection in IoV such as overtake illegally.

5   Conclusion and Future Work

In this paper, we proposed a temporal - spatial Petri net that can describe the driving process of a vehicle and detect events. In TSPN, we defined rules for transitions, structures and operations for units. Analysis process is also presented for event detection. Using TSPN, we can induce compound applications based on units for description when detecting event and implementing other requirements. In the case study, a bus driving process is described formally by TSPN and the tokens are verified by assigning constrains. The result shows that TSPN can describe the driving processes of vehicles in IoV and detect events effectively.

References

1. JGerla, M., Lee, E., Pau, G.: Internet of vehicles: from intelligent grid to autonomous cars and vehicular clouds. In: 2015 IEEE World Forum, pp. 241–246. IEEE, Seoul (2014)
2. Bosman, H., Iacca, G., Tejada, A., Heinrich, J.: Spatial anomaly detection in sensor networks using neighborhood information. Inf. Fusion **33**(1), 41–56 (2017)
3. Kang, M., Yu, H., Xiong, Q., Hu, H.: Spatial-temporal correlative fault detection in wireless sensor networks. Int. J. Distrib. Sens. Netw. **2014**, 1–16 (2015)
4. Man, K., Krilaviius, T., Vallee, T., Leung, H.: A formal analysis tool for wireless sensor networks. Int. J. Res. Rev. Comput. Sci. **1**, 24–26 (2009)
5. Liu, K., Lin, H., Fei, Z., Liang, J.: Spatially-temporally online fault detection using timed multivariate statistical logic. Eng. Appl. Artif. Intell. **65**(1), 51–59 (2017)
6. Olveczky, P., Thorvaldsen, S.: Formal modeling and analysis of wireless sensor network algorithms in real-time Maude. In: 20th IEEE International Parallel and Distributed Processing Symposium, pp. 122–140. IEEE, Rhodes Island, Greece (2007)
7. Agha, G., Meseguer, J., Sen, K.: Maude: rewrite-based specification language for probabilistic object systems. Electron. Notes Theor. Comput. Sci. **153**(2), 213–239 (2006)
8. Riaza, S., Afzaala, H.: Formalizing mobile ad hoc and sensor networks using VDM-SL. Procedia Comput. Sci. **63**, 148–153 (2015)
9. Silva, D.S., Resner, D., de Souza, R.L., Martina, J.E.: Formal verification of a cross-layer, trustful space-time protocol for wireless sensor networks. In: Ray, I., Gaur, M.S., Conti, M., Sanghi, D., Kamakoti, V. (eds.) ICISS 2016. LNCS, vol. 10063, pp. 426–443. Springer, Cham (2016). https://doi.org/10.1007/978-3-319-49806-5_23
10. Testa, A., Cinque, M., Coronato, A., De, P., Augusto, J.: Heuristic strategies for assessing wireless sensor network resiliency: an event-based formal approach. J. Heuristics **21**(2), 145–175 (2015)
11. Wang, J., Li, D.: Resource oriented workflow nets and workflow resource requirement analysis. Int. J. Softw. Eng. Knowl. Eng. **23**(5), 677–693 (2013)
12. Tremblay, M.: Cutkosky.: Using sensor fusion and contextual information to perform event detection during a phase-based manipulation task. In: IEEE International Conference on Intelligent Robots and Systems, pp. 262–267. IEEE, Pittsburgh (1995)

13. Kapitanova, K., Sang, H.: A compact event description and analysis language for wireless sensor networks. In: 2009 Sixth International Conference on Networked Sensing Systems, pp. 1–4. IEEE Computer Society, Pittsburgh (2009)
14. Xiao, Q.: Bus Plan Research Based on GPS Data. Beijing Jiaotong University, Beijing (2009)
15. Guo, S., Wei, Y., Shi, W.: The statistics analysis of bus stop time. J. Gungxi Normal Univ. **24**(2), 5–9 (2006)

A Decentralized Deterministic Information Propagation Model for Robust Communication

Christopher Diaz[1], Alexander Nikolaev[1(✉)], and Eduardo Pasiliao[2]

[1] University at Buffalo, 312 Bell Hall, Buffalo, NY 14260, USA
{cmdiaz2,anikolae}@buffalo.edu
[2] Air Force Research Laboratory, Eglin AFB, Okaloosa, FL 32542, USA

Abstract. Many of the methods that are used to optimize network structure for information sharing are centralized, which is not always desirable in practice. Often, it is only feasible to have the communicating actors modify the network locally, i.e., without relying on the knowledge of the entire network structure. Such a requirement typically arises in establishing communication between actors (e.g., Unmanned Aerial Vehicles) that either do not have access to a central hub or prefer not to use this direct transmission channel even if available. This paper adopts an actor-oriented modeling approach to develop the Decentralized Deterministic Information Propagation (DDIP) model that enables the creation of networks that exhibit the properties desirable for efficient information sharing. Computational experiments showcase the ability of the DDIP model to form robust networks while being energy-conscious, i.e., without unnecessarily overloading any particular actor.

Keywords: Communication networks · Decentralized optimization
Stochastic actor-oriented modeling

1 Introduction

Consider a sensor network (or, more generally, a network of actors) comprised of a group of sensors (actors) that are linked by a wireless medium and tasked to perform distributed sensing, decentralized decision-making and/or inference tasks. In such networks, sensors (actors) gather information about the physical world, conduct analyses based on local information, and then perform the ensuing actions upon the environment, thereby enabling automated and remote interaction with the environment.

In the above, the meaning of term "actor" differs from the conventional notion where an object is restricted to "act" in a particular way. Instead, the said actor, besides being able to act continuously on the environment, is also a network entity that performs networking-related functions, i.e., those including receiving, transmitting, processing and relaying information. For example, a robot may

© Springer Nature Switzerland AG 2018
X. Chen et al. (Eds.): CSoNet 2018, LNCS 11280, pp. 235–246, 2018.
https://doi.org/10.1007/978-3-030-04648-4_20

interact with the physical environment; however, from a networking perspective, the robot constitutes a single entity that is referred to as actor.

Applications of wireless sensor and actor networks may include teams of mobile robots that perceive the environment from multiple different viewpoints based on the data gathered by sensor networks. However, due to the presence of actors (that are usually resource-rich devices equipped with better processing capabilities, stronger transmission powers and longer battery life), the wireless sensor and actor networks have some differences from wireless sensor networks [1]. Moreover, in the wireless sensor and actor networks, depending on the application there may be a need to rapidly respond to sensor input. To provide the right actions, sensor data must still be valid at the time of acting. Therefore, the issue of real-time communication is very important in the wireless sensor and actor networks since actions are often required to be performed on the environment immediately after the sensing takes place.

The number of sensor nodes deployed in typical conventional applications may be in the order of hundreds or thousands. However, such a dense deployment is not necessary for "actor" actors due to the different coverage requirements and physical interaction methods supporting the acting tasks. Hence, in the wireless actor networks, the number of actors is much lower [1]. Therefore, in order to provide effective sensing, coupled with acting or inference tasks, a distributed local coordination mechanism is necessary among sensors/actors. Building such a distributed coordination mechanism in uncertain environments requires broader studies, which examine actor-centered and actor-based network models.

Much research in the domains of network analysis and communication addresses the need to efficiently exchange and spread information throughout a network as seen in [12, 16]. This topic has been examined through a variety of methods such as in [5, 7], most of which focus on modifying certain structural properties of the network using a centralized approach. The centralized methods, however, are not always adequate for the task at hand, which can be when dealing with applications related to sensor networks as described in [1].

This paper presents a Decentralized Deterministic Information Propagation network formation model (DDIP model) where actors link to each other in a decentralized manner, and in doing so, build a network that provides each actor with an ability for robust reception and propagation of information across the network. The model of the actors' behavior, i.e., local decision-making, is similar in spirit to the work by [15] that develops a stochastic social network formation model using a decentralized approach, which they call "actor-oriented modeling".

The paper is organized as follows. Section 1 discusses the decentralized network formation problem. Section 2 provides a literature review which describes the current state of the art research that has been done in decentralized communication network analysis. Section 3 introduces and details the proposed DDIP parametric model. Section 4 describes an approach to evaluating the model performance – the experimental setup and performance metrics, – and presents the computational results obtained with synthetically generated data sets. Section 5 offers conclusions and discussion about the potential future directions of this research.

2   Literature Review

This section describes the current state of the art in the research areas relevant to decentralized methods of analyzing and building communication networks.

There have been a number of works published recently that focus on how information flows through networks. Currently, much of the research in this field focuses on how to maximize the spread of influence across networks. While this area is not of direct relevance to our problem, some papers from it are still worth mentioning. In [2], a framework is presented for modeling competitive diffusion in social networks, solving a set of Most Probable Interpretation problems to describe how influence propagates across networks. In [5], an innovation diffusion model is presented, that extends the actor-oriented modeling [15] towards studying how social influence affects network formation.

There are also articles within the realm of information propagation and diffusion that do not focus on maximizing or describing the effects of influence across networks. In, [12], several models are proposed to only explain how information spreads. In [18], a partially absorbing random walk is employed to model how information passing can be used to learn the structure of a network. In [4] a transduction process, also employing absorbing random walks, is developed to traverse graphs. In [7], an evolutionary game theoretic framework is offered to predict information diffusion across networks.

The literature on decentralized methods to improve communication efficiency is also relevant to this paper, particularly because it emphasizes network robustness. Most of the existing papers on decentralized methods for network modeling focus on achieving consensus in a network in an organized manner. The authors of [16] create sets of decentralized conventions that focus on forming consensus throughout a network. In [10], a more general framework is presented for analyzing multi-agent systems that enables the actors to reach consensus. In [13], the use of decentralized communication networks is analyzed in respect to controlling autonomous actors.

There is a gap in the body of literature that pertains to decentralized communication networks, as most papers are focused on how to create consensus as opposed to modeling information passing and building robust communication networks in the first place. This paper looks to fill that gap by relying on the recent advances in social network analysis.

The use of models to analyze and predict the formation of social networks is a large topic of research in social network analysis. Descriptive social network techniques were used in [8] in order to create new ways to manage crisis de-escalation techniques. The use of social network analysis with respect to engineering and construction project management is evaluated in [3]. In [17], a model is developed to predict how groups of unconnected agents form social networks, focusing on how the pattern of interaction between agents causes networks to form. In [6], the evolution of social and economic networks is studied, where the dynamics of the individuals that make up the network are of particular importance. The actor-oriented modeling ideas for social network formation are described, e.g., in [14,15]. In the latter, Snijders et al. introduced a model, in which individuals periodically make changes to their local networks, with each maximizing their own weighted "happiness function" value. There has been some research in the use of decentralized methods to ensure network connectivity, as seen in [11], which focuses on the use of a decentralized control algorithm to balance the edges of networks. The latter work, however, focused mainly on making sure that connectivity was preserved, and did not place emphasis on the information passing properties of the resulting graphs; the model presented in our paper fills this gap.

3   The Decentralized Deterministic Information Propagation Model for Network Formation

The Decentralized Deterministic Information Propagation model (DDIP model) for network formation, introduced here, prescribes a particular order of communication network evolution, i.e., change in its structure, over multiple time periods. In each period, all the actors participate in several network building-related activities, performed sequentially in stages. The stages include a message forwarding (propagation) stage, a weight and objective calculation stage, a network state estimation stage, and a network modification stage. This section describes the stages in detail.

3.1   DDIP Model Stages Overview

The actors' activities in each time period begin with the forwarding stage, in which each actor forwards out messages to their connected network neighbors. The messages are passed on (propagated) as a partially absorbing random walk; such a random walk has been recently used, e.g., in [9] to define entropy centrality, as well as in [18] to learn and exploring graph structures. Namely, once an actor receives a message, it is passed on with probability less than one. Using the information derived from the number and total proportion of the messages received from all other actors in the network, each actor is able to update its belief about how well-connected it is – this takes place in the next stage, the one devoted to the calculation of weights and objective values. These updates lead to the revisions of the actors' own weight functions and to the recalculation of their own objectives. Actors then estimate how the changes to their local network would affect their unique objective function in the network state estimation stage. Actors look to make such changes in the local connection structure that will allow them the largest increase in the reception of messages from all other actors in the network with a special emphasis on the messages from their estimated far-away peers, similar to the way actors make changes in [15]. After all the actors have made their decisions in a single time period in the network modification stage, the next period begins, and the message forwarding and update procedures are repeated until a pre-set stopping criterion, e.g., one based on the number of time periods allocated for network formation, is met.

3.2   DDIP Model Parameters and Variables

In this section, the notations for the variables, vectors, and parameters of the DDIP model are described. The parameters of the model are the inputs that determine how the model behaves, i.e., how the revisions to the network structure are carried out. The message count and weight variables are updated in every period, and thereby, provide the actors with an ability to assess the quality of their network positions in terms of embeddedness (proximity to peers).

The variables and parameters listed in Table 1 serve to rigorously present the framework and structure for how the DDIP model forms networks. The model creates and modifies a directed graph G, with n actors (nodes) and the edge list E of all the active edges. Set S defines the allowable ties: some actors are assumed to not be able to connect with certain peers, consistent with proximity restrictions where some actors may be too far away from each other to communicate directly. Algorithm 1 describes how the DDIP model runs.

3.3   Forwarding Stage: Message Passing Procedure

The DDIP model begins each period with a forwarding stage. The goal of the forwarding stage is to allow each actor to update its belief about its own position with respect to the rest of the network, in a way that is decentralized.

The actors simulate the passing of messages to "learn" which neighbors seem to be close and which neighbors seem to be further away, through the partially absorbing random-walk procedure. During each forwarding stage, each actor i will send off m messages. Each message is first sent with an equal probability to any one of actor i's out-directed neighbors. After being forwarded to a neighbor j, the message is either terminated with probability α, or sent to one of j's out-directed neighbors with probability $(1 - \alpha)$. The message continues to be forwarded between actors until it is terminated.

The process of message forwarding is used to update each actor's p_{ijk}^t (proportion of messages) variable, which gives the actor the information necessary to infer the quality of its network position with respect to the peers. Each message contains the information of the source (actor j), the last actor who sent it (actor k), and a unique identifier that tells actor i to not record a duplicate if such messages ever reach it; however; each duplicate will still be forwarded on with a probability α. Each time actor i receives a message from source actor j, through neighbor k, such that it has not been received before, the corresponding p_{ijk}^t variable increases. The value of p_{ijk}^t is then used to calculate the weights and objective function value for actor i. During each period, the value of p_{ijk}^t is reset and recalculated to allow each actor to re-evaluate their position in the network.

Table 1. Notation, variables, and parameters used in the DDIP model

n	The number of actors in graph G
t_{max}	The maximum number of periods to run the DDIP model
E	The collection of active edges of Graph G
S	The collection of all possible edges of Graph G
g_i^t	The local structure of actor i's graph at period t
s_i^t	The collection of possible edges for actor i at period t
α	The probability that a message is terminated
m	The number of messages each actor sends per period t
γ	The neighbor's cost for connection
l	The threshold of in-directed ties that an'un-isolated' actor has
w	The scaling parameter for cost
p_{ijk}^t	The proportion of messages actor i received from source j through neighbor k during period t
$\beta_{ij}^{own,t}$	actor i's own preference for messages from actor j, during period t.
$\beta_{ij}^{neigh,t}$	The average if the preferences if actor i's out-directed neighbors for messages form actor j during period t
$\beta_{ij}^{total,t}$	The overall preference that actor i has for messages from actor j at time t - a weighted average of $beta_{ij}^{own,t}$ and $\beta_{ij}^{neigh,t}$
ρ	The weight of an actor's own preferences against it's neighbors preferences
h_i^t	The number actor i's active in-directed ties at period t
Y_i^t	The set of actor i's out-directed neighbors at period t
Z_i^t	The set of actor i's in-directed neighbors at period t
d_i^t	The set of actor i's decisions and estimates at period t

For application purposes, the message forwarding procedure can be emulated by sending all messages at the same time: i.e., actor i would send each out-directed neighbor an equal fraction of the m messages. For example, if the actors are set to send $m = 1000$ messages per round, an actor with two outgoing ties would send 500 messages to each of these neighbors. Each actor would receive that fraction, reduce the number by the termination factor α, and in turn, forward the messages in an even fraction to their neighbors. Once the number of messages received falls under a certain threshold, the propagation is terminated. The p_{ijk}^t value can then be calculated by taking the number of messages that each actor i receives from a source actor j through a connected neighbor k, and dividing the result by the initial message count m. In the experiment, the proportions of messages each actors receive are estimated, so the exact number of messages sent at each round is not needed.

Algorithm 1. The DDIP Model Logic

1: $g^t = g^0$;   /*Initializes the starting graph at period 0*/
2: $S = S^0$;   /*Initializes the possible edge set for graph G*/
3: **for** actor $i \in g^0$ **do**
4:    **if** $g_i^0 = \emptyset$ **then**
5:       Select $j \in s_i^0$ w.p. $1/|s_i^0|$;
6:       $E \leftarrow (j,i) \cup E^0$;   /*has any unconnected actors connect to a possible neighbor*/
7:    **end if**
8: **end for**
9: **for** $t \leftarrow 0$ to t_{max} **do**
10:    **for** actor $i \in g^t$ **do**
11:       Propagate m messages;   /*Use Random Walk Method to Simulate Message Passing*/
12:       Update p_{ijk}^t;   /*Calculate the proportions of messages received in period t*/
13:       Calculate β's and $f_i(g_i^t)$;   /*Using p_{ijk}^t, calculate weights and objective for actor i*/
14:       **for** Possible Neighbor $j \in s_i^t$ **do**
15:          Calculate $f_i(g\prime_{ij}^t)$;   /*Estimate objective after connecting to j*/
16:          $d_i^t \leftarrow (j, f_i(g_{ij}'^t)) \cup d_i^t$;   /*Add addition decision and estimate to decision list*/
17:       **end for**
18:       **for** actor $j \in Z_i^t$ **do**
19:          Calculate $f_i(g_{ij}''^t)$;   /*Estimate objective after removing active neighbor j*/
20:          $d_i^t \leftarrow (j, f_i(g_{ij}''^t)) \cup d_i^t$;   /*Add subtraction decision and estimate to decision list*/
21:       **end for**
22:       $d_i^t \leftarrow (i, f_i(g_i^t)) \cup d_i^t$;   /*Add do nothing decision to decision list*/
23:    **end for**
24:    **for** actor $i \in g^t$ **do**
25:       **if** $(j, f_{max,i}(g_i^t)) \in Z_i^t$ **then**
26:          $g^t \leftarrow g^t - (j,i)$;   /*If the best move is to subtract edge, remove edge, if allowed*/
27:          $Z_i^t \leftarrow Z_i^t - j$ /*Remove j from i's in-directed neighbors*/
28:          $Y_j^t \leftarrow Y_j^t - i$ /*Remove i from j's out-directed neighbors*/
29:          $s_i^t \leftarrow j + s_i^t$;   /*Add j to i's possible neighbor set*/
30:       **else if** $(j, f_{max,i}(g_i^t)) \in s_i^t$ **then**
31:          $g^t \leftarrow (i, f_{max,i}(g_i^t)) \cup g^t$;   /*If best decision is add tie,add the tie to the graph*/
32:          $s_i^t \leftarrow s_i^t - j$ /*Remove j from i's potential neighbors list*/
33:          $Z_i^t \leftarrow Z_i^t + j$ /*Add j to i's connected neighbor set*/
34:          $Y_j^t \leftarrow Y_j^t + i$ /*Add i to j's out-directed neighbor list*/
35:       **else**
36:          continue   /*actor i chose to do nothing this period*/
37:       **end if**
38:    **end for**
39:    $p_{ijk}^t \leftarrow 0 \ \forall \ i,j,k$;   /* Reset message proportion variables*/
40:    $d_i^t \leftarrow \emptyset \ \forall i$;   /*Reset decision and bid lists for all actors*/
41:    $t \leftarrow t + 1$;   /*Move to next period*/
42: **end for**
43: **Return** $g^{t_{max}}$

3.4   Calculation of Weights and Objective Values

Using the proportion of message counts p_{ijk}^t obtained during the forwarding stage in a period, the actors calculate the weights used for their objective equation and the objective function value itself. The details about how the weights and objective equations are computed are provided below.

Before an actor calculates its objective value in a given period, it first must calculate its β weights as described in Table 1. The values of $\beta_{ij}^{total,t}$ are used in the model, but they are calculated by taking the weighted average of the values of $\beta_{ij}^{own,t}$ and $\beta ij^{neigh,t}$,

$$\beta_{ij,t}^{own} = e^{(1-(p_{ijk}^t))}, \tag{1}$$

$$\beta_{ij}^{neigh,t} = \frac{1}{n} \sum_{y \in Y_i} \beta_{yj}^{own,t}, \qquad (2)$$

$$\beta_{ij}^{total,t} = (\rho)\beta_{ij}^{own,t} + (1-\rho)\beta_{ij}^{nei,t}, \qquad (3)$$

These weights are re-evaluated in each period and are used to adjust the objective function equation to take into account the fact that each actor strives to be able to receive messages from every other actor in the network. The weight $\beta_{ij}^{own,t}$ decreases exponentially as more messages are received from source actor j, and increases exponentially as less messages are received from actor j. This allows for actor i to try to make decisions that result in an expected increase of the count of messages sourced by those actors from whom it does not receive many messages, given a current network structure. The $\beta_{ij}^{neigh,t}$ is an average of the weights that each out-neighbor of i contains: it reflects a kind of cooperation between actors. The inclusion of $\beta_{ij}^{neigh,t}$ allows each actor to make changes that benefit its neighbors as well as itself. The $\beta_{ij}^{total,t}$ is the weighted average of $\beta_{ij}^{own,t}$ and $\beta_{ij}^{neigh,t}$, weighted by the preference parameter ρ. Using the all the resulting values, each actor then calculates their own unique objective value,

$$f_i(g_i^t) = \sum_j \sum_k p_{ijk}^t(g_i^t)\beta_{ij}^{total,t} - w \sum_k \gamma |Y_k^t|, \quad \forall\, i, \qquad (4)$$

with this formula capturing how "happy" actor i is with its current local network structure. The larger the proportion of the messages that actor i receives from all other actors in the network, the larger the objective value is. In order to discourage overloading an actor with forwarding too many messages, there is a cost that is directly related to the number of the outgoing ties, Y_k^t, that each in-neighbor k of actor i possesses in time period t (immediately preceding the currently ongoing revision stage). This cost is expressed using parameters γ and w, and make up the right portion of the objective equation, as seen in 4. This cost is used to keep actors from having too many outgoing ties, without placing any absolute restrictions on the number of ties an actor can possess. The use of both parameters allow for tuning the different costs associated with the model, giving more flexibility to these parameters allow for a model that can create more robust networks. As actor i adds an incoming tie to its neighbor k who possesses more outgoing links, actor i's own cost will increase, which will decrease actor i's own objective value. In the next stage of DDIP, the actors will estimate how this objective value would change under each possible change of their incoming ties, informing the network-building actions.

3.5   Network Estimation Stage and Modification Stage

In each period, each actor has three different options: they can add an incoming tie to one of their eligible neighbors, delete a currently active incoming tie from one of their connected neighbors, or do nothing (an actor cannot simultaneously add and delete a tie in the same period). Each actor estimates how their objective might change from making a modification, with the help of the message passing process observations collected in prior stages; each actor shares their p_{ijk}^t value with the nearby unconnected neighbors. An actor i estimates the value gain that will result from adding an incoming tie to an eligible neighbor j by computing

$$f_i(g_{ij}^{\prime,t}) = f_i(g_i^t) + \frac{1}{|Y_j^t|+1} \sum_{u \in g} \sum_{k \in Z_j^t} p_{juk} - w\gamma(|Y_j^t|+1), \quad \forall\, i \in g,\ \forall\, j \in s_i^t, \quad (5)$$

which looks at the current objective value for actor i and adds the estimated increase due to the proportion of the messages that i would receive from each other actor in the graph if it were to connect to actor j (this is captured in the middle portion of (5)); then, the actor subtracts the cost of pulling messages from actor j. Similarly, the actor estimates the potential effect of disconnecting the each currently connected in-neighbor j by computing

$$f_i(g_{ij}^{\prime\prime,t}) = f_i(g_i^t) - \sum_{u \in g} \sum_{j} p_{iuj} + w\gamma|Y_j^t|, \quad \forall\, i \in g,\ \forall\, j \in Z_i^t. \quad (6)$$

Here, the actor takes the current objective value and subtracts the proportion of messages that were received from all actors $u \in g$ that came through actor j; then, the cost of pulling from actor j is subtracted (this cost would no longer be incurred). Note that the logic of (6) is not flawless, as actor i might be receiving a large proportion of the same messages, which came through j, from another actor u, so i would believe that losing j would be costly while it might not be the case.

The DDIP model imposes rules that actors follow when deciding what changes should be made to their local network. First, the actors that have any incoming ties under a certain limit l are considered isolated, and these actors are not allowed to lose out-directed ties to discourage complete isolation of actors. In the network modification stage, each actor will make the decision that leads to the largest increase in their personal objective. Once all actors have made their choices, the next period starts.

4   Experimental Evaluation of Model Performance

The experiments were set up to run the DDIP model on 20 sample networks of size $n = 10, 15$, and 20 actors each. Ten networks of each size were created using a synthetic unit-disk based method, which sets the node spatial positions uniformly over a given rectangular; then, if the Euclidean distance between a pair of actors was less than d, then an edge between these actors was declared allowable. The problem instances produced by this method were restricted to ensure that fully connected graphs were possible. The reason that such small networks were used in the experiments was to reflect the use case of modeling networks after sensor networks of UAVs, which tend to move in smaller formations.

Each DDIP model run was initialized with each actor connecting to one randomly chosen neighbor (if any). This was implemented to see how the DDIP model solutions vary with different initial connection setups.

4.1   Evaluation Metrics

We introduce three metrics for examining the quality of a given solution:

$$e_r = \frac{|E^{t_{max}}|}{|S^0|}, \ \mu^{-1} = \frac{1}{n}\frac{1}{n-1}\frac{1}{\sum_i\sum_{j\neq i}\pi_{(i,j)}}, \ \eta = \frac{e^{a\mu^{-1}}}{e_r}\frac{n}{|S|} = \frac{e^{a\mu^{-1}}}{|E^{t_{max}}|}. \quad (7)$$

The edge ratio, e_r, is used to describe the ratio of the number of active edges $|E|$ used in an output graph from the DDIP model to the number of possible edges $|S|$. A small e_r means that the resulting network of the DDIP model contained relatively few edges compared to the number possible ones. The average inverse distance, μ^{-1}, is equal to the average of the inverse of the sum of the lengths of the shortest paths π_{ij} between all pairs of actors i and j. As μ^{-1} increases, the average number of edges it takes to go from one actor to any other actor decreases. This statistic is useful for taking into account graphs that are not fully connected, since the inverse distance between a pair of unconnected actors is 0 $(1/\infty)$. The edge efficiency, η, combines the information captured in both e_r and μ^{-1} to evaluate the quality of solutions produced by the DDIP model. When evaluating solutions, resulting graphs with a higher value of η are preferred, as this favors graphs that achieve a smaller average distance between actors, while using a relatively few amount of edges.

4.2   Experimental Results

Multiple combinations of the DDIP model parameters were tested and best selections identified. For the test instances with the networks of size $n = 10, 15, 20$, the w parameters used were 0.642, 0.555, and 1.288, and the γ parameters used were 1.096, 1.210, and 0.863, respectively.

The DDIP instances were tested using Python 2.7 on a Dell Inspiron 15 7000 (2.3GHz Intel Core i5-6200U processor, 8GB RAM) for ten periods, ten times per sample generated input graph, per each sample graph size.

The values of the network performance metrics in (7) were calculated for all of the resulting networks that were formed with the DDIP model. The values of μ^{-1} and η were also computed for the fully connected instance, where $E = S$, of each sample graph that comprised the experimental testbed. Table 2 reports the average results for each performance metric, and compares the results of the DDIP model to the average metrics of the fully connected graphs for each graph size and type in the test bed.

The results in Table 2 indicate that the DDIP model is able to form networks that contain efficient structures for information propagation. As expected, for each graph size, the average inverse distance values μ^{-1} of the output networks were less than the average μ^{-1} values over fully connected graphs of the same size and type. Further, the resulting edge efficiency values η from the DDIP model networks were larger than the average η values for the fully connected networks. These results, combined with the low average edge ratio e_r values of the DDIP result networks, show that the model was able to form networks with relatively few ties but desirable connectivity properties.

Table 2. DDIP model results for different numbers of actors

Network Size, n	Average DDIP μ^{-1}	Average Fully Connected μ^{-1}	Average DDIP e_r	Average DDIP η	Average Fully Connected η
Unit Disk 10	0.54	0.76	0.50	2.28	2.23
Unit Disk 15	0.45	0.65	0.48	1.61	1.40
Unit Disk 20	0.35	0.58	0.39	1.30	1.04

5 Conclusion

The topic of spreading information across networks is widely studied in network science. Most works in the field of information passing, as it relates to social network analysis, focus on the spread of influence across networks and utilize centralized methods in order to find network formation solutions. In certain cases, such as deciding on how to form communication networks for autonomous UAVs, the use of centralized methods is not feasible. This paper thus opens a promising approach towards decentralized network formation modeling that leads to the creation of robust networks that contain structural properties suited for information passing.

The results of the DDIP model application showcase that this new modeling approach can be used to create robust networks. It does have limitations: e.g., as is, the model relies on deterministic rules, which limits its flexibility. Future extensions to this model should focus on the more organized methods for the DDIP model parameterization. From the analysis perspective, allowing the actors to change their physical positions in space (i.e., accounting for movement) and allowing for external changes to the possible edge set (i.e., accounting for adversarial attacks) would also offer interesting extensions.

Acknowledgments. This work was funded in part by the AFRL Mathematical Modeling and Optimization Institute, by the National Science Foundation Award No. 1635611, and by the U.S. Air Force Summer Faculty Fellowship (granted to the second author by the Air Force Office of Scientific Research).

References

1. Akyildiz, I., Kasimoglu, I.: Ad Hoc Netw. J. **2**(4), 351–367 (2004). https://bwn.ece.gatech.edu/surveys/actors.pdf
2. Broecheler, M., Shakarian, P., Subrahmanian, V.: A scalable framework for modeling competitive diffusion in social networks. In: 2010 IEEE Second International Conference on Social Computing (SocialCom), pp. 295–302, August 2010. https://doi.org/10.1109/SocialCom.2010.49

3. Chinowsky, P., Diekmann, J., Galotti, V.: Social network model of construction. J. Constr. Eng. Manag. **134**(10), 804–812 (2008). https://doi.org/10.1061/(ASCE)0733-9364(2008)134:10(804)
4. De, J., Zhang, X., Cheng, L.: Transduction on directed graphs via absorbing random walks. arXiv preprint arXiv:1402.4566 1402(4566) (2014). http://arxiv.org/abs/1402.4566
5. Greenan, C.C.: Diffusion of innovations in dynamic networks. J. Roy. Stat. Soc. Ser. A (Stat. Soc.) **178**(1), 147–166 (2015). https://doi.org/10.1111/rssa.12054/pdf
6. Jackson, M.O., Watts, A.: The evolution of social and economic networks. J. Econ. Theor. **106**(2), 265–295 (2002). https://doi.org/10.1006/jeth.2001.2903. http://www.sciencedirect.com/science/article/pii/S0022053101929035
7. Jiang, C., Chen, Y., Liu, K.: Evolutionary dynamics of information diffusion over social networks. IEEE Trans. Signal Process. **62**(17), 4573–4586 (2014). https://doi.org/10.1109/TSP.2014.2339799
8. Lanham, M., Morgan, G., Carley, K.: Social network modeling and agent-based simulation in support of crisis de-escalation. IEEE Trans. Syst. Man Cybern. Syst. **44**(1), 103–110 (2014). https://doi.org/10.1109/TSMCC.2012.2230255
9. Nikolaev, A.G., Razib, R., Kucheriya, A.: On efficient use of entropy centrality for social network analysis and community detection. Soc. Netw. **40**, 154–162 (2015). http://www.sciencedirect.com/science/article/pii/S0378873314000550
10. Olfati-Saber, R., Fax, A., Murray, R.M.: Consensus and cooperation in networked multi-agent systems. Proc. IEEE **95**(1), 215–233 (2007)
11. Sabattini, L., Secchi, C., Chopra, N.: Decentralized control for maintenance of strong connectivity for directed graphs. In: 21st Mediterranean Conference on Control and Automation, pp. 978–986, June 2013. https://doi.org/10.1109/MED.2013.6608840
12. Safar, M., Mahdi, K., Torabi, S.: Network robustness and irreversibility of information diffusion in Complex networks. J. Comput. Sci. **2**(3), 198–206 (2011). https://doi.org/10.1016/j.jocs.2011.05.005. http://www.sciencedirect.com/science/article/pii/S1877750311000482
13. Smith, B., Egerstedt, M., Howard, A.: Automatic deployment and formation control of decentralized multi-agent networks. In: IEEE International Conference on Robotics and Automation, ICRA 2008. pp. 134–139, May 2008. https://doi.org/10.1109/ROBOT.2008.4543198
14. Snijders, T.A.: The statistical evaluation of social network dynamics. Sociol. Methodol. **31**(1), 361–395 (2001)
15. Snijders, T.A., Van de Bunt, G.G., Steglich, C.E.: Introduction to stochastic actor-based models for network dynamics. Soc. Netw. **32**(1), 44–60 (2010). http://www.sciencedirect.com/science/article/pii/S0378873309000069
16. Villatoro, D., Sabater-Mir, J., Sen, S.: Robust convention emergence in social networks through self-reinforcing structures dissolution. ACM Trans. Auton. Adapt. Syst. **8**(1), 2:1–2:21 (2013). https://doi.org/10.1145/2451248.2451250. https://doi.org/10.1145/2451248.2451250
17. Watts, A.: A dynamic model of network formation. Games Econ. Behav. **34**(2), 331–341 (2001). https://doi.org/10.1006/game.2000.0803. http://www.sciencedirect.com/science/article/pii/S0899825600908030
18. Wu, X.M., Li, Z., So, A.M., Wright, J., Chang, S.F.: Learning with partially absorbing random walks. In: Advances in Neural Information Processing Systems, pp. 3077–3085 (2012). http://papers.nips.cc/paper/4833-learning-with-partially-absorbing-random-walks

Gaming Bot Detection: A Systematic Literature Review

Denis Kotkov, Gaurav Pandey, and Alexander Semenov$^{(\boxtimes)}$

University of Jyvaskyla, Faculty of Information Technology,
P.O. Box 35, FI-40014 Jyvaskyla, Finland
kotkov.denis.ig@gmail.com, {gaurav.g.pandey,alexander.v.semenov}@jyu.fi

Abstract. In online games, some players employ programs (bots) that allow them to bypass game routines and effortlessly gain virtual resources. This practice leads to negative effects, such as reduced revenue for the game development companies and unfair treatment for ordinary players. Bot detection methods act as a counter measure for such players. This paper presents a systematic literature review of bot detection in online games. We mainly focus on games that allow resource accumulation for players between game sessions. For this, we summarize the existing literature, list categories of games ignored by the scientific community, review publicly available datasets, present the taxonomy of detection methods and provide future directions on this topic. The main goal of this paper is to summarize the existing literature and indicate gaps in the body of knowledge.

Keywords: Online games · Bot detection · Machine learning

1 Introduction

Online games have millions of players and bring billions of dollars of revenue to game development companies [3]. In this paper, the term *player* refers to the individual, who plays the game [22]. Games can fall into one of the two categories: games that allow players to accumulate game resources between game sessions, such as MMORPGs (massively multiplayer online role-playing games) and games, where players gather game resources in every session from scratch, such as FPS (first-person shooter) games [25]. In this paper, we focus on online games that allow players to save gained resources between game sessions.

Players of these games spend days and sometimes even years building up their characters to compete or collaborate with other players and acquire access to new game content [4]. In this paper, the term *character* refers to an avatar controlled by the player in the virtual world of the game [22]. Game development companies benefit from players by selling to them game items or special abilities that players would spend a lot of effort to acquire.

Players can buy these products not only from game development companies, but also from other players [2]. Markets, where players buy and sell characters

X. Chen et al. (Eds.): CSoNet 2018, LNCS 11280, pp. 247–258, 2018.
https://doi.org/10.1007/978-3-030-04648-4_21

and game products are very popular among players, as they offer prices lower than that of game development companies and allow players to purchase products that game development companies do not sell. For example, more than half of total money exchange in the famous MMORPG game Aion is associated with real money transactions [12]. Many of these markets can be identified in search engines; for instance, market "G2G"[1] offers hundreds of thousands items for sale for World of Warcraft. China, up to 100,000 players are hired to build up their characters for selling [22]. Some player can even make a living just by building up their characters and selling them later [1].

Many players use bots for repetitive actions needed to gain resources or build up their characters. Bots appear in games for different purposes:

- A bot can be integrated in a game to play with human players. Usually, it is clear which character is a bot and these bots are not needed to be detected.
- A player can use a bot to access game content, which was unavailable earlier. For example, a player can implement a bot in the Sikuli[2] platform to access content in the puzzle game Bejeweled[3].
- A player can use a bot to gain social influence in a game. For example, a Counter Strike player can use a bot to win or gain an advantage over other players. Examples of such software are enablers of automatic cross-hair. In this case, the player does not receive any profit, but social influence.
- A player can use a bot to gain real life resources, such as real money or goods. For example, an Aion player can use a bot to bypass game routines and earn game resources. This player can sell the gained resources for real money later.

In this paper, we mainly focus on the detection of bots that appear in games to generate profit for their owners, as these kinds of bots harm both game development companies and players. Game development companies receive less revenue, as instead of buying products from the companies, players earn these products using bots. Ordinary players also suffer because of bots. This is because bots can play without break, build up their characters faster and cause inflation of the game currency by mining it with a much higher speed than ordinary players [22].

Bots are not the only way to cheat in games. Users can also use additional programs that simplify their gaming tasks. For example, a Counter Strike player can use a program that makes walls transparent, which allows this player to track characters of other players and gain an advantage in the game [20]. However, in this paper, we only focus on bots, which are computer programs that control a player's character and play the game unattended [22].

There are multiple bots available for different games; many of them claim that they are feature-rich very easy to use[4], and there are tens of thousands users discussing bot usage at the forums[5]. Typically bots aimed at mobile games require

---

[1] https://www.g2g.com/wow-us/Item-2299-19260.
[2] http://www.sikuli.org/.
[3] https://www.ea.com/games/bejeweled/bejeweled-blitz?setLocale=en-us.
[4] https://www.raccoonbot.com/.
[5] https://mybot.run/forums/.

Android OS emulator to be installed, and the bot software works inside the emulator. Some bots are free software, however, some require license fee[6]. Many bot manufacturers claim, that their software has *"advanced artificial intelligence that closely mimics a humans behavior"*[7]; thus, detection of the bots might be not a trivial task.

On the other hand, a lot of research is focused on creation of efficient AI for playing different games, such as poker [9]; and many other games [23]. Also, behavior of online game players was studied as a model for real-life people interaction [6].

The main goal of this paper is to summarize the existing literature on gaming bot detection and indicate gaps in the body of knowledge. The main contributions of this paper are summarized as follows.

- It reviews existing body of knowledge.
- It presents a taxonomy of bot detection methods.
- It provides future directions of the topic based on the literature review.

1.1 Methods and Logistics

This paper provides a literature review on bot detection in online games. We conducted a systematic literature review [21], which included screening (or gathering) related literature, processing (or analyzing) collected literature and communicating the results of the review. The key points followed in our review process are:

- **Literature Search.** We first looked for literature based on the following search queries: "game bot detection", "game bot security" and "game bot cheating detection". We analyzed the top twenty articles from results returned by Google Scholar[8] in response to each search query. We retrieved the search results twice: articles published overall and articles published starting from 2017 (to receive the most recent articles). Overall, we found 35 distinct articles.
- **Screening of Literature.** Our selection criteria for the literature was based on the JUFO ratings[9] of the articles. These ratings created by the Finnish scientific community, classify the publication channels into four levels: 0, 1, 2 and 3. The higher the level the higher the quality of the publication channel. We took into account only articles published in the publication channels of at least level 1. After filtering out articles that do not meet our requirements, we selected 12 key articles (See Table 1).

---

[6] https://wrobot.eu/store/category/2-wrobot/.
[7] https://wrobot.eu/.
[8] https://scholar.google.com/.
[9] https://www.tsv.fi/julkaisufoorumi/haku.php?lang=en.

1.2   Research Questions

In this paper, our literature review focuses on answering the following research questions:

RQ1: *What game categories have received low attention from the scientific community for bot detection?*
Our goal is to detect categories of games that are targeted by bots, but skipped by the scientific community, as these categories bring new challenges and need to be considered.

RQ2: *What are the publicly available datasets for bot detection?*
We aim to collect a list a datasets available for experiments.

RQ3: *How can we detect bots in online games?*
The purpose of this RQ is to review the state-of-the-art bot detection methods.

RQ4: *What are the future directions of bot detection?*
We aim to provide future directions of this topic.

The rest of the paper is organized as follows. We first discuss game categories in Sect. 2. We then list the publicly available datasets in Sect. 3 and review bot detection methods in Sect. 4. We also present future directions of the topic in Sect. 5. Finally we provide conclusion and future work in Sect. 6.

2   Studied Game Categories

In this section, we describe existing game categories and categories studied by the scientific community. Finally, we will answer RQ1 by indicating game categories disregarded by the selected studies.

Although games vary significantly, they can generally be classified in several categories. However, these categories are relative and a game can belong to several categories at the same time. We extended the categorization presented in [10] as follows:

– **Role playing games.** A player controls their character and explores the virtual world of the game. These games usually involve earning resources, such as items or game currency and the enhancing character's abilities. A subcategory of these games is massively multiplayer online role-playing games (MMORPGs), e.g. World of Warcraft[10].
– **Action games.** A player navigates their character in the game world by avoiding or destroying obstacles on its way. The emphasis of these games is on the player's hand-eye coordination. A typical example of an action game is Super Mario Bros[11].

---

[10] https://worldofwarcraft.com/en-us/.
[11] https://www.joy.land/super-mario-bros.html.

- **Adventure games.** A player navigates their character in the game and solves puzzle like problems on their way. The abilities of the character usually stay fixed. The focus of this category of games is on the story line. An example from this category is Syberia[12].
- **Strategy games.** It is common that in games of this category, a player controls a population of characters and makes decision for them. The focus of this category is on tactic and strategy. A famous example from this category is StarCraft[13].
- **Music games.** A player needs to imitate playing a musical instrument or dance to earn game points. The focus of this category is on the consistency of music and player's movements. An example from this category is Guitar Hero[14].
- **Shooting games.** Normally, a player controls a character armed with a weapon, which is often a gun to destroy other characters. A famous example from this category is the first person shooting (FPS) game Quake[15].
- **Fighting games.** A player controls a character in a combat against one or more other characters. A famous fighting game is Mortal Kombat[16].
- **Puzzle games.** In this category, a player does not normally control any characters. The focus of this category is on puzzle solving. A famous example from this category is Tetris[17].
- **Gambling games.** These games always include consideration, chance and prize. A player bets something of value, such as money on a random event and wins the prize according to the consideration depending on the result of the event. One of the most common example of the game from this category is Roulette[18].

According to our literature review (Table 1), most research on bot detection focuses on MMORPG and FPS. Studies target MMORPG, because in the games of this category, bots are used by certain players for gaining profit. This discourages other ordinary players to play the game and financially hurts the game development companies. Studies also target FPS games, as the case study that can be generalized to other kinds of games [11]. The rest of categories received low attention from the scientific community, while games belonging to these categories also suffer from bots in the same way as MMORPG. For example, the famous strategy mobile game Clash Royale[19] has more than 27 million players[20] and some of these players use bots[21] to improve their characters and sell them later.

---

[12] http://www.syberia.microids.com/EN/.
[13] https://starcraft.com/en-us/.
[14] https://www.guitarhero.com/.
[15] https://quake.bethesda.net/en.
[16] http://www.mortalkombat.com/.
[17] https://tetris.com/.
[18] https://www.casinotop10.net/free-roulette.
[19] https://supercell.com/en/games/clashroyale/.
[20] https://toucharcade.com/2017/08/29/clash-royale-saw-27-million-players-enter-its-crown-championship-fall-season/.
[21] http://clashroyalebot.com.br/.

3   Datasets for Bot Detection

In this section, we answer RQ2 by listing publicly available datasets based on our literature review. We also discuss the methods to collect datasets, that can be utilized for bot detection tasks.

Researchers collect various datasets for bot detection tasks, but most of them remain publicly unavailable (as we can see that most of the datasets in Table 1 are private). Based on our literature review, we have identified the following datasets:

- **Quake 2 Datasets.** Quake 2 allows to record a log of the game, which can later be used to watch and analyze the recorded game [11]. The logs contain character movements and game events, such as picking game items, shootings and destroying a character. Players share their game recordings on the number of websites, such as Planet Quake[22] or Demo Squad[23].
- **Aion Dataset**[24]. The dataset contains action logs performed by 49,739 characters in the famous MMORPG Aion from April 9 till July 5, 2010 [16]. The dataset also contains the list of banned users verified by human labor, which is useful for testing bot detection algorithms.

In situations, when datasets suitable for researchers' needs are publicly unavailable, researchers employ the following data collection methods:

- **Tracking events.** The researchers could track events (such as clicks and keyboard buttons) in the client application of the game. Gianvecchio et al. [14] developed a program that runs concurrently with the game client application and tracks keyboard and mouse events.
- **Developing a game.** The researchers could develop their own games that suit their needs and track events in them. Alayed et al. [7] developed an FPS game and tracked players' actions in this game.
- **Dataset generation.** In order to generate botnet datasetm Shiravi et. al [26] analyzed real packet traces to create profiles for agents generating real traffic. Then they generated malicious traffic by exploring multi-stage attack scenarios. Similar approach can be followed specifically for bot detection.

There are many bot software packages available, and for collection of the dataset it could be possible to run the bot at controlled environment; but in this case it is not possible to collect data from the game without specific reverse-engineering (or packet sniffing), since main game software is closed and located at the servers controlled by game-developer.

---

[22] http://planetquake.gamespy.com/.
[23] http://q2scene.net/ds/.
[24] http://ocslab.hksecurity.net/Datasets/game-bot-detection.

Table 1. A summary of articles

Article	Category	Game	Dataset
Chen et al. [11]	Trajectory	FPS (Quake 2)	Game traces publicly available at five websites dedicated to Quake
Kang et al. [16]	Action frequency & Social activity	MMORPG (Aion)	A public Aion dataset
Kang et al. [18]	Action frequency & Social activity	MMORPG (Aion)	A private Aion dataset
Mitterhofer et al. [22]	Trajectory	MMORPG (World of Warcraft)	A private dataset collected from World of Warcraft (only trajectories)
Bernardi et al. [8]	Action frequency & Social activity	MMORPG (Aion)	A public Aion dataset
Gianvecchio et al. [14]	Action frequency	MMORPG(World of Warcraft)	A private dataset (keyboard and mouse events)
Alayed et al. [7]	Action frequency	FPS (Trojan Battles, developed for this research)	A private dataset (game events)
Kang et al. [17]	Social activity	MMORPG (Aion)	A private dataset (game events and chatting activity)
Kwon et al. [19]	Social activity & Network-side	MMORPG (Aion)	A private dataset (trade log)
Thawonmas et al. [28]	Action frequency	MMORPG (Cabal Online)	(event log)
Tao et al. [27]	Action frequency	NetEase MMORPG	A private dataset (event log)
Chung et al. [13]	Action frequency	MMORPG (Yulgang Online)	A private dataset (event log)

4   Bot Detection Methods

In this section, we answer RQ3 by classifying methods used for detection of gaming bots.

4.1   Supervised and Unsupervised Learning Methods

Most methods employ machine learning for bot detection. [5,8,16,24]. These methods can employ a supervised learning algorithm or an unsupervised learning algorithm.

In case of supervised machine learning methods (specifically, classification algorithms), the software needs a *ground truth* dataset: with instances labeled as bots or ordinary users. Using such dataset, a bot classifier model can be trained. For an unknown instance, this trained model in turn is used to estimate the probability that the instance is a bot. If the probability is beyond a certain threshold, the instance is classified as a bot.

Unsupervised methods used for bots detection do not require learning a model using a training dataset. A popular unsupervised method is *anomaly detection*; they aim to detect rare or abnormal activity by the bots. Moreover, clustering of players can also be used for bot detection [27]. Here, the human players that are typically the majority of players in the gaming system, would form larger clusters than players suspected to be bots.

4.2   Method Classification Based on User Behavior

Figure 1 demonstrates the taxonomy of bot detection methods on the basis of user behavior. Bot detection methods can be classified into three categories [16]: client-side, network-side and server-side.

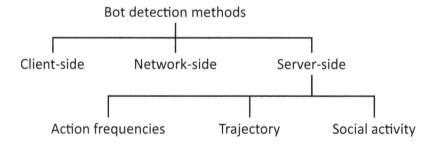

Fig. 1. Taxonomy

- **Client-side.** Client-side methods function similarly to anti-viruses. Players install these programs to their computers and the programs detect bots by monitoring information regarding processes that are being executed.
- **Network-side.** Network-side methods are based on analysis of the network traffic.
- **Server-side.** Server-side methods are based on behavior of players in the game. Server-side methods usually involve machine learning algorithms and can be classified based on the used features: action frequencies [14], character trajectory [11] and social activity [17].

- **Action Frequencies.** Action frequency features are based on the number of times a character performed a particular action. For example, an action frequency feature can be a number of times an FPS character hit the target [7].
- **Trajectory.** Character trajectory features are based on the movements of the character in the game, such as a trace generated by the character in Quake 2 [11].
- **Social Activity.** Social activity features are based on social interactions between characters. There can be trades between characters [19] or messages sent from one character to another [17].

Table 1 summarizes the reviewed literature in terms of the presented taxonomy and our research questions. The majority of selected studies employ action frequency features, while some use both action frequency and social activity feature spaces. Trajectory features are the least popular according to the selected literature.

The reviewed bot detection methods are based on machine learning, either supervised or unsupervised. Most of the studies employ neural networks [8,14] common classification algorithms, such as logistic regression [7], support vector machines [7] or naive Bayesian classifier [11].

Studies on bot detection also differ in terms of tasks:

- Detecting bots one by one. The majority of studies develop a method which classifies each character as a bot or a real user. For example, Thawonmas et al. [28] proposed a method to detect if a particular character is a bot.
- Detecting groups of bots. Kwon et al. [19] developed a method of detecting gold farming groups in World of Warcraft. These groups consist of several bots, where each of them plays one of the three roles: a gold farmer, a merchant or a banker. Gold farmers destroy monsters, collect game resources, such as money and items and pass them to merchants. Merchants items from game money and deliver them to bankers. Bankers sell game money for real money to other players.

Note: We notice that game bot detection methods are similar to methods for the detection of fake accounts on the social media sites [15], as fake account detection methods use the same fundamental assumption that the behavior of fake accounts is different from that of real users.

5 Future Directions

In this section, we address RQ4 and identify the following future directions for the detection of gaming bots on the basis of literature review:

- The studies on gaming bot detection mostly focus on MMORPG and disregard other game categories, such as strategy or action. Online games that belong to these genres also allow to accumulate resources between user sessions and suffer from bots. For example, the game Clash of Clans[25] is populated with bots[26]. Games of disregarded categories bring new challenges to the scientific community, as their game mechanics are different from that of MMORPG.

– Another future direction is the expansion of the types of machine learning models used for the detection of bots. For example, Markov Decision Process could be used to develop a model particularly for the detection of bots in online games.

– The majority of the review studies used up to two feature spaces (for example, action frequency and social activity). Meanwhile, employing a wider variety of features spaces has a potential to increase the detection accuracy. However, handling more feature spaces in many cases is more challenging than dealing only with a single feature space.

6   Conclusion and Future Work

Some online players use bots to gain virtual resources, without making efforts in gaming. This often results in negative effects on the revenue for the game development companies as well as dissatisfaction of the ordinary players. In this paper, we conducted a systematic literature review and focused mainly on games that allow accumulation of resources in subsequent session. We answered the following research questions:

– *RQ1. What game categories have received low attention from the scientific community for bot detection?*
  We found that the selected studies mostly target MMORPG and FPS games and disregard other categories of games, such as strategy, action and fighting.
– *RQ2. What are the publicly available datasets for bot detection?*
  We indicated two publicly available datasets: the Quake 2 dataset and the Aion dataset. Both datasets contain data on players' actions in the games, but majority of the datasets are not publicly available
– *RQ3. How can we detect bots in online games?*
  We presented a taxonomy of bot detection methods: client-side, network-side and server-side, which can be based on action frequencies, social activity or character trajectory. To detect bots, the reviewed studies used common classification algorithms and neural networks.
– *RQ4. What are the future directions of bot detection?*
  We indicated three future directions: targeting more game categories, the expansion of methods for detection bots and the combination of different feature spaces.

In our future work, we are planning on extending this literature review with comparison of studies on the topic in terms of methodologies. Our future work also includes design of bot detection methods.

---

[25] https://supercell.com/en/games/clashofclans/.
[26] https://www.raccoonbot.com/.

References

1. Ways to Make Money Playing Video Games. https://ivetriedthat.com/7-ways-to-make-money-playing-video-games/. Accessed 14 Sept 2018
2. G2G Corporate—Gaming For A Living. https://corp.g2g.com/. Accessed 14 Sept 2018
3. Global Games Market Revenues 2018—Per Region & Segment—Newzoo. https://newzoo.com/insights/articles/global-games-market-reaches-137-9-billion-in-2018-mobile-games-take-half/. Accessed 14 Sept 2018
4. I will game: anatomy of MMO addiction. https://www.cnet.com/news/i-will-game-anatomy-of-mmo-addiction/. Accessed 14 Sept 2018
5. Ahmad, M.A., Keegan, B., Srivastava, J., Williams, D., Contractor, N.: Mining for gold farmers: automatic detection of deviant players in MMOGs. In: 2009 International Conference on Computational Science and Engineering, pp. 340–345. IEEE (2009)
6. Ahmad, M.A., Srivastava, J.: Behavioral data mining and network analysis in massive online games. In: Proceedings of the 7th ACM International Conference on Web Search and Data Mining, WSDM 2014, pp. 673–674. ACM, New York (2014). https://doi.org/10.1145/2556195.2556196
7. Alayed, H., Frangoudes, F., Neuman, C.: Behavioral-based cheating detection in online first person shooters using machine learning techniques. In: 2013 IEEE Conference on Computational Intelligence in Games (CIG), pp. 1–8. Citeseer (2013)
8. Bernardi, M.L., Cimitile, M., Martinelli, F., Mercaldo, F.: A time series classification approach to game bot detection. In: Proceedings of the 7th International Conference on Web Intelligence, Mining and Semantics, p. 6. ACM (2017)
9. Brown, N., Sandholm, T.: Superhuman AI for heads-up no-limit poker: libratus beats top professionals. Science (2017). https://doi.org/10.1126/science.aao1733. http://science.sciencemag.org/content/early/2017/12/15/science.aao1733
10. Chen, C.L., Ku, C.C., Deng, Y.Y., Tsaur, W.J.: Automatic detection for online Games Bot with APP. In: 2018 Third International Conference on Fog and Mobile Edge Computing (FMEC), pp. 289–294. IEEE (2018)
11. Chen, K.-T., Liao, A., Pao, H.-K.K., Chu, H.-H.: Game Bot detection based on avatar trajectory. In: Stevens, S.M., Saldamarco, S.J. (eds.) ICEC 2008. LNCS, vol. 5309, pp. 94–105. Springer, Heidelberg (2008). https://doi.org/10.1007/978-3-540-89222-9_11
12. Chun, S., Choi, D., Han, J., Kim, H.K., Kwon, T.: Unveiling a socio-economic system in a virtual world: a case study of an MMORPG. In: Proceedings of the 2018 World Wide Web Conference on World Wide Web, pp. 1929–1938. International World Wide Web Conferences Steering Committee (2018)
13. Chung, Y., et al.: Game Bot detection approach based on behavior analysis and consideration of various play styles. ETRI J. **35**(6), 1058–1067 (2013)
14. Gianvecchio, S., Wu, Z., Xie, M., Wang, H.: Battle of Botcraft: fighting bots in online games with human observational proofs. In: Proceedings of the 16th ACM Conference on Computer and Communications Security, pp. 256–268. ACM (2009)
15. Gurajala, S., White, J.S., Hudson, B., Matthews, J.N.: Fake Twitter accounts: profile characteristics obtained using an activity-based pattern retection approach. In: Proceedings of the 2015 International Conference on Social Media & Society, p. 9. ACM (2015)
16. Kang, A.R., Jeong, S.H., Mohaisen, A., Kim, H.K.: Multimodal game bot detection using user behavioral characteristics. SpringerPlus **5**(1), 523 (2016)

17. Kang, A.R., Kim, H.K., Woo, J.: Chatting pattern based game BOT detection: do they talk like us? KSII Trans. Internet Inf. Syst. **6**(11), 2866–2879 (2012)
18. Kang, A.R., Woo, J., Park, J., Kim, H.K.: Online game bot detection based on party-play log analysis. Comput. Math. Appl. **65**(9), 1384–1395 (2013)
19. Kwon, H., Mohaisen, A., Woo, J., Kim, Y., Lee, E., Kim, H.K.: Crime scene reconstruction: online gold farming network analysis. IEEE Trans. Inf. Forensics Secur. **12**(3), 544–556 (2017)
20. Laurens, P., Paige, R.F., Brooke, P.J., Chivers, H.: A novel approach to the detection of cheating in multiplayer online games. IEEE (2007)
21. Levy, Y., Ellis, T.J.: A systems approach to conduct an effective literature review in support of information systems research. Inf. Sci. **9** (2006)
22. Mitterhofer, S., Krügel, C., Kirda, E., Platzer, C.: Server-side bot detection in massively multiplayer online games. IEEE Secur. Priv. **7** (2009)
23. Ontan, S., Synnaeve, G., Uriarte, A., Richoux, F., Churchill, D., Preuss, M.: A survey of real-time strategy game AI research and competition in starcraft. IEEE Trans. Comput. Intell. AI Games **5**(4), 293–311 (2013). https://doi.org/10.1109/TCIAIG.2013.2286295
24. Prasetya, K., Wu, Z.D.: Artificial neural network for bot detection system in MMOGs. In: Proceedings of the 9th Annual Workshop on Network and Systems Support for Games, p. 16. IEEE Press (2010)
25. Rocha, J.B., Mascarenhas, S., Prada, R.: Game mechanics for cooperative games. ZON Digital Games **2008**, 72–80 (2008)
26. Shiravi, A., Shiravi, H., Tavallaee, M., Ghorbani, A.A.: Toward developing a systematic approach to generate benchmark datasets for intrusion detection. Comput. Secur. **31**(3), 357–374 (2012)
27. Tao, J., Xu, J., Gong, L., Li, Y., Fan, C., Zhao, Z.: NGUARD: A Game Bot Detection Framework for NetEase MMORPGs (2018)
28. Thawonmas, R., Kashifuji, Y., Chen, K.T.: Detection of MMORPG bots based on behavior analysis. In: Proceedings of the 2008 International Conference on Advances in Computer Entertainment Technology, pp. 91–94. ACM (2008)

Graph-Based Comparison of IoT and Android Malware

Hisham Alasmary[1], Afsah Anwar[1], Jeman Park[1], Jinchun Choi[1,2],
Daehun Nyang[2(✉)], and Aziz Mohaisen[1(✉)]

[1] University of Central Florida, Orlando, FL 32816, USA
{hisham,afsahanwar,parkjeman,jc.choi}@Knights.ucf.edu,
mohaisen@ucf.edu
[2] Inha University, Incheon, Republic of Korea
nyang@inha.ac.kr

Abstract. The growth in the number of android and Internet of Things (IoT) devices has witnessed a parallel increase in the number of malicious software (malware) that can run on both, affecting their ecosystems. Thus, it is essential to understand those malware towards their detection. In this work, we look into a comparative study of android and IoT malware through the lenses of graph measures: we construct abstract structures, using the control flow graph (CFG) to represent malware binaries. Using those structures, we conduct an in-depth analysis of malicious graphs extracted from the android and IoT malware. By reversing 2,874 and 201 malware binaries corresponding to the IoT and android platforms, respectively, extract their CFGs, and analyze them across both general characteristics, such as the number of nodes and edges, as well as graph algorithmic constructs, such as average shortest path, betweenness, closeness, density, etc. Using the CFG as an abstract structure, we emphasize various interesting findings, such as the prevalence of unreachable code in android malware, noted by the multiple components in their CFGs, the high density, strong closeness and betweenness, and larger number of nodes in the android malware, compared to the IoT malware, highlighting its higher order of complexity. We note that the number of edges in android malware is larger than that in IoT malware, highlighting a richer flow structure of those malware samples, despite their structural simplicity (number of nodes). We note that most of those graph-based properties can be used as discriminative features for classification.

Keywords: Malware · Android · IoT · Graph analysis

This work is supported by the NSF grant CNS-1809000, NRF grant 2016K1A1A2912757, Florida Center for Cybersecurity (FC2) seed grant, and support by the Air Force Research Lab. This work would not have been possible without the support of Ernest J. Gemeinhart.

X. Chen et al. (Eds.): CSoNet 2018, LNCS 11280, pp. 259–272, 2018.
https://doi.org/10.1007/978-3-030-04648-4_22

1 Introduction

Internet of Things (IoT) is a new networking paradigm interconnecting a large number of devices, such as voice assistants, sensors, and automation tools, with many promising applications [1]. Each of those devices runs multiple pieces of software, or applications, which increase in complexity, could have vulnerabilities that could be exploited, resulting in various security threats and consequences. As a result, understanding IoT software through analysis, abstraction, and classification is an essential problem to mitigate those security threats [1,2].

There has been a large body of work on the problem of software analysis in general, and a few attempts on analyzing IoT software in particular. However, the effort on IoT software analysis has been very limited with respect to the samples analyzed and the approaches attempted. Starting with a new dataset of IoT malware samples, we pursue a graph-theoretic approach to malware analysis. Each malware sample can be abstracted into a Control Flow Graph (CFG), which could be used to extract representative static features of the application. As such, graph-related features from the CFG can be used as a representation of the software, and classification techniques can be built to tell whether the software is malicious or benign, or even what kind of malicious software it is (e.g., malware family level classification and label extrapolation).

The limited existing literature on IoT malware, and despite malware analysis, classification, and detection being a focal point of analysts and researchers [3–6], points at the difficulty, compared to other malware type. Understanding the similarity and differences of IoT malware compared to other prominent malware type will help analysts understand the differences and use them to build detection systems upon those differences. To understand how different the IoT malware is from other types of emerging malware, such as mobile applications, we perform a comparative study of those graph-theoretic features in both types of software to highlight the control flow graph shift in IoT malware to android application malware.

Contributions. In this paper, we make the following contributions. First, building on the existing literature of mobile apps analysis and abstraction using CFGs, we look into analyzing CFGs of emerging and recent IoT malware samples. Then, using various graph-theoretic features, such as degree centrality, betweenness, graph size, diameter, radius, distribution of shortest path, etc., we contrast those features in IoT malware to those in mobile applications, uncovering various similarities and differences. Therefore, the findings in this paper can be utilized to distinguish between IoT malware and android malware.

Organization. The rest of this paper is organized as follows. In Sect. 2 we review the related work. In Sect. 3 we introduce the methodology and approach of this paper, including the dataset, data representation and augmentation, control flow graph definition, and graph theoretic metrics. In Sect. 4 we present the results. In Sect. 5 we present discussion and comparison, followed by concluding remarks in Sect. 6.

2   Related Work

The limited number of works have been done on analyzing the differences between android (or mobile) and IoT malware, particularly using abstract graph structures. Hu *et al.* [7] designed a system, called SMIT, which searches for the nearest neighbor in malware graphs to compute the similarity across function using their call graphs. They focused on finding the graph similarity through an approximate graph-edit distance rather than approximating the graph isomorphism since few malware families have the same subgraphs with others. Shang *et al.* [5] analyzed code obfuscation of the malware by computing the similarity of the function call graph between two malware binaries – used as a signature – to identify the malware. Christodorescu and Jha [8] analyzed obfuscation in malware code and proposed a detection system, called SAFE, that utilizes the control flow graph through extracting malicious patterns in the executables. Bruschi *et al.* [9] detected the self-mutated malware by comparing the control flow graph of the malware code to the control flow graphs for other known malware.

Tamersoy *et al.* [10] proposed an algorithm to detect malware executables by computing the similarity between malware files and other files appearing with them on the same machine, by building a graph that captures the relationship between all files. Yamaguchi *et al.* [11] introduced the code property graph which merges and combines different analysis of the code, such as abstract syntax trees, control flow graphs and program dependence graphs in the form of joint data structure to efficiently identify common vulnerabilities. Caselden *et al.* [12] generated a new attack polymorphism using hybrid information and CFG, called HI-CFG, which is built from the program binaries, such as a PDF viewer. The attack collects and combines such information based on graphs; code and data, as long as the relationships among them.

Wuchner *et al.* [13] proposed a graph-based detection system that uses a quantitative data flow graphs generated from the system calls, and use the graph node properties, i.e. centrality metric, as a feature vector for the classification between malicious and benign programs. In addition, Jang *et al.* [14] used a behavioral representation of the programs as quantitative data flow graphs to classify the malware families based on their system call structures by using multiple graph characteristics, such as degree centrality, graph density, etc., as a feature vector.

Android Malware. Gascon *et al.* [15] detected android malware through classifying their function call graphs. They found the reuse of malicious codes across multiple malware samples showing that malware authors reuse existing codes to infect the android applications. Zhang *et al.* [16] proposed a detection system for the android malware by constructing signatures through classifying the API dependency graphs and used that signature to uncover the similarities of android applications behavior.

3   Methodology

The goal of this study is to understand the underlying differences between modern android and emerging IoT malware through the lenses of graph analysis. The abstract graph structure through which we analyze malware is the control flow graph (CFG), previously used in analyzing malware as shown above. Unique to this study, however, we look into various algorithmic and structural properties of those graphs to understand code complexity, analysis evasion techniques (decoy functions, obfuscation, etc.).

Towards this goal, we start by gathering various malware samples in two datasets, IoT and android. For our IoT dataset, we utilized samples gathered through the IoTPOT honeypot [17]. For our android dataset, various recent android malware samples, due to Shen *et al.* (obtained from a security analysis vendor) are utilized [18]. For our analysis, we augment the datasets by reversing the samples to address various analysis issues. Using an off-the-shelf tool, we then disassemble the malware samples to obtain the CFG corresponding to each of them. We use the CFG of each sample as an abstract representation and explore various graph analysis measures and properties. The rest of this section highlights the details of the dataset creation and associated analysis.

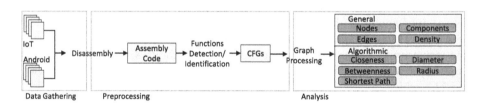

Fig. 1. Data flow diagram for the analysis process for the CFGs.

3.1   Dataset Creation

Our IoT malware dataset is a set of 2,874 malware samples, randomly selected from the IoTPOT [17], a telnet-based honeypot which is now extended to other services. Additionally, we also obtained a dataset of 201 android malware samples from [18] for contrast. These datasets represent each malware type. We reverse-engineered the malware datasets using *Radare2* [19], a reverse engineering framework that provides various analysis capabilities including disassembly. To this end, we disassemble the IoT binaries, which in the form of Executable and Linkable Format (ELF) binaries, as well as the Android Application Packages (APKs) using the same tool, *radare2*. *Radare2* is an open source command line framework that supports a wide variety of malware architecture and has a python API, which facilitated the automation of our analysis.

Labeling. To determine if a file is malicious, we uploaded the samples on *Virus-Total* [20] and gathered the scan results corresponding to each of the malware. We observe that each of the IoT and android malware is detected by at least one of the antivirus software scanners listed in VirusTotal, whereas the android dataset has a higher rate.

Differences. We notice that while the android malware samples are detected by almost every antivirus software, the IoT malware has a low detection rate, which is perhaps anticipated given the fact that the IoT malware samples are recent and emerging threats, with fewer signatures populated in the antivirus scanners, compared to well-understood android malware. To further examine the diversity and representation of the malware in our dataset, we label them by their family (class attribute). To do so, we use *AVClass* [21], a tool that ingests the *VirusTotal* results and provides a family name to each sample through various heuristics of label consolidation. Table 1 shows the top seven family labels and their share in both the IoT and android malware datasets. Overall, we noticed that the IoT malware belong to seven families, while the android malware belong to 39 unique families, despite the clear imbalance in the number of samples.

Processing. In a preprocessing phase, we first manually analyzed the samples to understand their architectures and whether they are obfuscated or not, then used *Radare2*'s Python API, *r2pipe*, to automatically extract the CFGs for all malware samples. Then, we used an off-the-shelf graph analysis tool, *NetworkX*, to compute various graph properties. Using those calculated properties, we then analyze and compare IoT and android malware. Figure 1 shows the analysis workflow we follow to perform our analysis.

Table 1. Top 7 android and IoT families with their number of malware samples.

Android Family	# of samples	IoT Family	# of samples
Smsreg	72	Gafgyt	2,609
Smspay	34	Mirai	185
Dowgin	14	Tsunami	64
Zdtad	9	Singleton	7
Kuguo	9	Hajime	7
Revmob	8	Lightaidra	1
Smsthief	6	Ircbot	1

Program Formulation. We use the CFGs of the different malware samples as abstract characterizations of programs for their analysis. For a program P, we use $G = (V, E)$ capturing the control flow structure of that program as its representation. In the graph G, V is the set of nodes, which correspond to the functions in P, whereas E is the set of edges which correspond to the call relationship between those functions in P. More specifically, we define $V = \{v_1, v_2 \ldots, v_n\}$ and $E = \{e_{ij}\}$ for all i, j such that $e_{ij} \in E$ if there is a flow from v_i to v_j. We use $|V| = n$ to denote the size of G, and $|E| = m$ to denote the number of primitive flows in G (i.e., flows of length 1). Based on our definition of the CFG, we note that G is a directed graph. As such, we define the following centralities in G. We define $A = [a_{ij}]^{n \times n}$ as the adjacency matrix of the graph G such that an entry $a_{ij} = 1$ if $v_i \to v_j$ and 0 otherwise.

3.2   Graph Algorithmic Properties

Using this abstract structure of the programs, the CFG, we proceed to perform various analyses of those programs to understand their differences and similarities. We divide our analysis into two broader aspects: general characteristics and graph algorithmic constructs. To evaluate the general characteristics, we analyze the basic characteristics of the graphs. In particular, we analyze the number of nodes and the number of edges, which highlight the structural size of the program. Additionally, we evaluate the graph components to analyze patterns between the two malware types. Components in graphs highlight unreachable code, which are the result of decoys and obfuscation techniques. Moreover, we assess the graph algorithmic constructs; in particular, we calculate the theoretic metrics of the graphs, such as the diameter, radius, average closeness centrality etc. We now define the various measures used for our analysis.

Definition 1 (Density). *Density of a graph is defined as the closeness of an edge to the maximum number of edges. For a graph $G = (V, E)$, the graph density can be represented as the average normalized degree, such as: $Density = 1/n \sum_{i=1}^{n} \deg(v_i^{f_i})/n - 1$ for a benign graph. Other for the IoT and android graph are defined accordingly.*

Definition 2 (Shortest Path). *For a graph $G = (V_i, E_i)$, the shortest path is defined as: $v_i^x, v_i^{x_1}, v_i^{x_2}, v_i^{x_3}, \ldots v_i^y$ such that $length(v_i^x \to v_i^y)$ is the shortest path. It finds all shortest paths from $v_i^x \to v_i^y$, for all $v_i^{x_j}$, which is arbitrary, except for the starting node v_i. The shortest path is then denoted as: $S_{v_i^x}$.*

Definition 3 (Closeness centrality). *For a node v_i, the closeness is calculated as the average shortest path between that node and all other nodes in the graph G. This is, let $d(v_i, v_j)$ be the shortest path between v_i and v_j, the closeness is calculated as $c_c = \sum_{\forall v_j \in V / v_i} d(v_i, v_j)/n - 1$.*

Definition 4 (Betweenness centrality). *For a node $v_i \in V$, let $\Delta(v_i)$ be the total number of shortest paths that go through v_i and connect nodes v_j and v_r, for all j and r where $i \neq j \neq r$. Furthermore, let $\Delta(.)$ be the total number of shortest paths between such nodes. The betweenness centrality is defined as $\Delta(v_i)/\Delta(.)$.*

Definition 5 (Connected components). *A connected component in graph G is a subgraph in which two vertices are connected to each other by a path, and which is connected to no additional vertices in the subgraph. The number of components of G is the cardinality of a set that contains such connected components.*

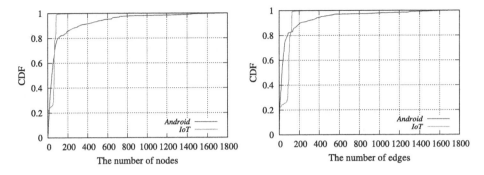

Fig. 2. CDF for the Nodes   **Fig. 3.** CDF for the Edges

Definition 6 (Diameter and Radius). *The diameter of a graph* $G = (V, E)$ *is defined as the maximum shortest path length between any two pairs of nodes in the graph, while the radius is the smallest shortest path length among any two pairs of nodes in* G. *More precisely, let* $d(v_i, v_j)$ *be the shortest path length between two arbitrary nodes in* G. *The diameter is defined as* $\max_{\forall i \neq j} d(v_i, v_j)$ *while the radius is defined as* $\min_{\forall i \neq j} d(v_i, v_j)$.

In this work, we use a normalized version of the centrality, for both the closeness and betweenness, where the value of each centrality ranges from 0 to 1.

4   Results

4.1   General Analysis

Figures 2 and 3 show the difference between the android and IoT malware in terms of two major metrics of evaluation of graphs, namely the nodes and edges.

Nodes. It can be seen in Fig. 2 that the top 1% of the android and IoT malware samples have at least 1,777 and 367 nodes, respectively. We note that those numbers are not close to one another, highlighting a different level of complexity and the flow-level. In addition, as shown in Fig. 2, we also notice a significant difference in the topological properties in the two different types of malware at the node count level. This is, while the android malware samples seem to have a variation in the number of nodes per sample, characterized by the slow growth of the y-axis (CDF) as the x-axis (the number of nodes) increases. On the other hand, the IoT malware have less variety in the number of nodes: the dynamic region of the CDF is between 1 and 60 nodes (slow curve), corresponding to [0.2–0.3] of the CDF (this is, 10% of the samples have 1 to 60 nodes, which is a relatively small number). Furthermore, with the android malware, we notice that a large majority of the samples (almost 60%) have around 100 nodes in their graph. This characteristic seems to be unique and distinguishing, as shown in Fig. 2.

Edges. Figure 3 represents the top 1% of the android and IoT malware samples, 1,707 and 577 edges, respectively, which shows a great difference between them. In particular, this figure shows that differences at the edges count as well. The android samples have a large number of edges in every sample that can be shown from the slow growth on the y-axis. Similar to the node dynamic region for the IoT, the IoT samples seem to have a smaller number of edges; the active region of the CDF between 1 to 85 edges correspond to [0.2–0.4] (about 20% of the samples). Additionally, we notice that the smallest 60% of the android samples (with respect to their graph size) have 40 edges whereas the same 60% of the IoT samples have around 95 edges.

This combined finding of the number of edges and nodes in itself is very intriguing: while the number of nodes in the IoT malware samples is relatively smaller than that in the android malware, the number of edges is higher. This is striking, as it highlights a simplicity at the code base (smaller number of nodes) yet a higher complexity at the flow-level (more edges), adding a unique analysis angle to the malware that is only visible through the CFG structure.

Density. Figure 4 shows the density of the datasets, where we notice almost 90% of the IoT samples have a density around 0.05 whereas the android samples have a diverse range of density over around 0.15. By examining the CDF further, we notice that the density alone is a very discriminative feature of the two different types of malware: if we are to use a cut-off value of 0.07, for example, we can successfully tell the different types of malware apart with an accuracy exceeding 90%.

Graph Components. Figure 5 shows a boxplot illustration of the number of components in both the IoT and android malware's CFGs. We notice that 3.23% of the IoT malware, corresponding to 93 IoT samples, have more than two components, which indicates that a large percentage of the IoT samples have one component that represents the whole control graphs for the samples. These samples have a range of file sizes from 56, 500–266, 200 Bytes. We notice that 526 (18.3%) of the IoT samples, on the other hand, have only one node, with file sizes in the range of around 2,000–350,000 bytes.

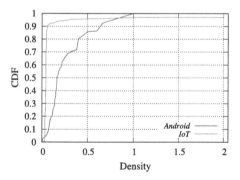

Fig. 4. The distribution of density. Notice that the density is discriminative, where one can tell the two types of malware apart with high accuracy (90%) for a fixed density.

The android malware have a large number of components. We find that 4.47%, or 9 android samples, have only one component, where their size ranges from around 16,900–240,900 bytes. On the other hand, 192 samples (95.5%) have more than one component. We note that the existence of multiple components in the CFG is indicative of the unreachable code in the corresponding program (possible a decoy function to fool static analysis tools). As such, we consider the

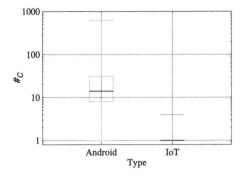

Fig. 5. The distribution of the number of components in CFGs. Notice that $\#_C$ means the number of components. The box represents the distribution from the upper quartile to the lower quartile, and the black bar represents the median value.

largest component of these samples for the further CFG-based analysis. However, we notice that 20 android samples have the same node counts in the first and second largest components. Furthermore, we find 14 samples that have the same number of node and edge counts in the first and second largest components. The number of nodes and edges in these samples range from 0–5, but the file sizes range from around 118,000–3,300,000 bytes.

Root Causes of Unreachable Code/Components. Figure 5 shows the box-plot of the number of components for both the android and IoT malware. The boxplot captures the median and 1st and 3rd quartile, as well as the outliers. We notice that the median of the number of components in IoT samples is 1, whereas the majority of android malware lies between 8 and 18, with median of 14 components. We notice this issue of unreachable code to be more prevalent in the android malware but not in the IoT malware, possibly for one of the following reasons. (1) The android platforms are more powerful, allowing for complex software constructs that may lead to unreachable codes, whereas the IoT platforms are constrained, limiting the number of functions (software-based). (2) The android Operating System (OS) is advanced and can handle large code bases without optimization, whereas the IoT OS is a simple environment that is often time optimized through tools that would discard unreachable codes before deployment.

4.2 General Algorithmic Properties and Constructs

Closeness. Figure 6 depicts the CDF for the average closeness centrality for both datasets. To reach this plot, we generalize the definition in 3 by aggregating the average closeness for each malware sample and obtaining the average. As such, we notice that around 5% of the IoT and android have around 0.14 average closeness centrality. This steady growth in the value continues for the android samples as shown in the graph; 80% of the nodes have a closeness of less than

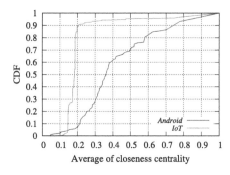
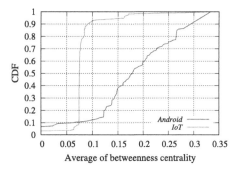

Fig. 6. The average of closeness centrality in the largest component of each sample.

Fig. 7. The average of betweenness centrality in the largest component of each sample.

0.6. On the other hand, the IoT samples closeness pattern tend to be within the small range: the same 80% of IoT samples have a closeness of less than 0.19, highlighting that the closeness alone can be used as a distinguishing feature of the two different types of malware.

Betweenness. Figure 7 shows the average betweenness centrality for both the datasets. The average betweenness is defined by extending Definition 4 in a similar way to extending the closeness definition. Similar to the closeness centrality, 10% of the IoT and android samples have almost 0.07 average betweenness centrality, which continues with a small growth for the android malware to reach around 0.26 average betweenness after covering 80% of the samples. However, we notice a significant increase in the IoT curve where 80% of the samples have around 0.08 average betweenness that shows a slight increase when covering a large portion of the IoT samples. This huge gap that we notice in Figs. 6 and 7 is quite surprising although explained by correlating the density of the graph to both the betweenness and the closeness: the android samples tend to have a higher density, thus an improved betweenness, which is not the case of the IoT.

Diameter, Radius, and Average Shortest Path. Figure 8 shows the diameter of the graphs. Almost 15% of the IoT samples have a diameter of around 12 that can be noticed from the slow growth in the CDF, whereas the android malware have around 0.1. After that, there is a rapid increase in the CDF curve for the diameter in the 80% of both samples, reaching 9 and 17 for the android and IoT, respectively. Similarly, Fig. 9 shows the CDF of the radius of the graphs. We notice that 15% of the android samples have a radius of around 1, while the IoT samples have around 6. In addition, 80% of the android samples have around 4 while the IoT have around 8. This shows the significant increase for both datasets. As a result from these two figures, we can define a feature vector to detect the android and IoT samples, where we can use the value of 10 for the diameter and 5 for the radius to tell different malware types apart.

Figure 10 represents the average shortest path for the graphs. Similar to the other feature vectors, we notice almost 80% of the IoT malware have an average shortest path greater than 5, whereas the android malware have an average less than 5.

5   Discussion and Comparison

We conduct an empirical study of the CFGs corresponding to 3,075 malware samples of IoT and android. We generate the CFGs to analyze and compare the similarities and differences between the two highly prevalent malware types using different graph algorithmic properties to compute various features.

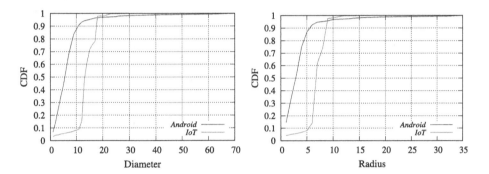

Fig. 8. The distribution of diameter.   **Fig. 9.** The distribution of radius.

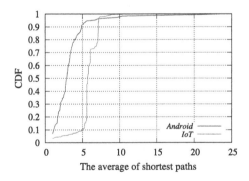

Fig. 10. The average of the lengths of shortest paths.

Based on the above highlights of the CFGs, we observe a major difference between the IoT and android malware in terms of the nodes and edges count, which are the main evaluation metric of the graph size. Our results show that unlike the android samples, the IoT malware samples are more likely to contain a lesser number of nodes and edges. Even though around 21% of the IoT malware, or 603 samples, have less than two nodes and edges, we notice they have various file sizes ranging from around 2,000 to 350,000 bytes per sample. This finding can be interpreted by the use of different evasion techniques from the malware authors in order to prevent analyzing the binaries statically. We notice these malware samples correspond to only one component except for one malware sample that corresponds to two components.

With the high number of nodes and edges in the android malware, and unlike the IoT samples, we observe that the CFGs of almost 95.5%, or 192 android samples, have more than one component, which shows that the android malware often uses unreachable functions. This is shown when using multiple entry points for the same program, and the multiple components (unreachable code) is a sign of using decoy functions or obfuscation techniques to circumvent the static analysis. In addition, the prevalence of unreachable code indicates the complexity of the android malware: these malware samples have a file size ranging from 118,500 to 29,000,000 bytes, which is quite large in comparison to the IoT malware (2k–350k, as shown above).

After analyzing different algorithmic graph structures, we observe a major variation between the IoT and android malware graphs. We clearly notice a cut-off value for the density, average closeness, average betweenness, diameter, radius, and average shortest path for both datasets that can be applied to the detection system and reach an accuracy range around 80%–90% based on the feature vector being applied. We notice that those differences in properties are a direct result of the difference in the structural properties of the graphs, and can be used for easily classifying different types of malware, and showing their distinctive features.

In most of the characterizations we conducted by tracing the distribution of the properties of the CFGs of different malware samples and types, we notice a slow growth in the distribution curve of the android dataset, whereas a drastically increase for the IoT dataset. These characteristics show that the android malware samples are diverse in their characteristics with respect to the measured properties of their graphs, whereas the IoT malware is less diverse. We anticipate that due to the emergence of IoT malware, and expect that characteristic to change over time, as more malware families are produced. We also observe that the IoT malware samples are denser than the android malware. As shown in Fig. 4, we observe that 75 IoT malware, or almost 2.6%, have a density equal to 2. By examining those samples, we found that they utilize an analysis circumvention technique resulting in infinite loops.

Our analysis shows the power of CFGs in differentiating android from IoT malware. It also demonstrates the usefulness of CFGs as a simple high-level tool before diving into lines of codes. We correlate the size of malware samples with the size of the graph as a measure of nodes and edges. We observe that even with the presence of low node or edge counts, the size of malware could be very huge, indicative of obfuscation.

6   Conclusion

In this paper, we conduct an in-depth graph-based analysis of the android and IoT malware to highlight the similarity and differences. Toward this goal, we extract malware CFGs as an abstract representation to characterize them across different graph features. We highlight interesting findings by analyzing the shift in the graph representation from the IoT to the android malware and tracing size (nodes, edges, and components). We observe decoy functions for circumvention, which correspond to multiple components in the CFG. We further analyze algorithmic features of those graphs, including closeness, betweenness, and density, which all are shown to be discriminative features at the malware type level, and could be used for classification.

References

1. Gerber, A.: Connecting all the things in the Internet of Things. https://ibm.co/2qMx97a. Accessed 2017
2. Harrison, L.: The Internet of Things (IoT) Vision. https://blog.equinix.com/blog/2015/03/12/the-internet-of-things-iot-vision/. Accessed 2015
3. Mohaisen, A., Alrawi, O., Mohaisen, M.: AMAL: high-fidelity, behavior-based automated malware analysis and classification. Comput. Secur. **52**, 251–266 (2015)
4. Mohaisen, A., Alrawi, O.: AV-Meter: an evaluation of antivirus scans and labels. In: Dietrich, S. (ed.) DIMVA 2014. LNCS, vol. 8550, pp. 112–131. Springer, Cham (2014). https://doi.org/10.1007/978-3-319-08509-8_7
5. Shang, S., Zheng, N., Xu, J., Xu, M., Zhang, H.: Detecting malware variants via function-call graph similarity. In: Proceedings of the 5th International Conference on Malicious and Unwanted Software, MALWARE, pp. 113–120 (2010)
6. Mohaisen, A., Alrawi, O.: Unveiling Zeus: automated classification of malware samples. In: Proceedings of the 22nd International World Wide Web Conference, WWW, pp. 829–832 (2013)
7. Hu, X., Chiueh, T., Shin, K.G.: Large-scale malware indexing using function-call graphs. In: Proceedings of the ACM Conference on Computer and Communications Security, CCS, pp. 611–620 (2009)
8. Christodorescu, M., Jha, S.: Static analysis of executables to detect malicious patterns. In: Proceedings of the 12th USENIX Security Symposium (2003)
9. Bruschi, D., Martignoni, L., Monga, M.: Detecting self-mutating malware using control-flow graph matching. In: Büschkes, R., Laskov, P. (eds.) DIMVA 2006. LNCS, vol. 4064, pp. 129–143. Springer, Heidelberg (2006). https://doi.org/10.1007/11790754_8
10. Tamersoy, A., Roundy, K.A., Chau, D.H.: Guilt by association: large scale malware detection by mining file-relation graphs. In: Proceedings of the the 20th ACM International Conference on Knowledge Discovery and Data Mining, KDD, pp. 1524–1533 (2014)
11. Yamaguchi, F., Golde, N., Arp, D., Rieck, K.: Modeling and discovering vulnerabilities with code property graphs. In: Proceedings of the IEEE Symposium on Security and Privacy, SP, pp. 590–604 (2014)

12. Caselden, D., Bazhanyuk, A., Payer, M., McCamant, S., Song, D.: HI-CFG: construction by binary analysis and application to attack polymorphism. In: Crampton, J., Jajodia, S., Mayes, K. (eds.) ESORICS 2013. LNCS, vol. 8134, pp. 164–181. Springer, Heidelberg (2013). https://doi.org/10.1007/978-3-642-40203-6_10
13. Wüchner, T., Ochoa, M., Pretschner, A.: Robust and effective malware detection through quantitative data flow graph metrics. In: Almgren, M., Gulisano, V., Maggi, F. (eds.) DIMVA 2015. LNCS, vol. 9148, pp. 98–118. Springer, Cham (2015). https://doi.org/10.1007/978-3-319-20550-2_6
14. Jang, J.-W., Woo, J., Mohaisen, A., Yun, J., Kim, H.K.: Mal-Netminer: malware classification approach based on social network analysis of system call graph. In: Mathematical Problems in Engineering (2015)
15. Gascon, H., Yamaguchi, F., Arp, D., Rieck, K.: Structural detection of android malware using embedded call graphs. In: Proceedings of the ACM Workshop on Artificial Intelligence and Security, AISec, pp. 45–54 (2013)
16. Zhang, M., Duan, Y., Yin, H., Zhao, Z.: Semantics-aware android malware classification using weighted contextual API dependency graphs. In: Proceedings of the ACM Conference on Computer and Communications Security, CCS, pp. 1105–1116 (2014)
17. Pa, Y.M.P., Suzuki, S., Yoshioka, K., Matsumoto, T., Kasama, T., Rossow, C.: IoTPOT: a novel honeypot for revealing current IoT threats. J. Inf. Process. JIP **24**, 522–533 (2016)
18. Shen, F., Vecchio, J.D., Mohaisen, A., Ko, S.Y., Ziarek, L.: Android malware detection using complex-flows. In: Proceedings of the 37th IEEE International Conference on Distributed Computing Systems, ICDCS, pp. 2430–2437 (2017)
19. Developers: Radare2. https://www.radare.org/r/. Accessed 2018
20. Developers: VirusTotal. https://www.virustotal.com. Accessed 2018
21. Sebastián, M., Rivera, R., Kotzias, P., Caballero, J.: AVCLASS: a tool for massive malware labeling. In: Monrose, F., Dacier, M., Blanc, G., Garcia-Alfaro, J. (eds.) RAID 2016. LNCS, vol. 9854, pp. 230–253. Springer, Cham (2016). https://doi.org/10.1007/978-3-319-45719-2_11

Revisiting of 'Revisiting the Stop-and-Stare Algorithms for Influence Maximization'

Hung T. Nguyen[1,2], Thang N. Dinh[1(✉)], and My T. Thai[3]

[1] Virginia Commonwealth University, Richmond, VA 23284, USA
{hungnt,tndinh}@vcu.edu
[2] Carnegie Mellon University, Pittsburgh, PA 15213, USA
[3] University of Florida, Gainesville, FL 32611, USA
mythai@cise.ufl.edu

Abstract. SSA/DSSA were introduced in SIGMOD'16 as the first algorithms that can provide rigorous $1 - 1/e - \epsilon$ guarantee with fewer samples than the worst-case sample complexity $O(nk\frac{\log n}{\epsilon^2 OPT_k})$. They are order of magnitude faster than the existing methods. The original SIGMOD'16 paper, however, contains errors, and the new fixes for SSA/DSSA, referred to as SSA-fix and D-SSA-fix, have been published in the extended version of the paper [11]. In this paper, we affirm the correctness on accuracy and efficiency of SSA-fix/D-SSA-fix algorithms. Specifically, we refuse the misclaims on 'important gaps' in the proof of D-SSA-fix's efficiency raised by Huang et al. [5] published in VLDB in May 2017. We also replicate the experiments to dispute the experimental discrepancies shown in [5]. Our experiment results indicate that implementation/modification details and data pre-processing attribute for most discrepancies in running-time. (We requested the modified code from VLDB'17 [5] last year but have not received the code from the authors. We also sent them the explanation for the gaps they misclaimed for the D-SSA-fix's efficiency proof but have not received their concrete feedback.)

Keywords: Influence maximization · Stop-and-Stare
Approximation algorithm

1 Introduction

Given a network $G = (V, E)$ and an integer k, the *influence maximization* (IM) asks for a subset of k nodes, called seed set, that can influence maximum number of nodes in the network under a diffusion model. The problem has produced a long line of research results, e.g., those in [1,3,6,11,16] and references therein.

RIS Framework. A key breakthrough for the problem is the introduction of a novel technique, called *reverse influence sampling* (RIS), by Borgs et al. [1]. The RIS framework, followed by all works discussed in this paper [5,11,16], will

© Springer Nature Switzerland AG 2018
X. Chen et al. (Eds.): CSoNet 2018, LNCS 11280, pp. 273–285, 2018.
https://doi.org/10.1007/978-3-030-04648-4_23

- Generate a collection $\{R_1, R_2, \ldots, R_T\}$ of *Reversed Reachability Sets* (or RR sets). Each RR set R_i is generated by selecting a random node u and perform a reversed traversal from u to include into R_i all nodes that can reach to u, i.e., can influence u.
- Find a subset S of k nodes that can cover a maximum number of RR sets using the greedy algorithm for the maximum coverage problem.
- The returned solution S will be a $(1 - 1/e - \epsilon)$ solution, for large T.

Worst-Case Sample Complexity. The sample complexity, i.e., the number of RR sets to guarantee a $(1 - 1/e - \epsilon)$ approximation factor is shown to be $\theta(k, \epsilon) = O(nk \frac{\log n}{\epsilon^2 \mathsf{OPT}_k})$ [17] where OPT_k denotes the expected influence of an optimal solution. Unfortunately, $\theta(k, \epsilon)$ depends on OPT_k, an unknown, thus, it is challenging to know whether or not $\theta(k, \epsilon)$ samples have been generated.

Tang et al. [16] proposed IMM algorithm that stops when $\theta(k, \epsilon)$ samples have been generated. Recently, a flaw in the analysis of IMM has been pointed out by Chen [2] together with a fix for IMM. Independently, we proposed in [13] BCT, an algorithm that also stops within $O(\theta(k, \epsilon))$ samples for generalized versions of IM, with heterogeneous cost and influence effect.

Unfortunately, even meeting the sample complexity $\theta(k, \epsilon)$ is not efficient enough for billion-scale networks. In several weighted models, such as Trivalency or constant probability [11,14,15], IMM (and BCT) struggles for the largest test networks such as Twitter and Friendster datasets. The main reason is that $\theta(k, \epsilon)$ is a **worst-case** sample complexity, thus, it is *very conservative* in practice. The θ threshold needs to hold for all "hard" inputs, which rarely happens in practice. Can we achieve $(1 - 1/e - \epsilon)$ approximation guarantee with fewer than $\theta(k, \epsilon)$ samples?

Stop-and-Stare and Instance-specific Sample Complexity. SSA and D-SSA were introduced in our SIGMOD'16 [8] as the first algorithms that can guarantee $(1 - 1/e - \epsilon)$ optimality with fewer than $\theta(k, \epsilon)$ samples. For each specific instance $\Pi = (G = (V, E), k, \epsilon)$ of IM, SSA and D-SSA aim to reduce the sample complexity to some instance-specific thresholds. Unlike the worst-case threshold θ, instance-specific thresholds adapt to the actual complexity of the input including the information contained in network structure and influence landscape. Thus, those thresholds can be several orders of magnitude smaller than θ, especially, for 'easy' instances of IM. Consequently, algorithms that meet this new thresholds are potentially 1,000 times (or more) faster than IMM [16] and BCT [13].

Specifically, SSA and D-SSA were designed to provide $1 - 1/e - \epsilon$ guarantees using only $O(N_{min}^{(1)}$ and $O(N_{min}^{(2)}$ samples where $N_{min}^{(1)} > N_{min}^{(2)}$, termed Type-1 and Type-2 minimum thresholds [8], respectively. $N_{min}^{(1)}$ and $N_{min}^{(2)}$ are instance-specific lower-bounds on the number of necessary samples and can be many times smaller than $\theta(\epsilon, k)$ in practice. Specifically, they are the lower-bounds for IM's algorithms following "out-of-sample validation" approaches that: (1) continuously, generating two pools (of increasingly sizes) of samples, one for finding a candidate solution and one for 'validating' the candidate solution; and

Table 1. Summary of papers related to **SSA** and **D-SSA** algorithms

Papers	Date	Contribution
Nguyen et al. SIGMOD'16 [8]	25 May 2016	Stop-and-Stare algorithms SSA/D-SSA proposed
Personal communication	Jul. 2016	We identified the issues in the proof of SSA/D-SSA thanks to anonymous reviewers for IEEE/ACM ToN. The reviewers pointed out a similar mistake in our submitted manuscript [10]
Nguyen et al. ArXiv-v2 [9]	7 Sep 2016	SSA-fix provided (D-SSA remained broken)
Huang et al. VLDB [5] early version	15 Jan. 2017	Identified the errors in proofs for approximation factor and sample efficiency for SSA and D-SSA and provided a similar SSA-fix
Nguyen et al. ArXiv-v3 [11]	22 Feb 2017	Provided D-SSA-fix and correct proofs for approximation factor and sample efficiency for SSA-fix and D-SSA-fix
Huang et al. VLDB'17 [5]	May 2017	Adding a claim on the flaw in the proof for D-SSA-fix's sample efficiency in [11]. No concerns raised for the proof on SSA-fix/D-SSA-fix approximability and SSA-fix's sample efficiency
This paper	Oct. 2018	Affirmed the D-SSA-fix's sample efficiency, rejecting the doubt raised in Huang et al. [5]

(2) stop when the discrepancies in the estimations of the candidate in the two pools are sufficiently small. Unlike $\theta(\epsilon, k)$, our new lower bounds $N_{min}^{(1)}$ and $N_{min}^{(2)}$ still vary widely among inputs that share the parameters n, k, and OPT_k.

In summary, the key contribution in [11] is that SSA/D-SSA are not only $(1 - 1/e - \epsilon)$ approximation algorithms but also are asymptotically optimal in terms of the proposed instance-specific sample complexities.

Our work in [8] consists of 4 major proofs:

- **SSA 's and D-SSA 's approximability:** showing that SSA and D-SSA return $1 - 1/e - \epsilon$ solutions with high probability (2 proofs).
- **SSA's and D-SSA's efficiency:** showing that SSA and D-SSA using only cT_1 and cT_2 samples where $\theta(k, \epsilon) \gg T_1 > T_2$ are instance-specific sample complexities and c is a fixed constant (2 proofs).

Errors in Our Proofs [8] and Fixes. Our proofs contain flaws which comes from the *applying of concentration inequalities in which the parameters, such as ϵ, δ and the number of samples, may depend on the generated samples.*

The errors were brought to our attention through two channels: (1) the same flaw pointed out by anonymous reviewers for one of our submission (not the published version) to IEEE/ACM Transaction to Networking [10] in Jul. 2016 and (2) an early manuscript of Huang et al. [5] in Jan. 2017 and concerns on the martingales sent to us by the authors of [5].

Upon discovering the errors, we uploaded the fix for SSA, called SSA-fix, on Arxiv on Sep. 2016 [9] and the fix for D-SSA, called D-SSA-fix, with corrected proofs in Feb. 2017 [11].

The final version of Huang et al. [5], while not giving any comments on the 3 proofs for SSA-fix's approximability, SSA-fix's efficiency, and D-SSA-fix's approximability, claims *"important gaps"* in our proof for D-SSA-fix's efficiency. While we appreciated the errors pointed out in Huang et al. [5] for our original paper in SIGMOD'16 [8], we found the claim on "important gaps" of D-SSA-fix's efficiency is a misclaim.

This paper aims to affirm the correctness of D-SSA-fix's efficiency in [11], explaining the 'important gaps' claimed in Huang et al. [5] (and their extended version [4]) and explain the discrepancies in experiments claimed by Huang et al. [5]. We summarize the timeline of publication and correspondence in Table 1.

Organization. We first summarize our fixes for SSA/DSSA in our Arxiv [11]. Then we provide justification for the claimed by [5] on the "important gaps" for D-SSA-fix's efficiency. Finally, we present the experiment to explain the observed discrepancies in [5].

Algorithm 1. SSA-fix

Input: Graph G, $0 \leq \epsilon, \delta \leq 1$, and a budget k
Output: An $(1 - 1/e - \epsilon)$-optimal solution, $\hat{S}_k$ with at least $(1 - \delta)$-probability

1 Choose $\epsilon_1, \epsilon_2, \epsilon_3$ satisfying Equation 18 in [11];
2 $N_{max} = 8 \frac{1-1/e}{2+2\epsilon/3} \Upsilon\left(\epsilon, \frac{\delta}{6}/\binom{n}{k}\right) \frac{n}{k}$; $i_{max} = \lceil \log_2 \frac{2 N_{max}}{\Upsilon(\epsilon_3, \delta/3)} \rceil$;
3 $\Lambda_1 \leftarrow (1 + \epsilon_1)(1 + \epsilon_2)\Upsilon(\epsilon_3, \frac{\delta}{3 i_{max}})$
4 $\mathcal{R} \leftarrow$ Generate Λ_1 random RR sets
5 **repeat**
6 | Double the size of $\mathcal{R}$ with new random RR sets
7 | $<\hat{S}_k, \hat{\mathbb{I}}(\hat{S}_k)> \leftarrow$ Max-Coverage($\mathcal{R}$, k, n)
8 | **if** $\text{Cov}_{\mathcal{R}}(\hat{S}_k) \geq \Lambda_1$ **then**   ▷ Condition C1
9 | | $\delta'_2 = \frac{\delta_2}{3 i_{max}}$; $T_{max} = 2|\mathcal{R}| \frac{1+\epsilon_2}{1-\epsilon_2} \frac{\epsilon_3^2}{\epsilon_2^2}$
10 | | $\mathbb{I}_c(\hat{S}_k) \leftarrow$ Estimate-Inf($G, \hat{S}_k, \epsilon_2, \delta'_2, T_{max}$)
11 | | **if** $\hat{\mathbb{I}}(\hat{S}_k) \leq (1 + \epsilon_1)\mathbb{I}_c(\hat{S}_k)$ **then**   ▷ Condition C2
12 | | | **return** $\hat{S}_k$
13 **until** $|\mathcal{R}| \geq N_{max}$;
14 **return** $\hat{S}_k$

Algorithm 2. The original D-SSA algorithm [8]

Input: Graph G, $0 \leq \epsilon, \delta \leq 1$, and k
Output: An $(1 - 1/e - \epsilon)$-optimal solution, $\hat{S}_k$

1   $\Lambda \leftarrow 2c(1+\epsilon)^2 \log(\frac{2}{\delta})\frac{1}{\epsilon^2}$

2   $\mathcal{R} \leftarrow$ Generate Λ random RR sets by RIS

3   $<\hat{S}_k, \hat{\mathbb{I}}(\hat{S}_k)> \leftarrow$ Max-Coverage$(\mathcal{R}, k)$

4   **repeat**

5       $\mathcal{R}' \leftarrow$ Generate $|\mathcal{R}|$ random RR sets by RIS

6       $\mathbb{I}_c(\hat{S}_k) \leftarrow \text{Cov}_{\mathcal{R}'}(\hat{S}_k) \cdot n/|\mathcal{R}'|$

7       $\epsilon_1 \leftarrow \hat{\mathbb{I}}(\hat{S}_k)/\mathbb{I}_c(\hat{S}_k) - 1$

8   **if** $(\epsilon_1 \leq \epsilon)$ **then**

9          $\epsilon_2 \leftarrow \frac{\epsilon - \epsilon_1}{2(1+\epsilon_1)}$, $\epsilon_3 \leftarrow \frac{\epsilon - \epsilon_1}{2(1 - 1/e)}$

10         $\delta_1 \leftarrow e^{-\frac{\text{Cov}_{\mathcal{R}}(\hat{S}_k) \cdot \epsilon_3^2}{2c(1+\epsilon_1)(1+\epsilon_2)}}$

11         $\delta_2 \leftarrow e^{-\frac{(\text{Cov}_{\mathcal{R}'}(\hat{S}_k) - 1) \cdot \epsilon_2^2}{2c(1+\epsilon_2)}}$

12   **if** $\delta_1 + \delta_2 \leq \delta$ **then**

13   **return** $\hat{S}_k$

14       $\mathcal{R} \leftarrow \mathcal{R} \cup \mathcal{R}'$

15       $<\hat{S}_k, \hat{\mathbb{I}}(\hat{S}_k)> \leftarrow$ Max-Coverage$(\mathcal{R}, k)$

16   **until** $|\mathcal{R}| \geq (8 + 2\epsilon)n\frac{\ln\frac{2}{\delta} + \ln\binom{n}{k}}{k\epsilon^2}$;

17   **return** $\hat{S}_k$

Algorithm 3. D-SSA-fix

Input: Graph G, $0 \leq \epsilon, \delta \leq 1$, and k
Output: An $(1 - 1/e - \epsilon)$-optimal solution, $\hat{S}_k$

1   $N_{max} = 8\frac{1 - 1/e}{2 + 2\epsilon/3}\Upsilon\left(\epsilon, \frac{\delta}{6}/\binom{n}{k}\right)\frac{n}{k}$;

2   $t_{max} = \lceil \log_2(2N_{max}/\Upsilon(\epsilon, \frac{\delta}{3})) \rceil$; $t = 0$;

3   $\Lambda_1 = 1 + (1+\epsilon)\Upsilon(\epsilon, \frac{\delta}{3t_{max}})$;

4   **repeat**

5       $t \leftarrow t + 1$;

6       $\mathcal{R}_t = \{R_1, \ldots, R_{\Lambda_1 2^{t-1}}\}$;

7       $\mathcal{R}_t^c = \{R_{\Lambda_1 2^{t-1}+1}, \ldots, R_{\Lambda_1 2^t}\}$;

8       $<\hat{S}_k, \hat{\mathbb{I}}_t(\hat{S}_k)> \leftarrow$ Max-Coverage$(\mathcal{R}_t, k)$;

9   **if** $\text{Cov}_{\mathcal{R}_t^c}(\hat{S}_k) \geq \Lambda_1$ **then**   ▷ Condition D1

10         $\mathbb{I}_t^c(\hat{S}_k) \leftarrow \text{Cov}_{\mathcal{R}_t^c}(\hat{S}_k) \cdot n/|\mathcal{R}_t^c|$;

11         $\epsilon_1 \leftarrow \hat{\mathbb{I}}_t(\hat{S}_k)/\mathbb{I}_t^c(\hat{S}_k) - 1$;

12         $\epsilon_2 \leftarrow \epsilon\sqrt{\frac{n(1+\epsilon)}{2^{t-1}\mathbb{I}_t^c(\hat{S}_k)}}$; $\epsilon_3 \leftarrow \epsilon\sqrt{\frac{n(1+\epsilon)(1 - 1/e - \epsilon)}{(1+\epsilon/3)2^{t-1}\mathbb{I}_t^c(\hat{S}_k)}}$;

13         $\epsilon_t = (\epsilon_1 + \epsilon_2 + \epsilon_1\epsilon_2)(1 - 1/e - \epsilon) + (1 - \frac{1}{e})\epsilon_3$;

14   **if** $\epsilon_t \leq \epsilon$ **then**   ▷ Condition D2

15   **return** $\hat{S}_k$;

16   **until** $|\mathcal{R}_t| \geq N_{max}$;

17   **return** $\hat{S}_k$;

2 Summary of **SSA**-fix and **D-SSA**-fix [11]

First, we summarize the errors and our fixes for SSA/D-SSA algorithms and refer to the extended version of our SIGMOD paper in [11] for complete proofs.

2.1 Fixes for **SSA** algorithm

The main idea of SSA (and the Stop-and-Stare framework) is to (1) generate a collection of samples $\mathcal{R}$ and find a candidate solution $\hat{S}_k$ using the greedy algorithm; (2) measure the difference between (biased) influence of $\hat{S}_k$ with samples in $\mathcal{R}$ and an unbiased estimation of $\hat{S}_k$ on another set of samples; and (3) the algorithm stops if the difference is small enough, otherwise, it doubles the number of generated samples.

Summary of Errors for SSA. The influence for candidate solution $\hat{S}_k$ is estimated multiple times. And the error probability did not take this fact into the account.

Summary of Changes in SSA-fix. As highlighted in Algorithm 1, to account for the multiple influence estimates by Estimate-Inf procedure, we decrease the error probability by a factor $i_{max} = O(\log n)$. Specifically, Algorithm 1 introduces the factor i_{max} and divides the probability guarantee δ_2 by i_{max} in Lines 2 and 9. Through union bound, we can show that this sufficiently accounts for the cumulative error in Estimate-Inf while insignificantly affecting the number of samples.

Note that [5] provides the same fix by decreasing the error probability by a factor $O(\log n)$.

2.2 Fixes for **D-SSA** Algorithm

Summary of Errors for D-SSA. In the original D-SSA, presented in Algorithm 2, the computations of δ_1 and δ_2 depend on ϵ_1, ϵ_2 and ϵ_3, which, in turn, depend on the generated samples. This dependency on the generated samples make the proof incorrect as the of Chernoff's inequality.

Summary of Changes in D-SSA-fix. Our D-SSA-fix, shown in Algorithm 3, set $\delta_1 = \delta_2 = c'\delta$ for a fixed constant c'. The Chernoff's bounds are applied to bound the errors ϵ_1 and ϵ_2 at the fixed points when the number of samples are $\Lambda_1 2^i$, for $i = 1, 2, \ldots, \lceil \log N_{max} \rceil$. This change is reflected in the Lines 9–14.

We compute ϵ_1, the discrepancy of estimating using two different collections of RR sets, i.e. $\mathcal{R}$ and $\mathcal{R}'$; ϵ_2 and ϵ_3 bound the maximum estimation errors with high probability. At a first glance, ϵ_2 and ϵ_3 still seem to depend on the generated RR sets in $\mathcal{R}_t^c$. However, $\frac{\mathbb{I}_t^c(\hat{S}_k)}{1+\epsilon}$ serves as a lower-bound for $\mathbb{I}(\hat{S}_k)$ with high probability and can be used in the bounding of ϵ_2 and ϵ_3.

3   Affirming the Correctness in **D-SSA**-fix's Efficiency [11]

The final version of Huang et al. [5] claims *"important gaps"* in our proof for *D-SSA-fix's efficiency*. Here we provide the details showing this misclaim and affirm the correctness for D-SSA-fix's efficiency proof.

3.1   Gap in Showing $\epsilon_2 \leq \epsilon_0/3$ and Explanation

Gap Claimed by Huang et al. [4,5]. The first gap claimed by Huang et al. [4] (Page 14, B.1 Misclaim) is about Eqs. (93) and (94), in the proof of Theorem 6, in [11]. Below we quote those two equations in [11].

Apply the inequalities $2^{t-1} \geq \alpha \frac{n}{\text{OPT}_k}$ [a], Eq. (88),

and $\mathbb{I}(\hat{S}_k) \geq (1 - 1/e - \epsilon)\text{OPT}_k$, Eq. (87).

For **sufficiently large** $\alpha > \frac{9(1+\epsilon)}{(1-1/e-\epsilon)}$, we have

$$\epsilon_2 = \epsilon\sqrt{\frac{n(1+\epsilon)}{2^{t-1}\hat{\mathbb{I}}_t^c(\hat{S}_k)}} \leq \epsilon_0/3 \leq \epsilon_b^*/3 \qquad (93)$$

$$\epsilon_3 = \epsilon\sqrt{\frac{n(1+\epsilon)(1-1/e-\epsilon)}{(1+\epsilon/3)2^{t-1}\hat{\mathbb{I}}_t^c(\hat{S}_k)}} \leq \epsilon_0/3 \leq \epsilon_b^*/3 \qquad (94)$$

---

[a] The Eq. (88) in [11] states $2^{t-1} \geq \alpha \frac{n}{\text{OPT}_k} \frac{\epsilon^2}{\epsilon_0^2}$. Here, the factor $\frac{\epsilon^2}{\epsilon_0^2}$ were missed due to a typo.

Fig. 1.1. Proof of Theorem 6 in [11]. Huang et al. [4] claimed important gaps for Eqs. (93) and (94).

Huang et al. raised the concern that their derivation using Eqs. (87) and (88) do not lead to Eqs. (93) and (94).

Our Response. The omitted detail is that $\hat{\mathbb{I}}_t^c(\hat{S}_k)$ is an unbiased estimator of $\mathbb{I}(\hat{S}_k)$, thus, its value concentrates around $\mathbb{I}(\hat{S}_k)$. In fact, from Eq. (89), $\tilde{\epsilon}_t \leq \frac{\epsilon_0}{3}$, and Eq. (90), $\hat{\mathbb{I}}_t^c(\hat{S}_k) \geq (1 - \tilde{\epsilon}_t)\mathbb{I}(\hat{S}_k)$, it follows that

$$\hat{\mathbb{I}}_t^c(\hat{S}_k) \geq (1 - \frac{\epsilon_0}{3})\mathbb{I}(\hat{S}_k) \geq (1 - \frac{\epsilon}{3})\mathbb{I}(\hat{S}_k) \quad \text{(since } \epsilon_0 = \min\{\epsilon, \epsilon_b^*\}) \qquad (1)$$

Thus, picking a sufficiently large constant $\alpha = \frac{100(1+\epsilon)}{(1-1/e-\epsilon)}$, we have

$$\epsilon_2 = \epsilon\sqrt{\frac{n(1+\epsilon)}{2^{t-1}\hat{\mathbb{I}}_t^c(\hat{S}_k)}} \leq \epsilon\sqrt{\frac{n(1+\epsilon)}{2^{t-1}(1-\frac{\epsilon}{3})\mathbb{I}(\hat{S}_k)}} \leq \epsilon\sqrt{\frac{n(1+\epsilon)}{\alpha\frac{n}{\text{OPT}_k}\frac{\epsilon^2}{\epsilon_0^2}(1-\frac{\epsilon}{3})\mathbb{I}(\hat{S}_k)}} \text{(by Eq. 88)}$$

$$< \frac{\epsilon_0}{3}\sqrt{\frac{(1-1/e-\epsilon)\text{OPT}_k}{\mathbb{I}(\hat{S}_k)}} \leq \frac{\epsilon_0}{3} \text{ (by Eq. 87)} \qquad (93)$$

Since $\epsilon_3 < \epsilon_2$, we also have $\epsilon_3 \leq \epsilon_0/3 \leq \epsilon_b^*/3$, i.e., Eq. (94) follows.

...

In addition, the proof assumes that we can set the constant α to be larger than $\frac{9(1+\epsilon)}{(1-1/e-\epsilon)}$, but this assumption does not always hold. In particular, as shown in Equation 27, α must ensure that $2^{t-1} \geq \alpha \frac{n}{\mathsf{OPT}_k} \frac{\epsilon^2}{\epsilon_0^2}$, which leads to

$$\alpha \leq \frac{2^{t-1}\mathsf{OPT}_k \epsilon_0^2}{n\epsilon^2}. \tag{2}$$

Therefore, we can set $\alpha \geq \frac{9(1+\epsilon)}{(1-1/e-\epsilon)}$, only if

$$\frac{9(1+\epsilon)}{(1-1/e-\epsilon)} \leq \frac{2^{t-1}\mathsf{OPT}_k \epsilon_0^2}{n\epsilon^2}. \tag{3}$$

This inequality is never established in the proof.

Fig. 1.2. Argument in [4] on the gap of setting constant α

3.2   Gap on Setting of α and Explanation

Gap Claimed by Huang et al. [4]. The second gap is shown in Fig. 1.2. Huang et al. raised the concern that the constant α may not exist due to bounded range between $\frac{9(1+\epsilon)}{(1-1/e-\epsilon)}$ and $\frac{2^{t-1}\mathsf{OPT}_k \epsilon_0^2}{n\epsilon^2}$.

Our Response. We first select a fixed and sufficiently large constant α, e.g., setting $\alpha = \frac{100(1+\epsilon)}{(1-1/e-\epsilon)}$. There is no need to choose α to satify the inequality $2^{t-1} \geq \alpha \frac{n}{\mathsf{OPT}_k}$. Indeed, for a fixed constant α at some sufficiently large iteration t such that $|\mathcal{R}| = \Lambda 2^{t-1} \geq T_{\text{D-SSA}} \geq \alpha \Upsilon(\epsilon_0, \frac{\delta}{3t_{max}})\frac{n}{\mathsf{OPT}_k}$, the inequality $2^{t-1} \geq \alpha \frac{n}{\mathsf{OPT}_k}$ will hold. The alternative will be the algorithm stops 'early' due to the condition $|\mathcal{R}_t| \geq N_{max}$ on line 16, Algorithm 3, thus, $T_2 = O(N_{max}) = O(\theta(k,t))$ and we can still conclude the efficiency of D-SSA-fix.

4   Experimental Discrepancies and Explanations

Huang et al. [5] shown some discrepancies in our experiments in [8]. We replicate the modifications in [5] and rerun all experiments in [8] and conclude that most anomalies found in [5] are *attributed to different experimental settings and data processing*. We were unable to reproduce some results in [5] due most likely to unknown modifications in [5].

4.1   Experimental Settings

We follow the settings in [5] with the following exceptions:

- **Modifications of SSA and D-SSA.** We sent a request to the authors of [5] for the modifications they made on SSA and D-SSA, however, we have waited for 5 months without responses. Following [5], we removed all the practical optimizations we made in our code and only kept exactly what are described in our paper [8] including the larger constants, adding RIS samples one by one (not in batch of fixed size as before), starting the number of samples from Υ_1. We published our implementation in [12] for reproducibility purposes.
- **Experiment Environment.** We ran all the experiments in our Linux machine which has a 2.30 Ghz Intel(R) Xeon(R) CPU E5-2650 v3 40 core processor and 256 GB of RAM.
- **5 runs of each experiment:** We repeat each experiment 5 times and report the average.
- **New results of SSA and D-SSA fixes:** We also include new results for the fixes of SSA and D-SSA algorithms. The modified implementation can be found in [12].

Formating the Input Networks. We download most of the raw networks from the well-known Stanford SNAP dataset collection except the large network Twitter that was obtained from [7] when it was still available for download. In our original experiments in SIGMOD'16 [8], we directly took the networks and compute the edge weights according to the Weighted Cascade (WC) model. In addition, instead of using the plain-text format, we convert the network to binary format for fast I/O communication (a significant speedup, e.g. 2 min to read the whole Twitter network compared to almost an hour for IMM using plain-text). The performance for all comparing IM algorithms on those weighted networks are presented subsequently. Note that, we did not add the I/O time to the results on running time.

Later, we noticed that on some large undirected networks, e.g. Orkut, only one direction of the edge is stored in the raw data. However, for smaller networks, e.g. NetHEPT, NetPHY, both directions are kept. We run our experiments again and found certain matching results with [5] and suspect the discrepancies in [5] are partially caused by the data formatting. Nevertheless, all the algorithms are run on the same data set and fair comparisons are made. Note that [5] also ignored the data formatting details.

4.2   Experiments Rerun

To confirm the experimental results in both our original work in SIGMOD'16 [8] and the discrepancies found in VLDB'17 [5], we replicate both of these experiments following exactly their settings as described as follows:

- **SIGMOD'16 - Rep:** Rerun of experiments in our work SIGMOD'16 [8] where the original implementations of SSA and D-SSA are used.

- **VLDB'17 -Rep:** Rerun of experiments in VLDB'17 paper [5] where we follow their descriptions to modify SSA and D-SSA algorithms, i.e. removing all the optimization we made in our original implementations.
- **VLDB'17 -Rep (undirected):** Also a rerun of experiments in VLDB'17 paper [5] but the network input is formated as undirected, i.e. for each edge (u, v), add the other direction (v, u).

For comparison, we add the results in our SIGMOD'16 paper [8] and VLDB'17 paper [5] and denote them as **SIGMOD'16** [8] and **VLDB'17** [5], respectively in our results.

4.3   Possible Explanations for the Discrepancies

We compare the experiments' settings between our paper [8] and [5] and found the following mismatches:

- **Code modifications:** A major point is that the authors of [5] has modified our code, thus, affected the performance of our code. Since we did not received the modified code from [5] after 5 months of waiting, we follow the description in [5] to modify SSA and D-SSA.
- **Directed/Undirected network formats:** The Orkut and Friendster networks are undirected networks downloaded from SNAP library but we treat them as directed networks. All algorithms (IMM, TIM+) were run on this same directed network and, thus, the comparison were fair. The oversight of treating Orkut/Friendster as directed networks is due to the expectation that the edges in those networks are doubled, i.e., both (u, v) and (v, u) are present in the input. Unfortunately, unlike other smaller undirected networks, this is not the case for Orkut and Friendster.
- **Measures of the number of samples:** We measure the number of samples used by each algorithm. For SSA, we show the number of samples used in finding the max-coverage.

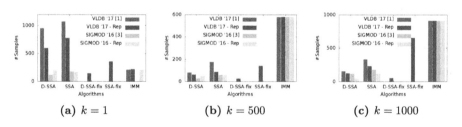

(a) $k = 1$ (b) $k = 500$ (c) $k = 1000$

Fig. 1. Number of samples generated on Enron network (See Subsect. 4.2 for legend details)

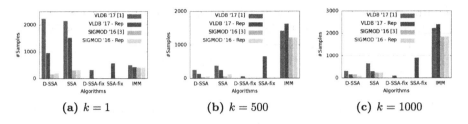

Fig. 2. Number of samples generated on Epinions network (See Subsect. 4.2 for legend details)

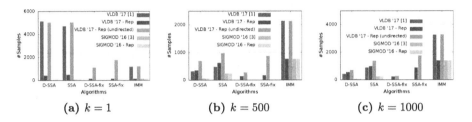

Fig. 3. Number of samples generated on Orkut network (See Subsect. 4.2 for legend details)

4.4 Experimental Results

We replicate two sets of experiments in [5] based on which they claimed the discrepancies in our experiments in [8]. The first set focuses on the number of RR sets generated by different algorithms on three networks, i.e. Enron, Epinions and Orkut, and the results are presented in Figs. 1, 2 and 3. The second set of experiments is solely about the running time of IM algorithms on the case $k = 1$ and tests on 6 networks, namely NetHEPT, NetPHY, Epinions, DBLP, Orkut and Twitter. The results for these experiments are shown in Table 2. Based on our results, we draw the following observations:

Table 2. Relative running time of **SSA**, **D-SSA**, **SSA fix** and **D-SSA fix** to **IMM** for $k = 1$

Nets	LT model					IC model				
	SSA	D-SSA	SSA fix	D-SSA fix	IMM	SSA	D-SSA	SSA fix	D-SSA fix	IMM
NetHEPT	4.1	2.1	1.0	0.9	1	4.9	3.7	2.6	1.1	1
NetPHY	5.4	3.5	1.3	1.2	1	4.9	4.1	2.5	2.0	1
Epinions	3.0	2.2	1.3	1.0	1	4.3	4.0	1.2	0.9	1
DBLP	4.5	2.7	1.2	1.0	1	5.4	5.0	1.3	1.1	1
Orkut	2.1	1.4	0.7	0.7	1	5.3	4.5	1.2	1.0	1
Twitter	**0.7**	**0.6**	0.4	0.4	1	5.7	3.6	1.3	1.3	1

- **Our results in the SIGMOD'16 paper** [8] **are reproducible given specific implementation settings.** The results in Figs. 1, 2 and 3 show that our primary experimental results in SIGMOD'16 paper [8] are very similar to our rerun. Here we used exactly the same implementation published online in [12]. There is slight random fluctuation due to the fact that in [8], we only run each experiment once but on our rerun, we take the average over 5 runs.

- **Data processing has substantial impact on the experimental results and may cause the discrepancies found in** [5]. From Fig. 3 on Orkut network that we had the network format problem, we see the sharp differences when the network is formated as directed and undirected. This explains the discrepancies on Orkut found in the VLDB'17 paper [5]. Moreover, when formating correctly as an undirected network, our results largely agree with those in [5] on Orkut dataset.

- **Some experimental results in** [5] **are not replicable:** From Figs. 1, 2 and 3, we see that compared to the results reported in [5], our rerun of [5] are 2 times smaller on Enron and Epinions datasets. These differences can only be explained by the unknown modifications made in [5] that were not documented in their paper and unknown to us.

On the case of $k = 1$, in [5], the authors show that IMM always runs faster than SSA and D-SSA, however, from Table 2, on the largest network, i.e. Twitter, SSA and D-SSA are faster than IMM under LT model.

The number of samples generated by SSA and D-SSA in our reruns are several times higher than that reported in our conference paper [8]. This is totally expected since we ignore all the optimizations made in our prior implementations.

- **New results: D-SSA fix, SSA fix and IMM for** $k = 1$ **have similar running time.** From Figs. 1, 2 and 3, we also include the results for SSA fix and D-SSA fix and observe that SSA fix and D-SSA fix use fewer samples than IMM even for $k = 1$. For larger value of k, SSA fix and D-SSA fix are significantly more efficient than IMM in sample usage. From Table 2, we see that namely SSA fix and D-SSA fix use roughly the same amount of time as IMM for $k = 1$ and run faster than IMM on large networks, e.g. Orkut, Twitter, on the LT model.

References

1. Borgs, C., Brautbar, M., Chayes, J., Lucier, B.: Maximizing social influence in nearly optimal time. In: Proceedings of the Twenty-Fifth Annual ACM-SIAM Symposium on Discrete Algorithms, pp. 946–957. SIAM (2014)
2. Chen, W.: An issue in the martingale analysis of the influence maximization algorithm IMM. arXiv preprint arXiv:1808.09363 (2018)
3. Chen, W., Lakshmanan, L.V., Castillo, C.: Information and influence propagation in social networks. Synth. Lect. Data Manag. 5(4), 1–177 (2013)
4. Huang, K., Wang, S., Bevilacqua, G., Xiao, X., Lakshmanan, L.V.S.: Revisiting the Stop-and-Stare Algorithms for Influence Maximization. https://sites.google.com/site/vldb2017imexptr/

5. Huang, K., Wang, S., Bevilacqua, G., Xiao, X., Lakshmanan, L.V.S.: Revisiting the stop-and-stare algorithms for influence maximization. Proc. VLDB Endow. **10**(9), 913–924 (2017)
6. Kempe, D., Kleinberg, J., Tardos, É.: Maximizing the spread of influence through a social network. In: Proceedings of the Ninth ACM SIGKDD International Conference on Knowledge Discovery and Data Mining, pp. 137–146. ACM (2003)
7. Kwak, H., Lee, C., Park, H., Moon, S.: What is Twitter, a social network or a news media? In: WWW, pp. 591–600. ACM (2010)
8. Nguyen, H.T., Thai, M.T., Dinh, T.N.: Stop-and-stare: optimal sampling algorithms for viral marketing in billion-scale networks. In: Proceedings of the 2016 International Conference on Management of Data, pp. 695–710. ACM (2016)
9. Nguyen, H.T., Thai, M.T., Dinh, T.N.: Stop-and-stare: optimal sampling algorithms for viral marketing in billion-scale networks. arXiv preprint arXiv:1605.07990v2 (2016). Accessed 7 Sep 2016
10. Nguyen, H.T., Thai, M.T., Dinh, T.N.: A billion-scale approximation algorithm for maximizing benefit in viral marketing. IEEE/ACM Trans. Netw. (TON) **25**(4), 2419–2429 (2017)
11. Nguyen, H.T., Thai, M.T., Dinh, T.N.: Stop-and-stare: optimal sampling algorithms for viral marketing in billion-scale networks. arXiv preprint arXiv:1605.07990 (2017). Accessed 22 Feb 2017
12. Nguyen, H.T., Thai, M.T., Dinh, T.N.: SSA/DSSA Implementations. https://github.com/hungnt55/Stop-and-Stare (2018). Accessed 16 May 2018
13. Nguyen, H.T., Dinh, T.N., Thai, M.T.: Cost-aware targeted viral marketing in billion-scale networks. In: INFOCOM 2016-The 35th Annual IEEE International Conference on Computer Communications, pp. 1–9. IEEE (2016)
14. Nguyen, H.T., Nguyen, T.P., Phan, N., Dinh, T.N.: Importance sketching of influence dynamics in billion-scale networks. arXiv preprint arXiv:1709.03565 (2017)
15. Tang, J., Tang, X., Yuan, J.: Influence maximization meets efficiency and effectiveness: a hop-based approach. In: Proceedings of the 2017 IEEE/ACM International Conference on Advances in Social Networks Analysis and Mining 2017, ASONAM 2017, pp. 64–71. ACM, New York (2017). http://doi.acm.org/10.1145/3110025.3110041
16. Tang, Y., Shi, Y., Xiao, X.: Influence maximization in near-linear time: a martingale approach. In: Proceedings of the 2015 ACM SIGMOD International Conference on Management of Data, SIGMOD 2015, pp. 1539–1554. ACM, New York (2015). http://doi.acm.org/10.1145/2723372.2723734
17. Tang, Y., Xiao, X., Shi, Y.: Influence maximization: near-optimal time complexity meets practical efficiency. In: Proceedings of the 2014 ACM SIGMOD International Conference on Management of Data, pp. 75–86. ACM (2014)

An Issue in the Martingale Analysis of the Influence Maximization Algorithm IMM

Wei Chen$^{(\boxtimes)}$

Microsoft Research, Beijing, China
weic@microsoft.com

Abstract. This paper explains a subtle issue in the martingale analysis of the IMM algorithm, a state-of-the-art influence maximization algorithm. Two workarounds are proposed to fix the issue, both requiring minor changes on the algorithm and incurring a slight penalty on the running time of the algorithm.

1 Introduction

Tang et al. design a scalable influence maximization algorithm IMM (Influence Maximization with Martingales) in [17], and apply martingale inequalities to the analysis. In this paper, we describe a subtle issue in their martingale-based analysis. The consequence is that the current proof showing that the IMM algorithm guarantees $(1-1/e-\varepsilon)$ approximation with high probability is technically incorrect. We provide a detailed explanation about the issue, and further propose two possible workarounds to address the issue, but both workarounds require minor changes to the algorithm with a slight penalty on running time. Xiaokui Xiao, one of the authors of [17], has acknowledged the issue pointed out in this paper.

1.1 Background and Related Work

Influence maximization is the problem of given a social network $G = (V, E)$, a stochastic diffusion model with parameters on the network, and a budget of k seeds, finding the optimal k seeds $S \subseteq V$ such that the influence spread of the seeds S, denoted as $\sigma(S)$ and defined as the expected number of nodes activated based on diffusion model starting from S, is maximized. The influence maximization is originally formulated as a discrete optimization problem by Kempe et al. [13], and has been extensively studied in the literature (cf. [3] for a survey). One important direction is scalable influence maximization [1,5–7,9,10,12,15,17,18], which focuses on improving the efficiency of running influence maximization algorithms on large-scale networks. The early studies on this direction are heuristics based on graph algorithms [5–7,10,12] or sketch-based algorithms [9]. Borgs et al. propose the novel reverse influence sampling (RIS) approach, which achieves theoretical guarantees on both the approximation ratio and near-linear expected running time [1]. The RIS approach is further improved

© Springer Nature Switzerland AG 2018
X. Chen et al. (Eds.): CSoNet 2018, LNCS 11280, pp. 286–297, 2018.
https://doi.org/10.1007/978-3-030-04648-4_24

in [15,17,18] to achieve scalable performance on networks with billions of nodes and edges. The IMM algorithm we discuss in this paper is from [17], which uses the martingales to improve the performance, and is considered as one of the state-of-the-art influence maximization algorithms. However, we show in this paper that the algorithm has a subtle issue that affects its correctness. The IMM algorithm has been used in later studies as a component (e.g. [4,16,19]), so it is worth to point out the issue and the workarounds for the correct usage of the IMM algorithm. The SSA/D-SSA algorithm of [15] is another state-of-the-art influence maximization algorithm, but the original publication also contains several analytical issues, which have been pointed out in [11].

2   Description of the Issue

2.1   Brief Description of the RIS Approach

At the core of the RIS approach is the concept of reverse-reachable (RR) sets. Given a network $G = (V, E)$ and a diffusion model, an RR set $R \subseteq V$ is sampled by first randomly selecting a node $v \in V$ and then reverse simulating the diffusion process and adding all nodes reached by the reverse simulation into R. Such reverse simulation can be carried out efficiently for a large class of diffusion models called the triggering model (see [13,17] for model details). Intuitively, each node $u \in R$ if acting as a seed would activate v in the corresponding forward propagation, and based on this intuition the key relationship $\sigma(S) = n \cdot \mathbb{E}[\mathbb{I}\{S \cap R \neq \emptyset\}]$ is established, where $\sigma(S)$ is the influence spread, $n = |V|$, and $\mathbb{I}$ is the indicator function. The RIS approach is to collect enough number of RR sets $\mathcal{R} = \{R_1, R_2, \ldots, R_\theta\}$, so that $\sigma(S)$ can be approximated by $\hat{\sigma}(S) = n \cdot \sum_{i=1}^{\theta} \mathbb{I}\{R_i \cap S \neq \emptyset\}/\theta$. We call $R_i \cap S \neq \emptyset$ as S covering R_i. Thus, the original influence maximization problem is converted to finding k seeds S that can cover the most number of RR sets in $\mathcal{R}$. This is a k-max coverage problem, and a greedy algorithm (referred to as the NodeSelection procedure in IMM [17]) can be applied to solve it with a $1 - 1/e$ approximation ratio.

Implementations of the RIS approach differ in their estimation of the number of RR sets needed. IMM algorithm [17] iteratively doubles the number of RR sets until it obtains a reasonable estimate LB as the lower bound of the optimal solution OPT, and then apply a formula $\theta = \lambda^*/LB$, where λ^* is a constant dependent on the problem instance, to get the final number of RR sets needed (See Fig. 1 for the reprint of the Sampling procedure of IMM).

2.2   Summary of the Issue

The main issue of the IMM analysis in [17] is at its correctness claim of Theorem 4, which shows that the output of IMM gives a $1 - 1/e - \varepsilon$ approximate solution with probability at least $1 - 1/n^\ell$. The proof of this part is very brief, containing only one sentence as excerpted below, which combines the result from Theorems 1 and 2.

"*By combining Theorems 1 and 2, we obtain that Algorithm 3 returns a $(1 - 1/e - \varepsilon)$-approximate solution with at least $1 - 1/n^\ell$ (probability)*."

At the high level, Theorem 1 claims that if NodeSelection procedure is fed with an RR set sequence of length at least $\theta \geq \lambda^*/OPT$, then with probability at least $1-1/n^\ell$, NodeSelection outputs a seed set that is a $1 - 1/e - \varepsilon$ approximate solution. Then Theorem 2 claims that the Sampling procedure outputs an RR set sequence of length at least λ^*/OPT with probability at least $1-1/n^\ell$. It may appear that we could use a simple union bound to combine the two theorems to show that IMM achieves the $1 - 1/e - \varepsilon$ approximation with probability at least $1 - 2/n^\ell$. Finally, we just need to reset $\ell = \ell + \log 2/\log n$ to change the probability from $1 - 2/n^\ell$ to $1 - 1/n^{\ell}.^1$

However, with a closer inspection, Theorem 1 is true only for each **fixed length** $\theta \geq \lambda^*/OPT$, but the Sampling procedure returns an RR set sequence of **random length**. Henceforth, to make the distinction explicit, we use $\tilde{\theta}$ to denote the random length returned by the Sampling procedure. Technically, this $\tilde{\theta}$ is a *stopping time*, a concept frequently used in martingale processes [14]. Thus, what Theorem 2 actually claims is $\Pr\{\tilde{\theta} \geq \lambda^*/OPT\} \geq 1 - 1/n^\ell$. Due to this discrepancy between fixed length and random length in RR set sequences, we cannot directly combine Theorems 1 and 2 to obtain Theorem 4 as in the paper. This is the main issue of the analysis in the IMM paper [17].

In the next two subsections, we will provide more detailed discussion to illustrate the above issue. In Sect. 2.3, we first make it explicit what is the exact probability space we use for the analysis of the IMM algorithm. Then in Sect. 2.4, we go through lemma by lemma on the original analysis to make the distinction between the fixed length θ and the random stopping time $\tilde{\theta}$ explicit, so that the issue summarized above is more clearly illustrated.

2.3   Treatment on the Probability Space

For the following discussion, we will frequently refer to certain details in the Sampling procedure of IMM, namely Algorithm 2 of IMM in [17] (see Fig. 1).

To clearly understand the random stopping time $\tilde{\theta}$, we first clarify the probability space upon which $\tilde{\theta}$ is defined. We first note that from the algorithm, the maximum possible number of RR sets the algorithm could generate is $\lceil \lambda^* \rceil$ (defined in Eq. (6)). Thus we view the probability space as the space of all $\lceil \lambda^* \rceil$ RR set sequences $R_1, R_2, \ldots, R_{\lceil \lambda^* \rceil}$, where each R_i is generated i.i.d. We denote this space as Ω. Then in one run of the IMM algorithm, one such RR set sequence $\mathcal{R}_0$ is drawn from the probability space Ω. In the i-th iteration of the Sampling procedure, the algorithm gets the prefix of the first θ_i (θ_i is defined in line 5 of Algorithm 2) RR sets in the above sequence $\mathcal{R}_0$, and based on certain condition about this prefix the algorithm decides whether to continue the iteration or stop; and when it stops, it determines the final number $\tilde{\theta} = \lambda^*/LB$ of RR sets needed,

---

[1] The original paper has a typo here. It says to reset ℓ to $\ell(1 + \log 2/\log n)$, but this is not necessary. Only resetting ℓ to $\ell + \log 2/\log n$ is enough.

Algorithm 2: Sampling $(G, k, \varepsilon, \ell)$

---

1 Initialize a set $\mathcal{R} = \emptyset$ and an integer $LB = 1$;
2 Let $\varepsilon' = \sqrt{2} \cdot \varepsilon$;
3 **for** $i = 1$ *to* $\log_2 n - 1$ **do**
4 $\quad$ Let $x = n/2^i$;
5 $\quad$ Let $\theta_i = \lambda'/x$, where λ' is as defined in Equation 9;
6 $\quad$ **while** $|\mathcal{R}| \leq \theta_i$ **do**
7 $\quad\quad$ Select a node v from G uniformly at random;
8 $\quad\quad$ Generate an RR set for v, and insert it into $\mathcal{R}$;
9 $\quad$ Let $S_i = $ NodeSelection($\mathcal{R}$);
10 $\quad$ **if** $n \cdot F_{\mathcal{R}}(S_i) \geq (1 + \varepsilon') \cdot x$ **then**
11 $\quad\quad$ $LB = n \cdot F_{\mathcal{R}}(S_i)/(1 + \varepsilon')$;
12 $\quad\quad$ **break**;
13 Let $\theta = \lambda^*/LB$, where λ^* is as defined in Equation 6;
14 **while** $|\mathcal{R}| \leq \theta$ **do**
15 $\quad$ Select a node v from G uniformly at random;
16 $\quad$ Generate an RR set for v, and insert it into $\mathcal{R}$;
17 **return** $\mathcal{R}$

Fig. 1. Algorithm 2 (Sampling procedure) of IMM as in the original paper [17].

and retrieves the prefix of $\tilde{\theta}$ RR sets from $\mathcal{R}_0$. Note that $\tilde{\theta}$ here is the θ used in line 13 of Algorithm 2, but we explicitly use $\tilde{\theta}$ to denote that it is a random variable (because LB is a random variable), and its value is determined by the prefix of RR sets in $R_1, R_2, \ldots$. In contrast, for a fixed θ such as the θ used in Theorem 1, it simply corresponds to the θ RR sets in the sequence sample $\mathcal{R}_0$. For convenience, we use $\mathcal{R}_0[\theta]$ to denote the prefix of $\mathcal{R}_0$ of fixed length θ, and $\Omega[\theta]$ to be the subspace of all RR set sequences of length θ. Note that we use Ω and $\Omega[\theta]$ to refer to both the set of sequences and their distribution.

2.4   Detailed Discussion by Revisiting All Lemmas and Theorems

Hopefully we clarify the distinction between the fixed-length sequence R_1, R_2, $\ldots, R_\theta$ and the actual sequence $R_1, R_2, \ldots, R_{\tilde{\theta}}$ generated by the sampling phase with a random stopping time $\tilde{\theta}$. We now revisit the technical lemmas and the theorems of the paper to explicitly distinguish between the usage of fixed length θ and random length $\tilde{\theta}$.

First and foremost, the martingale inequalities summarized in Corollaries 1 and 2 should only work for a fixed constant θ, not for a random stopping time, because they come from standard martingale inequalities as summarized in [8], which deals with martingales of fixed length. However, the authors introduce these inequalities in the context of RR set sequence generated by the Sampling procedure (see the first sentence in Sect. 3.1 of [17]). As we explained, the RR set sequence generated by the Sampling procedure has random length $\tilde{\theta}$, so Corollaries 1 and 2 should not be applied to such random length sequences. This is the source of confusion leading to the incorrectness of the proof of Theorem

4. Henceforth, we should clearly remember that Corollaries 1 and 2 only work for fixed length θ.

Next, for Lemmas 3 and 4, the θ there should refer to a fixed number, because their proofs rely on the martingale inequalities in Corollaries 1 and 2, which are correct only for a fixed θ.

For Theorem 1, same as discussed above, if we view θ as a fixed constant, then Theorem 1 is correct. We need to remark here that Theorem 1 talks about the node selection phase, so its exact meaning is that if we feed the NodeSelection procedure with an RR set sequence of **fixed length** θ, randomly drawn from the space $\Omega[\theta]$, then the node selection phase would return an approximate solution. Therefore, it is not applicable when the NodeSelection procedure is fed with the RR set sequence generated from the Sampling procedure, since this sequence has a random length and is not drawn from the space $\Omega[\theta]$ for a fixed θ.

Lemma 5 and Corollary 3 are still correct, since they are not related to the application of martingale inequality. For Lemmas 6 and 7, again they are correct when θ is a fixed number satisfying inequality (8).

For Theorem 2, as already mentioned in Sect. 2.2, it is about the RR set sequence $\mathcal{R} = \{R_1, R_2, \ldots, R_{\tilde{\theta}}\}$ generated by the Sampling procedure, with random length $\tilde{\theta}$, and its technical claim is

$$\Pr\left\{\tilde{\theta} \geq \frac{\lambda^*}{OPT}\right\} \geq 1 - \frac{1}{n^\ell}, \tag{1}$$

where the probability is taken from the probability space Ω, the random sample $\mathcal{R}_0$ of which determines the actual random length of output $\tilde{\theta}$. The proof of Theorem 2 uses Lemmas 6 and 7. When it uses Lemmas 6 and 7, it is in the context of the Sampling procedure, and the θ used for Lemmas 6 and 7 in this context is exactly the $\theta_i = \lambda'/x_i$ defined in line 5 of algorithm, where λ' is a constant defined in Eq. (9), and $x_i = n/2^i$, and i refers to the i-th iteration in the Sampling procedure. Therefore, θ_i indeed is a constant that does not depend on the generated RR sets, and the applications of Lemmas 6 and 7 is in general appropriate. However, the original proof of Theorem 2 is brief, and there is a subtle point that may not be clear from the proof, and thus some extra clarification is deserved here.

The subtlety is that, Lemmas 6 and 7 are correct when the NodeSelection procedure is fed with a fixed length RR set sequence sampled from $\Omega[\theta]$. However, in the i-th iteration of the Sampling procedure, the actual RR set sequence fed into NodeSelection is *not* sampled from the space $\Omega[\theta_i]$. This is because the fact that the algorithm enters the i-th iteration implies that the previous RR set sequence failed the coverage condition check in line 10 in the previous iterations, and thus the actual sequence fed into NodeSelection in the i-th iteration is a biased sample. This subtlety makes the rigorous proof of Theorem 2 longer, but does not invalidate the Theorem. Intuitively, for a random sample $\mathcal{R}_0[\theta_i]$ drawn from $\Omega[\theta_i]$, even if $\mathcal{R}_0[\theta_i]$ would not make the algorithm survive to the i-th iteration, we could still treat it as if it is fed to NodeSelection in the i-th iteration, and use Lemmas 6 and 7 to argue that some event $\mathcal{E}_i$ only occurs with a small probability δ_3. Then the event that both algorithm enters the i-th iteration and $\mathcal{E}_i$ occurs must be also smaller than δ_3. For completeness, in [2], we provide a more rigorous technical proof of Theorem 2 applying the above idea.

Continuing to Lemmas 8 and 9, similar to Lemmas 6 and 7, it is correct when we treat θ as a constant. For Lemma 9, it uses Lemma 8, and if we treat the application of Lemma 8 in the same way as we treat the application of Lemmas 6 and 7 in the proof of Theorem 2, then Lemma 9 is correct. Lemma 10 and Theorem 3 are independent of the application of martingale inequalities and are correct.

Finally, we investigate the proof of Theorem 4, in particular the part on the correctness of the IMM algorithm. As outlined in Sect. 2.2, a direct combination of Theorems 1 and 2 is problematic. We now discuss this point with more technical details.

For Theorem 1, based on our above discussion, it works for a fixed value of θ. More precisely, when we use the setting discussed after Theorem 1, what it really says is that, for all fixed $\theta \geq \lambda^*/OPT$, if we use a random sample $\mathcal{R}_0[\theta]$ drawn from distribution $\Omega[\theta]$, then when we feed the NodeSelection procedure with $\mathcal{R}_0[\theta]$, the probability that NodeSelection returns a seed set that is a $(1-1/e-\varepsilon)$ approximate solution is at least $1 - 1/n^\ell$. To make it more explicit, let $S_k^*(\mathcal{R})$ be the seed set returned by NodeSelection under input RR set sequence $\mathcal{R}$. Let $Y(S)$ be an indicator, and it is 1 when seed set S is a $(1 - 1/e - \varepsilon)$ approximate solution, and it is 0 otherwise. Then, what Theorem 1 says is,

$$\forall \theta \geq \lambda^*/OPT, \Pr_{\mathcal{R}_0[\theta]\sim\Omega[\theta]}\{Y(S_k^*(\mathcal{R}_0[\theta])) = 1\} \geq 1 - \frac{1}{n^\ell}. \tag{2}$$

Next, as discussed above, what Theorem 2 really says is given in Eq. (1). Also to make it more precise and use the same base sample from the probability space, let $\mathcal{R}_0$ be the sample drawn from Ω, and let $\mathcal{R}(\mathcal{R}_0) = \{R_1, R_2, \ldots, R_{\tilde{\theta}}\}$ be the sequence generated by the Sampling procedure, and $\tilde{\theta}(\mathcal{R}_0)$ denote its length. Thus by definition, $\mathcal{R}(\mathcal{R}_0)$ is the first $\tilde{\theta}(\mathcal{R}_0)$ RR sets of $\mathcal{R}_0$. Then Theorem 2 (and Eq. (1)) is restated as

$$\Pr_{\mathcal{R}_0\sim\Omega}\left\{\tilde{\theta}(\mathcal{R}_0) \geq \frac{\lambda^*}{OPT}\right\} \geq 1 - \frac{1}{n^\ell}. \tag{3}$$

For Theorem 4, we want to bound the probability that using the Sampling procedure output $\mathcal{R}(\mathcal{R}_0)$ to feed into NodeSelection, its output fails to provide the $1 - 1/e - \varepsilon$ approximation ratio, that is,

$$\Pr_{\mathcal{R}_0\sim\Omega}\{Y(S_k^*(\mathcal{R}(\mathcal{R}_0))) = 0\} \leq \frac{2}{n^\ell}. \tag{4}$$

The following derivation further separates the left-hand side of Eq. (4) into two parts by the union bound:

$$\Pr_{\mathcal{R}_0 \sim \Omega} \{ Y(S_k^*(\mathcal{R}(\mathcal{R}_0))) = 0 \}$$

$$\leq \Pr_{\mathcal{R}_0 \sim \Omega} \left\{ \tilde{\theta}(\mathcal{R}_0) < \frac{\lambda^*}{OPT} \vee \left(\tilde{\theta}(\mathcal{R}_0) \geq \frac{\lambda^*}{OPT} \wedge Y(S_k^*(\mathcal{R}(\mathcal{R}_0))) = 0 \right) \right\}$$

$$\leq \Pr_{\mathcal{R}_0 \sim \Omega} \left\{ \tilde{\theta}(\mathcal{R}_0) < \frac{\lambda^*}{OPT} \right\} + \Pr_{\mathcal{R}_0 \sim \Omega} \left\{ \tilde{\theta}(\mathcal{R}_0) \geq \frac{\lambda^*}{OPT} \wedge Y(S_k^*(\mathcal{R}(\mathcal{R}_0))) = 0 \right\}$$

$$\leq \frac{1}{n^\ell} + \Pr_{\mathcal{R}_0 \sim \Omega} \left\{ \tilde{\theta}(\mathcal{R}_0) \geq \frac{\lambda^*}{OPT} \wedge Y(S_k^*(\mathcal{R}(\mathcal{R}_0))) = 0 \right\}, \tag{5}$$

where the last inequality is by Theorem 2 (Eq. (3)). To continue, we want to bound

$$\Pr_{\mathcal{R}_0 \sim \Omega} \left\{ \tilde{\theta}(\mathcal{R}_0) \geq \frac{\lambda^*}{OPT} \wedge Y(S_k^*(\mathcal{R}(\mathcal{R}_0))) = 0 \right\} \leq \frac{1}{n^\ell}. \tag{6}$$

However, the above inequality is incompatible with Inequality (2), because Inequality (2) holds for **each fixed** $\theta \geq \frac{\lambda^*}{OPT}$, but Inequality (6) is for **all** $\tilde{\theta}(\mathcal{R}_0) \geq \frac{\lambda^*}{OPT}$. This is where the direct combination of Theorems 1 and 2 would fail to produce the correctness part of Theorem 4.

3   Possible Workarounds for the Issue

It is unclear if the analysis could be fixed without changing any aspect of the algorithm. In this section, we propose two possible workarounds, both of which require at least some change to the algorithm and incur some running time penalty.

3.1   Workaround 1: Regenerating New RR Sets

One simple workaround is that in the IMM algorithm, after determining the final length $\tilde{\theta}$ of the RR set sequence, regenerate the entire RR set sequence of length $\tilde{\theta}$ from scratch, and use the newly generated sequence as the output of the Sampling algorithm and feed it into the final call to NodeSelection. That is, after line 13 of Algorithm 2, regenerate $\tilde{\theta}$ RR sets instead of lines 14–16.

Intuitively, this would feed the final call of NodeSelection with an unbiased RR set sequence so that Theorem 1 can be applied. We represent this new unbiased sequence as a new independent sample $\mathcal{R}_0'$ from the probability space Ω, and then taking the prefix of $\mathcal{R}_0'$ with $\tilde{\theta}(\mathcal{R}_0)$ RR sets, where $\tilde{\theta}(\mathcal{R}_0)$ is the number of RR sets determined from sequence $\mathcal{R}_0$ that is needed for the final call of NodeSelection. Thus we use the notation $\mathcal{R}_0'[\tilde{\theta}(\mathcal{R}_0)]$ to represent the RR set sequence that is fed into the final call of NodeSelection. The correctness can be rigorously proved as follows. First, Eq. (4) for Theorem 4 is changed to:

$$\Pr_{\mathcal{R}_0 \sim \Omega, \mathcal{R}_0' \sim \Omega} \{ Y(S_k^*(\mathcal{R}_0'[\tilde{\theta}(\mathcal{R}_0)])) = 0 \} \leq \frac{2}{n^\ell}. \tag{7}$$

To show the above inequality, following a similar derivation as in Eq. (5), what we need to show is the following instead of Eq. (6):

$$\Pr_{\mathcal{R}_0 \sim \Omega, \mathcal{R}_0' \sim \Omega} \left\{ \tilde{\theta}(\mathcal{R}_0) \geq \frac{\lambda^*}{OPT} \wedge Y(S_k^*(\mathcal{R}_0'[\tilde{\theta}(\mathcal{R}_0)])) = 0 \right\} \leq \frac{1}{n^\ell}. \tag{8}$$

This can be achieved by the following derivation:

$$\Pr_{\mathcal{R}_0 \sim \Omega, \mathcal{R}_0' \sim \Omega} \left\{ \tilde{\theta}(\mathcal{R}_0) \geq \frac{\lambda^*}{OPT} \wedge Y(S_k^*(\mathcal{R}_0'[\tilde{\theta}(\mathcal{R}_0)])) = 0 \right\}$$

$$= \Pr_{\mathcal{R}_0 \sim \Omega, \mathcal{R}_0' \sim \Omega} \left\{ \bigvee_{\theta = \lceil \frac{\lambda^*}{OPT} \rceil}^{\lceil \lambda^* \rceil} \tilde{\theta}(\mathcal{R}_0) = \theta \wedge Y(S_k^*(\mathcal{R}_0'[\tilde{\theta}(\mathcal{R}_0)])) = 0 \right\}$$

$$\leq \sum_{\theta = \lceil \frac{\lambda^*}{OPT} \rceil}^{\lceil \lambda^* \rceil} \Pr_{\mathcal{R}_0 \sim \Omega, \mathcal{R}_0' \sim \Omega} \left\{ \tilde{\theta}(\mathcal{R}_0) = \theta \wedge Y(S_k^*(\mathcal{R}_0'[\tilde{\theta}(\mathcal{R}_0)])) = 0 \right\} \quad \{\text{union bound}\}$$

$$= \sum_{\theta = \lceil \frac{\lambda^*}{OPT} \rceil}^{\lceil \lambda^* \rceil} \Pr_{\mathcal{R}_0 \sim \Omega, \mathcal{R}_0' \sim \Omega} \left\{ \tilde{\theta}(\mathcal{R}_0) = \theta \wedge Y(S_k^*(\mathcal{R}_0'[\theta])) = 0 \right\}$$

$$= \sum_{\theta = \lceil \frac{\lambda^*}{OPT} \rceil}^{\lceil \lambda^* \rceil} \Pr_{\mathcal{R}_0 \sim \Omega} \left\{ \tilde{\theta}(\mathcal{R}_0) = \theta \right\} \cdot \Pr_{\mathcal{R}_0' \sim \Omega} \left\{ Y(S_k^*(\mathcal{R}_0'[\theta])) = 0 \right\} \quad \{\text{see note below}\}$$

$$\tag{9}$$

$$= \sum_{\theta = \lceil \frac{\lambda^*}{OPT} \rceil}^{\lceil \lambda^* \rceil} \Pr_{\mathcal{R}_0 \sim \Omega} \left\{ \tilde{\theta}(\mathcal{R}_0) = \theta \right\} \cdot \Pr_{\mathcal{R}_0'[\theta] \sim \Omega[\theta]} \left\{ Y(S_k^*(\mathcal{R}_0'[\theta])) = 0 \right\}$$

$$\leq \sum_{\theta = \lceil \frac{\lambda^*}{OPT} \rceil}^{\lceil \lambda^* \rceil} \Pr_{\mathcal{R}_0 \sim \Omega} \left\{ \tilde{\theta}(\mathcal{R}_0) = \theta \right\} \cdot \frac{1}{n^\ell} \quad \{\text{Eq. (2) of Theorem 1}\}$$

$$= \frac{1}{n^\ell}. \quad \{\text{note: independence of } \mathcal{R}_0 \text{ and } \mathcal{R}_0'\}$$

The key step is Eq. (9), where because $\mathcal{R}_0'$ is independent of $\mathcal{R}_0$ (we regenerate a new RR set sequence for the last call to NodeSelection), we can represent the probability $\Pr_{\mathcal{R}_0 \sim \Omega, \mathcal{R}_0' \sim \Omega} \left\{ \tilde{\theta}(\mathcal{R}_0) = \theta \wedge Y(S_k^*(\mathcal{R}_0'[\theta])) = 0 \right\}$ as the product of two separate factors. Therefore, the correctness part of Theorem 4 now holds. Note that within the Sampling procedure, we do not need to regenerate RR set sequences from scratch (before line 9 of Algorithm 2), because by our detailed discussion in Sect. 2.4, even without regenerating RR sets, Theorem 2 still holds with a more careful argument.

In terms of the running time, this workaround at most doubles the number of RR sets generated, and thus its running time only adds a multiplicative factor of 2 to the original result. Therefore, the asymptotic running time remains as $O((k + \ell)(n + m) \log n/\varepsilon^2)$ in expectation.

3.2   Workaround 2: Apply Union Bounding with Larger ℓ

The second workaround is by directly bounding Eq. (6) by a union bound, as shown in the derivation below.

$$\Pr_{\mathcal{R}_0 \sim \Omega} \left\{ \tilde{\theta}(\mathcal{R}_0) \geq \frac{\lambda^*}{OPT} \wedge Y(S_k^*(\mathcal{R}(\mathcal{R}_0))) = 0 \right\}$$

$$= \Pr_{\mathcal{R}_0 \sim \Omega} \left\{ \bigvee_{\theta = \lceil \frac{\lambda^*}{OPT} \rceil}^{\lceil \lambda^* \rceil} \tilde{\theta}(\mathcal{R}_0) = \theta \wedge Y(S_k^*(\mathcal{R}(\mathcal{R}_0))) = 0 \right\}$$

$$\leq \sum_{\theta = \lceil \frac{\lambda^*}{OPT} \rceil}^{\lceil \lambda^* \rceil} \Pr_{\mathcal{R}_0 \sim \Omega} \left\{ \tilde{\theta}(\mathcal{R}_0) = \theta \wedge Y(S_k^*(\mathcal{R}(\mathcal{R}_0))) = 0 \right\}$$

$$= \sum_{\theta = \lceil \frac{\lambda^*}{OPT} \rceil}^{\lceil \lambda^* \rceil} \Pr_{\mathcal{R}_0 \sim \Omega} \left\{ \tilde{\theta}(\mathcal{R}_0) = \theta \wedge Y(S_k^*(\mathcal{R}_0[\theta])) = 0 \right\}$$

$$\leq \sum_{\theta = \lceil \frac{\lambda^*}{OPT} \rceil}^{\lceil \lambda^* \rceil} \Pr_{\mathcal{R}_0 \sim \Omega} \left\{ Y(S_k^*(\mathcal{R}_0[\theta])) = 0 \right\} \tag{10}$$

$$= \sum_{\theta = \lceil \frac{\lambda^*}{OPT} \rceil}^{\lceil \lambda^* \rceil} \Pr_{\mathcal{R}_0[\theta] \sim \Omega[\theta]} \left\{ Y(S_k^*(\mathcal{R}_0[\theta])) = 0 \right\}$$

$$\leq \sum_{\theta = \lceil \frac{\lambda^*}{OPT} \rceil}^{\lceil \lambda^* \rceil} \frac{1}{n^\ell} \qquad\qquad \text{\{by Theorem 1, Eq. (2)\}}$$

$$\tag{11}$$

$$\leq \frac{\lceil \lambda^* \rceil}{n^\ell}. \tag{12}$$

Comparing the above derivation with the similar one for workaround 1, the key difference is between Eqs. (9) and (10). In Eq. (9), we could keep $\Pr_{\mathcal{R}_0 \sim \Omega}\{\tilde{\theta}(\mathcal{R}_0) = \theta\}$ because the event $\{\tilde{\theta}(\mathcal{R}_0) = \theta\}$ is independent of the event $\{Y(S_k^*(\mathcal{R}_0'[\theta])) = 0\}$ in the second term. But in Eq. (10), we cannot extract $\Pr_{\mathcal{R}_0 \sim \Omega}\{\tilde{\theta}(\mathcal{R}_0) = \theta\}$ because the event $\{\tilde{\theta}(\mathcal{R}_0) = \theta\}$ is correlated with the event $\{Y(S_k^*(\mathcal{R}_0[\theta])) = 0\}$ in the second term. Thus we have to simply drop the event $\{\tilde{\theta}(\mathcal{R}_0) = \theta\}$, causing the bound to be inflated by a factor of $\lceil \lambda^* \rceil$.

Using Inequality (12), our second workaround is to enlarge ℓ to ℓ' so that $\lceil \lambda^* \rceil / n^{\ell'} \leq 1/n^\ell$. However, λ^* is also dependent on ℓ. To make it clear, we write it as $\lambda^*(\ell)$. What we want is to set $\ell' = \ell + \gamma$, such that

$$\frac{\lceil \lambda^*(\ell') \rceil}{n^{\ell'}} = \frac{\lceil \lambda^*(\ell + \gamma) \rceil}{n^{\ell + \gamma}} \leq \frac{1}{n^\ell}. \tag{13}$$

This means we want $\lceil \lambda^*(\ell + \gamma) \rceil \leq n^\gamma$. From Eqs. (5) and (6) in [17], we have

$$\lambda^*(\ell) = 2n \left(\frac{e-1}{e} \sqrt{\ell \log n + \log 2} + \sqrt{\frac{e-1}{e} \left(\log \binom{n}{k} + \ell \log n + \log 2 \right)} \right)^2 \varepsilon^{-2}$$

$$\leq 8n(k + \ell + 1) \log n \cdot \varepsilon^{-2} - 1,$$

where the relaxation in the inequality above is loose, involving relaxing the first square root term to the second one, relaxing $(1 - 1/e)$ to 1, relaxing $\binom{n}{k}$ to n^k, relaxing $\log 2$ to $\log n$, and thus the -1 above can be certainly compensated by the relaxation, and it is used for relaxing the $\lceil \lambda^*(\ell + \gamma) \rceil$ next. Thus, to achieve $\lceil \lambda^*(\ell + \gamma) \rceil \leq n^\gamma$, we just need $8n(k + \ell + \gamma + 1) \log n \cdot \varepsilon^{-2} \leq n^\gamma$. Asymptotically, $\gamma > 1$ would be fine for large enough n. For a conservative bound, it is very reasonable to assume that $\varepsilon^{-1} \leq n$, $k + \ell + \gamma + 1 \leq n$, then we just need $8 \log n \leq n^{\gamma - 4}$, which means setting $\gamma \geq 4 + \log(8 \log n) / \log n$ is enough. Thus γ is essentially a small constant.

In practice, γ could be computed by a binary search once the parameters n, k, ℓ and ε of the problem instance are given. Then we can set $\ell = \ell + \log 2 / \log n + \gamma$ in the algorithm. By increasing ℓ with a small constant γ (e.g. $\gamma = 2.5$), the running time increases from $O(k + \ell)(m + n) \log n / \varepsilon^2)$ to $O(k + \ell + \gamma)(m + n) \log n / \varepsilon^2)$, so the running time penalty is likely to be smaller than that of the first workaround. Our experimental results below validate this point.

3.3 Experimental Evaluation

We evaluate the two workarounds and compare them against the original IMM algorithm on two real world datasets: (a) NetHEPT, a coauthorship network with 15233 nodes and 31373 edges, mined from arxiv.org high energy physics section, and (b) DBLP, another coauthorship network with 655K nodes and 1990K edges, mined from dblp.uni-trier.de. We use independent cascade model with edge probabilities set by the weighted cascade method [13]: edge (u, v)'s probability is $1/d_v$ where d_v is the in-degree of v. These datasets are frequently used in other influence maximization studies such as [4,5,17].

We use IMM, IMM-W1, and IMM-W2 to denote the original IMM, the IMM with the first and the second workarounds, respectively. For IMM-W2, we use binary search to find an estimate of γ satisfying $\lceil \lambda^*(\ell + \gamma) \rceil \leq n^\gamma$. We set parameters $\varepsilon = 0.1$, $\ell = 1$, and influence spread is the average of 10000 simulation runs. We test the algorithms in seed set sizes $k = 50, 100, \ldots, 500$. The code is written in C++ and compiled by Visual Studio 2013, and is run on a Surface Pro 4 with dual core 2.20 GHz CPU and 16 GB memory.

The influence spread and running time results are shown in Fig. 2. As expected, all three algorithms achieve indistinguishable influence spread, since the two workarounds are to fix the theoretical issue on the dependency of RR sets, and should not affect much on the actual performance of the IMM algorithm. In terms of running time, also as expected, IMM-W1 has the worst running time, but is within twice of running time of the IMM algorithm. IMM-W2 has much

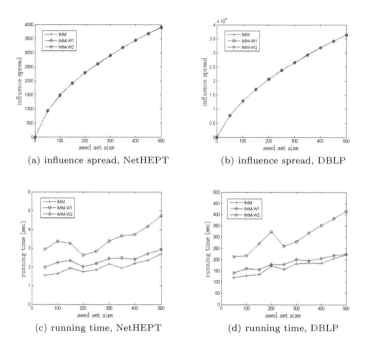

Fig. 2. Influence spread and running time results.

closer running time to IMM, though is still in general slower. We further observe that the γ value used for IMM-W2 is within 2.5 for the NetHEPT dataset and within 2 for the DBLP dataset. Therefore, it looks like that we can use the second workaround to provide a rigorous theoretical guarantee while achieving similar running time as the original IMM.

4   Conclusion

In this paper, we explain the issue in the original analysis of the IMM algorithm [17]. Two workarounds are proposed, both of which require some minor changes to the algorithm and both incur a slight penalty in running time. Since the IMM algorithm as a state-of-the-art influence maximization algorithm provides both strong theoretical guarantee and good practical performance, many follow-up studies in influence maximization use IMM algorithms as a template. Thus, it is worth to point out this issue so that subsequent follow-ups will correctly use the algorithm, especially if they want to provide theoretical guarantee. It remains an open question if the issue can be fixed without changing the original algorithm, or if a workaround with an even less impact to the algorithm and its running time can be found.

Acknowledgment. The author would like to thank Jian Li for helpful discussions and verification on the issue explained in the paper.

References

1. Borgs, C., Brautbar, M., Chayes, J., Lucier, B.: Maximizing social influence in nearly optimal time. In: SODA (2014)
2. Chen, W.: An issue in the martingale analysis of the influence maximization algorithm IMM. Technical report arXiv:1808.09363 (2018)
3. Chen, W., Lakshmanan, L.V.S., Castillo C.: Information and Influence Propagation in Social Networks. Morgan & Claypool Publishers, San Rafael (2013)
4. Chen, W., Teng, S.-H.: Interplay between social influence and network centrality: a comparative study on shapley centrality and single-node-influence centrality. In: WWW, pp. 967–976 (2017)
5. Chen, W., Wang, C., Wang, Y.: Scalable influence maximization for prevalent viral marketing in large-scale social networks. In: KDD (2010)
6. Chen, W., Wang, Y., Yang, S.: Efficient influence maximization in social networks. In: KDD (2009)
7. Chen, W., Yuan, Y., Zhang, L.: Scalable influence maximization in social networks under the linear threshold model. In: ICDM (2010)
8. Chung, F., Lu, L.: Concentration inequalities and martingale inequalities: a survey. Internet Math. **3**(1), 79–127 (2006)
9. Cohen, E., Delling, D., Pajor, T., Werneck, R.F.: Sketch-based influence maximization and computation: scaling up with guarantees. In: CIKM, pp. 629–638 (2014)
10. Goyal, A., Lu, W., Lakshmanan, L.V.S.: SIMPATH: an efficient algorithm for influence maximization under the linear threshold model. In: ICDM (2011)
11. Huang, K., Wang, S., Bevilacqua, G.S., Xiao, X., Lakshmanan, L.V.S.: Revisiting the stop-and-stare algorithms for influence maximization. PVLDB **10**(9), 913–924 (2017)
12. Jung, K., Heo, W., Chen, W.: IRIE: scalable and robust influence maximization in social networks. In: ICDM (2012)
13. Kempe, D., Kleinberg, J.M., Tardos, É.: Maximizing the spread of influence through a social network. In: KDD (2003)
14. Mitzenmacher, M., Upfal, E.: Probability and Computing. Cambridge University Press, New York (2005)
15. Nguyen, H.T., Thai, M.T., Dinh, T.N.: Stop-and-stare: optimal sampling algorithms for viral marketing in billion-scale networks. In: SIGMOD, pp. 695–710 (2016)
16. Sun, L., Huang, W., Yu, P., Chen, W.: Multi-round influence maximization. In: KDD (2018)
17. Tang, Y., Shi, Y., Xiao, X.: Influence maximization in near-linear time: a martingale approach. In: SIGMOD (2015)
18. Tang, Y., Xiao, X., Shi, Y.: Influence maximization: near-optimal time complexity meets practical efficiency. In: SIGMOD (2014)
19. Yang, Y., Mao, X., Pei, J., He, X.: Continuous influence maximization: what discounts should we offer to social network users? In: SIGMOD (2016)

A Stochastic Model for File Lifetime and Security in Data Center Networks

Quan-Lin Li$^{(\boxtimes)}$, Fan-Qi Ma, and Jing-Yu Ma

School of Economics and Management Sciences, Yanshan University,
Qinhuangdao 066004, China
liquanlin@tsinghua.edu.cn

Abstract. Data center networks are an important infrastructure in various applications of modern information technologies. Note that each data center always has a finite lifetime, thus once a data center fails, then it will lose all its storage files and useful information. For this, it is necessary to replicate and copy each important file into other data centers such that this file can increase its lifetime of staying in a data center network. In this paper, we describe a large-scale data center network with a file d-replication policy, which is to replicate each important file into at most $d - 1$ other data centers such that this file can maintain in the data center network under a given level of data security in the long-term. To this end, we develop three relevant Markov processes to propose two effective methods for assessing the file lifetime and data security. By using the RG-factorizations, we show that the two methods are used to be able to more effectively evaluate the file lifetime of large-scale data center networks. We hope the methodology and results given in this paper are applicable in the file lifetime and data security study of more general data center networks with replication mechanism.

Keywords: Data center · Replication mechanism · File lifetime
Data security · Markov process · RG-factorization

1 Introduction

Data center networks are an important infrastructure for various applications of modern information technologies. However, not only does each data center have a finite lifetime, but it is also possible to suffer from natural disasters and man-made damages. Once a data center fails, then it will lose all its storage files and useful information. In practice, such a data center failure has caused key innovation in design and management of large-scale data center networks, one of which is how to keep that no important file is lost in a data center network in the long-term. To do this, it is necessary to increase file and data availability by

Q.-L. Li was supported by the National Natural Science Foundation of China under grant No. 71671158 and No. 71471160, and by the Natural Science Foundation of Hebei province under grant No. G2017203277.

means of file replications as far as possible. In this case, a file copy redundancy technology is developed as a simple and effective mode that each important file is replicated into a subset of data centers according to a comprehensive consideration for departments and/or geographical environment, together with emergency responses for natural disasters and man-made damages. Therefore, during the last decade considerable attention has been paid to developing stochastic model analysis for assessing file lifetime and data security in large-scale data center networks with file replication mechanism. Also see Picconi et al. [11,12], Kersch and Szabo [5] and Feuillet and Robert [4] for more details.

Little work has been done on how to establish stochastic models (e.g., Markov processes, queueing theory and stochastic game) to assess the file lifetime and data security in a large-scale data center network with file replication mechanism. Intuitively, such a study is more interesting, difficult and challenging due to the fact that the mathematical modelling is based on reliability and security analysis of large-scale stochastic networks. Based on this, important topics include failure prediction for data centers, how to control new data centers joining this network, how to design and optimize file replication mechanism. In addition, there are still some interesting issues, such as cost analysis of recovering lost data, effect of file replication mechanism and bandwidth limitation, durability and availability of data, and how to control the file lost probability. Readers may refer to recent publications for details, among which, *data storage systems* by Blake and Rodrigues [2], Utard and Vernois [18], Lian et al. [7], Chun et al. [3] and Ramabhadran and Pasquale [14–16]; *DHT replication* by Picconi et al. [11,12], Kersch and Szabo [5], Pace et al. [10] and Kniesburges et al. [6]; *failure prediction* by Pinheiro et al. [13]; and *large-scale stochastic networks with unreliable processors* by Feuillet and Robert [4], Sun et al. [17] and Aghajani et al. [1].

The main contributions of this paper are twofold. The first one is to describe a large-scale data center network, in which each data center may fail and new data centers can join this network, and a file d-replication policy is proposed to increase file lifetime and data security. The second one is to develop three relevant Markov processes, which lead to two effective methods for assessing the file lifetime and data security in the data center network. By using the *RG*-factorizations of any absorbing Markov process, we show that the two methods can be very effective in file lifetime analysis of more general data center networks with file replication mechanism. In addition, we use numerical examples to indicate impact of the file d-replication policy on the file average lifetime of the data center network.

The remainder of this paper is organized as follows. Section 2 describes the data center network with file replication mechanism. Section 3 develops two relevant Markov processes to give an approximate method for assessing the file average lifetime. Section 4 establishes a QBD process to propose a two-dimensional method for assessing the file average lifetime, and uses numerical examples to indicate impact of the file d-replication policy on the file average lifetime of the data center network.

2   Model Description

In this section, we describe a large-scale data center network with file replication mechanism, in which each data center may fail and new data centers can join this network, and a file d-replication policy is proposed to increase the file lifetime and data security in the data center network.

For a large-scale data center network, we describe its physical structure, main random factors and system parameters as follows:

(1) **The physical structure:** There are many data centers distributed in parallel a physical network with different departments and/or geographical environment. For simplicity of analysis, we assume that all the data centers are identical and are operated independently.

(2) **The lifetime:** Each data center in this network may be failure. We assume that the lifetime X of each data center follows an exponential distribution with failure rate $\lambda > 0$, that is, $P\{X \leq t\} = 1 - e^{-\lambda t}$. Obviously, $E[X] = 1/\lambda$. If there are k data centers in this network, then the failure rate of the data center network is $k\lambda$ due to the exponential lifetime of each data center.

(3) **A joining process of new data centers:** Since the data center networks not only have fast developed in the last over ten years but also each data center may be failure, new data centers need to continually join to the network such that the data center network can maintain a development of sustainability through many incessant equipment replacements. We assume that the inputs of new data centers to the data center network are a Poisson process with arrival rate $\beta > 0$.

(4) **A file d-replication policy:** We assume that each file is stored in at most $d \geq 1$ data centers in this network. Once the copy number of the file is less than d and there also exists an available data center without storing the file, then the file will fast replicated to the data center. We assume that the copy time Y of the file replicated to the available data center follows an exponential distribution with copying rate $\mu > 0$, that is, $P\{Y \leq t\} = 1 - e^{-\mu t}$. Obviously, $E[Y] = 1/\mu$. If there are k identical copy files be being duplicated to k different data centers, then the copy time distribution of the k identical copy files is exponential with copying rate $k\mu$.

(5) **The file lost process:** Once a data center fails, then all its files and useful information in the data center will be lost immediately.

We assume that all the random variables involved in the data center network are independent of each other.

3   An Approximate Assessment Method of File Lifetime

In this section, we first set up a birth-death process to study the steady state probability distribution of the number of available data centers in the data center network. Then we establish another birth-death process to give an approximate assessment method of file lifetime in the data center network with file d-replication policy.

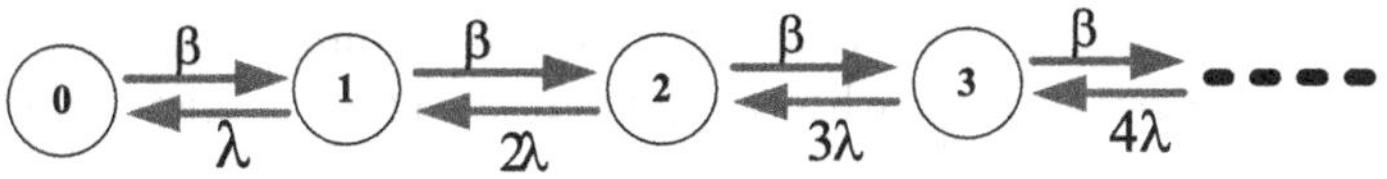

Fig. 1. State transition relation of a birth-death process

3.1   The Number of Available Data Centers

In this data center network, each data center may fail, and its lifetime of staying in the network follows an exponential distribution with failure rate λ. On the other hand, new data centers continuously join to the data center network, and their inputs are a Poisson process with arrival rate β.

Let $N(t)$ be the number of available data centers normally operating in the data center network at time t. Then $\{N(t) : t \geq 0\}$ is a birth-death process on state space $\Omega = \{0, 1, 2, ...\}$ whose state transition relation is shown in Fig. 1.

From Fig. 1, the infinitesimal generator of the birth-death process $\{N(t) : t \geq 0\}$ is given by

$$Q = \begin{pmatrix} -\beta & \beta & & \\ \lambda & -(\lambda + \beta) & \beta & \\ & 2\lambda & -(2\lambda + \beta) & \beta \\ & & \ddots & \ddots & \ddots \end{pmatrix}.$$

Since the two numbers λ and β are fixed, there must exist a positive integer $n_0 > \lfloor \beta/\lambda \rfloor + 1$ such that when $n > n_0$, we have $\lambda n > \beta$, where $\lfloor x \rfloor$ is the maximal integer part of the real number x. Thus, by using the mean-drift condition, it is easy to see that the birth-death process $\{N(t) : t \geq 0\}$ is irreducible, aperiodic and positive recurrent.

Let

$$\mathbf{N} = \lim_{t \to +\infty} N(t),$$

$$\theta_k = P\{\mathbf{N} = k\}, \quad k = 0, 1, 2, \ldots,$$

$$\theta = (\theta_0, \theta_1, \theta_2, \theta_3, \ldots).$$

Then it is clear that $\theta Q = 0, \theta e = 1$, where e is a column vector with each element one.

Theorem 1. *In this data center network, the steady state number $\mathbf{N}$ of available data centers operating normally follows a Poisson distribution with parameter β/λ, that is*

$$\theta_k = \exp\left\{-\frac{\beta}{\lambda}\right\} \frac{1}{k!} \left(\frac{\beta}{\lambda}\right)^k, \quad k = 0, 1, 2, \ldots.$$

Proof. By solving the linear equations $\theta Q = 0, \theta e = 1$, we get

$$\theta_k = \exp\left\{-\frac{\beta}{\lambda}\right\} \frac{1}{k!} \left(\frac{\beta}{\lambda}\right)^k, \quad k = 0, 1, 2, \ldots.$$

Thus the steady state number $\mathbf{N}$ of available data centers operating normally follows a Poisson distribution with parameter β/λ. This completes the proof. $\square$

It is seen from Theorem 1 that the Poisson random variable $\mathbf{N}$ provides useful information to understand the file d-replication policy. For example, the probability that no file can be successfully duplicated to a data center is given by $P\{\mathbf{N} = 0\} = \exp\{-\beta/\lambda\}$.

3.2　An Approximate Assessment for File Lifetime

In this subsection, we first correct the copying rate of the files to the data center network by means of the steady state (Poisson) probability θ_k for $k \geq 0$. Then we establish a new finite-state birth-death process to provide an approximate assessment for the file lifetime.

By using Theorem 1 and

$$\theta_k = \exp\left\{-\frac{\beta}{\lambda}\right\} \frac{1}{k!} \left(\frac{\beta}{\lambda}\right)^k, \quad k = 0, 1, 2, \ldots,$$

thus we can correct the copying rate of the files to the data centers as follows:

(a) If there is only one copy of a file in the data center network, then the file has the copying rate to another data center, given by

$$\mu_1 = \mu \sum_{j=2}^{\infty} \theta_j = \mu \sum_{j=2}^{\infty} \exp\left\{-\frac{\beta}{\lambda}\right\} \frac{1}{j!} \left(\frac{\beta}{\lambda}\right)^j.$$

That is, the copy time of this file follows an exponential distribution with copying rate μ_1.

(b) If there are k identical copies of a file (i.e., a file has been duplicated to k different data centers) in the data center network for $2 \leq k \leq d-1$, then the k identical files have the copying rate to another data center, given by

$$\mu_k = k\mu \sum_{j=k+1}^{\infty} \theta_j = k\mu \sum_{j=k+1}^{\infty} \exp\left\{-\frac{\beta}{\lambda}\right\} \frac{1}{j!} \left(\frac{\beta}{\lambda}\right)^j.$$

That is, the copy time of the k identical files to the other data center follows an exponential distribution with copying rate μ_k.

In the data center network, we denote by $M(t)$ the number of identical copies of one file at time t, then $\{M(t) : t \geq 0\}$ is a birth-death process on a finite state space $\mathbf{E} = \{0, 1, 2, \ldots, d-1, d\}$ whose state transition relation is depcited in Fig. 2.

Let

$$\eta = \inf\{t \geq 0 : M(t) = 0\},$$

Then η is the lifetime of a file which stays in the data center network. Of course, it is also the first lost time of the file which will possibly disappear in the data center network.

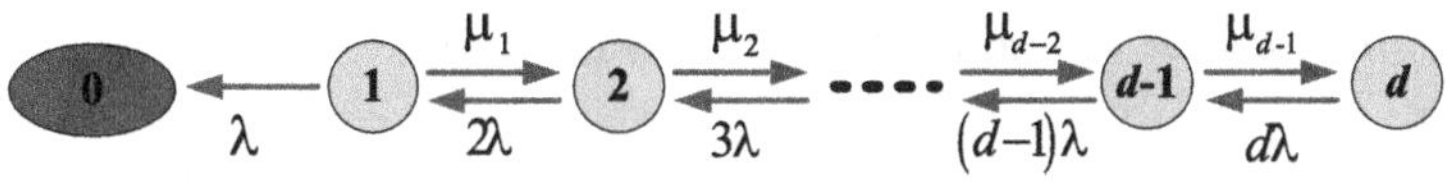

Fig. 2. State transition relation of a file replicated process

We write

$$S = \begin{pmatrix} -(\lambda + \mu_1) & \mu_1 & & & \\ 2\lambda & -(2\lambda + \mu_2) & \mu_2 & & \\ & \ddots & \ddots & \ddots & \\ & & (d-1)\lambda & -((d-1)\lambda + \mu_d) & \mu_d \\ & & & d\lambda & -d\lambda \end{pmatrix}, \quad S^0 = \begin{pmatrix} \lambda \\ 0 \\ \vdots \\ 0 \\ 0 \end{pmatrix}.$$

Also, we take the initial probability $(\widetilde{\gamma}, \gamma_0)$, where $\widetilde{\gamma} = (\gamma_1, \gamma_2, \ldots, \gamma_d)$, $\gamma_0 \in [0,1]$, and $\widetilde{\gamma}e = 1 - \gamma_0$.

Theorem 2. *In this data center network, the lifetime η of a file follows a PH distribution of size d with an irreducibility representation $(\widetilde{\gamma}, S)$. Also, the Markov process $(S + S^0\widetilde{\gamma})$ is irreducible. Further, the kth moment of the lifetime η of the file is given by*

$$E\left[\eta^k\right] = (-1)^k \, k! \widetilde{\gamma} S^{-k} e, \quad k = 1, 2, 3, \ldots.$$

Proof. It is easy to check that the infinitesimal generator of the birth-death process $\{M(t) : t \geq 0\}$ on state space $\mathbf{E} = \{0, 1, 2, \ldots, d-1, d\}$ is given by

$$\mathbf{Q} = \begin{pmatrix} S & S^0 \\ 0 & 0 \end{pmatrix}.$$

Obviously, the lifetime η of a file follows a PH distribution of size d with an irreducibility representation $(\widetilde{\gamma}, S)$. Also, the Markov process $(S + S^0\widetilde{\gamma})$ is irreducible. In addition, some simple computation can lead to the kth moment of the lifetime η. This completes the proof. □

Note that the matrix S is the infinitesimal generator of a birth-death process, thus we can give expression for the inverse of matrix S. To this end, we write

$$S^{-1} = \begin{pmatrix} s_{1,1} & s_{1,2} & \cdots & s_{1,d-1} & s_{1,d} \\ s_{2,1} & s_{2,2} & \cdots & s_{2,d-1} & s_{2,d} \\ \vdots & \vdots & & \vdots & \vdots \\ s_{d-1,1} & s_{d-1,2} & \cdots & s_{d-1,d-1} & s_{d-1,d} \\ s_{d,1} & s_{d,2} & \cdots & s_{d,d-1} & s_{d,d} \end{pmatrix},$$

It is easy to check from $SS^{-1} = I$ that the first column of S^{-1} is given by

$$s_{j,1} = -\frac{1}{\lambda}, \quad 1 \leq j \leq d,$$

and for $2 \leq k \leq d$, the kth column of S^{-1} is given by

$$s_{1,k} = -\frac{\prod\limits_{j=1}^{k-1} \mu_j}{k!\lambda^k}, s_{2,k} = -\frac{(\lambda + \mu_1)\prod\limits_{j=2}^{k-1} \mu_j}{k!\lambda^k}, s_{3,k} = -\frac{2!\lambda^2 + (\lambda + \mu_1)\prod\limits_{j=3}^{k-1} \mu_j}{k!\lambda^k},$$

$$\cdots, s_{k-1,k} = -\frac{\left[(k-2)!\lambda^{k-2} + (k-3)!\lambda^{k-3}\mu_{k-2} + \cdots + \lambda\prod\limits_{j=2}^{k-2} \mu_j + \prod\limits_{j=1}^{k-2} \mu_j\right]\mu_{k-1}}{k!\lambda^k},$$

and for $k \leq j \leq d$,

$$s_{j,k} = -\frac{(k-1)!\lambda^{k-1} + (k-2)!\lambda^{k-2}\mu_{k-1} + \cdots + \lambda\prod\limits_{j=2}^{k-1} \mu_j + \prod\limits_{j=1}^{k-1} \mu_j}{k!\lambda^k}.$$

Thus we obtain

$$E[\eta] = -\sum_{j=1}^{d}\sum_{i=1}^{d} \gamma_i s_{i,j}.$$

4   A Two-Dimensional Assessment of File Lifetime

In this section, we establish a two-dimensional Markov process by means of the number of available data centers and the number of identical copies of one file. Based on this, we propose a two-dimensional assessment method for the file lifetime of the data center network.

In the data center network, as seen above, let $N(t)$ and $M(t)$ be the numbers of available data centers and of identical copies of one file at time t, respectively. Obviously, $N(t) \in \{0, 1, 2, \ldots\}$ and $M(t) \in \{0, 1, 2, \ldots, d\}$. It is seen from the exponential and Poisson assumptions that $\{N(t), M(t) : t \geq 0\}$ is a two-dimensional Markov process, and further a QBD process, whose state transition relation is depicted in Fig. 3.

It is seen from Fig. 3 that the state space of the QBD process $\{N(t), M(t) : t \geq 0\}$ is expressed as

$$\Theta = \Delta \cup \Theta_1 \cup \Theta_2 \cup \Theta_3 \cup \cdots = \Delta \cup \left(\bigcup_{k=1}^{\infty} \Theta_k\right),$$

where $\Delta = \{(k, 0) : k = 0, 1, 2 \ldots\}$ is a set of all the absorption states, which are written as an absorbing state Δ^*. Observing the columns in Fig. 3, we write

Level $k \in \{1, 2, 3, \ldots, d-1\}$: $\Theta_k = \{(k, 1), (k, 2), \ldots, (k, k)\}$;
Level $l \in \{d, d+1, d+2, \ldots\}$: $\Theta_l = \{(l, 1), (l, 2), \ldots, (l, d)\}$.

From these levels, the infinitesimal generator of the QBD process $\{N(t), M(t) : t \geq 0\}$ on sub-state space $\bigcup_{k=1}^{\infty} \Theta_k$ is given by

$$T = \begin{pmatrix} A_{1,1} & A_{1,2} & & \\ A_{2,1} & A_{2,2} & A_{2,3} & \\ & A_{3,2} & A_{3,3} & A_{3,4} \\ & & \ddots & \ddots & \ddots \end{pmatrix}$$

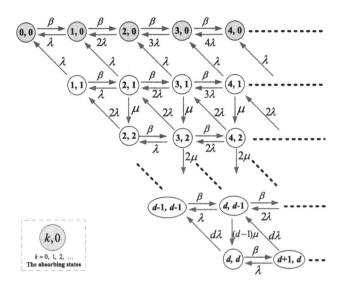

Fig. 3. State transition relation of a QBD process

where $\zeta_j(k) = k\lambda + \beta + j\mu$, and

$$A_{1,1} = -(\lambda + \beta), \quad A_{1,2} = (\beta, 0);$$

for $2 \le k \le d$,

$$A_{k,k-1} = \begin{pmatrix} (k-1)\lambda & & & & & \\ 2\lambda & (k-2)\lambda & & & & \\ & 3\lambda & (k-3)\lambda & & & \\ & & & \ddots & \ddots & \\ & & & & (k-1)\lambda & \lambda \\ & & & & 0 & k\lambda \end{pmatrix},$$

$$A_{k,k} = \begin{pmatrix} -\zeta_1(k) & \mu & & & \\ & -\zeta_2(k) & 2\mu & & \\ & & \ddots & \ddots & \\ & & & -\zeta_{k-1}(k) & (k-1)\mu \\ & & & & -\zeta_0(k) \end{pmatrix}, \quad A_{k,k+1} = \begin{pmatrix} \beta & & & & \\ & \beta & & & \\ & & \beta & & \\ & & & \beta & \\ & & & & \beta & 0 \end{pmatrix};$$

and for $l \ge d+1$,

$$A_{l,l-1} = \begin{pmatrix} (l-1)\lambda & & & & \\ 2\lambda & (l-2)\lambda & & & \\ & 3\lambda & (l-3)\lambda & & \\ & & & \ddots & \ddots & \\ & & & & (d-1)\lambda & (l-d+1)\lambda \\ & & & & d\lambda & (l-d)\lambda \end{pmatrix},$$

$$
A_{l,l} = \begin{pmatrix} -\zeta_1\,(l) & \mu & & & \\ & -\zeta_2\,(l) & 2\mu & & \\ & & \ddots & \ddots & \\ & & & -\zeta_{d-1}\,(l) & (d-1)\,\mu \\ & & & & -\zeta_0\,(l) \end{pmatrix}, \quad A_{l,l+1} = \begin{pmatrix} \beta & & & & \\ & \beta & & & \\ & & \beta & & \\ & & & \beta & \\ & & & & \beta & 0 \end{pmatrix}.
$$

Further, the infinitesimal generator of the QBD process $\{N(t), M(t) : t \geq 0\}$ on a modified state space $\mathbf{\Delta}^* \cup (\bigcup_{k=1}^{\infty} \Theta_k)$ is given by

$$
\mathbf{Q} = \begin{pmatrix} T & T^0 \\ 0 & 0 \end{pmatrix},
$$

where

$$
T^0 = -Te = (\lambda; \lambda, 0; \lambda, 0, 0; \lambda, 0, 0, 0; \lambda, 0, 0, 0, 0; \ldots)^T,
$$

and a^T represents the transpose of the row vector a.

Let

$$
\chi = \inf \{t \geq 0 : M\,(t) = 0, N\,(t) \in \{0, 1, 2, \ldots\}\},
$$

Then the random variable χ is the first passage time that the QBD process $\{N(t), M(t) : t \geq 0\}$ reaches the absorption state $\mathbf{\Delta}^*$ for the first time. That is, the random variable χ is the lifetime of a file of staying in data center network.

To use the PH distribution, we take an initial probability vector $\alpha = (\alpha_{\mathbf{\Delta}^*}, \alpha_1, \alpha_2, \alpha_3, \ldots)$, and $\alpha_{\mathbf{\Delta}^*} \in [0, 1]$. For $1 \leq k \leq d$,

$$
\alpha_k = (\alpha_{k,1}, \alpha_{k,2}, \cdots, \alpha_{k,k-1}, \alpha_{k,k}),
$$

and for $l \geq d + 1$,

$$
\alpha_l = (\alpha_{l,1}, \alpha_{l,2}, \cdots, \alpha_{l,d-1}, \alpha_{l,d}).
$$

Theorem 3. *In this data center network, the first passage time χ is an infinite-dimensional PH distribution with an irreducible representation $(\widetilde{\alpha}, T)$, where $\widetilde{\alpha} = (\alpha_1, \alpha_2, \alpha_3, \cdots)$, $\widetilde{\alpha}e = 1 - \alpha_{\mathbf{\Delta}^*}$. Also, the Markov Process $T + T^0\widetilde{\alpha}$ is irreducible. Further, the kth moment of the first passage time χ is given by*

$$
E\left[\chi^k\right] = (-1)^k\, k!\widetilde{\alpha}T^{-k}e, \quad k = 1, 2, 3, \ldots.
$$

Proof. Corresponding to the modified state space $\mathbf{\Delta}^* \cup (\bigcup_{k=1}^{\infty} \Theta_k)$, the infinitesimal generator of the QBD process $\{N(t), M(t) : t \geq 0\}$ is given by $\mathbf{Q}$. Thus it is clear that the first passage time χ is an infinite-dimensional PH distribution with an irreducible representation $(\widetilde{\alpha}, T)$. Also, the Markov Process $T + T^0\widetilde{\alpha}$ is irreducible, and the kth moment of the first passage time χ is also obtained. This completes the proof. □

It is necessary to show that the RG-factorizations by Li [8] can be applied to effectively deal with the infinite-dimensional PH distribution. Now, we calculate the mean $E[\chi]$. To this end, we first need to derive the inverse matrix of the matrix T by using the RG-factorizations.

we define the $U-$measure as

$$\mathbf{U}_0 = A_{1,1},$$

and for $k = 1, 2, 3, \ldots,$

$$\mathbf{U}_k = A_{k+1,k+1} + A_{k+1,k}(-\mathbf{U}_{k-1})^{-1}A_{k,k+1}.$$

We respectively define the $R-$ and $G-$measures as

$$\mathbf{R}_k = A_{k+1,k}(-\mathbf{U}_{k-1})^{-1}, \ k = 1, 2, 3, \ldots;$$

$$\mathbf{G}_l = (-\mathbf{U}_l)^{-1}A_{l+1,l+2}, \ l = 0, 1, 2, \ldots.$$

By using Sect. 2.7 of Li and Cao [9], the RG-factorization of matrix T is given by

$$T = (I - \mathbf{R}_L)\,\mathbf{U}_D\,(I - \mathbf{G}_U),$$

where

$$\mathbf{U}_D = \mathrm{diag}(\mathbf{U}_0, \mathbf{U}_1, \mathbf{U}_2, \ldots),$$

$$\mathbf{R}_L = \begin{pmatrix} 0 & & & \\ \mathbf{R}_1 & 0 & & \\ & \mathbf{R}_2 & 0 & \\ & & \mathbf{R}_3 & 0 \\ & & & \ddots & \ddots \end{pmatrix}, \quad \mathbf{G}_U = \begin{pmatrix} 0 & \mathbf{G}_0 & & \\ & 0 & \mathbf{G}_1 & \\ & & 0 & \mathbf{G}_2 \\ & & & 0 & \ddots \\ & & & & \ddots \end{pmatrix}.$$

By means of Appendix A.3 of Li and Cao [9], we have obtain

$$T^{-1} = (I - \mathbf{G}_L)^{-1}\,\mathbf{U}_D^{-1}\,(I - \mathbf{R}_L)^{-1}.$$

Let

$$X_k^{(l)} = \mathbf{R}_l\mathbf{R}_{l-1}\cdots\mathbf{R}_{l-k+1}, \quad 1 \le k \le l,$$

$$Y_k^{(l)} = \mathbf{G}_l\mathbf{G}_{l+1}\cdots\mathbf{R}_{l+k-1}, \quad 0 \le l \le k.$$

Then

$$\mathbf{U}_D^{-1} = \mathrm{diag}(\mathbf{U}_0^{-1}, \mathbf{U}_1^{-1}, \mathbf{U}_2^{-1}, \ldots),$$

and

$$(I - \mathbf{G}_L)^{-1} = \begin{pmatrix} I & Y_1^{(0)} & Y_2^{(0)} & Y_3^{(0)} & \cdots \\ & I & Y_1^{(1)} & Y_2^{(1)} & \cdots \\ & & I & Y_1^{(2)} & \cdots \\ & & & I & \cdots \\ & & & & \ddots \end{pmatrix}, \quad (I - \mathbf{R}_L)^{-1} = \begin{pmatrix} I & & & & \\ X_1^{(1)} & I & & & \\ X_2^{(2)} & X_1^{(2)} & I & & \\ X_3^{(3)} & X_2^{(3)} & X_1^{(3)} & I & \\ \vdots & \vdots & \vdots & \vdots & \ddots \end{pmatrix}.$$

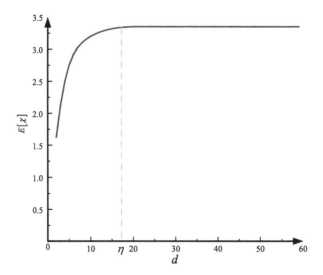

Fig. 4. The file lifetime depends on the key parameter d

Let

$$T^{-1} = (I - \mathbf{G}_L)^{-1} \mathbf{U}_D^{-1} (I - \mathbf{R}_L)^{-1} = \begin{pmatrix} T_{0,0} & T_{0,1} & T_{0,2} & \cdots \\ T_{1,0} & T_{11} & T_{1,2} & \cdots \\ T_{2,0} & T_{2,1} & T_{2,2} & \cdots \\ \vdots & \vdots & \vdots & \ddots \end{pmatrix}.$$

Then the mean of the first passage time χ is given by

$$E[\chi] = -\sum_{j=0}^{\infty} \sum_{i=0}^{\infty} \alpha_{i+1} T_{i,j} e.$$

Finally, we use a simple example to illustrate how the file lifetime χ depends on the maximum number of identical backups: $d \in (2, 59)$. Let $\lambda = 1$ and $\beta = 4$. As seen from Fig. 4, the mean $E[\chi]$ increases, as d increases. In addition, when d increases to a certain value, the mean $E[\chi]$ will no longer change significantly. Such a phenomenon will be very useful in design and optimization of the data center network with file replication mechanism.

References

1. Aghajani, R., Robert, P., Sun, W.: A large scale analysis of unreliable stochastic networks. Ann. Appl. Prob. **28**(2), 851–887 (2018)
2. Blake, C., Rodrigues, R.: High availability, scalable storage, dynamic peer networks: pick two. In: The 9th Workshop on Hot Topics in Operating Systems, vol. 3, pp. 18–21 (2003)

3. Chun, B.G., et al.: Efficient replica maintenance for distributed storage systems. In: The 3rd Symposium on Networked Systems Design & Implementation, vol. 6, pp. 45–58 (2006)
4. Feuillet, M., Robert, P.: A scaling analysis of a transient stochastic network. Adv. Appl. Probab. **46**(2), 516–535 (2014)
5. Kersch, P., Szabo, R.: Mathematical modeling of routing in DHTs. In: Shen, X., Yu, H., Buford, J., Akon, M. (eds.) Handbook of Peer-to-Peer Networking. Springer, Boston (2010). https://doi.org/10.1007/978-0-387-09751-0_14
6. Kniesburges, S., Koutsopoulos, A., Scheideler, C.: CONE-DHT: a distributed self-stabilizing algorithm for a heterogeneous storage system. In: Afek, Y. (ed.) DISC 2013. LNCS, vol. 8205, pp. 537–549. Springer, Heidelberg (2013). https://doi.org/10.1007/978-3-642-41527-2_37
7. Lian, Q., Chen, W., Zhang, Z.: On the impact of replica placement to the reliability of distributed brick storage systems. In: The 25th IEEE International Conference on Distributed Computing Systems, pp. 187–196. IEEE (2005)
8. Li, Q.L.: Constructive Computation in Stochastic Models with Applications: The RG-Factorizations. Springer, Berlin (2010). https://doi.org/10.1007/978-3-642-11492-2
9. Li, Q.L., Cao, J.: Two types of RG-factorizations of quasi-birth-and-death processes and their applications to stochastic integral functionals. Stoch. Models **20**(3), 299–340 (2004)
10. Pace, A., Quema, V., Schiavoni, V.: Exploiting node connection regularity for DHT replication. In: The 30th IEEE Symposium on Reliable Distributed Systems, pp. 111–120. IEEE (2011)
11. Picconi, F., Baynat, B., Sens, P.: An analytical estimation of durability in DHTs. In: Janowski, T., Mohanty, H. (eds.) ICDCIT 2007. LNCS, vol. 4882, pp. 184–196. Springer, Heidelberg (2007). https://doi.org/10.1007/978-3-540-77115-9_19
12. Picconi, F., Baynat, B., Sens, P.: Predicting durability in DHTs using Markov chains. In: The 2nd International Conference on Digital Information Management, vol. 2, pp. 532–538. IEEE (2007)
13. Pinheiro, E., Weber, W.D., Barroso, L.A.: Failure trends in a large disk drive population. In: The 5th USENIX Conference on File and Storage Technologies, vol. 7, No. 1, pp. 17–23 (2007)
14. Ramabhadran, S., Pasquale, J.: Analysis of long-running replicated systems. In: INFOCOM 2006, pp. 1–9 (2006)
15. Ramabhadran, S., Pasquale, J.: Durability of replicated distributed storage systems. ACM SIGMETRICS Perform. Eval. Rev. **36**(1), 447–448 (2008)
16. Ramabhadran, S., Pasquale, J.: Analysis of durability in replicated distributed storage systems. In: IEEE International Symposium on Parallel & Distributed Processing, pp. 1–12. IEEE (2010)
17. Sun, W., Feuillet, M., Robert, P.: Analysis of large unreliable stochastic networks. Ann. Appl. Probab. **26**(5), 2959–3000 (2016)
18. Utard, G., Vernois, A.: Data durability in peer to peer storage systems. In: IEEE International Symposium on CLUSTER Computing and the Grid, pp. 90–97. IEEE (2004)

The Design of Real Time Recording System for Electric Spark Source Parameters Based on the Internet of Things

Mingzhang Luo[1,2], Hao Zhang[1], Qiang Liu[3(✉)], Yang Xu[1], Chong Luo[4], and Zhongyuan Wang[1]

[1] National Demonstration Center for Experimental Electrical and Electronic Education, Yangtze University, Jingzhou 434023, China
lmz@yangtzeu.edu.cn
[2] Electronics and Information School, Yangtze University, Jingzhou 434023, China
[3] State Key Laboratory for Performance and Structural Safety of Petroleum Tubular Goods and Equipment Materials, CNPC Tubular Goods Research Institute, Xi'an 710077, Shanxi, China
liuqiang030@cnpc.com.cn
[4] Management School, Yangtze University, Jingzhou 434023, China

Abstract. The electric spark source is widely used in the fields of shallow surface exploration and earthquake prediction because of its environmental protection, rich spectrum and good consistency. However, most electric spark source is short of real time recording and control system for power parameters, so that its failure rate is quite high. This paper introduces a real-time power parameter recording system of electric spark source. It has the advantages of failure detection, fast fault location, and network extension. It can realize the remote control and monitoring, and has a strong popularization value.

Keywords: Electric spark source · Power parameter recording
Internet of things

1 Introduction

The electric spark source is a manual controlled seismic source with the advantage of greens environmental protection, which is mainly used in the field of shallow surface geophysical exploration, such as petroleum exploration and civil engineering exploration. In the past few years, the electric spark source has been gradually replacing the explosive source which is extremely dangerous. It is need to ensure the safety of transporting and storing the explosive source, and requires professional blasting personnel when it is used. The cost of supervision and operation is

This work was supported by the China National Petroleum Corporation essential research and strategic reserve technology research fund project (grant No. 2017Z-05).

very high. In addition, the regional limits of explosives are relatively higher, and the excitation effect is difficult to control, so that the parameters of each excitation wave are slightly different, including the energy, time delay and the frequency of seismic impulses. However, the electric spark source has the advantages of controllable excitation energy, good consistency of excitation, accurate delay time and no geographical limitation. The electric spark source was first developed by the western countries. In 1957, the Alps geophysics company developed the world's first electric spark source system [1]; In the early 60s, the United States began to develop land and marine sparks. In 1966, Miller got the patent of the land electric spark source, and Wayna et al achieved the patent of marine electric spark source. In 1973, Barbier reported a coded electrical spark source for marine exploration. The domestic electric spark source started a little late. In 80s and 90s, the Institute of Electrical Engineering, Chinese Academy of Sciences, and the Geophysical Exploration Department of Dagang Oilfield, China National Petroleum Corporation, successfully developed the vehicle electric spark source for land oil and gas exploration. In 2004, the first Institute of Oceanography of the National Oceanic Administration successfully designed a kind of intelligent controlled complex coherent electric spark source device [2].

In 2013, Dai et al. [3] introduced a focused electric spark source used as a non-contact acoustic source to excite stress waves in solids. The source consists of an electric spark source located at the near focus of an ellipsoidal reflector that focuses the acoustic disturbance generated by the spark source to the far focal point. In 2016, Fan et al. [4] introduced a set of single channel electric spark source system, which mainly includes two units of charging and discharging. By using the ORIGIN data analysis software, the variation trends of the plasma channel resistance and the discharge power in the time domain are observed. At the same year, Fan et al. [5] developed a kind of multi-channel electric spark source system, a number of single-channel electric spark sources are assembled in the construction site, using the ARM processor and the host computer to control them assembly, solving the difficult problems that the traditional high energy electric spark source system is difficult to carry out the exploration in mountainous areas; Liu et al. [6] established a pressure sensor based blast wave pressure field measurement system and a schlieren technique based blast wave propagation history measurement to study the characteristics of electric spark induced blast wave. In 2017, Xu et al. [7] presented a non-contact acoustic spark source for NDT applications. The acoustic pressure wave generated by an electric spark is focused by an ellipsoidal reflector from the inner focus of the reflector to the far focus. The focused spark source has high pressure amplitude and broad bandwidth.

Over the past ten years, Geophysical instruments team of Yangtze University developed the CD-2 portable electric spark source successfully, which is easy to carry, stable and the seismic data obtained is quite good. At present, the electric spark source manufacturers are all seeking the stable operation of the electric spark source equipment. The closed loop control of the electric spark source has not yet been reported.

This paper proposed a solution based on power electronic technology and the Internet of things, and realize an electric spark source product with closed-loop remote control. Using frequency conversion technology, the high-voltage DC energy from 220 V or 380 V AC power supply, has been stored in the high-voltage capacitor group. The voltage value is controlled by the microcontroller through a closed-loop system. When the voltage reaches a certain value or receives the trigger signal from the seismograph, the high-voltage spark switch is turned on, and the electric energy stored in the capacitor is instantaneously discharged in the medium through the cable and the discharge electrode, and produces shock waves. The remote terminal is connected with the underlying system through WiFi system, the data stored in SD card is transmitted to the remote monitoring terminal through the transmission module, and the real-time data display can be realized. The state data of the electric spark source are recorded in real time and uploaded to the cloud, so the engineer can analyze the state of the electric spark source remotely, and make a judgment of possible failure, and decide whether to maintain the equipment. It can further improve the stability and safe operation of the electric spark source equipment, and realize the remote monitoring and control of the electric spark source.

2   Requirement Analysis

2.1   The Basic Principle of the Electric Spark Source

The electric spark source is a seismic wave launcher that uses a discharge electrode to discharge in a liquid and converts the electric energy stored in a high voltage capacitor into a seismic wave. The schematic diagram of the basic principle of the electric spark source is as shown in Fig. 1.

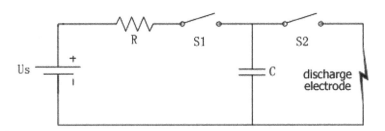

Fig. 1. The schematic diagram of the basic principle of the electric spark source

Us is the source charging system, when switch S1 is closed, and the switch S2 is disconnected, the charging system begin to recharge the capacitor C. After completing recharge, the switch S1 is disconnected and the switch S2 is closed. The capacitance C discharges instantaneously through the discharge electrode to ionize and vaporize the water around the electrode, and the electrical energy is converted into seismic wave energy, accompanied by heat energy and light energy. The CD-2 electric spark source using frequency-inverting and voltage-inverting working mode. By changing the frequency of the inverter to control the output voltage, and then changing the voltage value across the capacitor at both ends, the process of recharge is realized. After completing recharge, the charging switch is cut off, the discharge switch is closed, the power energy is discharge through the transmitter with two electrodes immersed in water, and the energy conversion process is completed.

2.2 Demand Analysis of Real Time Recording of Electric Spark Source Power Parameters

The CD-2 electric spark source adopt frequency-inverting and voltage- inverting working mode to realize the recharging process, and the charge time is about 30 s. The first parameter to be considered in this design is the change of the charge current in the charging process by monitoring the change of the charge current in real time to determine whether the charging process is normal. Once an exception occurs, such as a sudden increasing of charging current, the fuse in the protection circuit will be broken down, the whole system will stop working so as to avoid excessive current burning other modules. During the process of charging the capacitor, the voltage between the two electrodes of the capacitor increases continuously. To prevent overcharging of the capacitor, the voltage should be monitoring. At the same time, the output voltage frequency of the inverter is increasing. In order to dynamically observe the frequency change of the inverter, we need to monitor the working frequency of the converter in real time. All the data can be saved to the local SD card, and it can be transferred to the remote monitoring terminal through the WiFi.

3 System Design

Block diagram of real time recording system for electric spark source parameters is as shown in Fig. 2. The system is composed of voltage/current acquisition module, SD card storage module, inverter working frequency measuring module, energy storage voltage measuring module, WiFi transmission module and remote monitoring terminal. The STM32F407 is the main controller. Since the measured parameters are heavy current and high voltage, in order to ensure the system safety and steady, the industrial measurement module is used [8]. The data of the electric spark source is exchanged with MCU through serial port. The frequency is measured directly through frequency output port reserved on the inverter. The electric spark source output is voltage, which has a linear relationship with the frequency, through A/D converter and related mathematical operations [9], the values of frequency is obtained. The energy storage voltage measuring module is used to measure the voltage between the two electrodes of the capacitor. Due to the limited data storage of MCU, the measured current, voltage and frequency are stored in the SD card, and all data are transmitted to the remote monitoring terminal through WiFi.

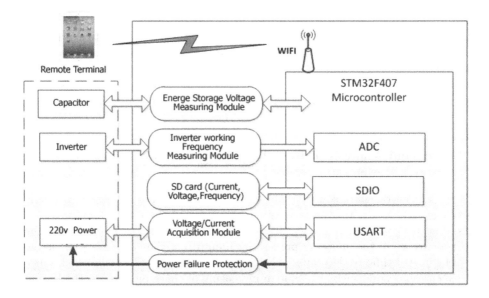

Fig. 2. Block diagram of real time recording system for electric spark source parameters

4   Module Function

4.1   Energy Storage Voltage Measuring Module

The energy storage voltage is the voltage up to 10000 V between the two electrodes of the high energy capacitor. The function of this module is to measure the charge voltage and upload it to the MCU (STM32F407) in real time. The OWON series is used to measure the high voltage, through the resistance divider, the measuring voltage range is between 0–10 V. Considering the safety of measurement, adopt Bluetooth to effectively isolate the high-voltage measuring module and MCU (STM32F407), so as to ensure the safety of high-voltage measurement and data communication.

4.2   Voltage/Current Acquisition Module

In general, the input voltage of the electric spark source is 50 Hz/220 V, it is usually derived from the DC generator or battery-inverter. Its input current is 2–3 A, an industrial voltage/current measuring module is used to monitoring of the output parameters of power. The module is equipped with a serial port, which can be directly connected with MCU. After the hardware connection completed, the MCU sends the command directly, and then the corresponding data can be obtained. There are 6 kinds of module command, so that 6 parameters can be obtained. This design only needs to obtain the voltage and current data.

4.3 Charging Frequency Measuring Module

The frequency signal is provided by the inverter, the control circuit terminal provides a frequency output interface, it output an analog voltage that has a linear relationship with the frequency, the corresponding frequency values can be obtained by AD acquisition and related mathematical operations. Using stm32 MCU internal AD module [10], 12 bit resolution, reference voltage Vref = 3.3 V for AD acquisition. The amplitude of the inverter output voltage is adjustable (0–10 V), default gain is 100%, the corresponding frequency is 0–400 Hz. According to the reference voltage of the AD module, the gain is set to 33%, then the output voltage is 0–3.3 V, so that the AD module can collect frequency range in 0–400 Hz. The relationship between frequency and output voltage is as following,

$$f = 132 * v \tag{1}$$

The impedance of the inverter output terminal is 100 K, the maximum external input impedance of the AD module is 50 K, In order to accurately detect the analog voltage, a voltage follower between the inverter and the AD module. In addition, the voltage follower also plays an impedance matching function, at the same time, the anti-interference ability of the whole system is also increased.

4.4 Data Storage and Transmission Module

Data storage medium is SD card, its working voltage is 2.7−3.6 v, SPI or SD working mode [11], the host can choose any mode to communicate with the SD card. SD mode allows 4 lines of high speed data transmission, SPI mode is slower than the SD mode [12]. The Stm32f407 MCU has the SPI and the SD interface, which can be used in both modes, this design uses the faster SD mode. The transmission module is responsible to transfer the acquired data to the remote monitoring terminal, so that the terminal can display the data in real time, the remote terminals connect with the underlying system through WiFi, realizing the function of data transmission.

5 Test and Adjusting

In order to avoid interference, the whole system is mounted on a metal shield and connected to the existing electric spark source system. The terminal display interface is as shown in Fig. 3.

The left curve indicates the power supply voltage of the electric spark source, the single charge current, the single charge frequency and the change trend of the single charge voltage respectively. In this test, the electric spark source works with 220 V voltage, the charging current reaches about 2 A, the inverter frequency changes in 0–300 Hz, and the charge voltage reaches 5000 v. The above parameter change trend reflects the condition of the normal working of the electric spark source. When the electric spark source appears abnormal, such as out of phase, the charge voltage will increase quickly. It is reflected on the terminal

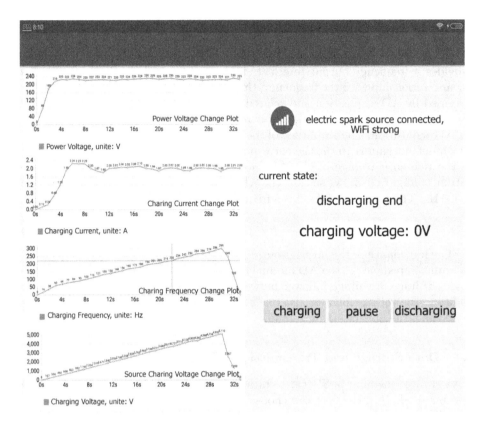

Fig. 3. The terminal display interface

that the slope of the charging voltage curve will be very high, so as to realize the function of fast locating the fault. On the right side, there are the control buttons and the related state of the charge and discharge of the electric spark source. Control buttons include charging, discharging, and pause. The display state include the connection state of the electric spark source and the remote control terminal, the current state of the electric spark source(charging, pause, and the end of discharging), and the real time display of charge voltage.

6   Conclusion

An electric spark source power parameter recording system based on the internet of things is designed for the electric spark source, the real-time monitoring and recording of charging and discharging process of the electric spark source can be carried out. There are 3 innovation points as following.

1. The electric spark source power voltage value is controlled by the microcontroller through a closed-loop system, the charging and discharging process can be precisely controlled.

2. With the idea of internet of things, the traditional electric spark source equipment has the function of interconnecting, and can communicate with the intelligent terminal through the WiFi, the data can be monitored through remote system.
3. The real-time monitoring and recording of the working state of the electric spark source is beneficial to the fault diagnosis of the system and the rapid positioning of the fault. Therefore, the system has great application and promotion value.

References

1. Pei, Y.L., Wang, K.Y., Liu, C.G., Li, X.S., Li, Z.G.: The sparker source charging technique. Ocean Technol. **26**(03), 73–76 (2007)
2. Wu, X.L., Wang, J.M.: Research and Design of High Power Sparker. Yangtze University (2016)
3. Dai, X., Zhu, J., Haberman, M.R.: A focused electric spark source for non-contact stress wave excitation in solids. J. Acoust. Soc. Am. **EL134**(6), 513 (2013)
4. Fan, A.L., Sun, Y.H., Xu, Z., et al.: Single channel electric spark source and discharge experimental study. Advanced Technology of Electrical Engineering & Energy (2016)
5. Fan, A., Sun, Y., Yan, P., et al.: Design on a kind of multi-channel electric spark source system. In: Industrial Electronics and Applications, pp. 2391–2394. IEEE (2016)
6. Xu, X., Sun, Y., Fu, R., et al.: Development of the solid-state modular land electric spark source. High Volt. Appar. **53**(4), 36–40 (2017)
7. Liu, Q., Shao, H., Zhang, Y.: Study on shock waves induced by electric spark discharge. China Science paper (2016)
8. Yang, Z.Y., Xu, Z.L.: The digital measurement and wireless data transmission for power parameter. Electr. Meas. Instrum. **42**(472), 34–37 (2005)
9. Guo, Y., Fu, Z.X.: Frequency measurement of AC sampling and implementation of tracking phase-locked method. Zidonghua Yu Yiqi Yibiao **12**(03), 17–19 (2002)
10. Ye, J.Z., Yin, X.: Development and application of the power load parameter recording and monitoring system. Comput. Eng. **32**(05), 247–248 (2006)
11. Zhang, C., Zhang, C.J., Wu, X.G.: Design and implementation of simple SD card driven method in MCU system. **28**(04), 479–481+499 (2011)
12. Li, S.Q., Dong, H.B., Li, R.S.: Design of SD memory card based on FatFs file system. Meas. Control Technol. **30**(12), 79–80 (2011)

App Tamper Detection and Retrospective Program Research

Wenrong Jiang[✉]

School of Computer and Information, Shanghai Polytechnic University,
Shanghai, China
wrjiang@sspu.edu.cn

Abstract. In recent years, the rapid development of mobile Internet, the arrival of 3G, 4G era, the decline in the cost of production of smart mobile terminals, smart phones in people learning, work and life in the penetration rate is higher and higher. But some of the free open source platform features not only give developers a broader space for development, but also to the user to add a lot of security risks, especially the risk of APP to tamper-based. Based on the research of APP tampering detection and retrospective research, this paper elaborates its research background and significance, and introduces the present situation of mainstream protection technology. Then, it introduces the reliable identification of APP tampering, tampering with APP's retrospective and tampering with APP risk surface Evaluation, probe SDK self-protection technology program design, and the program to test the environment deployment, display functional effects.e sheet.

Keywords: APP tamper detection
Tampering with the retrospective of APP
APP tamper with the reliable knowledge
Tampering with APP's risk assessment

1 Introduction

In recent years, due to the rapid development of mobile Internet, some free open source platform features not only give developers a broader development space, but also add a lot of security risks and application compatibility, user experience, network delay, plug-in security issues And other issues for user.

According to the monitoring of the National Internet Emergency Center, the main risks of mobile applications include: source code decompilation, server-side control, data storage, inadequate protection of the transport layer, data leakage, client injection, and non-trusted input security decisions; The mobile Internet malware samples number by National Internet Emergency Center capture and obtaining through vendor exchange was 2053, 501 in 2016.

Therefore, how to improve the APP in the tamper identification, tamper with the retrospective of APP, tamper with the APP's risk assessment and other aspects of technical improvement is even more urgent.

© Springer Nature Switzerland AG 2018
X. Chen et al. (Eds.): CSoNet 2018, LNCS 11280, pp. 318–329, 2018.
https://doi.org/10.1007/978-3-030-04648-4_27

1.1   Research Significance

In this paper, through the study of APP tamper detection and retrospective program, we can provide security construction ideas for all mobile application security vendors and APP developers, sort out and abandon the disadvantages of existing mobile APP security reinforcement, at the same time, according to the actual business needs of mobile APP industry using the latest development standards and popular technology research, the introduction of probe SDK and APP tamper detection and traceability system, the maximum extent to solve the problem of APP protection process for the entire mobile application security industry Innovation and establish a benchmark, so as to promote the development of APP security technology differentiation.

1.2   Research Status

The current marketplace existing APP tamper detection and retraining programs are proposed by the mobile application security vendors, which are specialized in the reinforcement of the main products manufacturers: love encryption, Na Jia, Bang Bang as the representative, the following manufacturers of tampering detection and retrospective technology for easy analysis.

(1) APP tamper detection status
   In the reinforcement of the manufacturers to strengthen the security at the same time, will be written in the APP to strengthen the protection of the core library files used to identify malicious attacks tampering logic, so as to maximize the reinforcement strength.
   However, the protection logic of the various manufacturers can be malicious attackers through technical means to remove, and online a large number of tools and tutorials against APP reverse, resulting in the overall security reinforcement protection failure.
(2) APP tampering with the status
   In the entire mobile application life cycle, generally divided into "before, after, after" three stages, and APP tampering is often classified as "after" stage, at present, the mobile security vendors or take the more traditional reptile technology on domestic and foreign mainstream application market and developer forum, paste it to crawl mobile APP information, and then the original package, tampering package comparison, and thus locate the tampering application.
   However, for the reptile technology corresponding to the anti-reptile protection means has been the company's business sector attention, The mobile application market in order to maintain the core competitiveness will introduce the corresponding protective measures, resulting in reptile techniques used to trace the possibility of failure of APP. And the existing retrospective program only stay in the APP was tampered with, can not be prevented in advance.

2   Program Formulation

2.1   Overall Technical Framework

The overall APP tamper detection and traceback scheme is implemented through the front-end SDK and the back-end server linkage, where the tamper recognition and traceability module is integrated into the mobile client via the SDK, tampering data collected through the encrypted channel to the back-end server for data analysis and risk assessment.

2.2   Reliable Identification of APP Tampering

After the common behavior analysis of the attacker, the attacker on the purpose of tampering with APP mainly for:

(1) Modify the APP code
   The code in the key to modify the code, the code used to restrict the use of APP code to delete or modify.
(2) Add other code
   In a normal APP to allow the attacker to benefit from the advertising SDK, data acquisition SDK and so on.
(3) Modify/add APP network access
   Dumping its data to an attacker server.

The means by which an attacker could steal an APP would include:

(1) For APK
   (a) Decompile the APK using the APKTOOL tool
   (b) Tampering with the resources, configuration files, and code that are decompiled
   (c) Use the class APKTOOL tool to compile the tampered file
   (d) Re-ssign APK
   (e) Get a tamper with APP
(2) For Classes.dex
   (a) Unzip the Classes.dex file from APK
   (b) Use Baksmali.JAR to decompile the Classes.dex file
   (c) Modify the anti-compiled get. Smi file
   (d) Use Smali.JAR to recompile into the Classes.dex file
   (e) Compile the compiled Classes.dex into APK
   (f) Re-sign APK
   (g) Get a tamper with APP

Based on the above analysis, the attacker on the APP to complete the tamper with the reinstallable after the implementation of the APP must be compiled and re-signed two processes, so the Eclipse tampering reliable identification technology can be based on the recognition of these two technical points to complete.

2.3   Tampering with the Retrospective of APP

Tampering with APP's retrospective means that when the APP was tampered, through the technical means to tamper with the APP running terminal environment, the problem vector APP information, time, geographical location and other data, through the intelligent analysis of the data obtained, the depth of mining and then reverse the use of tampering APP technical means, combined with large data platform in the historical data on the tampering risk factor calculation.

(1) Probe technology
   Probe technology that mobile tampering event monitoring and data collection technology collectively, the development of a mobile APP probe SDK, the SDK can be achieved from the integrity of the verification and signature verification to monitor whether the two aspects of the occurrence of tampering, If the occurrence of tampering on the terminal environment, the occurrence of tampering APP anomaly analysis and other data acquisition and collection, and then get the data encryption sent to the server by the server for data analysis and mining retroperformed APP events.
(2) Big data analysis technology
   For unknown APP tampering attacks can be monitored by the probe, but it is necessary to establish a large data platform, the probe to monitor the data to share, data mining, data modeling and other technical means can be more accurate trace back to the source of the incident and other more specific information.

2.4   Tampering with APP Risk Assessment

(1) The core business code is tampered
   (a) Authority tampering
       Through the code of the core business code to tamper with, in the function of counterfeiting false return value and parameter values to fraud in the implementation of the business code snippet, through the behavior of free experience of paid features, low-level user experience advanced users and other functions.
   (b) Data fraud
       APP's core business module usually produces core business data that associates more core business functions (Eg, location, account information, cell phone information, etc.), to tamper with the APP to forgive the data to deceive the server or subsequent business functions.
(2) Code carrying the virus
   (a) Privacy snooping and stealing
       APP is injected into the malicious code is usually a secret collection code, parasitic in an APP, through the APP is installed to the phone to collect mobile phone users' privacy information and snooping.

(b) Malicious promotion

Parasitic to the APP in the malicious code will be malicious to promote pop-up ads, download extra APP and install to lead to cell phone carton, traffic waste, poor use and other issues.

(3) Risk data assessment

Tampering with APP's risk assessment is subsequent risk factor rating carried by Tampering with the APP event, this requirement is based on the information in the retrospective solution of the APP to obtain the detailed information of the event of tampering with the APP risk, and then the secondary data mining and the data combination of the data acquired by the large data platform, thus converting the risk coefficient level.

2.5   Probe SDK Self-protection

The probe SDK is used as a third-party APP to use tamper event monitoring and data acquisition plug-ins because third-party APP is unknown, and it is important to ensure that all aspects of the SDK are stable and functioning properly. The complex mobile APP domain SDKs face the risk points that include the following:

(a) SDK is spread and exploited maliciously

SDK as a third party APP used by the plug-in, if not with the application of binding verification, then there will be malicious spread and malicious use of the risk.

b) Core code leaked

SDK positioning in a mobile end APP common and core business module, to achieve the core business module code is very important, if the code is not reinforced or confused then the core code will be exposed risk.

(1) SDK and APP validation technology

Mobile APP as a file that the existence of MD5 value of the file, in the formal translation of the APP in the case of not being tampered with its MD5 will not be replaced, So the probe SDK and APP verification technology includes the specified APP file MD5 check; And each formal APP has its own signature file, by binding in the probe SDK target APP signature information in the normal operation of the SDK to verify the caller APP signature information, verify the success of the normal use.

(2) Code Enclosure Technology

Mobile APP Android SDK code files include JAR files, SO files, which interact with the APK interface is the most important JAR file. JAR file is written in JAVA code compiled by other JAVA / Android program reference file, the file if not protected by the jd-gui tool to view the code and decompile and so on.

JAR code shell technology is to JAR as the goal, the JAR core code fragments in the extraction, reinforcement, dump, to be run when the program self-decryption.

(3) Code confusing technology

Mobile APP Android SDK business core functions commonly used C/C++ prepared to the SO file format provided to the JAR call, mobile APP iOS SDK code using C/C++/OC code to write, this type of language is high threshold of attack, but because it is the preparation of the core business module, so there are targeted attacks attack the object, So the code to move the APP need to be code-obfuscated, through the code confused to achieve the program code basic block division, the program code control flow introduction, the program code jump instruction introduction, program code control flow flat, program code string encryption, Equivalent conversion, program export function confusion to protect the SDK code security.

3   Experimental Research

3.1   Research and Development

In order to verify the feasibility of the program, based on C/C++ developed a "APP tamper detection and traceability system", the platform contains the probe SDK (support Andrews and iOS platform), in the APP tamper detection and traceability based on the platform after the integration of the corresponding SDK can be effective tamper detection and traceability (Tables 1, 2, 3, 4).

3.2   Program Deployment

Environmental Preparation.

(1) Server-side hardware preparation

Table 1. Server hardware resource preparation

Usage	Platform	Processor	Memory	Disk
Control center	VMware	4 Core	2 G	300 G
Database	VMware	8 Core	16 G	500 G

(2) Server-side software preparation

Table 2. Server-side software preparation

Usage	Operating system	Required application
Control center	CentOS 7.1	APP tampering detection and routing system
Database	CentOS 7.1	Microsoft SQL 2008 R2

(3) Test APP preparation
(4) Test model preparation
(5) Tampering tool preparation

Table 3. Test APP list

Name	Required application
Testing DEMO	Android and Apple APP
Probe APP	APP tampering detection and routing

Table 4. Test machine list

Name	Required application
Testing DEMO	Android APP

Install the Configuration. Note: The following provides only the key step information, the other is not listed in the installation and configuration information are subject to default (Fig. 1 and Table 5).

(1) Database server
  – Using Microsoft SQL Server 2008 R2 installation media, select "New installation or add functionality to existing installation"
  – Select all features
  – Set the sa password
  – Verify that the installation results are successful
  – After installation, use the sa account to log in to the management control center, create a new TEST instance for the APP tamper detection and trace system configuration and information storage
(2) Control center
  (a) Fixed Control Center server IP address (S.S.S.S) and computer name
  (b) Double-click "APP Tamper Detection and Traceability System" to install

Table 5. Tamper tools list

Name	Usage
GdbServer	Testing Tool
IDA	Static decompiling Software
Zjdorid	Dynamic reverse analysis models based on Xposed framework
Substrate	HOOK tool
Interface hijacking tool	Testing interface hijacking

Use environment and equipment

Terminal environment	Device Information	Geographic location	SIM/Network		
Operator				Connection channel	wifi
Cellphone number				Country	CN
Voice	zh			IP	15.152.16.172
Wifi BSSID	08:62:66:84:72:7E			Wifi signal strength	4
Wifi status	3				

Fig. 1. APP tamper detection and traceability control center

Fig. 2. Probe SDK download

(c) During the installation process, configure the database address and instance name, SA password for database link

(d) After installation, open IE visit: http://.S.S.S//users/exit.do, enter the user name and password, you can access the platform (as shown in Fig. 6)

(3) Probe SDK integration

    (a) Download the probe SDK via the platform (as shown in Fig. 2)

    (b) Complete the APP integration according to the SDK integration manual

    (c) After the integration of the normal signature can be installed to test the phone

3.3 Show Results

(1) Reliable identification of APP tampering

After testing the APP into the probe SDK, the overall APP is operational at the time of integrity, signature verification, any tampering on the protection of APP, in the APP run-time will be effectively detected, after the protection of APP after tampering directly flashed.

(2) Tampering with the retrospective of APP

Test DEMO APP to test all data back to the control center via the probe SDK by simulating tamper attacks on the test model. Test DEMO by 55 tamper attacks (as shown in Fig. 3), click on the specific "SUBSTRATE plug-in perception" (as shown in Fig. 4) view details.

Basic Data

Equipment Quantity	Environmental risk equipment	Cumulative perceptual
26	24	55

Environmental risk

24	1	1
Among my users	Among my users	Among my users
Number of ROOT devices	Number of simulator devices	Number of malicious program devices

Fig. 3. Tampering with APP retrospective data display

Use environment and equipment

Terminal environment	Device Information	Geographic location	SIM/Network		
Simulator operation	Yes			ROOT\Jailbreak	Yes
Signature kernel state	Unbroken			Device information tampering	No
Virus information	0 Show∧			LIBC kernel destruction	No

Fig. 4. Overview of tamper attack behavior

System version	All versions					
Application version	All versions					
Attack type	All	Interface hijacking	Ida debugging	Gdbserver debugging	Hijack injection	Inject injection
	Xposed plugin /zjdorid	Substrate plugin	Other injection			

Attack type

Application equipment	Device system version	Application version	Attack time	Operating
Substrate plugin	S55t	4.42	0.0.8	

Fig. 5. Tampering with APP terminal environment information

Use environment and equipment

Terminal environment	Device Information	Geographic location	SIM/Network		
Vendor	Sony			Device ID	354192061823552
Model	S55t			Operating system	Android
System version	4.4.2			IMEI	354192061823552
				MAC	30:75:12:ae:7b:f9
CPU Architecture	armeabi-v7a			Resolution	1280*720
Device local time	2017-05-23 15:00:33				

Fig. 6. Tampering with APP device information

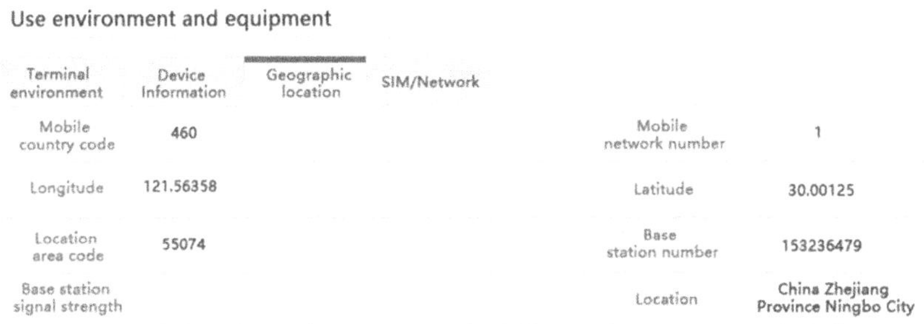

Use environment and equipment

Terminal environment	Device Information	Geographic location	SIM/Network		
Mobile country code	460			Mobile network number	1
Longitude	121.56358			Latitude	30.00125
Location area code	55074			Base station number	153236479
Base station signal strength				Location	China Zhejiang Province Ningbo City

Fig. 7. Tampering with APP geography

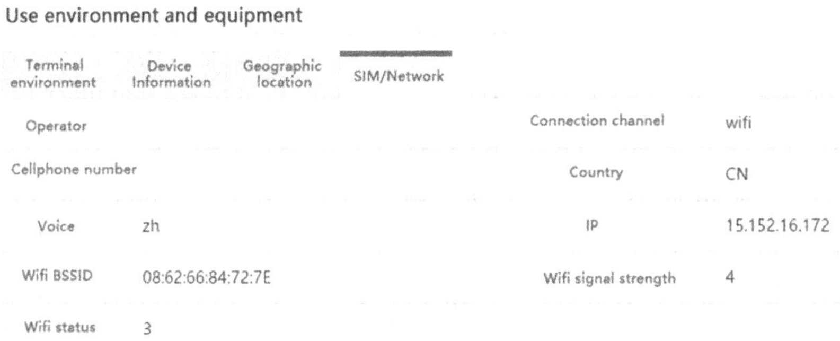

Use environment and equipment

Terminal environment	Device Information	Geographic location	SIM/Network		
Operator				Connection channel	wifi
Cellphone number				Country	CN
Voice	zh			IP	15.152.16.172
Wifi BSSID	08:62:66:84:72:7E			Wifi signal strength	4
Wifi status	3				

Fig. 8. Tampering with APP network/SIM information

You can see the detailed tampering of the APP runtime terminal environment (shown in Fig. 5), the device information (shown in Fig. 6), the geographic location (shown in Fig. 7), the SIM / network (shown in Fig. 8), etc. Effectively retraining APP on the tampering.

(3) Tampering with APP's risk assessment

By assessing the risk of tampering with APP, the risk of tampering with APP can be rated as "safe application", "low risk application", "high risk application", "malicious application".

(4) Probe SDK self-protection Test APP can be run normally by testing the probe SDK and testing APP; and when using other APP into the probe SDK for integration, the APP runtime can not function properly with the Probe SDK function. For the probe SDK itself, due to the shell and confuse protection, can effectively prevent the core industry logic is reverse view (as shown in Fig. 9)

Fig. 9. SDK post-protection tool reverse effect

4   Conclusion

In this paper, through the background of APP tampering detection and retrospective program, the related basic theory, the core technology manufacturers and other angles to elaborate its technology to discuss the shortcomings of the existing technical solutions, finally, the research of APP tamper detection and retrospective system is studied, and the design of the whole research scheme is expounded in detail. The architecture and the simple test are carried out to verify the feasibility of APP tamper detection and traceability, and to abandon the existing mobile manufacturers APP tampering detection and retroactive protection of the shortcomings, So as to solve the APP developers existing APP was tampered with and can not trace the practical problems, but also for domestic mobile security vendors should provide a new way to protect and promote the healthy development of the industry as a whole.

Acknowledgement. This work is supported by the Key Disciplines of Computer Science and Technology of Shanghai Polytechnic University under Grant No. XXKZD1604 and supported by the Shanghai Alliance Program under Grant No. LM201673.

References

1. Becher, M.: Computer Security Art and Science. Addison-Wesley Longman Publishing Co., Inc., Boston (2003)
2. Jiang, W., Lin, S.: Exploration and practice of various forms in university-enterprise cooperation model on colleges and universities. In: 2012 International Conference on Education Reform and Management Innovation (ERMI 2012), vol. 2012, no. 12, pp. 403–408. Information Engineering Research Institute, Shenzhen (2012)
3. Enck, W., Ongtang, M., McDaniel, P.: Understanding android security. IEEE Secur. Priv. Mag. **7**, 50–57 (2009)
4. Ongtang, M., McLaughlin, S., Enck, W., McDaniel, P.: Semantically rich application-centric security in Android. Secur. Commun. Netw. **5**, 658–673 (2012)
5. Eswaraiah, R., Reddy, E.S.: A fragile ROI-based medical image watermarking technique with tamper detection and recovery. In: Fourth International Conference on Communication Systems and Network Technologies. IEEE Computer Society (2014)
6. Piao, Y., Jung, J.H., Yi, J.H.: Server-based code obfuscation scheme for APK tamper detection. Secur. Commun. Netw. **9**, 457–467 (2016)
7. Jiang, W., Wang, A., Wu, C., Chen, J., Yan, J.: Approach for name ambiguity problem using a multiple-layer clustering. In: The 2009 IEEE International Conference on Social Computing (SocialCom-09) (2009)
8. Bang, J., Cho, H., Ji, M., et al.: Tamper detection scheme using signature segregation on android platform. In: IEEE International Conference on Consumer Electronics (2016)
9. Suh, G.E., Fletcher, C., et al.: Author retrospective AEGIS: architecture for tamper-evident and tamper-resistant processing (2014)

Deep Self-Taught Learning for Detecting Drug Abuse Risk Behavior in Tweets

Han Hu[1], NhatHai Phan[1(✉)], James Geller[1], Huy Vo[2], Bhole Manasi[1],
Xueqi Huang[2], Sophie Di Lorio[1], Thang Dinh[3], and Soon Ae Chun[4]

[1] New Jersey Institute of Technology, Newark, NJ 07102, USA
phan@njit.edu
[2] The City College of New York, New York, NY 10031, USA
[3] Virginia Commonwealth University, Richmond, VA 23284, USA
[4] City University of New York, Staten Island, NY 10314, USA

Abstract. Drug abuse continues to accelerate toward becoming the most severe public health problem in the United States. The ability to detect drug abuse risk behavior at a population scale, such as among the population of Twitter users, can help us to monitor the trend of drug-abuse incidents. Unfortunately, traditional methods do not effectively detect drug abuse risk behavior, given tweets. This is because: (1) Tweets usually are noisy and sparse; and (2) The availability of labeled data is limited. To address these challenging problems, we proposed a deep self-taught learning system to detect and monitor drug abuse risk behaviors in the Twitter sphere, by leveraging a large amount of unlabeled data. Our models automatically augment annotated data: (i) To improve the classification performance, and (ii) To capture the evolving picture of drug abuse on online social media. Our extensive experiment has been conducted on 3 million drug abuse-related tweets with geolocation information. Results show that our approach is highly effective in detecting drug abuse risk behaviors.

Keywords: Deep learning · Self-taught learning · Drug abuse · Tweets

1 Introduction

Abuse of prescription drugs and of illicit drugs has been declared a "national emergency" [12,17]. This crisis includes the misuse and abuse of cannabinoids, opioids, tranquilizers, stimulants, inhalants, and other types of psychoactive drugs, which statistical analysis documents as a rising trend in the United States. The most recent reports from the National Survey on Drug Use and Health (NSDUH) [27] estimate that 10.6% of the total population of people ages 12 years and older (i.e., about 28.6 million people) misuse illicit drugs in 2016, which represents an increase of 0.5% since 2015 [26]. According to the Centers for Disease Control and Prevention (CDC), opioid drugs were involved in 42,249 known deaths in 2016 nationwide [10]. In addition, the number of heroin-involved deaths has been increasing sharply for 5 years, and surpassed the number of firearm homicides in 2015 [22].

© Springer Nature Switzerland AG 2018
X. Chen et al. (Eds.): CSoNet 2018, LNCS 11280, pp. 330–342, 2018.
https://doi.org/10.1007/978-3-030-04648-4_28

In April 2017, the Department of Health and Human Services announced their "Opioid Strategy" to battle the country's drug abuse crisis [12,17]. In the Opioid Strategy, one of the major aims is to strengthen public health data collection, in order to inform a real-time public health response, and to improve the timeliness, as the epidemic evolves. Given its 100 million daily active users and 500 million daily tweets [11], Twitter has been used as a sufficient and reliable data source for many detection tasks, including epidemiology [30] and public health [1,4,5,15,21,28], at the population scale, in a real-time manner. Motivated by these facts and the urgent needs, our goal in this paper is to develop a large-scale computational system to detect drug abuse risk behaviors via Twitter sphere.

Several studies [5–7,18,28,29] have explored the detecting of prescription drug abuse on Twitter. However, the current state-of-the-art approaches and systems are limited in terms of scales and accuracy. They applied strictly keyword-based approaches to collect tweets explicitly mentioning specific drug names, such as Adderall, oxycodone, quetiapine, metformin, cocaine, marijuana, weed, meth, tranquilizer, etc. [5,7,28,29]. That may not reflect the actual distribution of drug abuse risk behaviors on online social media, since: (1) The expressions of drug abuse are often vague, in comparison to common topics, i.e., a lot of slang is used; and (2) Strictly keyword-based approaches are susceptible to lexical ambiguity in natural language [21]. In addition, the drug abuse-related Twitter data usually is very imbalanced, i.e., dominated by non-drug abuse tweets, such as reports, advertisements, etc. The limited availability of annotated drug abuse-related tweets makes it even more challenging to distinguish drug abuse risk behaviors from drug-related advertisements, social discussions, reports, and news. However, existing approaches [5–7,18,28,29] have not been designed to address these challenging issues for drug abuse detection on online social media.

Contributions: To address these challenges, our main contributions are to propose: (**1**) A large-scale drug abuse-related tweets collection mechanism based on supervised machine learning and data crowd-sourcing techniques; and (**2**) A deep self-taught learning algorithm for drug abuse-related tweet detection.

We first collect tweets by filtering tweets through a filter, in which a variety of drug names, colloquialisms and slang terms, and abuse-indicating terms (e.g., overdose, addiction, high, abuse, and even death) are combined together. We manually annotate a small number of tweets as seed tweets, which are used to train machine learning classifiers. Then, the classifiers are applied on unlabeled data to produce machine-labeled tweets. The machine-labeled tweets are verified again by humans on Mechanical Turk, i.e., a crowd-sourcing platform, with good accuracy but at a much lower cost. The new labeled tweets and the seed tweets are combined to form a sufficient and reliable labeled data set for drug abuse risk behavior detection, by applying deep learning models, i.e., convolution neural networks (CNN) [16], long-short term memory (LSTM) models [14], etc.

However, there is still a large amount of unlabeled data, which can be leveraged to significantly improve our models in terms of classification accuracy. Therefore, we further propose a self-taught learning algorithm, in which the training data of our deep learning models will be recursively augmented with a set of new machine-labeled tweets. These new machine-labeled tweets are generated by applying the previously trained deep learning models on a random sample of a huge number of unlabeled tweets, i.e., the 3 million tweets, in our dataset. Note that the set of new machine-labeled tweets possibly has a different distribution from the original training and testing datasets. An extensive experiment conducted on 3 million drug-abuse related tweets with geolocation information shown that our approach is highly effective in detecting drug abuse risk behaviors.

2   Background and Related Work

On the one hand, the traditional studies, such as NSDUH [23], CDC [10], Monitoring the Future [20], the Drug Abuse Warning Network (DAWN) [31], and the MedWatch program [33], are trustworthy sources for getting the general picture of the drug abuse epidemic. On the other hand, many studies that are based on modern online social media, such as Twitter, have shown promising results in drug abuse detection and related topics [1,4–7,15,18,21,28,29]. Butler et al. [18] measured online endorsement of prescription opioid abuse by developing an integrative metric through the lens of Internet communities. Hanson et al. [7] conducted a quantitative analysis on 213,633 tweets discussing "Adderall", a prescription stimulant commonly abused among college students. Hanson et al. [6,7] focused on how possible drug-abusers interact with and influence others in online social circles. Furthermore, Shutler et al. [29] performed a qualitative analysis of prescription opioid related tweets and found that indication of positive abuse was common.

Our previous work [24] showed the potential of applying machine learning models in drug abuse monitoring system to detect drug abuse-related tweets. Several other works also utilized machine learning methods in detecting and analyzing drug related posts on Twitter. For instance, Sarker et al. [28] proposed a supervised classification model, in which different features such as n-grams, abuse-indicating terms, slang terms, synonyms, etc., are extracted from manually annotated tweets. Then, these features are used to train traditional machine learning models to classify drug abuse tweets and non-abuse tweets. Chary et al. [5] discussed how to use AI models to extract content useful for purposes of toxicovigilance from social media, such as Facebook, Twitter, and Google+. Recently, Coloma et al. [8] illustrated the potential of social media in drug safety surveillance. Furthermore, Twitter and social media have been shown to be reliable sources in analyzing drug abuse and public health-related topics, such as cigarette smoking [1,21], alcohol use [15], and even cardiac arrest [4].

Although existing studies have shown promising approaches toward detecting drug abuse-related risk behavior and information in Twitter, their performance, in terms of accuracy and scales, is still limited. In this paper, we propose a deep self-taught learning system to leverage a huge number of unlabeled tweets. Self-taught learning [25] is a method that integrates concepts of semi-supervised and multi-task learning, in which the model can exploit examples that are unlabeled and possibly come from a distribution different from the target distribution. It has already been shown that deep neural networks can take advantage of unsupervised learning and unlabeled examples [2,34]. Different from other approaches mainly designed for image processing and object detection [3,9,13,35], our deep self-learning model shows the ability to detect drug abuse risk behavior given noisy and sparse Twitter data with a limited availability of annotated tweets.

3   Deep Self-Taught Learning System for Drug Abuse Risk Behavior Detection

In this section, we present the definition of the drug abuse risk behavior detection problem, our system for collecting tweets, labeling tweets, and our deep self-taught learning approach (Fig. 1).

Problem Definition: We use the term "drug abuse risk behaviors" in the wider sense, including misuse and use of Schedule 1 drugs that are illegal; and misuse of Schedule 2 drugs, e.g., Oxycodone, which includes the use thereof for non-medical purposes, and the symptoms and side-effects of misuse. Our task is to develop classification models that can classify a given unlabeled tweet into one of the two classes: a drug abuse risk behavior tweet (**positive**), or a non-risk behavior tweet (**negative**). The main criteria for classifying a tweet as drug-abuse related can be condensed into: *"The existence of abusive activities or endorsements of drugs."* Meanwhile, news, reports, and opinions about drug abuse are the signals of tweets that are not drug abuse-related.

3.1   Collecting and Labeling Tweets

In our crawling system, raw tweets are collected through Twitter APIs. For the collection of focused Twitter data, we use a list of the names of illegal and prescription drug [32] of drugs that have been commonly abused over time, e.g., barbiturates, OxyContin, Ritalin, cocaine, LSD, opiates, heroin, codeine, fentanyl, etc. However, the data is very noisy, since: (1) There was no indication of how to distinguish between drug abuse and legitimate use (of prescription drugs) in collected Tweets, and (2) A lot of slang terms are used in expressing drug abuse-related risk behavior. To address this problem, we added slang terms for drugs and abuse-indicating terms, e.g., "high," "stoned," "blunt," "addicted," etc., into our keyword search library. These slang terms are clearly expressing that the tweets in question were about drug abuse. As a result, most of the collected data is drug abuse-related.

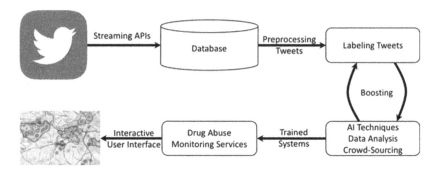

Fig. 1. Drug Abuse Detection System. There are 4 steps as follows: (1) Tweets will be collected through Twitter APIs. (2) Reprocessed tweets will be labeled by humans, AI techniques, and crowd-sourcing techniques. (3) Labeled tweets will be used to augment the training data of our AI models and data analysis tasks to identify drug abuse-related tweets, through a boosting algorithm. And (4) Trained systems will be used in different drug abuse monitoring services and interactive user interfaces.

To obtain trustworthy annotated data, there are two integrative steps in labeling tweets. In the first step, 1,794 tweets randomly chosen from collected tweets were manually classified into drug abuse tweets and non-abuse tweets by two professors and three students who have experience in drug abuse behavior study. Several instances of drug abuse tweets and non-abuse tweets are illustrated in Table 1. These labeled tweets are considered seed tweets, which then are used to train traditional binary classifiers, e.g., SVM, Naive Bayes, etc., to predict whether a tweet is a drug abuse-related tweet or not. The trained classifiers are applied on unlabeled tweets to predict their labels, which are called machine labels. In the second step, 5,000 positive machine-labeled tweets with high classification confidence are verified again on Mechanical Turk, which is a well-known crowd-sourcing platform, to improve the trustworthiness and to avoid bias in the annotated data. Our integrative labeling approach results in a reliable and well-balanced annotated data set, with 6,794 labeled tweets. In total, we have collected 3 million drug abuse-related tweets with geo-location, among which 6,794 tweets are labeled.

Tweet Vectorization: Raw tweets need to be first pre-processed, then represented as a vector, before they can be used in training machine learning models. In this study, we choose a commonly used pre-processing pipeline, followed by three different vectorization methods. The pre-processing pipeline consists of following steps:

– The tweets are tokenized and lower-cased. The special entities, i.e., including Emoji, URL, mentions, and hashtags, are removed or replaced with special wordings. The non-word characters, i.e., including HTML symbols, punctuation marks, and foreign characters, are removed. Words with 3 or more repeating characters are reduced to at most 3 successive characters.

– Stop-words are removed according to a custom stop-word list. Stemming is applied using the standard Porter Stemmer.

After the preprocessing steps, common vectorization methods are used to extract features from tweets, including: (1) Term frequency, denoted tf, (2) Tf-idf, and (3) Word2vec [19]. Word2vec is an advanced and effective word embedding method that converts each word to a dense vector of fixed length. We considered two different word2vec models: (i) Custom word2vec which is developed based on our 3 million drug abuse-related tweets, and the model contains 300-dimensional vectors for 1,130,962 words and phrases; and (ii) Google word2vec, which is a well-known pre-trained word2vec vectors built from part of Google News dataset with about 100 billion words, and the model contains 300-dimensional vectors for 3 million words and phrases.

3.2 Deep Self-Taught Learning Approach

By applying both traditional and advanced machine learning models, such as SVM, Naive Bayes, CNN, and LSTM, on the small and static annotated data, i.e., 6,794 tweets, we can achieve reasonable classification accuracies of nearly 80%. However, to develop a scalable and trustworthy drug abuse-related risk behavior detection model, we need to: (1) Improve classification models to achieve higher accuracy and performance; and (2) Leverage the large number of unlabeled tweets, i.e., nearly 3 million tweets related to drug abuse behaviors, to improve the system performance. Therefore, we propose a deep self-taught learning model by repeatedly augmenting the training data with machine-labeled tweets. The pseudo-code of our model is as follows:

Step 1: Initialize labeled data D consisting of 5,794 annotated tweets as the training set. Initialize a testing data T consisting of the remaining 1,000 annotated tweets.

Table 1. Instances of manually annotated drug abuse tweets and non-abuse tweets.

	Tweets
Abuse	Ever since my Acid trips like whenever I get super high I just start lightly hallucinating and it's tbh creepy.
	Drove like 10 miles on these icy ass roads all to get some weed if imma be locked up in my house for awhile imma need some weed.
	Smoking a blunt at home so much better than going to the woods in Brooksville and puking on yourself Bc you drank too much fireball.
Non-Abuse	Just watched Fear and Loathing in Las Vegas for the first time and I think I should have been on acid to fully understand it.
	Today I was asked if I do heroin because I went to Lancaster????
	Morgan told me my Bitmoji looks like a heroin addict?

Step 2: Train a binary classification model M using the labeled data D. M could be a CNN model or a LSTM model.

Step 3: Use the model M to label the unlabeled data, which simply consists of 3 million unlabeled tweets. The set of new labeled tweets is denoted as $\overline{D}$, which is also called machine-labeled data.

Step 4: Sample tweets from the machine-labeled data $\overline{D}$ with a high classification confidence, and then add the sampled tweets D^+ into the labeled data D to form a new training dataset: $D = D \cup D^+$. A tweet is considered to have a high classification confidence if it has a classification probability $p \in [0, 1]$ higher than a predefined boosting threshold δ.

Step 5: Repeat Steps 2–4 after k iterations, which is a user-predefined number. Return the trained model M.

With the self-taught learning method, the training data contains the annotated data D which is automatically augmented with highly confident, machine-labeled tweets, in each iteration. That have a great potential to increasing the classification performance of our model over time. In addition, the unlabeled data can be collected from the Twitter APIs in real time, to capture the evolving of drug abuse-related risk behaviors. In the literature, data augmentation approaches have been applied to improve the accuracy of deep learning models [3]. However, the existing approaches [3,9,13,35] are quite different from our proposed model, since they focused on image classification tasks, instead of drug abuse-related risk behavior detection as in our study. To ensure fairness, testing data T is separated from other data sources during the training process.

Baseline Model	Parameter Setting	
SVM	$C = 5.0, gamma = 0.01, kernel: rbf$	
Random Forest	$N\_estimators = 500, class\,weight = balanced, max\,depth = 20$	
Naïve Bayes (Gaussian)	default setting	
Naïve Bayes (Multinomial)	default setting	

Proposed Model	Layers	Parameter Setting
Self-Taught CNN (**b-CNN**)	embedding	size: 300, length: 20
	dropout	dropout rate: 0.2
	convolutional layer	kernel sizes: [2,3,4], number of kernels: 20 activation function: Relu, strides: 1
	max pooling	pool size: 2
	flatten	no parameters
	concatenate	no parameters
	dropout	dropout rate: 0.5
	two dense layers	dense layer 1, size: 520×500; dense layer 2, size: 500×2
Self-Taught LSTM (**b-LSTM**)	embedding	size: 300, length: 20
	dropout	dropout rate: 0.2
	LSTM	sequence output: False
	dropout	dropout rate: 0.5
	two dense layers	dense layer 1, size: 300×500; dense layer 2, size: 500×2

Fig. 2. Parameter settings.

4   Experimental Results

To examine the effectiveness and efficiency of our proposed boosting deep learning approaches, we have carried out a series of experiments using a set of 3 million drug abuse-related tweets collected in the past 4 years. We first elaborate details about our dataset, baseline approaches, measures, and model configurations. Then, we introduce our experimental results.

4.1   Experiment Settings

Dataset: In our first data-collecting session, 71,363 tweets were collected. Among them, 1,794 tweets were manually labeled as a **seed dataset**, by two professors and three students with experience in drug abuse behavior study. 280 drug abuse related tweets and 1,514 tweets not related to drug abuse were identified. The seed dataset was used for building the initial machine learning model (i.e., SVM), which was used to further classify the unlabeled 3 million tweets. These 3 million drug abuse-related tweets with geo-location information cover the entire U.S. We then selected 5,000 tweets labeled by the machine learning model (i.e., SVM) with a high confidence level, and rendered them verified by using Mechanical Turk. In total, the number of manually labeled tweets was 6,794, including 3,102 positive labels and 3,677 negative labels.

Baseline and Deep Learning Models: In our experiments, Random Forest (**RF**), Naive Bayes (**NB**), and **SVM** are employed as baseline approaches in the binary classification task, i.e., to classify whether a tweet is a drug abuse-related tweet or not. Figure 2 shows the parameter settings of baseline approaches and the proposed models. Note that for the Naive Bayes method, we use Gaussian Naive Bayes with word2vec embedding. Meanwhile, we use term frequency (i.e., tf) and tf-idf vectorizations for Multinomial Naive Bayes. This is because: (1) The vectors generated by term frequency-based vectorization had a very high number of dimensions and could be only represented by sparse-matrix, which was not supported by Gaussian Naive Bayes; and (2) The Multinomial Naive Bayes required non-negative inputs, but vectors generated by word2vec embedding had negative values. Regarding our self-taught CNN (**b-CNN**) and self-taught LSTM (**b-LSTM**) models, the Adam Optimizer algorithm with the default learning rate is used for training. The number of iterations k is set to 6. All the experiments have been conducted on a single GPU, i.e., NVIDIA GTX TITAN X, 12 GB with 3,072 CUDA cores.

Measures: Accuracy, recall, and $F1$-value are used to validate the effectiveness of the proposed and baseline approaches. Due to the small size and the imbalanced label distribution, we adopted the Monte Carlo Cross-Validation technique. In each run, a fixed number of data instances is sampled (i.e., without replacement) as the testing dataset, and the rest of the data as the training dataset. Multiple runs (i.e., 3 times) are generated for each model in each set of parameters and experimental configurations. We report the average of these runs as result.

4.2 Validation of the Deep Self-taught Learning Models

Our task of validation concerns three key issues: **(1)** Which parameter configurations are optimal for the baseline models, i.e., SVM, RF, and NB? **(2)** Which boosting model is the best in terms of accuracy, recall, and F1-value, given the 6,794 annotated tweets and the 3 million unlabeled tweets? and **(3)** Which vectorization setting is more effective? To address these concerns, our series of experiments are as follows:

Figure 3 illustrates the accuracy, recall, and F1-value of each algorithm with different parameter configurations, i.e., term frequency tf, tf-idf, and $word2vec$, on the (annotated) seed dataset. The term *"custom"* is used to indicate the word2vec embedding trained in our own drug abuse-related tweets, compared with the pre-trained Google News word2vec embedding, denoted as "google." It is clear that the SVM model using the custom-trained word2vec embedding achieves the best and the most balanced performance in terms of all three measures, i.e., accuracy, recall, and F1-value, at approximately 67%. Other configurations usually have a lower recall, which suggests that the decisions they make bias towards the major class, i.e., tweets that are not drug abuse-related or negative tweets. Note that Naive Bayes had a complete failure, i.e., no correct positive tweet prediction was made, when using tf-idf. Therefore, these results were not shown in Fig. 3. From the angle of classifiers, SVM model achieves the best overall performance. Random Forest has slightly less average accuracy than the SVM model, but worse recall and F1-value. Furthermore, from the view of vectorization approach, it is clear that word2vec embedding outperforms term frequency and tf-idf in most of the cases.

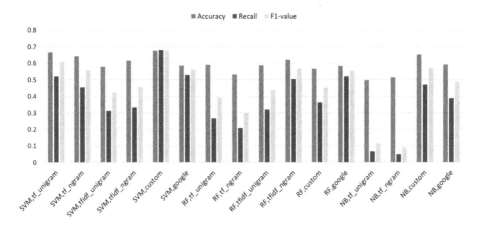

Fig. 3. Accuracy, recall, and F1-value of each baseline models on the seed dataset.

As shown in the previous experiment, SVM model using the custom-trained word2vec embedding achieves the best performance, we decided to apply the same model structure to compare with our deep self-taught learning approaches.

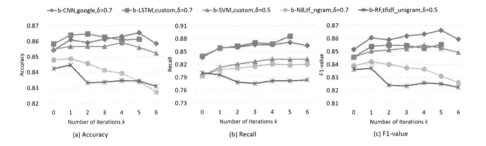

Fig. 4. Accuracy, recall, and $F1$-value of the five self-taught learning models, including b-CNN, b-LSTM, b-SVM, b-NB, and b-RF.

In this experiment, 1,000 labeled tweets were randomly sampled and held out from the 6,794 labeled tweets as testing set. The remaining 5,794 labeled tweets were used as the initial training dataset. At each epoch, 10,000 machine-labeled tweets were randomly sampled from 3 million unlabeled tweets and merged into the training set. Figure 4 shows the experimental results of the five self-taught learning models, including self-taught CNN (**b-CNN**), self-taught LSTM (**b-LSTM**), self-taught SVM (**b-SVM**), self-taught NB (**b-NB**), and self-taught RF (**b-RF**). All configurations of classifiers and vectorization methods are tested. For the sake of clarity, we only illustrate the best-performing setting for each model in Fig. 4. It is clear that our proposed deep self-taught learning approaches (i.e., b-LSTM and b-CNN) outperform traditional models, i.e., b-SVM, b-NB, and b-RF, in terms of accuracy, recall, and $F1$-value, in all cases. Our models achieve 86.53%, 88.6%, and 86.63% in terms of accuracy, recall, and $F1$-value correspondingly.

The impact of two different word2vec representations on b-CNN, i.e., the custom word2vec embedding we trained from our corpus, and pre-trained Google News word2vec embedding, is shown in Fig. 5. The Google News word2vec achieves 0.1%, 0.4%, and 0.3% improvements in terms of accuracy, recall, and $F1$-value (86.63%, 89%, 86.83%, respectively) compared with the custom trained

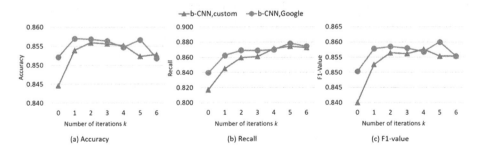

Fig. 5. Performance comparison between custom word2vec embedding and Google News word2vec embedding.

word2vec embedding. In addition, it is clear that Google News word2vec embedding outperforms the custom trained word2vec in most of the cases. This is because the Google News word2vec embedding was trained on a large-scale corpus, which is significantly richer in contextual information, compared with our short, noisy, and sparse Twitter datasets.

5   Discussion

According to our experimental results, our deep self-taught learning models achieved promising performance in drug abuse-related risk behavior detection in Twitter. However, many assumptions call for further experiments. First, how to optimize the classification performance by exploring the correlations among parameters and experimental configurations. For instance, for SVM and RF models, unigram feature works better than n-gram feature on term frequency; however, for tf-idf, it is the opposite situation. Second, the pre-trained Google News word2vec embedding performs better than the custom-trained word2vec embedding may also be situational. These findings indicate the necessity of leveraging size and quality of the training data for training word embedding, given that the available data may better fit the classification task but be short in quantity. Nevertheless, among the measures, recall receives a more significant boost than accuracy and F1-value. We may argue that the proposed deep self-taught learning algorithm helped correcting the bias in the classifiers caused by the imbalanced nature of the training dataset. However, more experiments need to be conducted to verify this interesting point.

6   Conclusion

In this paper, we proposed a large-scale drug abuse-related tweet collection mechanism based on supervised machine learning and data crowd-sourcing techniques. Challenges came from the noisy and sparse characteristics of Twitter data, as well as the limited availability of annotated data. To address this problem, we propose a deep self-taught learning algorithm to improve drug abuse-related tweet detection models by leveraging a large number of unlabeled tweets. An extensive experiment and data analysis were carried out on 3 million drug abuse-related tweets with geo-location information, to validate the effectiveness and reliability of our system. Experimental results shown that our models outperform traditional models. In fact, our models correspondingly achieve 86.63%, 89%, and 86.83% in terms of accuracy, recall, and F1-value. This is a promising result.

References

1. Aphinyanaphongs, Y., Lulejian, A., Penfold-Brown, D., Bonneau, R., Krebs, P.: Text classification for automatic detection of e-cigarette use and use for smoking cessation from twitter: a feasibility pilot. In: Pacific Symposium on Biocomputing, vol. 21, pp. 480–491 (2016)
2. Bengio, Y.: Learning deep architectures for AI. Found. Trends Mach. Learn. **2**(1), 1–127 (2009)
3. Bettge, A., Roscher, R., Wenzel, S.: Deep self-taught learning for remote sensing image classification. CoRR abs/1710.07096 (2017)
4. Bosley, J.C., et al.: Decoding twitter: surveillance and trends for cardiac arrest and resuscitation communication. Resuscitation **84**(2), 206–212 (2013)
5. Chary, M., Genes, N., McKenzie, A., Manini, A.F.: Leveraging social networks for toxicovigilance. J. Med. Toxicol. **9**(2), 184–191 (2013)
6. Hanson, C.L., Cannon, B., Butron, S., Giraud-Carrier, C.: An exploration of social circles and prescription drug abuse through twitter. J. Med. Internet Res. **15**(9), e189 (2013)
7. Hanson, C.L., Burton, S.H., Giraud-Carrier, C., West, J.H., Barnes, M.D., Hansen, B.: Tweaking and tweeting exploring twitter for nonmedical use of a psychostimulant drug (adderall) among college students. J. Med. Internet Res. **15**(4), e62 (2013)
8. Coloma, P.M., Becker, B., Sturkenboom, M.C.J.M., van Mulligen, E.M., Kors, J.A.: Evaluating social media networks in medicines safety surveillance: two case studies. Drug Saf. **38**(10), 921–930 (2015)
9. Dong, X., Meng, D., Ma, F., Yang, Y.: A dual-network progressive approach to weakly supervised object detection. In: Proceedings of the 2017 ACM on Multimedia Conference, MM 2017, pp. 279–287 (2017)
10. Northern Ireland on Drug Abuse: Overdose death rates, September 15, 2017. National Institute on Drug Abuse, 20 January 2018. https://www.drugabuse.gov/related-topics/trends-statistics/overdose-death-rates
11. Northern Ireland on Drug Abuse: Twitter by the numbers: stats, demographics and fun facts, 2018. Omnicore, 7 March 2018. https://www.omnicoreagency.com/twitter-statistics/
12. Ex-DEA Agent: Opioid crisis fueled by drug industry and congress. CBS 60 Minutes, 17 October 2017
13. Gan, J., Li, L., Zhai, Y., Liu, Y.: Deep self-taught learning for facial beauty prediction. Neurocomputing **144**, 295–303 (2014)
14. Hochreiter, S., Schmidhuber, J.: Long short-term memory. Neural Comput. **9**(8), 1735–1780 (1997)
15. Hossain, N., Hu, T., Feizi, R., White, A.M., Luo, J., Kautz, H.A.: Precise localization of homes and activities: detecting drinking-while-tweeting patterns in communities. In: ICWSM (2016)
16. Lecun, Y., Bottou, L., Bengio, Y., Haffner, P.: Gradient-based learning applied to document recognition. Proc. IEEE **86**(11), 2278–2324 (1998)
17. Marino, T.: Withdraws in latest setback for trump's opioid fight. New York Times, 17 October 2017
18. McNaughton, E.C., Black, R.A., Zulueta, M.G., Budman, S.H., Butler, S.F.: Measuring online endorsement of prescription opioids abuse: an integrative methodology. Pharmacoepidemiol. Drug Saf. **21**(10), 1081–1092 (2012)

19. Mikolov, T., Chen, K., Corrado, G., Dean, J.: Efficient estimation of word representations in vector space. CoRR abs/1301.3781 (2013)
20. Monitoring the Future: A continuing study of american youth. http://www.monitoringthefuture.org
21. Myslín, M., Zhu, S.H., Chapman, W., Conway, M.: Using twitter to examine smoking behavior and perceptions of emerging tobacco products. J. Med. Internet Res. **15**(8), e174 (2013)
22. National Institute on Drug Abuse: Gun violence archive, past summary ledgers. (n.d.). Gun Violence Archive, 20 January 2018. http://www.gunviolencearchive.org/past-tolls
23. National Poisoning Data System: National Poisoning Data System, 16 January 2017. http://www.aapcc.org/data-system/
24. Phan, N., Chun, S.A., Bhole, M., Geller, J.: Enabling real-time drug abuse detection in tweets. In: 2017 IEEE 33rd International Conference on Data Engineering (ICDE), pp. 1510–1514 (2017)
25. Raina, R., Battle, A., Lee, H., Packer, B., Ng, A.Y.: Self-taught learning: transfer learning from unlabeled data. In: Proceedings of the 24th International Conference on Machine Learning, ICML 2007, pp. 759–766 (2007)
26. SAMHSA: Key substance use and mental health indicators in the United States, 2015. SAMHSA (n.d.), 20 January 2018. https://www.samhsa.gov/data/sites/default/files/NSDUH-FFR1-2015/NSDUH-FFR1-2015/NSDUH-FFR1-2015.htm
27. SAMHSA: Key substance use and mental health indicators in the United States, 2016. SAMHSA (n.d.), 20 January 2018. https://www.samhsa.gov/data/sites/default/files/NSDUH-FFR1-2016/NSDUH-FFR1-2016.htm
28. Sarker, A., et al.: Social media mining for toxicovigilance: automatic monitoring of prescription medication abuse from twitter. Drug Saf. **39**(3), 231–240 (2016)
29. Shutler, L.: Prescription opioids in the twittersphere a contextual analysis of tweets about prescription drugs. Ann. Emerg. Med. **62**(4), S122 (2013)
30. Signorini, A., Segre, A.M., Polgreen, P.M.: The use of twitter to track levels of disease activity and public concern in the U.S. during the influenza a h1n1 pandemic. PLOS ONE **6**(5), 1–10 (2011)
31. Substance Abuse and Mental Health Services Administration Center for Behavioral Health Statistics and Quality (formerly the Office of Applied Studies): The dawn report: highlights of the 2009 drug abuse warning network (dawn) findings on drug-related emergency department visits, 28 December 2010
32. The National Center on Addiction and Substance Abuse: Commonly used illegal drugs, 16 January 2017. http://www.centeronaddiction.org/addiction/commonly-used-illegal-drugs
33. US FDA: Medwatch: the FDA safety information and adverse event reporting program, 16 January 2017. http://www.fda.gov/Safety/MedWatch/
34. Weston, J., Ratle, F., Collobert, R.: Deep learning via semi-supervised embedding. In: Proceedings of the 25th International Conference on Machine Learning, ICML 2008, pp. 1168–1175 (2008)
35. Yuan, Y., Liang, X., Wang, X., Yeung, D., Gupta, A.: Temporal dynamic graph LSTM for action-driven video object detection. CoRR abs/1708.00666 (2017)

Refined Weighted Random Forest and Its Application to Credit Card Fraud Detection

Shiyang Xuan, Guanjun Liu$^{(\boxtimes)}$, and Zhenchuan Li

Department of Computer Science and Technology, Tongji University,
Shanghai 201804, China
{xsyfor,liuguanjun,1510482}@tongji.edu.cn

Abstract. Random forest (RF) is widely used in many applications due to good classification performance. However, its voting mechanism assumes that all base classifiers have the same weight. In fact, it is more reasonable that some have relatively high weights while some have relatively low weights because the randomization of bootstrap sampling and attributes selecting cannot guarantee all trees have the same ability of making decision. We mainly focus on the weighted voting mechanism and then propose a novel weighted RF in this paper. Experiments on 6 public datasets illustrate that our method outperforms the RF and another weighted RF. We apply our method to credit card fraud detection and experiments also show that our method is the best.

Keywords: Random forest · Weighted decision tree
Credit card fraud

1 Introduction

Machine learning and data mining are becoming more and more important in many areas. For example, Recommender systems make a good recommendation for users [19], spam classifier protects our emails from spam [2], anomaly detection systems are to detect abnormal behaviours of systems [20], and fraud detection systems learn the features of transactions from lots of malicious data and then prevent a fraud transaction [8]. All these successful applications are owed to effective data and good models.

In these methods of machine learning, random forest [21] is studied and applied widely. It is a representation of bagging [25] which is one kind of ensemble learning [22] method based on the fact that the ensemble of multiple weak classifiers would be better than single classifier. Bagging assigns the same weight to every weak classifier. But we think that different weak classifiers should have different weights due to the random selection of data and features. Therefore, we put forward refined weighted random forests (RWRF).

© Springer Nature Switzerland AG 2018
X. Chen et al. (Eds.): CSoNet 2018, LNCS 11280, pp. 343–355, 2018.
https://doi.org/10.1007/978-3-030-04648-4_29

Credit cards are widely used with the development of commerce and the popularization of mobile phones, especially online transactions [1]. Credit card has made an online transaction easier and more convenient. However, there is a growing trend of transaction frauds resulting in a great losses of money every year [17,18]. Transaction fraud not only has a dramatic influence on economy but also makes people lose their confidence in enterprises [26]. It is estimated that losses are increased yearly at double digit rates by 2020 [5]. Hence, fraud detection is very necessary. In this paper, We use random forest and its improved version to train the normal and fraud behavior features.

The major contributions of this paper are summarized as follows. (1) We propose a new method that can assign different weights to different decision trees [23] in a random forest. (2) Our method is applied both the public data and our private transaction data that are provided by an e-commerce company in China. Experiments are conducted to compare the effectiveness of random forest, trees weighting random forest (TWRF) [27] and our RWRF. (3) From the result of experiments, some conclusions are made which would be helpful for future work.

The paper is organized as follows. Section 2 describes some related work about random forest and credit card fraud detection. Section 3 introduces traditional random forest and our improved random forest RWRF. The experiments and performance comparison are discussed in Sect. 4. Finally, some conclusions and future work are presented in Sect. 5.

2   Related Work

A comprehensive understanding of fraud detection could be helpful for us to solve the problem of credit card fraud. The work in [16] provides a comprehensive discussion on the challenges and problems of fraud detection research. Mohammad et al. [15] review the most popular types of credit card fraud and the existing nature-inspired detection methods that are used in detection methods. Basically, there are two types of credit card fraud: application fraud and behavior fraud [4]. Behavior fraud is that criminals steal the information of a card from the genuine cardholder and then use them to consume. Application fraud is that criminals get new cards from issuing companies by forging card information.

Recently, Checking behaviors of the cardholder is a popular kind of fraud detection method in many banks [10]. Almost all the existing work to detect credit card fraud is to capture the behavior patterns of the cardholder and to check legality of transactions based on these patterns. Srivastava et al. [8] using a hidden markov model (HMM) to model the sequence of transaction features and use it as the regular behavior of the cardholder. A transaction will be considered to be fraudulent if the current transaction is not accepted by the HMM with a high probability. However, they consider the transaction amount as the only feature and didn't make full use of other data of a transaction such as transaction time and transaction place. Amlan et al. [11] propose a method which uses two-stage sequence alignment to combine both anomaly detection and misued detection. Gabriel et al. [14] propose an alternative method to prevent fraud in E-commerce applications by using a signature-based method. They use it to establish a user's behavior deviations and consequently detect the potential fraud in time. Leila et al. [6] propose an aggregating profile which exploits the inherent patterns in time series of transactions, and the fraud detection is performed online at the end of a period respectively. Zheng et al. [7] consider the diversity of user's transaction behavior in credit card fraud detection.

Random forest has been used in many areas. In [28], it is used to solve the problem of cost-sensitive feature selection. The algorithm puts the features cost into the construction process of a basic decision tree, and then generates a low-cost feature subset. When constructing a base tree, features are randomly selected. The probability of the feature is inversely proportional to the cost associated with it. In [29], random forests are used in geophysical and geochemical sciences. They use random forest to predict the lithology of the Hearne Archean-Paleoproterozoic tectonic area. Harris et al. use the Mahin's parallel processing to construct a random-forest-based decision model, which is applied to quasi-real-time peer botnet detection [30]. [32] proposes a framework based on random forest for real-time head pose estimation from images and then extends it to a set of facial features located in 3D. The algorithm employs a voting method in which each patch extracted from the image can be directly voted for the head pose or each facial feature. Xuan et al. [12] make a comparison for different implementations of random forest for credit card fraud detection.

Winham et al. [33] put forward to a weighted random forest to improve predictive performance. They compute the weight based on the out-of-bag error of decision tree. Li et al. proposes TWRF method [27]. They employed it to classify high-dimensional noisy data. They add some noisy features to data so as to make it more difficult to deal with. As they said, it will be better to verify the effectiveness of their algorithm.

3   Random Forest and Refined Weighted Random Forest

Before introducing RWRF, we review random forest first.

3.1   Random Forest

Random forest, one of ensemble methods, is a combination of multiple tree predictors such that each tree depends on a random independent dataset and all trees in the forest are of the same distribution. It does not overfit as more trees are added, but produces a limiting value of the generalization error [21]. The superiority of random forest comparing to single decision tree is that it is insensitive to specific training data and is not easy to overfit [13]. The capacity of random forest not only depends on the strength of individual tree but also the correlation between different trees. The stronger the strength of single tree and the less the correlation of different tress, the better the performance of random forest.

The variation of trees comes from their randomness which involves bootstrapped samples and randomly selects a subset of data attributes. We make a brief introduction of random forest as shown in Fig. 1. At first, we get different bootstrap samples from our original data by sampling with replacement. Then, for each sample data, we train a decision tree which is CART (Classification and Regression Trees) [24] whose training set comes from bootstrapped samples. When predicting the class of new data instances, every tree gives a prediction. The final class is the majority voting of all decision trees.

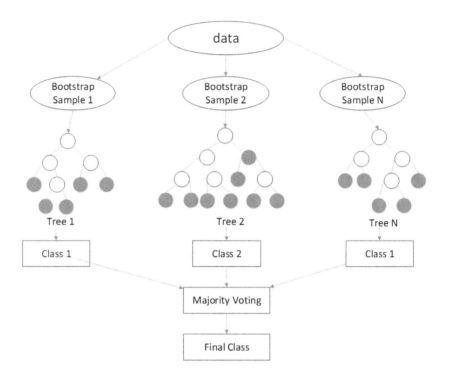

Fig. 1. Illustration of random forest.

For readability, some notations are introduced here. Considering a given dataset D with n examples (i.e. $|D| = n$), we denote: $D = \{(\boldsymbol{x}_i, y_i)\}$ where $i = 1, ..., n$, $\boldsymbol{x}_i \in X$ is an instance in the m-dimensional feature space $X = \{f_1, f_2, ..., f_m\}$ and $y_i \in Y = \{0, 1\}$ is the class label associated with instance $\boldsymbol{x}_i$.

At each node, CART splits dataset by choosing the best attribute from a subset of attributes according to Gini impurity which measures uncertainty of dataset. The subset of attributes are randomly selected from all attributes of the dataset. According to advices from Breiman, setting the size of the subset to the square root of the number of all attributes is a good choice [21]. The Gini impurity is defined in (1) and is described in (2) under the condition of feature x_i.

$$Gini(Node) = 1 - \sum_{k=1}^{C} p_k^2 \tag{1}$$

where C is the number of classes which is 2 in binary classification problem and p_k is the probability that a record belongs to class k.

$$Gini(Node, x_i) = \frac{|Node_l|}{|Node|} Gini(Node_l) + \frac{|Node_r|}{|Node|} Gini(Node_r) \tag{2}$$

where $Node_l$ is the left child of the current node and $|Node|$ represents the number of instances in the dataset w.r.t. the current node.

An example of CART is shown in Fig. 2. The internal nodes are represented by circles and the leaf nodes is represented by squares. The variable and number in circles are the best splitting attribute and its value, respectively. The number labeled on the left edge from an internal node means the value of this attribute greater than or equal to the splitting value, while the number labeled on the right edge means that the attribute has a less value. The number in a leaf node is the class label which the node belongs to.

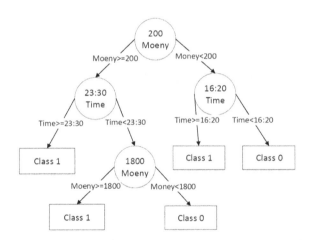

Fig. 2. Illustration of Classification and regression tree.

3.2   Refined Weighted Random Forest

Although random forest has good performance and has applied in many areas, there is still some room for improvement. Our RWRF focus on different impor-tance of every decision trees. The structure of each decision tree, the splitted attribute in each node and the number of instances in every leafs can be thought as the parameters of random forest [34]. Due to the randomization of bootstrap sample and attributes selecting, the parameters of different trees are not identical. Some trees may be more likely to learn the true distribution of data than others. These trees should be given more importance.

There are two literatures [27,33] which use the accuracy of out-of-bag (oob) data as a metric to compute the weights of base classifiers. One of them use the inverse of error rate of oob data and another one use the accuracy of oob data. Among them, TWRF is defined according to the form of (3). This method is easy and subtle. As they said, TWRF could be better than random forest in high-dimensional data. Let $\{Tree_i(x), Tree2(x), ..., Tree_t(x), x \in X\}$ denote the set of trees in a random forest.

$$f(x) = \sum_{i=1}^{t} weight_i * Tree_i(x) \tag{3}$$

where $weight_i$ represents the weight of $Tree_i$.

But in our opinion, there are still some problems in the method. The first problem is that it just uses the information of oob data. Different base classifiers have different oob data. It is not common to evaluate the performance of different models. The second problem is that although some base classifiers have the same accuracy of oob data, they may have different performance in predicting new instance. The phenomenon can be shown in the followed situation. Tree1 and Tree2 have the same accuracy in some specific dataset, but for most of instances Tree1 gets the right result with probability 0.8 and Tree2 gets the right result with probability 0.6. We have reasons to think that Tree1 should be more important than Tree2. We can also explain it from the point of view of entropy see Eq. (4). Tree1 has lower uncertainty than Tree2.

$$H = - \sum_{i}^{|c|} p_i \log p_i \tag{4}$$

Based on the two problems, we put forward our scheme of computing weights. To distinguish with TWRF which based on the accuracy of oob data, we called our random forest as refined weighted random forest (RWRF). The weights of RWRF are computed in (5)

$$weight_i = \sum_{i=1}^{n} [(p_{ci} - (1 - p_{ci})) * I(p_{ci} > (1 - p_{ci}))$$
$$+\alpha * (p_{ci} - (1 - p_{ci})) * I(p_{ci} < (1 - p_{ci}))] \tag{5}$$

where i is the index of instance, c is the class of x_i.

The improvements of our method include two aspects. First, the data we used is all training data including in-bag data and oob data. The reason is that the performance evaluation of different base classifiers should have the same evaluation dataset, in-bag data measures the converge degree of our model and oob data measures the generalization of our base classifiers. Second, we use the margin between probability of predicting true class and false class label. The margin measures the extent to which the expectation number of votes for the right class exceeds the expectation number of votes for other class. We accumulate correct prediction margin and penalize incorrect prediction with a hyper parameter α. The hyper parameter can be set according to validation set. It depends on the penalization to the base classifier when it make a wrong prediction. It varies in different dataset.

For large dataset and imbalanced data, we take a small step forward. In order to reflect the difference among different weights, we make the weights to be zero-mean-centering. Additionally, for the weights which are less or equal to zero, we just drop it. The reason behind it is that for large data set, the difference among different base classifiers is mainly reflected by the ability of distinguishing the samples closing to decision boundary. For most of data keeping away from the decision boundary, all base classifiers can classify them well. A base classifier which can distinguish data closing to decision tree should get more attention. For imbalanced data, we should decrease the effect of instances of majority class. Therefore, it is reasonable to make the weights to be zero-mean-centering. We also prove it by our experiments that zero mean centering could be better than the case without it. There are another benefit when we use zero-mean-centering of weights. We can just use half of trees we trained to predict new data instances. In the classification problem, all classification results of individual trees are combined to decide the final class which having the most votes.

Algorithm 1 describes the process of producing RWRF.

Algorithm 1. Refined weighted random forest.

Input:
D: the training data
t: the number of Trees
Output:
RWRF f
1: **for** $i = 1$ to t **do**
2:    Sample from training dataset D using bootstrap to get in-of-bag data;
3:    Use in-of-bag data to build decision tree;
4:    Use dataset D to compute $weight_i$ for $Tree_i$;
5: **end for**
6: Assemble $weight_i$ for $Tree_i$ to get f;
7: **return** f;

---

4   Experiment

This section shows the details and results of experiments. Firstly, performance measures and dataset we used are described. Then we make a comparison between random forest, TWRF and our RWRF in public dataset and our private bank dataset. Finally, the result of experiments is shown and explained. We conduct our experiments to compare our RWRF with classic random forest and TWRF. The implementation of random forest comes from scikit-learn, an open source python library for machine learning and data mining [36]. We implemented TWRF and our RWRF as a plug-in of scikit-learn and carried out all experiments in the same environment.

4.1   Performance Measures

Before we describe the experiment, we first describe the measures we used. For public dataset, we just use accuracy as performance measure. The basic measures are listed in Table 1. For our private data, accuracy is not suitable to measure the performance of these methods since it is a significantly imbalanced dataset [3,9]. For example, predicting all instances into the majority class will also have a high value of accuracy. Hence we also use precision, recall, F-measure and log loss as our performance measures. Precision is the percent of true positive guesses in all positive guesses. Recall is the fraction of positive guesses in all positive instances. F-measure is the harmonic mean of recall and precision. Log-loss is the mean of cross entropy between the distribution of the true labels and the predictions for all data instances.

$$accuracy = \frac{TP + TN}{TP + FP + TN + FN} \tag{6}$$

$$precision = \frac{TP}{TP + FP} \tag{7}$$

$$recall = \frac{TP}{TP + FN} \tag{8}$$

$$F - measure = \frac{2 \times precision \times recall}{precision + recall} \tag{9}$$

$$logloss = \frac{1}{n} \sum (y_i \log p_i + (1 - y_i) \log(1 - p_i)) \tag{10}$$

Table 1. basic measures

Predict	Real	
	Positive	Negative
Positive	True positives	False positive
Negative	False negative	True negative

4.2 Experiment I

The first dataset we used is 20news group which is classic dataset of text classification. Due to our RWRF is focus on binary classification problem. We choose several pair of news which are selected in 20news group. The pair we choose is showed in Table 2. In every pair, there are 1000 data instances and half of them is included in every class. To verify the effectiveness of our method, we have also used other public datasets as listed in Table 2. All of these datasets are from libsvm [31] and UCI [35] data repository. We split the dataset into training set and testing set according to the ratio of 3:1. The number of trees is set from 30 to 300 with an increment 30. We compute the mean of all these ten results. The detailed results of experiments are showed in Table 2.

Table 2. Accuracy Results of experiment I

Datasets	Methods		
	RF	TWRF	RWRF
alt.atheism-misc.forsale	90.55%	90.69%	**91.68%**
comp.graphics-comp.sys.mac.hardware	92.64%	92.64%	**93.65%**
sci.crypt-comp.windows.x	84.96%	85.08%	**85.97%**
sci.med-rec.motorcycles	81.11%	81.23%	**83.88%**
comp.graphics-comp.sys.mac.hardware	85.92%	85.92%	**86.43%**
talk.politics.guns-talk.religion.misc	75.45%	75.45%	**77.89%**
breast_cancer	94.15%	94.15%	**94.74%**
cod_rna	94.51%	94.55%	**95.19%**
occupy	94.93%	94.97%	**95.83%**
phishing	96.55%	**96.55%**	96.52%
diabetes	79.92%	79.52%	**80.32%**

From the results, we can find that our RWRF achieves the best result in all datasets except phishing.

4.3 Experiment II

In this experiment, We explore the effectiveness of RWRF in our private data which comes from a financial company of China. The dataset including 5 million transactions of B2C data. Each record is labeled by legal or fraud. There are only 150000 fraud transactions and the rest of data are legal transactions. This means that the dataset is extremely imbalanced and thus the relevant imbalanced problem should be considered. As fraud transactions in the dataset are limited, this experiment adopts the random under-sampling method [9] on legal transactions. The results are described in Table 3.

Table 3. Measures results of experiment II

Datasets	Methods				
	Accuracy	Logloss	Precision	Recall	F-measure
RF	97.11%	0.079	37.62%	**85.32%**	0.522
TWRF	97.11%	0.079	37.63%	**85.32%**	0.522
RWRF	**97.76%**	**0.075**	**44.50%**	84.68%	**0.583**

From Table 3, we can find that the performance our RWRF is better than RF and TWRF. Although our recall rate is a little small, our precision has a great improvement which means that RWRF has less false positive rate. The reason is that we penalize the classifier when it misclassified instances by setting α a big value. Because F-measure is the harmonic mean of recall and precision and the space is limited, we just draw the relation between the number of trees and the value of F-measure in Fig. 3. From it we find that RF and TWRF has almost the same results. The reason may be that the dataset is imbalanced and is not high-dimensional. Therefore, TWRF is not too suitable for such data, but RWRF is more suitable.

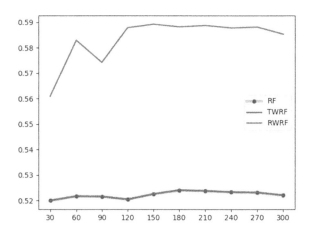

Fig. 3. F-measure results of experiment II.

We also apply other algorithms in our experiments, such as support vector machine, naive bayes an neural network. But the results of them are worse than random forest. Due to the limited space, we don't describe them here.

5   Conclusions

In this paper, we propose an improved random forest, RWRF, and compare it with random forest and TWRF. A B2C dataset on credit card transactions and other public datasets are used in our experiment. We just consider binary classification problem in this paper. In the future, we plan to apply it in multi classification problem.

Acknowledgments. Authors would like to thank reviewers for their helpful comments, and also thank Professor Changjun Jiang who provides authors a lot of assistance on data and experiments. This paper is supported in part by the National Natural Science Foundation of China under grand no. 61572360 and in part by the Shanghai Shuguang Program under grant no. 15SG18. Corresponding author is G.J. Liu.

References

1. Gupta, S., Johari, R.: A new framework for credit card transactions involving mutual authentication between cardholder and merchant. In: 2011 International Conference on Communication Systems and Network Technologies, pp. 22–26. IEEE (2011)
2. Thomas, K., Grier, C., Ma, J., Paxson, V., Song, D.: Design and evaluation of a real-time url spam filtering service. In: Security and Privacy, vol. 42, pp. 447–462. IEEE (2011)
3. Zhang, Y., Liu, G., Luan, W., Yan, C., Jiang, C.: An approach to class imbalance problem based on stacking and inverse random under sampling methods. In: 2018 IEEE 15th International Conference on Networking, Sensing and Control (ICNSC), pp. 1–6. IEEE (2018)
4. Bolton, R.J., Hand, D.J.: Unsupervised profiling methods for fraud detection. In: Credit Scoring and Credit Control VII, pp. 235–255 (2001)
5. Gmbh, Y., Co, K.G.: Global online payment methods: Full year 2016, Technical report (2016)
6. Seyedhossein, L., Hashemi, M.R.: Mining information from credit card time series for timelier fraud detection. In: 2010 5th International Symposium on Telecommunications (IST), pp. 619–624. IEEE (2010)
7. Zheng, L., Liu, G., Yan, C., Jiang, C.: Transaction fraud detection based on total order relation and behavior diversity. IEEE Trans. Comput. Soc. Syst. **99**, 1–11 (2018)
8. Srivastava, A., Kundu, A., Sural, S., Majumdar, A.: Credit card fraud detection using hidden Markov model. IEEE Trans. Dependable Secure Comput. **5**(1), 37–48 (2008)
9. Drummond, C., Holte, R.C.: C4.5, class imbalance, and cost sensitivity: why under-sampling beats oversampling. In: Proceedings of the ICML Workshop on Learning from Imbalanced Datasets II, pp. 1–8 (2003)
10. Quah, J.T.S., Sriganesh, M.: Real-time credit card fraud detection using computational intelligence. Expert Syst. Appl. **35**(4), 1721–1732 (2008)
11. Kundu, A., Panigrahi, S., Sural, S., Majumdar, A.K.: Blast-ssaha hybridization for credit card fraud detection. IEEE Trans. Dependable Secure Comput. **6**(4), 309–315 (2009)

12. Xuan, S., Liu, G., Li, Z., Zheng, L., Wang, S., Jiang, C.: Random forest for credit card fraud detection. In: 2018 IEEE 15th International Conference on Networking, Sensing and Control (ICNSC), pp. 1–6. IEEE (2018)
13. Bhattacharyya, S., Jha, S., Tharakunnel, K., Westland, J.C.: Data mining for credit card fraud: a comparative study. Decis. Support Syst. **50**(3), 602–613 (2011)
14. Mota, G., Fernandes, J., Belo, O.: Usage signatures analysis an alternative method for preventing fraud in E-Commerce applications. In: International Conference on Data Science and Advanced Analytics, pp. 203–208. IEEE (2014)
15. Behdad, M., Barone, L., Bennamoun, M., French, T.: Nature-inspired techniques in the context of fraud detection. IEEE Trans. Syst. Man Cyber. Part C **42**(6), 1273–1290 (2012)
16. Bolton, R.J., Hand, D.J.: Statistical fraud detection: a review. Stat. Sci. **17**(3), 235–249 (2002)
17. Chan, P.K., Fan, W., Prodromidis, A.L., Stolfo, S.J.: Distributed data mining in credit card fraud detection. IEEE Intell. Syst. Appl. **14**(6), 67–74 (2002)
18. Chen, R.C., Chen, T.S., Lin, C.C.: A new binary support vector system for increasing detection rate of credit card fraud. Int. J. Pattern Recognit. Artif. Intell. **20**(02), 227–239 (2006)
19. Mcdonald, D.W., Ackerman, M.S.: Expertise recommender:a flexible recommendation system and architecture. In: ACM Conference on Computer Supported Cooperative Work, pp. 231–240. ACM (2000)
20. Chandola, V., Banerjee, A., Kumar, V.: Anomaly detection: a survey. ACM Comput. Surv. **41**(3), 1–58 (2009)
21. Breiman, L.: Random forests. Mach. Learn. **45**(1), 5–32 (2001)
22. Dietterich, T.G.: Ensemble methods in machine learning. In: Kittler, J., Roli, F. (eds.) MCS 2000. LNCS, vol. 1857, pp. 1–15. Springer, Heidelberg (2000). https://doi.org/10.1007/3-540-45014-9_1
23. Quinlan, J.R.: Induction on decision tree. Mach. Learn. **1**(1), 81–106 (1986)
24. Breiman, L., Friedman, J.H., Olshen, R., Stone, C.J.: Classification and regression trees. Biometrics **40**(3), 358 (1984)
25. Breiman, L.: Bagging predictors. Mach. Learn. **24**(2), 123–140 (1996)
26. Albrecht, W.S., Albrecht, C., Albrecht, C.C.: Current trends in fraud and its detection. Inf. Syst. Secur. **17**(1), 2–12 (2008)
27. Li, H.B., Wang, W., Ding, H.W., Dong, J.: Trees weighting random forest method for classifying high-dimensional noisy data. In: IEEE, International Conference on E-Business Engineering, pp. 160–163. IEEE (2011)
28. Zhou, Q., Zhou, H., Li, T.: Cost-sensitive feature selection using random forest: selecting low-cost subsets of informative features. Knowl. Based Syst. **95**, 1–11 (2016)
29. Harris, J.R., Grunsky, E.C.: Predictive lithological mapping of Canada's North using random forest classification applied to geophysical and geochemical data. Comput. Geosci. **80**, 9–25 (2015)
30. Singh, K., Guntuku, S.C., Thakur, A., et al.: Big data analytics framework for peer-to-peer botnet detection using random forests. Inform. Sci. **278**(19), 488–497 (2014)
31. Chang, C.C., Lin, C.J.: LIBSVM: a library for support vector machines. ACM Trans. Intell. Syst. Technol. **2**, 27:1–27:27 (2011)
32. Fanelli, G., Dantone, M., Gall, J., et al.: Random forests for real time 3D face analysis. Int. J. Comput. Vis. **101**(3), 437–458 (2013)

33. Winham, S.J., Freimuth, R.R., Biernacka, J.M.: A weighted random forests approach to improve predictive performance. Stat. Anal. Data Min. ASA Data Sci. J. **6**(6), 496–505 (2013)
34. Friedman, J.H.: Greedy function approximation: a gradient boosting machine. Ann. Stat. **29**(5), 1189–1232 (2001)
35. UCI Homepage. http://archive.ics.uci.edu/ml/datasets.html
36. Scikit-learn Homepage. http://scikit-learn.org/stable/

A Congestion Control Protocol for Wireless Sensor Networks

Chuang Ma$^{(\boxtimes)}$

Shanghai Polytechnic University, Shanghai, China
machuang@sspu.edu.cn

Abstract. In Wireless Sensor Networks (WSNs), the congestion can increase the ratio of packet loss and reduce of the network throughput. In this paper, I study on the congestion problem between child and parent nodes in WSN, which typically faces of low power and resource constraint devices. I use game theory strategy to design a parent-change procedure which decides how nodes changing their next hop node to mitigate the effect of network congestion. The simulation results show that the protocol can achieve improvement in packet loss rate and throughput.

Keywords: Congestion control · Game theory
Wireless Sensor Networks

1 Introduction

Nowadays, Wireless Sensor Networks (WSNs) are used to connect industrial devices, hospital instruments, household appliances and other fields. With WSNs, people can receive data from sensors and send information by the wireless network everywhere. These systems usually include many end devices that conform to IEEE 802.15.4 standard and are often characterized by short transmission range, low data rate, low cost and low communication power. The Internet Engineer Task Force (IETF) working group has standardized an adaptive layer to use in the devices with IEEE 802.15.4 MAC/PHY called IPv6 over Low power Wireless Personal Network (6LoWPAN) [1]. With 6LoWPAN implementation, IEEE 802.15.4 devices will gain the ability to receive, process, and forward IPv6 packets. Based on 6LoWPAN, IETF further proposed IPv6 Routing Protocol for Low-power and Lossy Networks (RPL) [2].

RPL is a tree-like topology routing protocol supporting multiple point to single point, normally, the single node is the sink node, single point to multiple point and point-to-point traffic which can be used in the applications of WSNs. If an event occurs in the leaf node, all the nodes in the event region will send packets to sink and may cause network congestion towards sink node. In WSNs, congestion control contains congestion detection and congestion avoidance. In general, congestion detection adopts few metrics such as buffer occupancy, channel loading, and the ratio of packet inter-arrival time to packet service time to detect the presence of congestion [3,4]. When congestion is detected, I use the congestion

© Springer Nature Switzerland AG 2018
X. Chen et al. (Eds.): CSoNet 2018, LNCS 11280, pp. 356–367, 2018.
https://doi.org/10.1007/978-3-030-04648-4_30

avoidance mechanisms to mitigate the presence of congestion. Currently, there is no explicit mechanism to detect or to avoid congestion in RPL protocol. In fact, RPL protocol uses a simple parent selection mechanism to avoid selecting parents with lower link quality, larger hop count, or larger expected transmission count [5].

In this paper, I propose a congestion control protocol based on game theory to alleviate the effect of congestion. In my protocol, nodes are informed about the presence of congestion by their parent through control messages. A child node will decide whether it changes its parent or not based on the game theory strategy to eliminate congestion by changing parent with light load.

The rest of this paper is organized as follows. Section 2 introduces related work. The detail of my protocol is presented in Sect. 3. The simulation results are described in Sects. 4 and 5 concludes this paper.

2   Related Works

In [6], the authors proposed hop-by-hop congestion control and load balancing scheme called CONSEQ in WSNs. It uses special effective queue length (EQL) as metric of congestion degree. CONSEQ dynamically adjusts transmission rate according to degree of congestion of each node in its forwarding set which contains neighbor nodes with smaller hop count to sink. If congestion is not mitigated, each node will use fuzzy logic to reduce the transmission rate.

The authors in [7] proposed a Priority-based Congestion Control Protocol (PCCP). PCCP uses ratio of packet inter-arrival time to packet service time as a metric of congestion. Once the congestion is detected, nodes will use the transmission rate of upward nodes and priority of packet to adjust its transmission rate.

The authors in [8] proposed a priority based congestion control for heterogeneous traffic in multipath WSNs. The congestion is detected by packet service rate. When congestion is detected, it will adjust the transmission rate by considering priority and traffic rate of neighbors in next transmission period to mitigate congestion. This protocol does not take advantage of multipath routing, and it reduces the transmission rate of each node instead of rerouting and bypassing the congested path.

In [9], the authors proposed a new scheme called Siphon. Siphon uses special virtual sinks distributed in the whole network, which have more powerful radio than normal sensor nodes. When congestion is detected, sensor nodes will forward packets to near virtual sink and the virtual sink will forward the packets to real physical sink via other radio network such as Wi-Fi. However, it needs another connected radio network which is infeasible in both low power and low cost consideration WSNs.

A new concept of routing protocol with congestion alleviation called Traffic-Aware Dynamic Routing (TADR) is proposed in [10]. TADR considers network traffic pattern as a "bowl" with sink residing at the bottom, and all data packets flow down just like water along the surface of the bowl. TADR uses combination of depth field force and queue length potential force to indicate which neighbor should forward next. Although TADR guides node to detour the congestion path, it has high chance to form one or more routing loops and increases the end-to-end delay.

3 Congestion Control Protocol

In this paper, I mitigate congestion via alternative path selection mechanisms for the following reasons. In RPL, the network topology is a Destination Orientated Direct Acyclic Graph (DODAG). Each node will emit DODAG Information Object (DIO) packet to all its neighbors to maintain the network connectivity. The DIO packets are controlled by a polite gossip policy, where each node periodically broadcasts a DIO packet to local neighbors but stays quiet if it has recently heard a DIO packet sent by itself. The DIO packets are sent from nodes periodically, however, the overheads of the packets are less than other control data because of the less size and forwarding times even when congestion occurs.

The DIO packet includes RPLInstanceID which is a unique identity of the network, rank field i.e. the sender's rank, and the option field which is used to store optional information such as objective function of RPL. The objective function is used to calculate the rank of nodes. In our protocol, I use the first and second bits of rank field as Congestion Notification bits (CN bits) and I will store the sending node's children information, including their IP addresses and the sending rates of the sender into the option field. When a node receives a DIO packet, it will use the objective function and the rank of the DIO sender to calculate an expected rank. If the expected rank is smaller than its current rank, the node will consider changing its parent to the DIO sender.

For most applications in WSNs, traffic flow in a network is light for a long time until one of the predefined events occurs in the sensing region. When the source sensors begin to collect data, sensors in the region will start transmitting a large amount of packets. Once the packets number is large enough to form transient packet burst, it will possibly cause congestion on the path from source nodes towards the sink node. However, mitigating the congestion by reducing the rate of upstream node will violate fidelity level required by applications and decrease the throughput in RPL.

My protocol redirect the traffic flow to another path by parent-change procedure. In this procedure, nodes change their parents with maximum benefit such as fewer hop count and smaller buffer occupancy. After that, the traffic flow will be scattered. It will improve the throughput of communication and reduce the packet loss rate. In my protocol, each node will keep to read the CN bit in DIO packet from parent. On the other hand, I will try to find an alternative path to scatter the traffic flow when congestion is detected. In RPL network, DIO packets are used to maintain the network connectivity. Upon receiving a DIO packet, a node saves the sending rate and link quality into its neighbor table and check whether the DIO sender is its parent. If the DIO packet is sent from its parent, the node will check the CN bit first. If the CN bit is clear, it means there is no congestion and the child node will calculate its rank as regular. Otherwise, the child node knows that the congestion occurs on its parent. Therefore, all child nodes associated with the parent will use game theory based strategy to determine their new parents. If congestion cannot be mitigated through the parent-change procedure, each node will notify its children through the DIO packet with CN bits set and the congestion information will be broadcasted to all leaf nodes. After a child node switches from its current parent to another, the nodes will forward the sensing data and find new path to transfer, moreover, its new neighbor will receive the data and can recognize the new child including the new parent. However, when the congestion disappears also after the child node changes its parent, the new parent will sent the DIO packet again periodically, and new round of selection will be implemented.

3.1 Congestion Detection Metrics

In recent congestion control protocols, several congestion metrics were proposed such as queue occupancy, channel loading, ratio of packet inter-arrival time to packet service time. I use the net packet flow rate which is packet generation rate $r_{generation}$ subtracted by packet service rate r_{output} as metric for detecting the presence of congestion on parent node. We can define the congestion metric α as below.

$$\alpha = r_{generation} - r_{output} \tag{1}$$

The value of α can be treated as the buffer occupation growing rate. If α is greater than 0, the probability of congestion is considerable. Conversely, if α is less than or equals to 0, the probability of congestion is low. Moreover, the bigger the α is, the more probability of congestion occurs. We can define the metric as below.

1. No Congestions, $\alpha \leq 0$
2. Lower Congestions, $0 < \alpha \leq 0.1 \times r_{generation}$
3. Middle Congestions, $0.1 \times r_{generation} < \alpha \leq 0.25 \times r_{generation}$
4. High Congestions, $0.25 \times r_{generation} < \alpha$

When there is no congestions in wireless sensor networks, the CN bits will be set by 00; when the networks is in Lower Congestions status, the CN bits will be set to 01; when the networks is in Middle Congestions status, the CN bits will be set to 10; when the networks is in High Congestions status, the CN bits will be set to 11. In the protocol, I address the middle and lower congestions problem only. If the network is under the status of high congestions, the sink node will give an information to their child nodes to stop the sending.

In RPL standard, DIO packets can be used to disseminate the net packet flow rate. Furthermore, we can use DIO packets to inform the presence of congestion to all the neighbors by adding a CN bits.

3.2   Rank Value of Nodes

The most important part of my protocol is to decide the rank value of each node in a DODAG network. The rank value can directly influence the network topology and the performance of network because each node will select a parent to minimize its rank value. Many metrics and constraints were studied to calculate the rank of a node such as energy state, hop count, expected transmission count, delay, and throughput. In my protocol, we can describe the rank of nodes as below.

$$rank(n) = RI + rank_p \tag{2}$$

RI is a constant which represents a rank increasing between a node and its parent. The rank increasing is used to prevent routing loop and the value is varied by implementations. We can set RI to 256 in my protocol (same as Contiki [9]). And $rank_p$ is the rank of the candidate parent p. I assume the link quality from node n to p is good enough.

3.3   Parent-Change Procedure

When congestion is detected, each node in the congested area will start the parent-change procedure, although it does not mean that every node have to change their current parents. In parent-change procedure, each node uses the potential game theory method [11] to find a better parent to improve the network performance. Based on the potential game theory, we can converge to a stable state called Nash Equilibrium (NE) which is also the best parent allocation for whole nodes in the congested area. As we have discussed before, each node will select a parent which can minimize its rank. However, if too many nodes select the same parent, the load of this parent node will increase significantly to lead to even congestion. Thus, we can treat the behavior of parent selection as a game called parent-selection game. Parent-selection game is a game which each player (node) attends a competition of parent selection to minimize its rank. In this game, the action (a node makes its decision of parent selection) of each node will affect other node's utility (i.e. throughput). We will describe the mechanism of parent-selection game as follows.

My parent-change procedure starts with a parent node that sends a congestion message to its children through the DIO packet. In potential game theory, we can reach NE by restricting only one node from changing its parent with minimal utility at a time. We use a random timer to randomly diffuse the time of change of parent by every node. When node i changes its parent, it will broadcast a new DIO packet to notify other children and increase the rank of old parent by RI to avoid changing back to the old parent. Noting that, we can adjust the timer according to new metrics instead of random timer, such as we can generate the shorter timer for nodes with higher transmission rates to reach NE faster.

In game theory, each player's action will affect other player's utility. The difficulty in finding an optimal action is that each player only knows about the utility of itself. Thus, nodes cannot know which selection is better for the global interest. Fortunately, as a subset of game theory, potential game theory can be used to deal with this problem. A game is a potential game if the incentive of all players to change their selection can be expressed using a single global function called the potential function. With the aid of potential function, each node can determine whether a parent is worth changing or not by only considering its utility function. For the use of potential game, we will transform my parent-selection problem into a game representation and present the parent-change procedure. When congestion is detected by a node, it will set the CN bits in DIO packet, which contains the parent information, children list, corresponding transmission rate, and forward to all its children. The children nodes receiving this message will consider changing parents according to the potential function. The potential function is built from information in neighbor table of each node, and the table will be updated upon the node received DIO messages from its neighbors. Each node can use this potential function to find a new parent which can decrease the value of this function in each round towards NE according to two properties of potential game: Property (1) is that each ordinal potential game exists a NE. Property (2) is that if we limit only one node from changing its parent at a time, we can converge to NE.

We define the *parent-selection game* as $\Gamma = \langle N, A, u \rangle$, where N is the set of players, A is the set of actions and u is the utility function set. For each player n_i, we defined the following terms:

Player set N: *The player set is defined as all children nodes of the DIO sender. We denote player set as $N = \{n_1, n_2, \ldots, n_m\}$. The set N contains m children.*

Parent set P: *The parent set of n_i is defined as all neighbors of player n_i whose ranks are less than n_i. We denote parent set as $P_i = \{p_1, p_2, \ldots, p_g\}$ if there are g parents for player n_i. $P = \bigcup_{1 \leq k \leq m} P_k$ is the union of parents of the m children, assuming $|P| = q$.*

Action set A: *The action set A is composed of any possible actions of each player. For player n_i, $A_i = \{a_i \mid a_i \in B^q$, there is only one 1 among a_i with the rest are $0\}$ is used to represent the parent selection decision of n_i, where $B = \{0,1\}$. For instance, $a_i = (1,0,\ldots 0)$ represents that node n_i chooses node p_1 as its parent. The action set of this game is defined as $A=\{(a_1, a_2, \ldots, a_m)^T \mid \forall a_i \in A_i\}$. Therefore, each element in A is an $m \times q$ matrix which shows the decision of every player in N. Thus, $a_{i,j} = 1$ means that player i selects parent j as parent in action a_i. Noting that if $p_j \notin P_i$, $a_{i,j}$ will be 0.*

Utility function u: *For player n_i, utility function is defined as $u_i: A \to \mathbb{R}$. The utility function is used to represent how much node n_i cost to reach sink node for action a_i. Thus, the smaller value of utility is the better one. We define utility function of player n_i with action a as,*

$$u_i(a) = RI + rank(p_k) + \sum_{1 \leq j \neq i \leq m, a_{j,k}=1} rate(n_j) + N_k \times rate(n_i) \qquad (3)$$

where p_k is the parent candidate of player n_i ($a_{i,k} = 1$) and N_k is the number of children of parent p_k. The utility function of player n_i is composed of four terms: rank increase per hop, link quality between nodes n_i and p_k, rank of p_k and the sum of packet transmission rate of all children of p_k. In utility function (5), we consider the rank of candidate parent p_k and transmission rate of each child associating with p_k. Hence, the utility function is able to reflect the load of a candidate parent. Noting that, we multiply N_k to the transmission rate of node i ($rate(n_i)$) is to balance the number of children in each parent node. This is because selecting a parent with high N_k will increase the cost of utility function quickly. The *rank* is defined in Eq. (1) and the transmission rate function is defined in Eq. (4).

$$rate(n_i) = R \times RI/M \tag{4}$$

where R is the packet delivery rate and M is the maximum packet delivery rate of each node. When a node reaches its maximum rate, it will not be able to handle more data packet. Thus, we let the rate function equals to RI when it reaches the maximum packet delivery rate. This will lead nodes to select other parents when the load of the candidate parent is satisfied.

A game Γ is an ordinal potential game if it admits an ordinal potential function. A function $\Phi : A \rightarrow \mathbb{R}$ is an ordinal potential for Γ if for every $i \in N$ and for every $a_{-i} \in A_{-i}$,

where $A_{-i} = \{(a_1, a_2, \cdots, a_{i-1}, a_{i+1}, \cdots, a_q) | \forall a_j \in A_j, 1 \leq j \neq i \leq\}$ and the condition in Eq. (5) is satisfied, where $a_{-i} = (a_1, a_2, \cdots, a_{i-1}, a_{i+1}, \cdots, a_q)$ is the action without player i (i.e. $a = (a_1, a_2, \cdots, a_q) = (a_i, a_{-i})$

$$u_i(a_i', a_{-i}) - u_i(a_i, a_{-i}) < 0 \iff \Phi(a_i', a_{-i}) - \Phi(a_i, a_{-i}) < 0 \tag{5}$$

We define the ordinal potential function Φ as Eq. (6) and prove it will satisfy Eq. (5) in Theorem 1.

$$\Phi(a) = \sum_{j=1}^{m} \{N_k \times rate(n_j) + rank(p_k)\}, \text{ if } a_{j,k} = 1 \tag{6}$$

where $a \in A$. The potential function is able to reflect the global interest in a network. In Eq. (4), the potential function contains the rank of each node's parent, and the packet rate of each child multiplied by the number of children in its parent.

Theorem 1. *The parent-selection game is an ordinal potential game with ordinal potential function Φ.*

Proof: We need to prove that Φ is a potential function in parent-selection game which satisfies Eq. (6) above. Assuming that a player n_i changes its parent to $p_{l'}$ from p_l, it changes the action from a to a'. The difference of utility function is:

$$u_i(a') - u_i(a) = rank(p_{l'}) - rank(p_l)$$

$$+ \left(\sum_{1 \leq j \neq i \leq m, a_{j,l'}' = 1} rate(n_j) - \sum_{1 \leq j \neq i \leq m, a_{j,l} = 1} rate(n_j) \right)$$

$$+ N_{l'}' \times rate(n_i) - N_l \times rate(n_i)$$

Then the difference of potential function is:

$$\Phi(a') - \Phi(a) = rank(p_{l'}) - rank(p_l) + \sum_{j=1}^{m} N'_k \times rate(n_j) - \sum_{j=1}^{m} N_k \times rate(n_j),$$

where $a_{j,k} = 1$, for each j.

Let $C = rank(p_{l'}) - rank(p_l)$.

$$\Phi(a') - \Phi(a) = C + \sum_{j=1}^{m} N'_k \times rate(n_j) - \sum_{j=1}^{m} N_k \times rate(n_j)$$

$$= C + \sum_{j=1,a'_{j,l}=1}^{m} N'_l \times rate(n_j) + \sum_{j=1,a'_{j,l'}=1}^{m} N'_{i'} \times rate(n_j) \quad (7)$$

$$- \sum_{j=1,a_{j,l}=1}^{m} N_l \times rate(n_j) - \sum_{j=1,a_{j,l'}=1}^{m} N_{l'} \times rate(n_j)$$

Because only node i changed its parent from p_l to $p_{l'}$, we can only consider the column l and l' in a and a', respectively. Thus, the number of children of p_l in a is one less than in action a' and the number of children of $p_{l'}$ in a is one more than in action a'. Thus, we have $N'_l = N_l - 1$ and $N'_{l'} = N_{l'} + 1$, the Eq. (7) can be deduced as follows.

$$(7) = C + \sum_{1 \leq j \neq i \leq m, a'_{j,l'}=1} rate(n_j) + N'_{i'} \times rate(n_i)$$

$$- \sum_{1 \leq j \neq i \leq m, a_{j,i}=1} rate(n_j) - N_l \times rate(n_i) \quad (8)$$

$$= u_i(a') - u_i(a)$$

$\therefore \Phi(a') - \Phi(a) = u_i(a') - u_i(a)$ ∎

Theorem 1 shows that my parent-selection game is an ordinal potential game. Thus, we can reach NE by each node changing its parent with minimal utility at a time.

4 Performance Evaluation

In the related works, there are no research with congestion mechanism in RPL and also they do not consider at tree-like network topology. Thus, we compare the performance of my proposed protocol to ContikiRPL with OF0 denoted as CRPL-OF0 [12]. In CRPL-OF0, the ranks of each node are calculated using the metric of hop count and expected transmission times from source to sink, respectively. We evaluate the performance of the protocols on throughput, and packet loss rate by Cooja simulation tool in Contiki system [13].

Nodes in simulation are categorized into three types: sink node, relay nodes, and sensing nodes. We evaluate the performance of my protocol by two scenarios and their nodes deployments are shown in Fig. 1. In scenario, we deploy the sink node in the center of the sensing area to collect data. The sensing data will be created by sensor node and the relay node will forward the data, however most node in real scenario have both abilities of sensing and forwarding. In this paper, the two kinds of nodes are distinguished in order to describe the process clearly. Each sensing node has one or two parents. We use Unit Disk Graph Medium (UDGM) with distance lose module as radio interference. The success rate of transmission in UDGM module decreases as distance increasing. We set the packet size to 100 bytes to avoid packet fragmentation. This is because there is no retransmission mechanism in Contiki and it will cause entire packet retransmission even if only one fragment is lost. The area size is 220 m × 220 m, simulation time is 200 s, radio range is 50 m and the numbers of nodes are 26 and 22 in scenario.

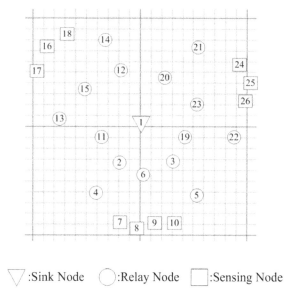

▽ :Sink Node   ◯ :Relay Node   ☐ :Sensing Node

Fig. 1. The nodes deployment in scenario

My metrics for performance comparison are the average packet loss rate, and average throughput. We simulate different transmission rate ranging from 2.5 to 18.2 packets per second for the above metrics. In the following simulations, we can reach NE within 13 times of parent changing.

In Fig. 2, the packet loss rate of my protocol is less than 25% while the loss rates of CRPL-OF0 is higher than 57% when the packet transmission rate of each node is equal to 10. When the transmission rate of node grows, the loss rates of CRPL-OF0 are significantly increasing. This is because nodes in CRPL-OF0 tend to select parent with fewer hop count to the sink. As the transmission rate grows, there are too many packets injected into the same candidate parent

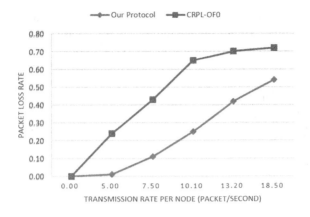

Fig. 2. Packet loss rate vs. transmission rate

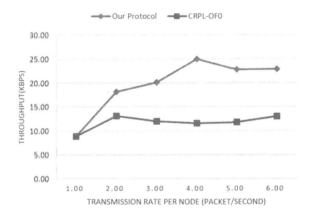

Fig. 3. Throughput vs. transmission rate

nodes than they can afford. On the other hand, nodes in my protocol can change their parents to keep the global load balance and avoid congested path, so that the lower loss rate are achieved.

Figure 3 shows the throughput with different packet transmission rates. When the transmission rate of each node grows, the throughput of my protocol is two times better than CRPL-OF0. Moreover, the peak throughput of CRPL-OF0 is around 7.5 packets per second and the peak throughput can extend to 10 packets per second in my protocol.

5   Conclusions

In traditional congestion control scheme, rate reducing mechanisms are used to mitigate the presence of congestion. However, rate reducing will degrade the throughput and lose the fidelity of application's request. In this paper, I proposed a novel congestion control protocol based on game theory over RPL to maximize the throughput. My protocol exploits a parent selection scheme which can improve the throughput of communication. When congestion occurred, nodes will change their parents according to the utility function in game theory to avoid the congested path. I implement my protocol in Contiki OS and evaluate the performance via simulator Cooja. It is shown that my protocol has two times improvement in throughput and less packet loss rate compared to ContikiRPL protocols with a little average hop count increasing to sink node.

References

1. Montenegro, G., Kushalnagar, N., Hui, J., Culler, D.: Transmission of IPv6 Packets over IEEE 802.15.4 Networks. RFC 4944 (Proposed Standard), Internet Engineering Task Force, September 2007. http://tools.ietf.org/html/rfc4944/
2. Winter, T., et al.: RPL: IPv6 Routing Protocol for Low-Power and Lossy Networks (RPL), RFC 6550 (Proposed Standard), Internet Engineering Task Force, March 2012. http://tools.ietf.org/html/rfc6550/
3. Kafi, M.A., Djenouri, D., Ben-Othman, J., Badache, N.: Congestion control protocols in wireless sensor networks: a survey. IEEE Commun. Surv. Tut. **16**(3), 1369–1390 (2014)
4. Iniya Shree, S., Karthiga, M., Mariyammal, C.: Improving congestion control in wsn by multipath routing with priority based scheduling. In: Proceedings of 2017 International Conference on Inventive Systems and Control (ICISC), Coimbatore, India, pp. 1–6, January 2017
5. Couto, D.D., Aguayo, D., Bicket, J., Morris, R.: A high-throughput path metric for multi-hop wireless routing. In: Proceedings of the 9th Annual International Conference on Mobile Computing and Networking, San Diego, USA, pp. 134–146, September 2003
6. Joseph Auxilius Jude, M., Diniesh, V.C.: DACC: dynamic agile congestion control scheme for effective multiple traffic wireless sensor networks. In: Proceedings of 2017 International Conference on Wireless Communications, Signal Processing and Networking (WiSPNET), Xiamen, China, pp. 1329–1333, October 2017
7. Kittali, R.M., Mahabaleshwar, S.K., Sutagundar, A.V.: Congestion controlled adaptive routing in wireless sensor network. In: Proceedings of 2016 International Conference on Signal Processing, Communication, Power and Embedded System (SCOPES), Odisha, India, pp. 1528–1532, October 2016
8. Sridevi, S., Usha, M., Lithurin, G.P.A.: Priority based congestion control for heterogeneous traffic in multipath wireless sensor networks. In: Proceedings of IEEE International Conference on Computer Communication and Informatics, Coimbatore, India, pp. 1–5, January 2012
9. Wan, C.Y., Eisenman, S.B., Campbell, A.T., Crowcroft, J.: Siphon: overload traffic management using multiradio virtual sinks in sensor networks. In: Proceedings of the 3rd International Conference on Embedded Networked Sensor Systems, San Diego, USA, pp. 116–129, November 2005
10. Ren, F., He, T., Das, S.K., Lin, C.: Traffic-aware dynamic routing to alleviate congestion in wireless sensor networks. IEEE Trans. Parallel Distrib. Syst. **22**(9), 1585–1598 (2011)
11. Monderer, D., Shapley, L.S.: Potential games. Games Econ. Behav. **14**(1), 124–143 (1996)

12. Tsiftes, N., Eriksson, J., Dunkels, A.: Poster abstract: low-power wireless IPv6 routing with ContikiRPL. In: Proceedings of the 9th ACM/IEEE International Conference on Information Processing in Sensor Networks, Stockholm, Sweden, pp. 406–407, April 2010
13. Atzori, L., Iera, A., Morabito, G.: From Smart objects to social objects: the next evolutionary step of the internet of things. IEEE Commun. Mag. **52**(1), 97–105 (2014)

Penalty Shutdown Mitigation in Wireless Sensor Networks Powered by Ambient Energy

Trong-Nhan Le, Tran-Huu-Nguyen Nguyen, Tan-Phuong Vo,
The-Duy Phan-Dinh, and Hoang-Anh Pham$^{(\boxtimes)}$

IoT Group, Faculty of Computer Science and Engineering,
HCMC University of Technology, VNU-HCM, Ho Chi Minh City, Vietnam
{trongnhanle,nthnguyen,vtphuong,duypdt,anhpham}@hcmut.edu.vn

Abstract. Wireless Sensor Networks (WSNs) have great attention in recent years due to their powerful advantages such as low-power, wireless communication and easy deployment, which are suitable for monitoring applications. Moreover, to support a long system lifetime and batteryless WSN nodes, a combination of harvested renewable energy and two layer-based energy storages (e.g., capacitors), working on a hysteresis comparator with two different thresholds, is integrated into a WSN node. However, this approach suffers from a penalty shutdown issue due to quickly decreasing voltage in the primary storage (PS) that directly powers the WSN node. This issue leads to the shutdown of a sensor node in a quite long period, even if there is still sufficient energy in the secondary storage (SS) that is responsible for charging the PS when the renewable sources are absent. In this paper, we propose two solutions to mitigate the penalty shutdown issue in a WSN node. The simulation on OMNeT++ demonstrates that our proposed approaches can increase the energy efficiency up to 61% compared to the traditional approach.

1 Introduction

Since the emergence of Internet-of-Things (IoT), many wireless objects equipped with unique identifiers can join the network and communicate with others through the Internet [1]. Leveraged by IoT networks, many smart applications, ranging from home automation, transportation and logistics, patient health-care, and smart environments (e.g., comfortable homes and offices) to futuristic robot taxi and city information model, are becoming popular in our living spaces. In IoT networks, physical objects can see, hear, think, perform jobs by having them "talk" together, to share information and to coordinate decisions [2]. The IoT transforms a physical object from being traditional to smart by exploiting its underlying technologies such as ubiquitous computing, embedded devices, communication technologies and especially, advanced data analytics. IoT embedded applications are playing a remarkable role to improve the quality of our lives, to reduce air pollution, and to improve agriculture and food supply.

© Springer Nature Switzerland AG 2018
X. Chen et al. (Eds.): CSoNet 2018, LNCS 11280, pp. 368–379, 2018.
https://doi.org/10.1007/978-3-030-04648-4_31

The rapid development of IoT objects has opened a significant proliferation of Wireless Sensor Networks (WSNs), which is composed of many wireless End Device (ED) nodes and a Base Station node (BST). It provides a ubiquitous sensing network and sensing data access through sensing-as-a-service [3]. These abilities of WSNs are suitable for monitoring spaces (e.g., environment and agriculture) or objects (e.g., human health-care and smart buildings). Indeed, many wireless sensor nodes are randomly deployed to cover the monitoring space and wirelessly send sensing data to a BST and ED nodes. Typically, a WSN application requires a long-term operation. However, the available energy from onboard batteries is usually limited, which is leading to a problem of battery maintenance and replacement if the deployment of wireless sensor nodes is in remote or large areas. Therefore, a WSN node is increasingly equipped with rechargeable energy storage devices coupled with an energy harvesting system that exploits the ambient energy from light, heat or vibration [4] to overcome the energy constraint.

Although ambient energy may be scavenged and the operations of a sensor node may last forever, the design of an energy efficient wireless sensor node that is powered by ambient energy has to cope with a big challenge. It is how to rapidly power-on the system from its empty energy state, so-called cool-booting issue [5]. It is evident that harvested energy may be absent in a sufficiently long period such as several days, leading to dry energy storage. For example, a solar-powered sensor node exhausts all of its buffered energy due to persistent poor weather conditions.

To support robust booting from total energy exhaustion, a double layers-based energy storage has been proposed [4]. The first one with small capacity so-called Primary Storage (PS) directly powers the whole system. The second one with larger capacity so-called Secondary Storage (SS) connects to the PS and is charged from harvested energy after the PS reaches its regulated voltage. This architecture benefits from a short charging time for the PS due to its small capacity and from considerable reserve energy in the SS. In this architecture, a hysteresis comparator with two different thresholds [4,5] activates a power enable (PE) signal for powering the sensor node. The PE signal is active when the PS voltage has reached a rising threshold (V_{THR}) and is inactive once the PS voltage is lower than a falling threshold (V_{THF}). Le et al. showed that this architecture provides fast booting time from the empty energy state (e.g., in order of seconds) compared to around half an hour in the system based on a standalone storage device. However, it has a drawback during the absence of harvested energy when the SS is responsible for charging the PS. The PS voltage will drop quickly if the sensor node has to perform some extra operations (e.g., packets retransmission due to collision). The problem becomes serious when the PS voltage drops under a falling threshold, which is leading to the system shutdown meanwhile the charge current from the SS is not enough to turn the sensor node back on. In other words, the sensor node is shut down even there is still an energy budget in the SS. This situation is called a penalty shutdown.

In this paper, we propose two approaches to mitigate the penalty shutdown problem for maximizing sensor node availability, thus improving the energy efficiency in an energy harvesting system. The first approach is to enhance the PE signal by considering both PS and SS voltages. Secondly, when harvested energy is absent, the SS directly supplies power to the sensor node instead of charging the PS. We simulate these approaches on OMNeT++ to evaluate the energy efficiency. The simulation results show that our solutions can increase the energy efficiency up to 61% compared to the traditional approach.

The remainder of this paper is organized as follows. Section 2 presents an overview of state-of-the-art harvested energy platforms for WSNs. The principle of the PE signal is analyzed with the explanations of the penalty shutdown problem in Sect. 3. The two proposed approaches are presented in Sect. 4 followed by the simulations of OMNeT++ in Sect. 5. Finally, the paper ends with remarkable conclusions.

2   State-of-the-Art Harvested Energy Platforms

Many energy harvesting wireless sensor network (EH WSN) platforms ranging from academia to industry have been proposed in recent years [4–7]. The independence of recharging or replacing batteries significantly increases the autonomy of the WSN nodes. This advantage makes EH WSN widely use in remote places where cables are becoming impractical and costly for deployment. The existing EH WSN platforms are classified into two categories, including single-path and dual-path architectures.

2.1   Single-Path Architecture

In the traditional single-path architecture shown in Fig. 1, each energy harvesting WSN node only contains an energy storage that can be a battery, a supercapacitor or both of them. Harvested energy from different renewable sources is used to charge the energy storage via an energy adapter that is required to adapt to different energy sources. For example, photovoltaic cells (PVs) provide high voltage but low current, thermal generators (TEGs) output low voltage but high current whereas wind turbines produce an AC output.

Many platforms using the single-path architecture have been studied and proposed. One of the first solar-powered WSN platforms, Heliomote platform [6],

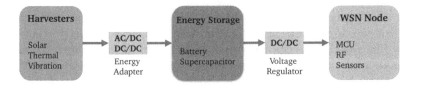

Fig. 1. Single-path architecture for an energy harvesting WSN node

use two small PVs connected directly to rechargeable batteries through a protection diode. However, if the batteries are recharged daily, the system lifetime is less than two years due to the limitation of battery recharge cycles. Therefore, a combination of a super-capacitor and a rechargeable battery was proposed in Prometheus platform [7] to enhance the system lifetime. When the super-capacitor is fully charged, the surplus energy charges the battery. When the super-capacitor voltage is below a predefined threshold, the demanded energy is driven from the battery. In this approach, the energy consumed by the WSN node is mainly served by the super-capacitor, resulting in a reduction of the battery usage. This solution takes advantage of more than half a million recharge cycles of a super-capacitor. Therefore, the battery life can be extended up to four years under an average of 10% load. Jiang *et al.* claimed that Everlast [8] can operate for an estimated lifetime of 20 years without any maintenance by removing batteries and using only super-capacitors for the energy storage.

Although this single-path architecture is simple and easy to implement, its main drawback is the delay due to the cool booting issue [4,5]. In order to overcome this drawback, the dual-path architecture has been proposed with the fundamental difference is that two energy storage devices, PS and SS, are used to buffer harvested energy rather than using only one storage.

2.2   Dual-Path Architecture

In the dual-path architecture shown in Fig. 2, an energy flow controller is added to drive the energy flow. When environmental energy is available, all harvested energy charges the PS for powering the WSN node. After the PS is fully charged, surplus energy is driven into the SS. Otherwise, when the environment energy is insufficient, the remaining energy is drawn from the SS to the PS for ensuring continuous operations of the WSN node. The advantage of the dual-path architecture is a fast booting from both empty PS and SS. Due to the PS small capacity, it is quickly charged to a minimum voltage that is sufficient to enable the voltage regulator to activate the WSN node, meanwhile the SS has a large capacity that provides long-term operations during the absence of harvested energy.

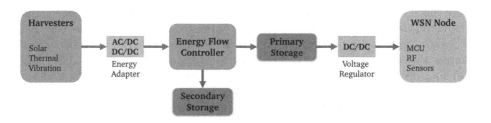

Fig. 2. Dual-path architecture for an energy harvesting WSN node

In DuraCap [5], harvested energy is firstly used to charge a small capacitor for booting the WSN node before fulfilling an array of larger super-capacitors. EscaCap [9] is an extended structure of DuraCap with a dynamic configuration for the SS that connects multiple super-capacitors in forms of serial or parallel utilizing a switch array. Experimental results showed that EscaCap efficiently reduces the leakage energy and improves the charging speed.

As for outdoor applications, the most popular energy sources are from solar and wind due to their high availability and high power. It seems to be a mutual complementarity between two sources, such as strong wind usually occurs when the weather is worse than in a sunny day, or during the night-time when solar energy is not available [10]. These reasons make solar and wind energy to be widely chosen in multi-source platforms such as Ambimax [11] and Capnet [12]. However, the booting time from exhausted energy is an issue when having only single energy storage as above-explained in Sect. 2.1. Therefore, many multi-source and multi-storage EH WSN platforms [4,13] have used the dual-path architecture, in which the operations of a sensor node rely on a PE signal that is used to turn it on or off.

3   Power Enable Signal and Energy Flows

Figure 3 depicts a system operation diagram that describes how the PE controls the power supply of a sensor node in the dual-path architecture. In the beginning, the sensor node is deployed with both empty storage devices. Harvested energy firstly charges the PS until the voltage of the PS V_{PS} reaches the rising threshold (V_{THR}). Then, the available energy in the PS is sufficient for booting the sensor node. Therefore, a comparator brings the power enable signal PE from low to high for powering the sensor node. However, the available energy in the PS at V_{THR} is only enough for booting the system and initializing some necessary modules of a microcontroller (MCU) such as I/O, Timer and ADC. Then, the MCU runs into sleep mode but periodically monitors V_{PS} using a low-power ADC until V_{PS} reaches the RF transmission threshold voltage (V_{RF}) to initialize the radio chip.

After booting, the energy flow controller keeps on charging PS to its regulated voltage (V_{Re}), then the SS is allowed to be charged. However, there is no more space for harvested energy after V_{SS} reaches its maximum voltage (V_{Max}). Therefore, the WSN node should utilize all harvested energy to increase the QoS and also avoid wasting energy [4]. When the harvested energy is absence, V_{SS} charges V_{PS} to V_{Re} as long as V_{SS} is still greater than V_{Re}. Otherwise, both V_{SS} and V_{PS} decrease together and the system is powered off once V_{PS} is under a falling threshold V_{THF}.

Since rechargeable batteries have a limited number of recharge cycles, super-capacitors opt for the energy storage as they are more durable and also have higher power density compared to rechargeable batteries [14]. Moreover, super-capacitors based systems also simplify the hardware design as charging circuits are not required. Then, it is easy to determine the charging state of

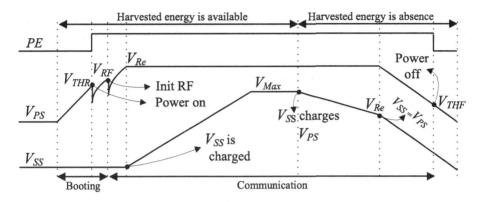

Fig. 3. A system operation diagram of the dual-path architecture

super-capacitor from its voltage [4]. However, when both PS and SS are super-capacitors in the dual-path architecture, they have to cope with a Paradox issue [15].

4   Proposed Solutions

Our solutions are proposed to improve the implementation of a harvested energy platform based on the dual-path architecture shown in Fig. 2, named Multiple Energy Sources Converter (MESC) [4]. As the schematic of MESC shown in Fig. 4, the main component LTC3108 plays a role of the energy flow controller that has two different outputs, including V_{OUT} and V_{STORE} having different charged priority. The V_{OUT} is firstly charged when harvested energy from V_{IN} is available. As soon as V_{OUT} is fully charged, V_{STORE} is allowed to charge. Therefore, V_{OUT} is connected to a primary storage (C_{PS}) while V_{STORE} is connected to a secondary one (C_{SS}). A hysteresis comparator using a nano-power MAX917 component with the rising and falling thresholds determined at the design phase

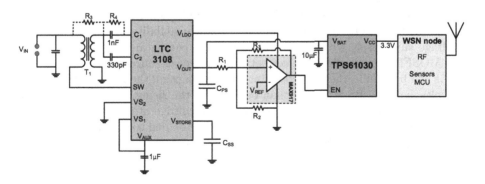

Fig. 4. Schematic of a dual-path architecture based on LTC3108

is used to implement the PE signal. Finally, this PE signal connects to a highly efficient power conversion product TPS61030 as a DC/DC converter block.

4.1   Power Enable Signal Enhancement

As aforementioned, the issue causing penalty shutdown is that the PE signal is activated by only considering the PS voltage. Therefore, in the first solution depicted in Fig. 5, the PE signal is modified in order to compare both V_{PS} and V_{SS} that are V_{OUT} and V_{STORE} as shown in Fig. 4, respectively. In order to reduce the cost of hardware components, the OR circuit of two diodes is used to select one of the input sources, which is fed into the comparator. Indeed, a source having a higher voltage is connected to the positive pin of the comparator, which can be a hysteresis op-amp circuit. Therefore, in the beginning, both V_{PS} and V_{SS} are empty, and the PE signal is low. As soon as the V_{PS} has been charged and passed through V_{THR}, the hysteresis comparator drives the output PE to high, enabling the power supply for the sensor node. The PE signal goes low only if V_{PS} and V_{SS} are both lower than the falling threshold (V_{THF}). This design not only guarantees the fast booting from the exhausted energy state but also overcomes the penalty shutdown issue.

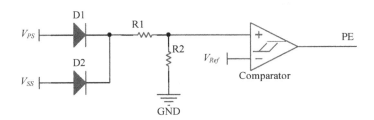

Fig. 5. Improve the PE signal by considering both voltage of PS and SS devices.

4.2   Energy Flow Optimization

To optimize the energy flow, we adopt a power multiplexer technique in a sensor node with the aims to maximize the sensor node availability. As shown in Fig. 6, a voltage supervisor, which is a voltage window comparator, provides a signal for a MOSFETs controller to select between the power sources of the PS and the SS. As can be seen in the corresponding timing diagram, the PS is selected when the voltage of the PS is higher than or equal to the rising threshold voltage of the PS (V_{THRPS}). The SS is selected when the voltage of the PS is lower than V_{THRPS}, and the voltage of the SS is higher than or equal to the falling threshold voltage of the SS (V_{THFSS}). Otherwise, the sensor node is off.

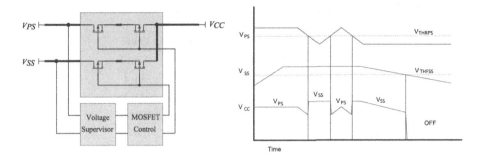

Fig. 6. Our proposed power multiplexer of V_{PS} and V_{SS} and its timing diagram

5   Network Simulations on OMNeT++

5.1   Simulation Setup

A network composed of N EDs and a BST is implemented in MiXiM version 2.1, which is a simulator for wireless and mobile networks running on the OMNeT++ version 4.4.1 framework. Our simulations are performed on a PC with Core i7 Intel CPU, 8G RAM, and 256G SSD HDD. The MSP430 microcontroller and the CC2420 2.4 MHz RF transceiver, which are already available on MiXiM 2.1, are equipped in a node. This network simulates a monitoring application for a 300 m × 300 m area. The BST is located in the middle of this area while EDs are randomly distributed around it. All EDs are equipped with two solar cells 4 × 6 cm in size. Each ED stores its harvested energy in a supercapacitor (C_S) initially charged to $V_0 = 2$ V. The minimum and maximum voltages for this storage device are $V_{Min} = 1.8$ V and $V_{Max} = 5.2$ V, respectively. The consumed energy profile of a wireless node is summarized in Table 1.

The battery model in MiXiM is modified to support two different capacitors used for the energy storage. A battery monitor controls the battery state of charge as follows. Every second, an amount of harvested energy charges the battery. According to the PS state of charge (SoC), this energy charges the PS until it is full before charging the SS. Whenever the node is active, the battery monitor updates the SoC of the PS by the amount of consumed energy for node's operations. Then, a part of the energy from the SS is fed to the PS. During the discharging process, if the SoC of the PS is lower than a minimum value (i.e., $V_{PS} < V_{THF}$), a reset signal is active to stop all operations of the node.

Communications between nodes rely on an asynchronous MAC protocol named RICER (Receiver Initiated Cycled Receiver) [17], which is well adapted to WSNs powered by ambient energy compared to synchronous protocols [18]. The main reason is due to the energy and complexity overhead by regularly performing a synchronization process. It means that synchronous protocols are relevant to networks having high traffic because of exchanged packets for the synchronization between many nodes. However, in the context of harvested energy WSNs with low data rate (e.g., packets are sent every 30 s), asynchronous MAC

Table 1. Consumed energy profile of a PowWow wireless node [16]

Description	Symbol	Value
Calculation Before Transmission	E_{CBT}	9.7 μJ
Transmit/Receive wake-up Beacon	E_{WUB}	51 μJ
Transmit/Receive ACK	E_{ACK}	51 μJ
Data Transmission	E_{DT}	80 μJ
Data Reception	E_{DR}	100 μJ
Clear Channel Assessment	E_{CCA}	18 μJ
Sensing from sensors	E_{SEN}	27 μJ
Transmission power	P_{Tx}	66.33 mW
Reception power	P_{Rx}	76.89 mW
Sleep power	P_{Sleep}	85.8 μW

protocols have shown their energy efficiency compared to synchronous protocols [19]. As asynchronous protocols usually adopt a non-scheduled preamble sampling scheme, both the transmitter and the receiver operate independently, and therefore they do not need to be synchronized. However, a rendezvous must be initiated either by the transmitter or the receiver to establish a communication.

In our simulation scenarios, all the nodes in the network periodically send their data to the BTS every 15 s. While the leaf nodes act as transmitters only, other relay nodes have to send their beacons whenever they wake-up since they are potential receivers. It is also required for multiple links capability and a routing process. In the beginning, we consider an existing low-cost flooding algorithm [20], in which the shortest path is usually selected to reduce the latency from leaf nodes to the BST. Consequently, some nodes acting as relay devices may have to forward packets from several nodes. In this case, the relay nodes have to perform some additional communications. If the penalty shutdown occurs, many links on the network are interrupted. This issue becomes critical if any relay node is a bottleneck node. Therefore, in this work, we modified the routing algorithm in order to select the path according to the available energy in each node as well as the total delay. In consequence, this policy can reduce the data congestion of relay nodes and balance the energy consumption among many nodes in the network.

In this work, we evaluate the penalty shutdown issue in terms of the average penalty shutdown period per day $\overline{T_{Pen}}$ defined by Eq. 1.

$$\overline{T_{Pen}} = \frac{\sum_{i=1}^{N} T_{Pen}(i)}{ND} \tag{1}$$

Where $T_{Pen}(i)$ (hours) is the total penalty shutdown period of an ED i^{th} during the whole simulation, N is the number of EDs and D is the number of simulation days (24 h per day). Our simulation duration is 120 h (i.e., $D = 5$) and N ranges from 5 to 25 nodes.

5.2 Simulation Results

Figure 7 shows our simulation results regarding average penalty shutdown periods of the three approaches including the related approaches [4,5] and our two proposed approaches. When the power enable signal considers the voltage of PS (V_{PS}) in the related approaches, the shutdown period is increased quickly when the network size increases from 5 to 20 nodes and reaches the saturation at $N = 25$ nodes. The main reason is that the number of neighbors around a relay node increases accordingly to the network size, and each relay node not only sends its packets to the BST but also forwards packets from their neighbors, which requires a burst of energy from PS to accomplish all of these tasks. Therefore, during the night, when the SS voltage is just lower than $V_{THR} = 2.9\,V$, the relay node is easily shutdown since its V_{PS} is lower than $V_{THF} = 1.8\,V$, leading to a high penalty shutdown period. With higher than 20 nodes (i.e., the network is dense), multiple relay nodes can forward a packet from a leaf node. Our modified routing algorithm can select the forwarding path according to the available energy in relay nodes, which helps to balance the consumed energy among many relay nodes in the network. Therefore, the penalty shutdown issues stop increasing quickly according to the size of the network which is higher than 20 nodes.

Our first proposed solution enhances the PE signal by considering both the PS and SS voltages. Even though the PS suddenly drops below V_{THF}, the wireless node is still powered by the SS as long as its voltage is higher than V_{THF}. Therefore, it reduces the penalty shutdown and consequently maintains the operations of the end device longer during the night when harvested energy is not available. Considering the average values derived from Fig. 7, the shutdown

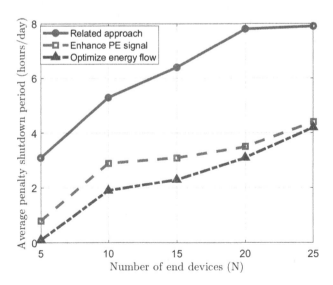

Fig. 7. Simulation results in terms of average penalty shutdown period

period by enhancing the PE signal is 2.94 h, which is reduced 51% compared to the related approach using MESC [4], with the shutdown period of 6.1 h. By applying our solution, the node only shuts down completely when both V_{PS} and V_{SS} are lower than V_{THF}. Although the shutdown period is reduced, the node has reset when V_{PS} is lower than V_{THF} even the PE is still enabled. This delay is small for the booting process, but it takes a few seconds (e.g., 30 s) for the node to initiate the whole system again before entering its sensing and communication states.

Our second proposed solution overcomes the reset issue in the first solution during the night when V_{PS} is lower than V_{THR} since the power supply of the end device is connected directly to V_{SS}. The simulation results show that the improvement in the second approach is 61% compared to the related approaches because of avoiding the leakage energy from PS and the paradox issue. It means that the ED has more budget energy for its operations during the night, leading to a shorter shutdown period.

6   Conclusions

In this paper, we proposed two solutions to significantly overcome the penalty shutdown issue in the dual-path architecture based harvested energy wireless sensor networks. The first solution produces an enhanced PE signal by considering both the PS and SS voltages. The simulation results show that the reduction of the penalty shutdown period is 51% compared to another related approach. However, the use of enhanced PE signal still produces a small reset period that is not ignorable for critical real-time monitoring applications. Our second proposed solution completely solves this reset issue by directly connecting both the PS and SS to the power supply of the sensor node and adding a voltage supervisor to maintain the operations of the sensor node continuously. As a result, it mitigates the leakage energy of the PS and the lost energy due to paradox issue to utilize more budget energy for communications. The simulation results show that the reduction of the penalty shutdown period is up to 61%. Future work focuses on implementing and validating the second approach of energy flow optimization in a real wireless sensor platform.

Acknowledgment. This work is partially supported by GDRI Sense-South Project (https://groupes.renater.fr/sympa/info/sense-south-gdri).

References

1. Whitmore, A., Agarwal, A., Da Xu, L.: The Internet of Things–a survey of topics and trends. Inf. Syst. Front. **17**(2), 261–274 (2015)
2. Al-Fuqaha, A., Guizani, M., Mohammadi, M., Aledhari, M., Ayyash, M.: Internet of Things: a survey on enabling technologies, protocols, and applications. IEEE Commun. Surv. Tutor. **17**(4), 2347–2376 (2015)
3. Deif, D.S., Gadallah, Y.: Classification of wireless sensor networks deployment techniques. IEEE Commun. Surv. Tutor. **16**(2), 834–855 (2014)

4. Le, T., Pegatoquet, A., Berder, O., Sentieys, O., Carer, A.: Energy neutral design framework for supercapacitor-based autonomous wireless sensor networks. ACM J. Emerg. Technol. 1–20 (2014)
5. Chen, C.-Y., Chou, P.H.: DuraCap: a supercapacitor-based, power-bootstrapping, maximum power point tracking energy-harvesting system. In: ACM/IEEE International Symposium on Low Power Electronics and Design (ISLPED), pp. 313–318 (2010)
6. Raghunathan, V., Kansal, A., Hsu, J., Friedman, J., Srivastava, M.: Design considerations for solar energy harvesting wireless embedded systems. In: International Symposium on Information Processing in Sensor Networks, pp. 457–462 (2005)
7. Jiang, X., Polastre, J., Culler, D.: Perpetual environmentally powered sensor networks. In: International Symposium on Information Processing in Sensor Networks, pp. 463–468 (2005)
8. Simjee, F.I., Chou, P.H.: Efficient charging of supercapacitors for extended lifetime of wireless sensor nodes. IEEE Trans. Power Electron. 23(3), 1526–1536 (2008)
9. Kim, S., Chou, P.H.: Energy harvesting by sweeping voltage-escalated charging of a reconfigurable supercapacitor array. In: IEEE/ACM International Symposium on Low-power Electronics and Design, pp. 235–240 (2011)
10. Liu, C., Chau, K., Zhang, X.: An efficient wind-photovoltaic hybrid generation system using doubly excited permanent-magnet brushless machine. IEEE Trans. Ind. Electron. 57(3), 831–839 (2010)
11. Park, C., Chou, P.H.: AmbiMax: autonomous energy harvesting platform for multi-supply wireless sensor nodes. IEEE Commun. Soc. Sens. Ad Hoc Commun. Netw. (SECON) 1, 168–177 (2006)
12. Ferry, N., Ducloyer, S., Julien, N., Jutel, D.: Power and energy aware design of an autonomous wireless sensor node. J. Adv. Comput. Sci. 2(4), 11–36 (2013)
13. Carli, D., Brunelli, D., Benini, L., Ruggeri, M.: An effective multi-source energy harvester for low power applications. In: Design, Automation Test in Europe Conference Exhibition (DATE), pp. 1–6 (2011)
14. Kailas, A., Brunelli, D., Weitnauer, M.A.: Comparison of energy update models for wireless sensor nodes with supercapacitors. In: ACM Workshop on Energy Neutral Sensing Systems, pp. 1–6 (2013)
15. Mita, K., Boufaida, M.: Ideal capacitor circuits and energy conservation. Am. J. Phys. 67(8), 737–739 (1999)
16. Alam, M., Berder, O., Menard, D., Anger, T., Sentieys, O.: A hybrid model for accurate energy analysis of WSN nodes. J. Embed. Syst. (EURASIP) 2011, 1–16 (2011)
17. Lin, E., Rabaey, J., Wolisz, A.: Power-efficient rendez-vous schemes for dense wireless sensor networks. In: IEEE International Conference on Communications, pp. 3769–3776 (2004)
18. Huang, P., Xiao, L., Soltani, S., Mutka, M.W., Xi, N.: The evolution of MAC protocols in wireless sensor networks: a survey. IEEE Commun. Surv. Tutor. 15(1), 101–120 (2013)
19. Kim, T., Kim, I.H., Sun, Y., Jin, Z.: Physical layer and medium access control design in energy efficient sensor networks: an overview. IEEE Trans. Ind. Inform. 11(1), 2–15 (2015)
20. Liang, O., Sekercioglu, Y., Mani, N.: A low-cost flooding algorithm for wireless sensor networks. In: IEEE Conference on Wireless Communications and Networking, pp. 3495–3500 (2007)

On Forwarding Protocols in Linear Topology Wake-up Wireless Sensor Networks

Jian Wang[1(✉)], Xiaolin Xu[1], Xiaoming Hu[1], and Wei Wayne Li[2]

[1] Shanghai Polytechnic University, Shanghai 201209, China
{wangjian,xlxu,xmhu}@sspu.edu.cn
[2] Texas Southern University, Houston, TX 77004, USA
wei.li@tsu.edu

Abstract. Wake-up radio (WuR) is a kind of ultra-low power transceiver that consumes energy at 1000 times lower in magnitude when compared to the main radio in traditional wireless sensors. When incorporated, traditional wireless sensor networks are possible to improve energy efficiency and packet delay simultaneously by mitigating idle listening and overhearing issues. In recent years, many works have designed and evaluated the performance of MAC protocols in WuR-enabled yet single-hop (i.e. star-shaped) wireless sensor networks. This paper moves to a multi-hop network and focuses on linear topology WuR-enabled WSNs. It makes practical sense as large-scale WSN topologies could be decomposed into multiple linear topologies. Based on WuR inherent characteristics and also signal interferences among adjacent sensors, we introduce some interesting design ideas and describe our proposed MAC protocol in detail. Analytical results on expected radio-on time of intermediate sensors when waken up are derived. Also numerical results based on normalized per-hop energy and delay ratios show the effectiveness of our protocol. It may serve as an interesting basis for potential researches into more realistically large-scale WuR-enabled WSNs.

Keywords: Wireless sensor network · Wake-up radio
Linear topology · MAC protocol · Energy efficiency

1 Introduction

Wireless sensor networks have found varied applications in environment monitoring, battlefield surveillance, industrial control, heath-care, and smart grid. They typically consist of many small low-cost wireless sensors. These sensors are in general battery-powered, bandwidth-constrained, and memory-limited. When deployed in the field, individual sensors continuously sense their surroundings.

This work is supported in part by Key Disciplines of Computer Science and Technology of Shanghai Polytechnic University under Grant No. XXKZD1604 and US National Science Foundation under Grant No. 1137732.

© Springer Nature Switzerland AG 2018
X. Chen et al. (Eds.): CSoNet 2018, LNCS 11280, pp. 380–391, 2018.
https://doi.org/10.1007/978-3-030-04648-4_32

As sensors have limited wireless communication ranges and often no communication infrastructure is available in the field, the sensors have to forward the generated data packets to the sink in a hop-by-hop manner by themselves.

The wireless sensor networks are desirable to operate unattendedly in months or even years. Thus it is necessary to conserve the limited energy when forwarding data packets. Typically duty-cycling [2] is an effective approach yet causing a large end-to-end packet delay, whereas always-on incurs considerable idle listening and overhearing issues. In recent years, ultra-low power wake-up radio (WuR) transceivers [12] have been designed and subsequently manufactured that have an energy consumption rate of around 1000 times smaller in magnitude [11] when compared to traditional radio transceivers, i.e. μW versus mW [9]. After they are incorporated into traditional sensors, it is possible to keep main radio transceivers asleep as long as possible and wake up them whenever needed via wake-up beacon packets. As such, dilemma of energy efficiency and end-to-end packet delay is mitigated, if not completely resolved, although the price of building WuR-enabled sensors would rise.

This work focuses on a multi-hop linear (i.e. chain-based) topology [13], which serves as the most fundamental building blocks of large-scale topologies. The sink is located at one end of the linear topology. The constituting sensors can be thought of as cluster-heads. They forward data packets towards the sink on behalf of their upstreaming sensors, as well as their own cluster-members. Each sensor comprises one main radio transceiver and another ultra-low power radio receiver (WuRx). The main radio transceiver remains asleep as long as possible. In contrast, the WuRx is always on. WuRx receives only wake-up beacon packets and no data packets. Moreover, WuRx cannot transmit packets. Wake-up beacon packets are generated and transmitted by the main radio transceiver with dynamic physical technologies. The wake-up beacon packets as well as data/acknowledgement packets share the same frequency band. Nevertheless, the wake-up beacon packets are transmitted at a lower bit rate yet with much stronger signal strength when compared to data/acknowledgement packets. This accounts for WuRx's lower signal sensitivity and slower signal processing capability.

Beacon packets are addressable. Specifically, each sensor gets its identification number at the initialization phase. When WuRx receives a wake-up beacon packet, it matches the identification number of its hosting sensor against that in the beacon packet. Whenever matched, a wake-up signal is generated and sent to the main controller of its hosting sensor. Subsequently, the main radio transceiver is switched on for exchanging wake-up acknowledgement, data, and data acknowledgement packets.

Wake-up radios have witnessed potential advantages in increasing energy efficiency and sustaining system performance simultaneously in wireless sensor networks. In general, related researching works can be categorized into either receiver-initiated (RI) or transmitter-initiated (TI) paradigms.

The receiver-initiated paradigm is suitable for data collecting applications, where wake-up beacon packets are to wake up neighboring senders who may possess interesting data packets. [7] presents and models a receiver-initiated consecutive packet transmission WuR MAC protocol, where multiple packet transmissions are packed into a single access winning competition. As such, losing senders avoid unnecessarily medium competitions in the multiple separate packet transmissions. Yet [7] only studies a single-hop network setting.

The transmitter-initiated paradigm is suitable for data reporting applications, where wake-up beacon packets are to wake up the relevant receivers (often sinks) that should get urgent data packets quickly. For instance, [5] introduces a backoff procedure before transmitting wake-up beacons in order to avoid potential collisions among wake-up beacons, and correspondingly removes backoff requirements from the main radios. It assumes the same contention window in every cycle with analysis based on discrete time Markov chain models. [6] presents and models performances of CCA WuR, CSMA WuR, and ADP WuR. It attempts to extend light traffic WuR-based MACs into varied heavy traffic scenarios. In contrast to previous always-on wake-up radios, [10] presents and optimizes a duty-cycled WuR-based MAC protocol, where the wake-up radio is duty-cycled in order to reach further higher energy efficiency. However, all these aforementioned TI works are still in single-hop networks.

As for formal analysis frameworks [3], [1] present absorbed Markov chain models to analyze TI works, where the number of transmission failures is assumed to follow a geometric distribution. However, both frameworks are based on the single sensor level, not on the MAC level competition in single-hop network, let alone on the multiple-hop network.

Mobile sinks [8] are used to collect data packets from adjacent sensors via transmitting on-demand wake-up beacons. In contrast, LoRa [4] combines long range wireless communication technologies to collect data packets directly (not by hops) from individual remote clusters that are equipped with wake-up radios.

Our work is obviously different from the previous ones, since we are focusing on designing MAC protocols in multiple-hop linear topology WuR-enabled wireless sensor networks, and may ignite potential researching interests shifting away from single-hop networks. The rest of the work is organized as follows: We introduce network background, design ideas, and present our MAC protocol in Sect. 2. Theoretical results on total en-route non-sleep time and simulation results on per-hop delay as well as energy consumption ratios are shown in Sects. 3 and 4, respectively. Finally, Sect. 5 concludes the work.

2   Proposed MAC Protocol in Linear Topologies

We first present background for multi-hop linear topology networks. Then we introduce design ideas of MAC protocol by exploiting characteristics of wake-up radios as well as the linear topology. Finally, we give the protocol details from an event-driven perspective in order to facilitate simulation implementation.

Background. Since the linear topology is considered in this work, all of the n sensors are positioned in a straight line with the distance between consecutive sensors being exactly the wake-up range. In particular, the sink is also on such a line, with the wake-up range being away from the nth sensor. In general, the main radio has better sensitivity and could detect much longer communication signals than WuRx. Yet in this work, these main radios are supposed to adjust their transmitting power to efficiently conserve limited onboard energy and also to match the wake-up range. In this way, the wake-up beacon packets and data packets can only reach the most adjacent sensors. The whole packet exchange between two consecutive sensors is as below: wake-up beacon, wake-up acknowledgement, data, and data acknowledgement. Note that all four kinds of packets are transmitted by the main radio. In contrast, except that wake-up beacon is received by WuRx, the remaining three are still received by the main radio. Recall that signals of the four kinds of packets occupy the same frequency band, it is possible to form collisions among them. Usually, the radio interference range of data and acknowledgement packets is longer than their communication range. As wake-up beacon has much stronger signal strength, its radio interference range is even longer than that of other three kinds of packets.

Each sensor on the linear topology, as well as its cluster-member sensors, continuously monitor their surroundings. Application-specific interesting data packets are obtained from time to time. Among them, delay-tolerant packets can be collected by duty-cycling methods or mobile sinks. Yet urgent packets, for instance, exceeding temperature threshold in fire detection and violating material concentration in environment monitoring, should be forwarded to the sink as quickly as possible. In realistic environments, the urgent data emerges randomly and significantly infrequently. It would be affordable by the wake-up based packet forwarding, because the wake-up beacons are much more energy consuming. Note that only the sensors constituting the linear topology are equipped with WuRx. Other cluster-member sensors in the sensor network are still traditional sensors. Once they have obtained the urgent data, they may wake up its belonging cluster-head sensor on the linear topology and then forwards its urgent data packets. Then the cluster-head sensor on the linear topology could wake-up its downstreaming sensor in turn. In this way, our linear topology network still has realistic application potentials, and also refrains from huge deployment cost.

As the same to the existing literature, urgent data packets in this paper on individual sensors are supposed to follow independent Poisson processes in temporal dimension. Each cluster-head sensor on the linear topology is supposed to have an aggregate urgent data rate of λ based on composition characteristics of Poisson data processes of individual cluster-member sensors. Hereafter, we investigate only cluster-head sensors, and postpone additional implications of wake-ups and data transmissions from cluster-member sensors in the future work.

Design Ideas. On the linear topology, it is intuitive for individual sensors to route the urgent data packets unidirectionally towards the sink, without any necessary complex routing decisions made on-the-fly. Thus, wake-up beacon packets are always towards the downstreaming sensors. The protocol stack would be mainly issues at the MAC layer. Besides the traditional CSMA rule, design ideas for our MAC protocol in the linear topology are as follows: (1) when the sensor receives a wake-up beacon packet while it is involved with forwarding packets

---

Algorithm 1. On generating a data packet

1: append the data packet into the transmitting queue
2: **if** timer_data, timer_ack, timer_channel, timer_forward are all off **then**
3:     switch on the main radio if it is asleep
4:     set timer_channel on with timeout being interval_cca
5: **end if**

Algorithm 2. On receiving a wake-up beacon packet

1: switch on the main radio if it is asleep
2: set timer_channel off if it is on
3: transmit a wake-ack packet
4: the main radio switches into receiving state
5: set timer_data on with timeout being interval_data

---

to its downstreaming sensor, it should prioritize upstreaming packet forwarding activities immediately; (2) the sensor wakes up its downstreaming sensor to forward packets only after the upstreaming sensor has finished transmissions of all available data packets; (3) the sensor should refrain from waking up its downstreaming sensor if its last data forwarding activity has not gone enough long time.

Due to inherent characteristics of linear topology, it should be better to gracefully give transmission privileges to other sensors when detecting channel busy. If downstreaming sensors get the channel, the urgent data packets will be forwarded to the sink quickly. If the upstreaming sensors get the channel, sooner or later the current sensor will get the channel via receiving wake-up beacon packets. As such, concurrent forwarding activities on the linear topology will be separated by at least some physical hops in spatial dimension. This contributes to both interference mitigation and energy conservation simultaneously.

Proposed MAC Protocol. Now, we give the detail of our MAC protocol. Specifically, from an event-driven perspective, the sensor state remains unchanged unless (1) the sensor generates an urgent data packet; (2) the wake-up radio receives a wake-up beacon packet; (3) the main radio receives a wake-up or data acknowledgement packet; (4) the main radio receives a data packet; (5) timeout on data packet arrivals, timeout on wake-up or data acknowledgement packet arrivals, channel being continuously idle sufficiently long, and last downstreaming packet forwarding gone long time. We present how the sensor copes with each aforementioned triggering event in the following.

Algorithm 1 copes with the case of the sensor that generates an urgent data packet. Specifically, the sensor first appends the data packet in the transmitting queue. Then it checks whether it is waiting for data packet, data or wake-up acknowledgement packet, channel being idle sufficiently long, or last downstreaming packet forwarding gone enough long time. If any of these four timers is on, then nothing needs to be done. Otherwise, the main radio is switched on if it is still asleep. Then the main radio conducts channel CCA via setting a timer

---

Algorithm 3. On receiving a wake-up or data acknowledgement packet

1: set timer_ack off
2: remove corresponding data packet from the transmitting queue if data-ack received
3: **if** the transmitting queue is empty **then**
4:     the main radio switches into sleep state
5:     set timer_forward on to suspend downstreaming packet forwarding temporally
6: **else**
7:     transmit the data packet at the head of the transmitting queue
8:     set timer_ack on, and the main radio switches into receiving state
9: **end if**

Algorithm 4. On receiving a data packet

1: append the data packet into the receiving queue if not duplicated
2: respond with a data acknowledgement packet
3: the main radio switches into receiving state
4: set timer_data on with timeout being interval_data, for waiting for next data packet

---

(i.e. timer_channel) with the channel continuously idle for at least interval_cca time. Timer_channel could simply become timeouts every interval_cca seconds.

Algorithm 2 copes with the case of the sensor that receives a wake-up beacon packet. Specifically, if the main radio is asleep, then the sensor switches on it. The sensor sets timer_channel off with the purpose that any pending downstreaming packet forwarding, if existing, should be suspended immediately. Subsequently, the sensor responds with a wake-up acknowledgement packet to the upstreaming sensor. As such, the upstreaming packet reception is prioritized immediately. Afterwards, the main radio listens for the channel and waits for receiving forthcoming data packets in interval_data seconds.

Algorithm 3 copes with the case of the sensor that receives a wake-up acknowledgement packet or data acknowledgement packet. Specifically, the sensor first sets off the corresponding timer (i.e. timer_ack). If a data acknowledgement packet is received, then the corresponding data packet is removed from the transmitting queue. Subsequently, if there is no data packet in the transmitting queue, the sensor switches the main radio off and also sets timer_forward on with timeout being interval_exchange. As such, consecutive downstreaming packet forwardings can be separated by sufficient long time. In case data packets exist in the transmitting queue, the sensor transmits the data packet at the queue head, sets on a timer (i.e. timer_ack) with timeout being interval_ack seconds that is to wait for data acknowledgement packet, and switches the main radio into receiving state.

Algorithm 4 copes with the case of the sensor that receives a data packet. Specifically, the sensor appends the received data packet into the receiving queue if not duplicated. Then the sensor responds with a data acknowledgement packet and the main radio switches into receiving state. Finally, the sensor sets on a timer (i.e. timer_data) with timeout being interval_data in order to determine whether the upstreaming sensor has finished all data packet forwardings.

Algorithm 5. On four kinds of timeouts

1: **if** timeout is from timer_data or timer_forward **then**
2:     set the corresponding timer_data or timer_forward off
3:     **if** timer_forward is off **then**
4:         **if** the receiving queue is nonempty **then**
5:             invoke **Algorithm 1** with each packet extracted from the receiving queue
6:         **else if** the transmitting queue is nonempty **then**
7:             set timer_channel on, with continuously idle being at least interval_cca
8:         **end if**
9:     **end if**
10: **else if** timeout is from timer_ack **then**
11:     set timer_ack off
12:     set timer_channel on with random-value timeouts, being idle at least interval_cca
13: **else if** timeout is from timer_channel **then**
14:     **if** channel continuously idle time is less than interval_cca **then**
15:         reset timer_channel on again with random-value timeouts
16:     **else**
17:         set timer_channel off
18:         **if** an expected data acknowledgement packet does not arrive **then**
19:             transmit a data packet at the head of the transmitting queue
20:             set timer_ack on, waiting for a data acknowledgement packet
21:         **else**
22:             transmit a wake-up beacon packet
23:             set timer_ack on, waiting for a wake-up acknowledgement packet
24:         **end if**
25:     **end if**
26: **end if**

Algorithm 5 copes with different cases of timeouts. Specifically, if the timeout is from timer_data or timer_forward, the sensor sets the corresponding timer off. Then it checks whether the timer_forward is off (i.e. last downstreaming packet forwarding has gone long time). If so, all of the data packets within the receiving queue is in turn extracted and fed to Algorithm 1. Otherwise, i.e. the receiving queue is empty, then the sensor starts a clear channel assessment process whenever the transmitting queue has pending data packets. If the timeout is from timer_ack, the sensor sets it off, and sets timer_channel on with the timeout being some randomly chosen large value (i.e. implementing backoff effects). In general, the range of the random timeout is multiple times of a single data packet forwarding. If the timeout is from timer_channel, the sensor checks whether the channel has been continuously idle for at least interval_cca. If not, the sensor resets the timer_channel and checks at its next timeout again. If so, the sensor sets timer_channel off. Depending on the current context, the sensor transmits a data or wake-up beacon packet and sets timer_ack on, waiting for corresponding acknowledgement packet.

3   Theoretical Results

The objective of this section is to derive average radio-on time interval for intermediate sensor when being waken up on the linear topology. In the following
theoretical analysis, we assume there is no signal interference among concurrent packet forwardings as well as channel errors for simplified derivations (The
simulation results in the next section will account for signal interferences, while
channel errors will be considered in the future). Recall that each sensor independently generates urgent data at λ packets/second, and these packets should
be forwarded towards the sink without en-route data aggregation.

Let τ denote time interval of one data packet transmission as well as
its acknowledgement packet. Suppose the intermediate sensor in question has
received k $(k = 1, 2, \cdots)$ data packets from the upstreaming sensor, and it needs
to forward these k packets towards the sink. We have the following major result.

Theorem 1. *Let $P_{j|k}$ denote the probability that given k packets in buffer, the
sensor forwards these k packets and then consecutively forwards j locally generated packets within one continuous forwarding activity, then*

$$P_{j|k} = \frac{\lambda^j}{j!} k\tau(k\tau + j\tau)^{j-1} e^{-\lambda(k\tau + j\tau)}, \ k = 1, 2, 3, \cdots, \ j = 0, 1, 2, \cdots. \quad (1)$$

Proof. Let X_i $(i = 1, 2, \cdots)$, denote the time interval between $(i-1)$th and ith
local data packets, we can easily know for any k $(k = 1, 2, 3, \cdots)$ that $P_{0|k} = P(X_1 \geq k\tau)$, and for any j $(j = 1, 2, \cdots)$ that

$$P_{j|k} = P\left(X_1 < k\tau, \cdots, \sum_{i=1}^{j} X_i < (k+j-1)\tau, \sum_{i=1}^{j+1} X_i \geq (k+j)\tau\right).$$

Denote by $P_0(x) = P(X_1 \geq x)$, and for any j $(j = 1, 2, \cdots)$ that

$$P_j(x) = P\left(X_1 < x, \cdots, \sum_{i=1}^{j} X_i < x + (j-1)\tau, \sum_{i=1}^{j+1} X_i \geq x + j\tau\right), \quad (2)$$

we use mathematical induction method to verify that for any $j \geq 0$ and $x > 0$

$$P_j(x) = \frac{\lambda^j}{j!} x(x + j\tau)^{j-1} e^{-\lambda(x+j\tau)}. \quad (3)$$

In fact, it is easy to verify that the result is true for the base $j = 0$ or $j = 1$.
Suppose the Eq. (3) is true for $j = n$, we need to verify that it is also true for
$j = n + 1$. Now, for any $x > 0$, we have

$$
\begin{aligned}
P_{n+1}(x) &= \int_0^x f(t) P_n(x + \tau - t) dt = \int_\tau^{x+\tau} f(x + \tau - y) P_n(y) dy \\
&= \int_\tau^{x+\tau} \lambda e^{-\lambda(x+\tau-y)} \cdot \frac{\lambda^n}{n!} y(y + n\tau)^{n-1} e^{-\lambda(y+n\tau)} dy \quad (4) \\
&= \frac{\lambda^{n+1} e^{-\lambda[x+(n+1)\tau]}}{(n+1)!} \cdot (n+1) \cdot \int_\tau^{x+\tau} y(y + n\tau)^{n-1} dy.
\end{aligned}
$$

It is obvious by a straightforward mathematical manipulation that

$$(n+1) \int_{\tau}^{x+\tau} y(y+n\tau)^{n-1} dy = x[x+(n+1)\tau]^n. \tag{5}$$

Substituting Eq. (5) into Eq. (4), we will have

$$P_{n+1}(x) = \frac{\lambda^{n+1}}{(n+1)!} e^{-\lambda[x+(n+1)\tau]} \cdot x[x+(n+1)\tau]^n, \quad x > 0. \tag{6}$$

This means that result (3) is also true for $j = n+1$, and therefore the theorem is verified by noting $P_{j|k} = P_j(k\tau)$ through mathematical induction method. $\square$

Remark 1. *When $j = 0, 1$, we have $P_{0|k} = e^{-\lambda k\tau}$ and $P_{1|k} = k\lambda\tau e^{-\lambda(k+1)\tau}$. This respectively represents the probability that after the sensor forwards all of k packets, no or only one local data packet is generated and forwarded.*

Based on the above main Theorem, we may have the follow direct corollary.

Corollary 1. *Denote by K the number of packets at the epoch of starting forwarding packets at any sensor and J_K is the number of total new packets forwarded from the starting epoch to the epoch when no packet is available in the given sensor. If the distribution of K is given by q_k ($k = 1, 2, ...$), then the average number, denote it by Φ, of packets forwarded in a cycle from starting epoch to the ending epoch for the specified sensor is given by*

$$\Phi = \sum_{k=1}^{\infty} \sum_{j=0}^{\infty} \frac{q_k \lambda^j}{j!} k(k\tau + j\tau)^j e^{-\lambda(k\tau+j\tau)}$$

Proof. By using the major result in the Theorem, we will have

$$\Phi = E[K + J_K] = \sum_{k=1}^{\infty} E[k + J_k] q_k = \sum_{k=1}^{\infty} \sum_{j=0}^{\infty} (k+j) P_{j|k} q_k$$

$$= \sum_{k=1}^{\infty} \sum_{j=0}^{\infty} \frac{q_k \lambda^j}{j!} k(k\tau + j\tau)^j e^{-\lambda(k\tau+j\tau)}$$

Considering the first sensor on the linear topology, its q_k when $k = 1$ is equal to 1. Then its $P_{j|1}$ is calculated. Considering the second sensor, its q_k, when $k = 1 + j$, is equal to $P_{j|1}$ multiplied by $q_1 = 1$ of the first sensor. Considering each other downstreaming sensor on the linear topology, its q_k is equal to the sum of $P_{k-\theta|\theta}$ multiplied by q_θ of its upstreaming sensor where $\theta = 1, 2, \cdots, k$.

Remark 2. *When accounting for time intervals of wake-up and wake-ack packet, let $\xi = T_{wakeup} + T_{wake\_ack}$ that is fixed and independent of τ, then the modified version of $P_{j|k}$, denote it by $P'_{j|k}$, is given by*

$$P'_{j|k} = P\left(X_1 < k\tau + \xi, \cdots, \sum_{i=1}^{j} X_i < (k+j-1)\tau + \xi, \sum_{i=1}^{j+1} X_i \geq (k+j)\tau + \xi\right).$$

With similar derivations, the modified version of Φ, denoted by Φ', can also be derived similarly. For each intermediate sensor on the linear topology, its radio-on time when waken up can thus be approximated by the τ multiplied by the sum of Φ' of the upstreaming sensor and current sensor. This expression is helpful for deployment where corresponding sensor density should be achieved for getting a balanced lifetime across different linear topology positions.

4 Simulation Results

We present simulation results of performance of our MAC protocol where packet forwarding undergoes signal interference that is neglected in the previous analysis results. We made a custom-built discrete-event simulator based on R programming language, strictly according to the aforementioned five algorithms. The relevant time instants and energy consumption of main radios are recorded until all data packets arrive at the sink. The default values of relevant parameters are shown in Table 1, which is referred to [5]. In addition, the interference range of data signals is twice of inter-sensor distance, while the interference range of wake-up beacon signals is four times of that distance. Each sensor produces data at a rate of 0.1 packet/second according to independent Poisson processes.

Table 1. Parameter configuration

Parameters	Data packet	ack packet	Data rate	cca interval	cca current	rx current
Value	35	5	20	128	20.28	18.8
Unit	bytes	bytes	kbps	μs	mA	mA
Parameters	Beacon packet	Beacon rate	Data tx current		Beacon tx current	
Value	6	8192	17.4		152	
Unit	bytes	bps	mA		mA	

In order to achieve comparable results among different scales of linear topology networks, we normalize performance results as follows. As data packets emerge randomly among individual sensors, we get the per-hop delay being total end-to-end delay of all data packets divided by their total hops. Then normalized per-hop delay ratio is obtained with the per-hop delay divided by the idealized one, which is equal to sum of time intervals for CCA, wake-up, wake-up acknowledgement, data and data acknowledgement packets. Similarly, normalized per-hop energy ratio is obtained with the per-hop energy consumption divided by the idealized one, which is equal to sum of energy consumption for conducting CCA, transmitting wake-up beacon packets, transmitting and receiving wake-up acknowledgement/data/data acknowledgement packets. Note that receiving wake-up packets is not accounted for, because WuRx is always on. The following plots are an average of 50 independent runs of simulations.

Figure 1 shows the per-hop delay ratio when varying number of sensors in the linear topology network, with total number of packets injected being 100. We

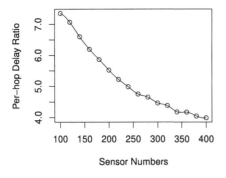

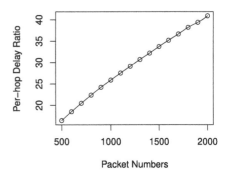

Fig. 1. Per-hop delay ratio vs sensors   **Fig. 2.** Per-hop delay ratio vs packets

observe that as the number of sensors increases, the per-hop delay ratio decreases. This is because the average spatial distance between data packets grows, which mitigates signal interference among packets. Figure 2 shows the per-hop delay ratio when varying number of packets injected into the network, with the number of sensors being 200. We can see that more packets injected, much larger the ratio becomes. A deep investigation reveals that some spatial-and-temporal adjacent data packets would pack together into single packet propagation process. Multiple packets may be forwarded in a single wake-up activity. Thus, delay accumulates quickly because the previously received packets in the queue cannot be forwarded further by the downstreaming sensor until all packets have received from the adjacent upstreaming sensor.

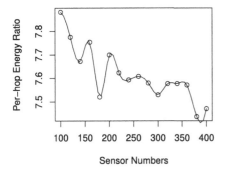

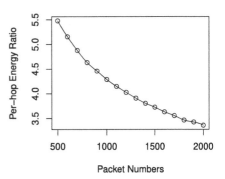

Fig. 3. Per-hop energy ratio vs sensors   **Fig. 4.** Per-hop energy ratio vs packets

Figure 3 shows the per-hop energy ratio when varying number of sensors, with packets injected being 100. We observe that the energy ratio fluctuates within a small value range, indicating the average per-hop energy consumption remains stable. Figure 4 shows the per-hop energy ratio when varying number of packets injected, with sensors being 200. We find that the per-hop energy ratio obviously goes down when more packets become available. This is due to chances of multiple data packets packed into wake-up batch forwarding activities.

5 Conclusions

This paper investigates how urgent data packets propagate on the linear topology WuRx-enabled wireless sensor networks. It presents some interesting design ideas, proposes detailed MAC protocol in event-driven processes, presents theoretical results on expected radio-on time of intermediate sensor when waken up without accounting for signal interferences, and shows numerical results on normalized per-hop delay and energy ratios upon a custom-built simulator with interferences implemented. It opens a new direction on evaluating WuR applications towards large-scale, multi-hop instead of single-hop (i.e. star-shaped) wireless sensor networks, especially when taking channel noise and non-independent urgent data process into account.

References

1. Ait Aoudia, F., Gautier, M., Magno, M., Berder, O., Benini, L.: A generic framework for modeling MAC protocols in wireless sensor networks. IEEE/ACM Trans. Netw. **25**(3), 1489–1500 (2017)
2. Alfayez, F., Hammoudeh, M., Abuarqoub, A.: A survey on MAC protocols for duty-cycled wireless sensor networks. Procedia Comput. Sci. **73**, 482–489 (2015)
3. Aoudia, F.A., Magno, M., Gautier, M., Berder, O., Benini, L.: Analytical and experimental evaluation of wake-up receivers based protocols. In: 2016 IEEE Global Communications Conference (GLOBECOM), pp. 1–7, December 2016
4. Aoudia, F.A., Gautier, M., Magno, M., Gentil, M.L., Berder, O., Benini, L.: Long-short range communication network leveraging LoRa and wake-up receiver. Microprocess. Microsyst. **56**, 184–192 (2018)
5. Ghose, D., Li, F.Y.: Enabling backoff for SCM wake-up radio: protocol and modeling. IEEE Commun. Lett. **21**(5), 1031–1034 (2017)
6. Ghose, D., Li, F.Y., Pla, V.: MAC protocols for wake-up radio: principles, modeling and performance analysis. IEEE Trans. Ind. Inform. **14**(5), 2294–2306 (2018)
7. Guntupalli, L., Ghose, D., Li, F.Y., Gidlund, M.: Energy efficient consecutive packet transmissions in receiver-initiated wake-up radio enabled wsns. IEEE Sens. J. **18**(11), 4733–4745 (2018)
8. Iwata, M., Tang, S., Obana, S.: Sink-based centralized transmission scheduling by using asymmetric communication and wake-up radio. In: 2017 IEEE Wireless Communications and Networking Conference (WCNC), pp. 1–6, March 2017
9. Magno, M., Jelicic, V., Srbinovski, B., Bilas, V., Popovici, E., Benini, L.: Design, implementation, and performance evaluation of a flexible low-latency nanowatt wake-up radio receiver. IEEE Trans. Ind. Inform. **12**(2), 633–644 (2016)
10. Mazloum, N.S., Edfors, O.: Influence of duty-cycled wake-up receiver characteristics on energy consumption in single-hop networks. IEEE Trans. Wirel. Commun. **16**(6), 3870–3884 (2017)
11. Oller, J., Demirkol, I., Casademont, J., Paradells, J., Gamm, G.U., Reindl, L.: Has time come to switch from duty-cycled MAC protocols to wake-up radio for wireless sensor networks? IEEE/ACM Trans. Netw. **24**(2), 674–687 (2016)
12. Piyare, R., Murphy, A.L., Kiraly, C., Tosato, P., Brunelli, D.: Ultra low power wake-up radios: a hardware and networking survey. IEEE Commun. Surv. Tutor. **19**(4), 2117–2157 (2017). Fourthquarter
13. Tang, S., Li, W.: QoS supporting and optimal energy allocation for a cluster based wireless sensor network. Comput. Commun. **29**(13), 2569–2577 (2006)

Effect of Topological Structure and Coupling Strength in Weighted Multiplex Networks

Rajesh Kumar[1(✉)], Anurag Singh[1(✉)], and Hocine Cherifi[2(✉)]

[1] Department of Computer Science and Engineering,
National Institute of Technology Delhi, New Delhi 110040, India
{rajeshkumar,anuragsg}@nitdelhi.ac.in
[2] University of Burgundy, LE21 UMR CNRS 6306, Dijon, France
hocine.cherifi@gmail.com

Abstract. Algebraic connectivity (second smallest eigenvalue of the supra-Laplacian matrix of the underlying multilayer network) and inter-layer coupling strength play an important role in the diffusion processes on the multiplex networks. In this work, we study the effect of inter-layer coupling strength, topological structure on algebraic connectivity in weighted multiplex networks. The results show a remarkable transition in the value of algebraic connectivity from classical cases where the inter-layer coupling strength is homogeneous. We investigate various topological structures in multiplex networks using configuration model, the Barabasi-Albert model (BA) and empirical data-set of multiplex networks. The threshold value d'_c is found smaller in heterogeneous networks for all the multiplex networks as compared to the homogeneous case. Experimental results reveal that the topological structure (average clustering coefficient) and inter-layer coupling strength has considerable effect on threshold values for the algebraic connectivity.

Keywords: Multiplex network · Algebraic connectivity
Coupling strength · Diffusion dynamics
Homogeneous and heterogeneous distribution of weights

1 Introduction

Most complex systems ranging from social, biological, physical, information and engineering, include multiple subsystems and layers of the connectivity among them. The approach of traditional complex network considers the case, where, each component is considered into a network's node, and interaction between these components is considered as a number, quantifying the weight of the corresponding link [4]. Therefore, it is important to take into account the 'multi-layer' nature of these systems for better understanding the dynamics on complex systems (diffusion, spreading process, congestion, etc.).

© Springer Nature Switzerland AG 2018
X. Chen et al. (Eds.): CSoNet 2018, LNCS 11280, pp. 392–403, 2018.
https://doi.org/10.1007/978-3-030-04648-4_33

The behavior of dynamical process on multiplex networks is related to algebraic connectivity which is also known as the second smallest eigenvalue (λ_2) of the supra-laplacian matrix of the underlying multiplex network [18]. Laplacian eigenvalues are more intuitive and very much important than the spectrum of the adjacency matrix [13]. Algebraic connectivity is a parameter that provides meaningful information about the diffusion properties of the network [9], its ability to synchronize [1] and its modularity [15]. Network characteristics (average degree of nodes, clustering coefficient, etc.) at each layer and interlayer coupling (homogeneous-linearly coupled, heterogeneous-non-linearly coupled) patterns have significant impact on the diffusion process in overall complex systems. In many cases abrupt change in values of (λ_2) is an indicator that the diffusion process is faster when the two-layers of the multiplex network superimpose on each other as compared to individual layer. These results are a direct impact of the emergence of more routes between every pair of nodes because of the multilayer structure [8].

In the existing literature, spreading processes studied by considering multiplex network with an homogeneous nature and assuming a random [14] network model, the BA model [2] or a combination of both models. However in many situations, multilayer networks are heterogeneous (i.e. they possess an heterogeneous pattern of interconnections). Most of the existing networks show a long-tailed degree distribution, approximated by a power-law distribution, $P(k) \sim k^{-\gamma}$. Therefore, it is important to have an algorithm in order to generate networks with such feature but random regarding other network properties. The BA model generates scale-free networks, but the value of the exponent γ cannot be controlled. On the other hand, the Configuration model generates a network with any given arbitrary degree sequence while enabling the control of the exponent value γ for networks with a power-law degree distribution. The Configuration may be applied, for example, to quantify the impact of the clustering over a particular dynamical process. Also there are consequences of addition of layer and non-homogeneous inter-layer coupling strength on dynamics on multilayer networks. Hence, it motivates us to propose a new model for heterogeneous multiplex networks and to study its dynamical behavior through the algebraic connectivity of the supra-Laplacian matrix. By tuning the degree-exponent γ, the threshold value of d_c for homogeneous network can be controlled thereby changing the average clustering coefficient.

1.1 Current State of the Art

Spectral properties of the combinatorial supra-Laplacian of underlying interconnected multiplex networks affects the dynamics of different types of diffusion processes [9,16]. Laplacian matrix, and its characteristics are greatly influenced by inter-layer coupling among layers. After changing in the second smallest eigenvalue of supra-Laplacian of an interconnected multiplex network, two distinct regimes can be observed and there is a structural transition phase between them [16]. The influence of inter-layer structure on the dynamical processes in the interconnected networks is studied in some of the recent works. Later,

Wang *et al.* showed that the inter-layer links based on the node's degree have less impact on the spreading size than the density of interconnections [19]. Saumell *et al.* found that the effect of correlations among the intra-layer and inter-layer degree [17]. The researchers revealed that outbreak is possible if the correlations among the nodes is high, even if the spreading threshold is not reached in any one of the network considered separately. Effect of the layer-switching cost on the spreading processes is studied by Cozzo *et al.* Layer-switching cost is defined by taking into account the difference between transmissibility (i.e., effective spreading rates) in the SIR model for intra and inter-layer connections. The researchers are shown that the outbreak state appears if the highest eigenvalue $\wedge$ of the Jacobian matrix is more than 1. Similar results are presented in [6], where the authors studied the SIS model in multiplex networks using a contact-contagion method with multiple spreading rates for intra and inter-layer links. They showed that the epidemic threshold of the entire network is controlled by the layer with largest eigenvalue.

In the existing literature, two distinct kind of dynamical processes on multilayer networks are discovered: (*i*) a single dynamical process which lies on the coupled structure of a multilayer network and (*ii*) 'mixed' or 'coupled' dynamics, iwhere, two or more dynamical processes are explained on each layer respectively and are coupled together by the presence of inter-layer connections among nodes [8]. The behavior of **single dynamical process** depends both on intra-layer structure and on inter-layer structure e.g., diffusion process. **Coupled dynamics** are coupled dynamical processes, which are critical for considering phenomena, e.g., the spreading dynamics of two simultaneous diseases in two-layer multiplex networks and disease spread may be coupled with the spread of information or behavior in the different layers of the network. In [3], the timescales associated with the global order parameters and the inter-layer synchronization of coupled Kuramoto oscillators on multiplexes has been investigated. It showed that the prior timescales are inversely proportional to the inter-layer coupling strength. Further, convergence of the global order parameter is faster than the inter-layer synchronization. In a recent work, diffusion dynamics on multiplex network is studied while considering the heterogeneous nature of multiplex networks [12].

1.2   Multilayer Networks

The complex systems may be represented by a network with one layer only (monoplex) and may have networks at multiple levels or with multiple types of edges at different layer among same number of nodes (or with other similar features). In these type of network we have layers other than the nodes and edges. In the most general **multilayer-network** framework, each node belongs to any subset of the layers, and we consider edges that encompass pairwise connections between all possible combinations of nodes and layers [10]. A node u in layer α can be connected to any node v in any layer.

Mathematically, a multilayer network is a pair, $\mathcal{M} = (\mathcal{G}, \mathcal{C})$, where, $\mathcal{G} = \{\mathcal{G}_\alpha; \alpha \in \{1, \dots, \mathcal{L}\}\}$ is a family of (directed or undirected, weighted or unweighted) graphs. $\mathcal{G}_\alpha = (\mathcal{X}_\alpha, \mathcal{E}_\alpha)$, where, $\mathcal{X}_\alpha$ is the set of nodes N of layer α

and $\mathcal{E}_\alpha \subseteq \mathcal{X}_\alpha \times \mathcal{X}_\alpha$ and represented by, $\mathcal{X}_\alpha = \{X_1^\alpha, X_2^\alpha \dots X_N^\alpha\}$. Set $\mathcal{G}$ is called layers of $\mathcal{M}$ and, $\mathcal{C}$ is the set of interconnections between nodes of different layers $\mathcal{G}_\alpha$ and $\mathcal{G}_\beta$ with $\alpha \neq \beta$,

$$\mathcal{C} = \{\mathcal{E}_{\alpha,\beta}; \alpha, \beta \in \{1, \dots, \mathcal{L}\}, \alpha \neq \beta\} \tag{1}$$

The elements of $\mathcal{C}$ are called crossed layers, and the elements of each $\mathcal{E}_\alpha$ are called intra-layer connections of $\mathcal{M}$ in contrast with the elements of each $\mathcal{E}_{\alpha\beta}(\alpha \neq \beta)$ that are called Inter-layer connections.

A **multiplex network** is a specific case of multilayer network where edges among layers only connect the mapping of the same node to the other layers [10]. For example, lets consider PNB-IOB banking multilayer network, where layer A contains the account holders of PNB Bank and layer B contains the account holders of IOB Bank. Without loss of generality, here, both layer contains the same number of nodes (accounts of the user) and here, any account holder may have accounts at both layer of the network (e.g., on A person has its current account on layer A and a saving account on layer B) (Fig. 1).

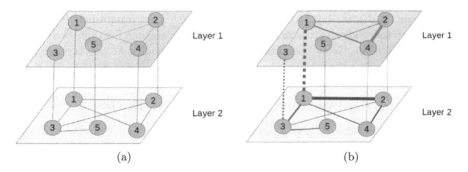

(a)   (b)

Fig. 1. (Left) A Multiplex Network (homogeneous) with two layers (Layer 1, Layer 2). Uniform thickness (weights) of edges (intra-layer, inter-layer) represent homogeneous nature. (Right) Heterogeneous multiplex network with non-uniform thickness (weights) of edges (intra-layer, inter-layer).

Note that connections in layer A do not necessarily represent the same type of connections that in layer B. Since one may have different transactions at each layer. Finally, inter-layer links are created between the two accounts of the same person, when a person transfer money to its own bank account at different layer (e.g., from current account of PNB to saving account of IOB) leading to a 2-layer multiplex network.

Topology and characteristics of the network at different layers in a multiplex network plays an important role not only in the coupling strength but also in diffusion process between the two layers. The research work presented in this paper emphasizes on the study of algebraic connectivity by considering heterogeneous nature of underlying multiplex networks. To study the effect of network topology and Inter-layer coupling strength on algebraic connectivity, the BA model and the Configuration model (with given power law degree sequence) are considered. Both models follow a power-law ($P(k) \sim k^{-\gamma}$) degree distribution, but in the Configuration model, various network properties can be tuned (e.g., degree exponent (γ), clustering coefficient). For heterogeneous networks, it is required to quantify the edge weights (intra-layer) and coupling strength (inter-layer), which enables to determine the capacity between pair of nodes. We made the choice of a two-layer multiplex network using data-sets of musical artists.

The rest of the paper is organized as follows: Sect. 2 discusses the proposed methodology. In Sect. 3 results of the analysis are reported. Finally, in Sect. 4, conclusions and future scope of the research are given.

2   Proposed Methodology

Network topologies, e.g., clustering coefficient, capacities of intra-layer links, inter-layer coupling strength plays an important role in the diffusion process. Therefore, edge weights ($\theta_{i,j}^{\alpha}$ (non-linearly coupled case)) between pair of nodes at any layer and inter-layer coupling strength ($\theta_{i,j}^{\alpha\beta}$) are quantified by taking into account the node degrees and similarity measure using *Pearson correlation* between them respectively then the intra-layer link weights at any layer α is,

$$\theta_{ij}^{\alpha} = (k_i^{\alpha} * k_j^{\alpha})^{\rho_{i,j}^{\alpha}} \tag{2}$$

The Pearson correlation coefficient of the layer α is given by [5],

$$\rho_{i,j}^{\alpha} = \frac{n \sum xy - \sum x \sum y}{(n \sum x^2 - (\sum x)^2)^{1/2} * (n \sum y^2 - (\sum y)^2)^{1/2}}, -1 \leq \rho_{ij}^{\alpha} \leq 1 \tag{3}$$

where, $\rho_{i,j}^{\alpha}$ is the similarity measure between nodes, i and j for any layer α. $\sum_{i,j} xy$ accounts for common neighbors of i and j, while $\sum x$, $\sum y$ represents the degree of node i and j for the layer α, k_i^{α}, k_j^{α} respectively.

The following examples illustrates how the edge weights are computed after considering a network of $n = 10$ nodes.

Case 1: $k_i = 5$, $k_j = 5$ and there are no common neighbors of i, j as shown in Fig. 2(a). In this case $\rho_{i,j} = -1$ and $\theta_{ij} = .04$ which clearly indicates that the capacity of link between nodes, i and j is low and diffusion will certainly be slow.

Case 2: $k_i = 5$, $k_j = 3$ and there are no common neighbors of i, j as depicted in Fig. 2(b). In this case $\rho_{i,j} = -0.65$ and $\theta_{ij} = .172$ which clearly indicates that the capacity of link between nodes, i and j is a little bit more as compared to **case** 1 and diffusion will be more.

Case 3: $k_i = 5$, $k_j = 5$ and there is one common neighbors of i, j. In this case $\rho_{i,j} = -0.6$ and $\theta_{ij} = .19$ as shown by thick edge in Fig. 2(c). Here, by introducing an alternate path (common neighbor) capacity of the link between nodes, i and j is considerably high as compared to **case 1**.

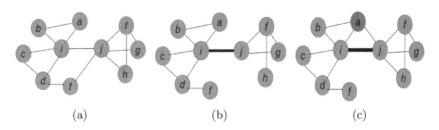

(a)   (b)   (c)

Fig. 2. Representation of how edge weights (intra-layer) are computed in all the above mentioned cases.

From the above observations, we find that by introducing common neighbors between nodes, i and j ($k_i \sim k_j$), there is an increase of the value of $\rho_{i,j}$ (in case 1 and case 3) which means there is an alternate path from node i to j via l leading to less congestion. Similar trend appears when there is considerable difference between degrees k_i, k_j (no common neighbors). Therefore, an increase in value of $\rho_{i,j}$ towards negative side reduces the intra-layer link capacity, while higher values of $\rho_{i,j}$ towards positive side indicates the rise in the value of $\theta_{i,j}^{\alpha}$.

While constructing the network layers by using the configuration model (with power-law degree sequence), more than one connected components are generated depending upon the number of nodes n degree exponent γ. Therefore, in order to obtain a single connected component, all the components are connected to the largest component by picking a random node from it. Edges are rewired in order to obtain higher number of triangles in the network layer. For linearly coupled ($w_{i,j}^{\alpha} = 1$) nodes in each layer, diffusion constant in a layer α d_x^{α} is taken as 1, and among nodes at layers α and β, diffusion constant has been taken as $d_x^{\alpha\beta}$. The coupled dynamical equation [9] representing the evolution of state of node x_i^{α}, in a multiplex network consisting of K networked layers is given by:

$$\frac{dx_i^{\alpha}}{dt} = d_x^{\alpha} \sum_{j=1}^{N} w_{ij}^{\alpha}(x_j^{\alpha}(t) - x_i^{\alpha}(t)) + \sum_{\beta=1}^{K} d_x^{\alpha\beta}(x_i^{\beta}(t) - x_i^{\alpha}(t)) \tag{4}$$

where, $w_{ij}^{\alpha} = \theta_{i,j}^{\alpha}/\langle\{\theta_{i,j}^{\alpha}\}\rangle$ is the effective edge weight. Similar kind of approach has been used to quantify $w_{ij}^{\alpha\beta}$.

The dynamical Eq. (4) can be casted in the usual form by defining the supra-Laplacian of the multiplex as an $KN \times KN$ matrix of the form:

$$\mathcal{L}^M = \mathcal{L}^K + \mathcal{L}^I \tag{5}$$

Where $\mathcal{L}^L$ depicts Laplacian of the independent layers and $\mathcal{L}^I$ is the Inter-layer Laplacian matrix.

$$\mathcal{L}^K = \begin{pmatrix} d_1 L^{(1)} & 0 & \cdots & 0 \\ 0 & d_2 L^{(2)} & \cdots & 0 \\ \vdots & \vdots & \ddots & \vdots \\ 0 & 0 & \cdots & d_M L^{(l)} \end{pmatrix} \tag{6}$$

Where, $K = \{1, 2, ...l\}$ is the number of layers of the multiplex network and N is the number of nodes in each network layer. The Laplacian matrix of each layer α is given by $L^\alpha = S^\alpha - W^\alpha$ where W^α is the weights matrix at layer α, and S^α is a diagonal matrix containing the strength of each node i at layer α, $(S^\alpha)_{ii} = \sum_j w_{ij}^\alpha$. The weighted matrix for Inter-layer network is given as

$$\mathcal{W}^I = \begin{pmatrix} 0 & X_{(1,2)}I & X_{(1,3)}I & \cdots & X_{(1,K)}I \\ X_{(1,2)}I & 0 & X_{(2,3)}I & \cdots & X_{(2,K)}I \\ X_{(1,3)}I & X_{(3,2)}I & 0 & \cdots & X_{(3,K)}I \\ \vdots & \vdots & & \ddots & \vdots \\ X_{(1,K)}I & X_{(2,K)}I & X_{(3,K)}I & \cdots & 0 \end{pmatrix} \tag{7}$$

Where, $X_{(\alpha,\beta)}$ is a vector of edge weights between node i at layer α and its replica at layer $\beta\{w_{ij}^\alpha, j = i\}$. Inter-layer laplacian $\mathcal{L}^I$ can be computed from $\mathcal{W}^I$. For linearly coupled case, $\{w_{ij}^{\alpha\beta} = 1, j = i\}$ and $K = 2$, $\mathcal{L}^I$ takes the form:

$$\mathcal{L}^I = \begin{pmatrix} d_{(1,2)}I & -d_{(1,2)}I \\ -d_{(1,2)}I & d_{(1,2)}I \end{pmatrix} \tag{8}$$

where, I is the identity matrix of $N \times N$. The second smallest eigenvalue (λ_2) of the Laplacian matrix considered as algebraic connectivity of the graph G because of the following proposition,

Let $G = (V, E)$ represent a network with V set of nodes and E set of edges with positive weights w_{ij}. The algebraic connectivity of the network G will be positive and have the minimum value of the function [7]

$$\phi(x) = n \frac{\sum_{i,j \in E} w_{ij}(x_i - x_j)^2}{\sum_{i,j \in E, i<j} w_{ij}(x_i - x_j)^2} \tag{9}$$

over all non-constant n-tuples $x = (x_i)$.

3   Results and Analysis

The following setup has been considered for studying the diffusion dynamics on two different weighted multiplex-networks: The first one is constructed using the Barabasi-Albert [2] model with 500 nodes at each layer. The second one is constructed using the Configuration model with power-law degree sequence

$(P(k) \sim k^{-\gamma})$, $\gamma = 2.1$, 2.2 for layer 1 and layer 2 respectively) and 500 nodes at each layer. For each of the multiplex network, the following scenario is considered:

- Nodes are non-linearly coupled ($w_{i,j}^{\alpha}$ is not identical) and Inter-layer coupling strength is non-uniform.
- Nodes are linearly coupled ($w_{i,j}^{\alpha} = 1$) and Inter-layer coupling strength is uniform ($w_{i,j}^{\alpha\beta} = 1$).
  Values of λ_2 (homogeneous inter-layer links) are computed by assuming all inter-layer link weights ($w_{i,j}^{\alpha\beta} = d_x$), while λ_2' (heterogeneous inter-layer links) is computed by setting weights to $w_{i,j}^{\alpha\beta} \times d_x$ respectively with changing the values of d_x from zero to 8 in steps of $d_x = 0.001$.

We analyze the effect of controlling the parameter d_x on diffusion dynamics in linearly coupled and non-linearly coupled cases (as mentioned in Sect. 4). Assuming $d_x = 0$, the spectrum of supra-Laplacian is given by $\wedge(\mathcal{L}^M) = \{0 = \lambda_1 = \lambda_2 < \lambda_3 \leq \lambda_4 \ldots \lambda_{2N}\}$ with $\lambda_3 = min(\lambda_2^1, \lambda_2^2)$ in both cases. Spectrum of Inter-layer Laplacian matrix is $\wedge(\mathcal{L}^I) = \{0, 2d_x\}$. In the absence of Inter-layer coupling, the two layers behave independently thus λ_1, $\lambda_2 = 0$ in the spectrum $\wedge(\mathcal{L}^M)$ indicates the existence of two independent connected components. The threshold value $d_x > d_c$ (d_c') as obtained in Figs. 3, 4 and 5, the effect of coupling strength in both cases comes into play and λ_2 (λ_2') suffers an abrupt change. Now there is a transition in the eigenvalues of supra-Laplacian matrix of underlying multiplex network. To illustrate our results, the evolution of eigenvalues of the supra-Laplacian of multiplex networks have been computed by considering the following network models:

(1) Multiplex network using BA model: From the experimental results, in the case of linearly coupled multiplex network the value of d_c is 0.450 and for non-linear, value of d_c' is 0.428 as shown in Table 1. In the regime where $(d_x > d_c(d_c'))$, $\lambda_2(\lambda_2')$ is controlled by monotonically increasing function that converges at λ_2 of $\{(\mathcal{L}^1 + \mathcal{L}^2)/2\}$ with $\{\mathcal{L}^1 + \mathcal{L}^2\}$ being the Laplacian matrix of aggregated network as shown in Figs. 3 and 5 respectively. The values of $\lambda_2(\lambda_2')$ saturates at $d_x > 8$. Values of threshold d_c (d_c') are obtained from experiments and shown in Fig. 3.

Table 1. Values of different parameters for the BA model

Parameter	Linearly coupled	Non-linearly coupled
Threshold value	0.450	0.428
Clustering coefficient (Layer 1)	0.0539	0.0539
Clustering coefficient (Layer 2)	0.0599	0.0599
λ_2 (Layer 1)	0.542	0.51
λ_2 (Layer 2)	1.31	1.25
$\lambda_2(L^1 + L^2)/2$	1.489	1.42

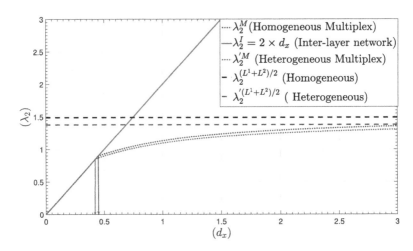

Fig. 3. Algebraic connectivity vs coupling strength d_x (For the BA model), which tunes the average weight of the inter-layer links. Magenta solid line represents λ_2 (inter-layer Laplacian) $= 2 \times d_x$ and Blue horizontal dotted line is λ_2 of the aggregate network (λ_2) $= \lambda_2 \{(\mathcal{L}^1 + \mathcal{L}^2)/2\}$ (homogeneous case), while brown horizontal dotted line corresponds to λ_2' (heterogeneous). (Color figure online)

(2) Multiplex using Configuration model: From the experimental results, the value of d_c (d_c') is obtained as 0.089 and 0.078 respectively as mentioned in Table 2. Two layers of multiplex network (heterogeneous) behave as a single layer when value of λ_2' of supra-Laplacian becomes 0.308 at $d_x = 0.365$ as shown in Fig. 4, while in homogeneous case λ_2 saturates ($\lambda_2 = 0.4$) at $d_x = 7.476$. This is due to the consequence of the higher value of the average clustering coefficients that can be observed from Tables 1 and 2. For larger value of clustering coefficient, there are more triangles in the network which enables the diffusion to take place at lower values of inter-layer coupling strength in the non-linear case. Whereas in the case of homogeneous, λ_2 saturates at higher values of $d_x > 8$.

Table 2. Values of different parameters for the Configuration model

Parameter	Linearly coupled	Non-linearly coupled
Threshold value	0.089	0.071
Clustering coefficient (Layer 1)	0.1665	0.1665
Clustering coefficient (Layer 2)	0.1623	0.1623
λ_2 (Layer 1)	0.118	0.079
λ_2 (Layer 2)	0.098	0.084
$\lambda_2(L^1 + L^2)/2$	0.40	0.308

(3) Multiplex network using Empirical data-set: The multiplex network has been constructed using the dataset representing the social network of a research department at Aarhus [11] (http://larica.uniurb.it/sigsna/data/). Two layers, Facebook and Lunch have been considered for the analysis as both layers contains the same numbers of nodes. Table 3 and Fig. 5 show that experimental results obtained using the empirical data-set are in agreement with the proposed methodology as discussed in Sect. 2.

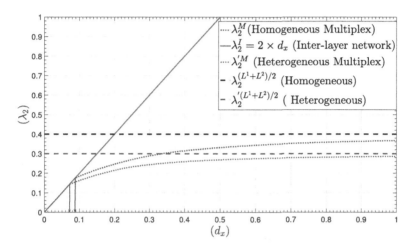

Fig. 4. Algebraic connectivities vs the coupling strength d_x (For Configuration model), which tunes the average weight of the inter-layer links. Magenta solid line represents λ_2 (inter-layer Laplacian) $= 2 \times d_x$ and Blue horizontal dotted line is algebraic connectivity of the aggregate network $(\lambda_2') = \lambda_2' \{(\mathcal{L}^1 + \mathcal{L}^2)/2\}$ (heterogeneous case), while Brown horizontal line corresponds to λ_2 (homogeneous). Red (Green) curved solid line represent λ_2' (λ_2) of supra-Laplacian matrix respectively. (Color figure online)

Table 3. Values of different parameters for the Empirical data-set

Parameter	Linearly coupled	Non-linearly coupled
Threshold value	0.081	0.008
Clustering coefficient (Layer 1)	0.67	0.67
Clustering coefficient (Layer 2)	0.63	0.63
λ_2 (Layer 1)	0.08	0.008
λ_2 (Layer 2)	0.76	0.11
$\lambda_2(L^1 + L^2)/2$	1.618	0.256

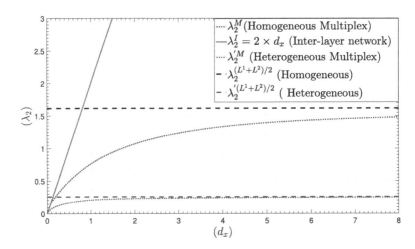

Fig. 5. Algebraic connectivity vs the coupling strength d_x (Empirical data-set), which tunes the average weight of the inter-layer links. Magenta solid line represents λ_2 (inter-layer Laplacian) $= 2 \times d_x$ and Blue horizontal dotted line is algebraic connectivity of the aggregate network $(\lambda_2') = \lambda_2' \{(\mathcal{L}^1 + \mathcal{L}^2)/2\}$ (heterogeneous case), while Brown horizontal line corresponds to λ_2 (homogeneous). Red (Green) curved solid line represent λ_2' (λ_2) of supra-Laplacian matrix respectively. (Color figure online)

4   Conclusion and Future Work

From the analysis done, it is found that network structure (individual layer) and heterogeneity play an important role in the diffusion dynamics on multiplex networks. Our experimental results reveal that in all the three taken multiplex networks the value of $d_c' < d_c$ as shown in Figs. 3, 4 and 5. Also from the Tables 1, 2 and 3 it can be observed that $d_c^{BA} > d_c^{Config.} > d_c^{Empirical}$ while, $Average\_clustering^{BA} < Average\_clustering^{Config.} < Average\_clustering^{Emp.}$. Therefore we conclude that experimental results are in good agreement with the theoretical framework. In the present work, we studied the behaviour of (λ_2) supra-Laplacian of multiplex networks consisting of two layers, by considering the BA model and the Configuration model. The results are validated by considering an empirical data-set. For the experimental analysis, it is assumed that each layer is a single connected component. In future work, further analysis may be done such as perturbation analysis, synchronization etc. for multiplex networks by considering multiple layers and real-world data-sets.

References

1. Aguirre, J., Sevilla-Escoboza, R., Gutiérrez, R., Papo, D., Buldú, J.: Synchronization of interconnected networks: the role of connector nodes. Phys. Rev. Lett. **112**(24), 248701 (2014)
2. Albert, R., Barabási, A.L.: Statistical mechanics of complex networks. Rev. Mod. Phys. **74**(1), 47 (2002)
3. Allen-Perkins, A., de Assis, T.A., Pastor, J.M., Andrade, R.F.: Relaxation time of the global order parameter on multiplex networks: the role of interlayer coupling in Kuramoto oscillators. Phys. Rev. E **96**(4), 042312 (2017)
4. Boccaletti, S., et al.: The structure and dynamics of multilayer networks. Phys. Rep. **544**(1), 1–122 (2014)
5. Royal Society (Great Britain): Proceedings of the Royal Society of London, no. v. 58. Taylor & Francis (1895). https://books.google.co.in/books?id=60aL0zlT-90C
6. Cozzo, E., Banos, R.A., Meloni, S., Moreno, Y.: Contact-based social contagion in multiplex networks. Phys. Rev. E **88**(5), 050801 (2013)
7. De Abreu, N.M.M.: Old and new results on algebraic connectivity of graphs. Linear Algebra Appl. **423**(1), 53–73 (2007)
8. De Domenico, M., Granell, C., Porter, M.A., Arenas, A.: The physics of spreading processes in multilayer networks. Nat. Phys. **12**(10), 901 (2016)
9. Gomez, S., Diaz-Guilera, A., Gomez-Gardenes, J., Perez-Vicente, C.J., Moreno, Y., Arenas, A.: Diffusion dynamics on multiplex networks. Phys. Rev. Lett. **110**(2), 028701 (2013)
10. Kivelä, M., Arenas, A., Barthelemy, M., Gleeson, J.P., Moreno, Y., Porter, M.A.: Multilayer networks. J. Complex Netw. **2**(3), 203–271 (2014)
11. Magnani, M., Micenkova, B., Rossi, L.: Combinatorial analysis of multiple networks. arXiv preprint arXiv:1303.4986 (2013)
12. Martínez, J.H., Boccaletti, S., Makarov, V.V., Buldú, J.M.: Multiplex networks of musical artists: the effect of heterogeneous inter-layer links. arXiv preprint arXiv:1805.08711 (2018)
13. Mohar, B., Alavi, Y., Chartrand, G., Oellermann, O.: The Laplacian spectrum of graphs. In: Graph Theory, Combinatorics, and Applications, vol. 2(871–898), p. 12 (1991)
14. Newman, M.E.: The structure and function of complex networks. SIAM Rev. **45**(2), 167–256 (2003)
15. Newman, M.E.: Modularity and community structure in networks. Proc. Natl. Acad. Sci. **103**(23), 8577–8582 (2006)
16. Radicchi, F., Arenas, A.: Abrupt transition in the structural formation of interconnected networks. Nat. Phys. **9**(11), 717 (2013)
17. Saumell-Mendiola, A., Serrano, M.Á., Boguná, M.: Epidemic spreading on interconnected networks. Phys. Rev. E **86**(2), 026106 (2012)
18. Sole-Ribalta, A., De Domenico, M., Kouvaris, N.E., Diaz-Guilera, A., Gomez, S., Arenas, A.: Spectral properties of the Laplacian of multiplex networks. Phys. Rev. E **88**(3), 032807 (2013)
19. Wang, Y., Xiao, G.: Effects of interconnections on epidemics in network of networks. In: 2011 7th International Conference on Wireless Communications, Networking and Mobile Computing (WiCOM), pp. 1–4. IEEE (2011)

A Single-Pair Antenna Microwave Medical Detection System Based on Unsupervised Feature Learning

Yizhi Wu[1(✉)], Bingshuai Liu[1(✉)], and Mingda Zhu[2]

[1] College of Information Science and Technology, Donghua University,
Shanghai 200051, China
yz_wu@dhu.edu.cn, bingshuai_liu@mail.dhu.edu.cn
[2] Department of Electrical Engineering and Computer Science, Syracuse University,
Syracuse, NY 13244, USA

Abstract. The microwave medical detection method is an emerging non-invasive technology, which starts showing great potential in microwave biomedical applications. However, the practical application of it still faces challenges such as the detection equipment is complicated and difficult to control, and various interferences in the empirical situation. The difference between the microwave signal of healthy organs and that of the patients with stroke is sometimes too subtle to be detected when there are various noises within the detecting environment. This paper designed a single-pair antenna microwave medical detection system based on unsupervised feature learning for stroke detection. The system uses unsupervised feature learning, principal component analysis (PCA), to extract features, and then uses support vector machine (SVM) to classify whether there is a stroke. The use of a single-pair antenna greatly reduces the dimensionality of the sample features and also eliminates the interference between antenna arrays. This paper also optimized the detection position of the single-pair antenna. The performance of the detection system was verified by simulation and experiment. The results show that in the case of random interference, the detection system will also achieve better results, and when the antenna is placed in the left and right of the brain, the best performance will be achieved.

Keywords: Microwave medical detection · Stroke
Single-pair antenna · PCA · SVM

1 Introduction

Nowadays, microwave (MW) medical detection has incited new researches in breast cancer and brain stroke due to its non-ionizing. Microwave-based devices

Supported by the Science and technology commission of Shanghai, China (SSTEC). No. 14510711600; the Fundamental Research Funds for Central Universities. No. 17D110417.

X. Chen et al. (Eds.): CSoNet 2018, LNCS 11280, pp. 404–414, 2018.
https://doi.org/10.1007/978-3-030-04648-4_34

are particularly suitable for prehospital use because they can be built in compact and portable formats at a relatively low cost and can also be easy to use [1]. Comparing to the breast cancer detection, the microwave stroke detection presents more challenges because of the complex brain structure and low difference of dialectical property between the stroke and healthy brain tissues [3,9,12,14]. The microwave imaging methods effectively used in breast cancer are not directly applicable in brain stroke. On the other hand, the microwave detection method based on classification and feature extraction shows its potentiality to be a promisingly alternative solution. Furthermore, due to the less bandwidth required from the classifying-based system, the proposed method would be helpful to minimize the problem of designing an ultra-wideband (UWB) antenna array and devices required from most microwave detection system nowadays [8,11,12]. Therefore, there are recent researches on the classification of microwave scattering signal. Methods in [1,12,15] differentiate the intracerebral hemorrhage (ICH) from the ischemic stroke (IS), while the hemorrhagic patients are distinguished from healthy volunteers by classifying high dimensional frequency microwave measurements. In [5], ensemble classifiers to fuse scattering signals from multiple microwave antennas are designed to detect abnormalities in the breast.

There are still serious challenges in classification-based microwave medical detection. First, microwave medical detection equipment is complex in structure and cumbersome to operate. To get omnibearing scattered MW wave signal, an antenna array is usually deployed around the brain and a radio frequency conversion device is provided to switch the signal source. Dozens of antenna and MW cables not only make the system bulky and also generate noise due to antenna and cable movements and discrepancies in antenna fabrication. Up to now the minimum number of antenna is 12 designed by Persson et al. [12]. Second, the microwave signals have high dimensions, which will introduce the following problems: redundant data which are irrelevant to the intrinsic characteristics, and data singularity problem. These may cause the non-effectiveness of the classification algorithms. Because of the subtle discrepancy between the microwave signal of the healthy subject and that of the patient with brain stroke, it is possible that the user response of the target is submerged in the noise and hard to be detected. Thus, effective feature learning is important to obtain valid features from the microwave signals.

To deal with the problems of microwave medical detection, we designed a single-pair antenna microwave medical detection system based on unsupervised feature learning. The use of a single pair of antennas simplifies the device architecture, eliminating the need for switching between antenna arrays and making it easier to operate. Moreover, using this architecture to collect microwave signals reduces the dimensionality of the features, and also eliminates the effects between antenna arrays. We adopt unsupervised feature learning, PCA, to extract features, which have good generalization ability and suitability because it can use un-labeled data samples for training. Moreover, we choose SVM to be the classifiers based on the learned features. And we optimized the measurement position of the antenna. The results are verified by both simulation data and experimental data, which show that we can obtain better performance when the antenna is placed in the left and right of the brain even in the presence of random noise interference.

This paper is organized as follows: In Sect. 2, the structure and theory of the single-pair antenna microwave detection system are introduced. Then, the simulation and experimental platform are introduced, and results are analyzed in Sect. 3. The Sect. 4 part is the conclusion.

2   Single-Pair Antenna Microwave Detection System

The single-pair antenna microwave detection system consists of two parts: single-pair antenna microwave measuring device, feature learning and classification module, as shown in Fig. 1. The microwave signal is transmitted through a pair of antennas to collect scattering information of the brain to generate sample data. Then, PCA is used to extract expressive features, and finally SVM is used to complete the recognition of stroke or not.

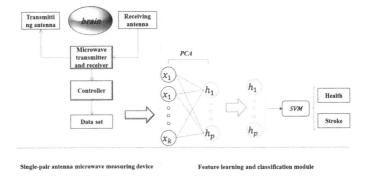

Fig. 1. Single-pair antenna microwave detection system

2.1   Single-Pair Antenna Microwave Measuring Device

Considering the current problems in microwave detection: system architecture complexity, high acquisition feature dimensions, and susceptible to interference. We designed a microwave measuring device based on a single-pair antenna. The model is shown in Fig. 2. The model uses a transmit antenna and a receive antenna, so we collect the microwave scattering parameter, S21, as the sample feature information. Using the step-frequency radar technique, the scattered signals are collected by the RF transceiver in the frequency-domain, and each collected signal data is a vector:

$$x_i \in C(f_l < f_m < f_h) \tag{1}$$

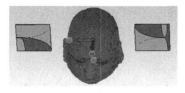

Fig. 2. Single-pair antenna measuring device model

Where f_m is one of the M frequency sampling points over the working bandwidth from f_l f_h, $m = 1, 2, 3...M$, and i is the is the sample number, $i = 1, 2, 3...n$. Each sample is a microwave scattering parameter, S21, collected by a pair of antennas, represented as a one-dimensional vector. Assuming we have collected n samples, the sample sets collected is expressed as follows:

$$[X] = \begin{bmatrix} x_1(f_1) & ... & x_1(f_M) \\ ... & ... & ... \\ x_n(f_1) & ... & x_n(f_M) \end{bmatrix}_{n \times M} \tag{2}$$

This microwave measuring device discards the complex antenna array structure and selects a simple pair of antennas to collect data. On the one hand, it simplifies the measurement architecture and makes it more convenient and efficient. On the other hand, it also reduces the characteristic dimension of information and also reduces noise interference. Taking into account the complex structure of the brain, the microwave signals collected by the antennas at different positions will also be different. Therefore, it is necessary to optimize the antenna placement, and we will discuss and analyze it in the following simulations.

2.2 Feature Learning and Classification Module

PCA. The principal component analysis (PCA) is a typical method of unsupervised feature learning utilized to reduce the dimensionality of data samples [10]. PCA can be defined as the orthogonal projection of the data into a lower dimensional linear space, known as the principal subspace where the variance of the projected data is maximized. The principal components are acquired by computing the eigenvectors and eigenvalues of the covariance matrix of the dataset. The eigenvectors corresponding to the directions of principal components of the original data and their statistical significance are given by their corresponding eigenvalues. To have dimensionality reduction, only a small part of the most significant eigenvectors is kept to compose the transformation matrix. Thus, PCA reduces dimensions using linear transformation in an unsupervised way. PCA is a classic simple model, take the data collected by our single-pair antenna measurement device as an example, we will briefly describe its process. Our sample set is M-dimensional with a total of n samples, recorded as $X = [x_M^1, ..., x_M^n]$.

First, centralize all samples:

$$x^i = x^i - \sum_{j=1}^{n} x^j \tag{3}$$

Second, calculate the sample covariance matrix $X_T X$ and do the singular value decomposition:

$$[USV] = SVD(X^T X) \tag{4}$$

Retrieve the eigenvectors $[w_1, .., w_k]$ corresponding to the largest k singular values to form a weight matrix W. And convert each sample x^i in the sample set into a new sample z^i.

$$z^i = W^T x^i \tag{5}$$

PCA model is simple, easy to optimize, and can effectively eliminate noise and redundancy, so, it meets the needs of our lightweight, convenient detection system.

SVM. The support vector machine is a classification model whose basic model is defined as the linear classifier with the largest interval in the feature space [6]. With SVM, the original input space is mapped into a higher dimensional dot-product space called a feature space. In the feature space, an optimal hyperplane is found that maximizes the generalization property of the classifier. Our goal is to identify healthy and stroke samples by training a sample set of completed feature learning, which is a two-category problem [4,6]. Consider the problem of separating the set of training data $(z^1, y_1), (z^2, y_2), ..., (z^n, y_n)$ into two classes, where $z^i \in R^k$ is a feature vector and $y_i \in -1, +1$ its class label. If we assume that the two classes can be separated by a hyperplane $w \cdot z + b = 0$ in some space H. Its classification decision function is:

$$f(z) = sign(w \cdot z + b) \tag{6}$$

The optimal hyperplane is the one which maximizes the margin γ.

$$\gamma = \frac{y \cdot f(z)}{\|w\|} \tag{7}$$

The optimization problem is:

$$max_{w,b} \quad \gamma s.t. \quad y_i \cdot f(z^i) \geq 1 \tag{8}$$

The optimal values for w and b can be found by solving a constrained minimization problem, using Lagrange multipliers.

3   Measurement Data and Results Analysis

3.1   Measurement Data

Simulation data. We use the electromagnetic simulation algorithm, Finite-Difference Time-Domain (FDTD), to generate a large amount of sample databasing on different brain phantoms. The simulated brain model is set up using MR image. As shown in Fig. 3. The electrical properties of different main tissues including skin, bone, fat, blood, dura, cerebral spinal fluid (CSF), grey and white matter can be found in [7], as shown in Table 1, and be initiated in the phantom. In the simulation, we choose Gaussian-modulated pulse with center frequency $f = 2\,\mathrm{GHz}$, and fractional bandwidth $B = 0.2\,\mathrm{GHz}$, as the excitation. Then one antenna emits microwaves, and the other antenna collects the microwave scattering parameter S21. In order to optimize the position of the antenna, we simulated the model of the antenna in front-back and left-right.

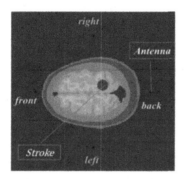

Fig. 3. The brain structure with the stroke used in simulation

Table 1. The electrical properties of different main tissues of the human body across the band 500 MHz–10 GHz

Tissues	ε	$\sigma(S/m)$
Dry skin	45–31.3	0.73–8
Bone	5.6–4.6	0.03–0.6
Fat	5.54–4.6	0.04–0.6
Blood	63.3–45.1	1.38–13.1
Dura	46–33	0.9–8.6
Cerebral Spinal Fluid (CSF)	70.1–52.4	2.3–15.4
Grey matter	58–38.1	0.8–10.3
White matter	41–28.4	0.47–7.3

Stroke-free simulated data is collected as Data1, by changing dielectric properties of brain tissues in the range of 10% to mimic the different complex dielectric constant (CDC) from person to person. The stroke-bearing data set, Data2, is collected not only by changing the CDC but also by adding blood clot to different position and size. Considering empirical application situation where the data may be polluted by several sources of noise, the data polluted by mechanical noise which results in slight movement of antenna position, are collected as Data3 and Data4 for stroke-free and stroke-bearing phantom respectively. Furthermore, white noise with SNR = 50 is added to produce stroke-free Data5 and stroke-bearing Data6, respectively. Both white noise and movement noise is further added to produce stroke-free Data7 and stroke-bearing Data8, which are the data set mostly close to the empirical situation. For each data set, we have collected microwave information about the antenna position at front-back and left-right.

Experiment data. We collected experimental data samples using brain phantoms with varying dielectric properties. The frequency band in the experiment is from 1.8 to 2.3 GHz. The brain phantoms are created from a mixture of glycerol, water, and ethanol. These are designed to mimic the dielectric properties of the skin and skull, average inner tissue, and white matter and grey matter, respectively, the stroke is caused by cerebral hemorrhage. This liquid brain stroke phantom is not fully realistic, however, it is a well-accepted design for simulation and early experiments [2,13].

We perform permittivity measurements on all of the liquid mixtures. Measurements are done with a dielectric probe kit (DAK3.5: 200 MHz–20 GHz) with 320 points recorded from 800 MHz to 4 GHz. The electrical properties of the average inner brain change in a small range. The positions of the stroke clot are also changed in the different phantoms. Our microwave experiment system is shown in Fig. 4. The system incorporates a pair of antenna held across a beaker full of liquid brain phantom, which located on an automatically circling supporter. For each phantom, we take three measurements and then average them to get rid of random interference. The comparison of the signal of stroke-bearing and health phantom shows the existence of the small variations of the signal. Since the experiment simplifies the brain model and uses a uniform medium to simulate the brain structure, the measurements of the antennas at different positions are the same. We performed experiments only on the presence or absence of stroke blood clots and obtained health datasets Data9 and stroke datasets Data10.

Fig. 4. The experiment platform

The frequency domain scattering parameters are shown in Fig. 5. The information is different. We need to extract it to complete the training identification.

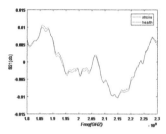

Fig. 5. Microwave signal of stroke and health samples collected from this platform

3.2 Results Analysis

Performance indicator. The essential task of microwave medical detection is to assign a label to each test data. A positive label indicates that there is no nidus in signal sample xi, and a negative label indicates the existence of a stroke. Minimizing the false positive rate, FP, is most important in reducing the chance of missed early detection. To prevent overdiagnosis the stroke, the false negative rate, FN, should also be controlled. We also use a scalar parameter e to measure average error, which could be used to estimate the overall performance of a classifier. The primary components of our classifier are feature extraction and classification. We address both the tasks and comparison of the above-mentioned combinations in the following section.

Results analysis. For both the simulation and experimental data set, we use about one-sixth as the test data and using the rest of the other as the training data. Health and stroke samples of each kind of data set is combined to set up four simulation datasets, Data1+2, Data3+4, Data5+6 and Data7+8 and one experimental dataset, Data9+10. For the simulation data, the grouping is the same for antenna position at front-back and left-right.

First, the validity of the feature learning and classification model in this system is verified. In order to verify the validity of the simple model PCA in feature learning, we compared it with another unsupervised feature learning sparse auto-encoder (SAE). SAE is a kind of unsupervised feature learning with neural network architecture. The purpose of feature learning is achieved by adjusting parameters such as sparse activation, hidden layer neurons, and loss functions. Because of its network architecture, optimization is more difficult. We use the PCA-SVM and SAE-SVM methods to train the data set and get the results, as shown in Table 2. The simulation dataset used is measured when the antenna is in the front-back position. From Table 2, it can be seen that the simple model PCA-SVM tends to show better performance than SAE-SVM on the dataset which is collected on single-pair antenna measurement device both in simulation and experiment.

Table 2. The comparison of results on different methods

Datasets	Methods	FN	FP	e
Data1+2	PCA-SVM	0.04	0	0.02
Data1+2	SAE-SVM	0.04	0.02	0.03
Data3+4	PCA-SVM	0	0.02	0.01
Data3+4	SAE-SVM	0.20	0.08	0.14
Data5+6	PCA-SVM	0.08	0.10	0.09
Data5+6	SAE-SVM	0.18	0.16	0.17
Data7+8	PCA-SVM	0.06	0.16	0.11
Data7+8	SAE-SVM	0.22	0.16	0.19
Data9+10	PCA-SVM	0.15	0.20	0.16
Data9+10	SAE-SVM	0.10	0.40	0.25

Table 3. The comparison of results on different measurement position

Datasets	Position	FN	FP	e
Data1+2	Front-back	0.04	0	0.02
Data1+2	Left-right	0.02	0	0.01
Data3+4	Front-back	0.12	0.02	0.07
Data3+4	Left-right	0.12	0	0.06
Data5+6	Front-back	0.08	0.10	0.09
Data5+6	Left-right	0.16	0	0.08
Data7+8	Front-back	0.06	0.16	0.11
Data7+8	Left-right	0.04	0.14	0.09

Next, we will further optimize the position selection of the antenna on the simulation data. We deployed the single-pair antenna measuring devices in different two position as shown in Fig. 3: front-back and left-right. The same data set are collected and their results under the PCA-SVM model are compared, as shown in Table 3. The performance of the system is different under different measurement positions. By comparing the results of different data sets, we can see that the left-right position measurement data are better than the data set measured in the front-back positions. In Data1+2, Data3+4, and Data5+6, the error rate is reduced by 0.01, and the error rate is reduced by 0.02 on Data7+8. It can be concluded that measuring on the left and right sides of the brain can provide better detection performance.

4   Conclusion

This paper designs a single-pair antenna microwave medical detection system based on unsupervised feature learning for stroke detection. The system is simple in structure and easy to control. We collected microwave signal through a pair of antennas while simplifying the apparatus, reducing the dimensions and interference. Then, PCA is used to extract features, and SVM is used to classify. We also optimized the measurement position of the antenna. Finally, our results show that the detection system is able to achieve better results in the case of random interference, and the signals collected by the antenna on the left and right sides of the brain are more conducive to stroke detection. And the following will further fine-tune the measurement position selection. In the next work, we will locate stroke lesions, and effective measurement locations will improve performance in the final positioning results.

References

1. Fhager, A., Candefjord, S., Elam, M., Persson, M.: Microwave diagnostics ahead: saving time and the lives of trauma and stroke patients. IEEE Microw. Mag. **19**(3), 78–90 (2018)
2. Gabriel, S., Lau, R.W., Gabriel, C.: The dielectric properties of biological tissues: II. Measurements in the frequency range 10 Hz to 20 GHz. Phys. Med. Biol. **41**(11), 2251–2269 (1996)
3. Guo, L., Abbosh, A.M.: Optimization-based confocal microwave imaging in medical applications. IEEE Trans. Antennas Propag. **63**(8), 3531–3539 (2015)
4. Huang, J., Shao, X., Wechsler, H.: Face pose discrimination using support vector machines (SVM). In: Proceedings of the Fourteenth International Conference on Pattern Recognition, vol. 1, pp. 154–156 (1998)
5. Li, Y., Porter, E., Santorelli, A., Popovi, M., Coates, M.: Microwave breast cancer detection via cost-sensitive ensemble classifiers: phantom and patient investigation. Biomed. Signal Process. Control. **31**, 366–376 (2017)
6. Mavroforakis, M.E., Theodoridis, S.: Support vector machine (SVM) classification through geometry. In: Proceedings of EUSIPCO (2010)
7. Mobashsher, A.T., Abbosh, A.M.: Artificial human phantoms: human proxy in testing microwave apparatuses that have electromagnetic interaction with the human body. IEEE Microw. Mag. **16**(6), 42–62 (2015)
8. Mohammed, B.J., Abbosh, A.M., Ireland, D.: Stroke detection based on variations in reflection coefficients of wideband antennas. In: Antennas and Propagation Society International Symposium, pp. 1–2 (2012)
9. Mohammed, B.J., Abbosh, A.M., Mustafa, S., Ireland, D.: Microwave system for head imaging. IEEE Trans. Instrum. Meas. **63**(1), 117–123 (2013)
10. Moore, B.: Principal component analysis in linear systems: controllability, observability, and model reduction. IEEE Trans. Autom. Control. **26**(1), 17–32 (2003)
11. Mustafa, S., Abbosh, A., Henin, B., Ireland, D.: Brain stroke detection using continuous wavelets transform matching filters. In: Biomedical Engineering Conference, pp. 194–197 (2012)
12. Persson, M., Fhager, A., Trefn, H.D., Yu, Y.: Microwave-based stroke diagnosis making global prehospital thrombolytic treatment possible. IEEE Trans. Biomed. Eng. **61**(11), 2806–2817 (2014)

13. Peyman, A., Rezazadeh, A.A., Gabriel, C.: Changes in the dielectric properties of rat tissue as a function of age atmicrowave frequencies. Phys. Med. Biol. **46**(6), 1617–29 (2001)
14. Semenov, S.Y., Corfield, D.R.: Microwave tomography for brain imaging: feasibility assessment for stroke detection. Int. J. Antennas Propag. **2008**(4), 264–276 (2008)
15. Yu, Y., Mckelvey, T.: A unified subspace classification framework developed for diagnostic system using microwave signal. In: Signal Processing Conference, pp. 1–5 (2014)

Forgetting Punished Recommendations for MOOC

Yanxia Pang[1,2(✉)], Liping Li[2], Wenan Tan[2], Yuanyuan Jin[1], and Ying Zhang[1]

[1] East China Normal University, Shanghai, China
yxpang@sspu.edu.cn
[2] Shanghai Polytechnic University, Shanghai, China

Abstract. Prerequisite inadequacy tends to cause more drop-out of MOOC. Recommendation is an effective method of learning intervene. Existing recommendation for MOOC is mainly for subsequent learning objects that have not been learned before. This paper proposes a solution called Forgetting-punished MOOC Recommendation (FMR). FMR combines the forgetting effect on learning score as a main feature for recommendation. It provides Prerequisite Recommendation (PR) for the unqualified learning objects and Subsequent Recommendation (SR) for the qualified objects. Experiments verify the accuracy improvement of PR and SR.

Keywords: MOOC · Recommendation · Prerequisite · Subsequent Location

1 Introduction

MOOC (Massive Open Online Course) develops rapidly in recent years, but the drop-out rate reaches 90% [1]. Kizilcec found that frustration is an important factor affecting learners' persistence in learning [2]. Pappano believes that MOOC learners are often frustrated for the inadequacy of prerequisite. The learner fails to keep pace and tends to drop out [3].

Prerequisite relationship between learning objects plays an important role for MOOC learning. Recommendation can effectively guide learners to learn. It is an effective mean to intervene in MOOC learning.

MOOC platforms pay effort on prerequisite for better learning. Figure 1 shows the learning content of math subjects on Khan Academy (https://www.khanacademy.orgn) which is one of the most popular MOOC platform. Usually, learners learn in order one by one. The previous knowledge provides prerequisites for further learning. Coursera (https://www.coursera.org) lists the prerequisite in course introduction. Khan Academy (https://www.khanacademy.org) lists the subject of the course according to the grade level of the target learners. Learners are asked to have a test. By this way, a suitable starting point will be found for them. But the MOOC platforms do not provide personalized recommendation on prerequisite. Existed MOOC recommendation is mainly about learning objects that were not learned before.

© Springer Nature Switzerland AG 2018
X. Chen et al. (Eds.): CSoNet 2018, LNCS 11280, pp. 415–426, 2018.
https://doi.org/10.1007/978-3-030-04648-4_35

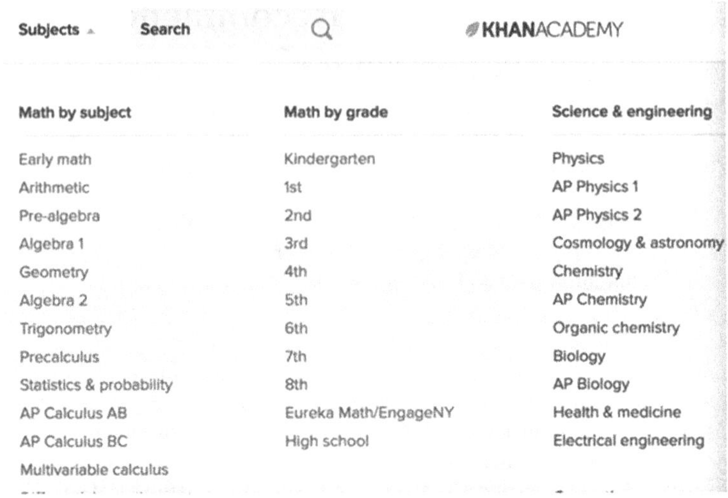

Fig. 1. Knowledge prerequisite of math subject on Khan Academy

This paper proposes a solution for MOOC recommendation on prerequisite and subsequent learning objects. Recommendations on Forgetting-punished MOOC Recommendation (FMR) recommends according to learners' learning situation. It diagnoses both qualified and unqualified location points on learning series (learning behaviors on the time series of the learner). Forgetting effect is combined for both correlation coefficient and recommendation feature measurement. For the unqualified learning objects, FMR recommends prerequisite according to learning series of learners who are qualified with the object. For qualified learning object, FMR recommends objects that take the qualified learning objects as prerequisite.

The main contributions are as follows:

- Learning location helps for adaptive recommendation according to learners' performance. The recommendation aims at the located qualified and unqualified learning objects.
- The forgetting effect is considered as punishment of learning score. It modifies the learning score with consideration on time decay for forgetting. Learning scores are adopted as features for recommendation. It is used to measure the prerequisite correlation. It reflects the effect of forgetting with time on.
- Experiments on realworld data show the improvement of FMR in accuracy. Especially the precision is improved obviously.

Section of Related Work is about research work of prerequisite and recommendation on learning series. The following section introduces FMR according to the work flow of recommendation. It includes prerequisite coefficient calculation and recommendation for prerequisite and subsequent learning. Experiments list the dataset and result of comparison with different recommendation methods. The last section is the summary.

2   Related Work

Prerequisite plays an important role in MOOC learning. In application, prerequisite is usually defined by expert labeling. Polyzou predicts academic performance based on the prerequisite relationship between courses which is achieved by expert annotation [4]. But manual labeling depends much on the experts. It cannot support massive recommendation.

In most research, prerequisite correlation is mainly calculated through knowledge based concepts analysis. Yang builds the concept map through the prerequisite relationship of the existing curriculum, which is used to predict the prerequisite [5]. Liu studies the learning dependence between knowledge points through text analysis [6]. Some research is based on the analysis of the concept map to establish the prerequisite relationship between the knowledge [7–9]. Wikipedia's content is mostly used for prerequisite training. Liang defines the prerequisite relationship between knowledge on links between pages of Wikipedia [10,11]. Wang adopts Wikipedia's links between knowledge concepts and establishes a concept map for teaching materials [12]. Agrawal extracts key concepts in the textbook and calculates prerequisite values between two concepts through the frequency and sequence of them [13]. These methods are all based on content. They are not personalized.

Sequential learning data is used for recommendation. Lu uses the association rule mining method to recommend courses and trains on other learners' learning paths [14]. Sun analyses learning path through metapath method, enriching the learner's portfolio [15]. Chen compares the homogeneity between the user and the item's image by path similarity [16]. Yu learned a similar user's behavioral sequence through collaborative filtering to make sequential recommendations [17]. These methods focus on prerequisite of knowledge, and do not recommend according to the situation of learners.

Yueh proposes a Markov-based recommendation on learning sequences and analyses the learning path from learner history [18]. Mi makes recommendations based on the context tree, focusing more on solution design than implementation [19]. Yu uses collaborative filtering to recommend in a game with storyline through other users' sequential actions [17]. Lee learns the sequence of behavioral learning courses through learners [20]. The recommendation considers only on subsequent recommendations and does not consider on relationship of prerequisite. And the feature is mainly on preference without consideration on learning performance.

We propose the solution FMR to recommend for prerequisite and subsequent learning objects with forgetting punishment.

3   Forgetting-Punished Recommendation on Prerequisite and Subsequent Learning Objects

Adaptive learning responds to learners according to their learning situation. It helps for less frustration and less drop-out [26]. To support adaptive learning better, RFP recommends according to situation of the learner. The situation is measured with learning location. Based on the location, the qualified and unqualified learning objects are detected. RFP recommends prerequisite learning objects for the unqualified learning objects and subsequent learning objects. Correlation of prerequisite on learning scores are adopted as features for recommendation. The effect of forgetting is combined to model the real learning better. According to the working flow of RFP, forgetting effect, prerequisite correlation and recommendation on prerequisite and subsequent learning are introduced in sequence.

3.1   Symbols

Before further discussion, some related symbols are listed with description in Table 1.

Table 1. Symbols

Symbol	Description
se_{si}	Score of learner s on learning object i
dis	Distance on time
$q(i, d_1)$	Prerequisite correlation coefficient between learning objects i and d_1
d_{si,sd_1}	Time distance between 2 learning behaviors of learner s on learning object i and d_1
I_{pr}	Learning object set for prerequisite recommendation
d_1	First unqualified learning object
d_2	Last qualified learning object
d_1	Any qualified learning object
sim_{sr}	Similarity between learner s and r
p_{ri}	Recommendation value of learning object i for learner r

3.2   Punishment of Forgetting Effect on Learning Score

German psychologist H. Ebbinghaus found that forgetting begins immediately after the learning behavior. The knowledge maintenance goes down with time on. The process of forgetting is not uniform. Ebbinghaus believes that the maintenance of mastered learning content is a function of time [22]. Table 2 lists Ebbinghaus's experimental results:

With the data of Table 2, Ebbinghaus proposes the forgetting curve as Fig. 2. It can be found that the memory is divided into short-term memory and long-term memory. The first memory zone is 5 min, the second memory zone is 30 min, and the third memory zone is 12 h. The first 3 memory zones belong to the category of short-term memory [23]. The fourth memory zone is 1 day, the fifth memory zone is 2 days, the sixth memory zone is 4 days, the 7th memory zone is 7 days, the 8th memory zone is 15 days, the last 5 memory zones are long-term memory [24].

Even for knowledge of science or engineering, although you will not forget so fast, the proficiency will low down like forgetting. Considering on the necessary of review, the learner still need practice repeatedly to strengthen the skills.

The learning score indicates knowledge maintenance. It is punished with time for forgetting. Even for the learning objects of science, the proficiency needs review with time on.

Table 2. Time points of Ebbinghaus's experimental results.

Days	Knowledge maintenance
0	0.33
0.33	0.582
1	0.442
8	0.358
24	0.337
48	0.278
144	0.254
720	0.211

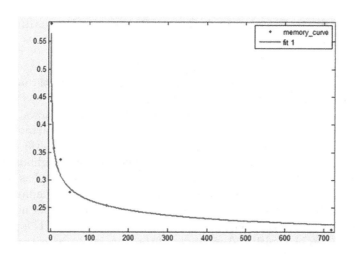

Fig. 2. Ebbinghaus forgetting curve

Matlab tools are used to model the forgetting function. By fitting the data of Table 2, the corresponding mathematical equation is as (2). It represents the score $se(si)$ decay with forgetting on time distance dis.

$$f(se_{si}, dis) = se_{si} * (0.34 * dis^{-0.2} + 0.13) \tag{1}$$

3.3   Prerequisite Correlation Coefficient Measuring

Breese made collaborative filtering recommendations based on correlation coefficients, vector comparisons, and Bayesian statistics. Correlation coefficient was found more accurate [25]. RFP defines the prerequisite correlation coefficient measurement with learning scores.

For two learning objects i and d_1, if scores of i and d_1 is positive correlated, the coefficient should be positive too. We calculate the correlation coefficient $q(i, d_1)$ by the Pearson correlation coefficient by learners' scores on the 2 learning objects.

The correlation between two learning behaviors is also affected by the time distance. If the time distance is long, the knowledge maintenance will decrease for forgetting. We suppose the behavior of learning object i takes place first. The maintenance of learning score on i after forgetting is punished at the time of learning behavior about d_1. $d_{(si, sd_1)}$ is the time distance between the two learning behaviors of learner s on learning objects i and d_1.

In order to keep the correlation values between 0 and 1, logic regression is adopted. The prerequisite correlation coefficient is calculated as (2) shows.

$$q(i, d_1) = \cfrac{1}{1 + e^{\left(\frac{\sum_{s=0}^{n_s}(f(se_{si}, d_{si,sd_1}) - \overline{se_l}) * (\overline{se_{d_1}} - se_{d_1})}{\sqrt{\sum_{s=0}^{n_s}(f(se_{si}, d_{si,sd_1}) - \overline{se_l})^2 \sum_{s=0}^{n_s}(se_{d_1} - \overline{se_{d_1}})^2}}\right)}} \tag{2}$$

3.4   Prerequisite Recommendation (PR) for the Unqualified Learning Object

According to the learning location, the first unqualified learning object d_1 needs prerequisite recommendation to the learner. RFP recommends through learning path of learner neighbors that is qualified in d_1. Their learning objects before d_1 become prerequisite candidates to be recommended as Fig. 3 shows.

The algorithm is shown in Algorithm 1. The algorithm recommends prerequisite learning object set I_{pr} for the target learner r. The first layer of the cycle goes through each similar learner s among qualified learner neighbor set S who are qualified in d_1. Learning objects of them before d_1 are adopted as recommendation candidates i. The second layer of the cycle is for each candidate I of the learner neighbor s. se_{ri} is the learning score of the qualified learner neighbor s on learning object i. sesi contribute to the recommendation value. The prerequisite correlation $q(i, d_1)$ is multiplied as weight of the learning score feature. After the cycle, the recommendation value is normalized.

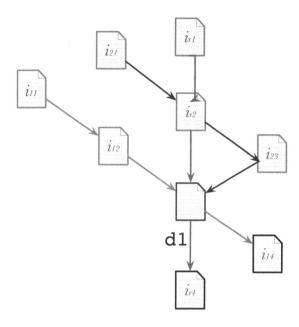

Fig. 3. Prerequisite recommendation candidates for d_1

seri is the learning score of the target learner r on learning object i. Considering on the necessity of review, it is in negative correlation with the recommendation value. For the forgetting after learning, it is punished with forgetting function $f(se_{ri}, dis(time(r, d_1), t_n))$. t_n is the system time of recommendation. $se_{r,d1}$ is the score of the target learner r on unqualified location d_1. $f(se_{ri}, dis(time(r, d_1), t_n))$ shows the inverse correlation of the score. It is in negative correlation with recommendation value for the review necessity. seri and ser, d1 are both considered for recommendation.

3.5 Subsequent Recommendation (SR) for the Qualified Learning Objects

The latest qualified learning object of the learner is defined as d_2. It means learning objects of the target learner before d_2 are all qualified. They are all indicated by symbol b. The subsequent learning objects with b as prerequisite should be recommended. The first learning object learned by qualified learner neighbors after d_2 is adopted as recommendation candidate as Fig. 4 shows. So are the qualified learning objects b.

The recommendation value is calculated according to the learning series of learner neighbors who are qualified in both d and following learning objects.

Qualified learner neighbors' learning scores on learning objects following b is adopted as one of the features for recommendation. The learning scores have similarity and prerequisite correlation coefficient as weights. The qualified learner

Algorithm 1. Prerequisite recommendation

Require: learner vectors $L\{l_1, l_2, \ldots, l_m\}$, the target learner r, unqualified location d_1;

Ensure: prerequisite recommendation result I_{pr};

1: get top similar d_1 qualified learner set $Ss_1, s_2, \ldots, s_{k1}$;
2: **for** EACH $s \in S$ **do**
3:     **for** EACH $i \in s\{i_1, i_2, \ldots, i_{index(d_1)}\}$ **do**
4:         $p_{ri}+ = sim_{sr} \times se_{si} \times q(i, d_1)$;
5:         $dec_{ri}+ = sim_{sr} \times q(i, d_1)$;
6: $p_{ri}/ = dec_{ri}$;
7: $p_{ri}+ = w_1 \times (100 - f(se_{ri}, dis(time(r, d_1), time(r, i)))) + w_2 \times (100 - se_{r,d_1}) + w_3 \times p_{ri}$;
8: select top k_2 p_{ri} for learner r, add i to I_{pr}
9: **return** I_{pr};

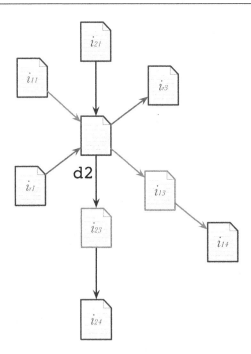

Fig. 4. Subsequent recommendation candidates for d_2

neighbor's learning score on prerequisite objects b and the learning score of the target learner on b are both combined as features for better performance of recommendation. The learning score of the target learner on b is punished by the forgetting function for better modeling of reality.

4   Experiment

The experiment is conducted on data recorded by the mic-video platform of ECNU[1]. It includes 686 learners, 136 mic-videos as learning objects and 7,163 related learning records.

The accuracy of recommendation is compared by precision, recall and f1-score. Experiments verify the improvement of accuracy on PR and SR.

k_1 is the number of selected top similar qualified learner neighbors for recommendation. k_2 is the top recommended items. The parameters of k_1 and k_2 were separately adjusted to test the performance. Weight parameters are assigned as 1 without loss of generality.

Different recommendation methods are compared under various k_1 and k2 combinations. One is collaborative filtering recommendation on interest CFPreference, and the other is a collaborative filtering recommendation on learning scores CFscore.

Figure 5 compares the precision between different k1 and k2 combinations. SR has the best performance in precision. It decreases the range of candidate learning objects. The learner neighbor's learning series is used for candidate selection. Only the first learning object after the qualified location is selected as a candidate for recommendation. The recommended results are more accurate. The precision of PR is better, The recommendation on prerequisite correlation has better performance.

Figure 6 is a comparison of recall under different combinations of k1 and k2. The performance of PR is relatively better. Its recommendation candidates cover all possible prerequisite learning objects of learner neighbors. The candidate of

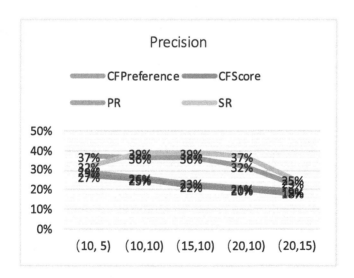

Fig. 5. Precision comparison between different recommendations

[1] http://jclass.pte.sh.cn.

SR cover only one learning object immediately following d. CF methods consider all learning objects of learner neighbors as candidates for recommendation. Compared with CF methods, the candidates of PR and SR is decreased. But the recall is not decreased. It shows the accuracy of PR and SR.

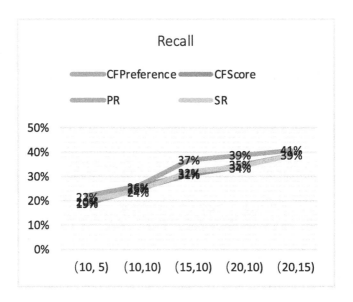

Fig. 6. Recall comparison of different recommendation

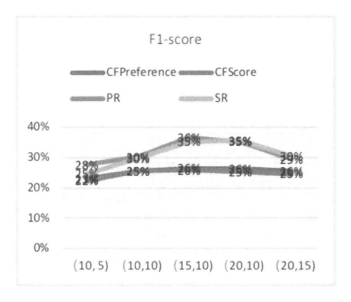

Fig. 7. f1-score comparison between different recommendations

Figure 7 compares f1-scores between different combinations of k1 and k2. Because the different performance on precision and similar performance on recall, and the comparison result on f1-score is similar to that on precision. The results of CFPreference and CFScore are similar, but not as good as PR and SR.

5   Summary

This paper proposes a Forgetting-punished MOOC Recommendation (FMR) on prerequisite. FMR recommends for qualified and unqualified learning objects that are diagnosed by location. Prerequisite learning objects are recommended for the unqualified locations, and subsequent learning objects are recommended for the qualified locations. The feature of learning score is punished for forgetting to model the reality better. It is different from normal MOOC recommendation on learning objects that are not learned before. Experiment verifies the improvement on accuracy by prerequisite recommendation (PR) and subsequent recommendation (SR). The prerequisite may be more than one learning object. The "and" relation between prerequisite learning objects deserves further research.

Acknowledgment. The work is funded by computer science and technology subject of Shanghai Polytechnic University with No. xxkzd1604.

References

1. Breslow, L., Pritchard, D.E., De Boer, J., Stump, G.S., Ho, A.D., Seaton, D.T.: Studying learning in the worldwide classroom: research into edX's first MOOC. Res. Pract. Assess. **8**, 13–25 (2013)
2. Kizilcec, R.F., Piech, C., Schneider, E.: Deconstructing disengagement: analyzing learner subpopulations in massive open online courses. In: Proceedings of the Third International Conference on Learning Analytics and Knowledge, pp. 170–179. ACM (2013)
3. Pappano, L.: The year of the MOOC. New York Times, New York (2012)
4. Polyzou, A., Karypis, G.: Grade prediction with course and student specific models. In: Bailey, J., Khan, L., Washio, T., Dobbie, G., Huang, J.Z., Wang, R. (eds.) PAKDD 2016. LNCS (LNAI), vol. 9651, pp. 89–101. Springer, Cham (2016). https://doi.org/10.1007/978-3-319-31753-3_8
5. Yang, Y., Liu, H., Carbonell, J., Ma, W.: Concept graph learning from educational data. In: Proceedings of the Eighth ACM International Conference on Web Search and Data Mining, pp. 159–168. ACM (2015)
6. Liu, J., Jiang, L., Wu, Z., Zheng, Q., Qian, Y.: Mining learning dependency between knowledge units from text. VLDB J. Int. J. Very Large Data Bases **20**(3), 335–345 (2011)
7. Huang, X., Yang, K., Lawrence, V.B.: An efficient data mining approach to concept map generation for adaptive learning. In: Perner, P. (ed.) ICDM 2015. LNCS (LNAI), vol. 9165, pp. 247–260. Springer, Cham (2015). https://doi.org/10.1007/978-3-319-20910-4_18
8. Scheines, R., Silver, E., Goldin, I.M.: Discovering prerequisite relationships among knowledge components. In: EDM, pp. 355–356 (2014)

9. Vuong, A., Nixon, T., Towle, B.: A method for finding prerequisites within a curriculum. In: EDM, pp. 211–216 (2011)

10. Liang, C., Wu, Z., Huang, W., Giles, C.L.: Measuring prerequisite relations among concepts. In: Proceedings of the 2015 Conference on Empirical Methods in Natural Language Processing, pp. 1668–1674 (2015)

11. Talukdar, P.P., Cohen, W.W.: Crowd sourced comprehension: predicting prerequisite structure in Wikipedia. In: Proceedings of the Seventh Workshop on Building Educational Applications Using NLP, pp. 307–315. Association for Computational Linguistics (2012)

12. Wang, S., et al.: Using prerequisites to extract concept maps from textbooks. In: Proceedings of the 25th ACM International on Conference on Information and Knowledge Management, pp. 317–326. ACM (2016)

13. Agrawal, R., Golshan, B., Terzi, E.: Grouping students in educational settings. In: Proceedings of the 20th ACM SIGKDD International Conference on Knowledge Discovery and Data Mining, pp. 1017–1026. ACM (2014)

14. Lu, Z., Pan, S.J., Li, Y., Jiang, J., Yang, Q.: Collaborative evolution for user profiling in recommender systems. In: IJCAI, pp. 3804–3810 (2016)

15. Sun, Y., Han, J., Yan, X., Yu, P.S., Wu, T.: Pathsim: meta path-based top-k similarity search in heterogeneous information networks. Proc. VLDB Endow. **4**(11), 992–1003 (2011)

16. Chen, Y., Zhao, X., Gan, J., Ren, J., Hu, Y.: Content-based top-N recommendation using heterogeneous relations. In: Cheema, M.A., Zhang, W., Chang, L. (eds.) ADC 2016. LNCS, vol. 9877, pp. 308–320. Springer, Cham (2016). https://doi.org/10.1007/978-3-319-46922-5_24

17. Yu, H., O'Riedl, M.: A sequential recommendation approach for interactive personalized story generation. In: Proceedings of the 11th International Conference on Autonomous Agents and Multiagent Systems, vol. 1, pp. 71–78. International Foundation for Autonomous Agents and Multiagent Systems (2012)

18. Huang, Y.-M., Huang, T.-C., Wang, K.-T., Hwang, W.-Y.: A Markov-based recommendation model for exploring the transfer of learning on the web. J. Educ. Technol. Soc. **12**(2), 144 (2009)

19. Mi, F., Faltings, B.: Adaptive sequential recommendation using context trees. In: IJCAI, pp. 4018–4019 (2016)

20. Lee, Y., Cho, J.: An intelligent course recommendation system. SmartCR **1**(1), 69–84 (2011)

21. Education Growth Advisors: Learning to adapt: understanding the adaptive learning supplier landscape. PLN/Bill and Melinda Gates Foundation (2013)

22. Ebbinghaus, H.: Memory: a contribution to experimental psychology. Ann. Neurosci. **20**(4), 155 (2013)

23. Schacter, D.L.: The seven sins of memory: insights from psychology and cognitive neuroscience. Am. Psychol. **54**(3), 182 (1999)

24. Averell, L., Heathcote, A.: The form of the forgetting curve and the fate of memories. J. Math. Psychol. **55**(1), 25–35 (2011)

25. Breese, J.S., Heckerman, D., Kadie, C.: Empirical analysis of predictive algorithms for collaborative filtering. In: Proceedings of the Fourteenth Conference on Uncertainty in Artificial Intelligence, pp. 43–52. Morgan Kaufmann Publishers Inc. (1998)

26. Clark, D.: Adaptive MOOCs. CogBooks adaptive learning. Copyright CogBooks (2013)

Internet Rurality: Developing an Index for Network Distance from Popular Internet Services

Thomas H. Yang[1(✉)], Franklin Liu[2], Weiguo Yang[3], and Hang Liu[4]

[1] North Carolina School of Science and Mathematics, Durham, NC 27705, USA
yang19t@ncssm.edu
[2] University of Illinois at Urbana-Champaign, Champaign, IL 61820, USA
[3] Department of Engineering and Technology, Western Carolina University,
Cullowhee, NC 28723, USA
[4] Department of Electrical Engineering and Computer Science,
The Catholic University of America, Washington DC, WA 20064, USA

Abstract. Based on the network structure of the Internet, we propose a locally measurable, global network structure-based performance measurement and develop the tools to measure the end user accessibility of a set of popular Internet services from various locations and the impact of user rurality on the network performance. The proposed Internet rurality measurement is defined by a composite index that accounts for both the number of hops and the round trip time (RTT) from the end user to several selected Internet services, including search engines (Google), social media (Facebook, Twitter), online news media (Times, Wall Street Journal, CNN), and e-commerce (Amazon). Over 60 runs were conducted over a period of three months and from six different end user locations across the United States utilizing varying Internet Service Provider (ISP) technologies, including both wireless and wired connections. The results show the viability of the proposed Internet Rurality Index (IRI) and demonstrate that a well-built local access service network plays an important role in the end user's Internet service performance; accordingly, the IRI does not closely correlate to the physical rurality of the end user location; rather, it appears to be connected to the ISP that the end user utilizes. This observation may have profound implications for the e-commerce and social media industries, as well as cloud computing, audio/visual streaming, and any other services that rely on efficiently transmitting large quantities data to the end user with minimal data loss. The efficiency of the Internet structure and precise areas of improvement, as well as further insights into local and global economies as a consequence of e-commerce and Internet infrastructure development, can be determined through the proposed Internet Rurality Index.

Keywords: Internet · Network distance · Internet rurality

© Springer Nature Switzerland AG 2018
X. Chen et al. (Eds.): CSoNet 2018, LNCS 11280, pp. 427–436, 2018.
https://doi.org/10.1007/978-3-030-04648-4_36

1   Background and Motivation

The Internet has profoundly changed the everyday lives of residents of econom-ically developed regions, offering new methods of communication, commerce, entertainment, and scholarship in ways unfathomable to previous generations. There has long been an economic divide between urban and rural regions, but the equality of resource access offered by the Internet may offer a means of bridging this gap. Studying the effect of physical location and local Internet infrastruc-ture in urban and rural regions is an important step in understanding the way that this evolving technology has changed and will change our world, especially the economic network connecting workers around the globe. Initial study of the business cycles that characterize a market economy dates back to the work of Wesley Mitchell and Arthur Burns for the U.S. National Bureau of Economic Research in the late 1930s [10], long before the development of the Internet, and this research laid the foundation for studying economic indicators, statis-tics often used to analyze current economic performance in an area or overall nationally. These indicators can also offer insights to forecast future economic performance. Three types of economic indicators based on time are: leading indicators, which are the first indications of economic changes; lagging indica-tors, which follow economic change; and coincident indicators, which approxi-mately coincide with changes in the economy [13]. For example, leading indi-cators include average weekly hours, vendor performance, money supply, and index of consumer expectations. Examples of lagging indicators include: dura-tion of unemployment, change in the CPI, value of outstanding commercial and industrial loans, and ratio of consumer credit to personal income. Additionally, there is another useful classification based on the correlation of the indicators to economic performance [11]. Procylical indicators indicate positive correlation with economy; countercyclical indicators indicate negative correlation with econ-omy. By analyzing these indicators, economists are capable of interpreting the current state of the economy and may forecast future economic trends. With the Internet becoming an increasingly large part of society and the economy, new tools and indicators become not only possible, but desirable.

Economic indicators serve important roles in monitoring and guiding a range of socioeconomic activities, from individual financial decisions to regional and federal fiscal and monetary policies. With the rapid development of e-commerce and social media networks in addition to the near-ubiquitous presence of the Internet around the world, it is widely accepted that Internet-based services are playing an increasingly vital role in economics and human society, and these innovations foreshadow and indicate new changes in the economy. For instance, a 2017 U.S. federal government report stated that e-commerce sales accounted for 7.2% of all retail sales in 2015, a significant increase from only 0.2% in 1998 [12]. According to the United States Census Bureau, in the first quarter of 2018, U.S. retail e-commerce sales totaled 114.4 billion dollars, accounting for an adjusted 9.3% of total retail sales [2]. A 2016 Pew Research Center study found that 79% of Americans make purchases online, up from 22% in June 2000, and that 15% buy online on a weekly basis [14]. The growth trend of the e-commerce industry in developed nations since its inception is clear, and it remains increasingly popular with younger demographics; 90% of U.S. adults aged 18 to 29 have expressed that they have purchased products online, the highest percentage in any polled demographic. Furthermore, the study found that frequent online shoppers are more likely to prefer online shopping to physical stores. E-commerce remains both a lucrative and relatively new industry, and new tools must be developed to reflect this new environment.

Social media is yet another innovation from the Internet that has grown immensely since its inception to become a near-ubiquitous part of life in developed nations. It is reported that the number of monthly active users worldwide on Facebook from 2008 to 2018 has grown from around 100 million to over 2.23 billion, nearly one third of the global population [1]. The number of monthly active Twitter users in the United States has also reached close to 70 million, which is over 20% of the total US population [3]. These online services have revolutionized everyday life and the business world, with huge implications for socioeconomic behavior at all levels, from the individual to the government to the global economy. The authors are particularly interested in finding out whether such a ubiquitous online presence can break down the traditional divide between urban and rural areas. The Internet may play a role in leveling the uneven playing field between rural and urban areas with its equality of opportunity in accessing online resources. We use the term "Internet rurality" to measure the end user accessibility to representative Internet services ranging from search engines to social media. We aim to develop a measure for Internet rurality based on the network structure of the Internet. We propose to use a composite index, the Internet Rurality Index, to measure the Internet rurality, which accounts for both the number of hops and the round trip time (RTT) from the end user to the Internet services. The following sections detail the formula and present the measurements from different locations across the United States.

2 Methodology and Related Work

Internet protocol, namely the TCP/IP, provides inherent tools for probing its network structure [7]. Ping, for instance, makes use of either an ICMP (Internet Control Message Protocol) echo or UDP (User Datagram Protocol) echo packets to reach a destination and return a round trip time (RTT). When the echo packets reach their destination, the destination interface will accordingly send back a packet to the originator. Based on the time the echo packet was sent and the time that the returned echoed packet was received, the RTT can be estimated. If the echo packet does not reach the destination within its maximum number of hops, as specified by the packet's Time-to-Live (TTL) flag – or the destination interface failed to return the echoed packet within the specified timeout – the destination is said to be unreachable.

Traceroute, on the other hand, utilizes the Ping program with incremental specified TTL. The Internet protocol specifies that when a packet is forwarded to an intermediate interface, its TTL flag will be modified and the TTL decreased by one. If a packet arrives with zero TTL, then the router will drop the packet and, as a courtesy, send an echohed packet back to the originator indicating that its packet has been dropped. From this echoed packet, the RTT can be determined, as can the identity of the intermediate node, which may then provide location and owner information for the node. When using Ping successively with incremental TTL, one can roughly trace the routes a packet took to reach its destination, revealing the structure of this Internet path. A typical traceroute output is shown below in Table 1. It can be seen that the hop numbers and the intermediate interfaces are reported for most cases. An intermediate router, however, does not always send a courtesy notification packet back to the originators when dropping packets with zero TTL. This would result in a "Request timed out" statement for those intermediate interfaces at certain hop number. Similarly, the intermediate router, when dropping packets with zero TTL, may deprioritize sending the courtesy notification packets back to the originators, increasing the determined RTT from the echo. This could result in the intermediate RTTs being unreliable for predicting the overall Internet service response time. The RTTs from the destination interface, however, are a much more reliable measure for that purpose, as it provides services to the end user and, therefore, prioritizes returning accurate data to inquisitive users attempting to access these services.

Ping and Traceroute utilities have been widely used to study the Internet. Previous works using similar TCP/IP utilities are focused on probing the larger network structure of the Internet such as ISP mapping of a significant

Table 1. Typical Traceroute output.

Tracing route to twitter.com [104.244.42.193] over a maximum of 30 hops			
1	5 ms	5 ms	5 ms	192.168.43.1
2	946 ms	*	1629 ms	66.174.175.255
3	775 ms	493 ms	1346 ms	69.83.61.228
4	1348 ms	379 ms	156 ms	69.83.60.34
5	229 ms	125 ms	204 ms	69.83.63.194
6	99 ms	136 ms	146 ms	69.83.32.172
7	154 ms	242 ms	157 ms	69.83.32.172
8	107 ms	99 ms	132 ms	69.83.32.65
9	695 ms	1098 ms	953 ms	204.148.39.13
10	225 ms	211 ms	283 ms	140.222.226.55
11	176 ms	122 ms	134 ms	204.255.168.70
12	160 ms	147 ms	120 ms	165.254.26.242
13	*	*	*	Request timed out
14	154 ms	182 ms	157 ms	104.244.42.193
Trace complete			

portion of the Internet [6,15,18]. End user experience related studies often focused on the overall Internet performance related impact on certain particular applications, such as audio/video streaming and teleconference services [5,16,17]. The impact of geographical location and economy of different regions on the end users' experience, however, can present unique opportunities to gain in-depth insights into regional economical development, as well as e-commerce and online social media activities. Here we wish to develop a viable measurement for the Internet rurality, which, as previously outlined, measures the end user accessibility to representative Internet services ranging from e-commerce to social media. To this end, we devise a measurement that traceroutes to a set of representative Internet services and analyze the results by identifying the Internet connections divided into four segments based on the Internet architecture [9]: (1) local area network (LAN): home/residential or campus network; (2) access ISP network (Access): from home/campus router to the local ISP cable headend/access router at the central office; (3) regional ISP network (Regional): from the local ISP cable headend to the ISP Internet gateway at a point of presence (PoP); (4) core Internet (Core): from the ISP gateway to the data center of the application service providers (ASP). By graphing the networks produced by the Traceroute utility in combination with geolocation based on IP address, these sections can be determined as shown in Fig. 1, offering insight into the origins of any variation in Internet rurality.

The raw data - RTT and number of hops to multiple popular Internet services - was collected via Traceroute commands executed via a client side Java program. This raw data was processed in Python to generate a weighted edge list of the network, weighted according to RTT. These files could be processed by the network software Gephi to visually produce the networks [4], displayed using the Yifan Hu Proportional layout algorithm [8]. By observing the structure shown in the network plots with geolocation by IP address and server identification, the four layers of the Internet connection (LAN, Access, Regional, and Core) can be identified, as shown in the two examples below in Fig. 1.

3   Measurements and Results

Significant variation in the Internet rurality index between rural and urban areas would likely arise in the access network connecting the router to the local ISP or the regional network connecting the local ISP to the point-of-presence (PoP). Upon reaching the core Internet, a rural/urban divide is unlikely to be the cause of any significant variation from location to location, as the distance traveled in the core Internet is chiefly determined by the ASP. Since we are more interested in the Internet Rurality of a given area, the exact nature and the structure of a local access network that comprises of the network within a home or a campus network were not counted when we calculate the Internet Rurality index. Furthermore, for the reasons discussed above, we only use the RTTs of the final step of the Traceroute, which reflects more reliably the response time from the

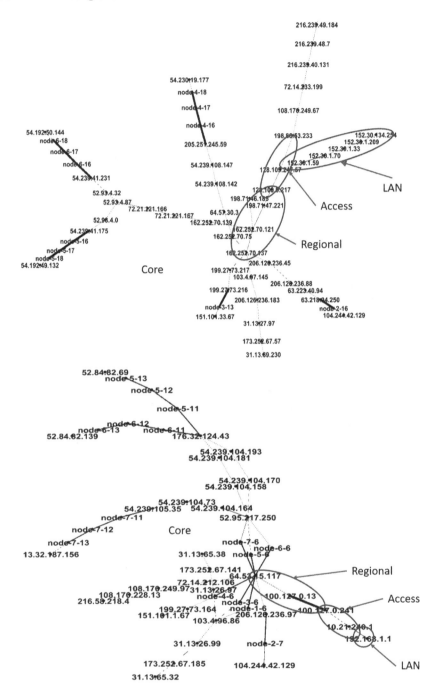

Fig. 1. Examples of Traceroute results illustrating the different sections of the Internet structure. Top: End-user originates from a campus network (WCU), which has five hops before reaching the access network. Bottom: End-user originates from a residential network, which only has one interface (home router) before reaching the ISP's access network.

Internet services requested. Accordingly, we define the Internet Rurality Index using the following formula:

$$\text{IRI} = n \log_{10} \text{ARTT} \tag{1}$$

where n is the average number of hops to reach the requested services excluding the hops within the LAN. The ARTT is the average RTT to reach the requested services. Rather than focusing on data or packet transmission over the Internet, the study seeks to develop a metric for describing how readily available modern Internet services are to the end user, with implications of describing potential structural inequalities in an increasingly interconnected Internet-based society. Table 2 shows the comparison of the average statistics of the Traceroutes to the selected Internet services from five different combinations of end user location and ISP technology. It can be seen that depending on the ISP connection technology that the end user used to access the Internet, the RTT can vary significantly, hence the choice of using a logarithmic scale to define the index measure. For the purpose of this pilot study, we try to capture representative samples focused on the traditional definition of the rural/urban divide. Over sixty tests were conducted from several selected locations around the United States over a period of three months. The results are plotted in Fig. 2. Due to the dynamic load balancing and routing, one can see that the IRI from a fixed location with the fixed ISP technology can still vary, but in a relatively narrow range, indicating that the proposed IRI can serve as a reliable measure for the Internet Rurality. It can be observed that the recorded LTE wireless connections had a greater IRI than other ISP connection technologies, with the greatest IRI being recorded for LTE wireless connections in rural Cullowhee, NC. However, the IRI

Table 2. Comparison of different end user location and ISP connection technology:

Location	Cullowhee NC	Cullowhee NC	WCU	Columbia SC	Washington DC
Connection	LTE Wireless	Wi-Fi	Wired	Wired	Wi-Fi
LAN Hops	1.0	1.0	5.0	1.0	1.0
LAN ARTT (ms)	4.8	2.6	8.8	2.9	21.8
Access Hops	1.0	1.0	1.9	1.0	1.0
Access ARTT (ms)	251.1	13.8	6.4	29.0	17.3
Regional Hops	7.0	3.0	2.0	4.0	4.0
Regional ARTT (ms)	314.0	15.7	11.4	39.9	77.4
Core Hops	6.4	6.4	8.0	8.1	7.6
Core ARTT (ms)	279.2	39.0	19.4	41.4	85.1
Total Hops	15.4	11.4	16.9	14.1	13.6
Final ARTT (ms)	281.6	28.0	19.2	49.4	56.8
IRI	35.3	15.1	15.2	22.3	22.1

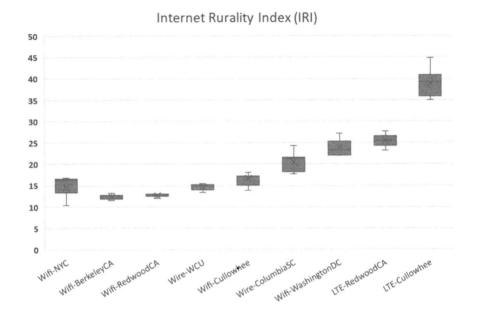

Fig. 2. IRI measurement results from over 60 runs from end user locations across the US.

of Wi-Fi connections in urban areas such as the New York City-Newark area and rural areas such as Cullowhee, NC are comparable. The more rural Cullowhee, NC returned lower Internet Rurality than certain metropolitan areas such as Columbia, SC and Washington, DC. This may indicate that significant variation in Internet Rurality is determined by the ISP connection technology and the associated Internet infrastructure in the area, which may vary greatly even within a single geographic region. For instance, data for the New York City area was collected in multiple locations throughout the metropolitan area, including Manhattan and the Newark International Airport, which may explain the large variation in the collected NYC data and offers evidence that the causes affecting Internet rurality may be more complex than the physical urban/rural divide.

4   Conclusions and Discussions

This study has demonstrated both the feasibility and effectiveness of utilizing the Internet Rurality index in analyzing Internet structure across the United States from the vantage point of the end user. Unlike current measurements of RTT in Internet-based studies, the proposed Internet Rurality index accounts for both the number of hops in the regional and core network and the average RTT to a basket of representative services, accounting for the geographical structure of the Internet and the role of service providers in connecting the end user to

Internet content. Initial forays into data analysis using IRI has indicated the possibility that population, as examined through the rural-urban divide, may not have a significant effect on the speed or efficiency of Internet connections as measured by the IRI. This has potential implications for media demanding fast and efficient data transmission over the Internet, such as audio or video calling via services like Skype or Google Hangouts, or audio and visual streaming companies. By extending and modifying the selected Internet services, subindices may be developed focusing on specific categories of Internet service, such as social media, e-commerce, audio/video streaming, and search engines, to name a few. There may also be potential for using the Internet rurality index as an economic indicator to account for the increasing role of the Internet in consumer activity. For example, the Internet rurality index in a region could serve as a coincident or lagging economic indicator, as investment in improving Internet infrastructure spurred by economic and business development may be observable through a changing IRI. Future implementation will be pursued with the aim of gathering significant amounts of data with service providers and end users anywhere with an Internet connection, with voluntary sharing of geolocation, Internet access technology, and the IRI. The findings of this study are insufficient to draw conclusions on the nature of the IRI as a potential economic indicator, but it lays the groundwork for future developments. New innovations in Internet connection technology and the role of the Internet in society by expanding the Internet into developing nations and research and development into smart technology and the Internet of Things only increases the need for the better understanding of Internet structure offered by the Internet rurality index.

References

1. Number of facebook users worldwide 2008–2018 — statistic. https://www.statista.com/statistics/264810/number-of-monthly-active-facebook-users-worldwide/
2. Quarterly retail e-commerce sales 1st quarter 2018. https://www.census.gov/retail/mrts/www/data/pdf/ec_current.pdf
3. Twitter MAU in the united states 2018 | statistic. https://www.statista.com/statistics/274564/monthly-active-twitter-users-in-the-united-states/
4. Bastian, M., Heymann, S., Jacomy, M.: Gephi: an open source software for exploring and manipulating networks. lcwsm, **8**, 361-362 (2009). http://www.aaai.org/ocs/index.php/ICWSM/09/paper/view/154
5. Bonfiglio, D., Mellia, M., Meo, M., Ritacca, N., Rossi, D.: Tracking down skype traffic. In: IEEE INFOCOM 2008 - The 27th Conference on Computer Communications, pp. 261–265 (2008). https://doi.org/10.1109/INFOCOM.2008.61
6. Burch, H., Cheswick, B.: Mapping the internet. Computer **32**(4), 97–98 (1997). https://doi.org/10.1109/2.755008
7. Comer, D.E.: Internetworking with TCP/IP, vol. 1. Pearson Higher Education, London (2013)
8. Hu, Y.: Efficient and high quality force-directed graph drawing. Math. J. **10**, 37–71 (2005)
9. Kurose, J.F., Ross, K.W.: Computer Networking : A Top-down Approach, vol. 4. Addison Wesley, Boston (2009)

10. Mitchell, W., Burns, A.: Statistical indicators of cyclical revivals. In: Statistical indicators of cyclical revivals. NBER p. 13 (1938). https://www.nber.org/chapters/c4251.pdf
11. Moffatt, M.: A Beginner's Guide to Economic Indicators (2018). https://www.thoughtco.com/beginners-guide-to-economic-indicators-1145901
12. Nicholson, J.R.: New insights on retail e-commerce, p. 14
13. Ray, M.A., Anderson, D.A., Krugman, P.R.: Krugman's economics for AP. Macmillan Higher Education, London (2011)
14. Smith, A., Anderson, M.: 1. online shopping and purchasing preferences (2016). http://www.pewinternet.org/2016/12/19/online-shopping-and-purchasing-preferences/
15. Spring, N., Mahajan, R., Wetherall, D., Anderson, T.: Measuring ISP topologies with rocketfuel. IEEE/ACM Trans. Netw. (TON) 12(1), 2–16 (2004). https://doi.org/10.1109/TNET.2003.822655
16. Tian, Y., Dey, R., Liu, Y., Ross, K.W.: China's internet: Topology mapping and geolocating. In: Proceedings IEEE INFOCOM, pp. 2531–2535 (2012). https://doi.org/10.1109/INFCOM.2012.6195646
17. Xu, Y., Yu, C., Li, J., Liu, Y.: Video telephony for end-consumers: Measurement study of google+, iChat, and skype 22(3), 826–839 (2014). https://doi.org/10.1109/TNET.2013.2260354
18. Yu, C., Xu, Y., Liu, B., Liu, Y.: Can you SEE me now? a measurement study of mobile video calls. In: IEEE INFOCOM 2014 - IEEE Conference on Computer Communications, pp. 1456–1464 (2014). https://doi.org/10.1109/INFOCOM.2014.6848080

Ranking Academic Advisors: Analyzing Scientific Advising Impact Using MathGenealogy Social Network

Alexander Semenov[1], Alexander Veremyev[2], Alexander Nikolaev[3], Eduardo L. Pasiliao[4], and Vladimir Boginski[2(✉)]

[1] University of Jyvaskyla, Faculty of Information Technology, 35, 40014 University of Jyvaskyla, Finland
`alexander.v.semenov@jyu.fi`
[2] University of Central Florida, 12800 Pegasus Dr., Orlando, FL 32816, USA
{`alexander.veremyev,vladimir.boginski`}`@ucf.edu`
[3] University at Buffalo, 312 Bell Hall, Buffalo, NY 14260, USA
`anikolae@buffalo.edu`
[4] Air Force Research Laboratory, Eglin AFB, Niceville, FL 32542, USA
`eduardo.pasiliao@us.af.mil`

Abstract. Advising and mentoring Ph.D. students is an increasingly important aspect of the academic profession. We define and interpret a family of metrics (collectively referred to as "a-indices") that can be applied to "ranking academic advisors" using the academic genealogical records of scientists, with the emphasis on taking into account not only the number of students advised by an individual, but also subsequent academic advising records of those students. We also define and calculate the extensions of the proposed indices that account for student co-advising (referred to as "adjusted a-indices"). Finally, we extend the proposed metrics to ranking universities and countries with respect to their "collective" advising impacts. To illustrate the proposed metrics, we consider the social network of over 200,000 mathematicians (as of July 2018) constructed using the Mathematics Genealogy Project data: the network nodes represent the mathematicians who have completed Ph.D. degrees, and the directed edges connect advisors with their students.

Keywords: Social networks · Big data · Scientific advising impact a-indices · Mathematics genealogy project

1 Introduction

In recent years, universities and other research institutions have put a lot of emphasis on assessing and enhancing the productivity of their faculty. One aspect that has been traditionally deemed important in these efforts is the number and quality of a researcher's publications. The popular metrics of publication productivity include various quantities based on an individual's citation record

© Springer Nature Switzerland AG 2018
X. Chen et al. (Eds.): CSoNet 2018, LNCS 11280, pp. 437–449, 2018.
https://doi.org/10.1007/978-3-030-04648-4_37

(e.g., total number of citations, weighted citations, i10-index, h-index, etc.), typically accounting for the "prestige" measures of publication outlets (e.g., journal impact factors, 5-year impact factors, SNIP, CiteScore, etc.) However, besides publication output, another – possibly equally important – aspect of the academic profession success is concerned with advising and mentoring Ph.D. students. One can argue that a successful academician is not only the one who publishes many highly-cited articles, but also the one who successfully advises students, and further, whose students in turn become successful academic advisors, thus ensuring the continuity and prosperity of an academic discipline. Indeed, in the modern era, many universities emphasize the importance of effective mentorship and post-graduation academic productivity of their Ph.D. students.

This paper makes methodological and applied contributions towards a systematic analysis of large-scale Ph.D. student advising data. We define and interpret a family of new metrics (collectively referred to as "a-indices") that can potentially be used for "ranking academic advisors" using the academic genealogical records of scientists. We rely on the well-known web-based Mathematics Genealogy project resource that has collected a vast amount of data on Ph.D. student advising records in mathematics-related fields.

Due to its popularity and public availability, MathGenealogy dataset has been used as a testbed in several previous studies. The basic characteristics of the MathGenealogy network snapshot from 2011, as well as those of the underlying network of countries, were presented in [1]. In [6], the authors analyzed the performance of students of those individuals who were near the beginning versus near the end of their academic careers and revealed interesting insights. Another study [8] used the data of Ph.D. degrees granted after 1973 and used it to compose a network of universities, where some of the universities were then labeled as strong sources ("authorities") of Ph.D. production, while the others were labeled as strong destinations ("hubs"). The authors of [4] presented a comprehensive analysis of the MathGenealogy network with respect to the classification of mathematical subjects, as well as most influential countries in terms of the Ph.D. graduates output. Further, they revealed the major "families" of mathematicians that originated in certain root nodes ("fathers" of mathematics' genealogical families), in the different times, covered by the project data. A new concept of eigenvector-based centrality was defined and tested on the MathGenealogy network in [10]. In [9], the authors proposed the so-called "genealogical index" for measuring individuals' advising records.

This paper takes a further step towards studying and ranking academic advising impact using MathGenealogy social network. The emphasis of this study is on taking into account not only the number of students advised by an individual but also subsequent academic advising records of those students, while providing the respective metrics that are easy to calculate, understand, and interpret.

The paper is organized as follows. In Sect. 2, we briefly describe the MathGenealogy dataset and provide its basic characteristics along with definitions and notations that will be used in the paper. In Sect. 3, we define and interpret the family of "a-indices" that we propose for ranking academic advisors. We extend these definitions to take into account co-advising in Sect. 4. Section 5 presents the results obtained on the MathGenealogy dataset. Section 6 offers concluding remarks.

2   Data Description, Notations, and Basic Characteristics of MathGenealogy Network

To facilitate further discussion, we first describe the MathGenealogy dataset and provide its basic characteristics, as well as define graph-theoretic concepts that will be used in the paper.

Data Description. The data were collected from the Mathematics Genealogy project website[1] using a web-crawler software. The dataset contains the records about nearly 231,000 mathematicians (as of July 2018). The information for each mathematician in the database includes name, graduation year, university, country, Ph.D. thesis topic and its subject classification, as well as the list of students advised by this individual. This available data allowed us to construct the directed network of advisor-advisee relationships.

Related Graph-Theoretic Concepts. Due to the fact that the considered dataset is a directed network, it is represented by a directed acyclic graph $G = (N, \mathcal{A})$, with a set of n nodes, $N = \{1, ..., n\}$, and a set of m arcs (links) $\mathcal{A}$ where the mathematicians represent the nodes of the graph, and the relation "i is an advisor of j" is represented by an arc from i to j. The in-degree ($deg^{in}(i)$) and out-degree ($deg^{out}(i)$) of node i are the numbers of arcs coming into and going out of node i, respectively. Clearly, the in-degree of node i is the number of this individual's Ph.D. dissertation advisors (equal to one for many nodes in the network, although a substantial fraction of nodes do have higher in-degrees), whereas the out-degree of node i is the number of Ph.D. students that this individual has successfully graduated. Node j is said to be reachable from node i if there exists a directed path from i to j. The number of links in the shortest path from i to j is referred to the distance between these nodes and denoted as $d(i, j)$ ($d(i, j) = +\infty$ if there is no such path). A group of nodes is said to form a weakly connected component if any two nodes in this group are connected via a path and no other nodes are connected to the group nodes, where the directions of arcs in a path are ignored.

The *harmonic centrality* of node i is defined as $C_h(i) = \sum_{j \in N} \frac{1}{d(i,j)}$ [2,7]. The *decay centrality* of node i is $C_d(i) = \sum_{j \in N} \delta^{d(i,j)}$ [5,11], where the parameter $\delta \in (0, 1)$ is user-defined, although it is often set at $\delta = 1/2$, which is the value used in this study (it is assumed that $1/d(i, j) = \delta^{d(i,j)} = 0$ if $d(i, j) = +\infty$).

---

[1] http://www.genealogy.ams.org/.

Basic Characteristics of MathGenealogy Network. The retrieved network had 12,263 weakly connected components, with the giant weakly connected component having 208,526 nodes and 238,212 arcs (thus containing about 90% of all the nodes in the network). All the computational results presented below were obtained for this giant component. Further in the text, we will use the term "network" implying the giant weakly connected component.

The analysis of many basic characteristics of an earlier snapshot of this network was conducted in [1]. Since such analysis is not the main focus of this study, we report only some of these basic characteristics for the most recent snapshot that are relevant to the material presented in this paper. The distribution of out-degrees in this network is presented in Fig. 1. As one can observe, it does resemble a power law, although it is not a "pure" power law, which is consistent with observations for many other real-world networks [3].

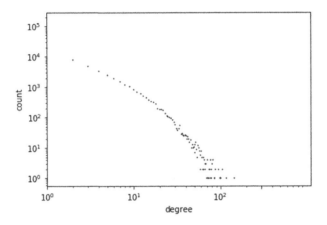

Fig. 1. Out-degree distribution (log-log scale) of the MathGeneaogy network.

The out-degree correlation for all the nodes in the considered network was calculated to be 0.055. This implies that on average there is a very minor correlation between the mentorship productivity of an advisor and a student. Therefore, we believe that in the proposed rankings of academic advisors it makes sense to "reward" those prolific advisors whose students are also successful academic mentors.

As for the in-degree distribution, it is not surprising that the majority of the nodes have in-degree equal to one. However, the network contains over 30,000 nodes with in-degree greater than 1, which means that a substantial fraction (about 15%) of mathematicians in the dataset had more than one Ph.D. advisor. Therefore, it is important to take into account the effects of co-advising, which is why we define "adjusted" versions of the proposed metrics (indices).

3   Advising Impact Metrics

In this section, we define four metrics ("*a*-indices") that we believe are appropriate for quantifying an individual's advising impact, with a focus on taking into account the mentoring success of an individual's students (going beyond just the number of the Ph.D. students that an individual has graduated). One way to address this is to consider the numbers of students and students-of-students, whereas another approach is to take into account all the academic descendants of an individual. These considerations are reflected in the following definitions.

Definition 1. *(a-**index**) The a-index of an individual i is the largest integer number n such that an individual has advised n students (Ph.D. graduates) each of whom has advised at least n of their own students (Ph.D. graduates). Equivalently, this is the largest number n of out-neighbors of node i in the directed network such that each of these neighbors has out-degree of at least n.*

Definition 2. *(a_∞-**index**) The a_∞-index of an individual i is the total number of their academic descendants, computed as the largest number of distinct nodes that are reachable from node i through a directed path.*

Definition 3. *(a_1-**index**) The a_1-index of an individual i is the harmonic centrality of the corresponding node i in the directed network: $a_1(i) = C_h(i) = \sum_{j \in N} \frac{1}{d(i,j)}$.*

Definition 4. *(a_2-**index**) The a_2-index of an individual i is the decay centrality (with $\delta = \frac{1}{2}$) of the corresponding node i in the directed network: $a_2(i) = C_d(i) = \sum_{j \in N} \frac{1}{2^{d(i,j)}}$.*

It can be seen from Definitions 1–4 that the *a*-index is a measure of the most "immediate" advising impact of an individual, which takes into account their advising success simultaneously with the advising success of their students.[2] Note that the *a*-index is similar to the *h*-index well-accepted for citations record evaluation; however, it turns out that it is rather hard to achieve a double-digit value of the *a*-index over one's academic career due to the fact that graduating a Ph.D. student is generally a less frequent event than publishing a paper. As it can be seen in Table 1, the highest *a*-index value in the considered dataset is 12 (achieved by only four mathematicians). Note that a relevant study [9] reported only one mathematician with the value of *a*-index ($g_{(1)}$ measure in their terminology) equal to 12. Overall, the *a*-index may be applicable as a metric of the advising impact for middle- to late-career academic scientists.

Note that the *a*-index can be extended in a straightforward fashion to reflect a more "long-term" advising impact of an individual by considering third, fourth,

---

[2] Of course, the out-degree of a node, that is, the number of advised students, is the simplest measure that assesses the more immediate advising impact; however, it is way too myopic. Indeed, the graduated students placed into an academic environment continue to boost the academic prowess of their alma-mater, compared, e.g., to the students who leave academia for the industry for good.

etc. generations of an individual's students as it was proposed in [9]. However, the main issue with this approach is that close to 100% of the mathematicians in the considered dataset would have zero values of such index, which would not allow one to effectively rank advisors' long-term impacts using this metric.

Therefore, in order to provide more practically usable quantifications of "long-term" advising impacts of individuals, especially for those scientists who are in the late stages of their careers and for those who have lived and worked centuries ago, we propose the a_1, a_2, and a_∞ indices. The a_∞-index essentially assigns equal weights to all the academic descendants of an individual, whereas the a_1 and a_2 indices prioritize (with different weights) the immediate (directly connected) students and students-of-students while still giving an individual some credit for more distant descendants. Possible practical interpretations of these indices are as follows.

The a_∞-index is appropriate for ranking the "root nodes" of the mathematics genealogy network, that is, nodes with zero in-degrees, which essentially correspond to "fathers" of mathematics' "genealogical families", such as those described in [4]. It is not practically significant to calculate this index for nodes with non-zero in-degrees, since their predecessors in the network would obviously have higher values of this index. Thus, the a_∞ index is interesting primarily from the perspective of history of mathematics, although it can certainly be calculated very easily for any contemporary mathematician.

On the other hand, the a_1-index and a_2-index do not necessarily possess the aforementioned property of the a_∞-index: the values of these indices may be higher for contemporary mathematicians than for the "fathers" of genealogical families due to the fact that an individual's immediate students and any other early-generation students attain higher index values than do any distant descendants. These indices are based on the well-known concepts of harmonic and decay centralities, which makes them easy to calculate and interpret, and hence, more attractive from a practical perspective. These indices can be applied to an academic advisor from any era, thus providing a universal tool of assessing the academic advising impact. However, it is still likely that the advisors in the late stages of their careers would have higher values of these indices (especially the a_1-index that gives higher weights to distant descendants) than those in early-to-mid-stages of their careers. This is not surprising, since these indices are designed to assess the long-term advising impact beyond the number of immediate students.

Further, note that there are several natural extensions of these definitions. First, all of these indices can be adjusted by taking into account the effects of co-advising, that is, giving a special treatment to the cases when multiple individuals have advised the same student j (that is, with node j having multiple incoming links). These particular extensions are addressed in more details in the next section. Second, the a-index can also be defined for a specific country or university (similarly to the h-index of a journal in citations metrics), that is, considering the respective country or university as a "super-node", with the outgoing links directed to all the Ph.D. graduates ever produced (or produced during a specific time frame) by this country or university, respectively. The resulting advising impact values for universities and countries, based on Math-Genealogy dataset, are also presented below.

4   Advising Impact Metrics Adjusted for Co-Advising

In this section, we define the extensions of our basic indices (Definitions 1–4) to handle the cases of co-advising, that is, the situations where one Ph.D. student was co-advised by more than one individual. It makes practical sense to introduce these definitions due to the fact that a substantial fraction of individuals in the considered dataset were advised by more than one advisor. The basic assumption that we make in the definitions below is that the credit for advising such a student is split equally between each of the co-advisors (i.e., if there are n listed co-advisors for a student, then each of the co-advisors receives $1/n$ credit for the graduation of the student).

4.1   Adjusted a_∞, a_1, a_2 Indices

The definitions of a_∞, a_1, a_2 indices can be modified to take into account co-advising in a rather straightforward fashion. The respective definitions are given below.

Definition 5. *(adjusted a_∞-index) The adjusted a_∞-index of an individual i is the total number of their academic descendants weighted by the reciprocals of their in-degrees, that is, $a_{\infty,adj}(i) = \sum_{j \in N} \frac{1}{deg^{in}(j)} \mathbb{1}_{\{d(i,j)<+\infty\}}$, where $\mathbb{1}_{\{d(i,j)<+\infty\}}$ is the indicator function corresponding to the condition that node j is reachable from node i through a directed path.*

Definition 6. *(adjusted a_1-index) The adjusted a_1-index of an individual i is defined as $a_{1,adj}(i) = \sum_{j \in N} \frac{1}{d(i,j)deg^{in}(j)}$.*

Definition 7. *(adjusted a_2-index) The adjusted a_2-index of an individual i is defined as $a_{2,adj}(i) = \sum_{j \in N} \frac{1}{2^{d(i,j)}deg^{in}(j)}$.*

As one can clearly see from these definitions, the values of these adjusted indices are always less than or equal to the respective values of their "regular" counterparts, as common sense would suggest.

4.2   Adjusted a-index

The above definition of a-index can also be modified to take into account co-advising, although this extension is not as straightforward as those in the previous subsection. The "adjusted a-index" of node i can be calculated as follows:

1. Calculate the "adjusted" out-degree of node i: $deg^{out}_{adj}(i) = \sum_{j:(i,j) \in \mathcal{A}} \frac{1}{deg^{in}(j)}$. Clearly, this value can be fractional and is reduced to simply the out-degree of node i if none of the students of the corresponding individual i were co-advised.

2. Compute and sort the adjusted out-degrees (defined as indicated above) of all nodes $\{j : (i,j) \in \mathcal{A}\}$ in the non-increasing order. Denote this sorted array as $D_1, D_2, \ldots$ and let D_k be the kth element of this array such that k is the largest integer satisfying $\lceil D_k \rceil \geq k$. Calculate $\min\{D_k, k\}$.
3. Calculate the *adjusted a-index* of node i $a_{adj}(i)$ as the minimum over the values obtained in steps 1 and 2.

The above procedure ensures that the adjusted a-index of any node i is always less than or equal to its "regular" a-index, whereas the possibility of fractional values of the adjusted a-index provides a more diverse set of its possible values. This would potentially allow one to create a more practically meaningful ranking of academic advisors based on their own productivity and productivity of their students, while taking into account co-advising.

5   Results for MathGenealogy Dataset

In this section, we present the results obtained on the MathGenealogy network using the metrics proposed above. Figure 2 shows the distribution of the values of the a-index and the adjusted a-index over the entire network. One can observe that while the "regular" a-index is always integer by definition, the adjusted a-index does often take fractional values, especially for lower values of the index, thus providing a more diverse set of possible values in a ranking. Further, Table 1 provides a ranking of top academic advisors with an a-index of at least 10, many of whom are prominent mathematicians from the 19th and 20th centuries (note that none of the mathematicians who worked before the 19th century made it into this ranking). Their respective adjusted a-index values are also given in the same table for comparison. One can observe that this ranking would change if it was done using the adjusted a-index, thus showing that co-advising is indeed a significant factor to consider in this context.

Table 2 presents the collective advising impact rankings of universities and countries based on their respective values of a-index. It can be observed that universities and countries with prominent reputation in mathematics-related research lead these rankings, which shows that (i) not surprisingly there is correlation between research and advising impacts, and (ii) the a-index is an appropriate metric for collective advising impact of a university or a country. Note that we do not consider adjusted a-index in this case (although it would be possible), since it is rare in the dataset that an individual's co-advisors come from different universities or countries.

Figure 3 shows the distribution of regular and adjusted a_1 and a_2 indices in the network. It appears that both of these distributions are close to power-law, whereas the range of values of the a_1-index is larger than that of the a_2-index, which follows from the respective definitions. Tables 3 and 4 present the rankings of top 25 advisors by regular versus adjusted a_1 and a_2 indices. For each index, mostly the same group of advisors appears in the regular versus adjusted index rankings, although their order slightly changes in both tables. Moreover, one can

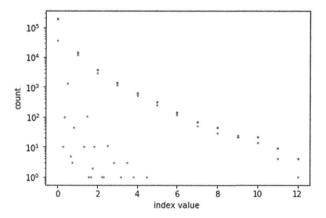

Fig. 2. The counts of individuals against their respective index values (blue for the a-index, orange for the adjusted a-index). (Color figure online)

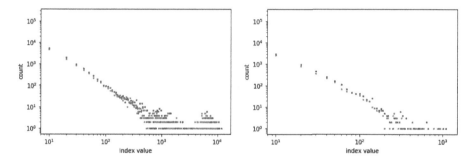

Fig. 3. The counts of individuals against their respective a_1 (left) and a_2 (right) index values (blue for the respective "regular" index, orange for the "adjusted" index), binned by ten consecutive index values per bin, plotted on a log-log scale. (Color figure online)

observe that the a_1-index-based ranking favors earlier generations of mathematicians (those from 16th, 17th, and 18th centuries), whereas the a_2-index-based ranking contains mathematicians from the 19th and the 20th centuries. This is a direct consequence of different weights given by these indices to distant academic descendants of an individual.

The detailed ranking of individuals with in-degree zero in the network (that is, "fathers" of genealogical families) by their a_∞ and adjusted a_∞-index values is not presented due to space limitations. The top-ranked scientist with respect to both of these indices is Sharaf al-Din al-Tusi, who lived in the 12th century and currently has 149,942 academic descendants.

Table 1. Top individuals by a-index, with the a-index of at least 10 and their corresponding adjusted a-index.

a-index	Name	Grad. Year	Country of Ph.D.	Adjusted a-index
12	Heinz Hopf	1925	Germany	11
12	Jacques-Louis Lions	1954	France	11
12	Mark Aleksandrovich Krasnoselskii	1948	Ukraine	12
12	Erhard Schmidt	1905	Germany	10
11	Andrei Nikolayevich Kolmogorov	1925	Russia	10
11	C. Felix (Christian) Klein	1868	Germany	10
11	Heinrich Adolph Behnke	1923	Germany	9
11	Karl Theodor Wilhelm Weierstrass	1841	Germany	9
11	John Torrence Tate, Jr.	1950	United States	11
11	Ernst Eduard Kummer	1831	Germany	10
11	Reinhold Baer	1927	Germany	8
11	Salomon Bochner	1921	Germany	11
11	David Hilbert	1885	Germany	10
10	Lothar Collatz	1935	Germany	9
10	Günter Hotz	1958	Germany	10
10	Pavel Sergeevich Aleksandrov	1927	Russia	10
10	Edmund Hlawka	1938	Austria	9
10	Phillip Augustus Griffiths	1962	United States	9
10	Michael Francis Atiyah	1955	United Kingdom	9
10	Haim Brezis	1972	France	10
10	Thomas Kailath	1961	United States	10
10	R. L. (Robert Lee) Moore	1905	United States	10
10	Alan Victor Oppenheim	1964	United States	10
10	Shiing-Shen Chern	1936	Germany	10
10	Elias M. Stein	1955	United States	10
10	Richard Courant	1910	Germany	9
10	Hellmuth Kneser	1921	Germany	9
10	Emil Artin	1921	Germany	10
10	Lipman Bers	1938	Czech Republic	9
10	Issai Schur	1901	Germany	8
10	Roger Meyer Temam	1967	France	9
10	John Wilder Tukey	1939	United States	9
10	Philip Hall	1926	United Kingdom	10
10	Beno Eckmann	1942	Switzerland	9
10	Oscar Ascher Zariski	1925	Italy	10

Table 2. Top universities and countries by a-index.

University Name	a-index
Harvard University	31
Princeton University	30
University of California, Berkeley	29
Massachusetts Institute of Technology	28
Stanford University	28
The University of Chicago	25
Lomonosov Moscow State University	25
University of Cambridge	24
Columbia University	24
ETH Zürich	24
Georg-August-Universitt Göttingen	22
University of Wisconsin-Madison	22
California Institute of Technology	22
University of Michigan	21
University of Oxford	21
Universiteit van Amsterdam	21
Yale University	20
University of Illinois at Urbana-Champaign	20
Universität Berlin	20
Ludwig-Maximilians-Universität München	20
Carnegie Mellon University	20

Country	a-index
United States	54
Germany	45
United Kingdom	33
Russia	31
Netherlands	29
France	26
Switzerland	25
Austria	22
Canada	21
Belgium	19
India	19
Sweden	18
Ukraine	17
Australia	17
Romania	17
Poland	17
Spain	17
Israel	17
Japan	16
Italy	15
Finland	15

Table 3. Top 25 individuals ranked by the a_1-index (left) and adjusted a_1-index (right).

Name	Year	a_1-index
Simeon Denis Poisson	1800	11800.58
Abraham Gotthelf Kästner	1739	10719.19
Joseph Louis Lagrange		10557.30
Pierre-Simon Laplace		10555.30
Jakob Thomasius	1643	10254.40
Leonhard Euler	1726	9969.036
Emmanuel Stupanus	1613	9907.44
Christian August Hausen	1713	9712.28
Johann Friedrich Pfaff	1786	9601.81
Friedrich Leibniz	1622	9569.92
Giovanni Beccaria		9556.55
Jean Le Rond d'Alembert		9555.55
Carl Friedrich Gauss	1799	9395.80
C. Felix (Christian) Klein	1868	9316.05
Petrus Ryff	1584	9245.31
Johann Bernoulli	1690	9126.35
Johann Andreas Planer	1686	8885.37
J. C. Wichmannshausen	1685	8882.86
Johann Elert Bode		8707.06
Felix Plater	1557	8669.28
Jacob Bernoulli	1676	8400.77
Nikolaus Eglinger	1660	8398.77
Julius Plücker	1823	8210.41
Johann Pasch	1683	8189.74
Rudolf Jakob Camerarius	1684	8189.74

Name	Year	Adj. a_1-index
Simeon Denis Poisson	1800	10486.00
Abraham Gotthelf Kästner	1739	9509.77
Joseph Louis Lagrange		9380.81
Pierre-Simon Laplace		9379.31
Jakob Thomasius	1643	9175.63
Emmanuel Stupanus	1613	8852.32
Leonhard Euler	1726	8836.15
Christian August Hausen	1713	8621.04
Friedrich Leibniz	1622	8565.26
Giovanni Beccaria		8491.40
Jean Le Rond d'Alembert		8491.15
Johann Friedrich Pfaff	1786	8479.49
Carl Friedrich Gauss	1799	8264.47
Petrus Ryff	1584	8262.28
C. Felix (Christian) Klein	1868	8111.17
Johann Bernoulli	1690	8090.71
Johann Andreas Planer	1686	7889.29
J. C. Wichmannshausen	1685	7887.46
Felix Plater	1557	7748.45
Johann Elert Bode		7693.68
Jacob Bernoulli	1676	7447.01
Nikolaus Eglinger	1660	7445.01
Johannes W. von Andernach	1527	7322.90
Guillaume Rondelet		7296.20
Otto Mencke	1665	7274.00

Table 4. Top 25 individuals ranked by the a_2-index (left) and adjusted a_2-index (right).

Name	Year	a_2-index
David Hilbert	1885	1099.72
C. Felix Klein	1868	1016.04
C. L. Ferdinand Lindemann	1873	907.25
Erhard Schmidt	1905	667.56
E. H. Moore	1885	639.77
Ernst Eduard Kummer	1831	636.78
K.T.W. Weierstrass	1841	575.10
Julius Plucker	1823	522.36
Solomon Lefschetz	1911	510.06
R. O. S. Lipschitz	1853	508.52
Oswald Veblen	1903	474.34
Richard Courant	1910	458.12
Heinz Hopf	1925	446.18
George David Birkhoff	1907	415.53
Jacques-Louis Lions	1954	385.92
Nikolai Nikolayevich Luzin	1915	366.49
Simeon Denis Poisson	1800	362.25
A. N. Kolmogorov	1925	361.89
Ferdinand Georg Frobenius	1870	354.50
Gaston Darboux	1866	346.64
Michel Chasles	1814	337.36
G. P. L. Dirichlet	1827	335.53
Ludwig Bieberbach	1910	334.29
Edmund Landau	1899	330.46
H. A. Newton	1850	323.17

Name	Year	Adj. a_2-index
David Hilbert	1885	949.74
C. Felix Klein	1868	873.30
C. L. Ferdinand Lindemann	1873	780.80
E. H. Moore	1885	597.00
Erhard Schmidt	1905	550.32
Ernst Eduard Kummer	1831	535.59
K.T.W. Weierstrass	1841	484.32
Solomon Lefschetz	1911	466.55
Julius Plucker	1823	449.19
R. O. S. Lipschitz	1853	436.90
Oswald Veblen	1903	431.94
Richard Courant	1910	400.25
George David Birkhoff	1907	388.12
Heinz Hopf	1925	349.33
Nikolai Nikolayevich Luzin	1915	335.95
Jacques-Louis Lions	1954	329.44
A. N. Kolmogorov	1925	326.89
Simeon Denis Poisson	1800	320.97
Gaston Darboux	1866	311.96
Michel Chasles	1814	309.62
H. A. Newton	1850	301.44
Ferdinand Georg Frobenius	1870	294.73
C. Emile Picard	1877	287.67
G. P. L. Dirichlet	1827	283.56
Edmund Landau	1899	280.94

6 Conclusion

We proposed a family of network-based advising impact metrics (a-indices) that are easy to calculate and interpret, as well as provide a flexible framework for ranking academic advisors from different eras and stages of their academic careers. Due to the fact that we focus on advising impact beyond the number of immediate students of an individual, the main limitation of this approach is its applicability to measuring advising impacts of early-career scientists (simply calculating an out-degree for "young" advisors would still be a viable option). However, one may argue that a true impact of an academic advisor is evident towards later stages of career when his/her students achieve their own advising success. Therefore, we believe that these indices can be used in practical settings, for instance, by universities in order to quantify and promote individual and collective advising successes of their faculty members. Further analysis and validation of these metrics on this and other datasets may be an interesting future research direction.

Acknowledgements. Work of A. Semenov was funded in part by the AFRL European Office of Aerospace Research and Development (grant no. FA9550-17-1-0030). This material is based upon work supported by the AFRL Mathematical Modeling and Optimization Institute.

References

1. Arslan, E., Gunes, M.H., Yuksel, M.: Analysis of academic ties: a case study of mathematics genealogy. In: GLOBECOM Workshops (GC Wkshps), pp. 125–129. IEEE (2011)
2. Boldi, P., Vigna, S.: Axioms for centrality. Internet Math. **10**(3–4), 222–262 (2014)
3. Broido, A.D., Clauset, A.: Scale-free networks are rare (2018). arXiv preprint arXiv:1801.03400
4. Gargiulo, F., Caen, A., Lambiotte, R., Carletti, T.: The classical origin of modern mathematics. EPJ Data Sci. **5**(1), 26 (2016)
5. Jackson, M.O.: Social and Economic Networks. Princeton University Press, Princeton (2010)
6. Malmgren, R.D., Ottino, J.M., Amaral, L.A.N.: The role of mentorship in protégé performance. Nature **465**(7298), 622 (2010)
7. Marchiori, M., Latora, V.: Harmony in the small-world. Phys. A: Stat. Mech. Appl. **285**(3–4), 539–546 (2000)
8. Myers, S.A., Mucha, P.J., Porter, M.A.: Mathematical genealogy and department prestige. Chaos Interdiscip. J. Nonlinear Sci. **21**(4), 041104 (2011)
9. Rossi, L., Freire, I.L., Mena-Chalco, J.P.: Genealogical index: a metric to analyze advisor-advisee relationships. J. Inf. **11**(2), 564–582 (2017)
10. Taylor, D., Myers, S.A., Clauset, A., Porter, M.A., Mucha, P.J.: Eigenvector-based centrality measures for temporal networks. Multiscale Model. Simul. **15**(1), 537–574 (2017)
11. Tsakas, N.: On decay centrality. BE J. Theor. Econ. (2016)

A Rich Ranking Model Based on the Matthew Effect Optimization

Jinzhong Li[1,2(✉)] and Guanjun Liu[3,4]

[1] Department of Computer Science and Technology, College of Electronic and Information Engineering, Jinggangshan University, Ji'an 343009, China
[2] Network and Data Security Key Laboratory of Sichuan Province, University of Electronic Science and Technology of China, Chengdu 610054, China
[3] Department of Computer Science and Technology, College of Electronic and Information Engineering, Tongji University, Shanghai 201804, China
[4] Key Laboratory of Embedded System and Service Computing, Ministry of Education, Tongji University, Shanghai 201804, China
1210510@tongji.edu.cn

Abstract. Most existing approaches of learning to rank treat the effectiveness of each query equally which results in a relatively lower ratio of queries with high effectiveness (i.e. rich queries) in the produced ranking model. Such ranking models need to be further optimized to increase the number of rich queries. In this paper, queries with different effectiveness are distinguished, and the queries with higher effectiveness are given higher weights. We modify the gradient in the LambdaMART algorithm based on a new perspective of Matthew effect to highlight the optimization of the rich queries and to produce the rich ranking model, and we present a consistency theorem for the modified optimization objective. Based on the effectiveness evaluation criteria for information retrieval, we introduce the Gini coefficient, mean-variance and quantity statistics to measure the performances of the ranking models. Experimental results show that the ranking models produced by the gradient-modified LambdaMART algorithm based on Matthew effect exhibit a stronger Matthew effect compared to the original LambdaMART algorithm.

Keywords: Learning to rank · Ranking model · Matthew effect
LambdaMART algorithm · Gradient

Supported by the National Natural Science Foundation of China under Grant Nos. 61762052 and 61572360, the Natural Science Foundation of JiangXi Province of China under Grant No. 20171BAB202010, the Opening Foundation of Network and Data Security Key Laboratory of Sichuan Province under Grant No. NDSMS201602, the Science and Technology Project of the Education Department of Jiangxi Province of China under Grant No. GJJ160746, and the Doctoral Scientific Research Startup Foundation of Jinggangshan University under Grant No. JZB1804.

© Springer Nature Switzerland AG 2018
X. Chen et al. (Eds.): CSoNet 2018, LNCS 11280, pp. 450–459, 2018.
https://doi.org/10.1007/978-3-030-04648-4_38

1 Introduction

Ranking is an important component that directly affects the performances of information retrieval systems such as search engines and recommendation systems. For instance, the underlying assumption of the PageRank algorithm [1] is that more important websites are likely to receive more links from other websites, it assigns a Web page with higher score if the sum of its corresponding backlinks is high. The PageRank algorithm exhibits the Matthew effect [2] to some extent, which refers to the phenomenon that the rich get richer and the poor get poorer. It is valuable since the PageRank algorithm evaluates the importance of web pages by the link analysis, and ranks web pages by the scores of the importance of web pages. Therefore, the Matthew effect is regarded as a desirable behavior of the ranking model.

Moreover, keywords ranking algorithm of Baidu, goods ranking rules of Taobao, and collaborative filtering algorithms for recommender systems are all showed the Matthew Effect to their respective degrees. Those ranked results of queries or recommendations at higher positions are likely to be the desired target pages of more number of people than those at lower positions, and the ranking of results exhibits the Matthew effect. Furthermore, it is necessary to consider the differences of different queries and to treat those queries distinctly when solving the ranking problem for information retrieval, due to the Matthew effects of the ranking. Therefore, it is a natural idea to distinguish the effectiveness scores of different queries in the training process of the ranking models.

Learning to rank for information retrieval refers to the machine learning techniques in order to train the ranking models in the ranking task. The existing approaches of learning to rank, such as LambdaMART [3,4], CCRank [5], ES-Rank, IESR-Rank and IESVM-Rank [6], Factorized Ranking SVM and Regularized Ranking SVM [7], all equally treat the effectiveness of each query in the optimization process of the ranking models, and these approaches do not distinguish the differences among the effectiveness of different queries. Here, we note that the effectiveness can be measured by any commonly-used information retrieval metrics (e.g. $NDCG$ [8] and ERR [9]). Due to the fact that the effectiveness of different queries may be different for the same ranking model, treating each query equally in the optimization process of the ranking models results in a relatively fewer number of rich queries. To this end, the ranking model needs to be further optimized to further increase the number of rich queries.

In this paper, we modify the gradient in LambdaMART algorithm based on Matthew effect from a new perspective. We describe how the gradient is modified, and present a consistency theorem. Based on the effectiveness evaluation criteria for information retrieval, we introduce the Gini coefficient, mean-variance and quantity statistics to measure the performances of the ranking models. Moreover, we conduct experiments to compare the performances of the ranking models between these models trained by the gradient-modified LambdaMART algorithm based on the Matthew effect (named as Matthew-λ-MART) and those models trained by the original one. The experimental results indicate that the Matthew-λ-MART exhibits a stronger Matthew effect.

2   Construction of the Rich Ranking Models via Matthew Effect

2.1   The Gradient of LambdaMART Algorithm

LambdaMART [3,4] is a state-of-the-art learning to rank algorithm, which has been proven to be very successful in solving real world ranking problems. An ensemble of LambdaMART rankers won the "2010 Yahoo! Learning to Rank Challenge".

The main feature of the LambdaMART [3,4] algorithm is the definition of the gradient function λ of the loss function without directly defining the loss function. λ quantifies the force of a 'to-be-sorted' document and points out the upward or downward adjustment direction in the next iteration. The two documents in each document pair are associated with a query have different relevance, and the gradients of the two documents are equivalent but their moving directions are opposite to each other. The gradient of the positive direction pushes the document toward the top of the ranked list, while the gradient of the negative direction pushes the document toward the bottom of the ranked list.

The LambdaMART [3,4] algorithm optimizes the gradient λ_i of each document d_i for each query q to train the ranking models. If the relevance judgement r_i between d_i and q is higher, and the ranked position of d_i is closer to the bottom of the ranked list for a given query q, then the positive value of λ_i indicates a push toward the top of the ranked list. Meanwhile, if the value of λ_i is bigger, then it shows that the force is stronger. If the relevance r_i between d_i and q is smaller, and the ranked position of d_i is closer to the top of the ranked list, then the negative value of λ_i indicates a push toward the bottom of the ranked list. Meanwhile, if the value of λ_i is smaller, then it shows that the force is stronger.

The LambdaMART [3,4] algorithm integrates the evaluation criteria ($NDCG$) of the information retrieval into the computation of the gradient. The gradient λ_i for each document d_i is obtained by summation of all λ_{ij} over all pairs of $<d_i, d_j>$ that d_i participates in for query q. Therefore, λ_i can be written as $\lambda_i = \sum_{j:\{i,j\}\in I} \lambda_{ij} - \sum_{j:\{j,i\}\in I} \lambda_{ij}$, where $\lambda_{ij} = -\frac{\beta}{1+e^{\beta \times (s_i - s_j)}} \times |\Delta M_{ij}|$, which denotes the gradient of the document pair $<d_i, d_j>$. In the formula $\lambda_{ij} = -\frac{\beta}{1+e^{\beta \times (s_i - s_j)}} \times |\Delta M_{ij}|$, β is a shape parameter for the sigmoid function, s_i and s_j represent the score assigned to d_i and d_j by the ranking model respectively, and ΔM_{ij} represents the change on effectiveness measure M by swapping the two documents d_i and d_j at rank positions i and j accordingly (while keeping the rank positions of all other documents unchanged). Therefore, ΔM_{ij} can be calculated by $\Delta M_{ij} = M_q - M_q^*$, where M_q denotes the effectiveness of query q for a ranked list of all documents w.r.t. q, M_q^* denotes the effectiveness of query q after swapping the documents d_i and d_j at the rank positions i and j for the ranked list, and M denotes the effectiveness evaluation criterion.

2.2   Modification of the Gradient of the LambdaMART Algorithm

The LambdaMART algorithm equally treats the effectiveness of each query in the training process of the ranking models. In order to discriminate the effectiveness score of each query, we assign different weights to different queries with unequal effectiveness scores for optimizing the gradients in the training process of the ranking models. In order to highlight the gradients of rich queries and enhance the effectiveness of rich queries, the weights of rich queries should be given the higher values based on the idea of the Matthew effect. We assign the effectiveness score of each query as the weight of the corresponding query. Therefore, the original effectiveness M is replaced by the new objective M^2 to modify the gradient of the original LambdaMART algorithm, thereby expanding the LambdaMART algorithm to optimize the rich ranking model. Therefore, ΔM_{ij} is replaced by ΔM_{ij}^* when λ_{ij} is computed, where $\Delta M_{ij} = M_q - M_q^*$ and $\Delta M_{ij}^* = (M_q)^2 - (M_q^*)^2$, which denotes the difference of the squared effectiveness scores of query q after swapping the two documents d_i and d_j at rank positions i and j (while keeping the rank positions of all other documents unchanged). In other words, $M_q - M_q^*$ is replaced by $(M_q)^2 - (M_q^*)^2$. The document pair $<d_i, d_j>$ for the same query is optimized according to the new gradient $\lambda_{ij}^{new} = -\frac{\beta}{1+e^{\beta \times (s_i - s_j)}} \times |\Delta M_{ij}^*|$, which strengthens the differences of upward or downward ranking force among the document pairs for different queries in the next iteration, and thus enhances the optimization of rich queries.

The gradient function of the LambdaMART algorithm is modified, and therefore, it is necessary to demonstrate that the Matthew-λ-MART algorithm can be used to train the ranking model for the learning to rank task. Now, we present that the new optimization objective M^2 satisfies the consistency property proposed in [4]: when swapping the ranked positions of two documents, d_i and d_j, in a ranked list of documents where d_i is more relevant than d_j but d_i is ranked after d_j, the optimization objective should be increased. In other words, for any document-pairs, the pairwise swap between correctly ranked documents d_i and d_j for the same query q must lead to a decrease of M^2, and the pairwise swap between the incorrectly ranked documents d_i and d_j for the same query q must lead to an increase of M^2.

Theorem 1. The   new   optimization   objective M^2 satisfies   the consistency property.

3   Evaluation Measures of Matthew Effect

A ranking model is richer than another model if (1) the former both has more rich queries and has more poor queries than the latter, or (2) the distribution of the effectiveness of queries of the former is more discrete than the latter. A richer ranking model is of a stronger Matthew effect. In order to measure the performances of the ranking model yielded by our modified approach, we introduce the following utility metrics to characterize the Matthew effect of ranking models from different perspectives. Based on the effectiveness evaluation criteria for information retrieval, we introduce Gini coefficient, mean-variance and quantity statistics to measure the performances.

3.1 Gini Coefficient

The Gini coefficient [10] is a measure of the statistical dispersion, which is intended to represent the income distribution of the residents in a nation, and is the commonly used as a measure of inequality of income or wealth. The Gini coefficient is calculated using the formula $G = \frac{\sum_{i=1}^{n} \sum_{j=1}^{n} |x_i - x_j|}{2n^2 \mu}$, where x_i denotes the income of individual i, $|x_i - x_j|$ denotes the absolute value of the difference between x_i and x_j, μ denotes the mean value of all individuals' incomes, and n denotes the total number of individuals. The smaller the inequality of income, the smaller the value of the Gini coefficient; and vice versa.

The Matthew effect is reflected by using Gini coefficients for the measurement in many economic areas, so Gini Coefficient can capture the Matthew Effect, which can be used to measure the performance of the ranking model. If we make an analogy with the distribution of the national income in the field of finance, the query in the learning to rank task resembles the individual in the distribution of the national income, and the effectiveness of the query resembles the income of the individual. Therefore, the Gini coefficient of learning to rank can be defined as follows:

$$Gini = \frac{\sum_{i=1}^{|Q|} \sum_{j=1}^{|Q|} |M_{q_i} - M_{q_j}|}{2|Q| \sum_{k=1}^{|Q|} M_{q_k}} \tag{1}$$

where, $q_i \in Q$ denotes the i-th query and $|Q|$ represents the total number of queries in query set Q.

$Gini$ is used to measure the degree of difference in effectiveness among all the queries in a ranking model, and to reflect the Matthew effect by comparing the $Gini$ of one ranking model with another. A higher Gini value represents a greater difference in effectiveness (i.e. effectiveness inequality) among all the queries in a ranking model. If the value of $Gini$ obtained by a ranking model is larger, then it indicates that the corresponding ranking model has a stronger Matthew effect.

3.2 Mean-Variance

In probability theory and mathematical statistics, mean is used to measure the average value of all random variables; Variance is used to measure the degree of deviation between a set of random variables and their mean, and it is an important and commonly used metric for calculating the discrete trend.

In order to observe the effectiveness of a ranking model, the mean μ of a ranking model is defined as follows:

$$\mu = \frac{1}{|Q|} \sum_{q \in Q} M_q \tag{2}$$

For a ranking model, the mean μ measures the average effectiveness (such as $NDCG$ and ERR) of all queries in a set of queries, i.e., it refers to the average effectiveness of the ranking model. The greater the mean μ, the better the average effectiveness of the ranking model; and vice versa.

In a ranking model, some queries are of high effectiveness but some are of low effectiveness. Therefore, in order to observe the degrees of their deviation, we divide the variance of a ranking model into the upside semi-variance V_{up} and the downside semi-variance V_{down}, which are defined as follows:

$$V_{up} = \frac{1}{|Q^+|} \sum_{q \in Q^+} (M_q - \mu)^2 \tag{3}$$

$$V_{down} = \frac{1}{|Q^-|} \sum_{q \in Q^-} (M_q - \mu)^2 \tag{4}$$

where, Q^+ and Q^- denote the set of queries with above-mean effectiveness and below-mean effectiveness in the query set Q respectively, and $|Q^+|$ and $|Q^-|$ denote the number of the set of queries Q^+ and Q^- respectively. The greater the variance, the greater the degree of deviation; and vice versa.

For a ranking model, the V_{up} and the V_{down} measures the discrete degree of effectiveness of the queries that are over and under the μ in the query set respectively. The Matthew effect of a ranking model is exhibited by comparing the V_{up} and the V_{down} of the ranking model to those of other ranking models respectively. If the values of both V_{up} and V_{down} of a ranking model are higher, then it indicates that the ranking model has a stronger Matthew effect; and vice versa.

3.3 Quantity Statistics

The range of values of the most commonly used effectiveness measures is between 0 and 1 in information retrieval, such as $NDCG$ and ERR. To compute the effectiveness distribution of all queries in a query set, the range of values of the effectiveness is divided into 5 intervals as $[0.0, 0.2]$, $(0.2, 0.4]$, $(0.4, 0.6]$, $(0.6, 0.8]$ and $(0.8, 1.0]$, respectively. We compute the number of queries distributed in these different intervals according to the effectiveness values of the queries in a given query set for different ranking models, and the purpose is to evaluate the strengths of their exhibited Matthew effect. We use an array $count$ to express the quantity statistics of different intervals for the effectiveness of queries, and the $count$ is defined as follows:

$$count[i] = \begin{cases} \sum_{M_q \in [0.0, 0.2], q \in Q} 1 & i = 0 \\ \sum_{M_q \in (0.2, 0.4], q \in Q} 1 & i = 1 \\ \sum_{M_q \in (0.4, 0.6], q \in Q} 1 & i = 2 \\ \sum_{M_q \in (0.6, 0.8], q \in Q} 1 & i = 3 \\ \sum_{M_q \in (0.8, 1.0], q \in Q} 1 & i = 4 \end{cases} \tag{5}$$

If the values of $count[0]$ and $count[4]$ obtained by a ranking model are larger, then the ranking model has a stronger Matthew effect.

4   Experiments

In order to verify the performances of the Matthew-λ-MART, we implement the algorithm based on the open-source RankLib library of learning to rank algorithms developed by Van Dang et al.[1] Based on the effectiveness measures $NDCG$ and ERR, we conduct experiments on Microsoft Learning to Rank dataset MSLR-WEB30K[2], which is the larger scale dataset of learning to rank and makes it possible to derive reliable conclusions. We report the total results of all five folds for the test dataset. The utility metrics used in our experiments are μ, V_{up}, V_{down}, $Gini$ and $count$ respectively, and their results are shown in Figs. 1, 2, 3, 4, 5 and 6.

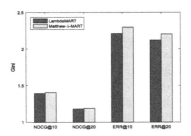

Fig. 1. $Gini$ of each algorithm on MSLR-WEB30K dataset

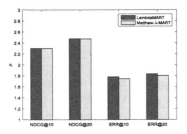

Fig. 2. μ of each algorithm on MSLR-WEB30K dataset

---

[1] http://sourceforge.net/p/lemur/code/HEAD/tree/RankLib/trunk/.

[2] http://research.microsoft.com/en-us/projects/mslr/download.aspx.

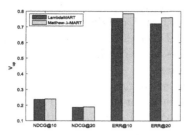

Fig. 3. V_{up} of each algorithm on MSLR-WEB30K dataset

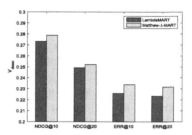

Fig. 4. V_{down} of each algorithm on MSLR-WEB30K dataset

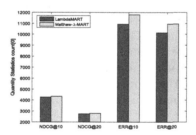

Fig. 5. $count[0]$ of each algorithm on MSLR-WEB30K dataset

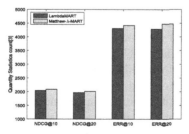

Fig. 6. $count[4]$ of each algorithm on MSLR-WEB30K dataset

From the perspectives of the Gini coefficient in Fig. 1, Matthew-λ-MART obtains the bigger *Gini* than LambdaMART on all effectiveness measures (including $NDCG@10$, $NDCG@20$, $ERR@10$ and $ERR@20$). These results show that the effectiveness across different individual queries in Matthew-λ-MART has a greater difference. Therefore, the ranking models trained by Matthew-λ-MART exhibit a stronger Matthew effect about *Gini*.

From the perspectives of mean-variance in Figs. 2, 3 and 4, although the μ obtained by the Matthew-λ-MART are smaller, the corresponding V_{up} and V_{down} are both bigger than the LambdaMART on all the above effectiveness measures. These results show that the effectiveness across different individual queries in Matthew-λ-MART has also a greater difference. Therefore, the ranking models trained by Matthew-λ-MART also exhibit a stronger Matthew effect about V_{up} and V_{down}.

From the perspectives of quantity statistics in Figs. 5 and 6, the $count[4]$ obtained by the Matthew-λ-MART w.r.t. rich queries and the corresponding $count[0]$ w.r.t. poor queries are both bigger than LambdaMART on all above effectiveness measures. These results of Matthew-λ-MART produce a relative polarization. Therefore, the ranking models trained by Matthew-λ-MART further exhibit a stronger Matthew effect about $count[0]$ and $count[4]$.

The primary reason for the above observations is that the gradient is modified by the Matthew effect in the original LambdaMART algorithm. Matthew-λ-MART highlights the corresponding differences of upward or downward ranking force between documents w.r.t. rich queries with high effectiveness and documents w.r.t. poor queries with low effectiveness in the next iteration. Therefore, the optimization of rich queries is strengthened and the optimization of poor queries is weakened accordingly. Therefore, more attentions are paid to optimize the ranked positions of the documents in the rich queries while less attentions for the poor queries. It leads to an increase in the corresponding numbers of both the rich queries and the poor queries respectively. Finally it increases the diversion or degree of difference in the effectiveness across all the queries in the ranking models.

5   Conclusion

To highlight the high effectiveness of the important queries and to abandon the average effectiveness across all the queries, the queries with different effectiveness are treated distinctly in our proposed approach, and they are assigned with different weights. Based on the new perspectives of Matthew effect, we modify the gradient in the LambdaMART algorithm by assigning higher weights for the gradients of the queries with higher effectiveness so as to highlight the optimization of these rich queries, and thereby produce the rich ranking model. We introduce the Gini coefficient, mean-variance, and quantity statistics to quantize the Matthew effect of the ranking models. In comparison with the original LambdaMART algorithm, the ranking models trained by the gradient-modified LambdaMART algorithm based on the Matthew effect exhibits a stronger Matthew effect.

It is obvious that different information has different popularity in different time periods, which causes the popularity of queries to change over time. Some of the queries (hot queries) gain a huge popularity with numerous searchers, while some of the queries (cold queries) are just opposite. Most existing approaches of learning to rank treat all the queries with equal weights and the popularity factor of the queries is neglected. Therefore, the hot queries and the cold queries are not treated differently. If the hot queries are not treated with higher priorities, then the huge number of users searching such hot queries may not be satisfied, which will degrade the overall user experiences. In order to increase the quality of user experiences, more weights should be assigned to the hot queries during the training process of the ranking models. As a future work, we plan to integrate the hot queries and the cold queries into the Matthew-effect-based gradient-modified LambdaMART algorithm to construct the ranking models. To make the rank of search results of hot query more effective, we will give more weights to the hot queries and less weights to the cold queries in the training process of the ranking models, so as to enhance the overall user experiences.

References

1. Page, L., Brin, S., Motwani, R., Winograd, T.: The pagerank citation ranking: bringing order to the web. Technical report, Stanford Digital Library Technologies Project (1999)
2. Merton, R.K., et al.: The matthew effect in science. Science **159**(3810), 56–63 (1968)
3. Wu, Q., Burges, C.J., Svore, K.M., Gao, J.: Adapting boosting for information retrieval measures. Inf. Retr. **13**(3), 254–270 (2010)
4. Burges, C.J.: From ranknet to lambdarank to lambdaMART: an overview. Microsoft Research Technical report MSR-TR-2010-82 (2010)
5. Wang, S., Wu, Y., Gao, B.J., Wang, K., Lauw, H.W., Ma, J.: A cooperative coevolution framework for parallel learning to rank. IEEE Trans. Knowl. Data Eng. **27**(12), 3152–3165 (2015)
6. Ibrahim, O.A.S., Landasilva, D.: An evolutionary strategy with machine learning for learning to rank in information retrieval. Soft Comput. **22**(10), 3171–3185 (2018)
7. Xu, J., Zeng, W., Lan, Y., Guo, J., Cheng, X.: Modeling the parameter interactions in ranking SVM with low-rank approximation. IEEE Trans. Knowl. Data Eng. (2018, in Press)
8. Järvelin, K., Kekäläinen, J.: Cumulated gain-based evaluation of IR techniques. ACM Trans. Inf. Syst. (TOIS) **20**(4), 422–446 (2002)
9. Chapelle, O., Metlzer, D., Zhang, Y., Grinspan, P.: Expected reciprocal rank for graded relevance. In: Proceedings of the 18th ACM Conference on Information and Knowledge Management, pp. 621–630. ACM (2009)
10. Dixon, P.M., Weiner, J., Mitchell-Olds, T., Woodley, R.: Bootstrapping the gini coefficient of inequality. Ecology **68**, 1548–1551 (1987)

A Load-Balanced and Low-Delay Data Collection for Wireless Sensor Networks

Xiaoyan Kui[1], Junbin Liang[2(✉)], Huakun Du[3(✉)], Shaojun Zou[2],
and Zhixiong Liu[4]

[1] School of Information Science and Engineering, Central South University,
Changsha 410083, China
xykui@csu.edu.cn
[2] Guangxi Key Laboratory of Multimedia Communications and Network Technology,
School of computer and electronics information, Guangxi University,
Nanning 530004, People's Republic of China
liangjb@gxu.edu.cn, 1115267041@qq.com
[3] School of Geosciences and Info-Physics, Central South University,
Changsha 410083, China
hkdu@csu.edu.cn
[4] School of Computer Engineering and Applied Mathematics, Changsha University,
Changsha 410022, China
lzxterry@163.com

Abstract. Energy consumption of nodes and delay in data collection are both important issues in large-scale wireless sensor networks. It is a challenging problem to achieve the goal of balancing energy consumption of nodes and shortening data collection delay at the same time. The paper utilizes a mobile data collector to collect data in the network and proposes a delay-constrained data collection algorithm named LAWA. LAWA constructs a shortest path tree (named load-balanced fat tree) according to the energy of nodes and the number of hops among nodes. Theoretical analyses and massive simulations show that, LAWA cannot only balance the energy consumption of nodes to prolong the network lifetime, but also shorten the path length of the mobile data collector and reduce the delay in data collection when compared with other existing algorithms.

Keywords: Wireless sensor networks · Data collection
Height-limited tree · Network lifetime

1 Introduction

With the rapid development of wireless communication technology, sensor technology, embedded technology and networking technology, wireless sensor networks (WSNs) have made great progress. Many applications associated with the sensor network have emerged in our life. As in public management applications, managers can use the information of the wireless sensor networks to monitor

© Springer Nature Switzerland AG 2018
X. Chen et al. (Eds.): CSoNet 2018, LNCS 11280, pp. 460–476, 2018.
https://doi.org/10.1007/978-3-030-04648-4_39

the surrounding environment. Based on the information obtained, the public management region can get the information whether there are security risks in environmental monitoring areas. In the applications of environmental monitoring and protection deployment, the sensor nodes monitored in the environment can organize themselves into networks and then send the collected data to the static Sink. By analyzing and processing the data collected by static Sink, people can take appropriate measure to protect environment.

One of the most important functions of the wireless sensor networks is to collect data. Based on whether the node can aggregate the received multiple data into one data, data collection can be divided into two types: data collection with aggregation and data collection without aggregation. A node can aggregate multiple received data and its own perception data under the type of data collection with aggregation, and then send the fixed-length data to its neighbors. Common aggregated data are temperature, humidity, air pressure and other numerical data; the data can be aggregated by the method of numerical calculation (such as the mean, variance, etc.). Under the type of data collection without aggregation, a node cannot aggregate multiple received data and perception data by itself, it can only transmit the original data, and under this type, the data sent by the nodes is equal to the sum of data perception and received by the node itself. Common non-aggregated data are video, audio, images and other non-numeric data, which is difficult to be aggregated. In this paper, we focus on the data collection protocol without aggregation.

2 Related Work

Many researchers have introduced the mobile node in the network to collect data [1–6] in recent years. The mobile node acts as a data collector role (Mobile Data Collector, named MDC) [7]. The paper used a mobile data collector to periodically collect data in a static multi-hop wireless sensor networks. However, the moving speed of mobile data collector is very low, without a good data collection protocol or mechanism; mobile data collector needs to walk a long time to collect all data perceived by nodes in the network, which leads to large data collection delay, and it is difficult to be applied in delay-sensitive environment, such as forest fire monitoring and gas monitoring applications in mines. In order to collect the perception data of all nodes within the shortest possible period, researchers need to consider both the energy consumption of nodes and the data collection delay to design effective data collection protocols.

The main researches in early stage are static WSNs (ie: nodes and sink are static after deployment). In the static WSN, neighboring nodes of sink need to forward large amounts of data to other nodes, often leading to excessive energy consumption of these nodes. As a result, the energy consumption of each node is unbalanced, which shortens the network lifetime [8]. In order to solve the unbalanced energy consumption problem, Shah et al. used mobile data collector to collect data in a sparse sensor networks [9], they noted that any moving object with a device of communication function can be used as a mobile data collector, such as people or animals or vehicles that carry a communication device.

Under the conditions of defined path length to achieve maximum lifetime, Hamidreza Salarian et al. proposed a data collection protocol named WRP [10] which based on weight. WRP used the iterative method to select collecting nodes until it cannot find the collecting nodes to satisfy the condition. Although WRP protocol could balance the energy consumption of nodes to a certain extent, but WRP [10] protocol did not consider energy level of nodes when calculating the weights, so it could easily cause the early death of some nodes due to excessive energy consumption and thereby reduce the network lifetime.

In order to balance the energy consumption of each node, some protocols used mobile data collectors to collect sensing data of nodes in the network. Mobile data collectors only saved sensing data of nodes temporarily, and the collected data will be finally uploaded to the static sink or base station. LBCDG [11], TPDG [12], SPT_DGA [13] are the typical data collection protocols with mobile data collectors.

The contribution of the paper can be listed as following:

(1) The proposed protocol LAWA in the paper uses a mobile data collector to collect data. LAWA is an energy-saving and time-saving data collection protocol in WSNs.
(2) LAWA selects the node with the highest energy in the two-hop range of static sink as the root of load-balanced fat tree to construct load-balanced fat tree. Taking into account the energy level of nodes and the location of sink, LAWA can avoid selecting the nodes with low energy as the root node, and also avoid the root node deviating too far from the sink, which can extend the network lifetime. Meanwhile, in the data collection process, LAWA can dynamically select the nodes with the high energy as the root of load-balanced fat tree based on current network conditions, so that each node can switch its role in different situations to balance the energy consumption of nodes.
(3) LAWA can reduce the number of stay nodes; shorten the length of the travel paths of the collector so as to shorten the data collection delay.
(4) By optimizing the height of height-limited trees, LAWA can make the nodes with higher energy to undertake more offspring nodes, which can balance the energy consumption of nodes and maximize the network lifetime.

3   System Model and Problem Statement

3.1   Network Model

Assume that there are n sensor nodes in the network that are labeled as $v_1, v_2, \cdots, v_n$, respectively. Denote the sink by v_0. All nodes are randomly deployed in an $A = M \times M$ field. The entire sensor network consisting of one or more undirected graph $G(V, E)$, where V is the set of nodes in G and E is the set of edges in G. Denoting the transmission range of sensor nodes and mobile collector as r, we assume that $r \ll M$. Nodes are assumed to be stationary after deployment. If v_i and v_j are within the communication radius of each other, then $(v_i, v_j) \in E$, the number of edge is denoted as $|E| = e$. Data size of sensing nodes is fixed and cannot be aggregated with the received data. There is only one mobile collector in the network and some congestion control strategies used to avoid congestion and data retransmission during transmission. Different nodes may have different initial energy and the energy cannot be supplied; the sink and the mobile collector are assumed to have infinite power supply and enough storage space. Furthermore, we assume that all nodes can be divided into three types: collector nodes, stay nodes and ordinary nodes. In particular, sink node belongs to stay node. Finally, we assume that nodes are not aware of their geographic locations.

3.2   Definitions

Definition 1. Construct many trees whose height does not exceed h, called the tree height-limited tree, where h is a positive integer.

Definition 2. Let root of height-limited tree be the collecting nodes.

Definition 3. In the process of data collection, if mobile collector moves to the location of node a for data collection, node a will be denoted as the stay node.

Definition 4. A round is defined as the process of gathering all the data from nodes to the static sink, mobile data collector traversing all the location of stay nodes to collect data from all nodes.

Definition 5. The energy dissipated of node v_i to deliver a packet of k bits from the source to the destination is defined as $C(v_i) = kE_r D(v_i) + kE_t(D(v_i) + 1)$, where E_r and E_t respect the energy dissipated in receiving and sending a packet of 1 bit. $D(v_i)$ represents the number of offspring nodes of v_i on the tree.

Definition 6. (surviving rounds of nodes). If the residual energy of node is greater than 0 after m rounds of data collection and the residual energy of node is smaller than 0 after $m + 1$ rounds of data collection, then the survival rounds of node v_i is denoted as m. Assume the energy of node v_i is $E(v_i)$, then the survival rounds of v_i in the tree can be computed by $S_{(node(v_i))} = [E(v_i)/C(v_i)]$, where the energy consumption of node v_i in a round to collect data is $C(v_i)$.

Definition 7. The network lifetime of height-limited tree T is usually defined as the survival rounds of the first node depletes its energy in height-limited tree T in the network. The network lifetime can be defined as: $L_{tree}(T) = \min_{m \in V_T} \{S_{node(v_m)}\}$, where the number of nodes in set in height-limited tree T is $V_T = k_1, k_2, \cdots, k_t$.

Definition 8. The network lifetime is defined as the minimum survival rounds of all nodes in the network.

Definition 9. Communication region is the area which uses the location of nodes to be the center and the radius of the covered area of the circle is r.

Definition 10. The number of node's hops is defined as the maximum number of hops that start from the node and then reach all offspring nodes in tree T.

Definition 11. The hop constrained in the network is defined as the maximum tree height of height-limited tree in the network.

Definition 12. The optimal height-limited tree of any height-limited tree in the network is determined by $T_{opt} = \{T | L_{tree}(T) = \max_{T' \in T_s(V_T))} L_{tree}(T)\}$. The optimal height-limited tree T_{opt} in Ts has the maximum lifetime, where r_t is the root of height-limited tree T, T' is the height-limited tree composed by V_T, and the root node is r_t, T_s is the set of all height-limited tree T.

Definition 13. The data is not correlated means that the data cannot be aggregated in WSNs. The amount of node's sending data is the sum of data sensed and received by node itself.

3.3   Problem Statement

For a connected network, if we construct a fat tree with all nodes in the fat tree, the sink can collect all the sensing data of nodes in a relatively short time. However, on one hand, in a complicated real environment (such as a severe forest), where the nodes cannot be deployed, it is difficult to ensure the connectivity of network, resulting in some nodes cannot sent the sensed data to the sink. On the other hand, though the network is connected, nodes around the sink need to forward a large amount of data, so that the energy consumption of these nodes is excessive and nodes are easily to die, thus shortening the network lifetime.

This paper takes full consideration of network connectivity and the energy consumption issue of nodes, as in literature [14,15], using a mobile data collector with large storage space and plenty of energy to complete the data collection. However, the data collector brings new challenges. Based on previous studies, the rate of nodes to send packets in WSNs is about several hundred meters per second [16,17], however the moving speed of a typical mobile system is approximately 0.1 to 2 meters per second [18]. Therefore, the sending rate of nodes is much faster than the moving rate of collector. If the mobile data collector can communicate directly with each node in the network, even though it can save much energy of nodes, however, mobile data collector requires to visit large number of nodes, resulting in the rapid growth of data collection delay, which is difficult to apply to delay-sensitive environment.

In order to improve the applicability and flexibility of data collection protocols, the paper takes into account different practical application scenarios, such as some delay-insensitive applications like monitoring in outdoor environment and some delay-sensitive applications like fire monitoring in forest. By setting hop constraint, the paper can meet different requirements for different practical application scenarios in data collection. For delay-insensitive applications, we can set a smaller hop constraint to make the amount of data received by the node cannot be too large, which will help to extend the network lifetime.

For delay-sensitive applications, set a larger hop constraint to make the mobile data collector visit less location and shorten the delay in data collection. The key problem of this paper is how to select suitable and reasonable stay nodes from the set of nodes in hop constraint environment. Good selection can make these stay nodes stay as closely as possible to shorten delay in data collection, and the energy consumption of nodes can be effectively balanced. To solve this problem, the paper proposes LAWA protocol.

3.4   Description of System Model

The paper proposed LAWA protocol to minimize length of path in data collection, which can be classified as an integer linear programming problem. In order to describe integer linear programming problem clearly, some notations and symbols are defined in Table 1 as below.

Table 1. Notations and symbols

symbols	meanings
v_0	Sink
$V = \{v_0, v_1, \cdots, v_{n-1}, v_n\}$	The set of nodes in the network
h	hop constraint
d_{ij}	The distance between v_i and v_j
$p_{ij} = \{0,1\}$	If the distance between v_i and v_j is covered in data collection path, then $p_{ij} = 1$, otherwise $p_{ij} = 0$
$t_{ij} = \{0,1\}$	If node v_i is on the height-limited tree rooted as v_j, then $t_{ij} = 1$, otherwise, $t_{ij} = 0$
$c_i = \{0,1\}$	If node v_i is the collecting node, then $c_i = 1$, otherwise, $c_i = 0$
$s_i = \{0,1\}$	If node v_i is the stay node, then $s_i = 1$, otherwise, $s_i = 0$
$t_{ij}^l = \{0,1\}$	If node v_i is on the first layer of height-limited tress v_j, then, $t_{ij}^l = 1$, otherwise, $t_i^l = 0$. When $i = j$, if there are nodes on the first layer of the height-limited tress rooted as v_i, then $r_{iik}^l = 1$, otherwise, $r_{iik}^l = 0$. Particularly, if node v_i is the collecting node, then, $r_{iik}^l = 1$
r_{ijk}^l	When $i \neq j$, if node v_i and v_j is on the l-1 layer and the first layer of height-limited tress rooted as v_k, respectively, and v_i is the father of node v_j, then, $r_{iik}^l = 1$. Otherwise $r_{iik}^l = 0$
$ns(i)$	The set of neighboring node of v_i

Objective function:

$$Minimize \sum_{i,j \in V \cup \{v_0\}} d_{ij} p_{ij} \tag{1}$$

Constraint:

$$\sum_{j \in V i \neq j} t_{ij} + c_i + s_i \qquad \forall i \in V \qquad (2)$$

$$c_i \times \sum_{j \in ns(i)} s_i \geqslant c_i \qquad \forall i \in V \qquad (3)$$

$$\sum_{j \in V i \neq j} t_{ij}^l \leqslant h \qquad \forall i \in V \qquad (4)$$

$$\sum_{j \in V i \neq j} r_{ijk}^l = r_{iik}^l \qquad \forall j, k \in V, j \neq k \qquad (5)$$

$$\sum_{i \in V \cup \{v_0\}} p_{ij} \times s_i = s_j \qquad \forall j \in V \cup \{v_0\} \qquad (6)$$

Formula (1) defines the objective function of how to find shortest path in data collection; formula (2) to (6) are the constraints of objective function.

Equality (2) bounds nodes or nodes on the height-limited tree (including the collecting nodes) or stay nodes. In particular, sink belongs to stay nodes.

Equality (3) bounds that there is at least one stay node in the communication range of each collecting node, which can ensure collecting nodes and stay nodes can send the sensed and received data to mobile data collector when mobile collector moves to the location of stay nodes.

Equality (4) bounds the height of arbitrary height-limited tree is not larger than h.

Equation (5) bounds that there are only one communication link for data transmission between any node on the h layer and the h-1 layer of height-limited tree [13].

Equation (6) bounds that the mobile data collector will only arrive stay node one time in the process of data collection of each round.

4   Design of LAWA

4.1   Basic Idea of LAWA

On one hand, LAWA uses fat-tree to shorten the delay for data collection and construct the height-limited tree. On the other hand, in the model of data collection without aggregation, the energy consumption of nodes on trees is proportional to the number of offspring nodes. In order to effective balance the energy consumption of nodes, nodes with high energy must be given more offspring nodes. LAWA first construct the load-balanced fat tree. In addition, if the number of access nodes is fewer and the nodes are more centralized, the mobile data collector will have a short path length to collect the data in a round, and then can shorten the delay in data collection.

In order to balance the energy consumption of each node and shorten the delay in data collection, LAWA protocol has four phases to complete the data collection. The first phase is the configuration of a set, which covers the load-balanced fat tree; the second phase is to construct height-limited tree; the third phase is to optimize the height-limited tree; the fourth phase is to calculate the path of data collection. These four phases are closely related to each other and the realization of each stage is based on the previous stage. Next LAWA will be described in detail.

4.2   Description of LAWA

First Phase of Constructing Load-Balanced Fat Tree. In order to construct a minimum height tree that can balance the energy consumption of nodes, the paper fully considers the energy level of nodes and the distribution of nodes in the WSNs to construct the load-balanced fat tree. Since the undirected graph G constituted by all nodes and edges in the network may contain one or more connected components, so the number of load-balanced fat trees may exceed one. The set of load-balanced fat trees can be denoted as FTs. In order to construct the set FTs, sink need to get the information about location and energy for each node. However, if the network formed by nodes is not connected, then the nodes not located in the same connected network as sink cannot send its information about position and energy to sink by other nodes. As a result, the sink cannot construct the set FTs of load-balanced fat tree. In order to solve the problem, LAWA uses one or more mobile data collectors to collect the information of position and energy of entire nodes [12]after the nodes are deployed in the network. Each node uses location technology (GPS) or positioning algorithm to obtain its own location, and then, the mobile data collector will send the information about location and energy of collected nodes to sink. Sink will construct the set FTs of load-balanced fat tree according to information about location and energy of each node. The process of how to construct a load-balanced fat tree is described in Fig. 1.

Second Phase of Constructing Height-Limited Tree. Height-limited tree will be constructed on the basis of the first phase of constructing set of load-balanced fat tree. The purpose to construct height-limited tree is to make the hop constraint not exceed a given positive integer h, so that the delay in data collection can be an acceptable range.

In practical application, the user can set the height h of limited tree according to the application. LAWA uses the same method to construct the height-limited tree in the same network topology. The greater of h, the less the number of nodes the mobile collector needs to visit, and more probability to obtain shorter path length in data collection. Thus, mobile data collector can have a high probability to finish the data collection within smaller delay. Conversely, the smaller of h, mobile collector often needs more time to complete the data collection. The problem of construct height-limited tree can be further divided into two sub-problems: (1) how to select the collecting nodes, and ensure the height of height-limited tree that uses collector as the root not exceed h. (2) how to select the

```
Function Construct Load-Balanced Fat Tree(node, n, rootNode, TDe, RDe)
              // construct the set of load-balanced fat tree
1. queue=rootNode;// root node is stored in the queue
2. m = 1;
3. while (m¡=length(queue))// all nodes in the same connected component are
                           added to the tree
4.a=queue(m);
5.if( isempty(node(a).neighbor))
6.fori=1:length(node(a).neighbor)
7.b=node(a).neighbor(i);
8.if(node(b).tree==0)//node is not added to the tree
9.nodeb selects the neighboring node c with the maximum number of survived
                  rounds in the tree as the father node
10.node(b).tree=1;
11.node(b).parent=c;
12.queue=[queue b];
13.end
14.end
15.end
16.m = m + 1;
17.end
```

Fig. 1. The algorithm for constructing load-balanced fat trees

access location for the mobile data collector to ensure that all the data sent by collecting nodes can be collected successfully, such that the mobile data collector only needs to access less to shorten the delay in data collection. The algorithm for construct height-limited fat tree is described in Fig. 2.

Third Phase of Optimizing Height-Limited Tree. After the operation in second-phase of constructing height-limited tree, the relevant information of each node changes, the information includes offspring nodes of the node, the number of node's hops and the hierarchical information of nodes in the tree. In this case, nodes with high energy may have small number of offspring nodes; in contrast, nodes with low energy may have a larger number of offspring nodes. However, in data collection without aggregation, the energy consumption of nodes is directly proportional to the number of their offspring nodes. In order to maximize network lifetime, we need to optimize the height-limited tree. The optimization issue of height-limited tree is further sub-divided into the following two questions: (1) which nodes need to be optimized? (2) How to optimize the nodes? The optimization algorithm is described in detail in Fig. 3.

Fourth Phase of Computing Path in Data Collection. The stay nodes have been selected in the second phase, and the height-limited tree has been

```
Function Construct Limited Tree(node, n, r, rootNode, hopCount, queue, TDe, RDe)
                    // construct height-limited tree
1. m = 1;
2. stack = queue;
3. while(m <= length(stack))//stack storage all the nodes in the tree,from small
            to large to storage nodes according to the hierarchy in the tree
4.a = stack(end);// leaf node in the farthest location
5.if(node(a).tree == 0)// node is not on the height-limited tree
6.if(a == rootNode)//node a is the root node
7.add root node a into the set of collecting nodes and the set of stay nodes;
9.break;
9.end
10.for i = 1:hopCount
11.w = a;// record current node
12.b = node(a).parent;// acquire node as father node b
13.a = b;
14.if(b == rootNode)// if node b is the root node, then jump out of the current cycle
15.break;
16.end
17.end
18.if(b == rootNode)
19.add root node b into the set of collecting nodes and the set of stay nodes;
20.break;
21.else
22.add root node b into the set of collecting nodes;
23.select node c on the load-balanced fat tree as the stay node that is in the
 communication range of node b, and it is nearest to the sink, its hop count
                of offspring nodes is not larger than h;
24.if(c = rootNode)// if stay node c is not the root node
25.remove node c from the load-balanced fat tree ;
26.end
27.add node c into the set of stay nodes;
28.select suitable collecting nodes in the communication range of stay nodes;
29.end
30.end
31.if(select root node as the collecting node)
32.break;
33.end
34.stack = stack(1 : end - 1);
35.end
```

Fig. 2. The algorithm for constructing height-limited trees

optimized in the third phase to extend network lifetime, then, LAWA will plan
the travel path for mobile data collector according to selected stay nodes for
data collection. However, while there are many algorithms of TSP, the path
length obtained by different algorithms are quite different, which affects delay
in data collection. In order to make the travel path of mobile data collector
achieve the optimal path, this paper uses the Christofides algorithm [19] to

```
Function Optimize Limited Tree(node, p, TDe, RDe, h)
1.update information about the tree and return the number of surviving node set
                    denoted as survivorSetSort
2.while( isempty(survivorSetSort))
3.select the node a with the minimum number of survival round;
4.transferFlag = 0;// transfer flag: 0 means cannot be transferred, 1 means can
                    be transferred;
5.if( isempty(node(a).descendant))
6.for i = 1:length(node(a).descendant)
7.b=node(a).descendant(i);
8.if(node c is within the communication range of node b, and after node b and its
   offspring nodes is transferred into node c, the height of tree cover node c is not
                    larger than h, then, the network lifetime will be extended)
9.add node c into the candidate set denoted as candidateNode;
10.end
11.end
12.if( isempty(candidateNode))
13.select node d as the target node in candidateNode, the new height-limited tree
                    will acquire the maximum
network lifetime after node b is successfully transferred.
14.node(d).children=union(node(d).children,b);// transfer to target node
15.node(b).parent=d;
16.node(a).children=setdiff(node(a).children,b);//remove node
17.update information of tree and return the set denoted as survivorSetSort;
18.transferFlag=1;
19.end
20.end
21.if(transferFlag==0)// if the child nodes of node a cannot be transferred,
       the optimization operation for height-limited tree will be terminated
22.break;
23.end
24.end
```

Fig. 3. The algorithm for optimizing height-limited trees

calculate the path of TSP algorithm, which is the best algorithm for TSP, and
the approximate rate is 3/2. Christofides algorithm executes as follows: firstly,
construct a load-balanced fat tree T' on the basis of a complete graph $G(V, E)$,
where V' is the set composed by all stay nodes and sink nodes, and E' is the set
of nodes Euclidean distance in V'; then, find the exact match with the smallest
value in V^0, where V^0 is the set of nodes that is covered in T' and their degree is
an odd number; then, based on the calculation in previous two steps, LAWA will
compute the Euler circuit using sink as a starting point and end point; finally, the
node repeated in Euler circuit will be removed to form Hamilton cycle. Hamilton
cycle can solve data collection path denoted as tour. Mobile data collector starts
from sink, walking along the data collection path of tour, and eventually returns
to sink to finish data collection of all nodes in the whole network.

4.3   Implementation of LAWA Algorithm

In the initial phase of network deployment, in order to select the collection nodes and stay nodes to construct an optimal height-limited tree, sink needs to gather all the distribution information of nodes. Distribution information includes the location, energy, and neighboring nodes of nodes. On the one hand, in the initial stage after network is deployed, nodes are deployed randomly and sink cannot acquire the distribution information about each node. On the other hand, node also cannot know the path to the sink; thus, the node cannot transmit its own distribution information accurately to the sink. A typical approach is to construct a hierarchy tree rooted as sink, and then uses a delivery mechanism to collect reliable distribution information, such as confirmation from one hop to another hop. However, this method is only applicable to the scenes that all nodes are in the same connected network topology. When the network is not connected, the node that is not in the same connected network as sink cannot send the distribution information to sink via wireless communication, thus cannot construct the optimal height-limited tree. In order to solve this problem, after the nodes are deployed, firstly, the mobile data collector will collect the distribution information of nodes in the whole network [12], and then, mobile data collector will send the distribute information to sink. Sink execute LAWA algorithm to obtain collection nodes, stay nodes, construct the optimal height-limited tree, and acquire the path information for data collection. Finally, mobile data collector will send the relevant information to all nodes in the network, and all nodes in the network will form a three-layer topology for data collection: the highest level is sink; the intermediate layer is collection nodes and stay nodes; the bottom is the common nodes. At this time, the initial phase of network deployment is finished and goes into the data collection phase.

5   Performance Evaluation

LAWA algorithm proposed in this paper focuses on issues of how to select the data transmission route in network and how to establish the route. In addition, we assume that the MAC layer has a reliable packet transport mechanism, and the problem of packet loss and congestion control issues at the network layer can be better solved. Since MATLAB can quickly build visible prototype systems, and it can analyze performance of the algorithm effectively, MATLAB meets the requirements of simulation experiments. Therefore, we chose MATLAB platform to evaluate performance of LAWA.

Hop constraints, communication radius and average density of network are the main factors that affect the performance of algorithm (ie, network lifetime and length of data collection path). In order to evaluate and analyze the performance of LAWA algorithm proposed in this paper, we compare LAWA with SPT_DGA [13] algorithm and use the same assumption of SPT_DGA. Node's sensing energy and calculating energy can be neglected [20]. In addition, nodes receive and broadcast a data request message only one time in process of each round of data collection. The size of data request message is very small and the number of data request message is also small, so the energy consumption of data request message can also be negligible. Therefore, energy consumption in transmission and receiving of data packets is the major communication consumption in WSNs. In order to make a fair comparison of LAWA and SPT_DGA, nodes use a fixed transmit power, and node's energy consumption in transmitting data is approximately two times of node's energy consumption in receiving data [21]. Some experimental parameters used in the paper are shown in Table 2.

Table 2. Experimental parameters

Parameter name	values
Area of target monitoring area	$400 \times 400 \ m^2$
Initial energy of node	$[0.5, 2] J$
Packet size	256 bit
Energy dissipated to deliver a packet of 1 bits	100 nJ/bit
Energy dissipated in receiving a packet of 1 bits	50 nJ/bit

The energy consumption of node is mostly used in sending and receiving data, thus in the entire process of data collection, algorithms only consider the energy consumption in sending and receiving data. For each parameter setting, we randomly generate 20 networks and report the average values.

5.1 Influences of Hop Constraints on Network Lifetime and the Length of Data Collection Path

This section will test how different values of hop constraints h influence the performance of LAWA and SPT_DGA in a randomly determined network. Assume that the network has 200 nodes randomly deployed in the target monitoring area, communications radius of node is 25 m, and other experimental parameters are shown in Table 2. We will test the performance of network lifetime and length of data collection path when the values of hop constraints are 1, 2, 3, 4, 5, 6, 7 and 8. Experimental results are shown in Fig. 4(a) and (b).

In Fig. 4(a), network lifetime of LAWA algorithm and SPT_DGA algorithm reduce constantly and LAWA algorithm achieves longer network lifetime than SPT_DGA algorithm when the number of hop constraints h becomes larger. There are three main reasons: (1) as the number of hops constraints h increases, the number of nodes on the height-limited tree increases both in LAWA and SPT_DGA. It will cause an increase in the energy consumption of the nodes, and thus shorten the network lifetime. (2) LAWA algorithm selects the collecting nodes within the communication range of stay nodes, and the hop count from its offspring nodes to collecting nodes is typically less than h, so there are a small number of nodes on the height-limited tree, which can preserve the energy of nodes effectively. (3) LAWA optimizes the height-limited tree effectively, and

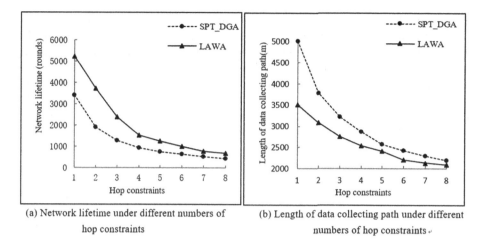

(a) Network lifetime under different numbers of hop constraints

(b) Length of data collecting path under different numbers of hop constraints

Fig. 4. The scene with different numbers of hop constraints

balances energy consumption of each node, therefore, LAWA achieves longer network lifetime than SPT_DGA.

In Fig. 4(b), as the number of hop constraints h increasing, length of data collecting path of LAWA and SPT_DGA are constantly decreasing, and length of data collecting path of LAWA is shorter than SPT_DGA. LAWA and data collection algorithms can achieve shorter path length. There are two main reasons: (1) as the number of hop constraints h increases, the number of stay nodes selected by LAWA and SPT_DGA are reducing, which can shorten the length of data collection path. (2) LAWA selects a part of nodes as the collecting nodes in the communication range of stay nodes, which can remove more nodes from the load-balanced fat tree. Thus, the number of stay nodes selected by LAWA is smaller than SPT_DGA, and LAWA can obtain a shorter path length for data collection.

5.2 Influences of Communication Radius on Network Lifetime and Path Length of Data Collection

The section will consider the area of target monitoring area, hop constraints, and the number of fixed nodes is fixed, network lifetime and path length of data collection will be tested under different communication radius of nodes. Assume hop constraints h is 4, and there are 400 nodes in the network; other experimental parameters are shown in Table 2. We will test network lifetime and path length of data collection under different communication radius of nodes, the communication radius is 15, 20, 25, 30, 35, 40, 45 and 50 m, respectively. Experimental results are shown in Fig. 5(a) and (b).

In Fig. 5(a), LAWA algorithm achieves longer network lifetime than SPT_DGA algorithm when communication radius of nodes is becoming larger from 15 m to 50m. For SPT_DGA, its network lifetime is becoming smaller when the communication radius of nodes is becoming larger. As the communication radius of node increases, the probability of the number of neighboring nodes in the communication radius of nodes is increasing, thus the number of nodes on height-limited tree will increase, which will shorten the network lifetime. However, with the increase of node's communication radius, the network lifetime obtained by LAWA will have a greater volatility. There are two main reasons: (1) nodes can be transferred between different height-limited tree when implementing optimization operation. When the communication radius of nodes increases, there will be more neighboring nodes within the communication ranges of nodes. Thus, the offspring nodes of bottleneck node can be transferred to nodes with higher energy, which can help to extend the network lifetime. Consequently, LAWA can usually achieve longer network lifetime under larger communication radius of node. (2) Network lifetime of LAWA is related not only to the communications radius of nodes, but also to the current network topology. Since the nodes in the network are deployed randomly, the network topology cannot be predicted, which easily leads to the fluctuations of network lifetime in the network.

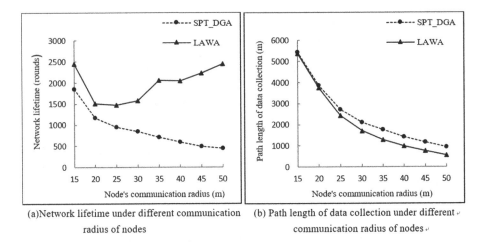

(a)Network lifetime under different communication radius of nodes

(b) Path length of data collection under different communication radius of nodes

Fig. 5. The scene with different communication radius of nodes

In Fig. 5(b), path lengths of data collection for LAWA and SPT_DGA are constantly decreasing, and length of data collecting path of LAWA is shorter than SPT_DGA. There are two main reasons: (1) with the increasing of node's communication radius, the height of shortest path tree constructed by SPT_DGA and the height of load-balanced fat tree configured by LAWA are usually decreasing, which helps to reduce the number of stay nodes in the network, so that each algorithm can obtain a shorter path length of data collection with a high probability. (2) The stay nodes selected by LAWA can be closer to sink with the increasing of node's communication radius, in addition, more collecting nodes can be selected in the communication range of stay nodes, and more nodes can be removed from the load-balanced fat tree. Thus, the number of stay nodes selected by LAWA will continue to decrease, so that LAWA can achieve a shorter path length than SPT_DGA in data collecting.

6   Conclusion

The paper presents an effective energy-saving method named LAWA to collect data in WSNs. Simulation results show that LAWA algorithm can achieve a greater advantage in network lifetime and path length in data collection compared with SPT_DGA algorithm, no matter how hops constraints, communication radius of nodes, and the number of nodes change in the network. In the next step, we will study how to use a distributed algorithm to construct height-limited tree and choose the stay nodes in order to better apply to the real environment.

Acknowledgement. This work is supported by the National Natural Science Foundation of China (Grant nos. 61502540, 61562005, 61502057), the Natural Science Foundation of Guangxi Province (Grant no. 2015GXNSFAA139286), The Cultivation Plan For One Thousand Young and Middle-Aged Backbone Teachers in Guangxi Higher Education School (Guangxi Education People (2017) No. 49), the National Science Foundation of Hunan Province (Grant no. 2015JJ4077), and the China Scholarship Council Project (Grant no. 2015 [3012]).

References

1. Yang, S., Adeel, U., Tahir, Y., et al.: Practical opportunistic data collection in wireless sensor networks with mobile sinks. IEEE Trans. Mob. Comput. **16**(5), 1420–1433 (2017)
2. Zhan, C., Zeng, Y., Zhang, R.: Energy-efficient data collection in UAV enabled wireless sensor network. IEEE Wirel. Commun. Lett. **7**(3), 328–331 (2017)
3. Choudhari, E., Bodhe, K.D., Mundada, S.M.: Secure data aggregation in WSN using iterative filtering algorithm. In: International Conference on Innovative Mechanisms for Industry Applications, pp. 1–5. IEEE (2017)
4. Gatti, R., Kumar, S.S., Kumar, K.S., Prasad, P.R., et al.: Improvement of speed in data collection rate in tree based wireless sensor network. In: IEEE International Conference on Recent Trends in Electronics, Information & Communication Technology, pp. 720–723. IEEE (2017)
5. Chen, C.C.: A novel data collection method with recharge plan for rechargeable wireless sensor networks. Wirel. Commun. Mob. Comput. **2018**, 1–19 (2018)
6. Takaishi, D., Nishiyama, H., Kato, N., Miura, R.: Towards energy efficient big data gathering in densely distributed sensor networks. IEEE Trans. Emerg. Top. Comput. **2**(3), 388–397 (2014)
7. Zhang, X.W., Dai, H.P., Xu, L.J., Chen, G.H.: Mobility-Assisted data gathering strategies in WSNs. Ruan Jian Xue Bao/J. Softw. **24**(2), 198–214 (2013). (in Chinese with English abstract). http://www.jos.org.cn/1000-9825/4349.htm
8. Olariu S, Stojmenovic I.: Design guidelines for maximizing lifetime and avoiding energy holes in sensor networks with uniform distribution and uniform reporting. In: Proceedings of the IEEE INFOCOM, pp. 1–12. IEEE Press, New York (2006)

9. Shah, R.C., Roy, S., Jain, S., Brunette, W.: Data mules: Modeling a three-tier architecture for sparse sensor networks. In: Proceedings of the ACM SNPA, pp. 30–41. IEEE Press, New York (2003)

10. Salarian, H., Chin, K.-W., Naghdy, F.: An energy-efficient mobile-sink path selection strategy for wireless sensor networks. IEEE Trans. Veh. Technol. **63**(5), 2407–2419 (2014)

11. Zhao, M., Yang, Y.Y.: A framework for mobile data gathering with load balanced clustering and MIMO uploading. In: Proceedings of the IEEE INFOCOM, pp. 2759–2767. IEEE Press, New York (2011)

12. Ma, M., Yang, Y.Y., Zhao, M.: Tour planning for mobile data-gathering mechanisms in wireless sensor networks. IEEE Trans. Veh. Technol. **62**(4), 1472–1483 (2013)

13. Zhao, M., Yang, Y.Y.: Bounded relay hop mobile data gathering in wireless sensor networks. IEEE Trans. Comput. **61**(2), 265–277 (2012)

14. Ma, M, Yang, Y.Y.: Data gathering in wireless sensor networks with mobile collectors. In: In: IEEE International Symposium on Parallel and Distributed Processing, IPDPS 2008, pp. 1–9 (2008)

15. Guo, S.T., Wang, C., Yang, Y.Y.: Mobile data gathering with wireless energy replenishment in rechargeable sensor networks. In: Proceedings of of the IEEE INFOCOM, pp. 1932–1940. IEEE Press, New York (2013)

16. Xing, G.L., Wang, T., Jia, W.J., Li, M.: Rendezvous design algorithms for wireless sensor networks with a mobile base station. In: Proceedings of the ACM MobiHoc, pp. 231–240. ACM Press, New York (2008)

17. Chipara, O., et al.: Real-time power-aware routing in sensor networks, In: 14th IEEE International Workshop on Quality of Service IWQoS 2006, pp. 83-92. IEEE (2006)

18. Pon, R., et al.: Networked infomechanical systems: a mobile embedded networked sensor platform. In: Proceedings of the IEEE IPSN, pp. 376–381. ACM/IEEE Press, New York (2005)

19. An, H.C., Kleinberg, R., Shmoys, D.B.: Improving christofides' algorithm for the s-t path TSP. In: Proceedings of the ACM STOC, pp. 875–886. ACM Press, New York (2012)

20. Heinzelman, W.R., Chandrakasan, A., Balakrishnan, H.: Energy-efficient communication protocol for wireless microsensor networks. In: Proceedings of the IEEE HICSS, pp. 1–10. IEEE Press, New York (2000)

21. Intanagonwiwat, C., Govindan, R., Estrin, D.: Directed diffusion: a scalable and robust communication paradigm for sensor networks. In: Proceedings of the ACM MobiCom, pp. 56–67. ACM Press, New York (2000)

Research on Telecom Flow Operation Based on User Profile

Feng Wang[1]([✉]), Weidong Huang[2], and Yuan Xu[2]

[1] Hohai University, Nanjing, China
18357825@qq.com
[2] Nanjing University of Posts and Telecommunications, Nanjing, China

Abstract. With the continuous development of science and technology in China, the concept of big data has gradually entered all walks of life and become an important scientific and technological force for industry transformation in China. Based on the background of big data development in China, this paper explores the formation conditions and evolutionary principles of big data in the drainage project, and designs and implements the front-end data interaction module, as well as the flow user data storage and analysis module based on the establishment of BDP large data flow management system model of telecom operators. The discussion in this paper will not only provide ideas for traditional operator flow management, but also provide guidance for big data applications in most other industries.

Keywords: Big data · BDP big data flow management system
Flow management

1 Introduction

In recent years, with the continuous development of telecommunication services, the demand of the communication industry has shifted from the demand for information technology to the demand for big data technology, and data as an asset has gradually become an important resource. Therefore, the demand for data information has become an essential factor in the transformation of the communications industry, for traditional structured data analysis has been unable to meet the needs of enterprises. In the traditional operator flow management system, grassroots technicians can only judge through the consumption activities and behaviors of the user at a certain stage, and there are many variable factors. The prediction results cannot be very accurate. Therefore, the flow pressure is also limited by the information collection and telephone return visits done by the front-end sales department. This inefficient, traditional, un-targeted,

Work described in this paper was funded by the National Natural Science Foundation of China under Grant No. 71671093. The authors would like to thank other researchers at Nanjing University of Posts and Telecommunications.

© Springer Nature Switzerland AG 2018
X. Chen et al. (Eds.): CSoNet 2018, LNCS 11280, pp. 477–486, 2018.
https://doi.org/10.1007/978-3-030-04648-4_40

and micro data-based business model cannot be supported by the big data flow model. Therefore, in order to solve this problem and ensure that the traditional operators improve the efficiency of data mining for user flows, it is necessary to establish a multi-dimensional information analysis model based on the user's consumption behaviors and habits, that is, to design a BDP big data flow management system that is powerful and takes into account all aspects of the user's needs to make up for these deficiencies.

2   Research Status at Home and Abroad on User Profile

User profile is also known as user persona, it is one of the effective methods for delineating users (user background, characteristics, personality tags, behavioral scenes, etc.) and analyzing user needs and satisfying the user's product design. It aims to analyze and extract the information about the user from the massive data, so as to help companies turn data into business value. In the field of communications industry operations, big data technology has shown a rapid development trend, and foreign scholars have also put forward many viewpoints in related literature and monographs. Spiekermann (2015) et al. put forward the idea of data analysis influence, trying to expand the influence of enterprises in the business environment [1]. After the inspection and development of the short-term market environment, many enterprise users have found that in addition to the continuous enhancement of collection capabilities, big data technology must have faster and more accurate analysis and response capabilities. On the one hand, it can increase the stickiness of enterprise users to the data analysis platform, and on the other hand, it can promote flow users to transform into consumer users. Therefore, based on the positioning of big data technology roles, the concept of data mining proposed by Wu, Zhu, Wu [2] (2014) has emerged. Big data mining is an exploratory concept, and how to mine is also a topic that foreign scholars have sharply discussed. Wamba, Akter [3], et al. (2015) analyzed the level of commercialization, patterns and user behaviors of online implementation, and it became an effective way to mine data in the field of commercialization. At the same time, with the expansion of the field of big data applications, the influence in the international community is also very obvious. Chen, Chiang [4] proposed an international type of agreement on big data technology in 2012, which was expected to coordinate the orderly development of big data in the international industry. Chinese government is also aware of the importance of the development of the big data industry and upgrades the industrialization of big data to a national strategy. As a hot concept in recent years, big data has high application prospects in market segmentation, satisfying user's requirements, providing enterprise decision-making basis, and upgrading business management.

3   Statement of Problem

At present, the decision of traditional operators has always been business-driven, that is, the application requirements of big data are completely proposed by the business department according to the data department. It is a big data application model that the data department completes the corresponding data analysis and mining according to the business requirements, and then returns the analysis results to the business department. The advantage of business-driven lies in that the business department is close to the front line of the business. The business departments have a better understanding of the development, the current difficulties and the development trend of the business. They must have a higher motivation to propose big data applications, which is conducive to the application of data analysis and mining results. The disadvantages of business-driven include the willingness and ability of the business departments putting forward demands is often highly correlated with their understanding of big data. At the same time, business departments are usually not familiar with the operator's own data, and do not know which data can be used to find something of value, which also affects the demand. The advantage of data-driven is that a data department has a higher understanding of big data, is more familiar with the data of the industry and external data sources, is more aware of data analysis and mining technology, and is more likely to propose more imaginative needs based on the perspective of data and methods. Therefore, it is necessary to design a platform for BDP big data flow management system that provides data multi-faceted services to solve these problems.

4   Design of BDP Model for Big Data Flow Exchange Platform

4.1   Overall Frame Design of BDP Model

The telecom operator's appeal to the BDP system design is that in the operator flow management system, the grassroots technicians can only judge through the consumption activities and behaviors of the user at a certain stage, and there are more variable factors, so the prediction on results still cannot be very accurate. Therefore, the flow pressure is also limited to the information collection and telephone return visits of the front-end sales department. This inefficient, traditional, un-targeted, and micro data-based business model cannot be supported by the big data flow model.

In order to ensure the efficiency of data mining for telecom operators to improve user flow, the construction of BDP platform will inevitably require a strong design framework that takes into account the needs of all aspects of users. In the industry, the requirements module for the design of the system include: Hadoop, HDFS, Hive, MongoDB technology front-end display platform development [5], flow event drive scheme, input and output system (i.e. I/O), Rserve exchange data service port, and so on. These technical factors are one of the important solutions for back-end mining data to the front-end display platform. After integrating the above technical factors, the overall framework constructed for the access layer, data analysis layer, application layer, and physical layer (see Fig. 1).

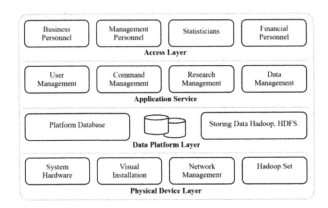

Fig. 1. A figure caption is always placed below the illustration. Please note that short captions are centered, while long ones are justified by the macro package automatically.

Access layer: It mainly provides the access capability to the platform for business personnel, managers, statisticians and financial personnel and other internal personnel of telecommunications operators. It can enable to manage content by unified identity authentication and different permissions on the data platform.

Application service layer: The application service layer mainly includes the management of program objects, including the management of a single user or a class of users, the input and feedback of the instructions of the flow management analysis, the integration of the platformized data to achieve the research effect of various management personnel on the realization of the user data stream, and the management of various types of data. Its main purpose is to meet the real-time management and monitoring of user data flow for various information personnel at the access layer, and realize the combination of big data analysis and business management analysis [6].

Data platform layer: The data layer is mainly composed of a database, in which MongoDB can directly store unstructured data in JSON format, and realize rapid retrieval and query of data through Simple System like operating system, and pass data to front-end users through traversing structures. In addition, the Hive function of the repository embedded in the data platform system is mainly responsible for analyzing the data, aiming at effectively processing massive unstructured data for data analysis and prediction in the whole platform [7].

Physical equipment layer: All physical equipments and equipments attached to the big data value chain, including infrastructure construction, belong to physical equipment layer. For telecom operators, it includes some business servers, system hardware, computer clusters, etc.

4.2 Functional Design of the BDP Database

From a technical perspective, the BDP management system is different from the traditional data management system. The main reason is that the data objects of its management system are mainly unstructured data. The traditional data processing methods such as traversal, selection, and looping can no longer satisfy the call, troubleshooting and selection of data objects by the BDP database. Therefore, the BDP database requires data collection, preprocessing, storage, mechanism, calculation mode, big data analysis and mining, big data visualization analysis, and big data security as important functional objects of the database operation process in the research and development stage.

In summary, domestic scholars have already published a number of articles in the core magazines of the telecommunications industry to elaborate [8]. This paper briefly draws the idea of the database modular operation framework as follows (see Fig. 2). The reference of these functional modules has certain similarities to other big data products. In general, the big data flow platform model should be divided into three modules, one is the flow information data source module; the second is the big data analysis system module; the third is the data clustering, analysis, coupling, and associated processing module [9].

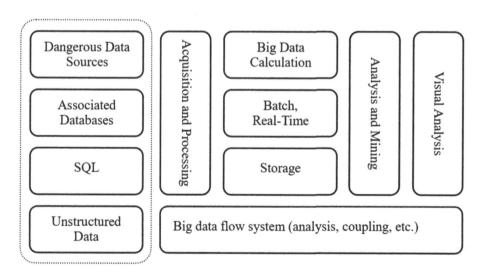

Fig. 2. Design framework for BDP database function module architecture

4.3   Functional Design of BDP Data Repository

Hive is a data repository built on a network cluster environment. Its storage functions and computing attributes are based on distributed files HDFS and MapReduce. This shows that BDP naturally has the big data computing function in the Hive attribute of data storage, thus effectively avoiding the development cost of the third-party data repository module. Therefore, BDP can realize the function of processing massive amounts of data more efficiently and conveniently by means of the related algorithms of the traditional SQL operating system. However, the data repository is the subject of user development needs, and it is necessary to adopt the multidimensional data model for design. This requires a logical structure level scheme.

The design of the logical structure model (see Fig. 3) is mainly to express the theme of user needs and business appeals in a linear way. This section briefly draws a diagram of its process structure. The goal is to reserve the usage habits and related information of the operators' user groups for their products, so that the consumer's consumption behavior can be directly or indirectly stored in the data platform layer of the operator's BDP directory. In this way, the user's behavior has the information waiting, thus forming the pre-processing of the data layer related modules, waiting for the implementation of other levels of instructions or calls.

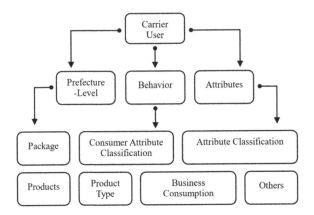

Fig. 3. User topic-oriented logical data warehouse model for BDP

4.4   Implementation of Flow User Data Storage Module

The first is the implementation of the front-end data interaction module. This article has little relevance to the analysis of big data flow users. Therefore, this paper just considers the debugging of Node.js2 as the necessary environment for database development. The login interface is primarily integrated with the Passport module, which is the authentication middleware for Node.js, it is flexible and easy to modularize, and very easy to integrate into any Express-based web application.

To put it simply, big data technology is different from traditional data storage, in that it is common that there are multiple data sources involved in the process. There are mainly two kinds of sources: the first is the local data source of traditional data, the second is the source of network data. Besides, data may also come from some organizations' own characteristic databases (for example, large public libraries, etc.). In this regard, we have developed the following program framework. First of all, the Hadoop distributed software architecture is used to access the system HDFS to achieve consistency between local data and externally imported data. Secondly, the Hive model of the data repository begins HQL query on HDFS, and the relevant instructions of the managers also perform a horizontal search on the data to distinguish the structure data from the unstructured data and generate functions such as calling and selecting. Finally, the job is performed on the MapReduce framework, and the R language and the Hive data repository are docked to achieve the "online and offline" storage effect on the user's naked eye. Specific flow chart as follows (see Fig. 4).

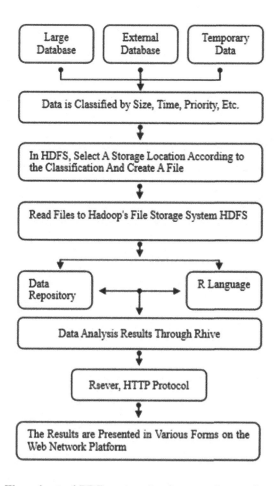

Fig. 4. Flow chart of BDP system implementation to data storage

4.5   Implementation of Flow User Data Analysis Module

The BDP data analysis module is mainly based on the R language as an analysis tool to conduct call analysis on the data stored by telecom operators. Then the resulting data is presented on the manager's PC terminal device from a human perspective, helping managers to supervise and make decisions.

As for the analysis module itself, BDP takes into account the setting of the data cloud analysis module in the process of development. Here, the user, that is, the management user, wakes up the previously set task ID by simply creating a task and creating a data packet on the WEB interface, of course, the data itself is still stored in the relevant database, and only the pointer retrieval changes. The ID setting starts working. Here, task users creation, data analysis, scripts, and existing scripts all have carrying capacity of response, that is, the data content carried in the flow is fragmented and processed into the HIVE information base for integration analysis. The specific flow chart is as follows (see Fig. 5).

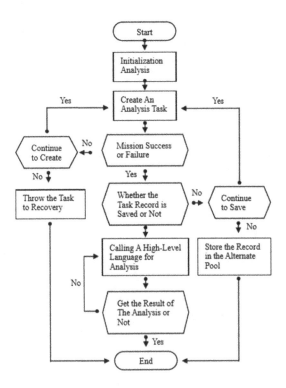

Fig. 5. Flow chart of BDP data analysis module system

5   Conclusion

With the advent of the big data era, many operators have used big data to reverse the low-margin space. They take big data as assets, innovate business models and profit models, and transform themselves into big data service providers. First of all, the main business content of the traditional communication industry is highly similar to that of modern large data drainage. The traditional operator communication management is to solve the problem of information interaction and transmission between users by using each user and the communication network as a medium. Big data management relies on the big data platform established by the operator network and business to solve the problem of enterprise demand and data connection. Communication users constitute a communication network, and enterprise users constitute a big data network. Second, big data management also has the same economic characteristics as the traditional network service. Driven by big data, it can effectively solve the current operational difficulties of telecom operators. Thirdly, we need to gradually develop big data capabilities, collect multi-party data through flow, and construct big data business model. Finally, the operator's data operation strategy can be divided into three steps: First, focus on the user scale and regard big data as core operational assets. The second is to build an end-to-end network infrastructure, because the network can integrate products and all kinds of own information data. In addition to combining the Internet, radio and television networks and other raw data also introduce data services for targeted industry applications. The third is to establish a big data service platform, expand the collection and distribution of P2P content generated by big data, and integrate the advantages of resources and CDN, so as to make it a direct source of profit, and a large-scale cross sectoral information sharing platform.

What's more, with the in-depth development of network convergence, integration of three networks has become imperative, and the popularity of mobile Internet and big data will inevitably lead to the overall trend of the future communication industry. Operators possess most of the resources of the communications industry through capital accumulation, so it is imperative to build big data services. Under the guidance of telecom operators, big data providers can effectively expand the number of customers, increase operating income, establish core strengths, and focus on business development. In the near future, the research and application of big data is the benchmark and direction for the transformation and development of telecom operators. Therefore, traditional operators should focus on this direction, and grasp the opportunities of industry development to strive to become a big data transmission operator and to serve more leading communication companies.

References

1. Spiekermann, S., Novotny, A.: A vision for global privacy bridges: technical and legal measures for international data markets. Comput. Law Secur. Rev. **31**(2), 181–200 (2015)
2. Wu, X., Zhu, X., Wu, G., et al.: Data mining with big data. IEEE Trans. Knowl. Data Eng. **26**(1), 97–107 (2014)
3. Wamba, S.F., Akter, S., Edwards, A.D., et al.: How 'big data' can make big impact: findings from a systematic review and a longitudinal case study. Int. J. Prod. Econ. **165**, 234–246 (2015)
4. Chen, H., Chiang, R.H., Storey, V.C., et al.: Business intelligence and analytics: from big data to big impact. Manag. Inf. Syst. Q. **36**(4), 1165–1188 (2012)
5. MEAN. https://github.com/linnovate/mean
6. Li, Z.Q., Chen, K., Wu, Y.W., Zheng, W.M.: Big data processing mode-system architecture, method and develop trend. J. Chin. Comput. Syst. **36**(4), 641–647 (2015)
7. Liu, L.Z., Deng, J.Y., Wu, Y.T.: Research on multi-class logistic regression algorithm based on hbase. Appl. Res. Comput. **10**, 1–3 (2018)
8. Zhang, H.P., He, H.Y., Chen, X.J.: Simulation of optimum identification in hierarchical classification of big data. Comput. Simul. **32**(10), 463–466 (2015)
9. Aisha, S., Ahmad, K., Abdullah, G.: BusiOverview of big data storage technologies. Front. Inf. Technol. Electr. Eng. **18**(8), 1041–1072 (2017)

Information Spreading in Social Network Through Explosive Percolation Theory

Xiaoxia Zhu, Jiaxin Song, Jianfang Meng, and Jia Liu[⊠]

School of Economic and Management Sciences, Yanshan University,
Qinhuangdao 066004, Hebei, China
liujia3891@163.com

Abstract. In this paper, we use the explosive percolation theory to set up an information spreading model. We analyze useful parameters in largest cluster and information spreading rates, and discuss some rules of sudden outbreaks of information. By using simulation experiments, it is easy to see that there exists a critical point in the outbreak of information, and that information is most infective in the early stage, and gradually weakened as the time increases. Also, this paper provides some new insights on governance of information spreading in social networks through observing the simulation results.

Keywords: Information spreading · Social network
Explosive percolation

1 Introduction

Information spreading in social networks has been an interesting topic for the last ten years. Social networks, especially Twitter and Facebook, have become the main places of public opinion expression, information release, marketing and so on. But at the same time, it also aggravates the possibility of large-scale information explosion in a short period of time. If the information spreading cannot be effectively controlled, it will easily trigger a crisis of public opinion and cause social unrest. Therefore, it has triggered an explosive attention in various disciplines, and several overview articles have reported on it, see the reference [1–3] for details. It is an important research direction for scholars to analyze the information spreading rules of a large number social networks, and then summarize the effective information spreading and prediction models.

Note that there is a natural similarity between information spreading and epidemic transmission, thus some studies used epidemic models. The warehouse model (SIR) proposed by Kermac and McKendrick [4] was a classical model to analyze the dynamics of infectious diseases. Daniel [5] proposed two propagation models in the SIS model from different priority levels. However, the research on information spreading based on the epidemic models not consider the role of network structure and social relations in the real social network system [6], which is insufficient to cope with the complex external environment.

© Springer Nature Switzerland AG 2018
X. Chen et al. (Eds.): CSoNet 2018, LNCS 11280, pp. 487–497, 2018.
https://doi.org/10.1007/978-3-030-04648-4_41

The complex network can fit the real network to a large extent [7]. In order to make the epidemic model more suitable for real social network systems, so as to better study the information spreading rules, Wang et al. [8], Zan et al. [9] and Zhao et al. [10] considered characteristics of network structure and used the complex network theory and SIR model to analyze the rumor spreading. With the development of study, scholars more and more clearly depict the mechanism of information spreading. And further research on mathematical analysis and calculation models are required.

Macroscopic emergence behavior (such as outbreaks of disease) has similarities with non-equilibrium phase transitions in statistical physics. Thus, phase transformation theory and percolation theory are applied to the study of the infectious diseases and information dissemination gradually [11–13]. This method introduces physical theory into the study of information spreading, and can effective in mathematical analysis and actual derivation of the information spreading model. Zhao [14], Wang et al. [15] applied the percolation theory to the SIR model, and calculated the spreading threshold and the maximum outbreak scale. Zhang [16] used bootstrap percolation theory in the empirical research, and found that as the change of the activity of nodes there is a critical value for the large-scale outbreak of rumors. Although, the classical percolation method is more accurate than the mean field method in the calculation of the epidemic model, the real-time dynamic and mutation behaviors in the network can not be captured properly.

Now, research on information spreading focuses on spreading mechanism and influencing factors. Epidemic model, complex network and percolation theory are a better combined method. This combined method can not only meet the consideration of the internal and external environmental factors of the complex social network system in reality, but also carry out mathematical analysis and practical derivation of the established information spreading model, so as to study the rules of information spreading more accurately, but there is very little research on the mechanism of the sudden outbreak of information. In fact, information is difficult to control is largely lies in its suddenness, which can quickly break out in a short time, and people hardly perceive it before the outbreak.

From the above perspective, this paper introduces the theory of explosive percolation to study the sudden outburst of information. According to the characteristics of information spreading, we use the explosive percolation theory to establish a information spreading model, and observe a critical point of information explosion from some simulation.

Classical percolation discusses the continuous and reversible phase transition. Achlioptas et al. [17] brought out a percolation model which showed an unexpected sharp transition, that is, the model was proved to be irreversible and discontinuous. Achlioptas's theory of explosive percolation provided a new idea for explaining the phenomenon of macro catastrophe. After then some authors have applied this model to research of many real systems, such as the homology of human protein [18], cascading failure [19], mobile phone call network (MPC) and large ArXiv cooperation network [20].

This paper has two main contributions. First, we discuss the sudden outbreak of information and use the explosive percolation theory to analyze the rule of information bursts. Second, we use this method to model information spreading in social networks and observe the critical point of information explosion by means of simulations. Furthermore we divide the information into different stages. Moreover, we explain why some information doesn't break out even though many people know it and why few times of spreading can lead to the explosion of information. We hope that our approach will help to further study the explosive percolation theory and information spreading in social networks.

The rest of the paper is organized as follows. In Sect. 2 we describe the explosive percolation algorithm for the 2D square lattices, and set up an information spreading model. In Sect. 3 we explain useful parameters of the model, and discuss the rules of the sudden outbreak of information. In Sect. 4 we give several useful results through simulation experiments. Finally, in Sect. 5 we provide some concluding remarks.

2   Information Spreading Model

In this section, we first describe the network of information spreading, and generalize the meaning of nodes and edges. Then we abstract the interpersonal relationships in the network as the neighbors, which are the receivers of information spreading. Furthermore, we introduce the SI model to describe the state of nodes in information spreading. Finally, using the explosive percolation theory, we propose a selection rule in neighborhood, and set up a information spreading model. The model is built as follows:

(1) Network, node and edge
   Modeling individuals and their behaviors, set $G = (V, E)$ where G represents the network, the entire information spreading system. V is a collection of all nodes v_i, which is an abstraction of potential recipients of information that may be accepted in the real world. E is a set of edges e_{ij}, denoting the propagation relationship between nodes. And the addition of edges indicates that information is propagated and exchanged once.

(2) Neighbors
   The definition of a neighbor is an abstraction of the interpersonal network in the real world, which refers to the potential recipients of information that has close interpersonal relationship between the nodes, and the nodes only exchange information with the neighbors. After the adjacent nodes obtain the information through the edge relationship, they merge into a cluster $c(v)$. A cluster is a collection of all nodes that can be reached from the node v via the edge, and the cluster size is the number of nodes included in the cluster. Considering the "six-degree segmentation theory", in order to make the model have small world effect better, this paper uses the von Neumann model, that is, the node takes neighboring four nodes (one on each of the upper and lower sides as neighbors).

(3) State

We assume that information that bursts in a short time cannot be effectively controlled. That is to say, there are no nodes that obtain information is immune or forgets to this information and restores to the unknown state in a short time. Therefore, according to the SI model, any node must be in one of the following two states: S - susceptible state (not receiving information state) and I - infection state (effective acquisition state). A node with a status of S indicates a potential recipient who has not received the information, and with a status of I indicates that the information has been accepted. Set the infection rate φ to 1, then $S + I \xrightarrow{\varphi} 2I$.

(4) Rules

Rules refer to the generalization and abstraction of the decisions and behaviors of individuals who have obtained information in the process of information spreading. Since the source of information is often an informal channel, its authenticity cannot be guaranteed, and individuals tend to disseminate this information to smaller groups when they obtain information. Inspired by the SR rule of the explosive percolation theory, this local decision rule is defined as follows: 1. Randomly select an individual as a party to information spreading. 2. Observe the surrounding four neighbors and calculate the cluster size of the four neighbors. 3. Select neighbors with smallest cluster sizes to propagate information.

We consider bond percolation on $L \times L$ square lattices with periodic boundary conditions in both directions, with $n = L \times L$ sites. One bond are added for each time step. The algorithm of information spreading is as follows:

(a) Starting from an empty network of $n = L \times L$ nodes.
(b) Randomly selecting any node v_i and the state of node v_i becomes I.
(c) Calculating the cluster size of four neighbor nodes.
(d) Choosing the neighbor v_j with the smallest cluster size, establish a link with v_i and update its state to I, and discard the other 3 nodes. If there is more

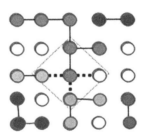

Fig. 1. Improved edge rules (For a more intuitive understanding, the 2D grid is hidden. The four neighbor nodes in the box are candidate nodes, while the clusters of the four neighbors are 2, 6, 1, and 3 respectively. In accordance with the rules, the node should be selected is right node, and the other three nodes are abandoned)

than one node with the smallest cluster size in the neighborhood, one of them is randomly selected and the rest are abandoned, as shown in Fig. 1.

(e) Repeating step 2, step 3 and step 4 until most nodes in the network are connected.

3   Process of Information Spreading

In this section, we mainly discuss the process of information spreading. We use the mean field theory to analyze the largest cluster and the spreading rate of information, and give the calculation method of the critical point of information explosion. The analysis shows that the transmission rate of information is decreasing, that is, information is most infectious at the initial stage.

3.1   Largest Cluster

The main study of percolation is the connectivity of the network. In this article, the cluster is considered to be a group that has obtained information, and the information is already shared within the group. Therefore, all nodes in the cluster are in the same state-infected state.

In the process of the information dissemination, different individuals have different perception of the connectivity of information transmission network. Individuals in the largest clusters are highly sensitive, which will be the first to perceive the outbreak of information.

In order to systematically study changes in the network, we monitor the changes in the largest cluster. We define the variation of the order parameter, i.e., the relative size of largest cluster with the increase of the added edge in the network, $P_{max}(t) = C_{max}/n$. Using the finite scale, P_{max} follows the scaling relation [21]:

$$P_{max} = n^{-\frac{\beta}{u}} F[(t - t_c)n^{-\frac{\beta}{u}}], \tag{1}$$

where n is the size of the system, F is a universal function, t is the control parameter (the evolution time of the system), i.e., the ratio of the number of edges to the total number of people. t_c is the critical point of the transition, β is the critical exponent of order parameter and u that of the correlation length, t_c is the critical value of the control parameter t. The susceptibility, i.e. the average cluster value reaches its maximum. It is also the point that the cluster size distribution becomes a power law.

The value t_c corresponds to the outbreak point of information, and it can be obtained by various methods. Besides the above two methods, it is also possible to find the maximum 'jump' time of the largest cluster C_{max}:

$$\Delta P(t) = \frac{1}{n} \max(C(T + 1) - C(T)). \tag{2}$$

Among the three methods we mentioned, due to the size of the network, the number of clusters in our network may not be enough to make it appear in a distributed shape, this is too inaccurate. Therefore, we will not discuss the second method here. Since it is not easy to directly analyze the largest cluster, many articles turn to the average size of the cluster, which is the first method.

According to D'Souza et al. [22], $x_i(G)$ represents the proportion of the total number of individuals (i.e., the number of people in the group) of I in the group size:

$$x_i(G) = \frac{1}{n}|\{v : c(v) = i\}|, \tag{3}$$

where, $c(v)$ is the group containing individual v, $|c(v)|$ is the group size. $x_i = in_i/n$, n_i is the number of clusters in the system of i. The above formula also means that the probability of the first node choosing the cluster size as i is x_i. Clearly, x_i is also a function of time. Thus the average cluster size is given by

$$W = \frac{1}{n}\sum_v |c(v)|, \tag{4}$$

where W is also a function of time, which describes the average size of a group, that is, the average size of the cluster in which any node is located at a certain time. It can also be written as

$$W = \sum_{i=1}^{n} ix_i = \frac{1}{n}\sum_{i=1}^{n} i^2 n_i. \tag{5}$$

Let $W* = W - \sum_{i=1}^{k} ix_i$. $W*$ correspond to the expected value of the group size greater than k. Order $s_j = 1 - \sum_{k<j} x_k$, s_j is the weight distribution of the group size starting from j. W (the size of the average group) changed, when the communication of information led to the merger of two groups of j and k, respectively. Thus we can get the rate of change of the expected value of the group size over time:

$$\frac{dW}{dt} = 2W\sum_{k=1}^{k} k(s_k^4 - s_{k+1}^4) + 2WW^*s_{k+1}^3. \tag{6}$$

D'Souza (2010) indicated that the differential equation can be roughly solved according to the Euler method, but the process is more complicated and also lose certain accuracy. In this paper, the simulation method is used to further obtain the explosion point by Eq. (2).

3.2   Propagation Rate of Information

Let $I(t)$ and $S(t)$ represent the proportion of the number of people in the information spreading state (infected state) and the unknown state of information (susceptible) at time t. Using mean field theory, the propagation rate of false information is defined as

$$r(t) = \frac{dI(t)}{dt} = -\frac{dS(t)}{dt}. \tag{7}$$

Obviously, $S(t)$ is the proportion of isolated nodes at time t in this model, $I(t)$ is the proportion of nodes in the cluster. From Eq. (2), when i takes 1, x_1 represents the ratio of the isolated nodes, that is, the proportion of nodes that are not infected. Initially, the value of x_1 is 1, which decreases with time gradually. Order $s_j = 1 - \sum_{k<j} x_k$, and s_j is the weight distribution of group size starting from j. The probability that the candidate neighbor nodes with a smaller cluster have a cluster size of j is $s_j^4 - s_{j+1}^4$. The differential equation is given by

$$\frac{dx_i}{dt} = -ix_i - i(s_i^4 - s_{i+1}^4) + i \sum_{j+k=i} x_j(s_k^4 - s_{k+1}^4). \tag{8}$$

The meaning of this differential equation is the average growth rate of the cluster whose size is I. Therefore, the spreading rate of false information can also be expressed as:

$$r(t) = -\frac{dS(t)}{dt} = -\frac{dx_1}{dt} = x_1 + s_1^4 - s_2^4. \tag{9}$$

From $s_1 = 1$, $s_2 = 1 - x_1$, which simplifies to:$r(t) = x_1 + 1 - (1 - x_1)^4$.
The derivative with respect to x_1, we get

$$\frac{dr(t)}{dx_1} = 1 - 4(x_1 - 1)^3. \tag{10}$$

Because $0 \le x_1 \le 1$, $r(t)$ is the increasing function of x_1. And x_1 is the decreasing function of time t, so $r(t)$ is decreasing in time. When x_1 takes a maximum of 1, it corresponds to the maximum value of $r(t)$ of 2, which is the fastest propagation rate when $t = 0$ at the beginning. The minimum value of x_1 is 0, when the $r(t)$ takes the minimum value of 0. This indicates that the false information is the most infectious when it is produced. At this time, the false information is novel and there is not enough evidence to be refuted, so it is easier to be believed and spread. The longer the false information appears, the less infectious it becomes.

4   Simulation Experiment

In this section, first, we simulate the model and observe the evolution process of the model, which shows that information spreading has a high degree of clustering. Then we record the maximum cluster and the propagation rate of information. Furthermore, we locate the critical point of information explosion and divide the stage of information spreading. Finally, we further discuss the law of information spreading.

Set the grid of $N = 101 \times 101$, and each grid represents a sustainable person. Using Netlogo for simulation, the edges are hidden and the nodes in the same cluster have the same pcolor and cluster-number attributes, and the cluster size is presented by the plabel. Attribute cluster-number is unique, that is, given any node it must have a corresponding cluster number. At each time step, only add one edge to the network, and the grid automatically updates its pcolor and cluster-number attributes. We monitor the growth of the largest clusters, the process of cluster merging and the rate of information spreading in this process, and the model evolution diagram is shown in Fig. 2:

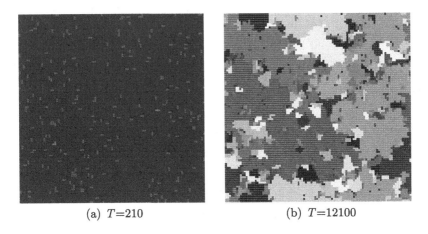

(a) T=210   (b) T=12100

Fig. 2. The model evolution diagrams in different time step

To observe the evolution process, the size of the cluster is mostly 2 in the initial stage. Over a long period of time, the growth of clusters is generally more balanced, and forming a large number of scattered clusters are formed. With the increase of time step, a large cluster suddenly appeared, and then almost all nodes in the network are connected rapidly in a short time. In this model, the propagation of false information of public crisis shows high clustering and network connectivity.

4.1   Simulation Analysis of Largest Cluster

The growth simulation of the largest cluster (as shown in Fig. 3) shows that the growth of the largest cluster has a longer "incubation period" and a shorter "outbreak period". The growth of the largest cluster is nearly zero before $t = 1.1$, and suddenly leaping when $t = 1.1$, presenting the explosive growth (note: with the increase of n, t can increase as the slightly, in general, do not break $t = 1.1$). When $t = 1.35$, 90% of nodes are in the largest cluster, and the whole network is connected. The time before $t = 1.1$ is considered as the incubation period of false information (the gestation period), the moment $t = 1.1$ is the beginning point of false information explosion, and the time $(1.1, 1.35)$ is the outbreak period of information. The average order parameter is $P_{max}(t) = 0.45$ when the average maximum outbreak point of information is at $t_c = 1.22$. Information spreading exists a threshold: when the spread degree is less than 1, information spreading is in the incubation period of information. At this time, information is only communicated at this time only in small group communication, and most

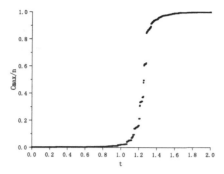

Fig. 3. Growth of the largest cluster

people do not perceive its the effect. When the spread propagation degrees more than exceeds 1, that information group in a short period of rapid growth for larger groups the group who knows the information grows into a larger group rapidly in a short time, and when the propagation degree reaches 1.22, in the transmission of 1.22, people can obviously perceive the influence the growth of the information influence. When the spread propagation degree exceeds is over 1.35, almost all individuals perceive the influence of information, and it is very easy to break out have a group events.

4.2   Simulation Analysis of Information Propagation Rate

The simulation results show that $S(t)$ is a curve whose slope decreases gradually, and finally becomes 0 (Fig. 4), which is consistent with the analysis of the average field theory. When the propagation degree reached 1.1, about 96% of the nodes have already obtained this information, but the information still did not explode. The increase in the number of infected people will affect the increase of network connectivity to some extent, but the existence of highly dispersed clusters weakens this effect. This also explains that there are a lot of information in life, which is very important to the masses, but it does not form an outbreak trend.

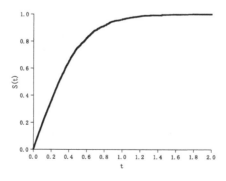

Fig. 4. The increase of infected population

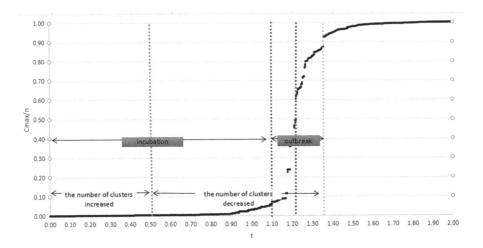

Fig. 5. False information propagation stage

4.3 Discussion

In general, with the control parameters as the evolution axis (as shown in Fig. 5), the information spreading has an long "latency period". During the incubation period, the dissemination of information forms a large number of scattered small groups, and the communication among groups forms the accumulation of medium-sized groups. Although a considerable number of people have been infected with information, it may not have caused the explosion of information. When the threshold value is exceeded, the medium group is merged into a large group, and the information suddenly erupts, and the less propagation makes the influence of the information increase sharply. Compared with the number of infected people, it is found that the outbreak of information is not the explosion of the number of infected people, but the mutation of the network connectivity of information spreading network.

5 Concluding Remarks

We apply the explosive percolation theory to the study of information spreading, study the rules of the sudden outbreak of information, and set up a model of information spreading. Moreover, we observe the critical point of information explosion by simulations and divide information spreading into several stages. Also, we find that the outbreak of information is not the explosion of the number of infected people, but the mutation of the network connectivity of information spreading network. This paper provides a new insight on how to use the explosive percolation theory and SI model to analyze information spreading. Along such a research line, there are still some interesting future directions that are worth studying, such as identifying information and making predictions before outbreaking.

References

1. Morales, A.J., Borondo, J., Losada, J.C., et al.: Efficiency of human activity on information spreading on Twitter. Soc. Netw. **39**(1), 1–11 (2014)
2. Martino, F., Spoto, A.: Social network analysis: a brief theoretical review and further perspectives in the study of information technology. Psychology J. **4**(1), 53–86 (2006)
3. Li, L., Sun, L., Yang, J.: Summary of social network research. Comput. Sci. **42**(11), 8–21 (2015)
4. Kermack, W.O., McKendrick, A.G.: A contribution to the mathematical theory of epidemics. Proc. R. Soc. Lond. A **115**(772), 700–721 (1927)
5. Trpevski, D., Tang, W.K., Kocarey, L.: Model for rumor spreading over networks. Phys. Rev. E Stat. Nolinear Soft Matter Phys. **81**(2), 1–11 (2010)
6. Wang, W., Jing, J.: Research on the Social Network-based Mechanism of public crisis information communication. Inf. Sci. **25**(7), 979–982 (2007)
7. Boccaletti, S., Latora, V., Moreno, Y., et al.: Complex networks: structure and dynamics. Phys. Rep. **25**(4), 175–308 (2006)
8. Wang, J., Zhao, L., Huang, R.: SIRaRu rumor spreading model in complex networks. Phys. Stat. Mech. Appl. **398**(15), 43–55 (2014)
9. Zan, Y., Wu, J., Li, P., et al.: SICR rumor spreading model in complex networks: counterattack and self-resistance. Phys. Stat. Mech. Appl. **405**(405), 159–170 (2014)
10. Zhao, L.J., Pan, W.: Rumor spreading model with variable spreading and removal rate. J. Univ. Shanghai Sci. Technol. **36**(4), 345–350 (2014)
11. Grabowski, A., Kosinski, R.A.: Percolation in real on-line networks. Acta Phys. Pol. **41**(5), 1135–1142 (2010)
12. Son, S.W., Bizhani, G., Christensen, C., et al.: Percolation theory on interdependent networks based on epidemic spreading. EPL **97**(1), 1–6 (2011)
13. Wang, X., Kang, L., Song, M., et al.: Interactive behavior characteristic mining based on percolation theory for information spreading. J. Comput. Inf. Syst. **11**(1), 133–140 (2015)
14. Zhao, D., Li, L., Peng, H., et al.: Multiple routes transmitted epidemics on multiplex networks. Phys. Lett. A **378**(10), 770–776 (2014)
15. Wang, X., Song, M., Guo, S., et al.: Information spreading in correlated microblog reposting network based on directed percolation theory. Acta Phys. Sin. **64**(4), 182–189 (2015)
16. Rui, Z.: Communication and management of public opinion based on complex network. Mod. Inf. **36**(04), 26–29 (2016)
17. Achlioptas, D., D'Souza, R.M., Spencer, J.: Explosive percolation in random networks. Science **323**(5920), 1453–1455 (2009)
18. Rozenfeld, H., Gallos, L., Makse, H.: Explosive percolation in the human protein homology network. Eur. Phys. J. B **75**(3), 305–310 (2010)
19. Pan, R.K., Kivela, M., Saramaki, J., et al.: Using explosive percolation in analysis of real-world networks. Phys. Rev. E Stat. Nonlinear Soft Matter Phys. **83**(2), 1–6 (2011)
20. Radicchi, F.: Percolation in real interdependent networks. Nat. Phys. **11**(7), 597–602 (2015)
21. Bastas, N., Kosmidis, K., Argyrakis, P.: Explosive site percolation and finite-size hysteresis. Phys. Rev. E Stat. Nonlinear Soft Matter Phys. **84**(6 Pt 2), 1–6 (2011)
22. D'Souza, R.M., Mitzenmacher, M.: Local cluster aggregation models of explosive percolation. Phys. Rev. Lett. **104**(19), 1–4 (2010)

A Novel Method for Detecting APT Attacks by Using OODA Loop and Black Swan Theory

Tero Bodström[(✉)] and Timo Hämäläinen

Faculty of Information Technology, University of Jyväskylä, P.O. Box 35,
Agora, 40014 Jyväskylä, Finland
`tetabods@student.jyu.fi`, `timo.hamalainen@jyu.fi`

Abstract. Advanced Persistent Threat (APT) attacks are a major concern for the modern societal digital infrastructures due to their highly sophisticated nature. The purpose of these attacks varies from long period espionage in high level environment to causing maximal destruction for targeted cyber environment. Attackers are skilful and well funded by governments in many cases. Due to sophisticated methods it is highly important to study proper countermeasures to detect these attacks as early as possible. Current detection methods under-performs causing situations where an attack can continue months or even years in a targeted environment. We propose a novel method for analysing APT attacks through OODA loop and Black Swan theory by defining them as a multi-vector multi-stage attacks with continuous strategical ongoing campaign. Additionally it is important to notice that for developing better performing detection methods, we have to find the most common factor within these attacks. We can state that the most common factor of APT attacks is communication, thus environment has to be developed in a way that we are able to capture complete network flow and analyse it.

Keywords: Advanced Persistent Thread (APT) · OODA loop
Black Swan theory · Network anomaly detection

1 Introduction

In this paper a novel approach for analysing APT attack kill chain and its life-cycle is proposed to gain deeper insights about the attacks and help the development of detection techniques. The number of these sophisticated attacks is increasing thus leaving societal infrastructures at more risk which can, in worst case, cause lost of human lives. The current attacks are already capable of hiding in cyber environments, bypassing firewalls as well as intrusion detection systems and other countermeasures effectively. The attackers are currently adopting Machine and Deep Learning based solutions to attack campaigns, especially in malware that modify attack vectors and behavioural patterns based on what the malware learns from the cyber environment, making the attacks more dangerous

© Springer Nature Switzerland AG 2018
X. Chen et al. (Eds.): CSoNet 2018, LNCS 11280, pp. 498–509, 2018.
https://doi.org/10.1007/978-3-030-04648-4_42

and unpredictable. To effectively protect systems against these above-mentioned campaigns, one must use similar techniques when developing countermeasures.

Our proposed approach studies APT attack's kill chain and lifecycle through OODA loop and Black Swan theory for describing how the attack behaves. Finally, we propose a method to detect APT attacks in an early phase of the campaign that can be adapted to Deep Learning.

The paper contains following structure: Sect. 2 presents definitions for APT kill chain and lifecycle from information security organizations and research community and Sect. 3 introduces the Black Swan theory and related research. In Sect. 4, the OODA loop is described and Sect. 5 explains thoroughly how the subjects from earlier sections are related to each other. Finally, Sect. 6 concludes and describes possible future works.

2 APT Attack, Kill Chain and Lifecycle

This section introduces APT attack and its kill chain utilising widely used definitions from research results and information security organizations.

2.1 APT Attack

APT attack is a sophisticated network attack which attempts to breach target networks and systems undetected in order to espionage or gain access to privileged information as long as possible. APT attacks can be also used to cause maximal destruction to target networks, systems, critical infrastructure or production. A commonly known malicious worm Stuxnet is an example of APT attack that targets production systems. The developers of these sophisticated attacks are skilled and well funded since they are tailor-made to the target networks and systems [1–5] - the cyber security risk at the targeted side is very high.

Ongoing APT attack uses multiple techniques to masquerade its activity in a network from detection. These attacks have the capability to hide in networks by mimicking legitimate traffic and modify itself during campaign by using random execution intervals and multiple legitimate protocols. The attack can also use more than one attack vectors simultaneously [1–10]. Another weakness that help attackers is the fact that 100% secure systems does not exist. Even well designed and protected systems and networks have their weak spots [8]. Moreover, the growing number of insider threats, where an individual with legitimate system access executes an attack, is a great concern [5,11].

2.2 Kill Chain

The term "kill chain" originates from military concept and it was adopted to information security as "Cyber Kill Chain" by Lockheed Martin. This commonly used kill chain describes seven stages for an attack, which are (i) Reconnaissance, (ii) Weaponization, (iii) Delivery, (iv) Exploitation, (v) Installation, (vi) Command and Control and (vii) Actions on Objective [1,2,7]. Few other similar *kill chain* definitions to mention are: (i) LogRhythm, (ii) Lancaster, (iii) SDAPT and (iv) BSI-model [7]. However, these models are practically mechanical execution flows and they do not take into account how sophisticated the attack may be or the fact that attack developers do not have any obligations to follow the phases described in models.

There exist research papers where improvements and different approaches in defining *kill chain* are proposed. Messaoud et al. used the term *"life cycle"* to describe the entire kill chain in their paper. The purpose was to improve earlier definitions by focusing on attack targets as well as different tactics, techniques and methods controlling impact of the attack. This way, instead of understanding only the early stages of the attack which is common, it is possible to understand the attack's life cycle as a whole. They stated that earlier defined *kill chain* falsely assumes that APT attacks are using the same seven phases every time in that exact order. To support this argument, for example Stuxnet has a mechanism to autonomously execute several tasks without command and control (phase vi) and thus it is not following the *kill chain* execution order. Therefore, the authors proposed a new model which is based on six phases, where *kill chain* phases are combined and considered from attackers intention [7]. Bhatt et al. proposed framework for detecting APT's and improvements to *kill chain* in their paper. The purpose was to focus on attack vectors' simultaneous dynamic behaviour and detect them before significant impact to the target. The framework consists of three separate methods: (i) multi-stage attack model, its core is based on seven-phase *kill chain*, (ii) layered security architecture to delay attack success, which increases detection time and (iii) event data collection from various sources and information analysis with Big Data technology. They stated that by using layered security, the entire *kill chain* has to be executed at least once in each layer which helps detection. For data collection they proposed separate sensors to each layer, configured to detect the ongoing *kill chain* phase [8].

Kill chain has not been the one and only approach on analysing APT attacks. For example, few recent papers [5,10,12] based their analysis on strategical game theory. Xiao et al. chose cumulative prospect theory (CPT) to improve APT attack detection dynamically. In their work attacker and defender are assumed to not know time intervals for the other opponent's actions, for example system scan for malware detection and attack execution intervals, which creates non-linear sequence of events. Both of the mentioned actions are strategic decisions with a different purpose. They stated that in both sides exists irrationality in strategic decision making under uncertain situations based on human subjective point of view, such as risk taking, thus strategic game theory fits well for APT detection and impact investigation [5,10]. Zhu et al. proposed combination of three strategic game models to detect APT behaviour and recognize correct countermeasures. APT was defined as a multi-stage and -phase attack and it was divided to three stages: (i) infection, (ii) stealthy infiltration and (iii) causing damage, and for each phase they selected different strategy, while between stages internal transition was implemented. Theory computes optimal behaviour for both sides, attacker and defender simultaneously, and the theory's main purpose was to *"capture the strategic interactions of an attacker with a sequence of agents in the system"*. The authors proposed *Gestalt Nash equilibrium* theory as a core of solution, as it provides a holistic risk assessment theory for APT attacks by adaptive learning methods and designing automated and optimal defence for multiple layers [12]. *Gestalt Nash equilibrium* theory was also analysed in [5] and identified as a best response strategy for opponents, optimizing their long-term objectives.

2.3   Lifecycle

The lifecycle of an APT attack begins when an attacker sets the target and intelligence gathering starts to find weak spots from the targeted cyber environment with methods such as open source intelligence, network scanning and social engineering [4, 7]. The lifecycle may end due to various reasons: the attack reaches its purpose, it is detected and interrupted or such countermeasures are implemented that it cannot fulfil its purpose and therefore ceases.

Intelligence gathering activities in a network, local and public, from anomaly detection point of view are difficult to detect, sometimes even impossible [6]. For example network scanning and open source intelligence can be executed completely outside of the target's cyber environment. Further, there can be multiple purposes for a network scanning, thus it is difficult to reason if it was executed by an APT or for some other purpose, even legitimate. Open source intelligence can be gathered from public records, such as DNS, whois records and so forth when targeted cyber environment is connected to public network, thus it does not create any communication to targeted environment. In addition, social engineering based attacks can be executed with methods that does not require access to target's cyber environment. Hence the critical point for network anomaly detection is, when a malware executes [8] first time and makes first communication or attempts it inside the target's cyber environment.

3   Black Swan Theory

According to Taleb's definitions, Black Swan is a surprising highly improbable consequential event, that can change the entire perspective to the subject in question. Black Swans are caused by *"severe limitation to our learning from observations or experience and the fragility of our knowledge"*, in other words, one single observation can completely invalidate earlier common beliefs. In addition, there exists positive and negative Black Swans and while effects of positive takes time to appear, effects of negative ones appear fast [13].

To be more precise, Black Swan is an event that has following three attributes, (i) it is an outlier that locates outside of the ordinary assumption, or outside of a *"tunnel"*, (ii) it causes extreme impact and (iii) after the event occurs, even being an extreme outlier, there exists a tendency to transfer the event from being unlikely to explainable and predictable one [13].

A rare event is same as uncertainty and to study those events we need to focus on extreme outliers, instead of focusing on normal events. These dynamical sudden events with low predictability and high impact can be seen also as events that should not happen, thus happened exactly because of that. There are multiple reasons for this phenomenon: (i) categorizing which reduces true complexity by ruling out sources of uncertainty, thus creating more misunderstanding, (ii) by focusing on causes of known Black Swans or a small number of sources of uncertainty, in other words on a *"tunnel"*, (iii) huge amount of data can be insignificant occasionally while one piece of data can be very significant, thus invalidate earlier beliefs, (iv) reducing dimensions, more random data has higher number of dimensions and it is more difficult to summarize. But as more data is summarized, less random it becomes thus leading to assumption that the environment is less random than it actually is, (v) learning is based on historical events at the expense of previously unknown events, leading to ignoring later ones before appearance, (vi) future predictions by using tools and methods which exclude rare events and (vii) with more detailed knowledge from environment, noise in knowledge increases thus creating false understanding of information. Furthermore, two important attributes which relate to Black Swan events are *"duration blindness"*, that is we cannot predict how long an event will last based on its history, and *"the curse of learning"*, that happens with overlapping information, where less learning happens while having more overlap in information. Above all, any event can have an infinite amount of possible causes [13].

While Black Swans are produced in a messy understanding of an environment, to be more precise, in a gap between what we really know and what we think we know, there are methods to make them predictable to a certain degree and turn unknown unknowns to *"Gray Swans"*. That is, they are somewhat tractable and by being aware of their existence, the element of surprise is lower. More specifically, the event is still rare but also expected. One way to reduce unknown is fractal randomness, it causes some Black Swan consequences to appear but does not give exact answers, in other words one can understand the consequence of an event without knowing the likelihood of an event. It is possible to infer such possible outcomes that are not directly visible in the data. However, instead of ignoring these deductions, they should be taken into account in the set of possible outcomes as well [13]. Zeng et al. proposed a hierarchical Bayesian reliability model framework to reduce unexpected failures in a process, which were presented as Black swans. Their mathematical model took all failures into account, expected and unexpected, and by increasing the knowledge of the environment their test results showed that probability of unexpected failures reduced. In addition, paper showed two important facts: (i) *"system complexity inherently hides unexpected failures"* and (ii) as the complexity of environment increases, possibility to unexpected failures increases also, thus *"the estimated reliability decreases"* [14]. Additionally Arney et al. stated that *"Through rare event scenarios that impact the global network, we see how different elements and entities interact with each other to produce even greater impact"*, that is small change in local condition can cause consequences to entire network [15].

4 OODA Loop

OODA loop, the decision cycle was presented by Colonel John Boyd and it was originally developed for observing and examining fighter pilots in aerial combat. Later on it has been adopted widely to business, law enforcement, military as well as to information security, as a decision making strategy [16–19].

Boyd stated that the people's ambiguity and the environments randomness creates a lot of uncertainty among us. However, the bigger problem is our inability to properly understand changing reality, that is, we find it difficult to change our perspectives according to prevailing conditions thus we tend to keep continuing with the existing mental concept. He also pointed out *"that trying to understand a randomly changing space with pre-existing mental concepts can only lead to confusion, ambiguity, and more uncertainty"*. Previous idea is based on three principles: (i) Gödel's Incompleteness theorem (ii) Heisenberg's Uncertainty Principle and (iii) 2nd Law of Thermodynamics. First, Gödel's Incompleteness theorem, states that every logical model of reality is incomplete, inconsistent and must adapt constantly to new observations. Second, Heisenberg's Uncertainty Principle, states that it is impossible to define the velocity and position of a particle at the same time. By applying this to environment, we will obtain more precise observations to exact domain but on the other hand we obtain more uncertainty to the other one. Third, 2nd Law of Thermodynamics, states that *"isolated system"* will have increasing entropy. By transferring this to organization, Boyd assumed that if individuals or organizations does not communicate with outsiders for getting new information, they will create mentally closed environment which leads to distorted perception of surroundings [16]. Therefore, it is important to frequently do situational assessments to gain awareness about the things that are going on in the environment [19].

The decision cycle has four phases, Observe - Orient - Decide - Act. Each phase in an OODA loop is a representation of a process, which is interacting with its environment. Its purpose is to resolve the earlier mentioned randomly changing space problem and increase awareness about the surrounding environment. Observe is a process for acquiring information about the environment through observing and interacting with it. It is guided and controlled by Orient while receiving feedback from Decide and Act. Orient is the process of filtering the information gathered in observe phase, taking into account the possible Orient-phases from previous loops. The filtering may include finding such correlations and dependencies that can be used in further decision making, therefore irrelevant information can be rejected. *"It shapes the way... we observe, the way we decide, the way we act"*. The process that selects which hypotheses will be executed based on environment's situation, is Decide. It is guided by input from Orient and delivers feedback to Observe. In Act-process, the selected hypotheses are tested by interacting with the environment. It is guided and controlled by Orient, it receives feedback from Decide and it provides feedback to Observe [16].

It is important to remember that both sides, attacker and defender in our case, are supposedly using their OODA loops or comparable decision making strategies [5]. Boyd emphasized that by operating in faster decision cycle tempo than an opponent, there the probability of winning is higher, or even better there exist a chance to get inside in an opponent's OODA loop. In other words, defender's cycle should perform with faster tempo than attackers [11,16,19]. Ma et al. pointed out that OODA loop is a robust encounter strategy for randomly changing environments and they also stated that effective OODA cycles generate encounter effectiveness [18]. Dapeng et al. executed OODA loop effectiveness simulation in their research. They stated that in theory, *"more timely and complete the information is more accurate and rapid the estimation, decision-making and action will be"*. That is, the opponent who gain more effective information, such that can be exploited on further attack phases, in certain time period, has more effective OODA cycle. Function table revealed that while gaining increasing amount of effective information, the accuracy of estimation increased as well. Their simulation showed that when opponents have the same tactical and technical performance, an opponent with more effective, or faster, OODA loop will win. An essential conclusion was, that it is more important to prevent the opponent gaining access to effective information than to improve tactical and technical performance [17]. However, Révay et al. stated that instead of faster OODA cycle tempo, Boyd actually meant rapid random changes in an OODA cycle tempo, which will create surprising and ambiguous behaviour thus confusing the opponent [16].

Fusano et al. tested OODA loop robustness with game theory by developing multi-agent combat simulation based on framework derived from game theory model and their multiple simulations conclusion supports Révay et al. lastly mentioned statement, opponent cannot win only by improving the performance based on observations of the other. To win, performance also requires modifications to the rules of orientation [20]. Another game theory research which supports same statement was simulated by Bilar et al., they developed a defence framework in order to identify malicious activities in a network. Their framework was based on fake targets: while the purpose was to detect suspicious behaviour, their intention was also to undermine opponents decision structure [21]. Thus OODA loop can be unified with a game theory in order to optimize own performance and create false understanding of the environment, which causes confusion to the opponent.

5   Deep Analysis of APT Attacks

In this paper, we propose a novel approach for evaluating the dynamics of APT attacks. Due to the complexity of attacks, our method tries to capture the multidimensionality of these attacks that multiple ongoing attack vectors, possibly in different stages, present. Instead of using strict flow controls or pure strategical theories we combine APT attack with OODA loop and Black Swan-theory in order to find the most common factor within these attacks.

5.1   APT Attack and Black Swan Theory

APT attack can be considered as a rare event, thus it can be considered as a Black Swan. Although APT attack numbers are growing, they continue to be rare and for this there are two possible reasons, (i) ongoing APT attacks are not detected or (ii) APT attack detections are not reported publicly. In this section we focus on the first reason, where ongoing Black Swans are not detected. By comparing Black Swan three attributes and APT attacks, we can state (i) APT attack locates outside of ordinary assumption, (ii) APT attack causes high impact to target on purpose and (iii) after discovery there exist a tendency to prove that APT attack is explainable and was predictable.

To detect these sophisticated attacks, we can consider Black Swan phenomenon reasons i-vii listed earlier in section III, *"duration blindness"* and *"the curse of learning"*. When considering a detection method, we must recognize earlier mentioned problems and develop a solution from a new perspective, that is, (i) keep true complexity of an environment, (ii) expand focus also to outside of a "tunnel", (iii) focus on all data, not just clusters, (iv) not reduce data dimensions in order to reduce computational complexity, (v) expand focus from historical events also to unknown events, (vi) develop new tools which does not exclude rare events and (vii) focus on data in original non-processed format. Even though there are known APT attacks that last from a month up to four years, it is not possible to predict with certainty that how long an attack continues. That is, the duration of one APT attack can be less than a day while another one may try to continue campaign as long as possible. Therefore, there does not exist a fixed duration for an attack campaign. To avoid *"the curse of learning"* a mechanism must be considered that learns from shorter time periods thus decreases overlap in information. Another important issue is that one has to know the environment correctly instead of making best guesses and creating countermeasures based on those.

5.2   APT Attack and OODA Loop

APT attack uses multiple simultaneous attack vectors which can be in different phases and different vectors may depend on the output of another vector. Therefore, we should think APT as multiple possibly dependent simultaneous OODA loops inside multiple attack vectors. This scheme is visualized in Fig. 1.

From the figure we can observe how these vectors 1-n have their dependent OODA loops. Timely execution of a vector's loop can depend on the results of earlier loop, the random execution interval of the vector and those loops from other attack vectors that send input data and execution commands. Before continuing to next stage, a vector can be in a halt until input from another vector arrives.

With this presented method, there is no necessity for knowing *"kill chain"* phases, thus we can observe that APT is a complex dynamical problem and we can state that APT a multi-vector multi-stage attack with continuous strategical ongoing campaign.

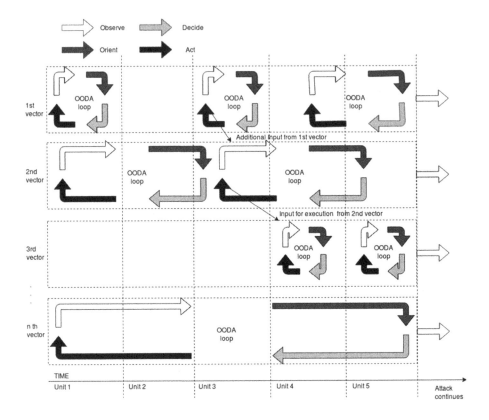

Fig. 1. Multi-vector multi-stage attack

5.3   From Black Swan to Strategic Decision

APT's were considered as a Black swans earlier, however, we can remove the surprise element, or at least reduce it with hypothesis *"we have an ongoing APT attack in a network"*. By being aware of the possibility of attacks, we transfer those to Grey Swans and thus make them somewhat predictable, that is, attacks continue to be unknown unknowns as there is no actual detection available, but it is possible to set detection methods in place.

Considering APT attack behaviour, it can be divided to two types: (i) programmed to fit environment, in other words tailored to known environment and (ii) programmed to learn from environment and modify itself during campaign to fit to the environment. Difference is that in the first option, attacker has to know the environment completely during the development of malware, Stuxnet is one example of this type attack. In the second option, with the help of machine or deep learning an attack learns and modifies itself during the campaign. Both of these has one common functionality, after the execution they start to follow campaign strategy, which can cause behavioural patterns that can be detected.

5.4   Performance Cost

When considering the proposed method from a technical point of view, we can state that it requires computational power, possibly a cluster of GPU's (Graphical Processing Unit) for running Deep Learning algorithms. Other resources include Random Access Memory (RAM) for buffering incoming network flow and also enough of hard disk space for saving outliers in a database.

As mirroring or replicating entire network flows require more network devices and planning, network capacity becomes also one concern. Furthermore, APT attacks are targeted to high value cyber environments thus it might not be beneficial to implement it to lower value environments until the prices of technical devices are low enough. In other words, cost benefit is an important factor when considering implementing the method.

6   Conclusion and Future Works

We can state as a fact that an APT attack uses some sort of communication in a network, otherwise malware would be an isolated malware in a hardware without further purpose defined for an APT. The communication can be, but not limited to, command & control to outside environment all the way to the attackers service. Campaign can also act independently inside a network and in this case, the communication happens between devices. However, communication is based on pre-programmed software logic, or logic through machine learning process from environment, and an APT starts to follow strategic instruction how to proceed with a campaign. Although an attack uses multiple simultaneous vectors with different phases, masquerades communication data, changes execution time intervals randomly, uses horizontal and vertical connections, mimics legitimate traffic, it communicates which leaves traces to network flow. Due to earlier mentioned sophisticated stealth techniques, an APT traffic can be statistically close to a normal traffic but it causes anomalies. However, it might be necessary to look deep into the binary level to find such anomalies. When detecting APT attacks, the focus should be in outliers, even in the tiniest ones, since an impact may cause huge damage to an environment.

We propose an approach to detect anomalies commonly present in APT attacks directly from network flow. When considering APT attacks, or more precisely their random execution intervals and long durations, real-time detection might not be possible nor necessary. Instead, the focus is to drop the detection time from years or months to an acceptable one, that is, days. To detect these complex attacks, there are few issues that must be considered: (i) dimension reduction and overlapping information may cause outliers to vanish and (ii) taking into account earlier detected outliers from historical data. Our earlier research results [22,23] showed that deep learning methods have a high potential to resolve the considerations (i) and (ii). One concern is to locate sufficient amount of good quality network data, for executing training and benchmarking tests.

Based on these observations, we can state also that the most common factor of APT attacks is communication, thus environment has to be developed in a way that we are able to capture complete network flow and analyse it for outliers. Additionally, we can setup decoys, for example honeypots, to create diversion from environment which can cause an attack to expose itself more easily. Furthermore, we have to consider how to detect attacks from legitimate outliers, to avoid false positives and even more serious false negative detections.

As a future works, we continue to study the proposed approach and to work on implementing such APT anomaly detection method that uses the ideas presented in the paper as well as determine which data types support detecting APT attack.

References

1. Brogi, G., Tong, V.V.T.: TerminAPTor: highlighting Advanced Persistent Threats through information flow tracking. In: 2016 8th IFIP International Conference on New Technologies, Mobility and Security (NTMS) (2016). https://doi.org/10.1109/NTMS.2016.7792480
2. Vukalović, J., Delija, D.: Advanced Persistent Threats - detection and defense. In: 2015 38th International Convention on Information and Communication Technology, Electronics and Microelectronics (MIPRO), pp. 1324–1330 (2015). https://doi.org/10.1109/MIPRO.2015.7160480
3. Chandran, S., Hrudya, P., Poornachandran, P.: An efficient classification model for detecting Advanced Persistent Threat. In: 2015 International Conference on Advances in Computing, Communications and Informatics (ICACCI), pp. 2001–2009 (2015). https://doi.org/10.1109/ICACCI.2015.7275911
4. Settanni, G., Shovgenya, Y., Skopik, F., Graf, R., Wurzenberger, M., Fiedler, R.: Acquiring cyber threat intelligence through security information correlation. In: 2017 3rd IEEE International Conference on Cybernetics (CYBCONF) (2017). https://doi.org/10.1109/CYBConf.2017.7985754
5. Hu, P., Li, H., Fu, H., Cansever, D., Mohapatra, P.: Dynamic defense strategy against Advanced Persistent Threat with insiders. In: 2015 IEEE Conference on Computer Communications (INFOCOM), pp. 747–755 (2015). https://doi.org/10.1109/INFOCOM.2015.7218444
6. Ussath, M., Jaeger, D., Cheng, F.: Advanced Persistent Threats: behind the scenes. In: 2016 Annual Conference on Information Science and Systems (CISS) (2016). https://doi.org/10.1109/CISS.2016.7460498
7. Messaoud, B., Guennoun, K., Wahbi, M., Sadik, M.: Advanced Persistent Threat: new analysis driven by life cycle phases and their challenges. In: 2016 International Conference on Advanced Communication Systems and Information Security (ACOSIS) (2016). https://doi.org/10.1109/ACOSIS.2016.7843932
8. Bhatt, P., Yano, E.T., Gustavsson, P.M.: Towards a framework to detect multi-stage Advanced Persistent Threats attacks. In: 2014 IEEE 8th International Symposium on Service Oriented System Engineering, pp. 390–395 (2014). https://doi.org/10.1109/SOSE.2014.53
9. Vance, A.: Flow based analysis of Advanced Persistent Threats detecting targeted attacks in cloud computing. In: 2014 First International Scientific-Practical Conference Problems of Infocommunications Science and Technology, pp. 173–176 (2014). https://doi.org/10.1109/INFOCOMMST.2014.6992342

10. Xiao, L., Xu, D., Mandayam, N.B., Poor, H.V.: Attacker-centric view of a detection game against Advanced Persistent Threats. In: IEEE Transactions on Mobile Computing (2018). https://doi.org/10.1109/TMC.2018.2814052
11. Eidle, D., Ni, S.Y., DeCusatis, C., Sager, A.: Autonomic security for zero trust networks. In: 2017 IEEE 8th Annual Ubiquitous Computing, Electronics and Mobile Communication Conference (UEMCON) (2017). https://doi.org/10.1109/UEMCON.2017.8249053
12. Zhu, Q., Rass, S.: On multi-phase and multi-stage game-theoretic modeling of Advanced Persistent Threats. IEEE Access **6**, 13958–13971 (2018). https://doi.org/10.1109/ACCESS.2018.2814481
13. Taleb, N.: The Black Swan: The Impact of the Highly Improbable. Random House, New York (2007)
14. Zeng, Z., Zio, E.: Modelling unexpected failures with a hierarchical Bayesian model. In: 2017 2nd International Conference on System Reliability and Safety (ICSRS), pp. 135–139 (2017). https://doi.org/10.1109/ICSRS.2017.8272809
15. Arney, C., et al.: Using rare event modeling & networking to build scenarios and forecast the future. In: 2013 IEEE 2nd Network Science Workshop (NSW), pp. 29–64 (2013). https://doi.org/10.1109/NSW.2013.6609191
16. Révay, M., Líška, M.: OODA loop in command & control systems. In: 2017 Communication and Information Technologies (KIT) (2017). https://doi.org/10.23919/KIT.2017.8109463
17. Dapeng, G., Jianming, H., Yuhu, Guoqian, X., Nainiang, Z.: Research on combat SD model based on OODA loop. In: 2015 2nd International Conference on Information Science and Control Engineering, pp. 884–888 (2015). https://doi.org/10.1109/ICISCE.2015.201
18. Ma, L., Zhang, M., Zhou, Z.: The OODA loop robustness evaluation based on OSOS combat network. In: 2014 International Conference on Information and Communications Technologies (ICT 2014) (2014). https://doi.org/10.1049/cp.2014.0583
19. Blasch, E.P., Breton, R., Valin, P., Bosse, E.: User information fusion decision making analysis with the C-OODA model. In: 14th International Conference on Information Fusion (2011)
20. Fusano, A., Sato, H., Namatame, A.: Study of multi-agent based combat simulation for grouped OODA loop. In: SICE Annual Conference 2011, pp. 131–136 (2011)
21. Bilar, D., Saltaformaggio, B.: Using a novel behavioral stimuli-response framework to defend against adversarial cyberspace participants. In: 2011 3rd International Conference on Cyber Conflict (2011)
22. Bodström, T., Hämäläinen, T.: State of the art literature review on network anomaly detection. In: Galinina, O., Andreev, S., Balandin, S., Koucheryavy, Y. (eds.) NEW2AN/ruSMART 2018. LNCS, vol. 11118, pp. 89–101. Springer, Cham (2018). https://doi.org/10.1007/978-3-030-01168-0_9
23. Bodström, T., Hämäläinen, T.: State of the art literature review on network anomaly detection with deep learning. In: Galinina, O., Andreev, S., Balandin, S., Koucheryavy, Y. (eds.) NEW2AN/ruSMART 2018. LNCS, vol. 11118, pp. 64–76. Springer, Cham (2018). https://doi.org/10.1007/978-3-030-01168-0_7

MLSPD - Machine Learning Based Spam and Phishing Detection

Sanjay Kumar$^{(\boxtimes)}$, Azfar Faizan, Ari Viinikainen, and Timo Hamalainen

Faculty of Information Technology, University of Jyvaskyla, Jyvaskyla, Finland
{sanjay.k.kumar,ari.viinikainen,timo.t.hamalainen}@jyu.fi,
azfar-faizan@hotmail.com

Abstract. Spam emails have become a global menace since the rise of the Internet era. In fact, according to an estimate, around 50% of the emails are spam emails. Spam emails as part of a phishing scam can be sent to the masses with the motive to perform information stealing, identity theft, and other malicious actions. The previous studies showed that 91% of the cyber attacks start with the phishing emails, which contain Uniform Resource Locator (URLs). Although these URLs have several characteristics which make them distinguishable from the usual website links, yet a human eye cannot easily notice these URLs. Previous research also showed that traditional systems such as blacklisting/whitelisting of IPs and spam filters could not efficiently detect phishing and spam emails. However, Machine Learning (ML) approaches have shown promising results in combating spamming and phishing attacks. To identify these threats, we used several ML algorithms to train spam and phishing detector. The proposed framework is based on several linguistic and URL based features. Our proposed model can detect the spam and phishing emails with the accuracy of 89.2% and 97.7%, respectively.

Keywords: Artificial Intelligence · Phishing · Spam emails
Supervised learning

1 Introduction

Spam is an unsolicited email usually from someone unknown, who tries to sell something or attract the user with advertisements. According to Statista [1], recent spam emails accounted for 48.16% of the total email traffic on the Internet. Figure 1, shows the current trends of spam emails. Although the primary goal of a spam email is not to steal the personal information, it could be used for different malicious purposes that include installing adware or malware. The spam email could be dangerous when it is part of a phishing scam that could lead to a phishing attack [2].

Phishing emails are used to steal personal information, identity theft or any other malicious purpose. Phishing attacks could be of several types, as they are not limited to emails. Most of the times, a phishing email contains links or

© Springer Nature Switzerland AG 2018
X. Chen et al. (Eds.): CSoNet 2018, LNCS 11280, pp. 510–522, 2018.
https://doi.org/10.1007/978-3-030-04648-4_43

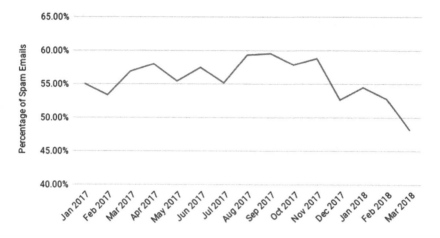

Fig. 1. Percentage of spam emails worldwide with period of time [1]

attachments, whereby, the recipient either has to click on a link or download an attachment for *more information*. The email usually looks like that it came from a reliable organization, for instance, it can be a password changing request from a bank or a note from the company. It is difficult to recognize these emails, and some of the recipients easily fall into the trap. The successful phishing attack can lead to several cybersecurity threats, such as personal information stealing, identity theft, installing malware including ransom-ware or crypto-jacking [3].

According to Darkreading [4], 91% of the cyber-attacks start with phishing emails containing URL. The main reasons that people become a victim of this threat include curiosity, fear, and urgency. The attacker usually set up a fake website such as bank webpage, that a user could easily trust and the URL link is somehow disguised to look legitimate. Volkmer et al. [5] deduced that the unawareness about the URLs is the main reason why people fell into the phishing trap. Most of the times, URL direct to another website and user inadvertently opens it. Even with good user awareness, nearly 30% of the phishing attacks are abstained by them [6]. Quite often, these URLs are found in the emails with the intriguing subject lines. Figure 2 shows the most clicked email subject lines worldwide. It can be seen that the most clicked email subject line is related to the password check, and it shows that the fear is the key factor which compels a user to open the email and click the link.

Filtering of spam emails is getting challenging and sophisticated, as the new methods and tricks have been adopted by the spammers to evade detection. The traditional phishing detection systems are usually based on the IP black-listing or whitelisting. Although these systems produce lower False Positive Rate (FPR), they fail to protect against unseen (zero-day) attacks [6]. In recent years, Artificial Intelligence (AI) became quite popular in the area of cybersecurity. There is a need for a robust AI based attack detection system, which can detect known and unknown spam and phishing threats accurately. To solve this issue, we

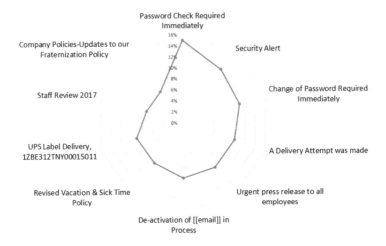

Fig. 2. Top 10 most-clicked general email subject lines globally [7]

propose ML based framework for spam and phishing system. More specifically, we offer a hybrid system which not only detects the spam emails, but also checks phishing URLs to combat phishing attacks. We have used several linguistic and URL based features to build the spam and phishing classifiers. We evaluated the performance for several ML algorithms and selected best two algorithms according to the several performance metrics such as accuracy, training time and True Positive Rate (TPR). Furthermore, we have used AutoWEKA [8] tool to tune and optimize the hyperparameters.

The rest of the paper is organized as follows: In Sect. 2, related work is discussed. Section 3 provides the overview of methods, dataset, and feature used in our experiments. In Sect. 4, we discussed performance metrics used in this study. In Sect. 5, we present the performance evaluation of classifiers. Finally, in Sect. 6, we provide conclusions and discuss future work.

2   Related Work

Spam and phishing detection using the ML methods are attracting research attention, due to their accuracy in detecting known and unknown attacks. In order to build an efficient ML model, proper feature extraction is needed [9]. Adversary usually changes its attack pattern to evade detection, so these ML models and features need to be updated to avoid concept drift [10].

Pan et al. [11] used a Support Vector Machine (SVM) algorithm by applying seven features. Few similar features used in our study are: "URL of Anchor", "Request URL" and "Server form handler". The study showed 84% of accuracy. McGrath et al. [12], performed the comparative analysis of Phishing URLs from several sources. Different features were taken into account during the study such as host-based, page based and lexical features of the URLs.

Xiang et al. [13] proposed CANTINA+ that uses SVM for phishing detection. The model was trained using 15 features from HTML, URL, Document Object Model (DOM) and using third-party services and search engines. The model produced TPR of 92%.

In 2015, Aydin et al. [14] used Naive Bayes (NB) and Sequential Minimal Optimization (SMO) algorithms to detect phishing URLs. Around 133 features were extracted from the URLs. Most of the features were the textual feature and from third party service providers such as "WhoIS". Due to a large number of features, correlation-based feature selection and consistency subset feature selection methods were used to reduce them. The highest accuracy of 95.39% was observed in experiments.

In 2017, Zouina et al. [15] proposed a phishing detection system that uses only six URL based features. Those features include the URL length, the number of hyphens, the number of dots, the presence of numbers or IP in the URL and the similarity index. All these six features are also used in our study. The author claimed the TPR of 95.80%.

In 2018, Jain et al. proposed a phishing detection system based on 14 URL based features. NB and SVM classifiers were used in their study, and they produced around 90% of accuracy [16]. Sahingoza et al. [17] proposed a phishing detection system which uses several Natural Language Processing (NLP) based, word vectors and hybrid features. The most of the NLP-based features used in the study are similar to that of URL based features in several other studies. The hybrid features were the combination of word vectors and NLP features. The highest accuracy of 96.36% was observed using Random Forest (RF).

3   Methodology

We proposed an intelligent ML-based framework to detect spam emails and phishing URLs. By analyzing various linguistic features in the email and the several features in the URL, ML algorithms can predict the spam and phishing emails. Figure 3 shows the proposed framework. The framework consists of classification models for spam and phishing detection, which were trained using two different datasets respectively.

The first dataset, which was used to train spam classifier, was built using the *CSDMC2010 SPAM corpus* [18]. It is one of the email dataset used for data mining competition with ICONIP 2010. The original corpus has around 2949 normal emails and 1378 spam emails. However, we used only 2500 emails to extract the features for generating the dataset. Subsequently, the data set is used to build a spam classification model. The features extracted from these emails are unique, as we used the IBM Watson Tone Analyzer (TA) API [19] to extract different linguistic tones. Three types of tones were detected by TA: Language tone, social tone, and emotional tone. According to TA, people show curious tones which make an impact in their daily communication [19]. Table 1 shows features extracted from this dataset using the TA API. The instances were labeled according to the email type (such as *SPAM* or *Normal*).

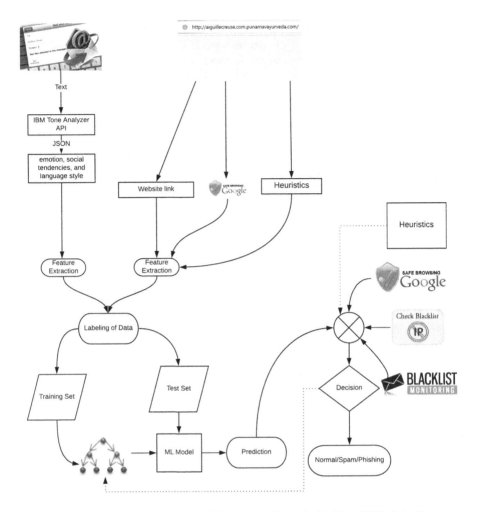

Fig. 3. Machine Learning based Spam emails and phishing URL detection

Another URL feature based dataset [20] was used to train phishing classifier. The dataset was obtained from the UC Irvine (UCI) ML repository
[21]. The dataset has around 11000 instances and 30 attributes, to decide if
it is a phishing website. The dataset has four types of attributes which are
extracted from the URLs, i.e., address bar based features, abnormal based features, HTML/JavaScript-based features and domain-based features [20]. Table 2
shows features used in this dataset, wherein, each feature is made up of the rule.
The complete description of the rules can be found at [22]. For example, the
feature (*URLLength*) is based on the rule that if the URL length is less than 54
characters, then the URL is legitimate. In contrast, if it URL length is greater
than 75 characters, then it is Phishing URL. If the URL length lies between 54

Table 1. Spam dataset feature list extracted by IBM Watson

Emotion tone features		
No.	Feature	Description
1	Anger	Active (Verbal or physical attack). Passive (Feels tension and hostility)
2	Fear	Fear can be a mild caution or extreme phobia
3	Disgust	Strong disapproval
4	Joy	Joy brings sense of inner-peace, commitment and safety
5	Sadness	It indicates a feeling of loss and disadvantage
Language tone features		
No.	Feature	Description
6	Analytical	It indicates person reasoning and analytical attitude about things
7	Tentative	It indicates person's degree of inhibition
Social tone features (*Big Five* personality theory)		
No.	Feature	Description
8	Openess	It shows frankness or lack of secrecy
9	Conscientiousness	Being careful, or vigilant
10	Extraversion	It indicates how social the person is
11	Agreeableness	It shows pro-social forms of behavior
12	Emotionalrange	It is the extent to which emotions are sensitive to the environment

and 75, then it is suspicious. Altogether 30 features based on rules decide to find the hidden patterns to classify phishing URL.

3.1 Working Principle

The model proposed in this study, comprised of two main components: Spam detector and phishing detector. Every email has to be pass through the spam detector, by first extracting the features using IBM Watson TA API and then the trained spam classifier makes the prediction. The system checks if the email contains any URL then several features (as mentioned in Table 2) will be extracted from that URL, before passing it to the trained model for phishing detection. The Algorithm 1, shows the basic working principle. There is also a decision function in our model (see Fig. 3) that decides the output by combining inputs from ML classifiers and other traditional systems. The decision function not only improve the accuracy of the system, but it also determines the retraining time of the ML model. The decision function acted as a black box in this study and considered as the future work.

Table 2. Phishing dataset feature list

Address bar based features		
No.	Feature	Description
1	HavingIPAddress	If the IP address is in the URL
2	URLLength	Long URL to hide suspicious part
3	ShortService	If URL shortening service used (such as TinyURL)
4	HavingAtSymbol	If URL has @ Symbol
5	DoubleSlash	If URL has "//" redirecting
6	PrefixSuffix	Domain seperated by (-) Adding Prefix or Suffix
7	HavingSubDomain	Sub-domain and multi sub-domains represented by dots in the URL
8	SSLFinalState	Certificate assigned with HTTPS (certificate issuer, certificate age)
9	DomainRegisterationLength	Domain registration rength in years
10	Favicon	Graphic image loaded from another domain
11	Port	If server is using any non-standard port
12	HTTPSToken	HTTPS token in the URL

Abnormal based features		
No.	Feature	Description
13	RequestURL	If images, videos, sounds are embedded in the same domain
14	URLOfAnchor	If the website and <a> tags have different domain names.
15	LinksInTags	Percentage of links in tags (<Meta>, <Script> and <Link>)
16	SFH	Server form handler
17	SubmittingToEmail	Submiting information to Email
18	AbnormalURL	Host name in URL (WHOIS database)

HTML and Java Script based features		
No.	Feature	Description
19	Redirect	Website forwarding/redirection
20	OnMouseover	"OnMouseover" event in the code
21	RightClick	Disabling right click by using "event.button" parameter
22	PopUpWidnow	Using pop-up Window
23	IFrame	IFrame redirection

Domain based features		
No.	Feature	Description
24	AgeOfDomain	Age of the domain extracted from WHOIS database
25	DNSRecord	DNS record from WHOIS database
26	Webtraffic	Website traffic by Alexa database (in top 100,000 websites)
27	PageRank	Page rank value
28	GoogleIndex	If webpage has a Google Index
29	LinksPointingToPage	Number of links pointing to page
30	StatisticalReport	Statistical-Report from PhishTank and Stopbadware

Result: Normal/Spam/Phish
if *Incoming Email* **then**
    Send Email to SpamDetector
    if *Email has URL* **then**
        Send URL to PhishDetector;
    end
end
if *User Click Link* **then**
    Send URL to PhishDetector;
end

Algorithm 1. Spam/Phishing detection algorithm

4 Performance Evaluation Metrics

In this section, several performance evaluation metrics used in this study are discussed. For spam/phishing detector, as shown in Table 3, *True Positive (TP)* represents spam/phishing instance classified as *"Spam/Phish"*. *False Positive (FP)* represents normal instance classified as *"Spam/Phish"*. *False Negative (FN)* represents spam/phishing instance classified as *"Normal"*. Finally, *True Negative (TN)* represents normal instance classified as *"Normal"*.

Table 3. Confusion matrix for spam/phishing detector

		Predicted	
		Spam/phish	Normal
Actual	Spam/phish	*True Positive*	*False Negative*
	Normal	*False Positive*	*True Negative*

Several metrics used for performance evaluation and comparison of results include TPR, FPR, True Negative Rate (TNR), False Negative Rate (FNR), Accuracy, Precision, F1 Measure and Area under ROC (AUC). All of these metrics have their importance in performance evaluation, and the equations for these metrics are mentioned below.

$$TPR = \frac{TP}{TP + FN} \tag{1}$$

$$FPR = \frac{FP}{FP + TN} \tag{2}$$

$$TNR = \frac{TN}{TN + FP} \tag{3}$$

$$FNR = \frac{FN}{TP + FN} \tag{4}$$

$$Accuracy = \frac{TP + TN}{TP + FP + TN + FN} \tag{5}$$

$$F1Measure = \frac{2 * (TPR * Precision)}{TPR + Precision} = \frac{2TP}{2TP + FP + FN} \tag{6}$$

5   Experiments and Results

We have performed several experiments using several ML algorithms and chose the best two algorithms for this study: RF and Multilayer Perceptron (MLP). The training set were used for training and validation of the classifiers, as WEKA [23] has an internal mechanism for validation. Therefore, there was no need for the separate validation set. The performance evaluation of the spam detector and the phishing detector was done separately using unseen test sets. In the end, AutoWEKA [8] was used to search for the best algorithm and tuned hyperparameters for the concerned dataset. AutoWEKA evaluated several ML algorithms with different hyperparameter settings automatically, and it used Bayesian optimization to find a strong instantiation for the given dataset.

5.1   Performance Evaluation of SPAM Detector

The dataset used to train SPAM detector has 2000 instances. Out of which 50% of the instances were extracted from the spam emails. The test set used to evaluate the performance of the classifier was based on 500 instances, wherein, 50% of the instances were from spam emails.

Table 4. Experiment 1: Performance evaluation of spam detector using test dataset

ML algorithm	TPR	FPR	TNR	FNR	Accuracy	F1 Measure	Precision	AUC
RF classifier	0.942	0.160	0.840	0.058	0.892	0.900	0.862	0.968
MLP classifier	0.922	0.184	0.816	0.078	0.871	0.880	0.841	0.937
AutoWEKA (SMO)	0.942	0.168	0.832	0.058	0.888	0.897	0.856	0.943

Table 4 shows the performance evaluation of SPAM detector. The best TPR was from the RF and the AutoWeka configuration. AutoWEKA chose Sequential Minimal Optimization (SMO) algorithm as the best fit for this dataset. However, RF performed better than SMO concerning FPR. Also, the accuracy and AUC measure were better in RF. RF produced the best result on the test data for default parameters. Figure 4 shows the ranking of the features using the RF algorithm. The higher value shows the importance of the feature in the prediction.

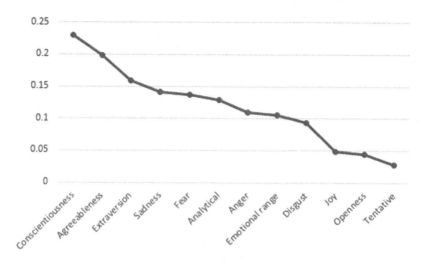

Fig. 4. Attribute ranking for the spam detector

5.2 Performance Evaluation of Phishing URL Detector

The dataset used to train Phishing detector has 8873 instances. Out of which 3050 instances were extracted from the phishing URLs, and the remaining ones were from the normal URLs. The test set used to evaluate the performance of the classifier was based on 2182 instances. The test dataset contains 1190 normal instances and remaining ones were phishing instances.

Table 5. Experiment 2: Performance evaluation of phishing detector using test dataset

ML algorithm	TPR	FPR	TNR	FNR	Accuracy	F1 Measure	Precision	AUC
RF classifier	0.967	0.014	0.986	0.033	0.977	0.975	0.983	0.997
MLP classifier	0.959	0.074	0.926	0.041	0.941	0.936	0.915	0.989
AutoWEKA	0.941	0.050	0.950	0.059	0.946	0.941	0.941	0.990

The Table 5 shows the performance of phishing detector. The RF algorithm produced the best result in terms of TPR, FPR, Accuracy, and AUC. AutoWEKA also chose RF using Bayesian optimization, but the selected hyperparameters were different from the default setting of RF. Figure 5, shows the ranking of the features used by phishing detector. The attributes are arranged according to their significance in identifying the phishing URLS.

5.3 Comparison of Results

We have also compared our model with several other works mentioned in Table 6 and found that our model has produced better results. We analyzed several

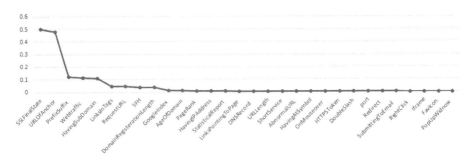

Fig. 5. Attribute ranking for the phishing detector.

models from 2006 to 2018. It can be observed that the accuracy of the models has been increased with the advent of time. We have also observed that SVM, SMO and RF are popular algorithms in phishing and spam detection.

Table 6. Comparison of results

Comparison of results of phishing URL detection

Author	ML algorithm	TPR	FPR	Accuracy	F1 Measure	Precision
Pan et al. [11]	SVM	0.882	0.290	0.836	0.888	0.895
Aydin et al. [14]	SMO	0.954	0.046	0.954	0.954	0.954
Zouina et al. [15]	SVM	0.958	-	-	-	-
Jain et al. [16]	SVM	-	-	0.900	-	-
Sahingoza et al. [17]	RF	-	-	0.964	0.964	-
MLSPD	RF	0.967	0.014	0.977	0.975	0.983

6   Conclusion

Phishing attacks are widespread nowadays, and it is getting challenging to detect them. ML and AI are becoming popular in spam and phishing detection, as the sophistication of threats is increasing. In this study, we proposed and evaluated ML-based spam and phishing detection system. The proposed model used several linguistic features from emails and URL based features to find hidden patterns in order to identify spam and phishing attacks. We evaluated several ML algorithms and RF produced the best accuracy of up to 97.7%. We have also analyzed the effect of various features and their importance in the prediction. Furthermore, we have compared our model with the work of several researchers in the field and found that ML-based phishing detection systems are getting efficient with the advent of time. But ML models need proper hyperparameter tuning and feature selection to predict efficiently on unseen data. Also, there is a need to retrain the model frequently to avoid concept drift situation. Our future work will be based on the hybrid model, which not only predict these threats more accurately and efficiently but also deal with concept drift situation. Moreover, new features will be added and feature reduction techniques will be used to improve the system.

References

1. Statista: Spam share of global email traffic 2014–2018. Technical report. https://www.statista.com/statistics/420391/spam-email-traffic-share. Accessed 1 Sept 2018
2. Kaspersky: What is spam and a phishing scam. Technical report. https://www.kaspersky.com/resource-center/threats/spam-phishing. Accessed 1 Sept 2018
3. CSO: What is cryptojacking? How to prevent, detect, and recover from it. Technical report. https://www.csoonline.com/article/3253572/internet/what-is-cryptojacking-how-to-prevent-detect-and-recover-from-it.html. Accessed 1 Sept 2018
4. Darkreading: 91% of cyberattacks start with a phishing email. Technical report. https://www.darkreading.com/endpoint/91-of-cyberattacks-start-with-a-phishing-email/. Accessed 1 Sept 2018
5. Volkamer, M., Renaud, K., Reinheimer, B., Kunz, A.: User experiences of TOR-PEDO: TOoltip-poweRED Phishing Email DetectiOn. Comput. Secur. **71**, 100–113 (2017)
6. Sheng, S., Holbrook, M., Kumaraguru, P., Cranor, L.F., Downs, J.: Who falls for phish?: a demographic analysis of phishing susceptibility and effectiveness of interventions. In: Proceedings of the SIGCHI Conference on Human Factors in Computing Systems, pp. 373–382. ACM (2010)
7. KnowBe4: Q2 2018 top-clicked phishing report. Technical report. https://www.knowbe4.com/press/knowbe4-releases-q2-2018-top-clicked-phishing-report. Accessed 1 Sept 2018
8. Kotthoff, L., Thornton, C., Hoos, H.H., Hutter, F., Leyton-Brown, K.: Auto-WEKA 2.0: automatic model selection and hyperparameter optimization in WEKA. J. Mach. Learn. Res. **18**(1), 826–830 (2017)
9. Kumar, S., Viinikainen, A., Hamalainen, T.: Machine learning classification model for network based intrusion detection system. In: Proceedings of the 11th International Conference for Internet Technology and Secured Transactions (ICITST), pp. 242–249, December 2016
10. Kumar, S., Viinikainen, A., Hamalainen, T.: A network-based framework for mobile threat detection. In: Proceedings of the 1st International Conference on Data Intelligence and Security (ICDIS), pp. 227–233, April 2018
11. Pan, Y., Ding, X.: Anomaly based web phishing page detection. In: Proceedings of the 22nd Annual Computer Security Applications Conference (ACSAC 2006), pp. 381–392, December 2006
12. McGrath, D.K., Gupta, M.: Behind phishing: an examination of phisher modi operandi. In Proceedings of the USENIX Workshop on Large-Scale Exploits and Emergent Threats (LEET) (2008)
13. Xiang, G., Hong, J., Rose, C.P., Cranor, L.: CANTINA+: a feature-rich machine learning framework for detecting phishing web sites. ACM Trans. Inf. Syst. Secur. (TISSEC) **14**(2), 21 (2011)
14. Aydin, M., Baykal, N.: Feature extraction and classification phishing websites based on URL. In: Proceedings of the IEEE Conference on Communications and Network Security (CNS), pp. 769–770, September 2015

15. Zouina, M., Outtaj, B.: A novel lightweight url phishing detection system using svm and similarity index. Hum. Centric Comput. Inf. Sci. **7**(1), 17 (2017)

16. Jain, A.K., Gupta, B.B.: PHISH-SAFE: URL features-based phishing detection system using machine learning. In: Bokhari, M.U., Agrawal, N., Saini, D. (eds.) Cyber Security. AISC, vol. 729, pp. 467–474. Springer, Singapore (2018). https://doi.org/10.1007/978-981-10-8536-9_44

17. Sahingoz, O.K., Buber, E., Demir, O., Diri, B.: Machine learning based phishing detection from URLs. Expert Syst. Appl. **117**, 345–357 (2018)

18. CSMINING CSDMC2010 SPAM corpus (2010, s.e.d., csdmc2010 and s. corpus). http://csmining.org/index.php/spam-mail-datasets.html. Accessed 1 May 2018

19. IBM: Watson tone analyzer. https://www.ibm.com/watson/services/tone-analyzer. Accessed 20 Aug 2018

20. Mohammad, R.M., Thabtah, F., McCluskey, L.: An assessment of features related to phishing websites using an automated technique. In: Proceedings of the International Conference for Internet Technology and Secured Transactions, pp. 492–497, December 2012

21. Dheeru, D., Karra Taniskidou, E.: UCI machine learning repository (2017). http://archive.ics.uci.edu/ml

22. Mohammad, R.M., Thabtah, F., McCluskey, L.: Phishing websites features. http://eprints.hud.ac.uk/id/eprint/24330/6/MohammadPhishing14July2015.pdf

23. Hall, M., Frank, E., Holmes, G., Pfahringer, B., Reutemann, P., Witten, I.H.: The weka data mining software: an update. ACM SIGKDD Explor. Newsl. **11**(1), 10–18 (2009)

Smart Crowdsourcing Based Content Review System (SCCRS): An Approach to Improve Trustworthiness of Online Contents

Kishor Datta Gupta[✉], Dipankar Dasgupta, and Sajib Sen

Department of Computer Science, University of Memphis, Memphis, USA
{kgupta1,ddasgupta,ssen4}@memphis.edu

Abstract. Online media is now a significant carrier for quicker and ubiquitous diffusion of information. Any user in social media can post contents, provide news blogs, and engage in debate or opinion nowadays. Most of the posted pieces of information on social media are useful while some are fallacious and insulting to others. Keeping the promise of freedom of speech and simultaneously no tolerance against hate speech often becomes a challenge for the hosting services. Some automated tools were developed for content filtering in industries. Also, companies are hiring specialized reviewers for accurate and unbiased reporting. However, these approaches are not achieving the goal as expected, on the other hand, new strategies are being adopted to tweak the automated systems. To face the situation, we proposed a smart crowdsourcing based content review technique to provide trustworthy and unbiased reviews for online shared contents. In this techniques, we designed an intelligent self-learned crowdsourcing strategy to select an appropriate set of reviewers efficiently which ensures reviewers' diversity, availability, quality, and familiarity with the news topic. To evaluate our proposed method, we developed a mobile app similar to popular social media (e.g., Facebook).

Keywords: Social network security and privacy · Big data analysis
Fake news · Crowd source · Social review system

1 Introduction

Deceptive news spreads through traditional news media or online social media, is a damaging publicity [1]. These news sources are composed and dispersed with the aim to cheat, keeping in mind the ultimate goal to harm an organization, element, or individual.

Deliberately altered news items are not as apparent as parody or mockery which is created to amuse, as opposed to deceiving its audience. Misleading news frequently utilizes eye-catching features or entirely manufactured news stories to expand readership, web-based sharing and Internet click income. This biased

© Springer Nature Switzerland AG 2018
X. Chen et al. (Eds.): CSoNet 2018, LNCS 11280, pp. 523–535, 2018.
https://doi.org/10.1007/978-3-030-04648-4_44

news additionally undermines the scope of genuine media and makes it more troublesome for writers to cover unique news stories [2]. Simple access to online notice income expanded political polarization, and the ubiquity of web-based social networking, principally the Facebook News Feed, have all been fascinated in the spread of false news [3,4], which have come to provide competition for legitimate news stories. Given the simplicity with which false news can be made and dispersed via web-based networking media stages [5], joined with our expanding propensity to expand news utilizing online networking [6], it is likely that we are being presented false news stories with substantially more prominent recurrence than before. An investigation of the best-performing news articles in the months paving the way to the election uncovered that the best deceptive news articles beat the best genuine news articles on Facebook (concerning likes, shares, and comments) [7]. One case is surprisingly successful, utterly deceitful site "Ending the Fed. It oversaw four of the ten main false election stories distinguished in the analysis, which were received nearly 180,000 more Facebook engagements than major news outlets [8]. Even though it is foggy to what degree false news affected the result of the presidential election [9], there is no doubt that many individuals were tricked by altogether manufactured (and frequently very whimsical) fake news stories C including, for instance, high-positioning government authorities, such as, Pakistan's defense minister [10]. Moreover, damaging elements amid Hurricane Sandy (2012) spread rumors and false pictures in real time [11,12], which went greatly viral on online web-based social networking and caused frenzy and disarray among the general population affected by the hurricane. A recently published article in the Los Angeles Times has shown how fake news in the previous century affected a large number of people in history whereas journalist earned much popularity of their paper through this fake news. Being moved by the adversary of false news, recently CEO of Facebook announced to fight against fake news to maintain meaningful interactions between members of its community. So, fighting against lousy content and misinformation in social media is now a global need.

2   Research Background

Content contamination has been seen in different applications, including email [13], web indexes [14], and blogs [15]. In this manner, various recognition and battling techniques have also been proposed. A couple of different techniques depending on image processing algorithms to identify spam in picture-based e-mails introduced in [16]. A classification model to distinguish fake images from real images of Hurricane Sandy presented in [17]. Authors in their work obtained 97%accuracy in predicting fake images from real. Corvey et al. [18] provided a crucial conclusion that during emergency situations users employ a specific vocabulary to convey tactical information on Twitter. Castillo et al. [19] achieved 70–80% accuracy using $J48$ decision tree classification algorithms to analyze twitter post. Authors in their work broke down the utilization of automated ranking strategies to quantify believability of data on Twitter for any given subject.

Canini *et al.* [20] demonstrated that significant parts of wellsprings of data are obscure and have low Twitter notoriety (fewer numbers of devotees) in breaking down tweets posted during the terrorist bomb blasts in Mumbai (India, 2011). The authors in their follow-up study [21] applied machine learning algorithms (*SVM* Rank) and information retrieval techniques (relevance feedback) to assess the credibility of content on Twitter. Donovan *et al.* [22] concentrated their work on discovering markers of the validity of tweets post, amid various circumstances (8 isolated occasion tweets). Their outcomes demonstrated that the best pointers of believability were URLs notices, re-tweets, and tweet lengths. Latest work on the fake news has recently been done by some college students at Yale University, developing a browser extension, which alerts users regarding fake or biased news and helps them towards more balanced coverage [23]. As their extension provides alternative news on other viewpoints based on logical consistency only, it is highly possible to have true negative and false positive news. So, to ensure the published news quality on social media a system of expert reviewers set need to be established. Based on the motivation we proposed a crowdsourcing approach for reviewers to validate news before posting. Three different line of research has already been done related to the above-stated review system. These include: content based, source based and review based.

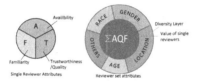

Fig. 1. Reviewers Attributes for an individual and as a reviewer set

The problem of content-based systems is that Natural Language Processing (NLP) and Machine Learning (ML) are still struggling to detect troll or sarcasm news with reasonable accuracy. Source base techniques are also impractical as its suffer from cold start problem. So, reviewer based systems are now being used due to its usability and better performance as well as its ability to face cold start problem. There are three types of reviewers based reporting system currently known. They are review content before publishing, review content after publishing, and review content only after get reported. In the beginning, most organizations used to practice single content reviewer policy. The main benefit is that it is faster than other processes. However, the problem is that the system becomes halt if a reviewer remains absent. Also, the question could come who will review the reviewer? A single reviewer may not know all relevant topics with that news item. We can quickly figure out that a single reviewer may also lack the necessary skill to review the news item. Maybe he knows some relevant topics well, but not all the content of the news. So, he may miss something very trivial which another reviewer might figure out without any effort. So, it is always better to have more than one reviewer to review news content. For example, one person may be knowledgeable about sports, and another person may be knowledgeable about medicine. If a news item comes out with the headline "Dope tests for football players are not reliable." The person who only knows football is not enough. We also need the person with medical knowledge too. For the above reason, the multiple reviewer concepts have been introduced. The main advantage of this concept is that if one of them is absent, the process can still process. The chance of missing any flaw in the news is little, as multiple people are reviewing with different knowledge sets. However, multiple review formats also have some issues. We have to decide how many reviewers are needed to review a news item. Will that number be static for a system or will this number be changing adaptively according to the news content? Another problem is how the reviewers will agree to accept the result of their review. Which way the reviewers will follow to agree to a single decision. How the news provider also responds to multiple reviewers concerns in this system. Also, all the reviewers may not have the same level of review power, as their skill and familiarity with the news may vary in different scales. The process to prioritize this issue is still a concern for multiple reviewer systems.

3   Our Proposed System

Based on the above discussion, it is obvious that we need to have a tool which can address the complex issues in multi reviewer systems. In short, this tool needs to maintain issues like as reviewers can not abuse the system. Their sarcastic reviews or bias reviews need to be disregarded. Then, reviewers will be weighted based on their quality. Diversity of reviewers need to be ensured. System should be able to find the reviewers who are available, have required skills and are familiarity with the news topic. Finally, system should possess a consensus model to reach a decision from a set of reviewers.

To address the above-stated requirements in a multiple reviewer news review system, we proposed a new tool for smooth and faster review process affirming

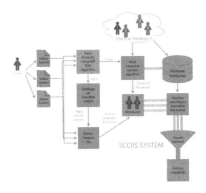

Fig. 2. SCCRS block diagram

the news quality and high-security level. We named this new tool as "SCCRS: Smart Crowd sourcing-based Content Review System." Here, we developed a content review system for online news/reports/messages and evaluated it with public data available. An intelligent algorithm has been used to find a reviewer set which satisfies [Availability, Quality, and Familiarity] AQF constrains for reviewer selection. We also used Multi-Objective Genetic Algorithm ($MOGA$) to select a diverse set of reviewers dynamically with optimal trustworthiness on news topics. At first, reviewers' profile will be built over a period through interactions and their feedback on the performance on classified documents. After that, each reviewer will also be evaluated independently based on their past performance, relevant knowledge, and their biases on news topics or content. In social media, users like to be involved through information sharing and posting comments. Using this vast source of the user base to review shared or posted content also increases their engagement in social media. In our method, we used weight-based reviewer's feedback system to reach consensus about reviews to ensure quality reports, so that false news does not get viral as it will go through multi-level crowd review, verification, and evaluation process. Figure 2 shows different components of the proposed Smart Crowd sourcing-based Content Review system (SCCRS).

4 Methodology: SCCRS

4.1 Formulation of The Methodology

Given a collection of news $\{N_j\}_{j\epsilon z+}$ in a news organization/social media or other content management system, having varying degrees of topics sensitivity $\{S_m\}_{m\epsilon z+}$ that require $\{P_m\}_{m\epsilon z+}$ number of reviewers to review it, such that if sensitivity S_m is higher than S_n then $P_m > P_n$, where reviewers activities are governed by their AQF [Availability, Quality and Familiarity] properties for accessing an news items. Assume, AQF pass value is C_{aqf} and the trustworthiness of the news represented by C_{news}, where $0.0 < C_{aqf} < 0.1$ and $0.01 < C_{news} < 0.99$. Assume, A_k, Q_k, and F_k represent each property of a reviewers, where $0.0 < k < 1.0$. So, a reviewer R_i, R_j to qualify, we need $k_r >= C_{aqf}$, where $K = \sqrt{\frac{\sum(K_j - K)^2}{N-1}}$. Let, $T = \{T_i\}_{i\epsilon z+}$ be the set of different topics, T_{wj} is the weight of topics in each news item, R_{wj} is the weight of reviewers in each news item. We need to find a few sets of R_s where R_s satisfies C_{aqf} constraints and can generate C_{news} with respect to T_{wj}. After we prepare the reviewer set we will try to improve the diversity factors. If the diversity factors are d_1, d_2, d_3 and their acceptable diversity factor values are d_{t1}, d_{t2}, d_{t3}, total diversity factor and rate will be $t_d = \sum_{n=1}^n d_{t_n}$ and $t_{dtr} = \frac{t_d}{t_n}$. Now, we have to make sure our selected set of reviewers among other sets has better td_{tr} value.

4.2   Methodology of SCCRS

In SCCRS, content are categorized in different categories. Each category is denoted as topics t_1, t_2, t_3. We also have a reviewer database where their past works on different topics and their session availability data are also present. From this data, we calculate each reviewer AQF value, and generate different sets of reviewers. After that, we calculate diversity factors in this sets. When we obtain an appropriate reviewer set, we provide them some already classified content and our target content. Based on their performance in already classified content, we accept their review in non-classified content.

Prepare Reviewer Data Set Model. Our first step is generating a set of reviewer modes keeping AQF properties. To generate this AQF value for each reviewer, we need to train our model with our test data which we gathered from the existing systems previous records and data sets. To avoid the cold-start problem, initially we will set default values as $A_{kj} = Q_{kj} = F_{kj} = 0.5$. Now, using training data or any new data we will determine value for A_k. Assume, total reviewers and total news as N_r and N_n.

Average logged in Rate for last N_x number news in N_n, $L_{ravg} = \sum_{i=0}^{n} \frac{L_r}{N_r}$.

Average Daily Retention rate for N_x number news in N_n, $D_{ravg} = \sum_{i=0}^{n} \frac{D_r}{N_r}$.

Average Response Rate for N_x number news in N_n, $R_{eavg} = \sum_{i=0}^{n} \frac{Re_r}{N_r}$.

Average Daily Session Rate for N_x number news in N_n, $S_{eavg} = \sum_{i=0}^{n} \frac{Se_r}{N_r}$.

Average Daily Session Length Rate for N_x number news in N_n, $Sl_{ravg} = \sum_{i=0}^{n} \frac{Sl_r}{N_r}$.

Average Wait rate for N_x number news in N_n, $Wt_{ravg} = \sum_{i=0}^{n} \frac{Wte_r}{N_n}$.

Now for each reviewer R_j to get N_x number of news in N_n time, where logged in rate $R_{jL} = \frac{L_{ravg}}{L_{rj}}$, daily retention rate $R_{jDr} = \frac{D_{ravg}}{D_{rj}}$, response rate $R_{jRer} = \frac{Re_{ravg}}{Re_{rj}}$, daily session rate $R_{jSer} = \frac{Se_{ravg}}{Se_{rj}}$, daily session length rate $R_{jSlra} = \frac{Sl_{ravg}}{Sl_{rj}}$, and wait rate $R_{jwt} = \frac{Wt_{ravg}}{Wte_{rj}}$. So, for R_j,

$$
A_{kj} = \frac{C_{x1} * R_{jL} + C_{x2} * R_{jDr} + C_{x3} * R_{jRer} + C_{x4} * R_{jSer}}{\sum_{c_x=1}^{6} c_x^2}
$$
$$
+ \frac{C_{x5l} * R_{jSlra} + C_{x6} * R_{jwt}}{\sum_{c_x=1}^{6} c_x^2}
\tag{1}
$$

where C_{xi} defined as $C_{x1} =$ weight value for logged in rate, $C_{x2} =$ weight value for daily retention rate, $C_{x3} =$ weight value for response rate, $C_{x4} =$ weight value for daily session rate, $C_{x5} =$ weight value for daily session length rate, $C_6 =$ weight value for wait rate. Now, to determine Q_k we will test reviewer with already determined news content. We also define the value of a Q_k using three metrics: Detection Rate (DR), False Alarm Rate (FAR), Testing Time (T_{rj}), where, DR $= \frac{TP}{TP+FN}$, FAR $= \frac{FP}{FP+TN}$, $T_{rj} = \frac{C_{er} * R_{jRer} + C_{wt} * R_{jwt}}{C_{er}^2 + C_{wt}^2}$. Now, for each reviewer

R_j we calculate

$$Q_{kj} = \frac{C_{DR} * DR + C_{FAR} * FAR + C_{trj} * T_{rj}}{C_{DR} + C_{FAR} + C_{trj}} \tag{2}$$

To calculate familiarity F_{kj} we have each topic weight in each news item T_{wi}, based on reviewers comment on existing topic news review. For each topic,

$$F_{kj} = \sum_{j=0}^{n} \frac{Q_{kjtw} * CT_W}{CT_W^2} \tag{3}$$

where Q_{kjtwi} defined as $Q_{kjtwi} = \frac{C_{DR} * DR_{twj} + C_{FAR} * FAR_{twj} + C_{trj} * T_{rjtwi}}{C_{DR}^2 + C_{FAR}^2 + C_{trj}^2}$. Now we will set the values of reviewer for a given topic as

$$T_{wi} R_{jAOF} = K_{rj} = K = \sqrt{\frac{\sum (K_j - K)^2}{N - 1}} \tag{4}$$

Algorithm: Prepare reviewer data set model:

1. Reviewer dataset train (Training Data T_d, Reviewer R_n, Constraint list C)
2. Calculate T_{avg} for all datatype
3. For each Reviewer R_j in R_n
4.   Calculate R_a with T_{avg} & C
5.   Calculate R_f with T_{avg} & C
6.   Calculate R_q with T_{avg} & C
7.   Calculate R_{afq}
8.   Add R_j in Reviewer dataset
9. Return Reviewer dataset

Prepare Diverse Set of Reviewers. The first step is to calculate the diversity factors. There are several methods to calculate diversity factors in a group. One of the known methods is using the *Gini coefficient*. This measures the inequality among values. There is also an index known as *Gini-Simpson* index $g_i = \sum_{i=1}^{n} p_i^2$, where $1 - \lambda = 1 - g_i = 1 - \frac{1}{2_D}$. Let, denote feature topic as F and sensitivity weight of each feature as Fs_w. We used the*Gini-Simpson* index for each of the diversity factors and calculated the diversity of each reviewer sets, and started a Multi-Objective Genetic Algorithm model ($MOGA$).

Prepare the Review Content List. After getting a reported content, for example X, and its category topic T_x, we will generate: X_1 number of True-positive T_x contents, X_2 number of False-positive T_x contents, X_3 number of True-negative T_x contents, X_4 number of False-positive T_x contents from database. Now, we will provide the reviewer a web form and will ask to review the total $t = \sum_{i=1}^{4} x_i + x$ number of reviews. We will calculate the weight of a single reviewer reviews from the performance of reviewing classified contents. If the reviewer fails to classify a M number of reviews, where $M < \frac{t}{k}$ and $k = $ value of reviewer performance threshold, we will reject this reviewer.

Fig. 3. User data sample

Fig. 4. Each review set attributes in demo application

5   Implementation

A steady state heuristic Multi-Objective Genetic Algorithm model has been used in SCCRS. We used visual studio $c\#$ to make our demo application. First, we picked a reviewer database of 9999 reviewers, which already have prior data of availability and familiarity and quality values. We normalize each data between 1 to 100 using equation $X_i = \frac{X_i - min_x}{max_x - min_x}$. Then, we randomly selected n number of reviewer sets with each consist of a k number of reviewers, where k is our expected number of reviewers for the content. So total number of reviewer is $n * k$. We consider this reviewer as our individual bit in chromosome and each reviewer set as a chromosome for our genetic algorithm and k is our initial population. We call this method as heuristic based because we select the best $n * k$ reviewers based on their harmonic mean of AQF values. Afterward, we calculated the diversity factors for age, gender, and race for each reviewer set using the equation $D_i = \frac{f(min_d) * d_{groupcount}}{100}$. After obtaining diversity, we calculate user harmonic mean to calculate total fitness using diversity, AQF values, and special weights. We also used the tournament selection technique and three-point crossover for the genetic algorithm. After each iteration diversity ratio increases while AQF values were consistent. When our best reviewer sets started to converge, we chose the reviewer sets. We conducted a study with a group of twenty reviewers in the system. We used a web admin panel to post news. The automated system extracted the topic and sent it to all reviewers. Based on the first fifty news review results, we trained our reviewer dataset and started selecting reviewer sets with our proposed genetic algorithm. We made a mobile app which has features like popular social media (e.g., Facebook), so reviewers got a user-friendly interface with which they were already familiar. We also provided points to the user as rewards and showed the best reviewer ranking list to give motivation to the reviewers. We then posted fifty more news items and calculated the reviewers feedback scores. For simplicity, we restricted the topics to three. Based on that we flagged the news as fake or normal. Later, we manually evaluated the results and determined the success rate. The purpose of using $NS3$ simulator in our implementation is to measure the delay times in sending and receiving the feedback from the reviewer. In Fig. 5, the $NS3$ simulation has been shown. A network with ten nodes had been categorized as requester, approver and control node by the color. Red as the requester, green for approver and yellow for control node. According to the procedure, the requester sends a packet to the selected approver via a router. In the meantime, this packet is checked by the control node and delivers the packet to its selected reviewer. After reviewing, the reviewer sends the packet back to the control node. The control node, through its internal ranking algorithm, provides an output, which is transmitted via router again. NetAnim has been used to see the $NS3$ simulation result. Ten nodes with different IP and MAC addresses in Fig. 5 indicates the different system configurations in the real world. Based on the application, two packets from the request side transmit to two different approvers.

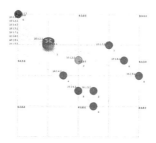

Fig. 5. Review process time in $NS3$ simulation (Color figure online)

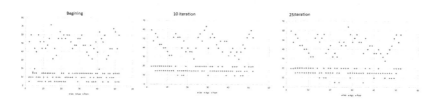

Fig. 6. Change of diversity elements over GA progress for each set

Fig. 7. Change of reviewer individual elements over GA progress for each set

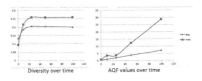

Fig. 8. Change of diversity and AQF values over GA progress

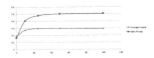

Fig. 9. Change of fitness over GA progress

6   Empirical Result and Performance Analysis

We compare our results of each reviewer sets over the generation time. If we closely look in Fig. 6 we will see gender, age and race factors are increasing over time after twenty-five iterations and almost all age and rage diversity grows up to ten to twenty. It is noticeable that in gender diversity it does not show any improvement. As from the beginning it was the best score. Now, if we see in Fig. 7 we will see the familiarity, availability, and quality factors are increasing over time after fifty iterations. It goes from 100 to 2000 level, and after 100 iterations it is close to 4000. Now, if we compare the fitness and diversity factor over generation time and their harmonic mean which is out of fitness value, we will see after a few iteration AQF values started to get higher, but as the diversity score increased slowly fitness value remained in lower range. It is visually more clear in Figs. 8 and 9. In Fig. 8 we can see convergence with time, where after an initial boost up its progress gets slow. The generation time for getting a reviewer set decreases as the system gets more and more news items, but it reaches a saturation point if the new topics not introduced in the system before. In the case of adding new topics, generation time will increase, and it will again decrease to a saturation point, and after that, it will remain more or less constant. In the beginning, the performance rate was high due to its measuring rate from training data which was one. After it had progressed with test data, rates fell sharply, but after a while, it started to improve its performance again.

The benefit of applying a *AQF* model is overwhelming. As we took the last N time availability, the system was getting a better available review set, and the chance of an inactive reviewer was getting lower by time. Using the quality properties for reviewers gave us an extra edge to select reviewers who have more success and failure rates than others. We can use failure rates as negative weights and success rates as positive weights to determine the validity of a news item. In this way, we will not lose the big portion of reviewers due to biases and less quality. Instead, we are using biased reviewers to determine news items which have the probability to be biased or not.

7   Conclusion and Future Work

In this paper, we proposed a smart crowd-sourcing approach to ensure the trustworthiness of news content providing unbiased reviews by appropriate reviewers. Our method has the flexibility to integrate and implement into many large and complex systems such as social media (e.g., Facebook, YouTube), health care system, code control tools, app review process, paper reviews system, etc. Uses of ML approach with this method provides an extra layer of security and integrity. Moreover, based on the weight-based calculation for all reviewersto reach consensus on a news topic provided us a platform to normalize the small biases of the reviewer as well as ensured reviewers' availability. In response to trolls/fake reviews, our method detects biased reviewers first and uses their property to detect news biases. Besides, uses of the genetic algorithm also helped the method to provide the best possible reviewer set. One application of our method can be in the medical field. For example, analyzing a patients report requires doctors who have the required necessary skills as well as familiarity with the report. So our method can provide the best possible set of doctors with the patients report to review with any human intervention, which concurrently makes it also *HIPPA* compliant. In future, we have a plan to apply a reward-based rating system which will be consistent with reviewer performances and will provide them a rating creating competition to make them more active. For the reward based system, we have a plan to go with the crypto currency-based reward system. In the proof of stake concept, we can reward the active user with more coins than another user. As decentralization will also help the full system to be faster, so a blockchain-based reward system will be a good incentive for the reviewers and making the system more robust.

References

1. Leonhardt, D., Thompson, S.A.: Trump's lies. New York Times, June 2017. https://www.nytimes.com/interactive/2017/06/23/opinion/trumps-lies.html. Accessed 30 Sept 2018
2. Carlos, M.: Millonario negocio fake news. Univision Noticias (2017). https://www.univision.com/noticias/america-latina/el-millonario-negocio-detras-de-los-sitios-de-fake-news-en-mexico. Accessed 30 Sept 2018

3. Hunt, E.: What is fake news? How to spot it and what you can do to stop it. The Guardian, January 2017. https://www.theguardian.com/media/2016/dec/18/what-is-fake-news-pizzagate. Accessed 30 Sept 2018

4. Woolf, N.: How to solve Facebook's fake news problem: experts pitch their ideas. The Guardian, January 2017. https://www.theguardian.com/technology/2016/nov/29/facebook-fake-news-problem-experts-pitch-ideas-algorithms. Accessed 30 Sept 2018

5. Shane, S.: From headline to photograph, a fake news masterpiece. New York Times, May 2016. https://www.nytimes.com/2017/01/18/us/fake-news-hillary-clinton-cameron-harris.html. Accessed 30 Sept 2018

6. Gottfried, J., Shearer, E: News use across social media platforms. Pew Research Center Journalism & Media, January 2016. http://www.journalism.org/2016/05/26/news-use-across-social-media-platforms-2016/. Accessed 30 Sept 2018

7. Silverman, C., Strapagiel, L., Shaban, H., Hall, E.: Hyperpartisan Facebook pages are publishing false and misleading information at an alarming rate. Buzzfeed (2016). https://www.buzzfeednews.com/article/craigsilverman/partisan-fb-pages-analysis. Accessed 30 Sept 2018

8. Craig, S.: Viral fake election news outperformed real news on Facebook? Buzzfeed (2016). https://www.buzzfeednews.com/article/craigsilverman/viral-fake-election-news-outperformed-real-news-on-facebook. Accessed 30 Sept 2018

9. Allcott, H., Gentzkow, M.: Social media and fake news in the 2016 election. National Bureau of Economic Research (2017). https://www.nber.org/papers/w23089. Accessed 30 Sept 2018

10. Goldman, R.: Reading fake news, Pakistani minister directs nuclear threat at Israel. New York Times (2016). https://www.nytimes.com/2016/12/24/world/asia/pakistan-israel-khawaja-asif-fake-news-nuclear.html. Accessed 30 Sept 2018

11. Melissa, K.: Fake-photos-hurricane-sandy. Yahoo News (2012). https://www.yahoo.com/news/blogs/trending-now/fake-photos-hurricane-sandy-flood-social-media-190021894.html. Accessed 30 Sept 2018

12. Guardian: Fake-photos-hurricane-sandy. Guardian (2012). https://www.theguardian.com/world/us-news-blog/2012/oct/30/hurricane-sandy-storm-new-york. Accessed 30 Sept 2018

13. Gomes, L.H., Cazita, C., Almeida, J.M., Almeida, V., Meira, W.: Workload models of spam and legitimate e-mails. Perform. Eval. **64**, 690–714 (2007)

14. Fetterly, D., Manasse, M., Najork, M.: Spam, damn spam, and statistics: using statistical analysis to locate spam web pages. In: 7th International Workshop on the Web and Databases: Colocated with ACM SIGMOD/PODS 2004, pp. 1–6 (2004)

15. Thomason, A.: Blog spam: a review. In: Conference on Email and Anti-Spam (CEAS), pp. 1–4 (2007)

16. Wu, C.T., Cheng, K.T., Zhu, Q., Wu, Y.L: Using visual features for anti-spam filtering. In: IEEE International Conference on Image Processing 2005, vol. 3, pp. III–509 (2005). http://citeseerx.ist.psu.edu/viewdoc/download?doi=10.1.1.88.4031&rep=rep1&type=pdf

17. Gupta, A., Lamba, H., Kumaraguru, P., Joshi, A.: Faking sandy: characterizing and identifying fake images on Twitter during hurricane sandy. In: 22nd International Conference on World Wide Web, pp. 729–736 (2013)

18. Corvey, W.J., Verma, S., Vieweg, S., Palmer, M., Martin, J.H.: Foundations of a multilayer annotation framework for Twitter communications during crisis events. In: 8th International Conference on Language Resources and Evaluation, pp. 1–5 (2012)

19. Castillo, C., Mendoza, M., Poblete, B.: Information credibility on Twitter. In: 20th International Conference on World Wide Web, pp. 675–684 (2011)
20. Canini, K.R., Suh, B., Pirolli, P.L.: Finding credible information sources in social networks based on content and social structure. In: IEEE Third International Conference on Privacy, Security, Risk and Trust, pp. 1–8 (2011)
21. Gupta, A., Kumaraguru, P.: Credibility ranking of tweets during high impact events. In: 1st Workshop on Privacy and Security in Online Social Media, pp. 2:2–2:8 (2012)
22. O'Donovan, J., Kang, B., Meyer, G., Hllerer, T., Adalii, S.: Credibility in context: an analysis of feature distributions in Twitter. In: 2012 International Conference on Privacy, Security, Risk and Trust, pp. 293–301 (2012)
23. Eaton-Robb, P.: College students come with plug combat fake news (2017). https://www.businessinsider.com/ap-college-students-come-up-with-plug-in-to-combat-fake-news-2017-12. Accessed 30 Sept 2018

Short Papers

Markov Decision Processes for Fake Accounts Detection

Alexander Semenov$^{(\boxtimes)}$, Gaurav Pandey, and Denis Kotkov

Faculty of Information Technology, University of Jyvaskyla, Jyväskylä, Finland
{alexander.v.semenov,gaurav.g.pandey}@jyu.fi, kotkov.denis.ig@gmail.com

Abstract. Detection of fake accounts on the Internet is usually considered as a one-time classification problem. However, with each subsequent action of the user, the chances of him to be considered as fake would change. Therefore, it is intuitive to see fake account detection as a sequential decision problem. Markov Decision Process (MDP) is an effective method for sequential decision making. In this paper, we define fake account detection as a sequential decision making problem and describe a MDP based definition for it.

Keywords: Fake account detection · Markov decision process
Machine learning

Extended Abstract

The use of fake identities presents a serious challenge for trustworthy information exchange on the Internet. Fake identity use refers to the use of such an identifier by a person to whom the identifier does not point to. This can be the result of identity theft or the creation of a fake identifier that does not point to any real person. State of the art methods of fake account detection typically involve application of supervised machine learning (where identities are classified as fake or benign), or anomaly detection algorithms; input data for these algorithms is particular set of features, depending on the application domain (such as texts posted by the user, his profile data, ego-network, etc).

Majority of current research presents fake account detection as one-time classification; however it is more natural to represent it as a sequential decision problem, where decision-maker performs certain actions that lead to identification of the fake account. This is because, with each action of a user (e.g. tweet content, frequency change of tweeting, addition of friends, etc.), the chances of him being a fake account can change. Therefore, we suggest to view fake account detection as a sequential decision problem, where actions of a *system* depend on the observed state of the identifier. Markov Decision Process (MDP) can be employed to model the problem, as it is a prominent model for sequential decision making. Article [3] applies Markov Reward process for sequential anomaly detection; reinforcement learning is applied to learn optimal customer interactions in [1].

© Springer Nature Switzerland AG 2018
X. Chen et al. (Eds.): CSoNet 2018, LNCS 11280, pp. 539–540, 2018.
https://doi.org/10.1007/978-3-030-04648-4

A Markov decision process is a 5-tuple $(S, A, P_a(S_i, S_j), R_a(S_i), \gamma)$, where S is a set of states, A is a set of actions, $P_a(S_i, S_j)$ is the probability that action a in state S_i will lead to S_j, $R_a(S_i)$ is the reward on taking action a on state S_i, γ is the discount factor [2]. The goal of decision maker is to find a *policy* $\pi(a|S_i)$ that defines behavior of the decision maker such that total cumulative reward will be maximized. We define following discrete time MDP notations for fake account detection:

Actions: Set of actions available to the decision maker that are aimed at helping to classify, or block the user. Examples of the actions are as follows: "Provide CAPTCHA test to use","Analyze CAPTCHA test response", "Block the user","Lock account for several minutes", "Unblock the user".

Observations: Actions of the user: send a message, like a post, repost a message, respond (or not) to CAPTCHA test

Rewards: Each action of the decision maker is associated with reward. Generally, reward is positive, when the user cannot pass the test, i.e. the bot was detected. Reward is negative when the user passes the test, since we cause inconvenience to a genuine user. Further, some actions (such as e.g. checking of the user by a human moderator) are considered expensive and incur negative reward. The best case is correct classification of all fake accounts.

History: sequence of interactions with a user: $\{o_1, a_1, ..., o_t, a_t\}$, where o_i represents and observation, and a_i represents an action. Examples: The user becomes active after locking period, The user changes his posting frequency, user abandons the account, etc.

States: We represent state of a single user as a full history of her interaction with the system. We assume the states as histories of all the users [1].

Transition Function: Transition function $P_a(S_i, S_j)$ is deterministically determined by the action and the change of states.

Objective: A policy $\pi(a|S_i)$ is the strategy that can be applied to any identity, based on all existing histories. The objective is to find an optimal policy π^*, maximizing cumulative reward, i.e. correct classification of all accounts with minimal false positives and "expensive" actions such as manual intrusion. In other words, we perform classification of a user based on histories of all users.

We defined MDP for fake account detection. Further, we will present algorithms for finding optimal policy, and compare it with supervised machine learning used for fake account classification. The learning process of the user in response to the actions taken by the system are not modeled in MDP. In future, we plan to look into stochastic games as a solution for fake account detection.

References

1. Silver, D., Newnham, L., Barker, D., Weller, S., McFall, J.: Concurrent reinforcement learning from customer interactions. pp. III-924-III-932. ICML (2013)
2. Szepesvári, C.: Algorithms for reinforcement learning. Synth. Lect. Artif. Intell. Mach. Learn. **4**(1), 1–103 (2010)
3. Xu, X.: Sequential anomaly detection based on temporal-difference learning: principles, models and case studies. Appl. Soft Comput. **10**(3), 859–867 (2010)

The Network of Causal Relationships in the U.S. Stock Market

Oleg Shirokikh[1], Grigory Pastukhov[2], Alexander Semenov[3], Sergiy Butenko[4], Alexander Veremyev[5], Eduardo Pasiliao[6], and Vladimir Boginski[5(✉)]

[1] Frontline Solver, Reno, NV, USA
olegshirokikh@gmail.com
[2] CSX Transportation, Jacksonville, FL, USA
grigoriypas@gmail.com
[3] University of Jyväskylä, Jyväskylä, Finland
alexander.v.semenov@jyu.fi
[4] Texas A&M University, College Station, TX, USA
butenko@tamu.edu
[5] University of Central Florida, Orlando, FL, USA
{Alexander.Veremyev,Vladimir.Boginski}@ucf.edu
[6] Air Force Research Laboratory, Eglin AFB, Valparaíso, FL, USA
eduardo.pasiliao@us.af.mil

Abstract. We propose a network-based framework to study causal relationships in financial markets and demonstrate the proposed approach by applying it to the entire U.S. stock market. Directed networks (referred to as causal market graphs) are constructed based on stock return time series data during 2001–2017 using Granger causality as a measure of pairwise causal relationships between all stocks. We consider the dynamics of structural properties of the constructed network snapshots, group stocks into network-based clusters, as well as identify the most "influential" stocks via a PageRank algorithm. The proposed approaches offer a new angle for analyzing global characteristics and trends of the stock market using network-based techniques.

Keywords: Stock market · Big data · Network analysis
Causal market graph · Granger causality

Extended Abstract

The modern stock market is a complex interconnected system, where various "local" factors can cause "global" changes in the behavior of the entire market. For instance, favorable or unfavorable economic conditions in certain countries, or in certain market segments, may affect other countries and industries and potentially cause positive or negative fluctuations that span the entire U.S. and international markets. The idea of describing causal relationships between different components of the market system has been addressed in several recent

© Springer Nature Switzerland AG 2018
X. Chen et al. (Eds.): CSoNet 2018, LNCS 11280, pp. 541–542, 2018.
https://doi.org/10.1007/978-3-030-04648-4

studies. The survey by [3] discussed the concept of *contagion* in financial markets, which essentially implies the propagation of impact (such as risk) between different components of the market. Clearly, a *network-based* model is a natural way to mathematically represent these "contagion" processes; however, the principles for constructing the networks that reflect certain types of processes may vary depending on the purpose of the study.

Possibly the most intuitive technique for constructing a network-based (or, graphical) model of the market is to represent its elements (e.g., stocks) as nodes and connect the nodes by links (arcs) based on pairwise correlations between the corresponding entities (i.e., the correlations between stock price fluctuations over a certain period of time). Such an approach was studied by [1, 2] in the context of identifying large correlated clusters and diversified portfolios in the U.S. stock market. Although the pairwise correlation measure has its merit in certain situations, its substantial drawback is in inability to produce *directed* links between entities, that is, establish the direction of "contagion" (i.e., the propagation from node i to node j vs. the propagation from node j to node i).

In this work, we construct and analyze a *directed* network model, which rigorously describes *causal relationships* between all pairs of stocks in the U.S. stock market using the concept of *Granger causality*. The motivation behind this approach was investigating the possibility of drawing meaningful conclusions about the behavior and trends of the entire market *solely* based on a rigorously defined quantitative causality measure, as an alternative to studying these causal relationships based on subjective criteria, such as analysts' opinions, etc., which may not be easily quantifiable. It should be noted that Granger causality, which will be formally defined later in this paper, can be used to determine whether the time series describing stock i is useful in predicting the behavior of stock j, which should not be confused with the statement "the increase/decrease in the price of stock i causes the increase/decrease in the price of stock j". Granger causality appears to capture certain structural properties of the stock market that reflect global tendencies in its behavior. In particular, we investigate various aspects of connectivity patterns and the dynamics of structural properties of the constructed network snapshots. Moreover, the proposed network representation is used to group stocks into network-based clusters and identify the most "influential" market entities (sectors, industries and individual stocks).

Acknowledgments. Work of A. Semenov was funded in part by the AFRL European Office of Aerospace Research and Development (grant no. FA9550-17-1-0030)

References

1. Boginski, V., Butenko, S., Pardalos, P.M.: Statistical analysis of financial networks. Comput. Stat. Data Anal. **48**, 431–443 (2005)
2. Boginski, V., Butenko, S., Pardalos, P.: Mining market data: a network approach. Comput. Oper. Res. **33**, 3171–3184 (2006)
3. Sowers, R., Giesecke, K.: Contagion. SIAM News p. 18 October 2011

Author Index

Printed in the United States
By Bookmasters